THE SUNDAY TIMES

ILLUSTRATED HISTORY OF FOOTBALL:
THE POST-WAR YEARS

THE SUNDAY TIMES

ILLUSTRATED HISTORY OF FOOTBALL:
THE POST-WAR YEARS

CHRIS NAWRAT & STEVE HUTCHINGS

CHANCELLOR
PRESS

First published in Great Britain in 1994 by Hamlyn

This abridged edition published in 1996 by Chancellor Press an imprint of Reed International Books Limited Michelin House, 81 Fulham Road, London SW3 6RB and Auckland, Melbourne, Singapore and Toronto

ISBN 1 85153 014 2

A CIP catalogue record for this book is available at the British Library

Produced by Mandarin Offset
Printed in Great Britain by The Bath Press, Avon

Contents

Nippy Carter unzips Charlton

WHEN the war ended the game faced enormous problems. Many players were still engaged on national service, grounds were bomb-damaged and petrol rationing restricted transport. So the League was divided into regional sections to reduce travel; promotion and relegation were suspended; the FA Cup was played on a two-leg home and away basis; and clubs were allowed to continue using guest players.

None of that stopped the crowds flocking back, and with the Leagues having an unreal feel to them most interest was concentrated on the FA Cup. The public were rewarded with a classic encounter between Derby and Charlton in the final.

For the first time in a Cup final, the ball burst minutes before the end of normal time when Jack Stamps, Derby's centre-forward, unleashed a fierce shot. There was another entry in the record books when Bert Turner of Charlton became the first man to score for both sides. He put Derby ahead when he deflected a shot into his own net, and seconds later he had a shot of his own deflected to give Charlton the equaliser.

In extra time Raich Carter showed that his skills were still as great as in the 1930s. Derby had shrewdly bought him from Sunderland for £6,000 in December and he had established a telling inside-forward partnership with Peter Doherty.

Doherty and the silver-haired Carter produced a quicksilver display which left the tiring Charlton defence floundering. Stamps scored twice and Doherty once as Derby's 4-1 victory convinced the crowd that football was back to its pre-war best.

Russians quit unbeaten

DYNAMO MOSCOW'S tour of Britain produced one of the strangest series of matches that anybody could recall. The Russians demanded that they should eat all their meals at the Soviet Embassy, and provide their own referee for at least one match. Then, in their first match against Chelsea, they presented each of their opponents with a bunch of flowers.

The press had written the visitors off as a group of pedestrian amateurs, but in front of 82,000 people their quick, precise football brought them back from 2-0 down against the run of play to a 3-3 draw.

Cardiff were destroyed 10-1 before a match with Arsenal, who played Stanley Matthews and Stan Mortensen as guests. The fog over White Hart Lane (Highbury was being rebuilt) was so thick that the Russian referee chose to patrol one touchline, with two English linesmen on the other sideline.

Both sides claimed that it was the other's fault that the game was not cancelled, and with nobody able to see more than five yards it was little wonder that hardly anybody knew exactly how the Russians came back from 3-1 down to win 4-3.

Moscow then played an ill-tempered 2-2 draw with Rangers, and were due to meet an FA XI at Villa Park. But just before that game was to be held they vanished, flying home without giving any reason.

Bert Turner, who scored for both teams, wins a corner for Charlton

Flower power: Chelsea were presented with bouquets by Dynamo Moscow

33 crushed to death at Bolton

THE second round FA Cup match between Bolton and Stoke on March 9 made it tragically apparent that war-scarred grounds could not cope with the crowds that were now flocking to matches. The official attendance at Burnden Park was put at 65,419, but it was estimated that nearer 85,000 people came to see whether Stoke could overcome a 2-0 deficit from the first leg.

With rationing still in force, a considerable number of policemen were guarding food in one of the stands. This was regarded as a more important duty than dealing with the gatecrashers who started climbing over the turnstiles in one corner of the ground.

As a result, part of the terracing became so overcrowded that the crush barriers collapsed. In the space of a few yards 33 people died and more than 500 were injured in the worst disaster in British football. The Home Office conducted an inquiry, which called for stricter safety standards at grounds but the recommendations were largely ignored.

FOR THE RECORD

■ Struggling Manchester United, £15,000 in debt and forced to share Maine Road with Manchester City, appointed Matt Busby their manager in February.

■ The FA Cup semi-final replay between Derby and Birmingham at Maine Road attracted a crowd of 80,407, a record for a midweek match between two clubs outside of Wembley. This caused the government to become so concerned about the effect of absenteeism on the efforts to rebuild the country that it soon banned midweek afternoon matches.

■ With huge crowds flocking to grounds, football clubs were making a fortune at the turnstiles. Players complained that they were not sharing in the bonanza, and threatened to go on strike unless their pre-war wages of £8 a week were raised. They won an increase to £9.

■ Aberdeen beat Rangers 3-2 in the final of the Scottish Southern League Cup. The following season the competition became the Scottish League Cup.

■ The FA persuaded all the British associations to rejoin FIFA.

League back with a storm

EVEN THE heavy rain on August 31 could not dampen the enthusiasm for the resumption of the League. Nearly a million people flocked to the 43 matches that day, which were identical fixtures to the first day of the short-lived 1939 season.

But the season was to become the longest on record as a bitter winter played havoc with fixtures. By January, so many pitches were white with snow and ice that the lines had to be marked out using red paint. More than 140 matches were postponed in three months.

In the end, everything hinged on two matches. Wolves, who had been 11 points clear at one stage, needed to win their last match against Liverpool to secure the title. But they lost 2-1, which gave the League leadership to Liverpool, a solid team built around Albert Stubbins, Billy Liddell and Bob Paisley.

Liverpool, though, had to wait a fortnight until June 14 when the final game of the season was Stoke's visit to Sheffield United. To the consternation of the fans and the players, Bob McGrory, Stoke's stubborn manager, had sold Stanley Matthews to Blackpool for £11,500 in May. Most thought the motive was McGrory's jealousy of Matthews' fame. It was a costly fit of pique. If Stoke had won they would have taken the title on goal average. But United's 2-1 victory gave the championship to Liverpool.

Old salts bale out sinking Arsenal

AFTER a third of the season the only thing that kept Arsenal off the bottom of the table was goal average. They lost nine of their first 14 matches and were heading for an unimaginable drop into the Second Division.

Up and coming young players were almost impossible to find, so Arsenal turned to a pair of old hands. Joe Mercer, 31 and suffering with a dodgy knee, was said to be contemplating retirement. But Arsenal persuaded him to play on for a little longer and paid £7,000 to Everton for their stalwart left half. Ronnie Rooke, at 35, was also said to be past it and could not command a place in the Fulham team. But Arsenal signed the veteran centre-forward in exchange for £1,000 and two of their reserve team players.

The rest of the country scoffed. Arsenal were clearly getting desperate. In fact, Arsenal were getting two bargains. Mercer, immediately made captain, brought authority to the side's play and Rooke showed that he had not lost his touch, scoring 21 goals in 24 matches. Arsenal only lost one of their next nine games as they hauled themselves clear of relegation.

Magical Mercer: the Arsenal captain steps out in style at Highbury

FOR THE RECORD

■ Len Shackleton scored six goals for Newcastle on his debut against Newport County in the Second Division after his £13,000 transfer from Bradford.

■ Sam Bartram, the Charlton goalkeeper, played with a hot poultice on his stomach to counter food poisoning in the FA Cup semi-final against Newcastle. Charlton went on to win the FA Cup and, amazingly, the ball burst for the second successive year during the final.

■ Neil McBain, New Brighton's 52-year-old manager, had to play in goal when the club's only regular keeper was injured. McBain became the oldest man ever to play in the League in a 3-0 loss to Hartlepools in the Third Division North.

■ Derby broke the British transfer record when they paid £15,500 for Billy Steel of Morton, the Scottish international inside-forward.

■ During the big freeze Portsmouth fans were so starved of action 10,000 watched a reserve game.

■ Doncaster Rovers set four records in the Third Division North: total points (72), away points (37), total wins (33) and away wins (18). They also equalled the division's record of only three defeats.

England favour Winterbottom

ENGLAND resumed playing internationals in September with a 7-2 victory in Belfast and life was looking good for the national side when they blasted eight goals past Holland.

But then England suffered an embarrassing 1-0 defeat by Switzerland in Zurich on May 18. That was enough to prompt Stanley Rous, the FA secretary, to have Walter Winterbottom, who had been appointed chief coach in 1946, made the first England team manager.

England bounced back by thrashing Portugal 10-0 in Lisbon on May 27. Stan Mortensen, nicknamed "the electric eel" for his ability to wriggle through defences, celebrated his debut with four goals.

The other great international of the season was played by Great Britain and the Rest of Europe at Hampden Park in May to celebrate the home nations rejoining Fifa. Mannion and Lawton both scored twice in the 6-1 victory over a scratch side led by Johnny Carey of Manchester United and Ireland that included players from 10 countries.

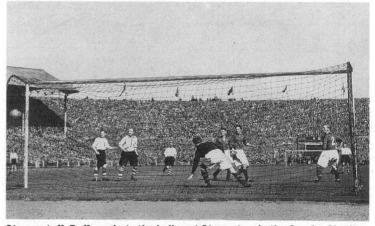

Strong stuff: Duffy rockets the ball past Strong to win the Cup for Charlton

Busby steadies United nerves

MATT BUSBY had learnt the manager's art during the war as a company sergeant-major in the army working with Tommy Lawton, Joe Mercer and Arthur Rowe.

With little money to spend at Manchester United, Busby invested his time in cultivating the latent talent at the club. His tactical vision and readiness to experiment produced a transformation.

The Irish international Johnny Carey was moved to right back from inside right, where the mercurial Johnny Morris took over. John Aston, the inside left, became the left back, making room for Stan Pearson to become the brains of the attack. With Jimmy Delaney, Jack Rowley and Charlie Mitten completing the forward line, United had a scintillating strike force.

Busby predicted that United would win the FA Cup, but they had to play a First Division team in every round. In the third round they were involved in an amazing match at Aston Villa – they conceded a goal straight from the kick-off, were ahead 5-1 at half-time, had their lead cut to 5-4 and finally prevailed 6-4.

At Wembley, United faced a resurgent Blackpool, who had reached the final for the first time. With Stanley Matthews and Stan Mortensen in tandem, Blackpool were 2-1 ahead with 20 minutes left. Blackpool were playing superbly, and any other team would have succumbed.

Not United. At half-time Busby and Carey had told the team not to panic and their riposte was sublime. Three goals came in 16 minutes and the crowd was left thrilled by a match that had been all-out attack from start to finish. The sergeant-major's team were truly on the march.

Arsenal do the business

TOM WHITTAKER the newly-appointed Arsenal manager, had his faith in Joe Mercer rewarded. Arsenal only dropped two points in their first 13 games and did not lose in the League until their 18th match.

The game was becoming more defensively minded and Arsenal were stuck with the label "lucky", because many people thought they played boring football and did not deserve to win.

But there was nothing lucky about their fine start, which was made without the Compton brothers, Denis and Leslie, who were helping Middlesex win cricket's County Championship. Nor did Arsenal fans care if their club was supposedly boring. The match at Chelsea brought traffic to a standstill for miles and touts were offering five-shilling tickets at 10 times the price; the meeting with Manchester United broke the League attendance record when 83,260 packed into Maine Road.

Arsenal had a solid, settled side and coasted to their sixth title with almost a month to spare. Mercer, again contemplating retirement, was persuaded to play on for another year.

Third Division go first class

A PAIR of audacious transfers created enormous interest in the Third Division. Tommy Lawton was determined to leave Chelsea, but they had rejected several offers before Notts County, a moderate Third Division North side, persuaded them to sell in November.

Meadow Lane was electrified by Britain's first £20,000 transfer. Lawton's debut was a sell-out, County's attendance record was broken within a few weeks and Lawton became the first Third Division player to appear for England.

Hull, too, wanted to improve themselves. In March they persuaded Derby to sell Raich Carter for a nominal fee. As well as playing, Carter would also be Hull's assistant manager. But when Major Frank Buckley resigned as manager within weeks to go to Leeds, Carter was given complete charge and Hull's attendances boomed.

Keeping his head: Jack Rowley rises above the Blackpool defence

---

FOR THE RECORD

■ Jack Fairbrother moved from Preston to Newcastle for £7,000, a record fee for a goalkeeper. The feeling that the transfer market was getting out of hand was increased when Charlton paid £6,000 for two non-League players from Dartford.

■ Millwall's ground was closed for seven days after crowd trouble.

■ Newcastle, with an average home crowd of more than 56,000, gained promotion to the First Division despite selling Len Shackelton to Sunderland in February. The deal raised the transfer record again, to £20,500.

■ Hibernian won the Scottish League title for the first time. Willie McCartney, who had assembled the side, died in January before he could enjoy the club's finest moment.

■ The total attendance for the season rose again, topping 40 million for the first time. In Scotland, 143,750 people saw Rangers beat Hibs in the Cup semi-final. And 133,570 attended the Scottish Cup final replay, a record for a midweek match.

■ The BBC claimed that 1 million people watched the Cup final on television.

■ Southern League Colchester reached the last 16 of the FA Cup. Then their M-plan for stopping Stanley Matthews backfired as Blackpool won 5-0. All of the goals were scored by players whose surname started with M.

Investment rewarded: Notts County fans flocked to watch Lawton

THE 1948-49 SEASON

Hull on top as Carter pulls it off

AS FAR as the people of Hull were concerned, Raich Carter became an instant hero in his first full season in charge. Patrolling the left wing, his skills were still, at 35, far superior to any other player's in the Third Division North.

Carter's emphasis on high-class football gave Hull a start of nine successive victories in the League, and after 13 away matches they had not been been beaten either. They also reached the quarter-finals of the Cup, where they were unlucky to lose 1-0 to Manchester United because their goal-keeper played most of the match with concussion.

It was little wonder that average attendances at Boothferry Park virtually doubled as Hull made their long-awaited return to the Second Division.

Carter: wily grey fox

Sunderland fall off Yeovil's cliff-hanger

ALEC STOCK, Yeovil's player-manager, ran the lowly Southern League club virtually single-handed – including cutting the grass of the soon to be famous pitch.

The press only started to pay attention to his team of part-timers when they reached the third round of the FA Cup and faced Second Division Bury. The media gave Stock a useful weapon; he talked up the 8ft slope on his pitch until, as he put it: "By the time Bury arrived the entire country thought we played on the side of a house."

Bury must have felt that way too as they fell 3-1. They probably did not know about Stock's other secret weapon either. His players were on a special diet – glucose, eggs and sherry – to give them strength.

Yeovil hit the jackpot when they were then drawn at home to mighty Sunderland. The First Division giants were out-run and out-fought as Stock put Yeovil ahead after 30 minutes. Sunderland managed to equalise and force extra time but it merely postponed the inevit-able. Bryant put Yeovil ahead again, Stock's diet gave his team the strength to survive the last 15 minutes and Yeovil were on their way to Manchester United.

It was the greatest day out Somerset had ever had and although Yeovil were crushed 8-0 Stock was pragmatic: "We just felt numb. But then we heard that our share of the gate (over £7,000) was more than our entire receipts for the previous season. Suddenly, what had happened on the field was of no significance."

Stock: crafty schemer

Pompey's senior service sail serenely to the title

SO MANY servicemen had been stationed on the south coast during the war that Portsmouth had been able to recruit the pick of the crop. But because their entire team had only cost a few thousand pounds they were not rated by the pundits.

However, it was Portsmouth's golden jubilee year and they wanted to celebrate the anniversary with a trophy. They also had a president who did not like losing, Field Marshal Montgomery. He was forever urging his players on in the way that he used to inspire his troops in battle. The Portsmouth captain received a missive from Montgomery suggesting it would be a good idea to hit Chelsea for six.

Portsmouth, not a team to disobey orders, obliged.

Portsmouth had their best ever start to the season and were on course for the Double but they were caught napping by Leicester in the FA Cup semi-final and the Second Division team, inspired by Don Revie, won 3-1. As often happens, being knocked out of the Cup concentrated the team's minds on the League.

The match that ultimately decided the League was at St James's Park in April, where Portsmouth's half-backs utterly stifled Newcastle to set up a 5-0 win. The title was theirs and Montgomery proudly received the trophy at Fratton Park.

Rangers grab their first treble chance

RANGERS made such a habit of winning the Scottish League and Cup that their fans expected nothing less. So they went one better and completed the first treble. Surprisingly, their rivals Celtic did not bother them in any of the competitions: Rangers won the League by one point from Dundee; beat Clyde 4-1 in the Cup final; and had a 2-0 victory over Raith in the League Cup final.

The Rangers team was built around the "Iron Curtain" defence. At its heart was the formidable George Young, who made more than 50 appearances for Scotland. He was ably supported by the hard tackling Willie Woodburn, Sammy Cox and Jock Shaw. But Rangers were not a purely defensive side, with the two Willies, Waddell and Thornton, keeping up a steady flow of goals.

THE 1949-50 SEASON

Scotland put pride before World finals

SCOTTISH supporters, still revelling in their 3-1 victory over England at Wembley last season, paid dearly for the arrogant attitude towards Fifa displayed by their FA.

Fifa were prepared to give the United Kingdom two places in the 1950 World Cup finals, with the winners and runners-up in the Home International championship qualifying. But the proud Scots insisted that they would only go to Brazil if they were actually to win the domestic tournament.

Both England and Scotland easily beat Wales and Northern Ireland, setting up a showdown at Hampden. England won 1-0 although Scotland were unlucky when Willie Bauld's shot bounced off the bar and hit the goal line but did not go in. A draw would have meant that Scotland, the previous year's champions, would have retained the trophy and gone to the World Cup.

Bauld: unlucky miss

Compton brothers saving double-act

Capital conquest: Arsenal won the FA Cup without leaving London

ARSENAL'S ageing stars proved they still had some life left in their legs with a resounding 2-0 victory over Liverpool in the FA Cup final. It was a fitting finale for Denis Compton, who was forced to stop playing at the end of the season by his knee injury.

Arsenal had Denis and his brother Leslie to thank for their appearance in the final. They were 2-1 down to Chelsea with seconds to go when Denis took a corner. Leslie ignored Joe Mercer's order not to join the attack and, as a result, was in just the right spot to score the equaliser.

The final was played in pouring rain on a strength-sapping pitch and at the interval Denis was exhausted. But revived by a large brandy he was able to set up the second goal that enabled Arsenal to withstand Liverpool's late rally.

While Arsenal were winning the Cup without ever having to play a game outside of London, their neighbours Tottenham were also attracting interest.

The Tottenham board were unhappy about their team never quite being good enough to get out of the Second Division, so they had recently appointed Arthur Rowe. The new manager told his team: "Make it simple, make it quick."

They did so with a vengeance, going 23 matches without defeat, topping the table throughout the season, and running away with the division by nine points. The team was talked about as the best side the club had ever produced, but Rowe disagreed – he knew they were capable of better things yet.

Championship just chimes again for Portsmouth

PORTSMOUTH won the League for the second year running, but this time the race was much closer, with several teams in the hunt and the title undecided until the end of the season.

Wolves, with their young team, made the early pace, not losing until their 13th match. They were overhauled by Liverpool, who went 19 matches before being beaten. Manchester United, who had just returned to Old Trafford, were as strong as ever and Portsmouth, Blackpool and Sunderland were not far behind.

Manchester United caught up with Liverpool in the spring and then faded, leaving Sunderland to edge in front at Easter. The international between England and Scotland was played on a Saturday, depriving several clubs of key players and giving Portsmouth a chance to go top for the first time.

Even then, only one point separated the top four clubs. And that was the way it stayed to the final Saturday, May 6. Portsmouth led Wolves on goal average and Sunderland were one point behind.

All three teams had emphatic wins: Portsmouth 5-1, Wolves 6-1 and Sunderland 4-1. It was enough to give Portsmouth the title by 0.4 goals, the first time the championship had been decided on goal average for a quarter of a century.

LEAGUE TABLES AND RESULTS 1945–1950

1945-46 | 1946-47 | 1947-48 | 1948-49 | 1949-50

WORLD CUP

1945-46	1946-47	1947-48	1948-49	1949-50
				Uruguay 2 Brazil 1

FA CUP

1945-46	1946-47	1947-48	1948-49	1949-50
Derby County 4 Charlton Athletic 1	Charlton Athletic 1 Burnley 0	Manchester United 4 Blackpool 2	Wolverhampton Wanderers 3 Leicester City 1	Arsenal 2 Liverpool 0

FIRST DIVISION

1946-47

	P	W	D	L	F	A	Pts
Liverpool	42	25	7	10	84	52	57
Man Utd	42	22	12	8	95	54	56
Wolves	42	25	6	11	98	56	56
Stoke	42	24	7	11	90	53	55
Blackpool	42	22	6	14	71	70	50
Sheff Utd	42	21	7	14	89	75	49
Preston	42	18	11	13	76	74	47
Aston Villa	42	18	9	15	67	53	45
Sunderland	42	18	8	16	65	66	44
Everton	42	17	9	16	62	67	43
Middlesbro	42	17	8	17	73	68	42
Portsmouth	42	16	9	17	66	60	41
Arsenal	42	16	9	17	72	70	41
Derby	42	18	5	19	73	79	41
Chelsea	42	16	7	19	69	84	39
Grimsby	42	13	12	17	61	82	38
Blackburn	42	14	8	20	45	53	36
Bolton	42	13	8	21	57	69	34
Charlton	42	11	12	19	57	71	34
Huddersfld	42	13	7	22	53	79	33
Brentford	42	9	7	26	45	88	25
Leeds	42	6	6	30	45	90	18

1947-48

	P	W	D	L	F	A	Pts
Arsenal	42	23	13	6	81	32	59
Man Utd	42	19	14	9	81	48	52
Burnley	42	20	12	10	56	43	52
Derby	42	19	12	11	77	57	50
Wolves	42	19	9	14	83	70	47
Aston Villa	42	19	9	14	65	57	47
Preston	42	20	7	15	67	68	47
Portsmouth	42	19	7	16	68	50	45
Blackpool	42	17	10	15	57	41	44
Man City	42	15	12	15	52	47	42
Liverpool	42	16	10	16	65	61	42
Sheff Utd	42	16	10	16	65	70	42
Charlton	42	17	6	19	57	66	40
Everton	42	17	6	19	52	66	40
Stoke	42	14	14	14	41	55	38
Middlesbro	42	14	9	19	71	73	37
Bolton	42	16	5	21	46	58	37
Chelsea	42	14	9	19	53	71	37
Huddersfld	42	12	12	18	51	60	36
Sunderland	42	13	10	19	56	67	36
Blackburn	42	11	10	21	54	72	32
Grimsby	42	8	6	28	45	111	22

1948-49

	P	W	D	L	F	A	Pts
Portsmouth	42	25	8	9	84	42	58
Man Utd	42	21	11	10	77	44	53
Derby	42	22	9	11	74	55	53
Newcastle	42	20	12	10	70	56	52
Arsenal	42	18	13	11	74	44	49
Wolves	42	17	12	13	79	66	46
Man City	42	15	15	12	47	51	45
Sunderland	42	13	17	12	49	58	43
Charlton	42	15	12	15	63	67	42
Aston Villa	42	16	10	16	60	76	42
Stoke	42	16	9	17	66	68	41
Liverpool	42	13	14	15	53	43	40
Chelsea	42	12	14	16	69	68	38
Bolton	42	14	10	18	59	68	38
Burnley	42	12	14	16	43	50	38
Blackpool	42	11	16	15	54	67	38
Birmingham	42	11	15	16	36	38	37
Everton	42	13	11	18	41	63	37
Huddersfld	42	12	10	20	40	69	34
Preston	42	11	11	20	62	75	33
Sheff Utd	42	11	11	20	57	78	33

1949-50

	P	W	D	L	F	A	Pts
Portsmouth	42	22	9	11	74	38	53
Wolves	42	20	13	9	76	49	53
Sunderland	42	21	10	11	83	62	52
Man Utd	42	18	14	10	69	44	50
Newcastle	42	19	12	11	77	55	50
Arsenal	42	19	11	12	79	55	49
Blackpool	42	17	15	10	46	35	49
Liverpool	42	17	14	11	64	54	48
Middlesbro	42	20	7	15	59	48	47
Burnley	42	16	13	13	40	40	45
Derby	42	17	10	15	69	61	44
Aston Villa	42	15	12	15	61	61	42
Chelsea	42	12	16	14	58	65	40
West Brom	42	14	12	16	47	53	40
Huddersfld	42	14	9	19	52	73	37
Bolton	42	10	14	18	45	59	34
Fulham	42	10	14	18	41	54	34
Everton	42	10	14	18	42	66	34
Stoke	42	11	12	19	45	75	34
Charlton	42	13	6	23	53	65	32
Man City	42	8	13	21	36	68	29
Birmingham	42	7	14	21	31	67	28

SECOND DIVISION

1946-47	1947-48	1948-49	1949-50
Champions: Manchester City Also promoted: Burnley Relegated: Swansea Town, Newport County	Champions: Birmingham City Also promoted: Newcastle United Relegated: Doncaster Rovers, Millwall	Champions: Fulham Also promoted: West Bromwich Albion Relegated: Nottingham Forest, Lincoln City	Champions: Tottenham Hotspur Also promoted: Sheffield Wednesday Relegated: Plymouth Argyle, Bradford Park Avenue

THIRD DIVISION SOUTH

1946-47	1947-48	1948-49	1949-50
Champions: Cardiff City Runners-up (not promoted): Queen's Park Rangers	Champions: Queen's Park Rangers Runners-up (not promoted): Bournemouth	Champions: Swansea Town Runners-up (not promoted): Reading	Champions: Notts County Runners-up (not promoted): Northampton Town

THIRD DIVISION NORTH

1946-47	1947-48	1948-49	1949-50
Champions: Doncaster Rovers Runners-up (not promoted): Rotherham United	Champions: Lincoln City Runners-up (not promoted): Rotherham United	Champions: Hull City Runners-up (not promoted): Rotherham United	Champions: Doncaster Rovers Runners-up (not promoted): Gateshead

SCOTTISH CUP

1946-47	1947-48	1948-49	1949-50
Aberdeen 2 Hibernian 1	Rangers 1 Morton 0, after 1-1	Rangers 4 Clyde 1	Rangers 3 East Fife 0

SCOTTISH FIRST DIVISION

1946-47

	P	W	D	L	F	A	Pts
Rangers	30	21	4	5	76	26	46
Hibernian	30	19	6	5	69	33	44
Aberdeen	30	16	7	7	58	41	39
Hearts	30	16	6	8	52	43	38
Partick	30	16	3	11	74	59	35
Morton	30	12	10	8	58	45	34
Celtic	30	13	6	11	53	55	32
Motherwell	30	12	5	13	58	54	29
T Lanark	30	11	6	13	56	64	28
Clyde	30	9	9	12	55	65	27
Falkirk	30	8	10	12	62	61	26
Q of South	30	9	8	13	44	69	26
Queen's P	30	8	6	16	47	60	22
St Mirren	30	9	4	17	47	65	22
Kilmarnock	30	6	9	15	44	66	21
Hamilton	30	2	7	21	38	85	11

1947-48

	P	W	D	L	F	A	Pts
Hibernian	30	22	4	4	86	27	48
Rangers	30	21	4	5	64	28	46
Partick	30	16	4	10	61	42	36
Dundee	30	15	3	12	67	51	33
St Mirren	30	13	5	12	54	58	31
Clyde	30	12	7	11	52	57	31
Falkirk	30	10	10	10	55	48	30
Motherwell	30	13	3	14	45	47	29
Hearts	30	10	8	12	37	42	28
Aberdeen	30	10	7	13	45	45	27
T Lanark	30	10	6	14	56	73	26
Celtic	30	10	5	15	41	56	25
Q of South	30	10	5	15	49	74	25
Morton	30	9	6	15	47	43	24
Airdrie	30	7	7	16	40	78	21
Queen's P	30	9	2	19	45	75	20

1948-49

	P	W	D	L	F	A	Pts
Rangers	30	20	6	4	63	32	46
Dundee	30	20	5	5	71	48	45
Hibernian	30	17	5	8	75	52	39
East Fife	30	16	3	11	64	46	35
Falkirk	30	12	8	10	70	54	32
Celtic	30	12	7	11	48	40	31
T Lanark	30	13	5	12	56	52	31
Hearts	30	12	6	12	64	54	30
St Mirren	30	13	4	13	51	47	30
Q of South	30	11	8	11	47	53	30
Partick	30	9	9	12	50	63	27
Motherwell	30	10	5	15	44	49	25
Aberdeen	30	7	11	12	39	48	25
Clyde	30	9	6	15	50	67	24
Morton	30	7	8	15	39	51	22
Albion	30	3	2	25	30	105	8

1949-50

	P	W	D	L	F	A	Pts
Rangers	30	22	6	2	58	26	50
Hibernian	30	22	5	3	86	34	49
Hearts	30	20	3	7	86	40	43
East Fife	30	15	7	8	58	43	37
Celtic	30	14	7	9	51	50	35
Dundee	30	12	7	11	49	46	31
Partick	30	13	3	14	55	45	29
Aberdeen	30	11	4	15	48	56	26
Raith	30	9	8	13	45	54	26
Motherwell	30	10	5	15	53	58	25
St Mirren	30	8	9	13	42	49	25
T Lanark	30	11	3	16	44	62	25
Clyde	30	10	4	16	56	73	24
Falkirk	30	7	10	13	48	72	24
Q of South	30	5	6	19	31	63	16
Stirling	30	6	3	21	38	77	15

SCOTTISH SECOND DIVISION

1946-47	1947-48	1948-49	1949-50
Champions: Dundee Also promoted: Airdrie	Champions: East Fife Also promoted: Albion Rovers	Champions: Raith Rovers Also promoted: Stirling Albion	Champions: Morton Also promoted: Airdrie

SCOTTISH LEAGUE CUP

1946-47	1947-48	1948-49	1949-50
Rangers 4 Aberdeen 0	East Fife 4 Falkirk 1, after 1-1	Rangers 2 Raith 0	East Fife 3 Dunfermline 0

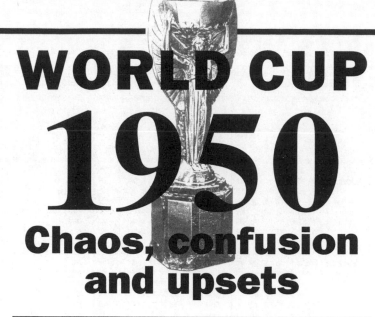

WORLD CUP 1950
Chaos, confusion and upsets

THE WORLD CUP in Brazil was the most chaotic, disorganised and ramshackle tournament in the event's history. It was marked by mass withdrawals, teams having to travel thousands of miles to fulfil fixtures in their own group, a structure that meant there was no official World Cup final and a showpiece stadium that was unfinished – even by the concluding match. But most of all it will be remembered for two of the most stunning upsets in World Cup history: England's defeat at the hands of the United States and Brazil's loss of the Jules Rimet Trophy when all they needed was a draw.

Because of the ravages of the Second World War there had not been a World Cup for 12 years (although the South Americans carried on with their own championships largely unaffected by outside events). Everything had augured well for the 1950 World Cup: the four British associations had finally rejoined Fifa in 1946 and would compete for the first time; the hosts were to build the biggest and greatest stadium the world had ever seen – the three-tiered, 200,000 capacity Maracana; and to celebrate the survival of the event the World Cup was renamed the Jules Rimet Trophy, after one of the initiators of the championship who had kept the trophy under his bed in France during the war lest the invading Germans found it and melted it down.

Almost immediately things started to go wrong. Czechoslovakia would not enter, nor would Hungary or the Soviet Union. So there were only 32 entries for the qualifying tournament. Then Argentina, Austria, Belgium, Burma, Ecuador, India, and Peru withdrew without playing a single match. Turkey pulled out after qualifying, as did Scotland.

The decision by the Scots was a classic example of cutting off your nose to spite your face. Fifa, delighted to have the four British associations back in the world family, had generously designated the home championships as a World Cup qualifying group, with two teams qualifying. Scotland arrogantly declared that they would only go to Brazil as British champions. England narrowly beat them 1-0 at Hampden, leaving the Scots in second place. Despite the protestations of the English and Scottish players, the Scottish Football Association stubbornly stayed at home.

It got worse. After Turkey, having qualified, withdrew Fifa invited France (who had been knocked out by Yugoslavia) to take their place. France accepted and then saw their itinerary, which involved thousands of miles criss-crossing Brazil. Their appeals against the schedule were rejected so they, too, withdrew. Portugal, also eliminated in the qualifying rounds, were offered Scotland's place – and they refused.

By the time the tournament got underway there was only a rump of 13 teams left, which were absurdly disorganised into two groups of four, one of three and one of two, these two being Uruguay and Bolivia, both of whom had qualified without playing a

match. Uruguay had thrashed Bolivia five times out of six and scored 27 goals. In Brazil they added another eight without reply. No other team would ever get such an easy ride to the final round.

The catalogue of fiascos was compounded by the well-meaning replacement of the simplistic knock-out structure of the previous three World Cups with leagues only, including the final round. But, amazingly, the organisers had omitted to schedule an actual World Cup final. Fortuitously, the gods rescued them when the concluding match of the tournament did decide the winners of the trophy (historians now refer to this match as a World Cup final).

Also, nobody had realised that groups should be centred on one, or

at most two, cities (only the Brazilians were to enjoy such an advantage) so that teams should not have to traipse all over the place playing matches hither and thither, often within days of each other. And this in a country as vast as Brazil, the fourth largest in the world covering nearly half the area of the whole of South America.

But out of this chaos came one of the most extraordinary tournaments. As Brazil were sweeping all before them with the sublime football that has made them world renowned, England, the nation that gave the game to the world, were to suffer the most humiliating result in their history in Belo Horizonte.

There was little indication that England were to fall flat on their faces. For the first time they had a full-time manager, Walter Winterbottom, and a team bristling with talent: Bert Williams in goal; Billy Wright and Alf Ramsey in defence; and an incomparable forward line of Tom Finney, Stan Mortensen, Wilf Mannion and Stanley Matthews. They were undoubtedly one of the favourites for the tournament, and some thought them the best side in the world.

England had won their first game unimpressively against Chile, and against the American minnows decided to stick with the same team – without Matthews – and treat it as practice match. And for the first half-hour that was what it appeared to be as England played virtually in the American half, shooting almost

Travelling hopefully: England arrived in Brazil full of confidence only to be sent packing by the Americans

at will, hitting the bar, and shooting over the bar. It seemed only time before the deluge came.

Then the unthinkable happened eight minutes before half-time. A shot from the left seemed well covered by the England goalkeeper when it was suddenly deflected by the head of the Haitian-born Larry Gaetjens. Nobody was sure whether he had hit it, or it hit him. Whatever, England were 1-0 down. And try as they might – including a dubiously disallowed goal from a Ramsey free-kick – the famous English forwards could not score.

When the result came over the wires in Britain some newspapers thought it a typing error and changed it 10-1. In Belo Horizonte the 10,000 crowd built bonfires on the terraces in celebration and carried the victorious Americans off shoulder high. "Bloody ridiculous," Mannion said. "Can't we play them again tomorrow?" England lost their next game, to Spain, and were on the boat home in ignominy.

In the final round Brazil had coasted through to the last match having scored 13 goals and conceded a mere two to amass four points. Uruguay, their opponents, had struggled to gain three. Brazil, therefore, only needed a draw to take the World Cup.

A world record crowd of 199,854 arrived at the Maracana to watch the inevitable. Before the match the Rio state governor proclaimed Brazil as champions. For the first half it looked that way as the Brazilians mounted wave after wave of attacks, and it seemed only time before their opponents would be overrun. But the first half was goalless and Brazil only scored, through Friaça, three minutes after the interval. Yet this did not break the Uruguayans' resolve. The now familiar trait of Brazilian over-confidence took over and, instead of falling back into defence, they continued to pour forward.

In the 66th minute Uruguay fashioned the equaliser when Schiaffino scored from a pass from Ghiaggia on the right wing. At this point Brazil were still winning the tournament but it seemed the strut had gone from their game. Sixteen minutes from time Ghiaggia again turned them on the wing, this time to score himself with a wonderful individual goal. The unimaginable had happened and the World Cup had returned to Montevideo.

Losing out: England (top) only won one match, against Chile; Billy Wright's men were to be shocked by defeat by the USA; the final attracted almost 200,000 spectators but they saw the hosts Brazil surprisingly beaten

THE 1950-51 SEASON

Rowe pushed slick Spurs to run rings round First Division

ARTHUR ROWE had spent time coaching in Europe and he brought the best of continental thinking to a Tottenham team that was just reaching maturity. Many of the players were the products of the Northfleet nursery, the Kent club that Spurs sent their young prospects to to finish their football education. All Rowe had to do was teach them to play his way.

He had a novel way of explaining what he wanted. Returning from one away match he used sugar cubes on the table of the train's dining car to illustrate why Tottenham's last-minute winning goal had been so brilliant.

"I spread the sugar out to map the moves," he said. "There were seven passes starting from our penalty area. I argued that if we could play like that, instead of just hoping for something to happen, we would score more often."

Rowe's theory was based on short passes and three-man triangles. It was dubbed "push and run", although Rowe did not like the term. But whatever it was called, his players relished following the Rowe style.

There was a great deal of speculation about how the First Division's upstarts would fare against more established sides. The answer was not long in coming. Five goals went past Portsmouth and, in November, Newcastle came to White Hart Lane and conceded seven, four of them before half-time.

A report of the Newcastle match said: "It is hard to imagine a more brilliant exposition of the game. This was vintage champagne, something to savour and remember. When the mechanism clicks at speed, with every pass placed to the last refined inch, there is simply no defence against it."

Tottenham won eight games in a row in the autumn and kept the momentum going just as spectacularly as they had done in the Second Division the previous season. They made sure of the title, the first in the club's history, in April – with a match still in hand.

Transfer fee ceiling spurned as clubs throw money around

PLAYERS finally won an improvement in their conditions with the establishment of a provident fund and an increase in their wages by a Labour Ministry tribunal, but elsewhere there was a feeling that the game had gone money mad.

The tribunal suggested limiting transfer fees to a maximum of £15,000 but the clubs swiftly rejected the idea. That was hardly surprising when Sunderland were prepared to spend a record £30,000 on Trevor Ford, the Aston Villa centre-forward. But despite having three forwards who cost a total of £70,000 Sunderland failed to score in nearly a third of their League matches.

The record did not last long. Minutes before the March transfer deadline Sheffield Wednesday paid Notts County £34,000 for Jackie Sewell, making the forward worth his weight in gold. Not that it did Wednesday any good – they were relegated on goal difference.

It was not only the big spending clubs that suffered. Brentford, despite an average home gate of 19,000, were losing money and forced to sell two of their best players, Jimmy Hill to Fulham and Ron Greenwood to Chelsea.

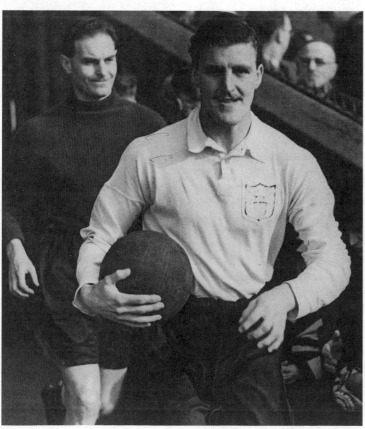

Making ends meet: Brentford were compelled to realise two of their key assets, Jimmy Hill (left) to Fulham and Ron Greenwood to Chelsea

Milburn rediscovers his lethal touch as Newcastle conquer Cup jitters

NEWCASTLE had gone from strength to strength since winning promotion and their fanatical supporters, remembering the club's great tradition, were keen for another trophy to come to St James's Park. Their wish was granted in the FA Cup, but not before Newcastle had had some scares on the way to Wembley.

In the fourth round they trailed Bolton 2-1 before scraping through 3-2, and then they had to ride out a series of storming attacks from Stoke to win 4-2. Their biggest fright came in the sixth round against the minnows of Bristol Rovers.

The entire Bristol Rovers side had cost £350 but they held Newcastle's £60,000 team to a 0-0 draw at St James's Park. Then Bristol Rovers had the temerity to take the lead in the replay before Newcastle won 3-1.

Newcastle also needed a replay to beat Wolves in the semi-final and then faced a nervous seven-week wait before the final. During this time their form deserted them.

They won only one League match out of 11, and "Wor" Jackie Milburn, their star striker, was dropped for one League game because he was suffering "a bad attack of

Wembley jitters". But Milburn rediscovered his composure in time for the final against Blackpool.

It was not a classic match because Blackpool, inexplicably, chose to play the offside trap.

They had had several close calls before Milburn started a run from the halfway line, with the Blackpool players appealing for offside again. But Milburn had timed his break to perfec-

Milburn: beat offside trap

tion and, unchallenged, he ran half the length of the pitch to slide the ball under the advancing goalkeeper George Farm.

There was no doubting his second goal four minutes later. He worked a quick one-two with Ernie Taylor and unhesitatingly hit the backheeled return pass. Farm had barely moved by the time the 25-yard angled shot went into the top corner of the net.

Little respite as England slip further

ENGLAND returned from the World Cup in Brazil painfully aware that they were no longer the pre-eminent football nation. And there were soon plenty of signs that British football was slipping behind the rest of the world.

England chopped and changed their side and gave away a 2-0 lead against Yugoslavia, who became the first continental team to draw a full international in England. Then England lost the decisive home international match against Scotland 3-2, and had to come from behind to beat Argentina.

England's only excuse was in the match against Scotland in April. Wilf Mannion was carried off with a suspected fractured skull after a terrible collision with Billy Liddell. Despite being reduced to 10 men for most of the match, England, for once, played with great resolve, even briefly taking the lead against the run of play.

Scotland also had their problems. They lost their first ever home match against a foreign team when Austria won 1-0 in December. The return fixture was even worse. Scotland lost 4-0 in Vienna in May, when Billy Steel became the first Scottish international to be sent off.

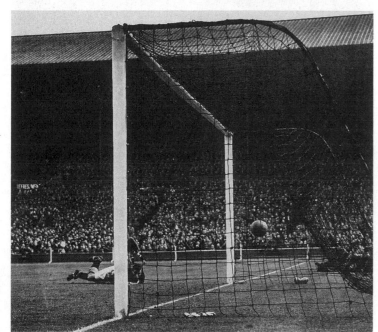

Master blaster: Milburn's second goal left the goalkeeper stranded

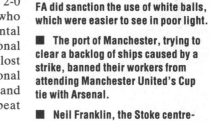

THE
1951-52
SEASON

Hot-shot United the top guns

An early glut of goals restored the public's faith in the quality of the English game and set the scene for an exciting season in which six different teams led the First Division.

Jackie Milburn set the ball rolling on the first Saturday with a hat-trick in Newcastle's six goal demolition of Stoke. His striking partner George Robledo was not to be outdone and hit a hat-trick in the first week of September when Newcastle humbled Tottenham, the stylish champions of the previous season, 7-2 at St James's Park. Robledo then added another four as Newcastle put seven goals past Burnley.

But the real hat-trick king was Jack Rowley of Manchester United, who had scored three hat-tricks by the first week of September, the fastest this had ever been accomplished in the First Division.

Nat Lofthouse was also among the goals for Bolton, Portsmouth with their all-international half-back line of Scoular, Froggatt and Dickinson were going well and Arsenal were as consistent as ever, especially at home.

After the Christmas holidays the top three teams in the First Division – Arsenal, Manchester United and Portsmouth – were all level on points. Arsenal were still disliked. People claimed they played negative football but this may have been prompted by jealousy at their continuing success – they were not beaten until the end of April.

Manchester United stayed in touch with them though. And when his team showed signs of going off the boil Matt Busby made a series of tactical switches. The two most important were moving John Aston from full-back to centre-forward and installing Roger Byrne on the left wing, where he scored seven goals in the last six matches.

With two matches to go Arsenal and Manchester United were level on points, with the mouth-watering prospect of the two clubs meeting in the final game of the season. But an ever-increasing injury list took its toll on Arsenal and, forced to play six reserves, they lost 3-1 to West Bromwich.

That left Arsenal needing to win 7-0 at Old Trafford to take the League on goal difference and keep their hopes of the Double alive. The task was clearly beyond them, and Manchester United celebrated their first title in more than 40 years with a 6-1 victory, Jack Rowley scoring yet another hat-trick.

Lionhearted Lofthouse waltzes around Vienna

Austria were widely regarded as the best team in Europe, so it was hardly surprising that their game against England was dubbed the "match of the century".

The match also provided a fascinating contrast in styles. Austria relied on a slow, measured build-up and their centre-half Ernst Ocwirk had a wide-ranging role as the team's playmaker. England still played the "old-fashioned" way with a traditional formation and the emphasis on speed and quick passing.

England took the match very seriously and, for the first time, arranged a full-scale practice session at Maine Road. But the contest at Wembley lost some of its edge when several leading players were injured in League matches the Saturday before forcing England to field a scratch side.

Austria struck first when Ocwirk set up Melchior with a long pass. But Alf Ramsey kept England in the game with a penalty and was instrumental in giving them the lead seven minutes from time when his free kick was headed in by Nat Lofthouse. Two minutes later though Austria equalised when Stojaspal scored a penalty awarded for handball.

The draw raised the expectations for the return match even higher and the game in Vienna six months later was labelled "the unofficial championship of Europe".

Nat Lofthouse gave England the lead after 20 minutes with a well-taken volley but Austria

Lofthouse: merry dance

were level almost immediately when Froggatt brought down Dienst and Huber scored the penalty.

Jackie Sewell quickly restored England's advantage but Dienst equalised again before the interval. The second half brought wave after wave of attacks from Austria and England only stayed on terms thanks to some excellent saves from Gil Merrick.

But Austria had left themselves open to counter-attacks and with less than 10 minutes left Lofthouse set off on a 50-yard solo run. The Austrian goalkeeper rushed off his line and Lofthouse shot just before the two players collided.

Lofthouse was knocked out by the impact and was lying unconscious on the ground as the ball crossed the goal line. He had to be carried off and was so dazed he could not play in the remainder of the match, but his brave-hearted effort earned him the title "The Lion of Vienna".

Hat-trick hero: Rowley shrugs off Ramsey's challenge

Adventure of the famous five

THE root of Hibernian's post-war triumphs could be traced back to one man, the incomparable Matt Busby. He had been stationed in Scotland during the hostilities and had played for Hibs as a guest, captaining a team of raw teenagers.

Managed by the late Willie McCartney and now by Hugh Shaw, Hibs had become the most powerful team in Scotland. They won the League for the third time in five years, and the second year running.

The key to their success was the "Famous Five" forward line of Eddie Turnbull, Bobby Johnstone, Gordon Smith, Lawrie Reilly and Willie Ormond, players whose skills complemented

each other perfectly. The versatile Bobby Coombe played in five different positions and Tommy Young kept goal despite having to do his national service. Hibs regarded Young as so valuable that they persuaded his regiment to let him fly home from Germany each weekend.

The season was also notable for being the first time since 1895 that neither Rangers nor Celtic won a trophy. Celtic's shock defeat by Third Lanark in the first round of the Cup was to have far-reaching consequences. Desperate to shore up their defence they turned to Llanelli, a far-flung outpost of the Welsh League, to sign the centre-half Jock Stein.

Dooley: inspired switch

Double blow for battling Arsenal

ARSENAL'S valiant attempt to do the Double ended with a second disappointment when Newcastle United became the first club to retain the FA Cup since 1891. But although Newcastle took the honours Arsenal won all the praise for their incredible spirit.

Arsenal's team was wracked by injuries; Ray Daniel played with his broken wrist in plaster, Doug Lishman had a cut that had turned septic and Jimmy Logie was suffering internal bleeding in a thigh injury.

To add to their misery, Wally Barnes, the right back, limped

off after a few minutes with torn ligaments when he twisted his right knee trying to make a quick turn on the lush turf. He returned with his knee heavily bandaged but could not continue, so Arsenal were forced to play most of the match with 10 men.

They mounted a brave rearguard action, with Don Roper holding his own as a makeshift defender and the indefatigable Joe Mercer appearing to be everywhere at once. As the minutes passed and Newcastle were kept at bay, the crowd warmed to Arsenal's heroic efforts.

They had even created the best chance of the match when Lishman hit the bar with an overhead kick.

But with less than 10 minutes to go Roper went down injured allowing Bobby Mitchell to cross to George Robledo, who headed the ball against the post and into the goal.

Newcastle's celebrations were muted because they appreciated the courage that Arsenal had shown. Tom Whittaker, the Arsenal manager, summed up the match when he said: "I have never been prouder of Arsenal than today."

Walking wounded: Lishman, playing with a septic cut, bravely attempts a shot at Newcastle's goal

Tragic end cuts short blossoming of Dooley

DEREK DOOLEY'S uncompromising play at centre-forward had worked wonders for Sheffield Wednesday as they won promotion but it was less well received in the First Division.

After three matches Wednesday left him out of the team "to emphasise our protest against the rough treatment he was getting from defences and for the marked-man attention from referees". Liverpool, the last team to play Wednesday, were incensed by the suggestion and retorted: "Dooley got no more than he gave."

There was no doubting, though, that Dooley's direct and unorthodox style was highly effective. He continued to pulverise opposing defences and had scored 16 goals in 29 games before his career was ended by a terrible accident.

Dooley was being touted as a prospect for England when Wednesday played at Preston in February. But he broke his right leg in the match when he challenged the goalkeeper for a 50-50 ball.

At first it seemed to be a straightforward injury, but Dooley had suffered a cut on the leg earlier. Just as he was about to leave hospital the cut became infected and then gangrene set in.

Doctors had no option but to amputate most of his leg and Dooley's career, which had seen him score 64 goals in 63 League matches, was over at the young age of 23.

Matthews casts a magic spell

WHEN Blackpool reached the Cup final again everybody in the country, apart from the residents of Bolton, were hoping that they would win. Stanley Matthews, at 38, was playing at Wembley for the third time and everybody believed that this was his last chance to collect a winner's medal.

Blackpool had enjoyed mixed fortunes on the way to Wembley. They had lost Allan Brown, who broke his leg as he scored the winner against Arsenal in the quarter-finals. Then they were lucky to beat Tottenham against the run of play in the semi-final when Alf Ramsey's terrible back pass let Jackie Mudie score with seconds remaining.

It looked as if Blackpool had used up all their luck as Bolton scored a soft goal in the second minute and led 3-1 after an hour. But Matthews was never a player to stop chasing lost causes. With 22 minutes left he made yet another run down the right wing, looped in a cross that Stan Hanson, the Bolton goalkeeper, fumbled and Stan Mortensen made it 3-2.

Blackpool played like a team possessed and the 100,000 crowd began to sense that the miracle might happen. But time was fast running out as Blackpool searched for the elusive equaliser.

There were only three minutes left when Mudie was fouled just outside the box. Mortensen, with one of the hardest shots in the game, studied the defensive wall, spotted the smallest of gaps and crashed the ball just inside the post to complete his hat-trick.

Now there was only going to be one outcome. As the players lined up for the kick-off Matthews looked at his team and clapped his hands three times. The ball was played out to Matthews and the maestro set off towards the goal, jinking this way and that.

Three Bolton defenders were left standing utterly confused by Matthews' trickery. And although he slipped slightly as he made his final pass into the penalty area the ball was still placed inch-perfect for Bill Perry to score the winning goal from 10 yards.

So dreams could come true after all. And although Mortensen had scored a hat-trick to go with the goals he had got in all the other rounds the final would always be remembered as "the Matthews final".

Crowning glory: Johnston holds the FA Cup aloft but the day belonged to the old maestro Matthews

Finishing touch: Perry latches on to an inch-perfect pass from Matthews for Blackpool's winning goal

Crowds flock to amazing amateur theatricals

THE LITTLE clubs enjoyed another good year in the FA Cup and their standard-bearer was Walthamstow Avenue, who became the first amateur side since Corinthians to reach the fourth round.

Their reward was a trip to Manchester United and thanks to some inspired goalkeeping they only trailed by one goal in the last 15 minutes. Then Trevor Bailey, the England cricketer, was fouled and Walthamstow scored an unexpected equaliser from the free kick. They lost the replay at Highbury 5-2 but the total crowd for the two matches was more than 85,000, earning the club £4,000.

The amateurs of Finchley were also involved in a replay, but in stranger circumstances. Thick fog blanketed their second round match and Crystal Palace had to field two youth

Howzat: Bailey, the Old Trafford hero, was caught out at Highbury

players when two of the first team could not reach the ground because of the weather.

Finchley were leading 3-1

when the match was abandoned after an hour. To prove that was not a fluke they won the replay by exactly the same score.

Busby's babes born in a baptism of fire

MANCHESTER UNITED, like Arsenal, were an ageing team. They started their campaign with the same side that had won the championship, but Matt Busby knew something had to be done.

When United slipped into the First Division basement in October Busby decided the time was right to start blooding his next crop of talent. Duncan Edwards was 15 when he made his debut, David Pegg was 17, Dennis Viollet was 19, Billy

Foulkes was 20. Tommy Taylor, bought from Barnsley for £30,000, was a comparatively "old" 21 but was picked by England within five weeks.

The combination of youth playing alongside experienced men served United well and they recovered to finish in eighth place. The rest of the country could only marvel at how Busby produced such great players, universally known as the Busby Babes before the season was out.

Busby: still ahead

Arsenal sneak home in tight finish

ARSENAL'S final match in the League on the Friday before the Cup final was every bit as dramatic as the events that unfolded at Wembley the next day.

For the second year in a row the First Division was a close-run thing which, in the final months, had four contestants – Arsenal, Burnley, Preston and Wolves. First Burnley then Wolves faded, reducing the field to a two-horse race.

When Preston beat Arsenal the Saturday before and con-

demned Derby to relegation on Wednesday they led the table by two points, with all their matches completed. Arsenal had to beat Burnley in their last match and then goal average would come into play.

Burnley were no pushovers and, in heavy rain, they took the lead at Highbury after eight minutes. Alec Forbes chose the perfect moment to score his first goal of the season for Arsenal and then Doug Lishman and Jimmy Logie put them firmly

on course with a 3-1 lead at half-time.

Arsenal then became complacent and allowed Burnley to cut the deficit. It needed all of Joe Mercer's experience to keep his side calm and stop them conceding another goal.

Arsenal and Preston finished with identical records (21 wins, 12 draws, nine defeats). But Arsenal won the title for a record seventh time by a tenth of a goal – their goal average was 1.51 to Preston's 1.41.

It was an emotional occasion at Highbury when Mercer came out to meet the joyous crowd massed outside the East stand. The man who was always going to play for "just one more season" said that he had finally decided to retire.

SIR STANLEY MATTHEWS
Wondrous winger
with the quicksilver touch

David Hunn

STANLY MATTHEWS and I were at Blackpool together, both claiming space along that right touchline. He was on one side of it in a tangerine shirt, I was on the other in Air Force blue. Every fortnight he seemed to have much less trouble securing his area than I did mine. He played at two speeds, an amble and a flash. The ball was always passed straight to him, and hard. He never wanted to run into space, somebody else might get there first. He wanted the ball at his feet. That way he knew he would beat one man, draw another, leave him and pop the ball over straight on to Stan Mortensen's head.

Matthews was the fastest man in football over 10 yards and those are the yards that matter. But the memory of him is of a meandering man, shorts a bit long and baggy, leaning over the ball as he caressed it up the touchline. The elbows were loose and the feet were pure magic.

Full-backs never knew what to do. Lunge in and you were done for. Matthews was away with the ball, and you never touched him. They would back off and back off, mesmerised, until they had to make a stand. He would show them the ball with one foot and take it away with the other. That body, which had seemed so idle, would shimmy to the left and ghost to the right, leaning so far over he should surely have fallen.

But it was the poor defender who bit the grass, heaving in frustration at a ball that was not there, at feet that had twinkled like stardust down the line. How the crowd loved it and loved Matthews, the greatest pure winger the game has ever seen. When we met for the first time, 46 years later, he was unmistakeable, the frame as spare as ever, his legs still threatening to deceive even as he crossed the road towards me. The same good old Stan, but white-haired now.

Even though he is, and has been for nearly 30 years, Sir Stanley Matthews, CBE, he is still Stan to the man in the street at Stoke. Twice he helped them to the Second Division championship and promotion – twice, 30 years apart. In the end they made him their president and erected a statue to him at Hanley, where he was born over a barber's shop. The statue showed him dribbling – what else – and recently the football was cut off it and stolen. At the Victoria Ground they would tell you that was the only time anybody got the ball off Stanley Matthews.

It takes dedication to be a successful genius.

Running rings round defenders: Matthews skips past Norman, the Tottenham centre-half

STANLEY MATTHEWS

Born February 1, 1915, Hanley, Staffordshire

PLAYING CAREER
Stoke City 1930-47, 1961-65
1930-47 203 pre-war appearances
Guested for Morton, Blackpool and others during the war
23 post-war appearances, 4 goals
1961-65 59 appearances, 3 goals
Played his last game against Fulham on February 6, 1965 and was the oldest player in the First Division at 50 years and 5 days
Honours Second Division: Winners 1933, 1963

Blackpool 1947-1961
379 appearances, 17 goals
Matthews was never booked throughout his entire career
Honours FA Cup: Winners 1953, Finalists 1948, 1951
League Championship: Runners-up 1956
Internationals England debut v Wales 1934
84 appearances (including twice for Great Britain), 11 goals (including goal on debut)

MANAGEMENT CAREER
Port Vale Manager 1965-68
Hibernian Manager 1970

Other career honours Knighted 1965. CBE 1957. European Footballer of the Year 1956. Footballer of the Year 1948, 1963. International Fair Play Committee award for services to sport 1987

Matthews never smoked, never drank, ate salads and fruit, starved on Mondays and still gets up before six every morning to exercise: "It somehow doesn't feel right later than that." At 50 he was as fit as a flea, and there was nothing fitter than his feet. "The Co-Op used to pay me £20 a week to wear their boots, and pretty early on I realised I didn't need these great stiff things with their rigid toecaps. So I went to the factory and got them to take the sole plate out and the toecap off and make me a really soft pair. It was the first time anybody had done that, and they were beautiful. I could fold them up and put them in my pocket. I got them to make me a white pair once, but I never wore them. Too embarrassed."

However many times you read the Matthews record, there seems little possibility that it can be true. He joined the Stoke ground staff at 15 on £1 a week, played his first Football League match for them six weeks after his seventeenth birthday and his last five days after his fiftieth. When he was 32 he began his 14 years with Blackpool, during which they reached three FA Cup finals. They won the last, in 1953 against Bolton, the match that the British football world will ever remember as the "Stanley Matthews Cup Final".

Blackpool were 3-1 down with 20 minutes to play; 3-2 down with three minutes left (a Matthews centre to Mortensen); and 3-3 (Mortensen's third) with less than one minute of injury time to the whistle. The ball went to Matthews on the wing. He beat the full-back and raced for the goalline. The Bolton centre-half abandoned his hope of halting him to cover Mortensen in the centre. Stan pulled the ball back behind Mort towards the penalty spot. Perry, the left wing, was there: 4-3 and delirium.

For England there were 84 internationals between 1934, when he was 19, and 1957, when

Still going strong: Matthews at 48

he was 42. You might think he was way past his best by then, but when he was two months short of his fortieth birthday West Germany came to Wembley and Matthews destroyed the left-back. Of that match the Daily Telegraph reporter wrote: "Through the changing scenes of international football, the genius of Stanley Matthews remains a radiant beacon. He won this match for England just as nearly 20 years ago he inspired the 3-0 defeat of Germany at Tottenham."

In the Mirror, Matthews was "immense, indescribable"; and in The Times "... a tour de force by the greatest player in football". Three months later he set up (according to Nat Lofthouse, the centre-forward) all seven goals that England scored against Scotland. The left-back that day, poor man, was Harry Haddock, aged 25. In David Miller's biography of Matthews, Haddock

vividly recreated the humiliations of that and many another day.

"He'd walk towards you with the ball on his right foot, feint to his left, and you'd go with him to your right. He'd touch the ball the other way, and be gone. You'd see it, and could do nothing. I knew that's what he'd do, and I wanted him to do it, because I thought I had the speed to stay with him. But he lost me."

Losing left-backs was Stanley's favourite pastime. He did it for 30 years on just about every ground he played. Football fans knew he was going to do it, and wherever he went they went too. In 1934 Stoke drew an average of more than 66,000 to six consecutive matches. It was small wonder that even at the age of 46, when he was slowing down a bit too much for First Division Blackpool, Stoke were glad to have him back.

In 1961 they had to pay Blackpool £3,500 for the privilege and they offered Matthews the highest wage he had ever known: £50 a week plus a £25 match fee. The week before his return, Stoke's home gate was 8,409. Two weeks later, with Matthews on the wing against Huddersfield (left-back, England's Ray Wilson) it was 35,288. "People told me I should have asked for £100," Matthews said. "But the money doesn't make you play better, does it? I was happy there. They were nice people. I had a lot of friends, thousands of them, on the other side of the touchline." In 1963 Stoke clinched promotion to the First Division once more. Matthews had played in 35 of their 42 matches, and he was 48 years old.

He never read the biography quoted above, excellent though it was. "I read the first page and to tell you the truth, David, I was embarrassed. I can't take people going on about how good I was. You just do your best, don't you?"

His genius was a "radiant beacon" for England

Wembley wizard: Matthews crosses for Perry to score the winning goal in the 1953 Cup final

THE 1953-54 SEASON

Joy at last for Cullis

ALL THE hard work that Stan Cullis had put in at Wolverhampton was repaid when his team won the League championship for the first time. The triumph was especially sweet because Cullis had suffered two great disappointments as a Wolves player – losing the 1939 FA Cup final and missing out on the championship in the 1946-47 season in his last match before he retired.

When Cullis took over as manager he continued the regime introduced by Major Frank Buckley, hard work in training, strict discipline at the club and all-out attack on the field. Wolves's critics argued that their reliance on long passes was no more than a glorified form of kick and rush. But Cullis argued that he was using basically the same approach as the mighty Hungarians, and the quicker and more often the ball was in the opponents' penalty area the more likely his team was to score.

Cullis used scientific research by Wing-commander Charles Reep to support his theory, and he silenced his critics when Wolves won the title by four points from West Bromwich, scoring 96 goals in the process.

Cullis: hard work pays off

Hungary hit England for six...

Taken apart 1: Grosics saves from Mortensen as the Mighty Magyars demolish England

IT HAD to happen sooner or later, but nobody could ever have been prepared for the scale of England's first home defeat by continental opposition. There had been enough warning signs in the past few years but hardly anybody was prepared to accept that England no longer ruled the world.

Until, that is, the fateful November afternoon when the Hungarian team, the 1952 Olympic champions and unbeaten in more than 20 matches, came to Wembley. It was not a case of England playing badly – by their standards they performed well. Ferenc Puskas and his Mighty Magyars were simply in a different class.

Hungary needed a mere 60 seconds to take the lead. Nandor Hidegkuti drew the defence out of position with a body swerve and swept a 20-yard shot through the gap and past the bewitched Gil Merrick.

The rest of the match followed the same pattern. England were out-played, out-passed and out-thought by a heady mixture of individual flair and clever teamwork. Hungary simply ran rings round a flat-footed and bemused England team.

Yesterday the inevitable happened. England at last were beaten by the foreign invader

THE TIMES

England were given a faint glimmer of hope when Jackie Sewell scored an equaliser after 15 minutes, but then they were destroyed in a breathtaking seven-minute spell. Hidegkuti scored again from close range, Puskas breezed past Billy Wright with brilliant trickery for the third goal and also scored the fourth from a free-kick.

Stan Mortensen brought the score back to 4-2 at half-time, but for every goal England got the Hungarians created two. First Bozsik struck, then Hidegkuti completed his hat-trick. Mercifully, the Hungarians eased up towards the end of the match and England added a third goal with a penalty from Alf Ramsey.

The headlines the next day said it all: "The New Wembley Wizards"; "Now It's Back To School For England – With Hungary The Soccer Masters" and "Make 'em Run – We Couldn't".

Worlds apart: Hungary ran England ragged at Wembley

. . . and then give them another painful lesson

ENGLAND had six months to reflect on the lessons they had been taught at Wembley before they went to Budapest to play Hungary again. At least, given the partisan attitudes displayed by some commentators, nobody tried to claim that the Wembley result was a fluke. The debate was whether English football had gone backwards or European football had progressed.

The England selectors had no real answer to the question other than to make seven changes to the team. They admitted that it was an experimental side, chosen to see if there was a better way of countering the Hungarians.

The answer, emphatically, was no. It soon became clear that nobody in England was a match for the Hungarians, and England were not going span the gulf in skills in such a short time.

This time they went down 7-1 in the People's Stadium, England's heaviest defeat ever. Hungary fielded 10 of the 11 players that had tormented England at Wembley and this time the torture was even worse. The Hungarians did not ease up late in the match and Puskas and company showed that they could turn on the style at will and there was nothing England could do about it.

Taken apart 2: England had no answers in Budapest

■ Alf Ramsey scored a penalty in the last minute to spare England's blushes as they came back from 3-1 down to salvage a 4-4 draw with the Rest of Europe in a match at Wembley as part of the FA's 90th anniversary celebrations.

■ Arsenal, despite saving a penalty in the second minute and then taking the lead, were beaten 2-1 at Highbury by Third Division Norwich in the fourth round of the FA Cup.

■ Arsenal signed the 34-year-old Tommy Lawton from Brentford to bolster their team and to coach their younger players.

■ Sam Bartram set a League record when he made his 500th appearance for Charlton on March 6.

■ Wolves beat Racing Club of Buenos Aires 3-1 in a friendly at Molineux in March.

■ Jimmy Delaney collected his third Cup-winners' medal in different countries with Derry City. He had already won the Scottish Cup with Celtic in 1937 and the FA Cup with Manchester United in 1948.

■ Uefa was formed at a meeting during the World Cup finals in Switzerland.

■ Scot Symon, the former East Fife manager who had guided Preston to the FA Cup final, took over as the manager of Rangers from Bill Struth in June. Symon, who had represented Scotland at football and cricket, was brought in to rebuild the club.

Unstoppable Port Vale take the League and Cup by storm

FORGET the wonderful Wolves, the team of the Midlands was surely Port Vale. They reached the semi-finals of the FA Cup, where they lost to West Bromwich Albion the eventual winners, and won the Third Division North championship by a street. Their Cup exploits meant they were the first Third Division side since the war to reach the semi-finals.

But in the League they were virtually unstoppable. They were the only team in all four divisions to be unbeaten at home; they lost a mere three matches away; they conceded a record low of only 21 goals in their 46 League matches while putting 74 past their opponents, and romped away with the championship 11 points clear of their nearest rivals.

Stein comes from nowhere to work wonders

CELTIC, who had not won the championship since 1938 and had won the Scottish Cup only once since that, ended their barren period by walking off with the Double. Even more remarkable was that the architect of their triumph was a veteran has-been, Jock Stein.

Stein, who had been the captain of Albion Rovers during their brief foray in the First Division in 1948-49, had been plucked from the obscurity of the Welsh non-League club Llanelli in December 1951 as a 29-year-old veteran. Celtic had recruited the solid, but slow centre-half simply to bolster the

reserve team and steady Celtic's youngsters. However a string of injuries accidentally propelled the bulky defender into the first team within two months.

Stein soon made the centre-half's position his own. Then when Sean Fallon, the captain, broke his arm Stein took his place. The promotion transformed Celtic. Stein was a born leader and his acute footballing brain soon became apparent both on and off the field. Celtic, who had finished eighth the previous season, made a dramatic charge on the championship and won 20 of their 30 League fixtures to capture the title, five

points clear of Hearts.

In the Scottish Cup Stein's rejuvenated side won a series of away ties, overcame Motherwell in the semi-final after a replay and faced Aberdeen, who had narrowly lost the Cup to Rangers the year before, in the final. Aberdeen gave away an unfortunate own goal shortly after the interval but equalised within a minute.

However, in the 63rd minute, Willie Fernie, one of Scotland's trickiest ball-players, set off on a mazy run that mesmerised the Aberdeen defence. So much so that Fallon, centre-forward for the day, was left unmarked.

Fernie slipped him the ball and Stein's miraculous rise from the depths of the Welsh valleys to the heights of the Double was complete.

Stein: born leader

23

THAT HUNGARY, unquestionably the greatest team in the world, lost the 1954 World Cup final was an even greater shock than Brazil losing to Uruguay four years earlier. Hungary, with Ferenc Puskas, Nandor Hidegkuti, Josef Bozsik, Sandor Kocsis and Zoltan Czibor, were a blend of artistry, intelligence and athleticism that neither Europe nor the world had ever seen. "The Magnificent Magyars" – as the British press dubbed them after their 6-3 and 7-1 drubbings of England in 1953 and 1954 – lost only one match between 1950 and 1956: the World Cup final in Switzerland. How they lost could be put down to two factors: the loopholes in the new structure that was introduced for the finals, and the utter cynicism of the West Germans who were eventually to triumph in the final.

The structures of the final stages of the past four World Cups had been deeply flawed (from straight knock-out to a simple League system without a designated final). On the face of it, the formula for the 1954 tournament ironed out many of the problems. Sixteen teams would qualify for the finals, they would be divided into four groups of four out of which eight teams would qualify for a straight knock-out tournament. This would be the structure for the next four World Cups.

However, in Switzerland, there was a bizarre bias added. In each group two teams would be seeded, and they would only play the unseeded teams. So each team only played two games not three, and the strongest only played the weakest. The formula was open to wicked exploitation.

West Germany were drawn against Hungary, Turkey and South Korea in group two with Hungary and, strangely, Turkey – who surprisingly had eliminated Spain in the qualifiers – as the the two seeds. West Germany's first match was against Turkey, a simple 4-1 runout. Their second was against Hungary. And now the devilry began.

The West Germans calculated that by losing to Hungary and then beating Turkey in the resultant play-off they could then avoid Brazil, one of the favourites, in the quarter-finals. They duly subsided 8-3 with virtually a reserve side. But worse than that, Puskas, Hungary's star player, was crocked in the process when he was deliberately

WORLD CUP 1954
Hungary fail the ultimate test

Battered into submission: Hungary's Magnificent Magyars (top) suffered at the hands of a cynical West German team

kicked on the ankle by the West German centre-half Werner Liebrich, and did not play again until the World Cup final. For the play-off against Turkey, the Germans made seven team changes and won 7-1.

But before the Germans and the Hungarians could meet in the final there were several strong, and talented teams, to overcome. Not least Uruguay, the holders and a country that had never lost a game in the World Cup. They had reached the

quarter-finals by humiliating Scotland 7-0 and then completed a British double by knocking out England 4-2. Gil Merrick, England's goalkeeper, should have saved at least two of the the Uruguayan goals but despite the skills in defence of Billy Wright, and in attack of Stanley Matthews, the Uruguayans prevailed to meet Hungary in the semi-finals. But only after Hungary had won the brutal "Battle of Berne" against Brazil.

That it became a match largely remembered for its physical side was a terrible indictment of two sides more renowned for their skills on the ball than their fouls off it. History has laid the principal blame at Brazil's door, not that the Hungarians – nor indeed Puskas, who wasn't even playing – were exactly innocent parties.

Hungary had begun in their usual madcap way and were two goals up in seven minutes. But a series of niggling fouls from the Hungarians disturbed the volatile South Americans and the rot began to set in. Then two penalties, the first for Brazil in the 18th minute, then one for Hungary in the 54th made the score 3-1.

With 24 minutes left Brazil made it 3-2 and were in the hunt. Within minutes, Bozsik and Nilton Santos were at each other's throats and both were sent off. Vicious tackling became the hallmark of the match. By the end, Hungary had a fourth goal in the 89th minute and another player was sent off, Humbert Tozzi of Brazil. There was an after-match brawl in which it was alleged that Puskas, only a spectator, had struck Pinheiro, the Brazilian centre-half, in the face with a bottle after the Brazilians had invaded the Hungarian dressing-room. Whatever the truth, Pinheiro left the ground with a bandaged five-inch head wound.

The quarter-final between Austria and Switzerland, the hosts, was just as extraordinary – but this time for the right reasons. It had been an extremely high-scoring tournament (by the finish 140 goals would have been scored in a mere 26 games) but the match in Lausanne took the biscuit. Austria were losing 3-0 after 23 minutes. Ten minutes later they were up 5-3. By half-time they were 5-4 in the lead, having missed a penalty. They were eventually 7-5 winners, with all 12 goals coming in the space of only 49 minutes of playing time.

Then in the semi-finals Austria, who were playing a West Germany that had out-muscled a delightful Yugoslavian side 2-0 in the quarter-final, simply collapsed. The Austrians were one of the most sublimely equipped teams in Europe and should, on paper, have beaten the nation that had so rudely taken them over in the Anschluss, yet they were swept aside 6-1 with their goalkeeper, Walter Zeman, making a string of disastrous errors. Zeman, who had been dropped because he was out of form, had been restored to the team only for this match.

By contrast the other semi-final, Hungary v Uruguay, was one of the most keenly contested matches ever witnessed in the World Cup finals, and some people have called it the finest game of football ever played. It pitted the best in the world (Hungary) against the twice world champions (Uruguay). Both sides were at their brilliant, mercurial best and the match swung like a pendulum.

Hungary went 2-0 up, but by full-time Uruguay, with Juan Schiaffino in scintillating form, had levelled the scores. But then a tiring Uruguay fell to the genius of Kocsis, who scored twice, and were eliminated 4-2. "We beat the best team we have ever met," Gyula Mandi, the Hungarian manager, said.

Now they were to be beaten by an inferior side, West Germany. But for the first 10 minutes of the World Cup final no bookmaker in the world would have thought it. In their inimitable fashion the Hungarians were 2-0 up within eight minutes despite the pouring rain. A predictable rout was on the cards.

But Hungary were vulnerable. Puskas, still suffering from the ankle injury he had received against the Germans in the early matches, had insisted on playing. Sadly the great player, despite scoring the opening goal, inevitably turned out to be a liability. Within eight minutes the West Germans had equalised and, with Puskas unbalancing the side, they scented an unprecedented triumph despite the Hungarians relentlessly attacking their goal.

Helmut Rahn and Toni Turek, the goalkeeper, were the West German heroes on the day. Turek, and the post, made save after save as the Hungarian forward line pounded them. Rahn, who had scored the equaliser in the 16th minute, then found himself in front of four defenders with seven minutes remaining. He went straight for goal and shot perfectly past Grosics into the corner for the winning goal.

Two minutes later Puskas thought he had equalised but the goal was dubiously ruled offside. Then Czibor fired a brilliant shot that Turek miraculously leaped to punch away. It was over, and the best team in the world had lost.

Hard times: England suffered from poor goalkeeping against Uruguay in the quarter-finals: Puskas suffered in the first round and was a shadow of his normal self in the final, allowing Walter, the West German captain, to collect the trophy

FOR THE RECORD

FIRST ROUND

POOL ONE	P	W	D	L	F	A	Pts
Brazil	2	1	1	0	6	1	3
Yugoslavia	2	1	1	0	2	1	3
France	2	1	0	1	3	3	2
Mexico	2	0	0	2	2	8	0

POOL TWO	P	W	D	L	F	A	Pts
Hungary	2	2	0	0	17	3	4
Turkey	2	1	0	1	8	4	2
W Germany	2	1	0	1	7	9	2
South Korea	2	0	0	2	0	16	0

Play off: Germany 7 Turkey 2
HT 3-1

POOL THREE	P	W	D	L	F	A	Pts
Uruguay	2	2	0	0	9	0	4
Austria	2	2	0	0	6	0	4
Czech.	2	0	0	2	0	7	0
Sweden	2	0	0	2	0	8	0

POOL FOUR	P	W	D	L	F	A	Pts
England	2	1	1	0	6	4	3
Italy	2	1	0	1	5	3	2
Switzerland	2	1	0	1	2	3	2
Belgium	2	0	1	1	5	8	1

Play off: Switzerland 4 Italy 1
HT 1-0

QUARTER-FINALS

West Germany 2 Yugoslavia 0
HT 1-0 Att. 17,000
Hungary 4 Brazil 2
HT 2-1 Att. 40,000
Austria 7 Switzerland 5
HT 5-4 Att. 29,000
Uruguay 4 England 2
HT 2-1 Att. 50,000

SEMI-FINALS

Hungary 4 Uruguay 2 aet
HT 1-0 Att. 37,000
West Germany 6 Austria 1
HT 1-0 Att. 58,000

THIRD PLACE PLAY-OFF

Austria 3 Uruguay 1
HT 1-1 Att. 31,000

FINAL

West Germany 3 Hungary 2
HT 2-2 Att. 60,000

Teams

West Germany Turek; Posipal, Kohlmeyer, Eckel, Liebrich, Mai, Rahn, Morlock, O. Walter, F. Walter, Schäfer
Hungary Grosics; Buzanszky, Lantos, Bozsik, Lorant, Zakarias, Czibor, Kocsis, Hidegkuti, Puskas, Toth

Leading goalscorers 11 Kocsis (Hungary); 6 Morlock (West Germany), Hugi (Switzerland); 5 Probst (Austria)
Total goals scored 140
Average per game: 5.38
Sendings-off Bozsik (Hungary) v Brazil, Santos (Brazil) v Hungary, Tozzi (Brazil) v Hungary; Referee: Arthur Ellis (England)
Number of players used by finalists 18 West Germany; 15 Hungary

THE
1954-55
SEASON

Reshuffled Celtic let lucky Clyde off the hook

CLYDE'S first triumph in the Scottish Cup final since 1939 was somewhat fortuitous. Trailing 1-0 to Celtic, to a goal scored by Walsh in the 38th minute, the little team from the East End of Glasgow squeezed an equaliser from Robertson with three minutes remaining. Thus, despite being outplayed by their illustrious rivals, Clyde had narrowly forced a replay.

The Celtic directors did not see it that way and foolishly decided to reshape the team, dropping the bustling Collins and disorientating the forward line by playing Fallon, a full back, at centre-forward. Wisely, Clyde stuck to the same 11 players.

Celtic's makeshift attack hardly bothered the Clyde defence, enabling Clyde to push men forward in numbers. The winning goal came in the 52nd minute from Clyde's left winger, Ring, and the team that had swept to the Double so brilliantly the previous season never looked like scoring an equaliser, and finished the season empty-handed.

With Aberdeen winning the championship and Hearts the Scottish League Cup, the two Old Firm clubs were left with nothing to show for their efforts. The best they could manage were the minor places in the League, Celtic finishing second, three points behind Aberdeen, and Rangers third, a further five points adrift. This was only the second season in history (the other was 1951-52) that neither Rangers nor Celtic had won a major trophy.

Whirlwind Wolves

World beater: Hancocks scored against Spartak and Honved

WOLVERHAMPTON proved that they had become a formidable team with two remarkable results against top European sides. Their series of friendlies against foreign opposition started in October, when First Vienna were lucky to get a draw at Molineux. A fortnight later Maccabi Tel Aviv found themselves thumped 10-0.

Floodlit matches against foreign teams were becoming the vogue and no game was more eagerly anticipated than the visit of Moscow Spartak in November. Spartak had already scored five goals against Arsenal in Moscow, and had just won the return fixture 2-1 at Highbury.

With fog swirling around a ground packed to the rafters there was no score for nearly an hour until Dennis Wilshaw gave Wolves the lead. But the final minutes of the match were electrifying. Johnny Hancocks put Wolves further ahead then, straight from the kick-off, Roy Swinbourne weaved through the entire Spartak team to score Wolves's third.

No sooner had the match restarted then the ball was in the net again, but Hancocks's effort was disallowed. Not to be deterred, he got Wolves's fourth goal less than a minute later. In little more than three minutes

Spartak had been torn apart in what one commentator described as "our greatest post-war victory."

But there was better still to come. A month later Wolves took on Honved, who had the incomparable Ferenc Puskas and several other members of the Hungarian national side in their ranks. Wolves trailed 2-0 at half-time and it looked as if the "Mighty Magyars" were about to teach English football another lesson.

Wolves were transformed by a stern lecture by Stan Cullis, their manager, at half-time and a switch in tactics. Cullis had noticed that the Hungarian team had a very square defence so he instructed his players to hit their long passes even longer.

With their wingers getting behind the Honved defence Wolves came storming back with a penalty from Hancocks and two goals in two minutes from Swinbourne. "Wolves the great!" the newspaper headline said the next day, and all the writers agreed that their victory was even better than the demolition of Spartak.

For Cullis, it was a vindication of his methods and he proudly boasted that Wolves were now the unofficial champions of the world, a claim that was to have far-reaching consequences.

Revie and Matthews rout Scots

SCOTLAND thought that they were the best team in Britain because they had only lost 4-2 to Hungary. Compared with England's suffering the previous season they regarded that as a moral victory. But when they came to Wembley for the Home international championships they received a rude awakening.

Duncan Edwards became the youngest player to represent England, making his debut at the age of 18, but the star of the show was the old man of the England team, Stanley Matthews.

Matthews was 40, but age had not blunted his skills. In tandem with Don Revie he simply shredded Scotland. England scored twice in under 10 minutes and the final tally was four goals for Dennis Wilshaw, two for Nat Lofthouse and one for Revie. Scotland were lucky that the 7-2 score did not reach double figures, because several other chances were missed.

Matthews left the pitch with the crowd's cheers ringing in his ears while Scotland slunk away knowing that they had suffered their worst ever defeat in the Home internationals. So much for them thinking that they were the best in Britain.

Matthews: still going strong

Newcastle's record run

Winning habit: Newcastle rewrote the FA Cup record books

NEWCASTLE blazed into the record books when they beat Manchester City 3-1 in the FA Cup final. They became the first team to win the Cup three times in five seasons; their sixth victory meant they equalled the Cup-winning records of Blackburn Rovers and Aston Villa and they were the first club to compete in 10 Cup finals. To cap it all their first goal, scored by Jackie Milburn in 45 seconds, was the fastest at Wembley.

Unfortunately their victory was soured by an injury to Manchester City's right-back Jimmy Meadows, who had to be taken off with badly wrenched ligaments of the knee and lower leg in the 18th minute leaving City with only 10 men. Ironically Meadows, injured himself yards from where Arsenal's Wally Barnes had suffered the same fate – in the same minute – in Newcastle's last Cup triumph, the 1952 final. And who were they both trying to tackle? The elusive Bobby Mitchell.

Mitchell proceeded to torment Billy Spurdle, who had been moved from the right wing into Meadows's position. In the second half – Bobby Johnstone having headed an equaliser a minute before the interval – Mitchell wrapped up the match for Newcastle.

In the 53rd minute, he latched on to a pass from White, left Spurdle for dead and virtually on the byeline, just as Traut-

mann was expecting a cross, the left-winger slotted the ball between the goalkeeper and the post. Seven minutes later Jimmy Scoular found Mitchell with a long pass over Spurdle's head. The left-winger placed the ball perfectly for George Hannah to give Trautmann no chance from 12 yards.

The advantage of playing against 10 men had virtually been cancelled out in the second half as both Milburn and Len White were clearly injured and continued only half-fit. Nonetheless, Newcastle were convincing winners, particularly given the battles they had endured getting to Wembley.

In the fifth round it had taken two replays to overcome Nottingham Forest; in the sixth round, a replay was required to dispatch Huddersfield and in the semi-final they came close to being embarrassed by York City. The Third Division club had been the revelation of the season, eliminating Blackpool and Spurs.

In the semi-final at Hillsborough they had the gall to go 1-0 up with a goal from Arthur Bottom until Vic Keeble forced another replay. Even then, at Roker Park, York battled away and Newcastle were mightily relieved not to go down in history as the side that allowed the first Third Division side to reach a Cup final. That was one record they didn't want.

Keeping it in the family: Len and Ivor Allchurch

Double act: John and Mel Charles also played for Wales

THE 1955-56 SEASON

Heroic Trautmann wins the Cup despite a broken neck

Walking wounded: Trautmann (right) did not discover his neck was broken until three days later

Brazil dazzled by Matthews

THERE WAS no stopping Stanley Matthews. He was the creator of almost all of England's attacks as Brazil were outshone under the Wembley floodlights.

Matthews's talents were more than a match for the Brazilians' skills and England led 2-0 after five minutes. But any ideas of a rout were dispelled when Brazil equalised in the second half. England finally ran out 4-2 winners, with Matthews creating three of the goals, but, amazingly they failed to score two penalties.

One produced a comic interlude. A Brazilian player, unhappy at the referee's decision, picked up the ball and marched off. He was chased by the referee who, in turn, was pursued by several other members of the Brazilian team, with Billy Wright, the England captain, following along behind. The crowd thought the game of "follow the leader" was hilarious.

One England player who followed Matthews's footsteps was Duncan Edwards. The youngster, fresh from Manchester United's triumph in the championship, gave a stirring performance during England's summer tour.

England were being run ragged by West Germany at the start of their match in Berlin. Edwards collected the ball in the heart of defence and set off on a storming run upfield. He swept imperiously past tackle after tackle before scoring with a thunderous 25-yard drive. The power of the shot so amazed the spectators that they started calling Edwards "Boom Boom".

The goal turned the tide in the match. Goals from Colin Grainger and Johnny Haynes gave England a 3-1 victory.

ALTHOUGH it was Don Revie's scheming brilliance that brought the FA Cup to Manchester City the year after their disappointment against Newcastle, the hero of the match was surely Bert Trautmann, City's blond German goalkeeper, and Footballer of the Year.

Twice Trautmann dived at the feet of onrushing forwards and twice he was injured. When he flung himself at Peter Murphy he received terrible blows on his head and neck and was knocked cold. Somehow he instinctively stopped the ball. Five minutes later he was in another collision, but he still got up to soldier on for the last 15 minutes of the match. The full extent of the former PoW's bravery was not known until three days later when, after complaining of recurring headaches, a second set of X-rays revealed that he had played on with a broken neck. Amazingly, the injury did not end Trautmann's career, and he returned to the team just before Christmas.

But if Trautmann should have sensibly left the field, half of Manchester believed Revie, who was playing only his second Cup game, should never have been on it at all. Revie had been in dispute with the club for much of the season and was only brought into the side on the eve of the match as City's manager, Les McDowall, reshuffled his forward line.

Revie had perfected the art of the deep-lying centre-forward, a strategy he had adopted from Ferenc Puskas, and it proved to be the undoing of Birmingham City, red-hot favourites to win the Cup. His impact was immediate. After three minutes Revie passed the ball from the half-way line to Roy Clarke on the left wing, raced to meet the return and cheekily backheeled the ball for Joe Hayes to score.

Birmingham's equaliser, after 15 minutes from Noel Kinsey, was never going to stop Revie's men. In five minutes in the second half they waltzed off with the Cup. Now the architect was the Scottish international Bobby Johnstone, another controversial selection because he was carrying an injury and playing out of position.

He started the move that led to Ken Dyson's 65th minute goal and, five minutes later, Johnstone raced from the wing to collect Dyson's through ball and fire the ball past Gil Merrick, to become the first man to score in successive Cup finals.

Chelsea denied a place in Europe

THE IDEA of staging a European Cup had been doing the rounds since the mid-1920s but the proposals had always received short shrift until Stan Cullis's boast that his Wolverhampton team were the best in the world stung the rest of Europe into action.

L'Equipe, the French sports newspaper, responded by inviting what they regarded as the top 18 clubs in Europe to a meeting in Paris. Sixteen teams attended, including Chelsea, the English League champions, and Hibs, who were regarded as having a better record in the past few season than Aberdeen, the Scottish champions.

The 16 readily agreed to a European Cup played on a home and away basis, and the tournament was sanctioned by Fifa on May 8, 1955, the tenth anniversary of VE Day. Fifa only imposed one restriction on the tournament, that all the entrants had to be approved by their national associations.

That ruling cost Chelsea their place. Although Chelsea were drawn against Djurgaarden of Stockholm they needed permission to play from the Football League. English football still had a very insular attitude to Europe, and the League's man-

Start of an era: Real Madrid win the first European Cup in Paris

agement committee decided to ask Chelsea to "reconsider" because the extra fixtures might be difficult to fulfil. Chelsea took the far from subtle hint and withdrew.

The Scottish authorities, with much more vision, allowed Hibs to take part. They beat Rot Weiss Essen 5-1 on aggregate in the first round, Djurgaarden 3-1 and 1-0 in the second round, but lost 3-0 overall to Rheims in the semi-final. The "extra" matches did not create any fixture congestion and left Hibs with a £25,000 profit.

The final, in Paris, was a sell-out and the crowd got their

money's worth. Rheims were two goals up against Real Madrid in little more than 10 minutes. But Real Madrid, for whom Alfredo di Stefano seemed to be able elude defenders at will, equalised after half an hour.

Rheims led again in the second half but Real Madrid were back on terms within five minutes. With di Stefano seemingly everywhere they scored the decisive goal in the 79th minute. Di Stefano had engineered all four goals in what was a great finish to what was going to turn out to be Europe's most prestigious competition.

Busby's Babes quickly come of age

MANCHESTER UNITED's fourth League championship began with a stuttering start but was eventually won at a canter. By November, United had lost four games, largely because of the absence of a settled side, but once Matt Busby found the right balance the side clicked into title form. They lost only three more League matches and were unbeaten at home with 18 wins and three draws to take the title by 11 points from Blackpool.

Ominously for the rest of the First Division – propitiously for United – the average age of the side was 23, one of the most youthful championship-winning sides in League history. Although United had last won

One of the secrets of Manchester United's success is that nearly all of us grew up together as boy footballers. The Manchester United way is the only way we know

ROGER BYRNE

Byrne: second championship

the title four years earlier, only two players, Roger Byrne and Johnny Berry, survived from that side. The rest, apart from three who were purchased from other clubs, were home-grown talent. Busby's Babes had quickly grown into a team to be reckoned with.

Falkirk spoil the party for Kilmarnock

FALKIRK, who had spent all season battling against relegation, stunned all of Scotland when they won the Scottish Cup for the second time in their history. Indeed, on the eve of the final it was still touch and go whether they would end up in the Second Division.

Managed by Reggie Smith, a Londoner who had played for Millwall, Falkirk were a bunch of misfits he had to knock into shape. While he was moderately successful in the League, inexplicably Falkirk were unstoppable in the Cup, knocking out Aberdeen, Clyde who were in blistering form in the Second Division, and Raith Rovers who finished fourth in the First Division, en route to Hampden.

Kilmarnock, their opponents in the final, were overwhelming favourites and had already laid on the civic reception to celebrate their triumph but, on the day, they seemed to panic. Toner, their centre-half, gave away a penalty in the 32nd minute and Prentice, the Falkirk captain, converted. Seconds before the interval Kilmarnock equalised with Curtlett heading in from a free kick. The second half was a goalless, mundane affair and Kilmarnock's celebrations were put on ice.

By contrast the replay was full of flowing football. Falkirk scored first in the 24th minute with Merchant heading in Murray's cross, but after fierce pressure in the second half Curtlett levelled the scores. In extra time, the favourites finally fell when Moran flicked a bouncing ball into the Kilmarnock goal.

Busby defies the League to enjoy a European adventure

Facing the challenge: Byrne and Busby with a memento from their match in Madrid

MANCHESTER UNITED as the League champions, were entitled to enter the fledgling European Cup and the club's board of directors unanimously accepted the FA's invitation to take part.

Matt Busby, the United manager, was keen to test his team. He thought that his young players would benefit from the experience, and that England had a lot to learn from Europe.

The Football League thought otherwise. As they had done with Chelsea last season, they tried to dissuade United. "United's participation was not in the best interests of the League," they wrote. But United refused to be bullied and Busby said: "Prestige alone demanded that the Continental challenge should be met, not avoided."

After winning 2-0 in Belgium, United had to play the return leg against Anderlecht at Maine Road because Old Trafford did not yet have floodlights. Manchester City scoffed and said

> *Some people called me a visionary, others a reactionary, while a few called me awkward or stubborn*
>
> MATT BUSBY

they did not expect more than 10,000 people to attend.

In fact, the crowd was more than 40,000 and they saw United record their biggest ever victory. United led 5-0 at half-time and kept going; Dennis Viollet scored four goals, Tommy Taylor got a hat-trick, Billy Whelan two and Johnny Berry one. When the score reached 10-0 United spent the rest of the match trying and failing to engineer a goal for David Pegg, who had created five chances for his colleagues and was the only United forward not to score.

After beating Borussia Dortmund 3-2 on aggregate in the next round, all the goals coming at Maine Road, United had a

real adventure in the quarter-finals.

Their flight to Bilbao was plagued by heavy snow and the plane had to land in a deserted field. Then, after losing 5-3, the United players had to help shovel the snow off the runway before the plane could return home. Undeterred, United made up the deficit at Maine Road and won 6-5 on aggregate.

Their reward was yet another trip to Spain in the semi-final. Again they returned home two goals adrift. But this time, with the prospect of an unbelievable treble on the horizon, they could only draw 2-2 with Alfredo di Stefano's Real Madrid at Old Trafford, where the floodlights had finally been installed, and were eliminated 5-3 on aggregate.

Busby was honest enough to admit that: "A great experienced side will always triumph over a great inexperienced side." But there was no doubt that United's exploits had captured the public's imagination.

Jinx dashes United's Double hopes

THE WEMBLEY jinx struck again, but this time not only did it deprive Manchester United of the FA Cup it also destroyed their ambitions of being the first club this century to win the Double. For the third time in five years a serious injury to a player had effectively reduced one team to 10 men and turned English football's most prestigious occasion into a farce.

This time it was Manchester United's goalkeeper, Ray Wood, who was laid low six minutes after the final had started by a foul challenge by Peter McParland. Four yards from the goal, Aston Villa's Irish international winger crashed into a stationary Wood, who had just collected McParland's header. Wood was taken off with a fractured cheek-bone, though he did return in the 33rd minute to limp along the right wing.

Jackie Blanchflower replaced him in goal with Duncan Edwards moving to centre-half and Frank Whelan, United's leading goalscorer, to left half. But although this makeshift United held out for nearly an hour, McParland was the man who once again did the damage scoring twice, in the 65th and 71st minutes.

When Tommy Taylor headed home Edwards's corner with seven minutes remaining, Roger Byrne, the United skipper, gambled everything on forcing a replay and Wood returned to play in goal. Now every Villa player was behind the ball, but United just could not find the crucial equaliser.

So Villa preserved their record as being the last club to win the Double, in 1897, and

Wood: fractured cheek-bone

broke another by winning the FA Cup for the seventh time. However it was a hollow victory and a hollow record. Amazingly the FA had discussed the use of substitutes 24 hours before the final and rejected the idea.

Charles seeks his fortune in Italy

Record-breaker: Juventus doubled the British transfer record to sign Charles from Leeds

SHOCK WAVES went through English football in April when Juventus, the extremely wealthy Italian club, purchased John Charles from Leeds United for £70,000, more than doubling the British transfer record. Charles was paid a £10,000 signing-on fee and £60 a week basic wages, four times the maximum permitted in England. Did this mean that there would be an exodus of stars to the Continent, or would players' wage demands in the Football League spiral out of hand?

Charles, a Welsh international, was an extremely popular and successful centre-forward with Leeds, where he had scored 151 goals in 297 games. In Italy he was equally successful and won three championships and two Italian Cups with Juventus. Charles, dubbed the Gentle Giant by his adoring Italian fans, was also versatile: during his career in Italy he showed he could equally well play as a centre-half.

WOLVES IN THE 1950s
The team that dominated a decade

James Wilson

SENTIMENT, 40 years on, should not blind one to how completely Wolves dominated their era and what a consistently great side they were. Three times within the decade they won the League, three times they were runners-up, and twice they won the FA Cup.

They had strong opposition as well: Manchester United, Manchester City, Arsenal, Chelsea, Tottenham, Blackpool and Burnley all had simultaneously memorable teams. So, too, in those days when the maximum wage still ruled, did Bolton and Wolves's local rivals West Bromwich Albion. If Everton and Liverpool were below their subsequent standards, Portsmouth and Newcastle United, three times the FA Cup winners in five seasons, more than made up for any temporary deficiencies on Merseyside. It was a period when the available talent was widely spread, which makes the Wolverhampton dominance even more remarkable.

The seeds of this greatness were sown in the late 1930s under a strong manager, Frank Buckley, who, skilfully trading in the transfer market, developed a homespun side at Molineux which, but for the war, might have become as dominant as the Wolves of the 1950s. Buckley was one of the first managers to appreciate the value of publicity. When he introduced injections for the Molineux playing staff the press maintained that this was "monkey gland" treatment, calculated to make Wolves, already well known as one of the fastest teams in the League, even quicker to the ball and in the way their movements developed. It was all nonsense of course. The injections were merely the primitive anti-flu affairs of those days and, in any event, the ploy sadly miscarried when Wolves, in 1939 the hottest favourites to win the Cup anybody can remember, went down 4-1 to Jack Tinn's spats and his unfancied but workmanlike Portsmouth.

Buckley's chief contribution to the subsequent Wolves success lay in his selection of Stan Cullis as captain of the club. Cullis, a natural leader of the old school, already believed in hierarchy and discipline, a faith further developed by his wartime service in the Army, first in the South Staffords and later as a formidable sergeant-major in the Army Physical Training Corps. When, in 1947, Cullis retired from active football he was the obvious choice to become the manager at Molineux. His were the standards and tactical concepts which underlaid the years of subsequent triumph.

If Cullis was a disciplinarian and determined to have his own way in football matters at Wolverhampton, he was also thoughtful and capable of a level of football analysis well ahead of his time. Characteristically, though he was as tough an individual as one could meet, he disliked bad language and never used it himself. His "tellings off" were legendary, but always couched in plain, correct terms – a technique he had doubtless mastered in the army.

Though there were many gifted individuals on the Wolves staff, the strength of Cullis's teams was always much greater than the mere sum of his chosen 11. The tactics were simple, so much so that those who did not understand their basis sometimes, mistakenly, dismissed them as "kick and rush". It was all based on pressure through teamwork, each player working to make the task of his colleagues as simple and easy as possible. Wolves were extremely fit, moved the ball quickly and ran brilliantly to support the player in possession. Cullis liked the ball moved quickly out of defence. Upfield players such as Swinbourne, the centre-forward, or those talented wingers Hancocks and Mullen were good enough to hold the ball until help arrived from behind, often in the shape of Broadbent, a wonderfully mobile inside-forward and instinctive reader of the game. The first support player to arrive always moved to help the player in possession, who, by using the easy option thus provided, retained possession for his own side.

The ultimate aim was to get a player to the byline; as a defender himself, Cullis realised how much more threatening a cross pulled back can prove than something directed vaguely forward from a midfield position. Wolves specialised in crosses – either delicate chips, a Hancocks speciality, or fast low ones, often converted at the far post by the timely arrival of whoever could get there first from midfield. The concept sounds, and was, simple. To execute it well, as Wolves did consistently, required great dedication and concentration, and especially an ability to control the ball quickly.

The real strength of the Wolves side lay in their half-backs, Wright, Flowers, Slater and Clamp to name four of the most distinguished. Wright, Cullis's choice of captain, played at No 5 for all of his later career. He had begun, however, as a wing-half, where he learnt to tackle and use the ball intelligently.

The half-backs were expected to win the ball in midfield; once they had done so they were able to exert the pressure on opponents which so often, especially in the second half, caused their downfall. Pressure exerted from midfield was, in fact, the main factor in Wolves's astonishing success. Their half-backs were skilful and adaptable. Slater, before coming to Wolverhampton, had played as an inside-forward for Blackpool, sometimes partnering Stanley Matthews. Later, his knowledge of the game and innate intelligence – he was a professor of physical education at Birmingham University – made him the obvious choice to succeed Wright when the latter retired as captain and wearer of the No 5 shirt. Flowers and Clamp were equally fine performers; all were expected to get forward whenever they saw a chance of doing so, and each reckoned to score a dozen or so goals in an average season.

Though Wolves were essentially an attacking side they were also solid at the back. In Bert Williams they had an outstanding goalkeeper; he won 24 caps for England and was unlucky not to have received more. Agility and athleticism (he

Molineux stretch: Booth missed but the ball went in off Bolton's Hennin in a 1959 Cup-tie

neither smoked nor drank) were his chief attributes, making up for his relative lack of height, only 5ft 10in. His successor, Finlayson, a Scot signed from Millwall, was also a sound goal-keeper even if he lacked Williams's personality and special abilities.

Wolves also had good full-backs such as Showell, Pritchard and Springthorpe, but Cullis did not like them to be spectacular. Overlapping was the province of the wing-halves, and Wright in the centre was the defender who mostly caught the eye.

It will be hard to overestimate Wright's contribution to Wolves, though this tends to be over-shadowed by his 105 caps for England. He was an outstanding captain leading by example. He did not believe in shouting if things went wrong on the field, preferring to concentrate on rectifying matters by restoring Wolves's pressure, which so often won them matches which otherwise, and with a lesser team spirit, would have been lost.

And one should not forget the Wolves crowd. Seldom less than 30,000, and for important games 40,000 or more, the sheer volume of noise they created was an important part of the pressure Wolves aimed to exert. The supporters were fine people, too, and knew their football; they were good to talk to before or after the match and one seldom left Wolverhampton without deepening one's knowledge of the game.

Could the Wolves style work successfully nowadays? Sadly, my conclusion is that it would be impossible, not least because modern players would never tolerate for long the Cullis code of discipline, or be able to generate the Molineux team spirit of the 1950s.

Though some of the Wolves players came from outside the Midlands they were essentially a Black Country team. There were few transfers over the period; as Broadbent said: "There was little point in leaving." When, unusually, Cullis attempted to strengthen his team by expensive imports from outside the newcomers often failed to settle. Henderson, from Portsmouth, and Hooper, from West Ham, both good players, were instances. Nor would the Wolves playing

style be effective against the present system of flat defences pressing forward to deny space to opponents. Goals were easier to score in the 1950s. There was more room and long balls into space were sensible tactics and unable to be dismissed as a last refuge of the incompetent. It was a different football world then; looking at things through the wrong end of a telescope is seldom profitable, and to attempt now to play like the Wolves of the 1950s would be a mistake.

Let nobody doubt that Wolves in those days were a great team, epitomising the additional strengths of the English game. Their famous victory over Honved, the Hungarian club side which included most of the players who so humiliated England at Wembley in 1953, went far towards restoring confidence in our style. Those like me who were privileged to have watched Wolves in their great days can, perhaps, be forgiven a grateful and nostalgic tear for the passing of the Molineux legend.

Wright: cool head in defence

Cullis's all-conquering team: Wolves won the FA Cup but the Double just eluded them in 1960

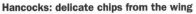

Hancocks: delicate chips from the wing

Pioneers: Broadbent scores against Vorwaerts

STAN CULLIS

Born October 25, 1915, Ellesmere Port

PLAYING CAREER
Wolverhampton Wanderers 1934-47
Honours FA Cup: Finalist 1939
League Championship: Runners-up 1938, 1939
Internationals England debut 1937
12 appearances. Also played in 20 war-time internationals

MANAGEMENT CAREER
Wolverhampton Wanderers Assistant Manager 1947-48; Manager 1948-64
Honours FA Cup: Winners 1949, 1960
League Championship: Winners 1954, 1958, 1959; Runners-up 1950, 1955, 1960

THE
1957-58
SEASON

Fiery Fernie runs rings round Rangers

WILLIE FERNIE was one of those absolutely infuriating players: when he was brilliant he was the greatest player on earth, and when he wasn't he was an utter liability. On October 19 Fernie woke up and he decided he was the former. Unfortunately for Rangers they were playing Celtic in the League Cup final that day.

Twisting, turning, spraying the ball about, there was nothing that Fernie touched that didn't turn to gold from his pivotal right-half position. At half-time the score was only 2-0, with goals from Sammy Wilson and Neil Mochan, but Celtic had hit the woodwork three times.

In the second half the floodgates opened and Celtic ran in another five goals. No matter how hard Rangers tackled Fernie, and some of the challenges were verging on the brutal, he was irrepressible. Mochan, on the left wing, and Charles Tully, on the right, ran the Rangers defence ragged creating the space for Fernie to exploit.

Billy McPhail was on the receiving end of many of Fernie's raking passes and he helped himself to a hat-trick in the second half, seemingly able to score at will. Mochan got another goal and it was Fernie himself who completed the rout, converting a penalty.

The 7-1 thrashing was the largest score in any British final. Heads had to roll. Poor Johnny Valentine, the centre-half who had been bought from Queen's Park at the beginning of the season, was made the chief scapegoat. It was his ninth and last game for the Rangers first team.

Munich air crash tragedy devastates Busby's Babes

Terrible toll: Back row: Tom Curry, Duncan Edwards and Mark Jones died; Ray Wood, Bobby Charlton, Bill Foulkes and Matt Busby survived. Front: John Berry survived; Bill Whelan, Roger Byrne, David Pegg and Eddie Colman died.

THE HEART was ripped out of English football in the snow at Munich airport on February 6. The aeroplane carrying the Manchester United team, attempting to take off for a third time, was unable to get enough height and hit a house at the end of a runway and crashed. Twenty-three of the passengers, including eight of the legendary "Busby Babes", died.

Manchester United were returning home from Yugoslavia where a 3-3 draw with Red Star Belgrade had qualified them for the semi-finals of the European Cup, and their plane had touched down to refuel. In appalling conditions the pilots attempted to get the plane home rather than stop over for a night.

Seven players, Geoff Bent, Roger Byrne, Eddie Colman, Mark Jones, David Pegg, Tommy Taylor and Billy Whelan died that night. Duncan Edwards, one of the most talented English footballers of the

century, was in a coma for a fortnight until he, too, passed away.

Matt Busby, whose chances were estimated at 50-50, managed to pull through. Two other "Babes", Jackie Blanchflower and Johnny Berry never played again. United's trainer, coach and secretary also perished, as did eight journalists, among them Frank Swift, the former Manchester City goalkeeper.

The whole country went into deep mourning at this sad loss of so many young lives. What was lost that fateful day was to be forever etched into the memories of all those that loved football. Except the Football League. When Wolves were crowned champions, Uefa – as a gesture of respect for their sorrow – invited Manchester United to enter the 1958-59 European Cup alongside Wolves.

The League, however, had never forgiven Busby for entering the competition against their express instructions in

1956 and so they refused to allow United's participation. The reason they gave was that it would be breaking Uefa's own rules, conveniently ignoring the fact that Uefa had already decided to waive its own rules.

Edwards: great talent lost

Lofthouse sinks makeshift United to dash the dream of a fairytale final

THE FA Cup final was always going to be a Manchester United fairytale ending, or the match Manchester United lost. Bolton couldn't win, even though they did, with two goals from England's lion-hearted centre-forward, Nat Lofthouse.

After the Munich aircrash, United had struggled to finish their season, slumping to ninth in the League, but in the Cup a tidal wave of emotion had carried them to the final. Matt Busby had somehow managed to survive, and was just passed fit to attend the final.

The mantle had passed to his assistant, Jimmy Murphy, who had managed to put together a scratch side made up of four of the "Busby Babes" that had survived, Bobby Charlton, Dennis Viollet, Harry Gregg and Billy Foulkes, first-team reserves and experienced players bought in.

Despite the weight of emotion hanging over the final, United were never really in it, espe-

Unhappy ending: Lofthouse, who scored both goals, challenges Gregg

cially after Lofthouse scored his first goal in the third minute. His second, in the 55th minute, was highly controversial as Lofthouse bundled goalkeeper Gregg over the line. The referee awarded a goal and there was no fairytale ending.

Terrible trio blast Hearts to the title

HEARTS' first championship this century was one of the most convincing ever witnessed in the British Isles. They lost only one of their 34 League matches, winning 29, scored a record 132 goals conceding a mere 29, leaving them with the staggering goal difference of 103. Rangers trailed in a sad second, 13 points behind.

The secret behind the Edinburgh club's success was their dynamic trio of Willie Bauld, Alfie Conn and Jimmy Wardhaugh in attack, and their human dynamo in midfield, Dave Mackay. With Mackay making the bullets the terrible trio could certainly fire them. Bauld was a tower in the air, Conn an industrious provider

and Wardhaugh the fastest thing on two legs.

Sadly for Hearts, in their annus mirabilis, the Double eluded them when their Edinburgh rivals, Hibernian, had the better of a seven goal thriller at Tynecastle in the third round of the Scottish Cup. Hearts had the last laugh though, Hibs lost 1-0 in the final to Clyde.

Quick-fire Summers revives Charlton

JOHNNY SUMMERS was a journeyman forward and Charlton were his fourth club. Aged 30, he was entering the twilight of his career, and on December 21 it became apparent that he was saving his best until the last.

Not that spectators at The Valley for the Second Division match against Huddersfield had any clue about what was coming. In fact, the only thing that

seemed to be coming was a whitewash.

Charlton lost Derek Ufton after 15 minutes when he broke his collar bone. They were only 2-0 down at half-time, but seven minutes after the interval they were 5-1 behind.

Then Summers, who was wearing a new pair of boots that he had not even broken in, went to work. He scored a hat-trick in

six minutes and then hit another two goals, all with his weaker right foot, to give Charlton a 6-5 lead.

Even then the drama was not over. Huddersfield equalised with two minutes left but Summers was not going to beaten. With the last move of the game he set John Ryan up for the winner in an almost unbelievable 7-6 match.

EDSON Arantes do Nascimento was just 17 when he played for Brazil in the 1958 World Cup finals in Sweden, the youngest player ever to play in the final stages. Pele, as he was now called, made his World Cup debut in Brazil's final game of the first round against the Soviet Union. Three matches and six goals later Brazil were the world champions and Pele was a household name worldwide.

The lithe, black teenager from impoverished Tres Corações had captured the hearts of everybody in the first World Cup to enjoy television coverage. Pele was blessed with everything: agility, athleticism, improbable ball skills, a powerful shot, unsurpassable heading skills, and – perhaps most importantly – the ability to read a game while in the thick of the action. Nobody had ever seen anything like it.

His first goal in the final best expressed his genius: 11 minutes after half-time, with Brazil only 2-1 ahead, Pele, in the midst of a melee in the Swedish penalty area and with his back to goal, trapped a high ball on his chest, lobbed it over his own head, spun round the defender and volleyed into the net. Any team would have been finished after a goal like that, and so it proved with the Swedes.

Not that the World Cup winners were a one-man show. Pele's divine talents were superbly complemented by an extraordinary Brazilian side, which, if it had not been for the emergence of Pele, could themselves have become as big superstars as the great man: Garrincha, Didi, Nilton Santos, Zito or Vava. Also Brazil played 4-2-4, then a revolutionary formation, that neatly expounded the artistry of their players while confounding their opponents. Yet strangely their team was only forged in the crucible of the final stages in Sweden. Indeed they almost did not qualify, only scraping through against Peru thanks to a Didi free-kick.

Brazil were not the only strong side to encounter problems in the qualifying rounds. Uruguay and Italy, both of whom had won the World Cup twice, fell to unfancied opposition, Paraguay and Northern Ireland respectively. Amazingly Spain, with Alfredo di Stefano and a clutch of the almighty Real Madrid team in their side, were eliminated by Scotland. Thus, by the time the World Cup began in

WORLD CUP 1958
Pele the master of the universe

Sweden on June 8, the 16 teams were an odd mix indeed.

Argentina, who had surprisingly lost the first World Cup final in 1930, had finally deigned to enter again and, despite the Italians poaching all their best players, had managed to qualify. But they were a debilitated side and probably wished they had not taken part, for when they returned home having won only one game they were pelted with rubbish. Hungary were no longer the force they had been in the previous World Cup after the Soviet invasion during the 1956 "revolution", and many of their key players, including Ferenc Puskas, Zoltan Czibor and Sandor Kocsis, defected to the West. Unsurprisingly, Hungary also failed to reach the quarter-finals.

Oddest of all were Wales, who had come second to Czechoslovakia in their qualifying group, yet still managed a back door entry to the finals thanks to Fifa's inexplicable political naivety. Despite the fact that Israel and Egypt had been at war in 1955, Israel were put into the African-Asian group. Inevitably Egypt, Indonesia, Sudan and Turkey withdrew one after the other, leaving Israel as qualifiers without having played a single game. As this was against Fifa rules they decided to draw lots among the teams that had finished second in their groups with the winner playing off against Israel. Wales won and promptly beat Israel home and away. With England also qualifying, all four home nations had reached the finals for the first time.

England were in disarray after the Munich air crash of February 1958 that had killed eight Manchester United players and ripped the heart out of both teams. The loss of the incomparable Duncan Edwards, Tommy Taylor and Roger Byrne was a blow from which England never recovered. Yet they compounded their problems by leaving out Stanley Matthews and Nat Lofthouse and bringing only 20 players, although they were permitted 22. Bobby Charlton was one of the 20, but was never selected.

Despite these setbacks they performed creditably: drawing 2-2 with the Soviet Union (but losing Tom Finney to injury in the process), 0-0 with Brazil and 2-2 with Austria in the strongest group in the tournament. They were the only team to stop Brazil scoring, and England should probably have been awarded a penalty. However they finished level with the Soviet Union and lost in the play-off for a place in the quarter-finals against Sweden.

Of the four home nations Scotland fared the worst, finishing bottom of their group with a solitary point. Northern Ireland and Wales proved to be the unlikely stars, both reaching the quarter-finals after play-offs.

Northern Ireland, under the inspirational managership of Peter Doherty, had been turned into more of a club side and with brilliant outfield players such as Danny Blanchflower, Billy Bingham and Jimmy McIlroy, and with Harry Gregg in goal, they ensured that they were never going to be pushovers – as the multi-talented Italy had learnt to their cost in the qualifiers.

Wales were of a similar ilk: an ebullient manager in Jimmy Murphy, a solid keeper in Jack Kelsey, Ivor Allchurch at inside-forward and the impressive John Charles at centre-forward. But in the quarter-finals both sides met formidable opposition. Wales, unfortunately without the injured Charles, only went down to Brazil when a 73rd minute goal from Pele ended their brave and resolute defence. Kelsey played magnificently in goal yet was eventually beaten by a deflection from one of his own defenders. Northern Ireland, ravaged by injuries, succumbed to France who scored four goals in a blistering 24 minutes, two of them from Juste Fontaine.

Fontaine, alongside Pele, was the other revelation of the tournament. He had come expecting only to be the reserve centre-forward, but after a training injury to the No1 choice he struck up a seemingly psychic understanding with the midfield impresario Raymond Kopa of Real Madrid and scored 13 goals in six matches, a World Cup record.

France, not particularly highly regarded before the tournament, went on to play attractive and entertaining football. However, in the semi-final, even a Fontaine goal after eight minutes was not going to upstage Brazil and Pele. A second-half hat-trick in 23 minutes from the 17-year-old maestro destroyed the French and set up the final against Sweden.

The Swedes had been lacklustre hosts and their attendances were

No stopping Brazil: even an injury to one of their players did not stop the flow of goals; Pele scored his second and Brazil's fifth as Sweden were swept aside in the final

pitiful. The highest, 51,000, was in Gothenburg for Brazil's first round match against the Soviet Union. For their semi-final against West Germany, however, they suddenly discovered their nationalism in Gothenburg, whipped up by the presence of cheerleaders on the pitch, and roared on their team, particularly after they fell behind.

A dubious equaliser, a German sent off, one injured and two goals in the last nine minutes and the hosts faced the exhilarating Brazilians in the final in Stockholm. But without the cheerleaders on the pitch, now banned, the crowd was strangely hushed. Sweden took the early lead they wanted, after four minutes. To no avail. Vava, Garrincha, Zagalo and, of course, Pele ran them ragged with a scintillating display. The best had proved they were the best.

THE
1958-59
SEASON

Wright rewrites the records

Ton up: Wright leads the team out in his 100th match for England

Quixall deal breaks bank

JOHN CHARLES'S record move to Juventus fuelled speculation about what would happen in the domestic market, and the answer was not long in coming. His brother Mel moved from Swansea to Arsenal for £40,000 and two players, but even that deal was nothing compared with the transfer of Albert Quixall.

Matt Busby knew that he had to reinforce his squad in the wake of the Munich disaster. The only answer was to make a rare foray into the transfer market. But other clubs, knowing his plight, and knowing that United had plenty of money, were asking ridiculous prices for moderate players. Busby was determined to spend his money wisely and in September he pounced, spending £45,000, a record deal between two British clubs, to buy Quixall, who was an England schoolboy and full international, from Sheffield Wednesday.

Both clubs were happy with the deal. It was the third time in under 10 years that Wednesday had sold a player for a record amount, and they still won the Second Division without Quixall. And United, with their new signing, finished a creditable second in the First Division.

Quixall: £45,000 transfer

BILLY WRIGHT became the first man in the world to play 100 times for his country when England beat Scotland 1-0 at Wembley on April 11.

It was a remarkable achievement by the Wolves centre-half, who had only missed three of England's 103 matches after the end of the Second World War. He had captained his country 85 times and the match at Wembley was a record 65th consecutive appearance for England.

Wright joined Wolves at the age of 14 and made his first-team debut in October 1939, at 15. Manager Major Frank Buckley was not over-impressed with his apprentice and threatened to send him home because he was too small at 5ft 3in. Fortunately for Wolves, Buckley relented.

Wright played alongside Stan Cullis and inherited the captaincy from him. By the age of 24, Wright had also been chosen to captain England for the first time, for the match against Ireland. Wright only heard the news when he was shown the stop press column in the local paper by a bus conductor.

With Cullis continuing the traditions established by Buckley at the club and Wright a model professional on the field, Wolves flourished and, after a shaky start, Wright had an unequalled record for England – 59 wins and 22 draws in the 100 matches that he played in.

After Buckley tried Wright in various positions in his early days (Wright thought his natural place was on the right wing) he established him as a wing-

half. But it was Cullis who made the transformation that was to enable Wright to enjoy such a long career.

Cullis, probably the finest centre-half to play for Wolves, realised that, at 30, Wright was losing some of his pace. So he convinced Wright to switch to centre-half. Despite his lack of height Wright soon adapted to the position, advised by Cullis on how to out-think the opposing centre-forward.

The change gave Wright a new lease of life as the linchpin of the defence and playmaker, and he went on to complete 105 matches for England, retiring on May 8 after the 8-1 victory over the United States. To add to his achievements, Wolves won the League championship again, scoring 110 goals.

Forest overcome final adversity

Breaking the jinx: Dwight gives Forest the lead before they were reduced to 10 men

ONCE AGAIN the FA Cup final was marred by an injury which reduced one team to 10 men – this phenomenon seems to be a hallmark of the 1950s – but for once the 11-man side didn't triumph. In the 32nd minute Roy Dwight, Nottingham Forest's right-winger, broke his right shin bone in a seemingly innocuous challenge with Luton's Brendan McNally. Dwight was carried off and watched the rest of the match on television from a hospital bed.

Fortunately for Forest they were 2-0 up at the time, Dwight having scored the first goal in the tenth minute when he hit Stewart Imlach's centre perfectly past Ron Baynham. Playing scintillating football, Forest added a second four minutes later when Imlach, from the left-back position, hit a glorious long pass to Billy Gray, whose diagonal ball to the far post was headed home by Tom Wilson. For the next 18 minutes Forest played Luton off the park. Then came the Dwight injury.

Luton now faced a team imbued with the Dunkirk spirit and despite the fillip of playing against 10 men could not even force a Forest save until six min-utes into the second half. However, in the 62nd minute, Luton got the goal they needed when Billy Bingham played a short corner to Ken Hawkes whose cross sailed past the Forest defence to give David Pacey a simple opportunity on the far post.

Still Forest hung on. Their worst moment came four minutes from time when Bingham swung in a cross from the right corner flag that Allan Brown, racing in with all the desperation of a man trying to catch a train, headed just past the post. The jinx was beaten.

Goals galore as Greaves starts with a bang and Clough keeps up his phenomenal strike rate

TWO HOTSHOTS were breaking all scoring records in the League, Jimmy Greaves and Brian Clough. Jimmy Greaves, who scored on his debut for Chelsea against Spurs in August 1957 when just 17, just kept rattling them into the back of the net.

A month later he scored on his debut for the England U-23 side against Bulgaria. In August he scored five for Chelsea against Wolves, the League champions, to become at 18 the youngest ever player to score five in a First Division match. Then, proving he was no flash in the pan, Greaves scored on his full England debut against Peru in Lima in May. Unsurprisingly, Greaves finished as the leading First Division scorer with 33 goals.

Brian Clough, five years older than Greaves, was also knocking the goals in for Middlesbrough in the Second Division. For the second consecutive year Clough was the division's leading scorer, with 42 goals. This was the third season Clough had averaged a goal a game, and he reached 100 League goals in fewer games than any previous player.

Greaves: debut goal

Clough: leading scorer

THE
1959-60
SEASON

Big clubs snub League Cup

THE FOOTBALL LEAGUE, who had opposed Chelsea's participation in the first European Cup in 1955 because of fixture congestion, performed a remarkable U-turn in June and launched a new domestic competition, the League Cup. Within days the leading clubs condemned it as an unnecessary burden on the players.

Wolves, Tottenham, West Brom, Arsenal and Sheffield Wednesday (four of which had finished in the top five that season) refused to take part. Bill Nicholson, the Spurs manager, was especially vociferous. He called for a smaller First Division with fewer games and condemned the League for demanding too much from the players.

England quick to drop Clough

BRIAN CLOUGH's scoring feats for Middlesbrough had not gone unnoticed and he was picked for the Football League against the Irish League.

He wasted no time in making his mark and scored all the goals in the 5-0 victory in Belfast on September 23. That performance undoubtedly helped him earn his first full England cap, against Wales. But a draw in Wrexham, and a defeat by Sweden at Wembley 11 days later, were enough to convince the selectors that Clough was not going to strike up a fruitful partnership with Jimmy Greaves.

Clough was dropped, and never played for England again. Undeterred, though, he kept on scoring goals for Middlesbrough. He finished the season with 39 League goals.

Real Madrid turn on the style

THE European Cup final between Real Madrid and Eintracht Frankfurt at Hampden Park in May has gone down in history not only as one of the greatest club games ever played, but also the match that forever changed British attitudes to Continental football. Its impact was as great as Hungary's rout of England at Wembley seven years earlier. And at the centre of the whirlwind, again, was Ferenc Puskas.

Puskas was now working in tandem with Alfredo di Stefano, the Argentinian maestro, and the pair, both 33, scored seven goals between them to dazzle the 127,000 spectators and millions more watching on television. Real's reputation was well known, they had won the European Cup every year since it started in 1955-56, but the performance they put on in Glasgow reached new heights.

Eintracht were no pushovers – they had annihilated Rangers 12-4 in the semi-final – and they showed as much by taking the lead in the 19th minute. That however simply set off the Madrid goal machine. Within 11 minutes di Stefano had put the European champions 2-1 up, then Puskas added one before the interval, and two shortly afterwards.

The match reached its breathtaking climax in the 70th minute. Puskas scored, Eintracht got another one back, di Stefano scored immediately after the re-start to complete his hattrick before Eintracht scored their third. Four goals in four minutes. Little wonder the awestruck Scottish crowd gave both teams an ovation when the referee blew the final whistle.

Opening the floodgates: di Stefano scores Real Madrid's first goal in their 7-3 victory

Burnley steal Wolves's thunder

IN A DRAMATIC finish to the season Burnley beat Manchester City 2-1 at Maine Road on the last day of the season to sneak past Wolves and snatch the League championship by a single point. It was the first time all season Burnley had led the table. If Burnley had drawn at Maine Road Wolves would have been the champions on goal difference.

Thus, by a whisker, Wolves were deprived not only of a League title, but of a memorable record that would have established them as the greatest, and most successful, club side in English football. The 1959-60 championship would have completed a hat-trick of successive League titles – to emulate Herbert Chapman's Huddersfield and Arsenal teams – and would have left them poised to achieve the elusive Double. Five days after losing the League title they were due to meet Blackburn in the FA Cup final and were widely expected to win (which they did).

However, the team that brought about Wolves' downfall was not Burnley but Tottenham, who went to Molineux in the penultimate match of the season. Danny Blanchflower, and Spurs, had their sights set on the Double as well – but for next season. Stopping Wolves would leave the way open for Spurs to grab the glory of being the first club this century to win the Cup and the League in a season.

Blanchflower held his team talk on the pitch, fired up his team and they beat Wolves 3-1. Burnley did their part by picking up maximum points in their last two matches and Wolves's extraordinary place in history slipped from their grasp. Sadly Wolves have not won the League or FA Cup since.

Angry fans pelt referee after 'Dustbin final'

Jeered off: Wolves's fierce tackles angered the crowd

AN INJURY turned the course of the Cup final once again and resulted in scenes the like of which had never been seen at Wembley. Blackburn Rovers had already been rocked by Derek Dougan demanding a transfer an hour before the kick-off and they were a goal down to Wolverhampton after 30 minutes when their full-back David Whelan broke his leg trying to tackle Norman Deeley.

A player short, Blackburn lost 3-0 as Deeley scored twice in the second half in a very poor match. The crowd were already incensed by Wolves's fierce tackling and the way Kevin Howley, the youngest person to referee a Cup final, had handled the match, and were booing long before the end of the game.

When Wolves tried to make their traditional lap of honour the spectators' anger boiled over and they pelted the players and the referee with orange peel, apple cores and rubbish. The press said that what should have been the season's show-piece match was so badly tarnished that it should have been called the "Dustbin final".

FOR THE RECORD

■ The Football League won a court case in July that established their copyright on fixture lists. The pools companies then signed a 10-year deal in which they agreed to pay the League half a percent of their gross takings after betting duty, with a guaranteed minimum of £245,000 a year.

■ The Football League moved its headquarters from Preston to Lytham St Annes. The new offices, formerly a small hotel, cost £11,000. Conversion of the building cost another £40,000 and took six months.

■ Joe Baker of Hibs became the first player at a Scottish club to represent England. He scored on his debut as England beat Northern Ireland 2-1 on November 18. His brother Gerry scored 10 goals when St Mirren beat Glasgow University 15-0 in the first round of the Scottish Cup.

■ Jock Stein took his first job as a manager, at Dunfermline in March. After he took over, the team won all of their last six matches to avoid relegation.

■ Cliff Holton, the League's leading scorer, hit hat-tricks on consecutive days for Watford in their Fourth Division matches against Chester and Gateshead. It was the first time this feat had been done since the war.

■ The drawn-out Fairs Cup was finally resolved when Birmingham lost 4-1 on aggregate to Barcelona. All the goals came in the second leg in Spain. The first European Nations Cup, which had started in 1958, was also decided when the Soviet Union beat Yugoslavia 2-1 in extra time in the final in Paris on July 10.

■ Denis Law's (above) move from Huddersfield to Manchester City in March was the first transfer between British clubs to exceed £50,000.

■ Real Madrid, the European Cup winners, beat Penarol, the South American champions, 5-1 on aggregate in the inaugural World club championship.

■ England were chosen to host the 1966 World Cup.

■ Tom Finney retired at the end of the season after 24 years, 472 matches and 76 appearances for England. A brass band played Auld Lang Syne and players and officials joined hands in the centre circle to salute him before Preston's match against Luton.

Cup exploits rewarded at last as the Posh step up in class

PETERBOROUGH were finally elected to the League on May 28 at the 21st attempt. There was no doubt that their exploits in the FA Cup in recent years helped their cause. In the past seven seasons they had reached the third round twice and the fourth round on two other occasions.

This season they had beaten Second Division Ipswich in the third round before going out to Sheffield Wednesday from the First Division. The other time they reached the fourth round,

they also beat another Second Division side, Lincoln, before losing to Huddersfield.

Another reason for Peterborough's being chosen to replace Gateshead was their determined approach. The Midland League team had been founded in 1923 and had been fully professional since the early 1930s. The club's 30,000 capacity stadium at London Road was the envy of many League clubs, and its facilities were so grand that the club were nicknamed "The Posh".

Fond farewell: Finney joins in the singing of Auld Lang Syne

LEAGUE TABLES AND RESULTS 1950 – 1960

1950-51

FA CUP
Newcastle United 2
Blackpool 0

FIRST DIVISION

	P	W	D	L	F	A	Pts
Tottenham	42	25	10	7	82	44	60
Man Utd	42	24	8	10	74	40	56
Blackpool	42	20	10	12	79	53	50
Newcastle	42	18	13	11	62	53	49
Arsenal	42	19	9	14	73	56	47
Middlesbro	42	18	11	13	76	65	47
Portsmouth	42	16	15	11	71	68	47
Bolton	42	19	7	16	64	61	45
Liverpool	42	16	11	15	53	59	43
Burnley	42	14	14	14	48	43	42
Derby	42	16	8	18	81	75	40
Sunderland	42	12	16	14	63	73	40
Stoke	42	13	14	15	50	59	40
Wolves	42	15	8	19	74	61	38
Aston Villa	42	12	13	17	66	68	37
West Brom	42	13	11	18	53	61	37
Charlton	42	14	9	19	63	80	37
Fulham	42	13	11	18	52	68	37
Huddersfld	42	15	6	21	64	92	36
Chelsea	42	12	8	22	53	65	32
Sheff Wed	*42*	*12*	*8*	*22*	*64*	*83*	*32*
Everton	*42*	*12*	*8*	*22*	*48*	*86*	*32*

SECOND DIVISION
Champions: Preston North End
Also promoted: Manchester City
Relegated: Chesterfield, Grimsby Town

THIRD DIVISION SOUTH
Champions: Nottingham Forest
Runners-up (not promoted): Norwich City

THIRD DIVISION NORTH
Champions: Rotherham United
Runners-up (not promoted): Mansfield Town

SCOTTISH CUP
Celtic 1
Motherwell 0

SCOTTISH FIRST DIVISION

	P	W	D	L	F	A	Pts
Hibernian	30	22	4	4	78	26	48
Rangers	30	17	4	9	64	37	38
Dundee	30	15	8	7	47	30	38
Hearts	30	16	5	9	72	45	37
Aberdeen	30	15	5	10	61	50	35
Partick	30	13	7	10	57	48	33
Celtic	30	12	5	13	48	46	29
Raith	30	13	2	15	52	52	28
Motherwell	30	11	6	13	58	65	28
East Fife	30	10	8	12	48	66	28
St Mirren	30	9	7	14	35	51	25
Morton	30	10	4	16	47	59	24
T Lanark	30	11	2	17	40	51	24
Airdrie	30	10	4	16	52	67	24
Clyde	*30*	*8*	*7*	*15*	*37*	*57*	*23*
Falkirk	*30*	*7*	*4*	*19*	*35*	*81*	*18*

SCOTTISH SECOND DIV
Champions: Queen of the South
Also promoted: Stirling Albion

SCOTTISH LEAGUE CUP
Motherwell 3
Hibernian 0

1951-52

FA CUP
Newcastle United 1
Arsenal 0

FIRST DIVISION

	P	W	D	L	F	A	Pts
Man Utd	42	23	11	8	95	52	57
Tottenham	42	22	9	11	76	51	53
Arsenal	42	21	11	10	80	61	53
Portsmouth	42	20	8	14	68	58	48
Bolton	42	19	10	13	65	61	48
Aston Villa	42	19	9	14	79	70	47
Preston	42	17	12	13	74	54	46
Newcastle	42	18	9	15	98	73	45
Blackpool	42	18	9	15	64	64	45
Charlton	42	17	10	15	68	63	44
Liverpool	42	12	19	11	57	61	43
Sunderland	42	15	12	15	70	61	42
West Brom	42	14	13	15	74	77	41
Burnley	42	15	10	17	56	63	40
Man City	42	13	13	16	58	61	39
Wolves	42	12	14	16	73	73	38
Derby	42	15	7	20	63	80	37
Middlesbro	42	15	6	21	64	88	36
Chelsea	42	14	8	20	52	72	36
Stoke	42	12	7	23	49	88	31
Huddersfld	*42*	*10*	*8*	*24*	*49*	*82*	*28*
Fulham	*42*	*8*	*11*	*23*	*58*	*77*	*27*

SECOND DIVISION
Champions: Sheffield Wednesday
Also promoted: Cardiff City
Relegated: Coventry City, Queen's Park Rangers

THIRD DIVISION SOUTH
Champions: Plymouth Argyle
Runners-up (not promoted): Reading

THIRD DIVISION NORTH
Champions: Lincoln City
Runners-up (not promoted): Grimsby Town

SCOTTISH CUP
Motherwell 4
Dundee 0

SCOTTISH FIRST DIVISION

	P	W	D	L	F	A	Pts
Hibernian	30	20	5	5	92	36	45
Rangers	30	16	9	5	61	31	41
East Fife	30	17	3	10	71	49	37
Hearts	30	14	7	9	69	53	35
Raith	30	14	5	11	43	42	33
Partick	30	12	7	11	48	51	31
Motherwell	30	12	7	11	51	57	31
Dundee	30	11	6	13	53	52	28
Celtic	30	10	8	12	52	55	28
Q of South	30	10	8	12	50	60	28
Aberdeen	30	10	7	13	65	58	27
T Lanark	30	9	8	13	51	62	26
Airdrie	30	11	4	15	54	69	26
St Mirren	30	10	5	15	43	58	25
Morton	*30*	*9*	*6*	*15*	*49*	*56*	*24*
Stirling A	*30*	*5*	*5*	*20*	*36*	*99*	*15*

SCOTTISH SECOND DIV
Champions: Clyde
Also promoted: Falkirk

SCOTTISH LEAGUE CUP
Dundee 3
Rangers 2

1952-53

FA CUP
Blackpool 4
Bolton Wanderers 3

FIRST DIVISION

	P	W	D	L	F	A	Pts
Arsenal	42	21	12	9	97	64	54
Preston	42	21	12	9	85	60	54
Wolves	42	19	13	10	86	63	51
West Brom	42	21	8	13	66	60	50
Charlton	42	19	11	12	77	63	49
Burnley	42	18	12	12	67	52	48
Blackpool	42	19	9	14	71	70	47
Man Utd	42	18	10	14	69	72	46
Sunderland	42	15	13	14	68	82	43
Tottenham	42	15	11	16	78	69	41
Aston Villa	42	14	13	15	63	61	41
Cardiff	42	14	12	16	54	46	40
Middlesbro	42	14	11	17	70	77	39
Bolton	42	15	9	18	61	69	39
Portsmouth	42	14	10	18	74	83	38
Newcastle	42	14	9	19	59	70	37
Liverpool	42	14	8	20	61	82	36
Sheff Wed	42	12	11	19	62	72	35
Chelsea	42	12	11	19	56	66	35
Man City	42	14	7	21	72	87	35
Stoke	*42*	*12*	*10*	*20*	*53*	*66*	*34*
Derby	*42*	*11*	*10*	*21*	*59*	*74*	*32*

SECOND DIVISION
Champions: Sheffield United
Also promoted: Huddersfield Town
Relegated: Southampton, Barnsley

THIRD DIVISION SOUTH
Champions: Bristol Rovers
Runners-up (not promoted): Millwall

THIRD DIVISION NORTH
Champions: Oldham Athletic
Runners-up (not promoted): Port Vale

SCOTTISH CUP
Rangers 1
Aberdeen 0, after 1-1

SCOTTISH FIRST DIVISION

	P	W	D	L	F	A	Pts
Rangers	30	18	7	5	80	39	43
Hibernian	30	19	5	6	93	51	43
East Fife	30	16	7	7	72	48	39
Hearts	30	12	6	12	59	50	30
Clyde	30	13	4	13	78	78	30
St Mirren	30	11	8	11	52	58	30
Dundee	30	9	11	10	44	37	29
Celtic	30	11	7	12	51	54	29
Partick	30	10	9	11	55	63	29
Q of South	30	10	8	12	43	61	28
Aberdeen	30	11	5	14	64	68	27
Raith	30	9	8	13	47	53	26
Falkirk	30	11	4	15	53	63	26
Airdrie	30	10	6	14	53	75	26
Motherwell	*30*	*10*	*5*	*15*	*57*	*80*	*25*
T Lanark	*30*	*8*	*4*	*18*	*52*	*75*	*20*

SCOTTISH SECOND DIV
Champions: Stirling Albion
Also promoted: Hamilton Academical

SCOTTISH LEAGUE CUP
Dundee 2
Kilmarnock 0

1953-54

WORLD CUP
West Germany 3
Hungary 2

FA CUP
West Bromwich Albion 3
Preston North End 2

FIRST DIVISION

	P	W	D	L	F	A	Pts
Wolves	42	25	7	10	96	56	57
West Brom	42	22	9	11	86	63	53
Huddersfld	42	20	11	11	78	61	51
Man Utd	42	18	12	12	73	58	48
Bolton	42	18	12	12	75	60	48
Blackpool	42	19	10	13	80	69	48
Burnley	42	21	4	17	78	67	46
Chelsea	42	16	12	14	74	68	44
Charlton	42	19	6	17	75	77	44
Cardiff	42	18	8	16	51	71	44
Preston	42	19	5	18	87	58	43
Arsenal	42	15	13	14	75	73	43
Aston Villa	42	16	9	17	70	68	41
Portsmouth	42	14	11	17	81	89	39
Newcastle	42	14	10	18	72	77	38
Tottenham	42	16	5	21	65	76	37
Man City	42	14	9	19	62	77	37
Sunderland	42	14	8	20	81	89	36
Sheff Wed	42	15	6	21	70	91	36
Sheff Utd	42	11	11	20	69	90	33
Middlesbro	*42*	*10*	*10*	*22*	*60*	*91*	*30*
Liverpool	*42*	*9*	*10*	*23*	*68*	*97*	*28*

SECOND DIVISION
Champions: Leicester City
Also promoted: Everton
Relegated: Brentford, Oldham Athletic

THIRD DIVISION SOUTH
Champions: Ipswich Town
Runners-up (not promoted): Brighton & Hove Albion

THIRD DIVISION NORTH
Champions: Port Vale
Runners-up (not promoted): Barnsley

SCOTTISH CUP
Celtic 2
Aberdeen 1

SCOTTISH FIRST DIVISION

	P	W	D	L	F	A	Pts
Celtic	30	20	3	7	72	29	43
Hearts	30	16	6	8	70	45	38
Partick	30	17	1	12	76	54	35
Rangers	30	13	8	9	56	35	34
Hibernian	30	15	4	11	72	51	34
East Fife	30	13	8	9	55	45	34
Dundee	30	14	6	10	46	47	34
Clyde	30	15	4	11	64	67	34
Aberdeen	30	15	3	12	66	51	33
Q of South	30	14	4	12	72	58	32
St Mirren	30	12	4	14	44	54	28
Raith	30	10	6	14	56	60	26
Falkirk	30	9	7	14	47	61	25
Stirling A	30	10	4	16	39	62	24
Airdrie	*30*	*5*	*5*	*20*	*41*	*92*	*15*
Hamilton	*30*	*4*	*3*	*23*	*29*	*94*	*11*

SCOTTISH SECOND DIV
Champions: Motherwell
Also promoted: Kilmarnock

SCOTTISH LEAGUE CUP
East Fife 3
Partick 2

1954-55

FA CUP
Newcastle United 3
Manchester City 1

FIRST DIVISION

	P	W	D	L	F	A	Pts
Chelsea	42	20	12	10	81	57	52
Wolves	42	19	10	13	89	70	48
Portsmouth	42	18	12	12	74	62	48
Sunderland	42	15	18	9	64	54	48
Man Utd	42	20	7	15	84	74	47
Aston Villa	42	20	7	15	72	73	47
Man City	42	18	10	14	76	69	46
Newcastle	42	17	9	16	89	77	43
Arsenal	42	17	9	16	69	63	43
Burnley	42	17	9	16	51	48	43
Everton	42	16	10	16	62	68	42
Huddersfld	42	14	13	15	63	68	41
Sheff Utd	42	17	7	18	70	86	41
Preston	42	16	8	18	83	64	40
Charlton	42	15	10	17	76	75	40
Tottenham	42	16	8	18	72	73	40
West Brom	42	16	8	18	76	96	40
Bolton	42	13	13	16	62	69	39
Blackpool	42	14	10	18	60	64	38
Cardiff	42	13	11	18	62	76	37
Leicester	*42*	*12*	*11*	*19*	*74*	*86*	*35*
Sheff Wed	*42*	*8*	*10*	*24*	*63*	*100*	*26*

SECOND DIVISION
Champions: Birmingham City
Also promoted: Luton Town
Relegated: Ipswich Town, Derby County

THIRD DIVISION SOUTH
Champions: Bristol City
Runners-up (not promoted): Leyton Orient

THIRD DIVISION NORTH
Champions: Barnsley
Runners-up (not promoted): Accrington Stanley

SCOTTISH CUP
Clyde 1
Celtic 0, after 1-1

SCOTTISH FIRST DIVISION

	P	W	D	L	F	A	Pts
Aberdeen	30	24	1	5	73	26	49
Celtic	30	19	8	3	76	37	46
Rangers	30	19	3	8	67	33	41
Hearts	30	16	7	7	74	45	39
Hibernian	30	15	4	11	64	54	34
St Mirren	30	12	8	10	55	54	32
Clyde	30	11	9	10	59	50	31
Dundee	30	13	4	13	48	48	30
Partick	30	11	7	12	49	61	29
Kilmarnock	30	10	6	14	46	58	26
East Fife	30	9	6	15	51	62	24
Falkirk	30	8	8	14	42	54	24
Q of South	30	9	6	15	38	56	24
Raith	30	10	3	17	49	57	23
Motherwell	30	9	4	17	42	62	22
Stirling A	30	2	2	26	29	105	6

SCOTTISH SECOND DIV
Champions: Airdrie
Also promoted: Dunfermline Athletic

SCOTTISH LEAGUE CUP
Hearts 4
Motherwell 2

	1955-56	1956-57	1957-58	1958-59	1959-60
WORLD CUP			Brazil 5 Sweden 2		
EUROPEAN CHAMPIONSHIP					USSR 2 Yugoslavia 1
EUROPEAN CUP	Real Madrid 4 Reims 3	Real Madrid 2 Fiorentina 0	Real Madrid 3 AC Milan 2	Real Madrid 2 Reims 0	Real Madrid 7 Eintracht Frankfurt 3
FAIRS CUP			Barcelona beat London 2-2 6-0		Barcelona beat Birmingham City 0-0 4-1
FA CUP	Manchester City 3 Birmingham City 1	Aston Villa 2 Manchester United 1	Bolton Wanderers 2 Manchester United 0	Nottingham Forest 2 Luton Town 1	Wolverhampton Wanderers 3 Blackburn Rovers 0

FIRST DIVISION

1955-56

	P	W	D	L	F	A	Pts
Man Utd	42	25	10	7	83	51	60
Blackpool	42	20	9	13	86	62	49
Wolves	42	20	9	13	89	65	49
Man City	42	18	10	14	82	69	46
Arsenal	42	18	10	14	60	61	46
Birmingham	42	18	9	15	75	57	45
Burnley	42	18	8	16	64	54	44
Bolton	42	18	7	17	71	58	43
Sunderland	42	17	9	16	80	95	43
Luton	42	17	8	17	66	64	42
Newcastle	42	17	7	18	85	70	41
Portsmouth	42	16	9	17	78	85	41
West Brom	42	18	5	19	58	70	41
Charlton	42	17	6	19	75	81	40
Everton	42	15	10	17	55	69	40
Chelsea	42	14	11	17	64	77	39
Cardiff	42	15	9	18	55	69	39
Tottenham	42	15	7	20	61	71	37
Preston	42	14	8	20	73	72	36
Aston Villa	42	11	13	18	52	69	35
Huddersfld	*42*	*14*	*7*	*21*	*54*	*83*	*35*
Sheff Utd	*42*	*12*	*9*	*21*	*63*	*77*	*33*

1956-57

	P	W	D	L	F	A	Pts
Man Utd	42	28	8	6	103	54	64
Tottenham	42	22	12	8	104	56	56
Preston	42	23	10	9	84	56	56
Blackpool	42	22	9	11	93	65	53
Arsenal	42	21	8	13	85	69	50
Wolves	42	20	8	14	94	70	48
Burnley	42	18	10	14	56	50	46
Leeds	42	15	14	13	72	63	44
Bolton	42	16	12	14	65	65	44
Aston Villa	42	14	15	13	65	55	43
West Brom	42	14	14	14	59	61	42
Birmingham	42	15	9	18	69	69	39
Chelsea	42	13	13	16	73	73	39
Sheff Wed	42	16	6	20	82	88	38
Everton	42	14	10	18	61	79	38
Luton	42	14	9	19	58	76	37
Newcastle	42	14	8	20	67	87	36
Man City	42	13	9	20	78	88	35
Portsmouth	42	10	13	19	62	92	33
Sunderland	42	12	8	22	67	88	32
Cardiff	*42*	*10*	*9*	*23*	*53*	*88*	*29*
Charlton	*42*	*9*	*4*	*29*	*62*	*120*	*22*

1957-58

	P	W	D	L	F	A	Pts
Wolves	42	28	8	6	103	47	64
Preston	42	26	7	9	100	51	59
Tottenham	42	21	9	12	93	77	51
West Brom	42	18	14	10	92	70	50
Man City	42	22	5	15	104	100	49
Burnley	42	21	5	16	80	74	47
Blackpool	42	19	6	17	80	67	44
Luton	42	19	6	17	69	63	44
Man Utd	42	16	11	15	85	75	43
Nottm F	42	16	10	16	69	63	42
Chelsea	42	15	12	15	83	79	42
Arsenal	42	16	7	19	73	85	39
Birmingham	42	14	11	17	76	89	39
Aston Villa	42	16	7	19	73	86	39
Bolton	42	14	10	18	65	87	38
Everton	42	13	11	18	65	75	37
Leeds	42	14	9	19	51	63	37
Leicester	42	14	5	23	91	112	33
Newcastle	42	12	8	22	73	81	32
Portsmouth	42	12	8	22	73	88	32
Sunderland	*42*	*10*	*12*	*20*	*54*	*97*	*32*
Sheff Wed	*42*	*12*	*7*	*23*	*69*	*92*	*31*

1958-59

	P	W	D	L	F	A	Pts
Wolves	42	28	5	9	110	49	61
Man Utd	42	24	7	11	103	66	55
Arsenal	42	21	8	13	88	68	50
Bolton	42	20	10	12	79	66	50
West Brom	42	18	13	11	88	68	49
West Ham	42	21	6	15	85	70	48
Burnley	42	19	10	13	81	70	48
Blackpool	42	18	11	13	66	49	47
Birmingham	42	20	6	16	84	68	46
Blackburn	42	17	10	15	76	70	44
Newcastle	42	17	7	18	80	80	41
Preston	42	17	7	18	70	77	41
Nottm F	42	17	6	19	71	74	40
Chelsea	42	18	4	20	77	98	40
Leeds	42	15	9	18	57	74	39
Everton	42	17	4	21	71	87	38
Luton	42	12	13	17	68	71	37
Tottenham	42	13	10	19	85	95	36
Leicester	42	11	10	21	67	98	32
Man City	42	11	9	22	64	95	31
Aston Villa	*42*	*11*	*8*	*23*	*58*	*87*	*30*
Portsmouth	*42*	*6*	*9*	*27*	*64*	*112*	*21*

1959-60

	P	W	D	L	F	A	Pts
Burnley	42	24	7	11	85	61	55
Wolves	42	24	6	12	106	67	54
Tottenham	42	21	11	10	86	50	53
West Brom	42	19	11	12	83	57	49
Sheff Wed	42	19	11	12	80	59	49
Bolton	42	20	8	14	59	51	48
Man Utd	42	19	7	16	102	80	45
Newcastle	42	18	8	16	82	78	44
Preston	42	16	12	14	79	76	44
Fulham	42	17	10	15	73	80	44
Blackpool	42	15	10	17	59	71	40
Leicester	42	13	13	16	66	75	39
Arsenal	42	15	9	18	68	80	39
West Ham	42	16	6	20	75	91	38
Man City	42	17	3	22	78	84	37
Everton	42	13	11	18	73	78	37
Blackburn	42	16	5	21	60	70	37
Chelsea	42	14	9	19	76	91	37
Birmingham	42	13	10	19	63	80	36
Nottm F	42	13	9	20	50	74	35
Leeds	*42*	*12*	*10*	*20*	*65*	*92*	*34*
Luton	*42*	*9*	*12*	*21*	*50*	*73*	*30*

	1955-56	1956-57	1957-58	1958-59	1959-60
SECOND DIVISION	Champions: Sheffield Wednesday Also promoted: Leeds United Relegated: Plymouth Argyle, Hull City	Champions: Leicester City Also promoted: Nottingham Forest Relegated: Bury, Port Vale	Champions: West Ham United Also promoted: Blackburn Rovers Relegated: Notts County, Doncaster Rovers	Champions: Sheffield Wednesday Also promoted: Fulham Relegated: Grimsby Town, Barnsley	Champions: Aston Villa Also promoted: Cardiff City Relegated: Hull City, Bristol City
THIRD DIVISION SOUTH	Champions: Leyton Orient Runners-up (not promoted): Brighton & Hove Albion	Champions: Ipswich Town Runners-up (not promoted): Torquay United	Champions: Brighton & Hove Albion Runners-up (not promoted): Brentford		
THIRD DIVISION NORTH	Champions: Grimsby Town Runners-up (not promoted): Derby County	Champions: Derby County Runners-up (not promoted): Hartlepools United	Champions: Scunthorpe United Runners-up (not promoted): Accrington Stanley		
THIRD DIVISION				Champions: Plymouth Argyle Also promoted: Hull City Relegated: Stockport, Doncaster Rovers, Notts County, Rochdale	Champions: Southampton Also promoted: Norwich City Relegated: York City, Mansfield Town, Wrexham, Accrington Stanley
FOURTH DIVISION				Champions: Port Vale Also promoted: Coventry City, York City, Shrewsbury Town	Champions: Walsall Also promoted: Notts County, Torquay United, Watford
SCOTTISH CUP	Hearts 3 Celtic 1	Falkirk 2 Kilmarnock 1, after 1-1	Clyde 1 Hibernian 0	St Mirren 3 Aberdeen 1	Rangers 2 Kilmarnock 0

SCOTTISH FIRST DIVISION

1955-56

	P	W	D	L	F	A	Pts
Rangers	34	22	8	4	85	27	52
Aberdeen	34	18	10	6	87	50	46
Hearts	34	19	7	8	99	47	45
Hibernian	34	19	7	8	86	50	45
Celtic	34	16	9	9	55	39	41
Q of South	34	16	5	13	69	73	37
Airdrie	34	14	8	12	85	96	36
Kilmarnock	34	12	10	12	52	45	34
Partick	34	13	7	14	62	60	33
Motherwell	34	11	11	12	53	59	33
Raith	34	12	9	13	58	75	33
East Fife	34	13	5	16	61	69	31
Dundee	34	12	6	16	56	65	30
Falkirk	34	11	6	17	58	75	28
St Mirren	34	10	7	17	57	70	27
Dunfermline	34	10	6	18	42	82	26
Clyde	*34*	*8*	*6*	*20*	*50*	*74*	*22*
Stirling A	*34*	*4*	*5*	*25*	*23*	*82*	*13*

1956-57

	P	W	D	L	F	A	Pts
Rangers	34	26	3	5	96	48	55
Hearts	34	24	5	5	81	48	53
Kilmarnock	34	16	10	8	57	39	42
Raith	34	16	7	11	84	58	39
Celtic	34	15	8	11	58	43	38
Aberdeen	34	18	2	14	79	59	38
Motherwell	34	16	5	13	72	66	37
Partick	34	13	8	13	53	51	34
Hibernian	34	12	9	13	69	56	33
Dundee	34	13	6	15	55	61	32
Airdrie	34	13	4	17	77	89	30
St Mirren	34	12	6	16	58	72	30
Queen's P	34	11	7	16	55	59	29
Falkirk	34	10	8	16	51	70	28
East Fife	34	10	6	18	59	82	26
Q of South	34	10	5	19	54	96	25
Dunfermline	*34*	*9*	*6*	*19*	*54*	*74*	*24*
Ayr	*34*	*7*	*5*	*22*	*48*	*89*	*19*

1957-58

	P	W	D	L	F	A	Pts
Hearts	34	29	4	1	132	29	62
Rangers	34	22	5	7	89	49	49
Celtic	34	19	8	7	84	47	46
Clyde	34	18	6	10	84	61	42
Kilmarnock	34	14	9	11	60	55	37
Partick	34	17	3	14	69	71	37
Raith	34	14	7	13	66	56	35
Motherwell	34	12	8	14	68	67	32
Hibernian	34	13	5	16	59	60	31
Falkirk	34	11	9	14	64	82	31
Dundee	34	13	5	16	49	65	31
Aberdeen	34	14	2	18	68	76	30
St Mirren	34	11	8	15	59	66	30
Third Lanark	34	13	4	17	69	88	30
Q of South	34	12	5	17	61	72	29
Airdrie	34	13	2	19	71	92	28
East Fife	*34*	*10*	*3*	*21*	*45*	*88*	*23*
Queen's P	*34*	*4*	*1*	*29*	*41*	*114*	*9*

1958-59

	P	W	D	L	F	A	Pts
Rangers	34	21	8	5	92	51	50
Hearts	34	21	6	7	92	51	48
Motherwell	34	18	8	8	83	50	44
Dundee	34	16	9	9	61	51	41
Airdrie	34	15	7	12	64	62	37
Celtic	34	14	8	12	70	53	36
St Mirren	34	14	7	13	71	74	35
Kilmarnock	34	13	8	13	58	51	34
Partick	34	14	6	14	59	66	34
Hibernian	34	13	6	15	68	70	32
Third Lanark	34	11	10	13	74	83	32
Stirling A	34	11	8	15	54	64	30
Aberdeen	34	12	5	17	63	66	29
Raith	34	10	9	15	60	70	29
Clyde	34	12	4	18	62	66	28
Dunfermline	34	10	8	16	68	87	28
Falkirk	*34*	*10*	*7*	*17*	*58*	*79*	*27*
Q of South	*34*	*6*	*6*	*22*	*38*	*101*	*18*

1959-60

	P	W	D	L	F	A	Pts
Hearts	34	23	8	3	102	51	54
Kilmarnock	34	24	2	8	67	45	50
Rangers	34	17	8	9	72	38	42
Dundee	34	16	10	8	70	49	42
Motherwell	34	16	8	10	71	61	40
Clyde	34	15	9	10	77	69	39
Hibernian	34	14	7	13	106	85	35
Ayr	34	14	6	14	65	73	34
Celtic	34	12	9	13	73	59	33
Partick	34	14	4	16	54	78	32
Raith	34	14	3	17	64	62	31
Third Lanark	34	13	4	17	75	83	30
Dunfermline	34	10	9	15	72	80	29
St Mirren	34	11	6	17	78	86	28
Aberdeen	34	11	6	17	54	72	28
Airdrie	34	11	6	17	56	80	28
Stirling A	*34*	*7*	*8*	*19*	*55*	*72*	*22*
Arbroath	*34*	*4*	*7*	*23*	*38*	*106*	*15*

	1955-56	1956-57	1957-58	1958-59	1959-60
SCOTTISH SECOND DIV	Champions: Queen's Park Also promoted: Ayr United	Champions: Clyde Also promoted: Third Lanark	Champions: Stirling Albion Also promoted: Dunfermline Athletic	Champions: Ayr United Also promoted: Arbroath	Champions: St Johnstone Also promoted: Dundee United
SCOTTISH LEAGUE CUP	Aberdeen 2 St Mirren 1	Celtic 3 Partick 0, after 0-0	Celtic 7 Rangers 1	Hearts 5 Partick 1	Hearts 2 Third Lanark 1

Player power forces League to abolish slavery contracts

Italy spends a fortune to buy Britain's best

ENGLISH football was only days away from its first national strike when the Football League backed down in its long-running dispute with the PFA.

THE moment that the maximum wage was abolished Tommy Trinder, the Fulham chairman, made Johnny Haynes the first £100 a week footballer in England.

That persuaded the England international not to seek his fortune abroad. But the debilitating effect of the maximum wage and restrictive contracts in Britain became clear when four more leading players followed John Charles's lead and were tempted by the lure of lira.

Joe Baker started the season by scoring nine times for Hibs in their 15-1 victory over Peebles Rovers in the first round of the Scottish Cup. But he soon went to Turin for £73,000.

Money was no object to foreign clubs determined to satisfy their fanatical supporters with the best players in the world, and Baker was joined in Italy by Denis Law of Manchester City, who also went to Turin for £100,000; Jimmy Greaves, who moved from Chelsea to AC Milan for £80,000 and Gerry Hitchens, who was transferred to their rivals Inter Milan for £80,000.

Greaves was in two minds but Milan made an unrefusable offer: £15,000 immediately and £40,000 over three years.

The arguments over players' wages and the terms of their contracts had dragged on for years. Professionals were restricted to a earning a maximum of £20 a week during the season and £17 in the summer. Although not a pittance by the standards of the wages paid in the early days of the League, it was far short of the money that players could make by moving abroad.

The players, led by Jimmy Hill, the PFA chairman, won their first breakthrough on January 9, when the maximum wage was abolished. But the League refused to budge on the contracts issue.

Players were not allowed to move to a club of their choosing when their contract expired, something that Hill described as a "slave contract". George Eastham, who wanted to move from Newcastle to Arsenal, was challenging his contract in court, arguing that it was a restraint of trade.

The PFA said it would call a strike, starting with the matches due to be played on Saturday, January 21. The League responded by ordering clubs to play their matches the day before to beat the strike. That ruling was greeted with derision —the Daily Mirror, in an editorial headlined "What a way to run a sport!", accused the League of being "idiotic".

It was apparent that most people supported the players' stance, and the League had to make a humiliating climbdown. After five hours of last-ditch talks at the Ministry of Labour on January 18, the League finally agreed to abandon the regulations that effectively tied a player to one club for life.

The players' victory was finally confirmed when Eastham's case reached the High Court, which ruled in his favour. At long last, football had been dragged, kicking and screaming all the way, out of the dark ages and into the modern era.

Fame and fortune: Baker is mobbed when he arrives in Rome

Demands met: Hill leaves the crisis talks at Ministry of Labour

England humiliate hapless Haffey

Unstoppable: England parade the Home International trophy after annihilating Scotland

■ Sir Stanley Rous (above) was elected the president of Fifa. Denis Follows replaced him as the secretary of the Football Association.

■ The Football League fined Burnley £1,000 for fielding 10 reserve-team players for their First Division match against Chelsea.

APRIL 15 was the worst day in Frank Haffey's life as his golden opportunity to shine for his country turned into a day of humiliation. Nothing could have prepared him for the 9-3 slaughter that England inflicted on their bitterest international rivals that day at Wembley. In his only other appearance for Scotland, the previous April, Haffey had played creditably and the only goal he conceded was a Bobby Charlton penalty as England scraped a 1-1 draw at Hampden.

Poor Haffey was not even Scotland's first-choice goalkeeper for the England match. Injuries to Bill Brown and Leslie had pushed the Celtic keeper into the team at the last minute, but it still was not a weak side that Scotland fielded that fateful afternoon. The lineup included such leading players as Denis Law, Dave Mackay, Billy McNeill and Ian St John. However England were on a roll: they had scored 23 goals in their previous four fixtures. Then against Scotland, England's attack moved up a gear.

Bobby Robson opened the scoring and by half-time England were 3-0 up. However, within six minutes of the second half Scotland had rallied and were only 3-2 down. Then the roof fell in. Jimmy Greaves helped himself to a hat-trick, Bobby Smith bagged a pair, as did Johnny Haynes, and one from Bryan Douglas completed the hammering. The English press were ecstatic, hailing England's forward line as their best ever and comparing them to Real Madrid, the kings of Europe.

Poor Haffey trudged off the field, head bowed, destined never to be picked to play for his country again. In England the match so captured the popular imagination that a long-playing record of the match commentary was released and endlessly played to taunt the hapless Scots. And, as if to prove it was no fluke, the next month England – without Greaves – trounced Mexico 8-0.

Rain robs Law of Cup record

DENIS LAW was left cursing the heavy rain that cost him a place in the record books.

Manchester City's fourth-round FA Cup tie against Luton should not have gone ahead because heavy storms had turned Luton's ground into a quagmire. In almost impossible conditions, the Second Division team took a 2-0 lead in the first 20 minutes.

The huge pools of water on the pitch did not hamper Law in the slightest and, despite the ball being almost unplayable, he hit six goals in succession to equal the FA Cup record.

Much to his chagrin though, the referee abandoned the match with just over 30 minutes remaining. Then, to make matters worse, Luton won the replay 3-1 with Law scoring City's consolation goal.

Revie sweet-talks Collins into saving Leeds

SOON AFTER he took charge of Leeds United, Don Revie made a secret visit to Old Trafford to seek Matt Busby's advice on how to be a good manager. The Manchester United manager's words almost certainly helped to keep Leeds out of the Third Division. "All you have to do is treat your players well. Be honest with them and never lie to them. In return they'll doing anything for you."

Leeds were staring relegation in the face in March when Revie bought Bobby Collins from Everton for £25,000, just days before the transfer deadline. But within days of arriving at Elland Road, Collins said that he wanted to leave.

But, recalling Busby's words, Revie persuaded the little inside-forward to withdraw his transfer request. Collins responded by guiding Leeds to safety. The team did not lose any of their last 10 League matches and when the chips were down in the final match of the season they won 3-0 at Newcastle to guarantee their survival.

THE
1960-61
SEASON

Football is not really about winning, or goals, or saves, or supporters – it's about glory. It's about doing things in style, doing them with a flourish; it's about going out to beat the other lot, not waiting for them to die of boredom; it's about dreaming of the glory that the Double brought

DANNY BLANCHFLOWER

Blanchflower: dream fulfilled

Glorious Double for Spurs

Double sealed: Gordon Banks dives in vain and Spurs' Double is nearly complete

EVERYBODY believed that the modern-day Double could not be done – apart from one man. So many teams had gone heart-breakingly close but failed at the final hurdle that it was almost established as a "fact" that the Double was a physical impossibility.

Danny Blanchflower, though, believed otherwise. As far back as 1958 he had said as much. On the flight home from the World Cup finals he had lectured Stan Cullis and Joe Mercer on the subject. "It is going to be done," Blanchflower said. "And Spurs will be the team to do it."

Quietly, and with very little fuss, Bill Nicholson had been staging a revolution at White Hart Lane. Just as Arthur Rowe had assembled the famous push-and-run team seemingly out of nowhere, Nicholson had built a formidable team around Blanchflower.

Just how all-powerful that team was was soon revealed.

Tottenham had a record-breaking start to the season, winning their first 11 League matches. They only dropped one point in their first 16 matches (a draw at home to Manchester City) and were so far ahead by Christmas that bookmakers refused to take any more bets on their winning the title.

By the turn of the year Spurs had 46 points from 25 matches and the only other blots on their copybook form were a defeat at Sheffield Wednesday, their nearest rivals, and a 4-4 draw at home to Burnley in a match which they had led 4-0. Only 27 goals were conceded while an enormous 82 were scored.

But still people thought that Tottenham, like the teams before them would crack. Some chance. The second half of the season was as much a procession as the first. Record after record tumbled as Tottenham marched to the title on April 17 with three games in hand when they beat Sheffield Wednesday in front of a rapturous crowd at White Hart Lane. Amazingly, Tottenham only had one player booked and only conceded one penalty all season.

Although Blanchflower's performances were crucial, Tottenham were far from a one-man band. Bobby Smith and Les Allen scored 51 goals between them; Cliff Jones and Terry Dyson dominated the wings; Dave Mackay was redoubtable in midfield and Bobby Brown was a safe pair of hands in goal

behind the defending of Peter Baker, Ron Henry and Maurice Norman.

Blanchflower was quick to acknowledge the importance of his team-mates, who gave him the time and the space needed to spur Tottenham's devastating attacks. As he said: "I could change the rhythm and change the pace, slow it down if necessary or speed it up when we needed to. I had the ball much more often than anybody else, so I should have done something with it, shouldn't I?"

By the standards of the rest of the season, Tottenham did not do a great deal in the FA Cup final. The burden of having everybody wanting them to win, but people still thinking that the Double could not be done, seemed to weigh heavily on Spurs.

Leicester dominated the early exchanges and created three good chances. But they were knocked out of their stride when Len Chalmers wrenched his right knee in a collision with Les Allen. The Leicester right-back limped on out on the wing, but was forced to come off just after Smith gave Tottenham the lead in the 69th minute.

With Leicester's defence in disarray Dyson added a second goal shortly afterwards. It was the seventh time in nine years that the Cup final had been affected by an injury, but not even that could take the gloss off Tottenham's "impossible" achievement.

How the double eluded clubs before Spurs in 1961

1904	*Manchester City*	League runners-up and FA Cup winners
1905	*Newcastle United*	League champions and FA Cup finalists
1913	*Sunderland*	League champions and FA Cup finalists
1913	*Aston Villa*	League runners-up and FA Cup winners
1928	*Huddersfield*	League runners-up and FA Cup finalists
1932	*Arsenal*	League runners-up and FA Cup finalists
1939	*Wolves*	League runners-up and FA Cup finalists
1948	*Manchester United*	League runners-up and FA Cup winners
1954	*West Bromwich Albion*	League runners-up and FA Cup winners
1957	*Manchester United*	League champions and FA Cup finalists
1960	*Wolves*	League runners-up and FA Cup winners

Treble eludes Rangers as sucker punches fell them at the final hurdle

RANGERS improved on their European performance of the previous season – a heavy defeat in the semi-finals of the Champions Cup – by reaching the final of the newly created European Cup Winners Cup.

It was the third of the European competitions to be launched and initially was seen very much as the poor relations to the Champions' Cup. Unlike Britain, where the domestic Cup competition predates the Leagues, many European countries did not have their own Cup and, if they did, its significance was not great. Thus only 10 clubs entered the inaugural European Cup-Winners' Cup.

After a shaky start against Ferencvaros in the preliminary round, Rangers scraped through 5-4 on aggregate, they strolled into the semi-finals by trouncing Borussia Moenchengladbach 11-0. There they met the once mighty Wolves who were now sadly entering a period of decline. A 2-0 victory at Ibrox proved too much for the English Cup winners to overhaul. They could only manage a 1-1 draw in the second leg at Molineux and Rangers became the first Scottish club to reach a European final.

A glittering treble was now possible as Rangers had won the Scottish championship by a point from Kilmarnock and beaten the same team 2-0 to capture the Scottish League Cup. However Italy's Fiorentina were too much for Rangers who, having acquired Jim Baxter from Raith Rovers, had developed into a highly skilled and attractive side.

The vagaries of European football were still new to the Scottish side and despite their constant raids on the the Italian goal they were unable to score at Ibrox. Instead Fiorentina's Milani caught them with two sucker punches, in the 12th and 88th minutes. In Florence Rangers again conceded a 12th minute goal to Milani but, despite an equaliser from Scott on the hour, Fiorentina were never going to surrender their aggregate lead. Four minutes from time Hamrin wrapped it up for the Italians.

Foreign fields: Greaves leaves London airport for Italy

■ Peterborough, in only their first season in the League, raced through the Fourth Division and were promoted as champions, having scored a record 134 goals. Terry Bly was their leading marksman with 52 goals in the League, which was a post-war record.

■ Ipswich, managed by Alf Ramsey, also scored 100 goals as they won the Second Division title. Ray Crawford's 39 goals made him the division's leading scorer.

■ Jimmy Greaves left England for Italy as the First Division's leading scorer, with 41 goals in the League.

■ Several famous clubs of the past fell on hard times. Preston were relegated to the Second Division after 10 seasons in the top flight, Newcastle went down after 13 seasons in the First Division, and Blackpool only escaped relegation by one point. Portsmouth also went down to the Third Division for the first time since the 1920s.

Stein works another miracle as Dunfermline hit the heights

JOCK STEIN was earning himself a reputation as a miracle worker in Scotland. Having amazingly saved Dunfermline from certain relegation the season before, he had now, in his first full season as the manager, guided the club to mid-table safety and their first major trophy, the Scottish Cup. To complete the fairy-tale their defeated opponents in the final had been Celtic, Stein's former club.

Bolstered by some astute purchases from England, Dunfermline breezed through the early rounds of the Cup, sweeping away Berwick and Stranraer. They stunned all of Scotland by beating Aberdeen 6-3 at Pittodrie in the third round. Alloa were brushed aside 4-0 in the next round, and in the semi-final – the furthest Dunfermline had ever gone in the Cup – St Mirren were eventually beaten 1-0 after a replay.

The final was where the bubble should have burst as Celtic mounted attack after attack. But even a late injury that saw them reduced to 10 men did not deter Dunfermline and they hung on to force a replay. Once again Dunfermline had to fight a rearguard action, but two breakaway goals from Thomson and Dickson gave the Fife club victory and the Cup. Was there any end to the miracles that Stein could work?

Stein: beat his old club in the Scottish Cup final

THE 1961-62 SEASON

Ramsey's yeomen march past the First Division aristocrats

IPSWICH, a team largely composed of non-entities and whom everybody outside of East Anglia had tipped for relegation, rocked the aristocrats of the First Division by winning the championship in their first ever season in the top flight. Alf Ramsey, a right back for Tottenham and England in the 1950s and now the Ipswich manager, was the guiding force behind this mind-boggling triumph.

Ramsey had taken the helm in 1955 when the club had just been relegated to the Third Division South. Their foray in the Second Division had been brief, just one season, but it had been the most the club had ever achieved. Ramsey, who had always been a thoughtful and deliberate footballer, got Ipswich back into the Second Division in 1957 and then spent the next three years assembling a close-knit squad of players loyal to him. Ramsey blended astute bargain basement purchases with younger players.

It was this squad that won Ipswich the Second Division championship in 1961 and, apart from the acquisition of Doug Moran from Falkirk for £12,000, it was the same squad that won the First Division championship. Ipswich thus emulated the Tottenham side of 1950 and 1951 who were the second club to win the Second and First Division championships in consecutive seasons. Ironically Ramsey had been a crucial member of those Tottenham teams.

Ipswich had achieved their extraordinary success because of Ramsey's tactical nous. He had two free-scoring strikers in Ray Crawford and Ted Phillips, and two wingers in Jimmy Leadbetter and Ray Stephenson. However Ramsey innovatively used his two wingers in midfield – a crude form of the 4-4-2 system that was to dominate English football by the end of the decade.

Ipswich had begun the season badly, taking only one point from their first three matches, but Ramsey stuck to his tactical guns and the results started coming. With Tottenham distracted by their European and FA Cup exploits and Burnley blowing up over the last seven League games, Ipswich stole home to take the title with a mere 56 points.

Stoke make a fortune from Matthews mania

Generation gap: Gerry Bridgwood, 17, welcomes Matthews

STOKE gave £3,500 to Blackpool to bring Stanley Matthews home, and paid the 46-year-old winger £50 a week, plus a £25 appearance fee. It was the best money the struggling Second Division club ever spent.

The match before Matthews arrived only drew just over 8,000 people to the Victoria Ground. The crowd attracted by his first home game was a staggering 35,288. The club was delighted and Matthews's teammates were equally happy – every week the attendance exceeded 12,000 they all received a bonus of £1 per thousand people.

Matthews made his debut against Huddersfield, who had the England international Ray Wilson at full-back. Stoke won 3-0 and Matthews was involved in all the goals, albeit with a little help from the referee who seemed to have been swayed by the occasion.

Wilson said: "Whenever the ball came to Matthews the crowd erupted. Once, I slid in quickly, got the ball from his foot and never touched him. But the whistle went. A foul!"

The fans flocked in week after week (the police had to impose a crowd limit of 50,000 for the FA Cup fourth round against Blackburn) and the money they spent enabled Stoke to strengthen their squad and finish the season in eighth place. There seemed to be no end to the magic that Matthews could work.

Unstoppable: Ray Crawford tormented First Division defences

European agony for Tottenham

Off target: Mackay heads the ball against the crossbar in the last minute of the semi-final at White Hart Lane

TOTTENHAM'S European Cup semi-final against the holders Benfica produced two of the most pulsating, dramatic, and ultimately heart-wrenching matches of the decade. The contest was given further edge as both managers believed the tie would provide the eventual winners with Real Madrid, the likely other finalists, clearly a waning force.

In the first leg, in Lisbon, Tottenham were in trouble after 20 minutes, Benfica having taken a 2-0 lead with goals from Aguas and Augusto. Bobby Smith reduced the arrears but Augusto restored their two-goal cushion for the return at White Hart Lane with a header. Tottenham had hauled back such a deficit before, notably in the preliminary round match against Gornik, but what really rankled was that the team believed that two good goals – one from Jimmy Greaves, the other from Smith – had been disallowed for offside.

Aguas made matters worse in the second leg improving Benfica's aggregate lead to 4-1 after 15 minutes. Then another Greaves goal was dubiously disallowed for offside. With three decisions going against him in the two legs it seemed as if Greaves's speed on the ball was just too fast for the officials to follow. Seven minutes before the interval Smith reduced the arrears and, four minutes into the second half Danny Blanchflower coolly stroked home a penalty. Spurs were now one goal behind on aggregate with 40 minutes left to play.

With the 65,000 crowd roaring them on and Dave Mackay playing like a man possessed, Tottenham threw everything at the Benfica goal. But it was not to be. Spurs hit both posts and, just before the final whistle, Mackay cracked one off the crossbar. It was a sad end to a glorious European campaign. Greaves also thought it was desperately unfair. Referring to the first leg in Lisbon, he said: "To this day I reckon the Swiss referee, Muellet, refereed us out of the final."

Nicholson saves a pound and spends a fortune on Greaves

TOTTENHAM strengthened their already formidable side when they brought Jimmy Greaves back from Italy in December for £99,999. The fee was deliberately £1 short of six figures because Bill Nicholson, the Spurs manager, did not want the England striker burdened with the label of Britain's first £100,000 footballer.

Greaves, who at 21 had been the youngest player to score 100 League goals, had been transferred from Chelsea to AC Milan in June for £80,000. Although he had settled well into his new team – scoring on his debut and amassing nine goals in 14 games – he had never settled into the Italian way of doing things. He resented the authoritarian style of management, bucked against their disciplinarian methods, and detested the negative tactics characteristic of Italian football.

Unfortunately for Spurs, because of the timing of his transfer, Greaves was not eligible to play in the European Cup for his new club until the semi-finals. Typically Greaves achieved what he always did when he arrived at a new club, scored in his first match.

Man apart: Greaves (back, second left) and ten others

Greaves's opening shots

1957	August 23	Tottenham v CHELSEA	Scored
1957	September 25	ENGLAND U-23 v Bulgaria	Scored twice
1959	May 17	Peru v ENGLAND	Scored
1961	June 7	MILAN v Botafogo	Scored
1961	December 16	TOTTENHAM v Blackpool	Scored hat-trick
1962	May 4	First Cup final. TOTTENHAM v Burnley	Scored
1970	March 20	Manchester City v WEST HAM	Scored twice

THE
1961-62
SEASON

Cup scant reward for Spurs

Finishing touch: Blanchflower's penalty made sure Spurs retained the Cup

Oxford step up as Accrington admit defeat

ACCRINGTON STANLEY finally admitted defeat in their fight for financial survival and resigned from the Football League on March 6. They had played 33 matches in the Fourth Division, but all their results were expunged.

Accrington's finances had declined along with their form. In 1955 they had attracted a crowd of more than 15,000 to one match as they just missed promotion to the Second Division. Now, struggling in the Fourth Division, their attendances were a fraction of that.

Matters were not helped by the club spending £14,000 to improve their ground by buying the grandstand used for the Aldershot military tattoo and erecting it as a new stand. Accrington's last League match was a 1-0 defeat at Crewe on March 2, and the club was wound up by the High Court.

Strangely, the little clubs who had complained so often about being kept out of the League by the end of season re-elections did not rush to take Accrington's place.

The League's annual meeting on June 2 only received two applications, from Oxford United and Wigan Athletic. Curiously, Oxford had enjoyed a huge improvement in their fortunes since the club was renamed from Headington United in 1960. After the change they won the Southern League two years in a row and that form, combined with a reasonable record in the FA Cup, was enough to win them a place in the Fourth Division by 39 votes to five.

TOTTENHAM'S season, which had looked so promising in March when they had the triple targets of the League title, FA Cup and European Cup in their sights, at last yielded one trophy: the FA Cup when they beat Burnley, the League runners-up, 3-1 in the final. Tottenham became only the second club this century to win the FA Cup in successive years, emulating Newcastle United's achievement exactly a decade earlier.

Burnley, whose form deserted them in the closing stages of the title race, were never really a match for a Spurs team now becoming past masters of Cup competitions. Jimmy Greaves, their expensive signing from Milan, had Burnley on the rack as early as the third minute when he scored a stupendous goal.

Smith had headed the ball down perfectly to Greaves who ran straight at the heart of Burnley defence. Just as he seemed to be surrounded by a posse of defenders Greaves stopped dead, wrong-footing all of them. He turned on the ball and slid a left-footed ground shot past the outstretched Adam Blacklaw.

Five minutes into the second half Jimmy Robson put Burnley briefly back into the game when he met Harris's deadly centre

Return trip: Spurs bring the Cup back again

with his shins. But within a minute Spurs had struck again. This time it was Smith who bamboozled the Burnley defence when, having trapped John White's cross, he turned and whacked the ball into the net. Ten minutes from time Danny Blanchflower delivered the coup de grace with a penalty after Tom Cummings had handled Terry Medwin's shot on the goal-line.

Tottenham's joy at retaining the Cup was muted. They had entertained high hopes of winning all three honours. Indeed they can trace their loss of the League championship to one

fateful match. On March 14, Spurs were at home to Ipswich and Bill Nicholson, the Spurs manager, raised with his players a change of tactics to counter Jimmy Leadbetter, Ipswich's deep-lying left-winger. However the players dissented and Nicholson, reluctantly, gave way. Spurs lost the match 3-1. If that result had been reversed Spurs would have won the Double again.

Nicholson proved his point in the Charity Shield at Portman Road in August. He insisted the players use the tactics they had spurned in March and Tottenham duly ran out 5-1 winners.

'The ball kept on hitting the net'

THE arrival of Jim Baxter in 1960 had galvanised Rangers. The team that had missed out on the treble last season showed every sign of being able to win all three honours this time, particularly with Davie Wilson in such prolific goalscoring form.

Wilson used to have a bet with his fellow forwards Jimmy Millar and Ralph Brand as to who would score first in each match. But Millar was not on hand to see one of Wilson's most spectacular performances.

Millar was injured so Rangers moved Wilson from the wing to replace him against Falkirk on March 17. The switch in position did not unsettle him and he scored six times - including three goals in eight minutes - in a 7-1 rout at Brockville. "The ball just kept on hitting the net," Wilson said modestly when asked about his feat.

Despite Wilson's goals – 28 in total – the Treble eluded Rangers once again. They retained the League Cup, although they were taken to a replay in the final by Hearts. The Scottish Cup, which had proved their downfall last season, was won at a canter.

Arbroath were hit for six in the second round, Aberdeen conceded five goals in the third round replay, Kilmarnock were brushed aside 4-2 and Motherwell, their conquerors in the Cup last season were dispatched 3-1 in the semi-final. The final was not particularly taxing either – Brand and Wilson shared the spoils in a 2-0 defeat of St Mirren.

Scot Symon's team, though could not retain the League title. Rangers lost the same number of matches as Dundee (five), but they drew three more games to hand Dundee their first championship.

Benfica's Eusebio upstages Puskas

BELA GUTTMANN was one of football's great nomads. He had played for Hungary in the 1924 Olympics, left home to coach in America and Holland, survived a Second World War concentration camp and returned to Hungary to take Ujpest to the national championship.

But his travels were far from over. He moved to Italy and guided AC Milan to the title, but was then sacked while his team were leading the League once again. Then he went to Brazil, where he took Sao Paulo to the top in 1958 and was credited with pioneering the 4-2-4 system that Brazil unveiled at the 1958 World Cup finals.

While Guttmann was working in Brazil he learnt to speak Portuguese, which explained why his next port of call was Benfica. And, as he had done everywhere else in the world, he had a winning team.

Benfica won the European Cup for the second year running and the final, in Amsterdam on May 2, showed that the balance of power in Europe was shifting. Bill Nicholson had watched Real Madrid during Tottenham's European campaign and was of the opinion that Real "were not the side they had been". Guttmann agreed with him.

It was hard to believe that Real were in decline when Fer-

Keeper of the faith: Pereira helped Benfica retain the trophy

enc Puskas scored a hat-trick in the first 38 minutes. But Benfica had pegged them back to 2-2 and equalised again early in the second half.

With Puskas's age and weight starting to take their toll it was time for him to make way for the next great player. Guttmann's wealth of experience enabled him to make the tactical changes that enabled the 20-year-old Eusebio to wrap up the game 5-3 with two goals in three minutes.

WORLD CUP 1962
Irresistible Brazil retain their trophy

THE SEVENTH World Cup, although full of drama, incident and surprises, is mostly remembered for what did not happen. Three of the world's greatest players were set to grace the world's greatest stage, and somehow didn't.

Pele, after one outstanding match in which he made one goal and scored the other having beaten four defenders, limped off in the second with a torn thigh muscle and was out of the tournament. At least he played; Alfredo di Stefano didn't. The world's most versatile forward used the excuse of a pulled muscle before the tournament began to fuel his personal row with Helenio Herrera, Spain's manager, and sullenly refused to kick a ball.

Lev Yashin, the world's No1 goalkeeper did play – after a fashion. His errors were so disastrous that the Soviet Union qualified for the quarter-finals despite him but then promptly lost 2-1 to unfancied Chile after Yashin inexplicably failed to save two speculative long shots. For Chile, the host nation, it was their finest hour. Because of Yashin's mishaps they had reached a semi-final against Brazil, the holders and the overwhelming favourites to retain their trophy.

That Chile even hosted the tournament in the first place was a minor miracle. They beat out bids from Argentina and West Germany, despite not having the stadiums nor the footballing tradition of either of the other candidates. Then there had been a devastating earthquake in 1960. But the zeal of the Chileans was not to be denied.

Carlos Dittborn, the president of the Chilean football federation, exemplified this when Fifa proposed to re-allocate the event. "We have nothing, that is why we must have the World Cup," he said. His cri de coeur spoke volumes and won the day. Two splendid stadiums were constructed and the tournament went off successfully. Sadly Dittborn, who had been the driving force behind the venture, died a month before the finals began.

However as some of the brightest stars faded, others shone. With Pele out injured, Brazil pulled another wonder out of their pocket: the 24-year-old "White Pele" Amarildo, another athletic genius who knew precisely where the goal was. As did Garrincha who blossomed into a truly world-class player in Pele's absence. Garrincha's sinuous runs and deadly crosses were now complemented by powerful shooting and strength in the air. He was certainly the man of the tournament as England found out to their cost.

England were the only home nation to qualify – Scotland were knocked out in a play-off match with Czechoslovakia and Wales were eliminated by Spain. Although England's approach to the finals was more organised than before (Walter Winterbottom had Jimmy Adamson, the Burnley captain, as his assistant) their build-up was far from perfect; a middle-aged Australian millionaire played in one practice match.

The team was built round its captain Johnny Haynes at inside-left, and the emphasis on one player was to prove England's undoing. The Yugoslav manager summed it up neatly: "Number 10 takes the corners. Number 10 takes the throw-ins. So what do we do? We put a man on number 10. Goodbye England."

And so it proved in the first match. Hungary's defence stifled Haynes and England were beaten 2-1 with Haynes complaining to a journalist: "You want us to lose." Alan Peacock replaced Gerry Hitchens at centre-forward for the next match and the switch helped England's forwards temporarily rediscover their touch as Argentine were easily beaten 3-1. But a poor performance against Bulgaria, and a 0-0 draw, left England second in their group and having to face Brazil in the quarter-finals.

Garrincha simply took England apart. The English defence had no answer to his penetrating runs and he gave Brazil the lead after half an hour with a soaring leap and header. Hitchens quickly equalised but Garrincha finished England off in the second half with a thunderous free-kick. The ball bounced off Ron Springett's chest and fell to Vava, who tucked away the easiest of chances. Six minutes later Garrincha hit a wicked, swerving long-range shot and Springett, whose eyesight was thought to be suspect, was completely wrong-footed.

Chile, Brazil's next opponents, were involved in one of the most disgraceful games ever seen at a World Cup finals. Their first round match with Italy was dubbed the "Battle of Santiago" after 90 minutes of brawling that the English referee Ken Aston could do little to prevent. He described the match as "uncontrollable". The tension was created by Italy's habit of poaching South American players and two intemperate articles written by Italian journalists claiming that Chile was a dreadful country.

Right from the kick-off the players were at each others' throats. Aston did not see the worst incident, which took place behind his back, but television viewers saw Leonel Sanchez, the son of a professional boxer, break Humberto Maschio's nose with a left hook. Amazingly neither linesman drew Aston's attention to what had happened.

Giorgio Ferrini, who seemed to be conducting a private war with Sanchez, was sent off for kicking Landa but refused to go. The match was stopped for 10 minutes, Italian officials were summoned on to the pitch, and Ferrini was finally marched away by a group of policemen. Then Mario David was dismissed for trying to kick Sanchez in the head and Italy, reduced to nine men, lost 2-0. Ferrini was banned for one match but, amazingly, David and Sanchez were let off by Fifa, who merely gave them "severe admonishment". The managers of all 16 countries were called to a meeting by the organising committee and warned about their teams' conduct.

After their victory over the Soviet Union, Chile were brought down to earth by Brazil in the semi-final. The Brazilians, with Garrincha rampant once again, played as if they were in a different class. Garrincha and Vava both bagged a pair as Chile were swept aside 4-2. Garrincha was sent off for retaliation late in the match, and was struck by a bottle thrown from the crowd as he left. Brazil feared that he would not be eligible for the final, but he was not suspended because he had been badly provoked throughout the match.

Brazil's opponents in the final, Czechoslovakia, had surprised

White Pele: Amarildo successfully stepped into the injured star's boots

everybody, including themselves, by progressing so far. That they did was due to the sublime goalkeeping of Wilhelm Schroiff. As Yashin waned, Schroiff waxed. His saves against the more fancied Hungary (in the quarter-final) and Yugoslavia (in the semi-final) were the stuff of legend. It seemed as if he was unbeatable no matter what was thrown at him. Schroiff's virtuosity was as vital to Czechoslovakia as was Garrincha's to Brazil. The Czechs were slow, precise and defensive minded, although in Josef Masopust they possessed a very inventive and cunning left-half.

Unfortunately for Czechoslova-kia and Schroiff, his form inexplicably deserted him in the final. The Czechs had taken a shock lead in the 16th minute when Masopust bisected the Brazilian defence and calmly slotted the ball home. But within two minutes Amarildo out-foxed Schroiff for the equaliser. As he cut in from the left, Schroiff guarded the near post only to watch helplessly as Amarildo's shot sailed in at the other end of the goal. In the second half Zito headed Amar-ildo's stunning cross into an open goal and Schroiff dropped Djalma Santos's lob into the path of the onrushing Vava for the brave Czechs to go down 3-1.

First blood: Chile strike first in the Battle of Santiago

Oops: Schroiff's gaffe allowed Vava to score Brazil's third goal

Twice winners: Brazil came from behind to retain the Jules Rimet trophy

FOR THE RECORD

FIRST ROUND

GROUP 1

	P	W	D	L	F	A	Pts
Soviet Union	3	2	1	0	8	5	5
Yugoslavia	3	2	0	1	8	3	4
Uruguay	3	1	0	2	4	6	2
Colombia	3	0	1	2	5	11	1

GROUP 2

	P	W	D	L	F	A	Pts
W. Germany	3	2	1	0	4	1	5
Chile	3	2	0	1	5	3	4
Italy	3	1	1	1	3	2	3
Switzerland	3	0	0	3	2	8	0

GROUP 3

	P	W	D	L	F	A	Pts
Brazil	3	2	1	0	4	1	5
Czech	3	1	1	1	2	3	3
Mexico	3	1	0	2	3	4	2
Spain	3	1	0	2	2	3	2

GROUP 4

	P	W	D	L	F	A	Pts
Hungary	3	2	1	0	8	2	5
England	3	1	1	1	4	3	3
Argentina	3	1	1	1	2	3	3
Bulgaria	3	0	1	2	1	7	1

QUARTER-FINALS

Chile 2   Soviet Union 1
HT 2-1 Att. 17,268

Yugoslavia 1   West Germany 0
HT 0-0 Att. 63,264

Brazil 3   England 1
HT 1-1 Att. 17,736

Czechoslovakia 1   Hungary 0
HT 1-0 Att. 11,690

SEMI-FINALS

Brazil 4   Chile 2
HT 2-1 Att. 76,594

Czechoslovakia 3   Yugoslavia 1
HT 0-0 Att. 5,890

THIRD PLACE PLAY-OFF

Chile 1   Yugoslavia 0
HT 0-0 Att. 66,697

FINAL

Brazil 3   Czochoslovakia 1
HT 1-1 Att. 68,679

Teams
Brazil Gilmar; D Santos, Oliveira, Zozimo, N Santos, Zito, Didi, Garrincha, Vava, Amarildo, Zagalo
Czechoslovakia Schroiff; Tichy, Pluskal, Popluhar, Novak, Kvasnak, Masopust, Popsichal, Scherer, Kadraba, Jelinek

Leading goalscorers 4 Valentin Ivanov (Soviet Union), Leonel Sanchez (Chile), Garrincha (Brazil), Vava (Brazil), Florian Albert (Hungary), Drazan Jerkovic (Yugoslavia); 3 Amarildo Tavares de Silveira (Brazil), Adolf Scherer (Czechoslovakia), Lajos Tichy (Hungary), Milan Galic (Yugoslavia)
Total goals scored 89
Average per game: 2.78
Sendings-off Vladimir Popovic (Yugoslavia) v Uruguay; Ruben Cabrera (Uruguay) v Yugoslavia; Referee: Karol Galba (Czechoslovakia). Giorgio Ferrini (Italy) v Chile; Mario David (Italy) v Chile; Referee: Ken Aston (England). Garrincha (Brazil) v Chile; Honorino Landa (Chile) v Brazil; Referee: Arturo Maldonado Yamasaki (Peru).
Number of players used by finalists
12 Brazil; 15 Czechoslovakia

● Four players have appeared for two nations in the World Cup final stages: Jose Altafini (then known as Mazzola) for Brazil in 1958 and Italy in 1962; Luis Monti Argentina 1930 and Italy 1962; Ferenc Puskas Hungary 1954 and Spain 1962; and Jose Santamaria Uruguay 1954 and Spain 1962.
● Vaclav Masek's goal for Czechoslovakia against Mexico was scored in 15 seconds, the fastest ever at the World Cup finals. However, his team lost the first round match 3-1 but still went on to the final.

THE
1962-63
SEASON

Genius Baxter and Rangers unstoppable

WITH Jim Baxter at his mercurial best, slicing defences open from midfield, the Rangers forwards were able to enjoy a field day. Ralph Brand, Jimmy Millar and Davie Wilson scored 105 goals between them, with the partnership of Millar and Brand doing most of the damage.

"We were just right for each other," Millar said. "Ralph was ahead of his time — always wanting to try out something new."

Millar was plagued by a bad back, and many people thought he was too small to play at centre-forward. But his timing was so good that he had no difficulty in out-jumping defenders and heading the ball on to Brand, who was no giant either.

Millar said that the Rangers team was "just about unbeatable in Scotland". There was no disputing his assessment as Rangers raced away with the League title, only losing two matches. Rangers finished nine points clear of Kilmarnock, and Millar was the division's leading scorer with 27 goals.

The Millar and Butler double act, known throughout Scotland as "a dose of M&B", was also the undoing Celtic in the Scottish Cup final replay.

Baxter, who took even more delight in running rings round Celtic than he did in tormenting other teams, produced a sublime display of skills.

Celtic were so bedazzled that Miller and Brand had no difficulty in applying the coup de grace — Brand scoring two goals and Millar one as Rangers collected the trophy for the third time in four years.

Ramsey vows: 'England will win the World Cup in 1966'

Three wise men: Ramsey with Denis Follows and Joe Richards at an FA committee meeting

THE FA and England entered a new era when Alf Ramsey was appointed to replace Walter Winterbottom as the manager of the national side. It was a critical appointment as England were the hosts for the 1966 World Cup and a repeat of their moderate performances in the previous four tournaments would be a public embarrassment. The post would now be full-time and Ramsey would decide all team selections. Under Winterbottom the team had been selected by an FA committee.

Ramsey had not been the obvious, or even first, choice. At Winterbottom's suggestion Jimmy Adamson, the Burnley manager, was offered the job but declined because he was reluctant to move South. Strangely the FA then turned to Ramsey rather than club managers with a more sustained run of success such as Bill Nicholson, of Spurs, or Stan Cullis, of Wolves. Ramsey was, after all, nothing more than a one-hit wonder and his championship-winning Ipswich were struggling to survive in the First Division.

Ramsey's first match in charge was an abject failure and England were eliminated from the European Nations Cup in the first round. In Paris in February England went 3-0 down to France, rallied with goals from Bobby Smith and Bobby Tampling but eventually succumbed 5-2, the first time England had conceded five goals for five years.

Ramsey's next two matches, against Scotland and Brazil, were little better but then, suddenly in the summer his team caught fire. Czechoslovakia were beaten 4-2 in Bratislava, East Germany 2-1 in Leipzig and Switzerland hammered 8-1 in Basle, Bobby Charlton scoring a hat-trick.

The press were effusive in their praise of the new regime and even Ramsey, normally dour, uncommunicative and deeply cautious, got carried away. "England will win the World Cup in 1966," he said. "We have the ability, strength, character and players with the right temperament." Brave words.

Winterbottom: replaced

Pools companies use experts to make up results and beat freeze

THE BIG FREEZE that gripped the country played havoc with football for months and forced the season to be extended by several weeks. On January 5, only three of 32 FA Cup third round matches and a handful of League games could be played. The following week was even worse, and only eight matches were played on January 19.

Clubs tried everything to beat the freeze – Blackpool used a flame-thrower on their ground and Leicester put a tent over their pitch – but to no avail. Nearly half of the Cup matches were postponed at least 10 times, and Lincoln only played Coventry at the 16th attempt.

The pools companies were forced to declare three successive coupons void, with the money carried forward to make the jackpot ever larger. Then, to keep the interest going, they hit on the idea of using a panel of experts to forecast the results. Four former players, Ted

Five wise men: the panel picked seven draws

Drake, Tom Finney. Tommy Lawton and George Young, and a former referee, Arthur Ellis, chose seven draws, eight away wins and 23 homes on January 26.

The results were announced on television and, not surprisingly, some punters who did not agree with the selections called

the process a farce. But the pools panel was here to stay.

The bad weather dragged on into February when, on the 9th, only seven out of 64 matches were played, a record low. The worst hit club of the lot, though, was Bolton who went a record time without a match, from December 8 to February 16.

FOR THE RECORD

■ Johnny Haynes (above), the Fulham and England inside-forward, missed almost all of the season when he was badly injured in a car crash in August.

■ John Charles returned to England when Don Revie signed him from Juventus for £53,000, at the start of the season. Charles could not settle and after playing 11 games for Leeds he returned to Italy, sold to Roma for £65,000.

■ Ipswich, playing in Europe for the first time, made a remarkable start, beating Floriana 14-1 on aggregate in the first round of the European Cup. Ipswich won 4-1 in Malta and then hit 10 at Portman Road with Ray Crawford scoring five of the goals.

■ Gravesend, of the Southern League, reached the fourth round of the FA Cup by beating Exeter, Wycombe and Carlisle. They held Second Division Sunderland to a 1-1 draw before losing the replay 5-2.

Dundee and Dunfermline come through their European baptism of fire in a blaze of glory

DUNDEE and Dunfermline, two of Scotland's less fashionable clubs, made successful forays into European competition. Indeed, the progress of both clubs was only halted when they were up against the eventual winners of their respective competitions.

In the European Cup, Dundee, the surprise champions of Scotland the season before, majestically reached the semi-finals, even sweeping away Anderlecht 4-1 in Belgium. But, as Ipswich had discovered in the second round, AC Milan were virtually unstoppable in their San Siro stadium.

Dundee's European hopes went crashing as they were trounced 5-1 in the first leg with four of Milan's goals coming in the second half. Dundee's lame excuse was that their goalkeeper, Bert Slater, had been unable to see the crosses from

Milan's sprightly wingers because he was dazzled by the flash bulbs of the photographers. In the return leg at Dens Park, Alan Gilzean scored the only goal of the game and then managed to get himself sent off for retaliation.

Milan went on to win the European Cup beating Benfica, the holders, at Wembley despite conceding a 19th minute goal to Eusebio. Two goals from Altafini in the second half were sufficient to give Italy its first European Cup.

In the Fairs Cup, Dunfermline drew Everton, who went on to win the League title, in the first round and a canny, tactical performance from Jock Stein's team at Goodison left Everton with only a slender 1-0 lead to defend in the second leg. A bravura performance in Scotland saw Dunfermline conquer Everton 2-0. It seemed that

Stein had grasped the knack of European competition.

Then Dunfermline faced Valencia, who had disposed of Celtic in the first round, and were shredded 4-0 in Spain. Somehow Stein inspired his players to reach unbelievable heights and at East End Park Valencia incredibly lost 6-2 to leave the tie level at 6-6. However in the replay, in Portugal, Valencia just managed to scrape a 1-0 victory.

The Spanish club then crushed Hibs in the quarter final and waltzed off with the trophy, even winning both legs of the final against Dynamo Zagreb. So there was some consolation for Stein: Dunfermline had been the only side to interrupt Valencia's steady progress to the Fairs Cup and two other Scottish clubs had proved to be mere cannon fodder for the Spaniards.

Eusebio: first blood

THE
1962-63
SEASON

Matthews the miracle worker

STANLEY MATTHEWS chose the perfect moment to score his first goal of the season for Stoke. They were leading 1-0 at home to Luton in their last match of the season, and Matthews's goal made sure of victory and the Second Division championship.

Although Matthews took a long time to get on the scoresheet he was a vital member of Stoke's side. Even though he was 48, he played in 35 League matches and his stylish performances created countless goals for the rest of the team.

Stoke's return to the First Division after a decade was a close thing, with Chelsea and Sunderland also vying for the two promotion places. The issue was not settled until the final matches of the season. When Stoke beat Chelsea in their penultimate match it appeared that they had done Sunderland a favour.

But Chelsea went to Sunderland and won 1-0, which left them needing to win their last match to overtake Sunderland on goal average. Chelsea made absolutely sure of promotion by thumping Portsmouth 7-0, their biggest win since the 1910-11 season.

Blanchflower talks Dyson into playing the game of his life

TOTTENHAM'S record-breaking start to the 1960s continued in Rotterdam on May 15 when they imperiously dismissed Atletico Madrid 5-1 to capture the European Cup Winners Cup and become the first British team to win a European trophy. It was a magnificent achievement. Atletico, the runners-up in the Spanish League, were the holders and Spurs were without their midfield dynamo Dave Mackay, who was unable to play because of a severe stomach upset.

Even Danny Blanchflower, their inspirational captain, was only partially fit and only played with the aid of a pain-killing injection. In a previous round against Rangers, Blanchflower had been sandwiched by two defenders seriously damaging his knee. The injury kept him out for 22 matches and he effectively had to play on one leg in Rotterdam. However, his influence on the field proved decisive, as did his dressing-room speech before the match.

The loss of Mackay seemed to have unnerved Bill Nicholson, the Spurs manager, and instead of a rabble-rousing team talk he spoke only of the quality of the opposition. After Nicholson had left Blanchflower took centre-stage and went through the Spurs team player by player. He convinced them that they were all world beaters, especially Terry Dyson, a winger not noted for his match-winning abilities.

Spurs had taken a 2-0 half-

Blanchflower's triumph: the first European trophy for a British club

time lead with goals from Jimmy Greaves and John White, but two minutes after the restart Ron Henry conceded a penalty and Atletico were back in the match battling for the equaliser. The next 20 minutes were frantic as Spurs desperately fought to preserve their lead. Then, in the 67th minute, out of the blue Dyson turned the match around.

The left winger hit a high cross into the Spanish penalty area that floated close to the keeper. Somehow he misread the flight of the ball and it sailed over his head and into the net. A fluke? Maybe, though Dyson claimed he had spotted the keeper off his line. Whatever, it galvanised Dyson to play the game of his life.

Thirteen minutes later Dyson crossed for Greaves to add a fourth, and with five minutes left Dyson scored a virtuoso goal, running 30 yards with the ball, outwitting defender after defender, before slamming a 25-yard shot into the goal. It certainly was the perfect game for the diminutive left winger. As Spurs left the field Bobby Smith advised Dyson to retire on the spot. Why? "Because you'll never play a better game," the centre-forward told him.

Matthews: vital goal

Everton go shopping and buy championship

DESPITE the weather, Everton cruised to their first League title since the war. But their success was not universally acclaimed. The club were labelled the "cheque book champions" because of the number of players their manager had bought.

Harry Catterick had spent £175,000 on five players last season and he added to his squad during Everton's enforced idle

spell in the depths of the big freeze by buying Tony Kay from Sheffield Wednesday for £60,000 and the Scottish international winger Alex Scott from Rangers for £40,000.

Everton's strength in depth enabled them to see off the challenge of Tottenham, Burnley and Leicester with games to spare. Everton regained the leadership of the First Division

in April when they beat Tottenham, and made sure of the title when they beat Fulham in their last game of the season.

The 4-1 victory meant that Tottenham, who lost to Manchester City that day, could not overhaul them, even though they had two more games to play. Tottenham only collected one point from those matches and finished a distant second.

Busby's swoops turn United around

Match winner: Denis Law (No 10) scored the first goal and sealed United's victory

MANCHESTER UNITED were a team still in transition after the Munich disaster. With no home-grown talent coming through the ranks Matt Busby was forced to continue buying players to keep his team afloat. Despite spending a small fortune, his team, which had cost close to a third of a million pounds, came very close to sinking into the Second division.

Before the season began Busby decided that he needed another goalscorer to sharpen his team's attack. He always wanted the best players, regardless of the cost, so he brought Denis Law back from Italy for £115,000. Law had walked out on Torino during an Italian Cup match when the team's coach forbade him from taking a corner.

After Law arrived at Old Trafford Busby decided that his forward was not getting enough chances created for him. So Busby plunged into the transfer market again to buy Pat Crerand from Celtic.

Despite the signings, United struggled terribly in the League. Their final match of the season, at Maine Road, would decide whether they, or Manchester City, were relegated. City

Match winner: Law's goal put Manchester United in the final

needed to win while a draw would suffice for United.

City led 1-0 in the second half until Law was brought down in the penalty area. Albert Quixall converted the penalty and the match finished 1-1. So, ironically, Law had played a large part in condemning his former club to the Second Division.

While his team had been struggling in the League Busby kept their spirits up by telling them that United were going to win the FA Cup. Because of fixture congestion United had to play three matches in 15 days.

Home wins against Huddersfield, Aston Villa and Chelsea took United to the quarter-finals.

United eased into the final by beating Third Division Coventry and Second Division Southampton. Their opponents at Wembley, Leicester, were the favourites because they had displayed much more consistent form in the League.

United had an early scare when their captain Noel Cantwell nearly headed a harmless cross into his own goal, but from that point on Law started to

repay a large slice of his record transfer fee.

Law produced a virtuoso performance. He scored the first goal after half an hour and his incessant attacking unsettled the Leicester defence enough for David Herd to add two more in the second half. The 3-1 victory was an emotional moment for Busby, who saw his team collect their first trophy since their blackest hour in 1958.

THE 1963-64 SEASON

Gentleman Jim a gent to end

Ten players in betting coup

FOOTBALL was rocked to its foundations on the morning of Sunday April 12 when a newspaper revealed that three Sheffield Wednesday players, two of them England internationals had fixed a match to stage a betting coup.

The People revealed that Peter Swan, the England centre-half, Tony Kay, who had also played for England after being transferred to Everton, and David Layne made sure Sheffield Wednesday were beaten 2-0 by Ipswich in December 1962. Each of them won £100 by betting on their team to lose.

Rumours had abounded for some time about matches being fixed, and the disclosures were just the tip of the iceberg. Jimmy Gauld, the former Everton and Charlton forward who was at the heart of the bribery scandal, revealed that two other

matches, between Lincoln and Brentford in the Third Division and York and Oldham in the Fourth Division, had been fixed on the same day.

Within weeks, the number of players implicated in the affair had more than trebled. Dick Beattie, who had played in goal for the Scottish Under-23 and Scottish League teams, was accused of being involved as were Walter Bingley (Halifax), Jackie Fountain (York), Harry Harris (Portsmouth), Ron Howells (Walsall), Bert Linnecor (Lincoln) and Peter Wraggs (Bradford).

The League suspended most of the players for life and 10 of them were convicted at Nottingham Assizes on January 26, 1965. Gauld received the heaviest sentence, four years in jail plus £5,000 costs. The other nine were also jailed for between four and 15 months.

Swan: bet on his team to lose

JIMMY DICKINSON finally retired at the age of 39, having made a record 764 League appearances for Portsmouth, his only club.

Dickinson was recruited during the war and turned professional while he was still serving in the Royal Navy. He was a key member of the team that won the championship in the 1948-49 season, Portsmouth's golden jubilee year, and retained it the following year.

Dickinson's cultured play for an unfashionable club brought him recognition by England, and he made 48 appearances at left-half for his country over nine years. He only lost his place in the national side after the emergence of Duncan Edwards and Portsmouth switched him to centre-half.

The finest achievement in Dickinson's career was to never fall foul of authority. In a career that spanned almost 20 years he was never spoken to by a referee, let alone booked, earning him the distinction of being known as "Gentleman Jim".

Little Luxembourg rock European big shots

THE Grand Duchy of Luxembourg (population 300,000) pulled off one of the greatest feats of giant-killing when they astounded Holland (population 12m) by knocking them out of the European championships in October. And it was no fluke – both legs were in Holland.

Normally Holland would field only a 'B' team against Luxembourg, but because of the importance of the tie they put out a full-strength side for the first game in Amsterdam in September. Everything seemed to be going to plan when Nuninga put Holland ahead after five minutes. However the expected flurry of goals never materialised and May levelled the scores in the 35th minute. Despite constant Dutch pressure there were no more goals.

In the second leg, in Rotterdam, the Dutch made wholesale changes bringing in the bulk of the Feyenoord side to avoid any further embarrassment. But to no avail. Dimmer gave Luxembourg the lead in the 20th minute, Kruiver equalised 10

minutes before half-time, and the Dutch play became frantic.

The Luxembourg goal was under constant barrage but it seemed that nothing could get past Nico Schmitt, the Duchy's goalkeeper. Dimmer provided the coup de grace with his second goal to put his country into a quarter-final tie against Denmark (population 4.7m).

Surely Luxembourg couldn't do it again? This time they played the first leg at home and, in the very first minute, Pilot shot them into the lead. Denmark, fearful of making the same mistake as Holland, piled on the pressure. The match seesawed back and forth to end 3-3, with Ole Madsen getting a hat-trick for Denmark.

If Denmark thought the second leg was going to be a doddle, Luxembourg soon shook them out of their complacency when Leonard gave them an early lead. Madsen, though, rose to the occasion, to equalise and then score again. But still Luxembourg would not lie down and Schmidt took the tie

into a third match with an equaliser six minutes from time.

Sadly for Luxembourg the bubble burst in the play-off in December in Amsterdam when Madsen scored his sixth goal against the Grand Duchy a minute before half-time. It was the only score of the match and the heroics of the Luxembourg national side were over.

But meanwhile Jeunesse Esch, their League champions, were upsetting the odds in the European Cup. In the first round the eight-times champions came back from a 4-1 defeat in Finland by Valkeakosken to register a thrilling 4-0 home victory that put them through to the second round – the first and only time a Luxembourg club had progressed that far.

They did not disgrace themselves either, astonishingly beating Partisan Belgrade 2-1 at home before losing 6-2 in Yugoslavia (population 18,500,000). To tiny Luxembourg it was their annus mirabilis: the year they tweaked the noses of the European big boys.

58

Heart and soul ripped out of Spurs

SADLY, Tottenham's fabulous Double side was disintegrating in front of Bill Nicholson's eyes. Terry Medwin, 30, had been injured on their summer tour to South Africa and missed the entire season. Nicholson also lost Dave Mackay, 29, in December when a broken leg kept him out for the rest of the season. Then Danny Blanchflower, 37, whose damaged knee had never fully recovered from the injury he had picked up against Rangers the previous season, announced his retirement. Bobby Smith, 31, was transferred to Brighton in May.

But the saddest blow of all came in July when John White, 27, was killed by lightning on a golf course while sheltering from a thunderstorm under a tree. Suddenly Spurs were deprived of one of the greatest midfield line-ups to grace an English pitch: Mackay, Blanchflower and White.

Blanchflower, whom Nicholson had inherited when he became the Spurs manager in October 1958, had joined the club in 1954, a £30,000 signing from Aston Villa. Mackay had been Nicholson's first major signing for the club when he snapped up the captain of Hearts and Scotland for £32,000 in March 1959. White followed in November of the same year, bought from Falkirk for £20,000. They were three of the most astute purchases Tottenham ever made.

As a threesome they could hardly be more different. Yet on the field they complemented each other wonderfully. Blanchflower was the most cultured, cerebral and elegant wing-half of the era. Mackay was tigerish, in the tackle and in the flesh. Nicholson called him the heartbeat of the team.

White, although slight in his frame, had been a cross-country champion and was a strong runner who had a knack of finding defence-splitting passes and also possessed a venomous shot. His ability to appear from nowhere earned him the nickname of "The Ghost".

It was surely the magic in midfield that these three players conjured up that was the key to Tottenham's winning the "impossible' Double in 1960-61. They were all irreplaceable.

Mackay: always the boss on the field for Tottenham

White: the ghost

When Bill Nicholson started to talk about identifying John White's body he broke down and had to go into the toilet. He never broke down like that

DAVE MACKAY
on how Nicholson broke the news of White's death to the Spurs players

United win the domestic battle but then lose the European war

TOTTENHAM'S defence of the European Cup Winners Cup did not last very long. After a bye in the first round, they were drawn against Manchester United in the second. Spurs won 2-0 at White Hart Lane on December 3 with goals from Dave Mackay and Terry Dyson. A week later they travelled to Old Trafford and walked into a double disaster.

Bobby Smith seemed to have got Tottenham off to the perfect start when he connected with Mackay's cross, but his header went directly to the keeper. Then Tottenham's night turned to dust. In the sixth minute David Herd met David Sadler's cross with a diving header to reduce the aggregate arrears. Seconds later, the heart was ripped out of Tottenham in the 20th minute when Mackay was carried off to hospital with a broken leg after a clash with Noel Cantwell. Mackay was out for the rest of the season.

Tottenham, with only 10 men, battled on and somehow managed to prevent United scoring again the first half. However, Herd scored a second early in the second half to level the scores. But still the Cup-holders refused to give in and a minute later they suddenly found themselves in the lead when Jimmy Greaves headed home a John White cross.

The fairytale ending was not to be. Bobby Charlton volleyed home the equaliser in the 78th minute and, with two minutes on the clock, he found the net again to knock Spurs out of Europe, and put his team into the quarter finals. There United met Sporting Club of Portugal, the eventual winners, who thrashed them 5-0 in Portugal and went through 6-4.

Capital's clubs turn the tide

From 1900 to 1960, the FA Cup was only won six times by clubs from London. But then the balance tipped firmly back in their favour.

Winners

1961 Tottenham	1970 Chelsea	1980 West Ham
1962 Tottenham	1971 Arsenal	1981 Tottenham
1964 West Ham	1975 West Ham	1982 Tottenham
1967 Tottenham	1979 Arsenal	

> *"I have never been as nervy during a match – even after I scored the first equaliser"*
>
> JOHN SISSONS

Sneaky Boyce breaks Preston's heart

ON PAPER, the Cup final was going to be one-sided. On the pitch it was anything but.

West Ham had reached Wembley the hard way, beating two other First Division teams, Burnley and Manchester United, in the quarter-finals and semi-finals. Second Division Preston North End, meanwhile, had beaten Fourth Division Oxford and Second Division Swansea.

The underdogs, though, took the lead after 10 minutes when Jim Standen could only parry Alec Dawson's shot and Doug Holden followed up. West Ham equalised within a minute with a goal from the 18-year-old John Sissons, who made a fine solo run past two defenders.

Preston played the far better football in the first half and Howard Kendall, the youngest player to appear in a Cup final this century (aged 17 years and 345 days), dominated midfield. Deservedly, Preston regained the lead five minutes before the interval. Standen slipped as he came out for a corner and Dawson was left unmarked for an easy header.

Bobby Moore, the Footballer of the Year, had been so ineffectual that Ron Greenwood, the West Ham manager, was forced to change his tactics to counter the threat posed by Kendall and Nobby Lawton. Their distribution was inch-perfect while West Ham's moves were breaking down too often as passes went astray.

West Ham began to get a grip on the midfield after the interval and Geoff Hurst just managed to score another equaliser.

His header hit the bar and Alan Kelly, the Preston goalkeeper, managed to get a hand to the rebound. The ball dropped behind Kelly and as he turned it trickled, agonisingly slowly, over the line.

There was further agony for Preston two minutes into injury time. Hurst made one last surging run and slipped the ball to Peter Brabrook. His cross sailed over the defence and Ron Boyce sneaked in unmarked on the blind side to head the winner.

It was a heartbreaking finish for Preston whose cultured play made a mockery of their underdogs label. Their contribution to the match had been so great, that the game was hailed by the press as being almost as exciting as the famous Matthews Cup final.

Moment of joy: Boyce scores the winning goal in the dying seconds

Rangers' greatest team rewarded with the Treble

THE TREBLE in Scotland (League, Scottish Cup and Scottish League Cup) was seen as an accomplishment as difficult as the Double in England. And since the inception of the Scottish League Cup in 1946-47 only one club had achieved it, Rangers in 1949. Then, gloriously, they did it again, with one of the greatest Ibrox teams ever to pull on the famous blue jerseys.

In Jimmy Millar, Ralph Brand and, occasionally Jim Forrest (who scored four goals in the Scottish League Cup final) they had a strike force second to none. To bolster their attack, Rangers also had Willie Henderson and Davie Wilson as marauding wingers. The midfield was also incomparable with the elegant Jim Baxter and his perfect foil, Ian McMillan. And all this in front of an unflappable defence composed of Bobby Shearer, David Provan, John Greig and Ron McKinnon. Little wonder that Scot Symon's team swept all before them.

Rangers demolished Morton 5-0 in the Scottish League Cup final, won the League in a canter, six points clear of Kilmarnock, and then Millar and Brand scored two goals in the last minute to win the Scottish Cup final against Dundee.

South Americans frighten Ramsey

Pick of the crop: di Stefano, Law and Lev Yashin turned out against England

FOR THE RECORD

■ Denis Law was chosen as the European Footballer of the Year.

■ Oxford's 3-1 defeat of Blackburn made them the first Fourth Division team to reach the quarter-finals of the FA Cup.

■ Jim Fryatt scored the fastest goal in first-class football on April 25. The referee's stopwatch timed his strike for Bradford Park Avenue against Tranmere at four seconds.

■ More than 300 people were killed in riots in Lima on May 25 after Peru had a goal disallowed in their match against Argentina.

ALF RAMSEY'S glorious summer extended into winter and then spring as England continued to rack up impressive victories. Wales were dispatched 4-0 in Cardiff, the Rest of the World – a team including fabulous players such as Alfredo di Stefano, Ferenc Puskas, Eusebio, Denis Law and Jim Baxter – 2-1 at Wembley, and then Northern Ireland were thrashed 8-3 with Jimmy Greaves scoring four times and Terry Paine helping himself to a hattrick.

There was a minor hiccup in Glasgow when Ramsey dropped Greaves for Roger Hunt and England lost 1-0 to Scotland, but once Greaves was restored to the side the victories continued. By the time England faced Brazil in Rio de Janeiro on May 30 in the four-country "Little World Cup" they had beaten Uruguay (2-1), Portugal (4-3 in Lisbon), the Republic of Ireland (3-1 in Dublin) and the USA (10-0 in New York). Confidence was sky high.

The Brazilians shattered England's aura of invincibility with scintillating football. England were outclassed in every department as Pele tore Ramsey's carefully selected side to shreds. The 5-1 scoreline could easily have been more. Shell-shocked, Ramsey dropped five players for the match against Portugal five days later in Sao Paulo and scraped a 1-1 draw.

If the Brazil match had shaken Ramsey's self-belief, then Brazil's subsequent 3-0 defeat at the hands of Argentina must have had him reaching for the cyanide. Merciless in their cynical and negative tactics, Argentina nullified Pele and reduced the apparently brilliant Brazilians to non-entities. England fared a little better when they met Argentina in Rio, only losing 1-0, but Ramsey's South American experience was a devastating blow to England's hopes for the World Cup in two years' time.

Shankly's silver tongue licks Liverpool into shape

BILL SHANKLY had played a canny game last season. He had used Liverpool's first year back at the top to convince his players that they were every bit as good as anybody else in the Division. "He's past it," Shankly would say. "He's nursing an injury. He's over-rated."

His players listened and learnt. Then they went out and put the lessons into practice. After an indifferent start, Liverpool took the First Division by the scruff of the neck. They beat Everton, the champions, 2-1 at Anfield in the tenth game of the season and never looked back.

The crowds flocked to Anfield to see teams taken apart. Ipswich were hit for six, as were Sheffield United, Stoke and Wolves. Aston Villa and Arsenal fared little better, both conceding five goals.

Roger Hunt was the club's leading scorer with 31 goals, many of which were created from the left wing by Peter Thompson, signed from Preston in August for a club record £40,000. Liverpool's strike rate was prodigious, particularly at home where they scored 60 goals.

Three straight wins over Easter virtually guaranteed Liverpool the title, which they won by four points from Manchester United. The Anfield faithful, who had started to doubt Shankly's ability in the Second Division were utterly convinced – Liverpool's average crowd for home games was only just short of 50,000.

Shankly: wise words

Thompson: shrewd purchase

TOTTENHAM IN THE 1960s
And the Spurs went marching on

Nick Pitt

THE GREAT teams have a life beyond their days on the field. Their innovations become the norm. The cheers that greeted them echo down the years. Their achievements inspire generations unborn.

But their legacy can also be curiously negative, and none has made life more difficult for their successors than the team that has come to be known as the Spurs Double team.

Since the early 1960s, when that team reigned supreme, there have been several worthy, even brilliant, Tottenham teams, many trophies won and a host of great individual players, including Osvaldo Ardiles and Glenn Hoddle. But each team has found itself compared to the Double team and has inevitably been found wanting.

At the time, the Double of the League and the FA Cup was a kind of holy grail. It had not been achieved in the 20th century, and although both Wolverhampton Wanderers and Manchester United had narrowly missed out on it in the late 1950s, many believed the Double to be impossible in modern times.

The man who built the Double team was Bill Nicholson. He had been a solid wing-half for Spurs, and had won one England cap. In October 1958 he was promoted from coach and assistant manager to manager. Nicholson was a dour, practical Yorkshireman, but he built a team in the best Tottenham traditions of stylish, attacking football. He was fortunate that several of the components of the team were already in place when his appointment was celebrated with a remarkable 10-4 win against Everton.

Already present were Bobby Smith, the burly, fearless centre-forward with a ferocious shot and surprising touch; Maurice Norman, a rock at centre-half; Cliff Jones, the brilliant Welsh winger noted for his greyhound speed and flying headers (though he had not yet been accepted by the ever-critical Spurs fans); and Danny Blanchflower, that most cultivated and original of wing-halves and, importantly, perhaps the greatest of all penalty-takers.

Nicholson entered the transfer market, and secured a series of bargains. From Hearts he bought the lion-hearted Dave Mackay; from Dundee the invariably secure goalkeeper Bill Brown; from Falkirk he bought the gifted John White, whose ability to create chances through stealth led him to be called The Ghost.

Rarely has a team achieved such balance. There was a spine of three uncompromisingly tough players: Smith, Mackay, Norman. There were two players with remarkable creative gifts: Blanchflower and White. The right flank was as strong as the left. The defence, typified by the full-backs, Peter Baker and Ron Henry, was strong but not showy; the attack scintillating.

It is hard to be sure exactly why a certain collection of individuals should function as a team, while another might not. But Spurs gloriously achieved the collective ideal, thanks to the team's balance and the influence of Blanchflower on the field and Nicholson off it. "I tried to keep our football as simple as possible," Nicholson recalled in the club's official history. "We had good players [a typical Nicholson understatement] but I didn't want them to indulge themselves too much as individuals. I used to tell them they had to be effective, not exhibition players."

In the summer of 1958 Blanchflower returned from playing for Northern Ireland in the World Cup, convinced that Spurs had a team that could achieve the elusive Double. In the 1959-60 League season Tottenham might have won but came third. In the Cup they had a remarkable tie against Crewe Alexandra, drawing 2-2 away before winning the replay 13-2. That match gave some idea of the attacking force Spurs would become. They led Crewe 10-1 at half-time and coasted the second half. But in the next round they were knocked out by Blackburn Rovers.

The following season, 1960-61, Spurs swept all before them. They opened their League campaign with a record: 11 consecutive victories, 36 goals for and 11 against. Such a run could not last forever. Spurs were held in their 12th game by Manchester City and were to lose seven times in their 42-match campaign. But their superiority to every other club was obvious and they won the championship by eight points from Sheffield Wednesday.

In the FA Cup, Tottenham defeated Charlton, Crewe, Aston Villa, Sunderland and Burnley to reach the final against Leicester. They were expected to win in style, but the final was a disappointment. Two late goals enabled Blanchflower, who 48 hours before had received the Footballer of the Year award, to climb the stairs of the Royal Box to claim the trophy and to fulfil the promise he had made to the Spurs chairman at the start of the season: the League and Cup Double. The glory days, and nights, were just beginning. The following season Jimmy Greaves, English football's greatest goalscorer, was bought from AC Milan for £99,999. His impact was immediate, not least in the Cup, which was retained with a 3-1 win against Burnley, Greaves scoring in the third minute.

But it was in the European arena that the Spurs Double side was to find its finest expression. European ties on Wednesday nights at White Hart Lane under the floodlights, with the

The Spurs go marching on: the team celebrates retaining the FA Cup in 1962

Hot shot: Greaves's arrival from AC Milan increased Tottenham's already formidable firepower

THE NICHOLSON YEARS

Born July 26, 1919, Scarborough

PLAYING CAREER
Tottenham 1936-55
He signed professional forms at 18 and made his League debut in 1938 as a full-back. After the war he became Tottenham's first choice centre-half, and moved to right-half in 1947, where he was an essential part of the team that won the League championship in 1951

Internationals One England cap v Portugal May 19, 1951

One goal (scored with his first touch after 19 seconds)

COACHING AND MANAGEMENT CAREER
First team coach 1955-58
Manager 1958-74
Honours European Cup: Semi-final 1962
European Cup Winners Cup: Winners 1963; Semi-final 1968; First round 1964
Uefa Cup: Winners 1972; Runners-up 1974; Semi-final 1973
League Championship: Winners 1961; Runners-up 1963; Third 1960, 1962, 1967, 1971; Fourth 1964
FA Cup: Winners 1961, 1962, 1967
League Cup: Winners 1971, 1973; Semi-final 1969, 1972

Other honours PFA Merit Award 1984

---

crowd singing "Glory, Glory, Hallelujah, the Spurs go marching on", became legendary. There always seemed a deficit to make up, and Spurs always seemed to make it up in style.

In their first European Cup match, against Gornik, the Polish champions, Tottenham trailed 4-2 after the first leg, but won 8-1 at home. Against Dukla Prague, the Czech champions, Spurs lost 1-0 away and won the second leg 4-2.

In the semi-final they faced Benfica of Portugal, having lost the first leg 3-1 with two goals disallowed. Benfica scored first but Tottenham attacked relentlessly, pulling back with a goal by Smith and a penalty by Blanchflower four min-utes after the interval. The final 40 minutes were frenzied. Spurs hit the woodwork three times but could not score the vital goal.

There was real consolation the following season, when Spurs won the European Cup Winners' Cup to become the first English team to win a European competition. On the way to the final they had lost their first-leg match against Slovan Bratislava 2-0 but won the second leg 6-0. In the final they defeated Atletico Madrid 5-1, belatedly proving themselves as good as any team in Europe in the early 1960s.

That was the Double team's glorious signing-off. Within a year the team's heart, its midfield, had been destroyed. Blanchflower, who had been suffering from injury, retired; White, a quiet player but considered by many to be the finest of them all, was killed by lightning while sheltering on a golf course; Mackay broke a leg in a match at Old Trafford.

Greaves and the others remained, soon to be joined by the wonderful Alan Gilzean. Over the next 30 years and more, Spurs would win many more cups, but never the League championship. And never again could they consistently achieve the sublime combination of breathtaking attack and certain defence that characterised the finest English club of them all.

Keeping it simple: Nicholson and Blanchflower emphasised attacking play

Smith: fearless forward with a fearsome shot

THE
1964-65
SEASON

Heartbreak for Leeds as United sneak home

FOR only the fourth time the League championship was decided on goal average, Manchester United pipping Leeds by 0.686 of a goal. Heart-breakingly, Leeds also lost the FA Cup final in extra time. So, by the slenderest of margins, the Double had slipped through their fingers.

Leeds had arrived in the First Division with a reputation as a hard and ruthless team and their performances did nothing to dispel this image. They won their first three League matches and by January were two points clear. By the spring the race was effectively between United and Leeds, who also met in the FA Cup semi-final.

The first match was an ugly goalless confrontation, and the replay, which Leeds won 1-0, was not much better. A fortnight later Manchester exacted their revenge in the League with a 1-0 victory at Elland Road. This result was the beginning of a marvellous run as United won six of their seven League matches after the semi-final. Their 3-1 defeat of Arsenal five days before the Cup final clinched their first title since 1957.

After Leeds lost the Cup final someone asked Bill Shankly, the Liverpool manager, if Don Revie's Leeds had failed. "Failed?" Shankly said. "Second in the championship. Cup finalists. Ninety per cent of managers would pray for 'failures' like that."

Liverpool gain as Byrne defies pain

Using his head: Ian St John's flying header past Gary Sprake in extra time crushes Leeds

Red machine: Liverpool won the FA Cup for the first time after two disappointments

ONE TROPHY had always eluded Liverpool, the FA Cup. They had been to the final twice before and lost on both occasions so against Leeds it was a case of third time lucky.

Liverpool were inspired by display of a raw courage by Gerry Byrne, who broke his collarbone after five minutes when he collided with Bobby Collins. With no substitutes allowed, Byrne insisted that he wanted to play on so that Leeds would not gain an advantage. Leeds never knew how badly he was hurt until after the match because, despite the pain, Byrne showed all his usual determination.

The final pitted two of the best defences in the country against each other so it was hardly surprising that the first 90 minutes were dour and goalless.

Byrne even created Liverpool's first goal in extra time. He resisted the temptation to try a shot from a narrow angle, instead slipping the ball across to give Roger Hunt the easiest of chances.

Leeds equalised two minutes later when Billy Bremner crashed a volley into the roof of the net. Liverpool, though, drew strength from Byrne's example. Ian St John glanced a header past Gary Sprake with nine minutes remaining and this time Liverpool were not going to be denied.

Matthews hits a half-century before bowing out a knight

STANLEY MATTHEWS finally retired at the end of the season, bringing to a close a wonderful career that had spanned more than 30 years.

His final game for Stoke was on February 6, when he created one of their goals in the 3-1 victory over Fulham. Matthews had just celebrated his birthday and the match made him the oldest player to appear in the First Division at the age of 50 years and five days.

Matthews had always placed great store by his fitness and he was asked what it was like to play when he was so old. "In my

> *Stanley Matthews knew exactly when, and where, to go. People could never tackle him, and nobody could touch him for speed over 10 yards. Even when he was nearing 50, he still had his magic*
>
> BOBBY CHARLTON

own mind I never had any doubts about my fitness," he said. "Stamina never worried me. I would never have played

had I not felt 100 per cent fit."

Many of his greatest adversaries from his days as an England player – Josef Masopust, Ferenc Puskas, Alfredo di Stefano and Lev Yashin – played for an International XI against Stoke in a special benefit match on April 28.

Yashin and Puskas carried him from the pitch on their shoulders in tribute, but by then Matthews had already received an even greater honour. Already a CBE, he was knighted in the New Year's honours list, the first footballer ever to receive this distinction.

■ When Jim Standen (above), the West Ham goalkeeper, reported for duty at the start of the season he had just topped the first-class bowling averages. He took 64 wickets for Worcestershire, who won the county championship for the first time.

■ Derek Forster, the Sunderland goalkeeper, was the youngest person to play in the First Division. He faced Leicester in August at the age of 15 years and 185 days.

■ Arthur Rowley, the Shrewsbury player-manager retired in February, having scored a record 434 goals in the League.

■ Gillingham's 1-0 defeat by Exeter on April 10 was the first time they had been beaten at home in 52 matches stretching back to April 1963.

Mackay's second leg injury adds to Spurs' woe

DAVE MACKAY'S and Tottenham's agony knew no bounds. Nine months after the ferocious midfielder broke his leg at Old Trafford in a European Cup-winners' Cup match, the old warhorse returned for his first

match, and broke the same left leg again.

Playing for the reserves against Shrewsbury in September at White Hart Lane he suddenly fell to the ground clutching his leg and clearly in severe pain.

It was typical of Mackay's indomitable spirit that his first thoughts were not whether his career was over, but of Bill Nicholson, his beleaguered manager, for whom nothing seemed to be going right.

Nicholson was experiencing major problems re-building his Spurs team as, one by one, the stars of the Double team were fading away. "Don't let Bill Nicholson know," Mackay said to those carrying him off the pitch, "not yet."

Past glories: Mackay's playing career seemed to be over

Sinking Celtic turn to Stein, the man with the Midas touch

JOCK STEIN, who had left Dunfermline to revitalise Hibs a year ago, was lured by ailing Celtic to revive their fortunes in February. Stein's magic touch had transformed Dunfermline and even in the short time Stein had been with Hibs he had turned the club around.

Celtic had not won a major trophy since 1958 – and that was only the Scottish League Cup – and were completely overshadowed by Rangers who had silverware galore in their trophy cabinet. Stein, who had captained Celtic to the Double in 1954, and seemed to have the

Midas touch when it came to winning trophies, was regarded as the perfect choice.

Curiously, the Scottish Cup semi-finals pitted Dunfermline against Hibs and Celtic v Motherwell. Celtic reached the final beating Motherwell 3-0, after a replay. Of his two former clubs, Dunfermline prevailed over Hibs 2-0.

In the final Stein's luck held good and Celtic were 3-2 winners at Hampden. Stein the miracle worker had done it again, within three months of taking over at Parkhead he had captured a major trophy.

THE
1964-65
SEASON

Limp England a sorry sight

ENGLAND'S torrid time in South America – where they were outclassed by Brazil and out-thought by Argentina – last summer seemed to have cast a cloud over Alf Ramsey's preparations for the World Cup next year. Although England were undefeated in their next nine internationals the opposition was generally modest, and four of the matches were unsatisfactory draws.

Narrow wins over Northern Ireland (4-3 in Belfast), Wales (2-1), Hungary (1-0) and Sweden (2-1 in Gothenburg) interspersed with scrappy draws with Belgium (2-2), Holland (1-1 in Amsterdam), Scotland (2-2) and Yugoslavia (1-1 in Belgrade) was hardly the form of world beaters. The very critics that had heaped such lavish praise on Ramsey a year earlier now claimed that England no longer had a realistic chance of winning the World Cup.

The one bright spot in all this gloom was the match between England and West Germany in Nuremberg in May. The Germans were considered one of the stronger sides in Europe and a Terry Paine goal gave England a much needed fillip as they won 1-0.

Paine: upstaged West Germany

Sheer perfection from Moore

Wembley wizards: West Ham return to collect another Cup

WEST HAM returned to Wembley for the second year running, for the final of the European Cup Winners Cup, and this time they showed none of the hesitation they had suffered in the FA Cup final against Preston last season.

They had made steady, if unspectacular progress in their first campaign in Europe. Most of their matches were won by the odd goal – Ghent were beaten 2-1 on aggregate in the first round, Sparta Prague 3-2 in the second round and Lausanne 6-4 in the quarter-finals.

In the semi-finals West Ham met Real Zaragoza, who had already eliminated Britain's two other representatives in the competition, Dundee in the second round and Cardiff in the quarter-finals. Once again, West Ham prevailed by a single goal, winning 2-1 at Upton Park then drawing 1-1 in Spain.

Bobby Moore, the West Ham captain, knew what had given his team the edge in all the matches – the presence of Martin Peters, who had just established himself in the side. "In Europe you need more skill," Moore said. "And Martin added an extra quality to our game."

West Ham had to reshuffle their team on May 19 because their two experienced forwards Peter Brabrook and Johnny Byrne were both injured. Ron Greenwood was forced to play the untested Alan Sealey, but he need not have worried about the winger's lack of experience.

Munich 1860 tried to match West Ham by playing attacking football themselves, and the entertaining game swung back and forth. Sealey decided the match with two goals in two minutes and Bobby Moore was able to lead his team up the steps once again to collect another trophy.

Moore thought it had been West Ham's best ever team effort. "There was a lot of good

Sealey: double strike

football and we played really well against a good side." Greenwood was much more succinct: "This was Bobby Moore's greatest game. Technical perfection."

Shankly fumes at daylight robbery

BILL SHANKLY was looking forward to pitting his wits against the best continental clubs in the European Cup, but the way that Liverpool were eliminated from the competition left him with a distrust of all things foreign.

Liverpool were only the second English team to reach the semi-finals and they had to face Inter Milan, the holders of the European Cup, days after winning the FA Cup. Their victory at Wembley enabled Shankly to employ a clever piece of gamesmanship.

Hours before the kick-off Anfield was packed solid, and everybody in the ground wanted to see the FA Cup. Shankly waited until Inter had gone out on to the pitch and told his team to wait in the dressing room. He then ordered two of his injured players to slowly parade the FA Cup around the touchline.

When Gerry Byrne and Gordon Milne lapped the ground Anfield erupted. The Inter players had to stand and fret in the middle of the pitch while the Liverpool fans went wild. The ploy worked and, with their nerves stretched to breaking point, Inter lost 3-1.

But Inter Milan's coach, the legendary Helenio Herrera, replayed the compliment in spades. The San Siro was a cauldron for the second leg; Liverpool were greeted by firecrackers, sirens, rockets, smoke bombs and a hail of bottles.

Worse, they were robbed by a series of dubious decisions by the referee. Inter led 3-0 after 20 minutes, but one of the goals appeared to have been scored straight from an indirect free kick. Another was allowed even though Tommy Lawrence, the Liverpool goalkeeper, was charged by an Inter player and had the ball kicked out of his hands.

Liverpool had a goal disallowed, at which point Tommy Smith threatened to punch the referee, and they were beaten 4-3 on aggregate. Shankly told his players that they were still the greatest team in the world. But he also believed that the referee had been bribed and the bitter experience meant that he never trusted a European team again.

Hearts lose out in numbers game

THE final day of the League season had dramatic consequences not just because one match would settle the outcome of the championship but also because it would lead to a fundamental change in the rules.

Kilmarnock went to Tynecastle needing to beat Hearts by two clear goals to pip them for the title on goal average. When the Ayrshire club duly won 2-0 and collected the championship, Hearts were understandably upset. The two clubs had exactly the same record (22 wins, 6 draws and 6 losses), but Hearts had scored 90 goals, conceding 49, whereas Kilmarnock had scored 62, conceding 33.

This gave Hearts a goal average of 1.837, and Kilmarnock a superior average of 1.879. However if goal difference had been used Hearts, with plus 41, would have been the champions instead because Kilmarnock's goal difference was only 29. Hearts' manifest disappointment at losing the title because of mathematical vagaries prompted them to propose to the Scottish Football League that goal difference, rather than average, should be used to separate teams on the same number of points, and this was adopted.

Fate however decided to be cruel to the Edinburgh club. The next time they came close to lifting the title – 21 years after Kilmarnock deprived them – Celtic pipped Hearts to the championship on the final day of the season . . . on goal difference. Ironically, if goal average had been used instead Hearts would have been the 1986 champions.

Ferencvaros finally prevail as the Fairs Cup becomes a farce

THIS SEASON'S Fairs Cup was probably the most chaotic and farcical competition Uefa had ever organised, even surpassing the inaugural tournament of 1955 which took three years to play 23 games.

Uefa's problems began when they accepted 48 entries and decided not to have any byes in the first round. If they had given 16 byes and played 16 ties they would have had a straightforward competition. Instead they ended up with six teams in the quarter finals and had to give two of them byes into the semi-finals.

To muddy the waters further Uefa had not devised a satisfactory way of deciding ties that finished all square. No fewer than nine ties went to a third match, and one had to be decided by the toss of a coin.

In the midst of all this confusion Manchester United and Everton, the two English representatives, progressed easily until they met each other in the third round where, in a tightly contested tie, United prevailed 3-2 on aggregate. In the six-team quarter-finals, however, United were unfortunately one of the teams not given a bye and had to play RC Strasbourg, who had eliminated Barcelona on the toss of a coin in the previous round.

A 5-0 thrashing at Old Trafford and a goalless draw in France pitted United against Ferencvaros in the semi-finals. Despite a battling performance by Matt Busby's team — the first two matches finished all square — they went out in the replay to the Hungarian club.

But Uefa still had one more idiosyncrasy to come before the competition was concluded. Instead of playing the one-match final on a neutral ground as they had the previous year, they elected to stage it in the Stadio Comunale in Turin, the home ground of the other finalist, Juventus. Ferencvaros had the last laugh though: Fenyvesi scored the only goal in the 74th minute and the Hungarians became the first club from the Eastern bloc to capture a European trophy.

No chance for Stein in selection nightmare

SCOTLAND'S determination to reach the World Cup finals in England had been demonstrated at the end of the previous season when the SFA had begged Celtic to allow Jock Stein to act as the caretaker manager of the national side. Their faith in the big man had soon been born out when Scotland drew 1-1 with Poland in Chorzow on May 23 and four days later beat Finland 2-1 in Helsinki.

However Scotland's hopes received a serious setback in October at Hampden when, without the brilliant Jim Baxter but leading 1-0 with a goal from Billy McNeill, they were beaten by Poland's two late goals which stole victory. Stein now had a formidable task on his hands: to beat Italy home and away. Scotland achieved the first objective with a John Greig goal in November, this left a tricky task in Naples – the graveyard of many visiting international sides – in December.

Stein's task was made virtually impossible by losing almost half his squad beforehand. Some were missing because their English clubs refused to release them; some were injured and some were not picked by the SFA. The list of the absent read like a who's who of Scottish talent: Baxter, Pat Crerand, Alan Gilzean, Denis Law and Dave Mackay. Conceding that his novice side would never beat a full-strength Italy, Stein aimed for a draw – gambling on a

Benfica led a merry dance by El Beatle's one-man band

BENFICA were undoubtedly the leading side in Europe. They had reached the final of the European Cup four times in the past five seasons, and had won the tournament twice. With Eusebio at the peak of his career they were content to leave Old Trafford 3-2 down after the first leg of their European Cup quarter-final against Manchester United.

The Portuguese team were convinced that they could easily make up the deficit at home. Matt Busby, the United manager, also knew that his team would face one of their toughest challenges ever. He ordered his players to contain Benfica for the first quarter of the match and then go in search of goals.

As Busby said afterwards, the precocious George Best "must have had cotton wool in his ears" during the team talk. The teenager was not going to hang around doing nothing for 20 minutes, he wanted to score goals.

Within 12 minutes he had put United 2-0 up. His first goal silenced the crowd, the second, a brilliant solo run, sent them into raptures. The rest of the team took their cue from Best and Busby's orders were ignored as United blitzed Benfica 5-1.

The Stadium of Light was dazzled by United, and particularly by Best. Every time Best touched the ball the crowd shouted "El Beatle" in unison. And, just like the pop stars, Best was mobbed at the end of the match. Busby was horrified when one Portuguese fan chased Best across the pitch, brandishing a knife. He needn't have worried – all that the man wanted was a lock of Best's hair.

A star is born: Best disobeyed orders and dazzled Benfica

Unfortunately for United, the happy ending did not last. Making their first appearance in the European Cup since the Munich disaster, they could not lay the ghosts of 1958 and were beaten by Partizan Belgrade in the semi-finals.

replay. Unfortunately it failed miserably, Italy hammered the Scots 3-0, and Stein's reign ended with him bitterly complaining of the lamentable national set-up.

None of the other Home countries managed to qualify either. Northern Ireland were only narrowly edged out by Switzerland, both sides beating each other at home, but Northern Ireland's two draws with Holland and Albania – giving the Eastern bloc country their only point – cost them a place in the finals. Wales won all three of their home matches, but also lost all three of their away games and the Soviet Union coasted to the finals.

Catterick buys the winning ticket

EVERTON had not conceded a goal on the way to Wembley, so they were doubly shocked to trail Sheffield Wednesday 2-0 in the FA Cup final. To add to their problems, they had hardly staged any penetrating attacks in the first half and their fans were getting restless, doubting the wisdom of dropping the experienced Fred Pickering for the young Mike Trebilcock.

Harry Catterick, the Everton manager, had come in for some stick from the club's supporters earlier in the season when he bought the little-known Trebilcock from Plymouth for £18,000. But even after Wednesday had scored their second goal in the 57th minute he said that he was not panicking.

Mike Trebilcock, too, had remained calm when it seemed that the unfancied Wednesday were going to run rings round Everton. A minute after David Ford had scored he crashed in a half-volley to give Everton hope. Five minutes later, with a tiring Wednesday starting to feel the effects of their exertions, he took advantage of a weak clearance by Sam Ellis to score another unstoppable goal.

Everton's decisive goal, in the 80th minute, was heartbreaking for Wednesday, and particularly Gerry Young. A long punt by the Everton goalkeeper should not have caused Young any problems. But, inexplicably, the left half let the ball run away from him. Quick as flash, Derek Temple whipped past him and ran on to score the winning goal.

Young was mortified by his mistake and slumped to the ground in despair. "I am inconsolable," he said. "Ninety-nine times out of a hundred I would have tamed that ball, but the hundredth time had to be in the Cup final."

■ Keith Peacock (above) became the first substitute to be used in the League when he came on for Charlton during their Second Division match against Bolton on August 21. At the end of the season the League decided that it was impossible for the referee to decide when a player was genuinely injured and a substitution should be allowed. So the rules were changed to allow substitutions to be made for any reason.

■ Roma were banned from the Fairs Cup for three years and fined £500 after Chelsea players were stoned during and after their match in Italy.

■ The third round Fairs Cup match between Leeds and Valencia at Elland Road became so ill-tempered that a policeman had to intervene to stop Jack Charlton attacking a Valencia player. The referee stopped the match for 10 minutes while tempers cooled and sent off three players, Charlton and two Spaniards.

■ Frank Saul ended a proud run on December 4 when he was the first Tottenham player sent off in a League match since October 1928.

Bringing home the bacon: Trebilcock rewarded Catterick's faith with the vital equaliser

Pickles finds World Cup to dig FA out of hole

THE FA were severely embarrassed when they lost the World Cup months before the finals were due to start.

Some time during the afternoon of Sunday March 20, a thief broke into Central Hall, Westminster, where the Jules Rimet trophy was on display at a stamp exhibition. He ignored all the rare stamps, with a value of at least £3m, and only took the trophy, worth £3,000 at most.

A £15,000 ransom demand was made but when the police arrested the culprit he turned out to be a hoaxer. Nobody knew what had happened to the Cup until a week after it had vanished, when David Corbett took his dog for a walk in Norwood, south London.

Pickles, a black and white mongrel, disappeared into some bushes and started digging furiously. He unearthed a brown paper parcel that contained the 12-inch high trophy.

Pickles had got the FA out of a pickle (they had started making emergency plans in case the trophy was not recovered) and was handsomely rewarded. When England won the World Cup Pickles was invited to the celebration banquet and allowed to lick the plates clean. His owner collected a £6,000 reward but the thief was never caught.

Pickles: celebration dinner

THE
1965-66
SEASON

Gento guides Madrid back to the heights

ONLY Francisco Gento, now 32 years old, remained of the fabulous Real Madrid side of the 1950s when they won five European Cups in succession with breathtaking football. The rebuilt Madrid team were criticised for being a shadow of their predecessors but then they would be: how can you replace a Puskas or a Di Stefano?

However their younger and more athletic successors took the famous club back to the top of the European summit when they beat Partizan Belgrade 2-1 in the European Cup final in Brussels.

Real's new stars were Amancio, Pirri and Velasquez. And it was Amancio who equalised after Vasovic had headed the Yugoslavs into the lead early in the second half. Serena, the right winger, thundered the winner from outside the penalty area six minutes from time.

For Gento, now Real's captain, it was a memorable occasion. It was his eighth European Cup final and the sixth time he was on the winning side, a record unlikely to be surpassed.

As a left-winger Gento was a wonder to behold. Jimmy Greaves held him in awe: "He was one of the fastest players I have ever seen. He streaked down the left wing like an Olympic sprinter, and even when at full pace managed to retain control of the ball. A small compact man with powerful thighs, Gento packed a thundering left-foot shot and his passes were always pin-pointed."

Gento retired in 1971 having played 761 matches and scored 253 goals for his club and helping them to 12 championships.

Shankly's luck finally runs out

Bad times 1: Liverpool were left disconsolate at Hampden Park

THE MANNER in which Liverpool dismissed the opposition to land their seventh League title had all the hallmarks of an emerging dynasty. Bill Shankly's team had assumed the leadership of the First Division at the end of November and simply raced away with the title, finishing six points clear of Leeds. It was their third major title in three seasons, and it equalled Arsenal's record of seven League championships.

Shankly had built a super-fit team that never seemed to suffer from injuries, indeed he had only used 14 players throughout the season and one of those made his one appearance in the final League game when the title was already secure. Shankly's defence, built around Ron Yeats and Tommy Smith, was resolute; his strike-force of Ian St John and Roger Hunt was prolific as they fed off the eager service of Liverpool's two wingers, Ian Callaghan and Peter Thompson.

Apart from their unexpected elimination in the third round of the FA Cup by Chelsea at Anfield, the only real disappointment in Liverpool's season was their failure to be the first British club to have completed a League and European double.

Liverpool's progress in the European Cup Winners Cup

Bad times 2: Held opens the scoring for Borussia Dortmund

had been impressive. They had disposed of Juventus, Standard Liege and Honved in successive rounds before meeting Celtic in the semi-final. In the first leg at Parkhead, Liverpool, without Hunt their leading scorer, struggled to withstand Celtic's attacking momentum and were fortunate to escape with a single goal defeat.

At Anfield the roles were reversed and by half-time Liverpool were still trailing to that single goal. A venomous free-kick from Smith levelled the scores. Geoff Strong, who had spent much of the half limping because of an injury, managed to find some extra spring in his legs and rose above the Celtic defence to score. With a minute

left it appeared Bobby Lennox had equalised, but the referee blew for offside.

Liverpool's opponents in the final at Hampden were Borussia Dortmund who had beaten West Ham, the holders, in the other semi-final. Siggy Held gave the West German club the lead just after the interval, Hunt equalised but then, with seconds left, failed with a simple chance and the match went into extra time. Liverpool were now faltering and in the 17th minute goalkeeper Tommy Lawrence, under pressure from Held, was forced to punch a ball from the edge of his area. Libuda pounced on the clearance and blasted the ball 40 yards past the stranded keeper.

Ramsey hones his grand plan to win World Cup

ENGLAND began their vital build-up to the summer's World Cup finals as badly as they had ended the previous season with a disappointing 3-2 defeat by nondescript Austria at Wembley in October. It later transpired that Jimmy Greaves, who had been out of sorts in the match, was suffering from jaundice and he did not return to the side until May.

With Greaves absent, Ramsey began to experiment with a 4-3-3 formation and, in December, England beat Spain 2-0 in Madrid, an extremely encouraging result. Although other results were patchy – notably a 1-1 draw with Poland at Goodison – there were more encouraging signs, including a 1-0 defeat of West Germany at Wembley in February with Geoff Hurst making a satisfactory debut. In April Hurst retained his place, and scored the first goal in a 4-3 defeat of Scotland at Hampden, England's first victory over the Scots in five years.

Ramsey now embarked on a wholesale series of changes in personnel and formations, searching not just for the right blend, but to create a squad flexible enough to cope with whatever problems other countries might create in the finals. He had not forgotten the harsh lessons the Argentinians had dished out in the "Little World Cup" in the summer of 1964.

Ramsey and his squad then retreated to Lilleshall, where he subjected them to a military-style regime designed to foster camaraderie and mould them into a team rather than a collection of gifted individuals. Fifteen days before the finals began, Ramsey and his team went on a whirlwind European tour. They played four matches in nine days, winning all of them with, once again, more team changes and experimentation. By the opening match, against Uruguay on July 11. Ramsey and England were now ready to face the best the world could throw at them.

Heading for the heights? Ramsey warms up for the World Cup finals

Wright: left Arsenal

■ Both Chester full-backs were carried off with broken legs during the Fourth Division match against Aldershot on January 1. Despite the setback, Chester still won 3-2.

■ Arsenal parted company with Billy Wright, their manager, at the end of the season.

■ Bradford Park Avenue were the second-highest scorers in the League with 102 goals. But they only finished 11th in the Fourth Division because they lost 20 matches and allowed their opponents to score 92 times.

■ Malcolm Allison teamed up with Joe Mercer at Manchester City and they guided the club back to the First Division.

■ Northampton, newly promoted to the First Division, went straight back down to the Second Division.

Dynamic duo: Mercer and Allison revived Manchester City

Stein takes charge and widens Celtic's horizons

BOLSTERED by his success in the Scottish Cup the previous season, Jock Stein set about realising his expansive ambitions for Celtic. First he refused to countenance a joint managership with Sean Fallon, and then he persuaded the club's board of directors that he would have a completely free hand in team selection. This was unheard of, but Stein got his way, the first Celtic manager to enjoy such power.

Although Stein, as the caretaker manager of the Scottish national side, was encumbered until December when they were eliminated from the World Cup finals, he soon had Celtic mounting a strong challenge for the championship. In January Celtic whipped Rangers 5-1 and, despite their Ibrox rivals chasing them for the rest of the season, that result was decisive. Celtic won the title two points ahead of Rangers, having scored a phenomenal 106 goals.

Celtic had also captured the Scottish League Cup beating Rangers 2-1. However Rangers denied Stein the satisfaction of a treble in his first full season in charge when, after a 0-0 draw, they took the Scottish Cup 1-0 in the replay. Stein's horizons were now wider than simply being the top dogs in Scotland. Perhaps foolishly, the Celtic boss announced that next season's priority was to win the European Cup, which no British club had ever come near winning.

WORLD CUP 1966

Wingless Wonders give England home win

ENGLAND'S victory in the World Cup final in 1966 will forever be remembered for two things: Kenneth Wolstenholme's immortal words at the end of extra time, and Geoff Hurst's controversial second goal that effectively won the trophy. In the dying seconds of the final, with England clinging on to a slender 3-2 lead against West Germany, Bobby Moore, instead of wildly clearing the ball, hit a precision pass to Hurst who raced upfield and unleashed a ferocious shot. The crowd, in anticipation of the final whistle, had begun to come on to the Wembley pitch. Wolstenholme remarked: "They think it's all over," just as Hurst's left-footed shot flew into the roof of the West German net. With the briefest pauses, Wolstenholme added: "It is now".

While those words have been fondly remembered ever since, England's third goal has been hotly debated ever since. Even today Germans will swear blind it was not a goal and film and photographic evidence have never given a conclusive answer. At the time two people were equally certain it was a goal: Roger Hunt and Backhramov, the Russian linesman.

Alan Ball had, somehow finding extra pace from his weary legs, latched on to Nobby Stiles's pass, raced past Karl-Heinz Schnellinger and crossed the ball to Hurst who was standing with his back to the goal. The West Ham striker controlled the ball, instantly turned and crashed it against the underside of the bar. The ball bounced on to the line and was cleared. Hunt, following up in the goalmouth, turned away, arms raised in celebration. But did the ball cross the line? The Germans thought not. Dienst, the Swiss referee, consulted his linesman and awarded the most controversial goal in the history of the World Cup.

It is a pity that the 1966 final will not properly be remembered for thrilling game it truly was. West Germany had taken an early lead in the 12th minute when a poor clearance from Ray Wilson was punished by Helmut Haller. Six minutes later a quickly-taken free-kick from Moore was headed in by Hurst.

England finally took the lead with 12 minutes remaining when Martin Peters scored from the rebound after Hurst's shot had been blocked. Seconds before the final whistle, West Germany conjured up a heart-breaking equaliser. From a dubious free-kick awarded against Jackie Charlton, Lothar Emmerich blasted the ball into the penalty area, it hit Schnellinger's back, fell to Held whose cross ricocheted off George Cohen's knee. Weber poked the ball in at the far post.

England's manager, Alf Ramsey, gave what was probably his most informal team talk ever during the break before extra time. "You've beaten them once," he told his weary men as they sprawled on the grass, "now you've got to do it again. Look at them. They're finished!"

Ramsey's speech was inspirational, even though most people perceived him as a man of few words. Ramsey was a first-rate motivator whose only problem was that he found it difficult to deal with the press. But out of the spotlight, working with players who always seemed to raise their game for him, he was a master tactician.

Ramsey had been appointed in 1962, and was the first England manager to have total control of team selection. And he made it very clear what his project was: to win the World Cup and win it his way. To this end Ramsey had worked unceasingly for the 1966 World Cup.

His way meant that for four years Ramsey experimented with formations and players to such an extent that players, press and public were bewildered. Ramsey also put a high premium on hard work and hard running, disposing of the wingers who historically had been the cornerstone of English football. This infuriated his critics, and few believed that England really could capture the ultimate prize.

However Ramsey knew exactly what he was doing: producing a world-beating team for the modern era. Although Ramsey's Wingless Wonders were vilified for their lack of flair and their emphasis on work-rate there was probably more talent in that England team than at any time since.

Ramsey was the most misunderstood of managers. Because of his dismissive, aloof personality he seemed to be a fish out water in the Swinging Sixties, but in reality he was a successful revolutionary. He was also his own man, something else that did not endear him to the public or FA officials. After the match against France in the first round Stiles perpetrated an horrendous tackle right in front of the Royal Box. Two FA bigwigs instructed Ramsey to drop Stiles for the next match. Ramsey refused and said that if Stiles did not play, he would resign. Such player loyalty was his hallmark and at Wembley on July 30 they repaid him handsomely.

England made an unconvincing start, but as their group was probably the weakest they easily qualified to meet Argentina in the quarter-finals. The South Americans were formidable opponents, but their undoubted skills were marred by a vicious streak of cynicism. Antonio Rattin, their captain, seemed to think he was above the rules of the game and beyond the referee's authority. While Kreitlein, the West German referee, was booking several of Rattin's teammates, Rattin was fouling with impunity.

Eventually the referee could stand it no more and sent him off. But Rattin refused to go and the referee was surrounded by the entire Argentine team, who threatened to walk off en masse. The game was delayed for 11 minutes before Rattin reluctantly left.

Ramsey was offended by the Argentinians' conduct and after England won 1-0 he raced on to the pitch to stop his players exchanging shirts with their opponents. Ramsey branded Argentina "animals", although he did apologise later for the remark.

Pele, too, was a victim of a series of harsh tackles. He was injured by a Bulgarian defender in the first round and missed the next match against Hungary. Then he was repeatedly scythed down as Portugal beat Brazil 3-1 to put them out of the competition. Pele returned to Brazil threatening never to play in the World Cup again.

Amid all the bitterness, the unlikely minnows from North Korea captured many hearts. Their team of tiny players had precious little international experience, but a goal from Pak Doo-ik, an army dentist, against Italy took North Korea into the quarter-finals at Italy's expense. The Italian team returned home in disgrace and were pelted with rotten fruit at Genoa airport.

North Korea almost pulled off another upset when they led Portugal 3-0 after 22 minutes. But their chances of reaching the semi-finals were undone by their lack of experience of how to shut a game down. Eusebio rallied Portugal with four goals in 32 minutes and although North Korea finally succumbed 5-3 their brave performances won them many friends.

However all of Eusebio's brilliance could not save Portugal in the semi-final against England and his penalty eight minutes from time was too late to overhaul Bobby Charlton's two brilliant goals. It was undoubtedly the match of the tournament ... until the final and the intervention of a Russian linesman.

High drama 1: Perfumo of Argentina and Haller of West Germany engage in aerial combat; North Korea gave several teams the fright of their lives; and Weber snatches a last-gasp equaliser in the final

FOR THE RECORD

FIRST ROUND

GROUP 1	P	W	D	L	F	A	Pts
England	3	2	1	0	4	0	5
Uruguay	3	1	2	0	2	1	4
Mexico	3	0	2	1	1	3	2
France	3	0	1	2	2	5	1

GROUP 2	P	W	D	L	F	A	Pts
W. Germany	3	2	1	0	7	1	5
Argentina	3	2	1	0	4	1	5
Spain	3	1	0	2	4	5	2
Switzerland	3	0	0	3	1	9	0

GROUP 3	P	W	D	L	F	A	Pts
Portugal	3	3	0	0	9	2	6
Hungary	3	2	0	1	7	5	4
Brazil	3	1	0	2	4	6	2
Bulgaria	3	0	0	3	1	8	0

GROUP 4	P	W	D	L	F	A	Pts
Soviet Union	3	3	0	0	6	1	6
North Korea	3	1	1	1	2	4	3
Italy	3	0	1	2	2	5	1
Chile	3	0	1	2	2	5	1

QUARTER-FINALS

England 1   Argentina 0
HT 0-0 Att. 90,584

West Germany 4   Uruguay 0
HT 1-0 Att. 33,751

Portugal 5   North Korea 3
HT 2-3 Att. 51,780

Soviet Union 2   Hungary 1
HT 1-0 Att. 26,844

SEMI-FINALS

West Germany 2   Soviet Union 1
HT 1-0 Att. 43,921

England 2   Portugal 1
HT 1-0 Att. 94,493

THIRD PLACE PLAY-OFF

Portugal 2   Soviet Union 1
HT 1-1 Att. 87,696

FINAL

England 4   West Germany 2 aet
HT 1-1 Att. 96,924

Teams
England Banks; Cohen, J Charlton, Moore, Wilson, Stiles, B Charlton, Ball, Hunt, Hurst, Peters
West Germany Tilkowski; Hottges, Schulz, Weber, Schnellinger, Haller, Beckenbauer, Seeler, Held, Overath, Emmerich

Leading goalscorers 9 Eusebio Ferriera da Silva (Portugal); 5 Helmut Haller (West Germany); 4 Geoff Hurst (England), Franz Beckenbauer (West Germany), Valeri Porkujan (Soviet Union), Ferenc Bene (Hungary)
Total goals scored 80
Average per game: 2.78
Sendings-off Jorge Albrecht (Argentina) v West Germany; Referee: Konstantin Zecevic (Yugoslavia).
Horacio Troche (Uruguay) v West Germany; Hector Silva (Uruguay) v West Germany; Referee: Jim Finney (England).
Antonio Rattin (Argentina) v England; Referee: Rudolf Kreitlein (West Germany).
Igor Chislenko (Soviet Union) v West Germany; Referee: Conceto Lo Bello (Italy).
Number of players used by finalists
14 West Germany; 15 England

● Over 40 nations have withdrawn from the World Cup for one reason or another. Egypt (1938, 1958, 1962 and 1966) have withdrawn the most often.

High drama 2: Hurst's second goal was surrounded by controversy

Moore the merrier: England's captain leads the celebrations

THE
1966-67
SEASON

Dynamic duo join Derby

SECOND DIVISION Derby County plucked the Hartlepools United managerial duo of Brian Clough and Peter Taylor out of the doldrums of the Fourth Division in the hope that the pair would soon restore them to the First Division. Clough, a prolific striker whose promising England career had been curtailed because of injury, had caused something of a stir when he took over at Hartlepools as the youngest manager in the League.

Sam Longson, Derby's chairman, had decided to gamble on the inexperienced Clough and Taylor, having been tipped off by Len Shackleton, the former England centre-forward turned journalist, that they were capable of rescuing a club who had finished 17th that season. Longson promised that £70,000 would be available to buy new players.

Clough: youngest manager

Taylor: valuable sidekick

Berwick make Rangers suffer the worst day of their lives

Worlds apart: Celtic were League champions again and Rangers finished nowhere

BERWICK 1 RANGERS 0 was the most sensational result in Scottish football history. Berwick, who had never finished higher than eighth in the Second Division, had bundled mighty Rangers, who had won the Scottish Cup four times in the previous five seasons, out of the Cup in the first round on January 28. The result sent shock waves through Scotland and rocked Ibrox to its foundations.

The hero of the day was Jock Wallace who combined the job of manager with that of goalkeeper. After Sammy Reid had put Berwick (whose ground is actually just in Northumberland) ahead in the 32nd minute Wallace pulled off save after save to the consternation of the Rangers players and fans. The repercussions from the match were extraordinary.

Jim Forrest and George McLean, the two strikers, were held entirely responsible for the debacle and never played for Rangers again. Forrest (145 goals in 164 games) was transferred in March to Preston for £38,000 and McLean (82 goals in 116 games) went to Dundee a month later in exchange for Andy Penman.

Scot Symon, the manager, did not fare much better. His 13-year reign – which included six Scottish championships, five Scottish Cups, four Scottish League Cups and two European Cup Winners Cup finals – came to an inglorious end in November when the Rangers chairman, John Lawrence, sent an intermediary to break the extraordinary news that he was sacked. Rangers were leading the table at time, having won six and

drawn two of their eight fixtures.

However between the end of January and the beginning of November Celtic had also rocked Scottish football. To their European Cup triumph, Rangers' bitter rivals had added the League, the Cup, the League Cup and the Glasgow Cup. An unbelievable year for Parkhead, a desperately embarrassing year for Ibrox, and so Symon was made the scapegoat.

David White replaced Symon but his two-year stint never put a dent in Celtic's stranglehold, and he had to give way to Willie Waddell who had achieved wonderful things with Kilmarnock. As he was to do with Rangers, especially with the appointment in June 1970 of a coach who had come a long way in a short time: Jock Wallace, formerly of Berwick Rangers.

Manchester United's winning ways put the smile back on Busby's face

ENGLAND'S triumph in the World Cup final brought a renewed sense of optimism to the game. The Daily Telegraph said: "England are now acknowledged as the leaders of world soccer. It is essential that we exploit a spirit of adventure and resist in the months ahead a temptation to resort to tactics of dreary defence."

Matt Busby, the Manchester United manager, needed no urging to play attractive football. But at the start of the season he was in despair. "We'll never win the European Cup now," Busby told Pat Crerand, reflecting on United's defeat in the semi-finals last season.

Then Denis Law demanded a big increase in his wages and a signing-on fee to renew his contract. Busby retaliated by putting his international striker on the transfer list.

But the crises passed. Law made his peace with the club and Busby set about taking United back into Europe. United were not beaten in the League after December 16 and, apart from being beaten at Old Trafford by Norwich in the fourth round of the FA Cup, were almost invincible at home.

They made sure of the title in convincing style, hammering the West Ham of Bobby Moore, Geoff Hurst and Martin Peters 6-1 at Upton Park in May. Bobby Charlton, Crerand and Bill Foulkes put United three up after 10 minutes and George Best added a fourth after 25 minutes. Law completed the rout with two goals in the second half.

One reporter wrote: "This was a triumph for that ever-diminishing school of managers who believe soccer is primarily an entertainment. Manchester United believe their customers should not only be granted the satisfaction of another victory, but should be delighted by the performance that earns it."

For Busby, who had even contemplated retirement at the start of the season, the European dream was alive once again.

Dazzling Baxter inspires Scotland to defeat the Auld Enemy and claim they are world champions

FOR SCOTLAND the "real" World Cup final was played on April 15, 1967 at Wembley, not July 30, 1966 – and they won it. England's victory the summer before rankled north of the border like no other result, especially as Scotland failed even to reach the finals. So to take on

> *If anybody had asked me who, out of all the teams in the world will come to Wembley and beat you, I would have said the Scots. It meant more for the Scots to beat the English than it did for the English to beat the Scots*
>
> BOBBY CHARLTON
> on England's defeat

the world champions on their own pitch and beat them was pure heaven.

Although Scotland's margin of victory was slender, 3-2, it was the style of it that enraptured Scottish fans. Jim Baxter was at his mercurial best, waltzing through an England team which,

Crowning glory: Jim McCalliog scores Scotland's winning goal at Wembley

apart from Jimmy Greaves in for Roger Hunt, was the same one that had defeated West Germany nine months earlier.

Baxter's dazzling cheek of taunting the England players and defying them to win possession of the ball was emulated by his teammates Denis Law, Billy Bremner and Tommy Gemmell.

It was sweet revenge as Scotland embarrassed the Auld Enemy and wiped out the bitter memory of their 9-3 humiliation six years ago to the day.

Mee rings the changes at Arsenal

THE WINDS of a quiet revolution seemed to be blowing through the marble corridors of Highbury. The sacking of Billy Wright in the summer of 1966 after four years as their manager was not really a surprise. After all Arsenal had not won anything since their championship victory in 1953 and in the meantime their deadly rivals, Spurs, had enjoyed spectacular success both at home and in Europe. But the appointment of Bertie Mee was.

Mee, the club's unassuming 46-year-old physiotherapist, was hardly the big-name appointment expected of a club as big as Arsenal. It even stunned Mee. "It was a surprise, but a very pleasant one," he said. "I had not planned to become a football manager."

Undeterred, Mee, with his coach Dave Sexton whom he had lured from Fulham, set about the job with gusto. By October he had sold the crowd-pleasing, but erratic, George Eastham to Stoke; exchanged Tommy Baldwin plus £50,000 for Chelsea's George Graham and bought Bob McNab from Huddersfield for £50,000 – a record for a full back.

Of course Mee was uniquely placed to put his finger on the pulse of the problem at Highbury. The Arsenal dressing-room had been his domain for the past six years as he worked to get the players fit. Known as a no-nonsense physio, he began the task of restoring Arsenal to their former glories with the advantage that the players respected him and knew that he was no pushover.

Stein and Celtic bring home the greatest prize in Europe

BY ALL footballing standards Celtic stood absolutely no chance of beating Inter Milan in the European Cup final. Inter, a collection of glittering internationals managed by the arch strategist of the era Helenio Herrera, had won the competition twice, in 1964 and 1965, and were the most sophisticated side in the world at gaining a 1-0 lead and then utterly closing the game down.

By contrast Celtic were an all-Scottish side unsophisticated in Continental ways, incapable of any master strategy and whose only tactic was out and out attack. Their domestic success was simply a product of the paucity of Scottish football. The Italian maestros would easily put the upstarts in their place. Anyway, that was the script.

Stein, of course, had other ideas. He knew that much of such criticism was valid but, if he could get his players to play above themselves and to play to their traditional strengths with marauding wingers providing the bullets for his front men to fire, then the Italians might well wilt under the barrage. He also had a few of his own tricks up his sleeve, if not on the field of play then away from it.

Typically, the Italian players were holed up in their camp and kept away from the press and hangers-on. Stein decided to build on the camaraderie his players shared by virtually running an open house at the team hotel, and kept his players in a permanently relaxed atmosphere. When the Celtic players went out on to the pitch they were noisily singing the Celtic song to the amazement of their Italian rivals. Stein even upstaged the great Herrera by stealing the bench he had earmarked for himself. Herrera was furious, but Stein would not give way. His players thought it was wonderful, knockabout stuff.

You'll be an immortal

BILL SHANKLY to JOCK STEIN
after the European Cup final

The first half followed the Herrera script. In the seventh minute Inter were awarded a penalty, Mazzola scored and, as expected, they promptly shut up shop. That, Herrera thought, was that. Stein was unfazed by the containing, counter-attacking game Herrera employed and the Celtic manager stuck to his guns. At half-time Stein exhorted his players to continue with their game-plan: to fire in accurate shot after accurate shot until the Italians cracked.

Luck seemed against them when Bertie Auld and Tommy Gemmell hit the bar, but the constant bombardment on the Inter goal never wavered. In the 63rd minute Celtic got their reward. Bobby Murdoch picked up Gemmell's pass, switched to Jim Craig on the right wing who found Gemmell with enough space in the middle to thunder the ball past the Italian keeper from 20 yards. With five minutes to go, and extra time on the cards, Gemmell was involved again, his left-wing pass to Murdoch was driven into the area and cannoned off Steve Chalmers for the winner.

Celtic had simply ripped the script into shreds. Jock Stein, manager for a little over two seasons, had taken Celtic to the pinnacle of club success, the European Cup, the first British side to mount the summit.

Gemmell: the match-winner

Against the odds: Celtic celebrate the winning goal in the European Cup final in Lisbon

West Brom caught napping by QPR

THE League Cup, once labelled "Hardaker's Folly", finally came of age thanks to two inspired changes to the competition. The final was made a single match and moved to Wembley, instead of being played over two legs home and away. And the winners would qualify for Europe, getting an automatic place in the Fairs Cup provided that they were a First Division team.

The incentive of European football persuaded several clubs that had spurned the competition previously to take part. Only Liverpool, the League champions, and Everton, the FA Cup holders, did not enter.

But things did not go quite to plan when First Division West Bromwich Albion succumbed to Third Division Queen's Park Rangers in the final. West Brom raced into a 2-0 lead before half-time with both goals scored by Clive Clark, a former QPR player.

But after the break West Brom's dominance evaporated. They played as if they were already day-dreaming about Europe and were comprehensively caught napping.

First Roger Morgan scored then, with 15 minutes remaining, Rodney Marsh equalised with a solo run and a shot that went in off the post. Still West Brom did not wake up and Mark Lazarus scored the winner for QPR late in the game.

QPR were denied a place in Europe but they had further cause for celebration when they ran away with the Third Division title by 12 points.

FOR THE RECORD

■ Blackpool sold Emlyn Hughes to Liverpool in March and finished bottom of the First Division by eight points, only winning one League match at home all season.

■ Derek Dougan (above) got a nasty shock when he scored a last-minute equaliser for Wolverhampton against Millwall in their Second Division match in April. Dougan turned to celebrate with a fan who had rushed on to the pitch, only to discover it was a Millwall supporter who promptly punched him in the face.

■ Billy Ferguson was the first Irish player to be sent off in an international, and the first player from any country to be sent off during the Home internationals, when Northern Ireland lost 2-0 to England.

Chelsea outflanked by Tottenham

Capital punishment: Bonetti is beaten for the second time in the first all-London Cup final

TOTTENHAM and Chelsea provided the first all-London FA Cup final this century, but that was all they had in common.

The contrast in styles between the two clubs was enormous. Tottenham had Bill Nicholson, one of the, if not the best, managers of the decade. Chelsea had the upstart Tommy Docherty in charge. Tottenham were a team with a common purpose. Chelsea were riven by internal disputes all season, and the wrangling over bonuses continued long into the night after the Cup final had ended. Tottenham had rebuilt their Double team. Chelsea were dependent on individual skills.

Before the match, Docherty said that Tottenham would only play as well as Chelsea allowed them to. But it was Docherty's decision to pack his midfield and employ a 4-4-2 formation that effectively handed the game to Tottenham.

Nothing epitomised Tottenham's spirit more than Dave Mackay, still soldiering on after injuries that would have finished the career of lesser men. What he lacked in pace he made up for in determination. And Mackay had, weeks before the match, pointed out the virtues of using wingers.

Tottenham, playing a classical 4-2-4 line-up had all the space they wanted to run at Chelsea. Jimmy Robertson made one wing his own and put Tottenham ahead on the stroke of half-time. Frank Saul, abetted by overlapping runs from the full-back Joe Kinnear, prowled the other flank and added a second goal with a stunning shot hit on the turn. Jimmy Greaves (with Mackay the only man to have played in Tottenham's last Cup-winning side) and Alan Gilzean tormented the heart of the Chelsea defence.

Against such an onslaught, Charlie Cooke's runs from midfield and Tony Hateley's efforts in attack were largely ineffectual. Bobby Tambling scored a consolation goal four minutes from time, but by then Tottenham's domination was such that they had been able to slow the game to almost walking pace.

The 2-1 scoreline hardly reflected Tottenham's superior tactics. But perhaps the greatest insight into the gulf between the two teams came at the post-match banquets.

One Chelsea player, complaining about his £50 loser's bonus said: "We are not money-grabbers. We are professionals and we believe that, for getting to Wembley, we deserve more."

Nicholson, meanwhile, was happy to do his job without so much as a contract. "I have all I want. What is the use of a contract? Your only security is your ability." The Double, two more FA Cups, and the European Cup Winners Cup said it all.

JOCK STEIN
A legend in his own lifetime

Roddy Mackenzie

The Big Man: Stein was a colossus in Scotland

FOR MANY Scots it was the day that football died. On the morning of September 11, 1985, Scotland should have been nursing a massive hangover after a 1-1 draw with Wales in Cardiff had secured qualification for the country's fourth successive World Cup finals. Instead, the nation shuffled to work gloomily.

Jock Stein, "The Big Man" of Scottish football, had died of a heart attack in the bowels of Ninian Park just minutes after masterminding another triumph the previous night. It was the way Stein would have wished to depart – in his working clothes and with football people watching over him.

Recalling that night, Roy Aitken, who played under Stein for Celtic and Scotland, was to recount: "In the dressing-room we should have been in celebratory mood at the end of the match. Scotland had made it to Mexico. But there was near silence as we changed and waited for more news. It must have been 20 minutes later that we were told. I looked at the physio Jim Steel's face and knew without any words that the worst had happened."

For a country which prides itself on its football, Stein had become a national hero. If it is said that most people can remember where they were when they heard of President Kennedy's assassination, then most Scots can tell you what they were doing when news of Stein's death came

through. It was felt that deeply. Ten thousand people lined the streets of Glasgow to pay their last respects as the funeral cortege made its way to Linn crematorium.

Scottish football had lost its leader, its ambassador and its keeper of dreams. Nobody has commanded the same respect since and the Scottish game is still coming to terms with the loss. "John, you're immortal," Bill Shankly told Stein after he had guided Celtic to the European Cup in 1967 and, in terms of Scottish football, it was no hyperbole.

Stein, from humble origins, was a man of the people who never lost the common touch. Raised in the Lanarkshire mining community of Burnbank, on the outskirts of Hamilton, it was obvious from an early stage of his football involvement that he would transcend barriers. Burnbank has yielded such football talent as Bobby Shearer, Jim Bett and Davie Cooper over the years. As Protestants, all took the natural path to Ibrox and Rangers. Stein, of the same faith, found his way to Celtic, a club with Roman Catholic roots.

He found his way to the club he was to make his name with as a player and a manager via the unglamorous route of Albion Rovers and the Welsh non-league side Llanelli. At Celtic Park he formed a formidable half-back line with Bobby Evans and Bertie Peacock and, as captain, led the club to a League and Scottish Cup double in 1954. He never pulled on the dark blue shirt of Scotland and an ankle injury led to his premature retirement from playing.

But it was to be on the coaching side of the game that Stein was to work his alchemy. Stein was one of the new breed of tracksuit managers in the British game and left no doubt that his place was on the shop floor with his workers.

Pat Stanton played under Stein at Hibernian and at Celtic. He remembers: "Stein had this knack of getting the best out of players, whatever their ability. He had some difficult players to deal with like Willie Hamilton at Hibs and Jimmy Johnstone at Celtic but he had his own methods. He was very much a man of the people and left you in no doubt that you were privileged to be a football player." I remember on one occasion the trainer at Hibs asked a couple of the players to help carry the kit hamper from the team bus. They thought this was beneath their dignity. But Stein intervened and reminded them that, had it not been for football, they could have been carrying bricks around for a living."

Stanton admits that he had one or two arguments with the manager in his time and points out: "He could be quite ruthless. Some of the players were frightened of him but they all respected him and his great knowledge of the game, and of human nature. Stein was not a man to hold grudges. Once he had made his point and told you what he felt, it was forgotten about." It is said that he would go to the extent of slapping his own face to make it red before he went into a dressing-room before a game to give the players the impression that he was in a rage, and that he would not tolerate a sub-standard performance. It is an example of the psychology and attention to fine detail that Stein employed to get a response from his players.

Stein was also one of the first managers to manipulate the media to his advantage. If one of the clubs he managed had played poorly on the Saturday, Stein would invariably stage a hastily-arranged press conference on the Sunday morning where he would "absent-mindedly" drop into conversation the fact that he was interested in signing such and such a player. The Monday newspapers would not be filled with an analysis of Celtic's defeat on the Saturday but with a positive Celtic story.

One of his typical coups came in the 10-month period he managed Hibernian in 1964-65. Hibernian's city rivals, Hearts, had qualified for the Fairs Cup so Stein, not to be outdone, arranged a challenge match for Hibs in Edinburgh – against Real Madrid, who had played in the European Cup final in seven out of the previous nine seasons.

Hibs drew 30,000 to the match, Hearts's European tie was eclipsed and, to top it all, Real Madrid were beaten 2-0. One local journalist had predicted a 7-0 win for the Spanish side and Stein, never one to miss a chance to make his point, dragged the sportswriter into the Hibs dressing-room afterwards to explain himself to the exuberant players.

Stein's first managerial charge was at Dunfermline between 1960 and 1964, where he helped the club win the Scottish Cup in 1961 and left a side which was still challenging for honours later in the decade. His sojourn with Hibs was followed by the inevitable return to Celtic Park

Simply the best: Gemmell and Johnstone

THE BIG MAN'S IMPACT

Born October 5, 1922, Blantyre, Lanarkshire

PLAYING AND MANAGEMENT CAREER

1942: Joined Albion Rovers from Blantyre Victoria while continuing to work in the local mine

1948: Won promotion to the Scottish First Division, but relegated the following year

1950: Signed full-time for Llanelli in the Welsh League

1951: Transferred to Celtic

1954: Won the championship and the Scottish Cup

1955: League runners-up and Scottish Cup beaten finalists

1956: Forced to retire by an ankle injury

1960: Appointed manager of Dunfermline Athletic

1961: Scottish Cup winners

1964: Left Dunfermline to manage Hibernian

1965: Appointed manager of Celtic

1966: Caretaker manager of the Scottish national team

1978: Left Celtic after he was denied a place on the board. Managed Leeds for 44 days before being appointed manager of the the Scottish national team

1982: Scotland qualified for the World Cup finals. Eliminated after the first round

CELTIC HONOURS

1966-78: Scottish League champions 10 times (won the First Division a record nine years in succession 1966-74 and won the Premier Division in 1977); Scottish Cup winners eight times (1965, 1967, 1969, 1971, 1972, 1974, 1975, 1977); Scottish League Cup winners six times (1966, 1967, 1968, 1969, 1970, 1975)

1967: European Cup winners

1970: European Cup beaten finalists

Died September 10, 1985

Crowning glory: Celtic celebrate the defeat of Inter Milan in the European Cup final

in 1965; to a club which had not won the league title since Stein's captaincy 11 years previously.

Stein's renewed liaison with the club was to bring 10 league titles (including a world record nine in succession between 1966 and 1974), eight Scottish Cups and six League Cups. The crowning glory was the European Cup when Celtic, competing in the event for the first time, beat Inter Milan 2-1 in the final in Lisbon in May 1967. In one fell swoop, Stein dismantled the Italian defensive system of cattenaccio, created by Inter's coach Helenio Herrerra, and the result was to change the face of the European game.

Stein also took Celtic to another European Cup final in 1970 but, on that occasion, the Scottish champions lost to Feyenoord 2-1, a result which signalled the start of the Dutch domination of the competition.

However, Celtic and Stein were to part company in 1978. Stein had almost lost his life in a car accident and it was taken for granted that when he recovered he would be offered a place on the Celtic board at a time when Billy McNeill, who captained Stein's European Cup winning side, was brought back from Aberdeen to fill the manager's chair. But Celtic had never had a Protestant director and Stein was, instead, offered a commercial position within the club. He regarded the offer as an insult and left to join Leeds United as manager.

That was to last only a matter of months as he was lured back to Scotland to take over as national team manager after the debacle of Argentina in 1978. Stein led Scotland to the 1982 World Cup finals in Spain – where they shared a memorable celebration of football in a match with Brazil in Seville – and then he masterminded the qualifying campaign for 1986 before his untimely death. Many have copied his methods, picked up his habits and employed his tactics since then. But Scottish football will never see his like again.

The team that Jock built: Celtic's squad in 1966. They went on to win the League a record nine years in a row

Leeds end their trophy famine and then do it again for good measure

Celtic's argy-bargy

Mayhem in Montevideo: riot police had to separate the brawling players

CELTIC'S clash with Racing Club for the world club championship was the unacceptable face of football at its very worst.

Celtic, the European Cup holders, beat the Argentine side in a niggling match at Hampden. But not even that could have prepared them for the reception they got in Buenos Aires on November 1.

As the team were led on to the pitch by a piper their goalkeeper, Ronnie Simpson, was felled by a stone and carried off barely conscious. When Celtic took the lead with a penalty the violence got even worse, with Jimmy Johnstone singled out as a target for particularly brutal treatment.

Half-time took on an air of farce when Celtic discovered that the water had been cut off in their dressing room. The interval lasted for 26 minutes because Celtic refused to resume the match until they had had a shower.

Racing Club put two goals past Celtic's stand-in goalkeeper Sean Fallon and Jock Stein foolishly agreed to a play-off match in Uruguay three days later.

This time both teams plumbed the depths, with the Celtic players determined to get their retribution in before they received any more punishment. Johnstone was sent off for elbowing an opponent, John Hughes was dismissed for kicking the Racing goalkeeper and Bobby Lennox also received his marching orders. Two Racing players were also sent off, and the violence got so bad that armed police had to separate the brawling players.

Towards the end of the match Celtic even had a fourth player dismissed. But amid the confusion nobody seemed to know that they had been ordered off so Celtic played on with eight men when they should have been reduced to seven.

Racing won 1-0 but the result did not matter. The world was horrified by the violence. Despite the fact that they had faced extreme provocation Stein fined all his players and publicly apologised for his team's misbehaviour.

FINALLY Don Revie's Leeds broke their duck and captured a major trophy. Leeds were in danger of forever being known as the nearly men. Since their return to the First Division in 1964 they had twice been runners-up (once on goal average), losing FA Cup finalists and losing Fairs Cup finalists. So when they faced Arsenal at Wembley in March in the revitalised League Cup final, the fear of failure hung over the Leeds players like a shroud.

Revie had considered winding his players up before the match by opening out a barren trophy case, but when he saw the jittery state they were in he hastily abandoned the idea. Not surprisingly football was the loser. Unimaginative Arsenal could find no way to break down the cautious and physical Leeds game plan. Terry Cooper, the Leeds full-back, provided the single bright spot in a dour match when he scored the only goal in the 20th minute, blasting a loose ball into the roof of the net.

In August Leeds, having disposed of three Scottish clubs in successive rounds (Hibs, Rangers and Dundee) found themselves in the Fairs Cup final for the second year in a row. Their opponents were Ferencvaros who came to Elland Road for the first leg with the most extraordinary strategy. They pulled shirts, kicked ankles, made little attempt to attack and always had at least eight men behind the ball.

Mick Jones scored an opportunist goal four minutes before half-time. Yet in the second half the Hungarians persisted with their negative tactics and if anything intensified their cynicism. Johnny Giles had to go off with concussion with Jones following him shortly after having been kicked in the groin. Leeds then went to Budapest in September protecting a 1-0 lead and missing Giles.

The Hungarians fought vainly to break down a determined Leeds defence in front of their fanatical 76,000 fans but Leeds had been battle-hardened in European competition and were able to cling on to their advantage and double the silverware in their trophy room.

Nearly men no more: Bremner brandishes the League Cup

Cardiff's starring role on the European stage

OUTSIDE of Wales, winning the Welsh Cup was seen as a back-door way into Europe. However, Cardiff City proved that they could do just as well on the international stage as any of the bigger clubs from England and Scotland.

Cardiff had already reached the quarter-finals of the Cup Winners Cup once before, in the 1964-65 season when they had knocked out the holders Sporting Lisbon. This time the struggling Second Division club went one better. It was particularly embarrassing for Aberdeen and Tottenham, both of whom were eliminated in the second round.

The finest performances produced by Jimmy Scoular's team came in the quarter-finals, which they reached by beating Shamrock Rovers and Breda. Thanks to Barrie Jones, Cardiff took a 1-0 lead over Torpedo Moscow to the Soviet Union. They hung on to lose only 1-0 in the depths of winter, necessitating a replay in West Germany.

Cardiff's team was devastated by injuries before the match on April 3. Scoular was forced to play five reserves, with Ritchie Morgan making his first-team debut at centre-half.

The new boys played like old hands and Cardiff won when the teenage John Toshack set up Norman Dean, the reserve centre-forward for the only goal of the match.

After a 1-1 draw in Hamburg Cardiff were only one match away from the final. But their brave run ended with a 3-2 defeat at home. Even so, they could hold their heads high as the most successful Welsh club in Europe of all time.

■ Pat Jennings (above), the Tottenham goalkeeper, scored a goal against Manchester United in the Charity Shield when his long, punted clearance was caught by the wind and bounced over Alex Stepney, the United goalkeeper.

■ Matt Busby was knighted.

■ Goalkeepers were limited to taking four steps with the ball by the International Board.

■ The government commissioned Norman Chester and a group of football experts to produce a report on the future of English football. Not surprisingly, its visionary recommendations were largely ignored by the League and the FA.

■ Arsenal had three players sent off in four days during two bad-tempered matches against Burnley. Bob McNab was dismissed in the League Cup quarter-final and Frank McLintock, the Arsenal captain, and Peter Storey were sent off in a League match.

■ Jimmy Scoular, the Cardiff manager, got a nasty shock when his team's match against Millwall was abandoned after half an hour. A visiting fan demanded a refund of his admission money and when Scoular explained that it was not possible he got punched in the face for his troubles.

White's black day as one slip deprives Rangers of the title

Winners lose: Rangers beat Celtic but lost the championship

DAVIE WHITE, the new man at the helm at Ibrox, soon discovered what an awesome task managing Rangers was. White had replaced Scot Symon in September and had guided the club to the final match of season unbeaten in the League. Unfortunately for White, a last-minute goal from Aberdeen gave them a 3-2 victory at Ibrox and certainly handed the title to Celtic.

The Rangers players left the field to a hail of abuse from their own supporters despite having taken 61 points from 34 games and having been the only team to have beaten Celtic in the League. The Ibrox fans obviously had short memories preferring to forget the glory days of the late 1950s and early 1960s and instead dwell on the current success enjoyed by Jock Stein and Celtic.

Extra special Astle

IT WAS certainly a dreadful FA Cup final, but West Bromwich Albion didn't care. Their 1-0 victory over Everton, the red-hot favourites, more than made amends for their embarrassing defeat the previous season at the hands of Third Division QPR in the League Cup final.

Jeff Astle scored the solitary goal in the third minute of extra time, amazingly with his left foot. As he said himself: "That's the dummy leg – the one that's just for standing on. My mates make a joke of it. Yet that's the third goal in a row it has brought me."

Astle broke the deadlock when his right-footed shot cannoned off Colin Harvey and rebounded to him. Without a single second's hesitation Astle whipped a shot from 20 yards into the far corner of the Everton goal. "You don't stop and think about what you're going to do in moments like that," he said. "You just hit the ball and hope for the best."

If Jimmy Husband had heeded Astle's advice it would have been Everton's name on the Cup, not West Brom's. Five minutes from the end of normal time Howard Kendall's cross was deflected to John Morrissey who brilliantly lobbed the ball into the open goal area. Husband, who was utterly unmarked, had all the time in the world to measure his header. Sadly for Everton he got his calculations wrong and sent it over the bar.

Everton pushed John Hurst up for the last 15 minutes but when he headed past the post it was all over.

On paper Everton had been dead certs for the Cup. Their midfield trio of Kendall, Harvey and Alan Ball was majestic, and with Brian Labone in defence and Joe Royle up front they were everybody's favourites. But Alan Ashman's unfashionable team closed them down, cluttered the midfield and Everton were not allowed to play the football of which they were capable.

Labone did a good job containing Astle. The West Brom striker only had two chances in the entire 120 minutes, but that was enough. Astle went into the final as the country's leading scorer with 34 League and Cup goals and had scored in every round, a record he maintained to blistering effect.

Lancashire's two-city dominance in the Swinging Sixties and the Beatles era		
League championship	**FA Cup:**	**In Europe:**
1963 Everton	1963 Manchester Utd	1966 Liverpool finalists Cup Winners Cup
1964 Liverpool	1965 Liverpool	1968 Manchester Utd winners European Cup
1965 Manchester Utd	1966 Everton	1970 Manchester City winners Cup Winners Cup
1966 Liverpool	1968 Everton runners-up	
1967 Manchester Utd	1969 Manchester City	*Of the 16 senior domestic trophies*
1968 Manchester City		*available in those eight years*
1970 Everton		*Lancashire clubs won 11 of them*

City's title tips Lancashire's balance of power

MANCHESTER CITY won the League championship for only the second time in dramatic style as they pipped their illustrious neighbours United on the very last day of the season. City had to win at Newcastle to take the title, a task that seemed awesome when, having taken the lead, City went in at half-time level at two apiece.

Malcolm Allison, the charismatic and visionary coach that the new manager Joe Mercer had hired in 1965 when City were in the doldrums of the Second Division, gave an inspired team talk. He said nothing. The team he had coached to super fitness and explosive speed knew what was expected of them and did it. Playing like men inspired, they stormed to a two-goal lead and a late Newcastle goal made no difference, the title was theirs.

It had been a close run race. Leeds and Liverpool had also been in contention until the final stages and when the dust settled a mere six points spanned the top five clubs. When the season began City had hardly looked contenders, taking only one point from their first three matches. Indeed, at one stage, United were five points clear of the pack.

Mercer and Allison reorganised their team, moving Mike Summerbee from the wing to centre-forward, and added Francis Lee to the forward line, at a cost of £60,000 from Bolton. A stirring derby at Old Trafford closed the gap when City gained a fully merited 3-1 victory. Then as the toll of United's European Cup campaign told, City became the principal beneficiaries.

With United lifting the European Cup, the axis of English football shifted from one part of Lancashire to another. Last year Merseyside had the top dogs with Liverpool as champions and Everton as the FA Cup winners. This year belonged to Manchester.

Mullery makes history as first dismissal puts paid to England's hopes

ENGLAND had mixed fortunes in their European championship campaign. True they finished a consoling third and had qualified by eliminating Scotland, cancelling out their embarrassing defeat at Wembley in 1967, but Alan Mullery's dismissal in the semi-final seriously dented England's international image.

The Home championships for this and the previous season had been designated as a qualifying group for the quarter-finals. Although Scotland had a clear advantage over England from their Wembley victory in 1967, their 1-1 draw with Wales left them needing to beat England at Hampden on February 24 to qualify. The Scots were missing Denis Law and Jim Baxter and, despite a virtuoso performance by Charlie Cooke, were fortunate to escape with a 1-1 draw.

England sailed past Spain to meet Yugoslavia in the semi-final in Florence on June 5. It was a bruising, cynical encounter that culminated in the second half with Mullery being sent off, the first time an England player had been dismissed. Mullery had his excuses – he had just been brought down with a late tackle by Trivic – but his retaliatory kick at the perpetrator, compounded by the forward's thespian display, left the referee with little choice.

Down to 10 men, England struggled to hold the young Yugoslav side and four minutes from time Dragan Dzajic, their outstanding winger, scored the only goal of the match. Three days later, in Rome, goals from Bobby Charlton and Geoff Hurst dispatched the Soviet Union to give England third place. In the final Yugoslavia took Italy, the hosts, to a replay before succumbing 2-0.

Moment of madness: Mullery foolishly retaliated and was sent off

United lay Munich ghosts to rest and make Manchester football's capital

TEN YEARS after the Munich disaster, Manchester United finally won the one trophy that mattered more to the club than any other, the European Cup.

Twice, though, it seemed that Matt Busby's long-held dream would turn into a nightmare once again. In the semi-finals United took a slender 1-0 to Real Madrid and, completely outplayed, were 3-1 down at half-time. Busby then gambled everything on all-out attack and, in a remarkable turn-around, goals from David Sadler and the Munich survivor Bill Foulkes took them through to the final against Benfica.

The match, at Wembley on May 29, was equally nerve-wracking. Bobby Charlton gave United the lead with a rare headed goal but Benfica equalised with 15 minutes to go.

Only seconds remained in the match when Eusebio burst through the United defence and had the goal at his mercy. Busby turned away in despair. All Eusebio had to was place the ball past Alex Stepney. Eusebio had rattled the crossbar with a fierce shot earlier, and once again he chose to hit the ball as hard as possible.

He blasted his shot too close to Stepney instead of tucking it into the corner. That mistake allowed Stepney to somehow get his fingertips to the ball and keep United's hopes alive with a reflex save. "Eusebio went for the glory," Nobby Stiles said. "He tried to break the net."

After 90 minutes, the United team were exhausted but Busby prepared them for extra time with a few simple words: "If you pass the ball to each other you will beat them." Stiles recalled the 1966 World Cup final. "Benfica were like the Germans – knackered."

Just how tired Benfica were became apparent in the third minute of extra time. Stepney's clearance was passed to George Best who, tired or not, took off on a 25-yard run. He beat one player, rounded another, and with the Benfica defence in disarray calmly sidestepped the goalkeeper and guided the ball into the net.

The goal lifted a huge burden from United's shoulders and from then on they were unstoppable. Their weariness was forgotten as Brian Kidd celebrated his 19th birthday by scoring a minute later, and Charlton scored a fourth goal soon afterwards. As Stiles had thought, it was like the World Cup final all over again.

When the final whistle blew Charlton collapsed exhausted and burst into tears. Overcome with emotion, Busby also wept when he joined his players on

---

It was like something from Roy of the Rovers

GEORGE BEST

---

the pitch. His grief over the Munich air crash eased.

"The moment when Bobby took the Cup it cleansed me," Busby said. "It eased the pain of the guilt of going into Europe. It was my justification."

Ten years on: Charlton hoists the European Cup a decade after Munich

FOR THE RECORD

Media man: Jimmy Hill joins the communications business

■ After five years as the hugely successful manager of Coventry, Jimmy Hill quit his post to work exclusively for television as a pundit. Hill steered the Midlands club from the Third Division to the First and gave the club a modern, go-ahead image. Noel Cantwell replaced Hill.

■ Port Vale were expelled from the Fourth Division for making improper payments to players. They were promptly re-elected. Peterborough had 19 points deducted for a similar offence, and were relegated from the Third Division as a result.

■ The British transfer record was broken twice, first when Martin Chivers moved from Southampton to Tottenham for £125,000 and then when Allan Clarke joined Leicester from Fulham for £150,000.

■ No team in the League managed to score 100 or more goals, the first time this had happened since the 1953-54 season.

■ Dave Mackay moved from Tottenham to Derby in July, saying: "I could do nothing more for them, nor they for me."

Mercer and Allison in overdrive as City's bandwagon keeps rolling on

MANCHESTER CITY'S revival under the managerial partnership of Joe Mercer and Malcolm Allison continued when they added the FA Cup to the League trophy they had won the previous season. Not bad for a team which four years earlier had finished 11th in the Second Division. Sadly for Leicester, the Wembley losers, they limped away from their Cup final defeat and failed to secure the seven points they needed from their last five League matches to avoid relegation to the Second Division.

But given the chances they had to win the Cup, it was not surprising they were League flops as well. Allan Clarke, their wonderfully gifted striker, had a magnificent shot pushed away for a corner in the 30th minute. Then Peter Rodrigues, Leicester's right-back, missed the opportunity of the match when he failed to connect feet from the goal.

Leicester's errors in front of goal continued in the second half. Andy Lochhead fluffed a simple chance from Clarke's header and then with 15 minutes remaining Lochhead blew another chance when he was hustled off the ball.

However, Manchester City were worthy winners. The forward line of Colin Bell, Francis Lee and Mike Summerbee in particular were a handful for Leicester throughout the 90 minutes. And Neil Young's goal in the 24th minute was the finest strike of the afternoon. The inside left latched on perfectly to Summerbee's pulled-back pass from the goal line to thump the ball past the hapless Peter Shilton. It was a goal worthy of a winner's medal, and so it proved.

City slickers: Oakes and Bell hoist the FA Cup

Busby bows out with every honour won

WITH HIS 60th birthday on the horizon, Sir Matt Busby announced his retirement on January 14. Manchester United were sixth from bottom of the First Division and Busby said that it was time for a younger man to take charge. In reality, with the European Cup won there was nothing else left for him to achieve.

Busby was the longest-serving manager in the League and,

> *I had never met anyone else like him in the game. The longer you knew him the more you felt for him, which was why he had everybody doing the things they did*
>
> DENIS LAW
> on Matt Busby

since the end of the war, he had overseen a remarkable transformation at Old Trafford. He had taken a club that was deep in debt and, by the sheer force of his personality, turned it around.

His first team was, by force of necessity, built from nothing. But Busby's determination to develop his own players rather than spend money in the transfer market laid the very foundations of the club.

With his post-war players ageing, Busby told his board of directors: "I am going to make the move which will make or break Manchester United." Overnight, half of the team were replaced by young reserves and the Busby Babes were born.

The gamble was the making of United, and also the breaking of the club's heart when so many brilliant careers were cut short one fateful night in Munich. Busby barely survived the plane crash, twice receiving the last rites, and was on the brink of quitting.

But urged on by his devoted wife Jean he fought back and rebuilt United yet again, although this time he was forced into the transfer market to replace his lost young stars.

Once again, Busby contemplated retirement when United were beaten by Partizan Belgrade in the semi-final of the

Midas touch: Busby parades one of the many trophies he won

European Cup. But his life's work was never going to be done until the emotional night that Bobby Charlton held the trophy aloft at Wembley.

Busby said that he would stay with the club as general manager, and there was feverish speculation about who would replace him. Don Revie was the bookmakers' favourite, but the methods he had used at Leeds were anathema to Busby.

Wilf McGuinness the assistant manager was a 6-1 outsider.

But once Busby discovered that Dave Sexton, the Chelsea manager, did not want to move north then McGuinness was his choice. Busby waited nearly three months, until he was sure United were in no danger of relegation, before making the announcement.

The first McGuinness knew about it was the day before, when he was told to wear a tie to work the following morning. He would soon discover that Busby was an impossible act to follow.

Arsenal's guns silenced by Rogers

DON ROGERS did next to nothing for the first 90 minutes of the League Cup final. The pitch was a muddy swamp but the Swindon winger started extra time with barely a mark on his shirt or shorts. Then he burst into life to scupper Arsenal with two goals.

Arsenal had been expected to stroll past Third Division Swindon but they did have their excuses. The pitch had been ruined by the International Horse of the Year show, and most of the team were still recovering from flu.

They hardly had any excuses for the way Swindon took the lead. Ian Ure's feeble back pass left Bob Wilson stranded and Roger Smart scored the easiest of goals. Arsenal then laid siege to the Swindon goal, but they were repeatedly beaten back by Peter Downsborough. During one frantic spell the Swindon goalkeeper faced nine corners in 10 minutes.

Another goalkeeping mistake, this time by Downsborough, let Bobby Gould force in an equaliser with four minutes remaining. But extra time was the last thing Arsenal wanted.

Heavy rain and the after-effects of the flu had sapped their strength while Rogers was still as fresh as a daisy.

He tucked a corner away to give Swindon the lead and then, in the last minute of the match, he made doubly sure. Starting from the half-way line, he ploughed through the mud to score a sparkling solo goal.

Swindon, as a Third Division club, were ineligible to take up a place in the Fairs Cup. But, like QPR, the last Third Division team to take the trophy, they won promotion instead.

■ The main stand at Nottingham Forest caught fire during the match against Leeds on August 24. The 34,000 spectators had to be evacuated, and Forest played the rest of their home games at Notts County's ground a few hundred yards away.

■ Geoff Hurst scored six times when West Ham beat Sunderland 8-0 in October and then admitted his first goal should have been disallowed because he scored it with his hand.

■ Rangers broke the Scottish transfer record when they bought Colin Stein from Hibs for £100,000 in October.

■ Jimmy Greaves scored his 200th goal for Tottenham in November. On the way, he scored three goals against Burnley in September, his first hat-trick in the League for four years. The 7-0 defeat of Burnley equalled Tottenham's record winning margin in the League.

White knight: Rogers (centre) did nothing apart from score two goals to capture the League Cup

Muddy heroes: the grimy Swindon players celebrate their dramatic victory in extra time at Wembley

United find argy-bargy strikes again

DESPITE the assaults Celtic had suffered in the world club championship last season, Matt Busby was determined that Manchester United were going to play in the competition. Like Jock Stein before him, after two maulings he probably wished he hadn't.

United went to Argentina for the first leg. The local press claimed that Nobby Stiles was "The Assassin", and even the match programme said he was a brute and a bad sportsman.

Not surprisingly, Estudiantes went out to get him. Stiles was the victim of a blatant head butt and was then sent off for dissent. Bobby Charlton was in the wars as well, needing several stitches in a deliberately inflicted leg wound.

The return leg, with Estudiantes holding a 1-0 lead, produced slightly better football in the 1-1 draw and even more violence. Denis Law was kicked so badly by the Argentinian goalkeeper that he had to be taken off and George Best was victimised throughout the match. His patience finally snapped and he was sent off with Medina for fighting.

Leeds tear up record books in relentless march to title

Tostao spoils England's summer trip

FRESH from having retained the Home international championships – beating Northern Ireland, Wales and Scotland in eight days in May – England enjoyed a reasonably successful tour to Latin America. Their first stop was Mexico City where the World Cup final will be next summer.

England found adjusting to the heat, humidity and altitude no easy matter and they laboured to achieve a goalless draw against the national side. Two days later England fared much better in Guadalajara when they beat a Mexican XI 4-0. Guadalajara is 2,000 feet lower than the capital and, fortunately for England, the site of their Group matches in the World Cup finals.

Colin Lee and Geoff Hurst both scored in England's next match in the tour, a satisfying 2-1 defeat of Uruguay in Montevideo. And with 10 minutes remaining of their final match – against Brazil in Rio de Janeiro – they seemed set to pull off a remarkable coup.

Colin Bell had put them ahead in the first half when he pounced on a deflection and their luck held when Gordon Banks saved Carlos Alberto's penalty. But Pele's team were in no mood to surrender meekly and a late rally broke a brave England visibly wilting in the heat.

Tostao equalised and two minutes from the end laid on a perfect pass for Jairzinho to score the winner. It was a cruel finish to the tour but Ramsey's men had held their own against the best in the world for 80 minutes.

LEEDS finally clicked into gear and won their first League championship in their 69-year history. It was no more than they had been threatening for the past five seasons, but somehow it had always eluded them. Almost certainly their success in winning the League Cup and the Fairs Cup the previous season had made all the difference. At last the monkey was off their shoulders: they had something to show for all their endeavours.

Don Revie and Leeds executed their championship pursuit in their inimitable, clinical fashion. They did it without breaking sweat and swept all setbacks aside. Even an incredible 5-1 defeat by Burnley was ignored (though they made sure to thump them 6-1 in the return) as Leeds proceeded to reel off 28 matches without defeat.

Their only other defeat in the League was at the hands of Manchester City on September 14, three days after the exertions of winning the Fairs Cup in Budapest. It was the only match that Leeds did not win in their first nine League fixtures. They began in magnificent style and maintained it throughout the season, breaking records galore.

To suffer only two defeats was a record; their final total of 67 points from 42 matches broke Arsenal's record of 1931; and, curiously, their goals tally – a mere 66 – was lower than any championship-winning side since the offside law was altered in 1925. To be fair it was an extremely low-scoring First Division, only two clubs scored more goals than Leeds.

Nor could Revie's team be justifiably criticised for negative play. Indeed he had deliberately set out to be more attack-minded because of the way Manchester City had won the title the previous season. City, he felt, had succeeded by attacking teams home and away and had arguably won the title from United by beating them 3-1 at Old Trafford.

For once bad luck ran Leeds'

Guiding force: Billy Bremner, the Leeds captain, inspired his team to their first League championship in the club's 69-year history

way with early defeats in the League Cup, FA Cup and Fairs Cup. Unlike previous seasons, where an ambitious assault on several fronts had stretched their resources and left them with nothing to show for it, in 1969 they had been left with a single objective: the championship. This time they got it.

QPR kick out Stock to start managerial musical chairs

In November Jim Gregory, the QPR chairman, sacked Alec Stock, the manager who had just guided them from the Third to the First Division in successive seasons. Incredibly it set off a chain reaction that by the end of the season resulted in 35 managerial changes.

Two days later Tommy Docherty left Rotherham to take over at QPR and Bill Dodgin was demoted to assistant manager. A fortnight later Ronnie Allen quit Wolves and Bill McGarry left Ipswich to replace him. The next day Bobby Robson was sacked at Fulham and Johnny Haynes was appointed player-manager with Dodgin as his assistant.

In December Nottingham Forest got rid of John Carey and installed Matt Gillies, who resigned from Leicester. Then Docherty walked out of QPR after a bust-up with Gregory leaving Les Allen as player-manager. Haynes continued the madness by packing in the manager's job after just four games. Dodgin stepped up.

The vacant spot at Leicester was taken by Torquay's Frank O'Farrell. Docherty quickly bounced back and was snapped up by Aston Villa. Stock also gained another job, just six weeks after his sacking at QPR, as Luton's manager. Stock also had the last laugh: QPR finished plumb bottom of the First Division and were relegated.

Newcastle belie their lowly status

NEWCASTLE confounded all the critics by romping away with the Fairs Cup, the fifth English club to win a European trophy since 1963. The criticism of Newcastle was nothing to do with the club, but the absurd way they had qualified for the tournament. Under Uefa's antiquated rules, adopted in 1955, the Fairs Cup was supposed to be for the benefit of European cities that organised trade fairs, and originally was supposed to be contested by a team drawn from all clubs in a city. This had soon fallen by the wayside, and instead a one city, one team policy obtained.

At the end of the 1968 season Newcastle had finished tenth with three London, and two Liverpool, clubs and the FA Cup winners above them. With Manchester City and United (as holders) in the European Cup; Liverpool, Leeds and Chelsea in the Fairs Cup; WBA in the Cup Winners Cup; the fourth Fairs Cup place fell to Newcastle by default.

Notwithstanding the amazing combination of circumstances that allowed Newcastle in through the back door, they grasped their golden opportunity with verve, scything their

Double top: Newcastle beat Ujpest Dozsa home and away

way through impressive European opposition. In successive rounds they eliminated Feyenoord, Sporting Lisbon, Real Zaragoza, Vitoria Setubal and Rangers.

In the final they scaled even higher peaks when they faced Ujpest Dozsa who had beaten Leeds in both legs in the quarter finals. At St James's Park, in the first leg, the Newcastle captain Bobby Moncur virtually won the tie single-handed. Frustrated by his team's inability to score against the Hungarians the defensive midfielder decided to throw himself into the attack, with immediate reward. Moncur scored two goals in the 63rd and 72nd minutes. They were Moncur's first goals in seven years. Jim Scott made it 3-0 seven minutes from time.

Moncur and Newcastle were no less impressive in the return in Budapest a fortnight later. Despite being 2-0 down at half-time, Moncur rallied his troops with a goal a minute after the restart and then Ben Arentfot and Alan Foggon completed a remarkable 3-2 away victory. Chastened critics now claimed that Newcastle's runaway success proved the strength in depth of the Football League.

World Cup sparks war in Honduras

THE semi-final matches between Honduras and El Salvador in the central and north American qualifying group for the World Cup finals were responsible for the start of a full-scale war between the two countries.

The two-legged semi-final went to a play-off after both teams won one match. There was rioting at all three games, which provoked skirmishes along the border between the two countries, which had been at loggerheads for some time. Hondurans claimed that their country was being over-run by migrant farmers from El Salvador, who in turn said that their people were being persecuted.

Soon after El Salvador finally won 3-2 in Mexico the two countries broke off diplomatic relations. A fortnight later, on July 14, El Salvador invaded Honduras, bombing military targets and the capital city's airport. Honduras retaliated with an immediate counter-attack and more than 2,000 people were killed in the fighting.

MATT BUSBY & GEORGE BEST
The dream team that fell to earth

Chris Nawrat

IN ITS own sweet way Matt Busby and George Best was a marriage made in heaven: Busby was the avuncular manager who simply adored footballers and loved it if they could express their skills in his teams. Best was the imp of the Sixties with a talent so outrageous that he captured not only Busby's heart, but the world's too.

Their two trajectories intersected at Wembley on May 29, 1968 when Manchester United gloriously captured the European Cup. For Busby, 59, it was the vindication of more than 20 years of steadfast devotion to United and exorcised the ghosts of the Munich air crash a decade earlier. For Best, 22, it was proof positive that he was the best player in Europe, if not on the earth. He had demonstrated that his talent was not so much errant, but beyond the comprehension of other mortals. It was to be only the beginning of even greater glories to come.

Busby's liaison with Manchester United began in the debris of the Second World War. Working with next to nothing more than the players on United's books he miraculously put together an FA Cup-winning side and a championship-winning side in the late 1940s and early 1950s built around Johnny Carey. Then, within a season, he transformed the club by introducing a host of home-grown teenagers, the Busby Babes, to replace his veteran side, including Carey. It was a bold, but realistic, gamble and it marked out Busby as a manager with the character for the big decisions. His reward was two further League titles and that his "unknowns" became household names, in particular Duncan Edwards.

That team, including Edwards, was cut down in 1958 in Munich when Busby himself was fortunate to escape alive. It was the worst moment in his life, his brilliant young team, his "Babes", destroyed because Busby wanted to pursue the future: success against Continental opposition. Busby dug into his soul, contemplated packing it in and came out fighting. He rebuilt United again, first with the cheque book, and then with what he loved best, Manchester United's own home-grown players.

In 1961, a frail 15-year-old Belfast kid arrived at Old Trafford for a trial. His name was George Best. Within 24 hours he was on the ferry back because he was homesick. Busby gave him another chance and Best returned a fortnight later. Despite the lack of size that had caused other professional clubs to reject him, Busby and United had instantly spotted Best's amazing talents. It is almost certain that if Best had gone to another club those talents would never have blossomed in the way they did. United never trained Best's ball skills out of him, as other clubs would have. Best's hallmarks – nutmegging opponents; shimmying, dazzling runs that left a host of defenders on their backsides; goalkeepers cheekily lobbed at the most ludicrous of angles – would have been consigned to the dustbin of the school playground.

But not at United. Busby allowed Best to indulge in the kind of football only found in kids' comics, and Best revelled in it. As Eamon Dunphy, a contemporary of Best's at Old Trafford, put it: "Footballers as people first, that was Busby's secret. Even the oldest of men were boys to him. His job was to facilitate their development as human beings, their innate talent would then blossom. That was his formula." Best concurred: "We never talked about how we were going to play. We just went out on to the pitch and got on with it. We were audacious and flamboyant, dangerous and unpredictable." None more so than Best.

By the mid-1960s Best was being hailed as the Fifth Beatle and was duly granted rock star status. For a quiet, shy lad from the back streets of Belfast who preferred the snooker hall, the pub and the bowling alley to the discotheque, the nightclub and the limelight it was an overwhelming experience. It had its advantages (Best was adored and chased by myriad women) and its disadvantages (the hangers-on and the demon drink) but it was the Swinging Sixties, so why not

Audacious: Law leads a United attack against Fulham in United's heyday

let the lad enjoy himself? By and large Busby and United turned a blind eye to Best's excesses and attempts to rein him in usually proved fruitless.

Best, Busby, Manchester United and the Swinging Sixties hit their apogee with the European Cup final. It was the crowning glory, the apex of achievement, like climbing Everest. But it meant different things to different people. Later Best realised that it had signalled the beginning of the end for him and his beloved United: "For Matt and Bobby Charlton, for Bill Foulkes, for Denis Law … they'd done it. And then they sat back and you could almost hear the energy and ambition sighing out of the club. It was like being in at the winding up of a company."

Best was still only 22, the rest of that United team were in the twilight of their careers and there were no more fabulous youngsters coming through on the legendary Old Trafford production line. Nor had Busby gone into the transfer market to strengthen his fading, ageing team. In the four years from 1964 to 1968 he had only bought one player, Alex Stepney, the goalkeeper. This was not the Busby of the 1950s and early 1960s always with an eye on the future, this was Busby sticking to the remnants of the 1958 side hoping against hope they could ease the pain of that horror on a Munich runway. Best understood this, but now that the European Cup had been finally won, he wanted wholesale changes.

Best confronted Busby in his office. He told the boss bluntly that Bobby Charlton (the two had hated each other from day one), Denis Law and Pat Crerand had to go. They were over the hill and holding the side back. The only solution,

Fateful flight: the Munich plane crash tore the heart out of Manchester United

Best told Busby, was to rebuild the side around him and make him the captain. Busby refused point blank, claiming that Best wasn't responsible enough. "Make me the captain and I will be responsible," was Best's retort. That exchange effectively ended the era of Busby and Best and saw Manchester United enter a downward spiral that would take more than a generation to reverse.

Six years later the club were relegated to the Second Division for the first time since 1938. Busby had retired in 1969, giving way to Wilf McGuinness but always leaving him in his shadow. Busby returned in 1970, retired again, this time handing over to Frank O'Farrell, but deposed him in 1972 and brought in Tommy Docherty. Throughout all this managerial mayhem Best had battled to hold a struggling side

together, battled to keep his personal life on an even keel, and battled to beat the bottle. He didn't win one of those contests. By 1973, having walked out and returned on numerous occasions, Best finally quit Old Trafford. The golden dreams that had beckoned so gloriously in 1968 had now turned to dust.

So did Busby fail a most precocious and extraordinary talent at the very zenith of his powers? Or did the boy wonder vaingloriously piss it all away in an orgy of self-indulgence?

Bob Paisley has this observation: "If you look at Matt and ask where he might have failed you immediately think of George Best. But could anybody have handled him? It's a shame that his talent wasn't fully used because after the age of 26 he just played around. But if Matt Busby couldn't handle him, nobody could."

SIR MATT BUSBY

Born May 26, 1909, Bellshill, Lanarkshire

PLAYING CAREER
Manchester City 1928-36
Over 200 appearances
Honours FA Cup: Winners 1934; Finalists 1933
Liverpool 1936-39
Internationals Played one full match for Scotland in 1933 and also captained the Scottish team during the war-time internationals

MANAGEMENT CAREER
Manchester United Manager 1945-69
Retired as team manager in 1969, but took charge temporarily in the 1970-71 season when Wilf McGuinness left the club
Appointed a director of Manchester United in 1971 and subsequently became the club's president
Honours European Cup: Winners 1968
FA Cup: Winners 1948; Finalists 1958
League: Winners 1952, 1956, 1957, 1965, 1967

Other honours Knighted 1968. CBE 1958
Football League vice-president 1982

Died January 20, 1994

Happy days: Crerand, Busby and Best

Tragic loss: Edwards died at Munich

THE
1969-70
SEASON

Revie: finished empty-handed

Leeds' treble turns to nought

LEEDS, under Don Revie, were without doubt the most unpopular side in the country. Their uncompromising – some would say ruthless – style of play won them few friends but many enemies. However the blows that fate dealt them in April surely melted the hardest of hearts.

On March 28 Leeds had played a total of 52 matches and lost only three. Within five weeks they played a further 10 matches but could only win one. In that terrible spell three prestigious trophies had slipped from their grasp: the League championship, the FA Cup and the European Cup. The impossible Treble had proved just that. Impossible.

First, on April 1, they lost the championship race to Everton, the team that had ended their unbeaten run of 34 League games in August. Leeds had taken over the First Division leadership in January but by mid-March Everton had regained it.

And on the same night Leeds went down 1-0 at Elland Road to Celtic in the European Cup semi-final, George Connelly scoring after 90 seconds. It was Leeds's eighth fixture in 22 days. In the return, a fortnight later, despite a thundering equaliser from Billy Bremner in the first quarter of an hour, the English champions could not

---

There is no doubt in my mind that they would have done that Treble had it been a normal season

BILL SHANKLY

---

hold the rampant Scottish champions. Two minutes into the second half John Hughes regained the lead for Celtic and then a dazzling, mazy run from Jimmy Johnstone, their quicksilver winger, set up Bobby Murdoch for the killing goal.

Four days earlier, on April 11, Leeds had met a robust Chelsea side in the FA Cup final and were held to a draw. In the replay at Old Trafford on April 29 once again Chelsea were their match. This time Chelsea prevailed in extra time and Leeds's last chance for honours had evaporated. It was a cruel way for the finest team in England to end the season: empty-handed.

So what went wrong? Two factors probably converged to wreck Leeds's season. First, because the World Cup was to be held in June, the season was foreshortened adding to fixture congestion and fatigue, particularly as Leeds were involved in so many competitions.

And second, the FA Cup semi-final against Manchester United certainly sapped their energy and playing resources. It took Leeds three matches, over 12 days, to shake off their rivals. The last match came two days before Leeds began their hectic Easter programme and the sheer volume of fixtures simply overwhelmed them.

Arsenal's barren years ended by the new kids on the block

ARSENAL produced a remarkable comeback on April 28 to end a long barren spell that had not seen a trophy come to Highbury since the League championship in 1953.

Their progress to the final of the Fairs Cup had been built on a series of resounding wins at home – 3-0 against Glentoran in the first round, a defeat of Sporting Lisbon by the same margin in the second round, a 7-1 thrashing of Dinamo Bacau in the quarter-finals, and yet another 3-0 win, against Ajax in the semi-finals.

But Arsenal's extraordinary defeat of Anderlecht in the final owed much to two of their teenagers, Ray Kennedy and Eddie Kelly.

Kennedy had signed for Arsenal the previous season and had yet to establish himself in the first team – starting only two League games and twice coming on as a substitute.

When he replaced Charlie George in the first leg of the final in Belgium on April 22, Arsenal were 3-0 down and looked to be on their way out. But five minutes from the end he scored with a header to give some hope to the 51,000 fans who packed into Highbury for the second leg.

Kelly, at 19, was just a few months older than Kennedy. He, too, was in his first season in the first team. But the young midfield player showed no signs of nerves when, in the 26th minute, he calmly trapped the ball and drove it into the net.

Arsenal were now only a goal behind and if they could score again they would take the Cup on the away goals rule. Roared on by the crowd they kept pressing forward, but Anderlecht would not succumb.

Finally, with just under 20

Flying high: McLintock launches himself at the Ajax goalkeeper

minutes remaining, Bob McNab looped a cross into the penalty area. John Radford produced a majestic leap to get to the ball and his header delivered the desperately needed goal. Then, a minute later, Jon Sammels clipped in a third goal to give Arsenal the outright victory and put the seal on a perfect night.

England go it alone as British sides join an illustrious list of failures in the World Cup

FROM the British Isles' point of view it was fortunate England had won the World Cup in 1966 because otherwise the home nations would have had no representatives in the 1970 finals in Mexico whatsoever. As holders, of course, England were spared the problems of qualification. It was a different story for Scotland, Wales and the two Irelands.

Scotland had much the best excuse. They had been drawn in the same group as West Germany, the beaten finalists in 1966, and Austria. Scotland's faint hopes disappeared when they drew 1-1 with West Germany at Hampden, lost 3-2 in Germany and 2-0 in Vienna. They did finish runners-up, edging out Austria by a point.

Wales also had a tough task: their opponents were Italy and East Germany. Predictably they lost all four games, conceding 10 goals and only scoring four. The

Finishing touch: Libuda scores for West Germany against Scotland

Republic fared little better as they scraped one point from six matches, and that a 1-1 draw at home to Denmark, as Czechoslovakia and Hungary slugged it out for the plane to Mexico. The Czechs eventually prevailed 4-1 in a play-off in Marseille.

Northern Ireland could not get past the Soviet Union, drawing at home and losing away. So for the third successive World Cup finals England were left to fly the flag on their own.

Not that the home nations were the only European casualties of note. Spain, Portugal and Yugoslavia also joined Hungary on the scrap heap of also-rans. There were upsets too in South America and Africa as Argentina, who had hoped to host the finals, were eliminated by Peru and Morocco, not Ghana, emerged as that continent's representatives. They were the first African side in the finals since 1934.

City capture a majority shareholding in two Cups

MANCHESTER CITY enjoyed their third season of success with a Cup double at home and abroad. And their first triumph, in the League Cup, was particularly sweet because it included a defeat of their illustrious neighbours Manchester United.

After an easy victory over Southport in the second round, City had to work harder in the next two stages, with home matches against First Division opponents each time – Liverpool were edged out 3-2 and Everton were dispatched 2-0.

City's finest victory was undoubtedly in the semi-finals, where they met their old rivals over two legs. The contest was effectively decided in the first match at Maine Road, which City won 2-1 thanks to a penalty scored by Francis Lee. They were able to hold on to their slender advantage at Old Trafford and a 2-2 draw was enough to take them to Wembley. It was

delicious revenge for United's 3-0 defeat of City in the fourth round of the FA Cup.

The final, on March 7, brought two of England's finest forwards, Lee and Jeff Astle, into opposition. Astle struck first, giving West Brom the lead in the first half. Lee, however, was not able to add to his tally and it was Michael Doyle who took the match into extra time and then Glyn Pardoe who scored the winner.

When it came to Cup matches it seemed that City were always saving their best for Maine Road, particularly in the European Cup Winners Cup. They had to play the first leg of every round away from home, and they only managed one win in four matches abroad.

But once they had got their opponents back to Manchester it was a different story, with four victories and 14 goals. City twice hit five goals, the most notable

Up for the Cup: Tony Book brandishes the European Cup Winners Cup

time being their 5-1 victory over Schalke in the semi-finals after a 1-0 setback in West Germany.

With their indifferent away form, the omens might not have appeared to be too good for their trip to Vienna to play the Polish side Gornik in the final.

But Lee, as happened so often, was irrepressible. In tandem with Neil Young he was responsible for both goals. The

first came early in the match when Lee's shot hit a post and Young scored from the rebound. Then, just before half-time, Young was brought down by the Polish goalkeeper and Lee converted the penalty.

Gornik scored a consolation goal in the second half but that was not going to stop City collecting their fourth trophy in the past three years.

Celtic fail Grand Slam test

LEEDS weren't the only British side to see their hopes of a Grand Slam of trophies turn to dust. Much the same thing happened to Celtic, Leeds's conquerors in the European Cup semi-final.

But in Celtic's case they had been chasing four trophies and won two, while Leeds had pursued three and lost the lot. In both cases fixture congestion and fatigue played a vital part in their downfall.

Celtic snapped up their first honour in October when they dispatched little St Johnstone in the Scottish League Cup final despite being without the injured Bobby Lennox, the suspended Willie Wallace and the disgraced Tommy Gemmell, who had been sent off for Scotland playing against West Germany. The 1-0 scoreline flattered St Johnstone.

Celtic's 25th League title was a one-horse race: the Parkhead side eventually finishing 12 points ahead of Rangers, having won 27 of their 34 League matches.

On April 11, Celtic went into the Scottish Cup final against Aberdeen at Hampden seemingly holding all the Grand Slam aces. They held a 1-0 lead against Leeds in the European Cup semi-final with the home leg to come the following Wednesday and were red-hot favourites to swagger past Aberdeen. That was the script, the reality was somewhat different.

Two incidents in the first half-hour probably turned the game Aberdeen's way. First the referee awarded a dubious penalty when Derek McKay's cross hit a defender's hand, Joe Harper converting, and then a Bobby Lennox "goal" was disallowed minutes later.

However, with seven minutes remaining, there had been no further goals until McKay pounced to give Aberdeen a 2-0 lead. Lennox got one back with two minutes to go, only for McKay to dash upfield and seal a famous 3-1 victory.

But there was still the European Cup, although Celtic were extremely fortunate to have reached the semi-final. In the second round in November Celtic had taken an impressive 3-0 lead to Benfica only to concede three goals themselves. With the scores tied at three apiece Celtic went through on the toss of a coin.

Against Leeds the 1-0 cushion

Israel: undid Celtic

they had from Elland Road was always going to be too much for Leeds who, despite levelling the scores after 13 minutes, succumbed 3-1 on aggregate.

Once again Celtic went into a final a shade too confident. This time the opponents were Feyenoord in Milan on May 6 and the Dutch champions proved to be more of a handful that Celtic had anticipated. Although Gemmell had given the Glasgow side the lead after half an hour with a powerful shot reminiscent of the goal in Lisbon that had won the European Cup three years earlier, the Dutch equalised minutes later. The scorer was Rinus Israel, their sweeper.

Israel was to prove the key to Celtic's undoing as Feyenoord were playing a sweeper system with a difference: the sweeper also attacked. Thus Israel stole out of defence to catch the Celtic defence unawares with a deft header.

Celtic, baffled by the Dutch style of play and with Jimmy Johnstone marked out of the game, failed to score and the match went into extra time. Four minutes from the end Billy McNeill handled the ball, the referee waved play on, and Ove Kindvall scored the winner as Feyenoord became the first Dutch club to win the European Cup.

Webb redeems himself

CHELSEA, who had finished third in the League, were probably the last team Leeds wanted to face in the FA Cup final after a long and grinding season. The London club were probably one of the few sides that could counter Leeds's steel with steel of their own. And so it proved.

The teams met at Wembley on April 11 just as the first two legs of Leeds's fabulous Treble, the League championship and the European Cup, were eluding them. It was a typical hard-fought battle with neither side giving any quarter.

A first-half header from Jack Charlton had given Leeds the lead before Peter Houseman levelled the scores. With six minutes remaining Leeds seemed finally to have one hand on the Cup when Mick Jones scored their second. But the fates hadn't finished with Leeds just yet. Two minutes later Ian Hutchinson levelled the scores and took the game into extra time. A barren half-hour necessitated a replay, the first since 1912.

Thus, a fortnight later, both teams travelled to Old Trafford.

The second match was, if anything, more brutal than the first. Peter Bonetti was virtually knocked out by a late charge from Jones and the match was held up for several minutes as the Chelsea goalkeeper received attention. Shortly afterwards a dazed Bonetti was unable to stop a Jones shot and Leeds were ahead for the third time.

But Chelsea just would not give up. Peter Osgood, with a magnificent diving header, put them back into contention with 12 minutes of normal time remaining.

And, one minute after the extra time interval, Chelsea took the lead for the first time after 226 minutes of play when David Webb, at the far post, contrived to bundle Hutchinson's long throw into the net.

Fate had dealt its final card. Webb had been dreadful in the first match – Eddie Gray had run the full back ragged – so much so that Chelsea had moved him into the centre of defence, but here was the Wembley "failure" turned Old Trafford hero. Cruel indeed.

Saved: Chelsea players embrace Osgood after his equaliser in the replay

Moore accused of jewel theft – charges vanish into thin air

DAYS before England were to play Romania in the first match of the World Cup finals in Mexico, Bobby Moore, their captain, was arrested for alleged theft in Bogotá, Colombia.

Moore was accused by a shop-girl, Clara Padilla, who worked in the Green Fire jewellery store in the hotel the England party were staying in, of stealing a £600 emerald and gold bracelet. Moore and Bobby Charlton had visited the shop but when they were asked to explain the disappearance of the bracelet they were astonished. Moore could not even recollect having looked at it. Moore and Charlton made statements to the police and thought nothing of it.

Then the England team, who were in South America to acclimatise for the finals, flew to Ecuador for a friendly match. On their return, en route to Mexico, they stopped over in Bogotá and Moore was put under house arrest. Apparently another "witness" had emerged. The England team were forced to depart without their captain and the incident became an international scandal.

For four days the controversy raged as diplomats were hauled in to clear up the matter. Harold Wilson, the Prime Minister, was in the throes of an election campaign but that did not deter him from applying political pressure on the Colombian authorities.

Gradually the case against Moore began to fall apart, particularly when it was discovered that other visiting celebrities such as bullfighters and singers had been similarly "stung" and had paid up to avoid publicity.

Moore was "bailed" to play in the finals and joined his teammates in Mexico. The case eventually subsided when the mystery witness disappeared and the perpetrators, Padilla and the owner of the shop, were charged with conspiracy in 1972.

FOR THE RECORD

Hundred up: Bobby Charlton and Terry Neill lead the teams out

■ Bobby Charlton captained England and scored a goal when he made his 100th international appearance, against Northern Ireland at Wembley on April 21.

■ England and Scotland's 0-0 draw at Hampden Park on April 25 was only the second time this result had occurred. The first was the inaugural match between the two countries in 1872.

■ Second Division Swindon won the end of season Anglo-Italian Cup. They were leading 3-0 at Napoli when the match was abandoned with 10 minutes still to play because of crowd trouble.

■ The annual meeting of the Football League decided to fix the minimum admission charge at six shillings.

■ Uefa decided to use penalty kicks, rather than the toss of a coin, to decide matches that finished all-square in the three Cup competitions.

■ Ronnie Simpson, the Celtic goalkeeper, retired in May. He had been playing since June 3, 1945, when he made his first appearance for Queen's Park.

Moore leaves court in Bogota after a four-hour investigation

Old guard bite the dust

SOME of the biggest names in England ended the season with a brutal reminder that their glory days were long past. Chief among them were Preston, the first ever winners of the Double, and Aston Villa, who occupied the bottom two places in the Second Division and were relegated – the first time that both clubs had ever sunk so low.

Sunderland and Sheffield Wednesday were also in decline, slipping out of the First Division. Sheffield Wednesday only had themselves to blame though. In their last match of the season they needed to beat Manchester City at home to condemn Crystal Palace in their place.

But they lost 2-1 and thus found themselves out of the top flight for the first time since the 1958-59 season. Huddersfield, another historic club, had been out of the First Division even longer.

They bounced back though, running away with the Second Division and finishing seven points clear of another famous club, Blackpool, who also reclaimed their place among the elite.

At the other extreme, the League finally bowed to pressure from non-League clubs, who felt that they were continually being denied a chance to prove themselves. Bradford Park Avenue failed to gain re-election and were replaced by Cambridge United, the Southern League champions. It was the first change that had been made since Oxford had replaced Accrington Stanley in 1962.

LEAGUE TABLES AND RESULTS 1960 – 1970

	1960-61	1961-62	1962-63	1963-64	1964-65
WORLD CUP		Brazil 3 Czechoslovakia 1			
EUROPEAN CHAMPIONSHIP				Spain 2 USSR 1	
EUROPEAN CUP	Benfica 3 Barcelona 2	Benfica 5 Real Madrid 3	AC Milan 2 Benfica 1	Inter Milan 3 Real Madrid 1	Inter Milan 1 Benfica 0
EUROPEAN CUP WINNERS CUP	Fiorentina beat Rangers 2-0 2-1	Atletico Madrid 3 Fiorentina 0, after 1-1	Tottenham Hotspur 5 Atletico Madrid 1	Sporting Lisbon 1 MTK Budapest 0, after 3-3	West Ham United 2 Munich 1860 0
FAIRS CUP	AS Roma beat Birmingham City 2-2 2-0	Valencia beat Barcelona 6-2 1-1	Valencia beat Dynamo Zagreb 2-1 2-0	Real Zaragoza 2 Valencia 1	Ferencvaros 1 Juventus 0
FA CUP	Tottenham Hotspur 2 Leicester City 0	Tottenham Hotspur 3 Burnley 1	Manchester United 3 Leicester City 1	West Ham United 3 Preston North End 2	Liverpool 2 Leeds United 1

FIRST DIVISION

1960-61

	P	W	D	L	F	A	Pts
Tottenham	42	31	4	7	115	55	66
Sheff Wed	42	23	12	7	78	47	58
Wolves	42	25	7	10	103	75	57
Burnley	42	22	7	13	102	77	51
Everton	42	22	6	14	87	69	50
Leicester	42	18	9	15	87	70	45
Man Utd	42	18	9	15	88	76	45
Blackburn	42	15	13	14	77	76	43
Aston Villa	42	17	9	16	78	77	43
West Brom	42	18	5	19	67	71	41
Arsenal	42	15	11	16	77	85	41
Chelsea	42	15	7	20	98	100	37
Man City	42	13	11	18	79	90	37
Nottm F	42	14	9	19	62	78	37
Cardiff	42	13	11	18	60	85	37
West Ham	42	13	10	19	77	88	36
Fulham	42	14	8	20	72	95	36
Bolton	42	12	11	19	58	73	35
Birmingham	42	14	6	22	62	84	34
Blackpool	42	12	9	21	68	73	33
Newcastle	*42*	*11*	*10*	*21*	*86*	*109*	*32*
Preston	*42*	*10*	*10*	*22*	*43*	*71*	*30*

1961-62

	P	W	D	L	F	A	Pts
Ipswich	42	24	8	10	93	67	56
Burnley	42	21	11	10	101	67	53
Tottenham	42	21	10	11	88	69	52
Everton	42	20	11	11	88	54	51
Sheff Utd	42	19	9	14	61	69	47
Sheff Wed	42	20	6	16	72	58	46
Aston Villa	42	18	8	16	65	56	44
West Ham	42	17	10	15	76	82	44
West Brom	42	15	13	14	83	67	43
Arsenal	42	16	11	15	71	72	43
Bolton	42	16	10	16	62	66	42
Man City	42	17	7	18	78	81	41
Blackpool	42	15	11	16	70	75	41
Leicester	42	17	6	19	72	71	40
Man Utd	42	15	9	18	72	75	39
Blackburn	42	14	11	17	50	58	39
Birmingham	42	14	10	18	65	81	38
Wolves	42	13	10	19	73	86	36
Nottm F	42	13	10	19	63	79	36
Fulham	42	13	7	22	66	74	33
Cardiff	*42*	*9*	*14*	*19*	*50*	*81*	*32*
Chelsea	*42*	*9*	*10*	*23*	*63*	*94*	*28*

1962-63

	P	W	D	L	F	A	Pts
Everton	42	25	11	6	84	42	61
Tottenham	42	23	9	10	111	62	55
Burnley	42	22	10	10	78	57	54
Leicester	42	20	12	10	79	53	52
Wolves	42	20	10	12	93	65	50
Sheff Wed	42	19	10	13	77	63	48
Arsenal	42	18	10	14	86	77	46
Liverpool	42	17	10	15	71	59	44
Nottm F	42	17	10	15	67	69	44
Sheff Utd	42	16	12	14	58	60	44
Blackburn	42	15	12	15	79	71	42
West Ham	42	14	12	16	73	69	40
Blackpool	42	13	14	15	58	64	40
West Brom	42	16	7	19	71	79	39
Aston Villa	42	15	8	19	62	68	38
Fulham	42	14	10	18	50	71	38
Ipswich	42	12	11	19	59	78	35
Bolton	42	15	5	22	55	75	35
Man Utd	42	12	10	20	67	81	34
Birmingham	42	10	13	19	63	90	33
Man City	*42*	*10*	*11*	*21*	*58*	*102*	*31*
Leyton O	*42*	*6*	*9*	*27*	*37*	*81*	*21*

1963-64

	P	W	D	L	F	A	Pts
Liverpool	42	26	5	11	92	45	57
Man Utd	42	23	7	12	90	62	53
Everton	42	21	10	11	84	64	52
Tottenham	42	22	7	13	97	81	51
Chelsea	42	20	10	12	72	56	50
Sheff Wed	42	19	11	12	84	67	49
Blackburn	42	18	10	14	89	65	46
Arsenal	42	17	11	14	90	82	45
Burnley	42	17	10	15	71	64	44
West Brom	42	16	11	15	70	61	43
Leicester	42	16	11	15	61	58	43
Sheff Utd	42	16	11	15	61	64	43
Nottm F	42	16	9	17	64	68	41
West Ham	42	14	12	16	69	74	40
Fulham	42	13	13	16	58	65	39
Wolves	42	12	15	15	70	80	39
Stoke	42	14	10	18	77	78	38
Blackpool	42	13	9	20	52	73	35
Aston Villa	42	11	12	19	62	71	34
Birmingham	42	11	7	24	54	92	29
Bolton	*42*	*10*	*8*	*24*	*48*	*80*	*28*
Ipswich	*42*	*9*	*7*	*26*	*56*	*121*	*25*

1964-65

	P	W	D	L	F	A	Pts
Man Utd	42	26	9	7	89	39	61
Leeds	42	26	9	7	83	52	61
Chelsea	42	24	8	10	89	54	56
Everton	42	17	15	10	69	60	49
Nottm F	42	17	13	12	71	67	47
Tottenham	42	19	7	16	87	71	45
Liverpool	42	17	10	15	67	73	44
Sheff Wed	42	16	11	15	57	55	43
West Ham	42	19	4	19	82	71	42
Blackburn	42	16	10	16	83	79	42
Stoke	42	16	10	16	67	66	42
Burnley	42	16	10	16	70	70	42
Arsenal	42	17	7	18	69	75	41
West Brom	42	13	13	16	70	65	39
Sunderland	42	14	9	19	64	74	37
Aston Villa	42	16	5	21	57	82	37
Blackpool	42	12	11	19	67	78	35
Leicester	42	11	13	18	69	85	35
Sheff Utd	42	12	11	19	50	64	35
Fulham	42	11	12	19	60	78	34
Wolves	*42*	*13*	*4*	*25*	*59*	*89*	*30*
Birmingham	*42*	*8*	*11*	*23*	*64*	*96*	*27*

	1960-61	1961-62	1962-63	1963-64	1964-65
SECOND DIVISION	Champions: Ipswich Town Also promoted: Sheffield United Relegated: Portsmouth, Lincoln City	Champions: Liverpool Also promoted: Leyton Orient Relegated: Bristol Rovers, Brighton & Hove Albion	Champions: Stoke City Also promoted: Chelsea Relegated: Walsall, Luton Town	Champions: Leeds United Also promoted: Sunderland Relegated: Grimsby Town, Scunthorpe United	Champions: Newcastle United Also promoted: Northampton Town Relegated: Swindon Town, Swansea Town
THIRD DIVISION	Champions: Bury Also promoted: Walsall Relegated: Tranmere Rovers, Bradford City, Colchester United, Chesterfield	Champions: Portsmouth Also promoted: Grimsby Town Relegated: Torquay United, Lincoln City, Brentford, Newport County	Champions: Northampton Town Also promoted: Swindon Town Relegated: Bradford Park Avenue, Brighton & Hove Albion, Carlisle United, Halifax Town	Champions: Coventry City Also promoted: Crystal Palace Relegated: Millwall, Crewe Alexandra, Wrexham, Notts County	Champions: Carlisle United Also promoted: Bristol City Relegated: Luton Town, Port Vale, Colchester United, Barnsley
FOURTH DIVISION	Champions: Peterborough United Also promoted: Crystal Palace, Northampton Town, Bradford PA	Champions: Millwall Also promoted: Colchester United, Wrexham, Carlisle United	Champions: Brentford Also promoted: Oldham Athletic, Crewe Alexandra, Mansfield Town	Champions: Gillingham Also promoted: Carlisle United, Workington, Exeter City	Champions: Brighton & Hove Albion Also promoted: Millwall, York City, Oxford United
LEAGUE CUP	Aston Villa beat Rotherham United 0-2 3-0	Norwich City beat Rochdale 3-0 1-0	Birmingham City beat Aston Villa 3-1 0-0	Leicester City beat Stoke City 1-1 3-2	Chelsea beat Leicester City 3-2 0-0
SCOTTISH CUP	Dunfermline Athletic 2 Celtic 0, after 0-0	Rangers 2 St Mirren 0	Rangers 3 Celtic 0, after 1-1	Rangers 3 Dundee 1	Celtic 3 Dunfermline Athletic 2

SCOTTISH FIRST DIVISION

1960-61

	P	W	D	L	F	A	Pts
Rangers	34	23	5	6	88	46	51
Kilmarnock	34	21	8	5	77	45	50
T Lanark	34	20	2	12	100	80	42
Celtic	34	15	9	10	64	46	39
Motherwell	34	15	8	11	70	57	38
Aberdeen	34	14	8	12	72	72	36
Hibernian	34	15	4	15	66	69	34
Hearts	34	13	8	13	51	53	34
Dundee U	34	13	7	14	60	58	33
Dundee	34	13	6	15	61	53	32
Partick	34	13	6	15	59	69	32
Dunfermline	34	12	7	15	65	81	31
Airdrie	34	10	10	14	61	71	30
St Mirren	34	11	7	16	53	58	29
St J'stone	34	10	9	15	47	63	29
Raith	34	10	7	17	46	67	27
Clyde	*34*	*6*	*11*	*17*	*55*	*77*	*23*
Ayr	*34*	*5*	*12*	*17*	*51*	*81*	*22*

1961-62

	P	W	D	L	F	A	Pts
Dundee	34	25	4	5	80	46	54
Rangers	34	22	7	5	84	31	51
Celtic	34	19	8	7	81	37	46
Dunfermline	34	19	5	10	77	46	43
Kilmarnock	34	16	10	8	74	58	42
Hearts	34	16	6	12	54	49	38
Partick	34	16	3	15	60	55	35
Hibernian	34	14	5	15	58	72	33
Motherwell	34	13	6	15	65	62	32
Dundee U	34	13	6	15	70	71	32
T Lanark	34	13	5	16	59	60	31
Aberdeen	34	10	9	15	60	73	29
Raith	34	10	7	17	51	73	27
Falkirk	34	11	4	19	45	68	26
Airdrie	34	9	7	18	57	78	25
St Mirren	34	10	5	19	52	80	25
St J'stone	*34*	*9*	*7*	*18*	*35*	*61*	*25*
Stirling A	*34*	*6*	*6*	*22*	*34*	*76*	*18*

1962-63

	P	W	D	L	F	A	Pts
Rangers	34	25	7	2	94	28	57
Kilmarnock	34	20	8	6	92	40	48
Partick	34	20	6	8	66	44	46
Celtic	34	19	6	9	76	44	44
Hearts	34	17	9	8	85	59	43
Aberdeen	34	17	7	10	70	47	41
Dundee U	34	15	11	8	67	52	41
Dunfermline	34	13	8	13	50	47	34
Dundee	34	12	9	13	60	49	33
Motherwell	34	10	11	13	60	63	31
Airdrie	34	14	2	18	52	76	30
St Mirren	34	10	8	16	52	72	28
Falkirk	34	12	3	19	54	69	27
T Lanark	34	9	8	17	56	68	26
Q of South	34	10	6	18	36	75	26
Hibernian	34	8	9	17	47	67	25
Clyde	*34*	*9*	*5*	*20*	*49*	*83*	*23*
Raith	*34*	*2*	*5*	*27*	*35*	*118*	*9*

1963-64

	P	W	D	L	F	A	Pts
Rangers	34	25	5	4	85	31	55
Kilmarnock	34	22	5	7	77	40	49
Celtic	34	19	9	6	89	34	47
Hearts	34	19	9	6	74	40	47
Dunfermline	34	18	9	7	64	33	45
Dundee	34	20	5	9	94	50	45
Partick	34	15	5	14	55	54	35
Dundee U	34	13	8	13	65	49	34
Aberdeen	34	12	8	14	53	53	32
Hibernian	34	12	6	16	59	66	30
Motherwell	34	9	11	14	51	62	29
St Mirren	34	12	5	17	44	74	29
St J'stone	34	11	6	17	54	70	28
Falkirk	34	11	6	17	54	84	28
Airdrie	34	11	4	19	52	97	26
T Lanark	34	9	7	18	47	74	25
Q of South	*34*	*5*	*6*	*23*	*40*	*92*	*16*
E Stirling	*34*	*5*	*2*	*27*	*37*	*91*	*12*

1964-65

	P	W	D	L	F	A	Pts
Kilmarnock	34	22	6	6	62	33	50
Hearts	34	22	6	6	90	49	50
Dunfermline	34	22	5	7	83	36	49
Hibernian	34	21	4	9	75	47	46
Rangers	34	18	8	8	78	35	44
Dundee	34	15	10	9	86	63	40
Clyde	34	17	6	11	64	58	40
Celtic	34	16	5	13	76	57	37
Dundee U	34	15	6	13	59	51	36
Morton	34	13	7	14	54	54	33
Partick	34	11	10	13	57	58	32
Aberdeen	34	12	8	14	59	75	32
St J'stone	34	9	11	14	57	62	29
Motherwell	34	10	8	16	45	54	28
St Mirren	34	9	6	19	38	70	24
Falkirk	34	7	7	20	43	85	21
Airdrie	*34*	*5*	*4*	*25*	*48*	*110*	*14*
T Lanark	*34*	*3*	*1*	*30*	*22*	*99*	*7*

	1960-61	1961-62	1962-63	1963-64	1964-65
SCOTTISH SECOND DIV	Champions: Stirling Albion Also promoted: Falkirk	Champions: Clyde Also promoted: Queen of the South	Champions: St Johnstone Also promoted: East Stirling	Champions: Morton Also promoted: Clyde	Champions: Stirling Albion Also promoted: Hamilton Academical
SCOTTISH LEAGUE CUP	Rangers 2 Kilmarnock 0	Rangers 3 Hearts 1, after 1-1	Hearts 1 Kilmarnock 0	Rangers 5 Morton 0	Rangers 2 Celtic 1

	1965-66	1966-67	1967-68	1968-69	1969-70
WORLD CUP	England 4 West Germany 2				Brazil 4 Italy 1
EUROPEAN CHAMPIONSHIP			Italy 2 Yugoslavia 0, after 1-1		
EUROPEAN CUP	Real Madrid 2 Partizan Belgrade 1	Celtic 2 Inter Milan 1	Manchester United 4 Benfica 1	AC Milan 4 Ajax 1	Feyenoord 2 Celtic 1
EUROPEAN CUP WINNERS CUP	Borussia Dortmund 2 Liverpool 1	Bayern Munich 1 Rangers 0	AC Milan 2 SV Hamburg 0	Slovan Bratislava 3 Barcelona 2	Manchester City 2 Gornik Zabrze 1
FAIRS CUP	Barcelona beat Real Zaragoza 0-1 4-2	Dynamo Zagreb beat Leeds United 2-0 0-0	Leeds United beat Ferencvaros 1-0 0-0	Newcastle United beat Ujpest Dozsa 3-0 2-3	Arsenal beat Anderlecht 1-3, 3-0
FA CUP	Everton 3 Sheffield Wednesday 2	Tottenham Hotspur 2 Chelsea 1	West Bromwich Albion 1 Everton 0	Manchester City 1 Leicester City 0	Chelsea 2 Leeds United 1, after 2-2

FIRST DIVISION

1965-66
	P	W	D	L	F	A	Pts
Liverpool	42	26	9	7	79	34	61
Leeds	42	23	9	10	79	38	55
Burnley	42	24	7	11	79	47	55
Man Utd	42	18	15	9	84	59	51
Chelsea	42	22	7	13	65	53	51
West Brom	42	19	12	11	91	69	50
Leicester	42	21	7	14	80	65	49
Tottenham	42	16	12	14	75	66	44
Sheff Utd	42	16	11	15	56	59	43
Stoke City	42	15	12	15	65	64	42
Everton	42	15	11	16	56	62	41
West Ham	42	15	9	18	70	83	39
Blackpool	42	14	9	19	55	65	37
Arsenal	42	12	13	17	62	75	37
Newcastle	42	14	9	19	50	63	37
Aston Villa	42	15	6	21	69	80	36
Sheff Wed	42	14	8	20	56	66	36
Nottm F	42	14	8	20	56	72	36
Sunderland	42	14	8	20	51	72	36
Fulham	42	14	7	21	67	85	35
Northampton	*42*	*10*	*13*	*19*	*55*	*92*	*33*
Blackburn	*42*	*8*	*4*	*30*	*57*	*88*	*20*

1966-67
	P	W	D	L	F	A	Pts
Man Utd	42	24	12	6	84	45	60
Nottm F	42	23	10	9	64	41	56
Tottenham	42	24	8	10	71	48	56
Leeds	42	22	11	9	62	42	55
Liverpool	42	19	13	10	64	47	51
Everton	42	19	10	13	65	46	48
Arsenal	42	16	14	12	58	47	46
Leicester	42	18	8	16	78	71	44
Chelsea	42	15	14	13	67	62	44
Sheff Utd	42	16	10	16	52	59	42
Sheff Wed	42	14	13	15	56	47	41
Stoke	42	17	7	18	63	58	41
West Brom	42	16	7	19	77	73	39
Burnley	42	15	9	18	66	76	39
Man City	42	12	15	15	43	52	39
West Ham	42	14	8	20	80	84	36
Sunderland	42	14	8	20	58	72	36
Fulham	42	11	12	19	71	83	34
Soton	42	14	6	22	74	92	34
Newcastle	42	12	9	21	39	81	33
Aston Villa	*42*	*11*	*7*	*24*	*54*	*85*	*29*
Blackpool	*42*	*6*	*9*	*27*	*41*	*76*	*21*

1967-68
	P	W	D	L	F	A	Pts
Man City	42	26	6	10	86	43	58
Man Utd	42	24	8	10	89	55	56
Liverpool	42	22	11	9	71	40	55
Leeds	42	22	9	11	71	41	53
Everton	42	23	6	13	67	40	52
Chelsea	42	18	12	12	62	68	48
Tottenham	42	19	9	14	70	59	47
West Brom	42	17	12	13	75	62	46
Arsenal	42	17	10	15	60	56	44
Newcastle	42	13	15	14	54	67	41
Nottm F	42	14	11	17	52	64	39
West Ham	42	14	10	18	73	69	38
Leicester	42	13	12	17	64	69	38
Burnley	42	14	10	18	64	71	38
Sunderland	42	13	11	18	51	61	37
Soton	42	13	11	18	66	83	37
Wolves	42	14	8	20	66	75	36
Stoke	42	14	7	21	50	73	35
Sheff Wed	42	11	12	19	51	63	34
Coventry	42	9	15	18	51	71	33
Sheff Utd	*42*	*11*	*10*	*21*	*49*	*70*	*32*
Fulham	*42*	*10*	*7*	*25*	*56*	*98*	*27*

1968-69
	P	W	D	L	F	A	Pts
Leeds	42	27	13	2	66	26	67
Liverpool	42	25	11	6	63	24	61
Everton	42	21	15	6	77	36	57
Arsenal	42	22	12	8	56	27	56
Chelsea	42	20	10	12	73	53	50
Tottenham	42	14	17	11	61	51	45
Soton	42	16	13	13	57	48	45
West Ham	42	13	18	11	66	50	44
Newcastle	42	15	14	13	61	55	44
West Brom	42	16	11	15	64	67	43
Man Utd	42	15	12	15	57	53	42
Ipswich	42	15	11	16	59	60	41
Man City	42	15	10	17	64	55	40
Burnley	42	15	9	18	55	82	39
Sheff Wed	42	10	16	16	41	54	36
Wolves	42	10	15	17	41	58	35
Sunderland	42	11	12	19	43	67	34
Nottm F	42	10	13	19	45	57	33
Stoke	42	9	15	18	40	63	33
Coventry	42	10	11	21	46	64	31
Leicester	*42*	*9*	*12*	*21*	*39*	*68*	*30*
QPR	*42*	*4*	*10*	*28*	*39*	*95*	*18*

1969-70
	P	W	D	L	F	A	Pts
Everton	42	29	8	5	72	34	66
Leeds	42	21	15	6	84	49	57
Chelsea	42	21	13	8	70	50	55
Derby	42	22	9	11	64	37	53
Liverpool	42	20	11	11	65	42	51
Coventry	42	19	11	12	58	48	49
Newcastle	42	17	13	12	57	35	47
Man Utd	42	14	17	11	66	61	45
Stoke	42	15	15	12	56	52	45
Man City	42	16	11	15	55	48	43
Tottenham	42	17	9	16	54	55	43
Arsenal	42	12	18	12	51	49	42
Wolves	42	12	16	14	55	57	40
Burnley	42	12	15	15	56	61	39
Nottm F	42	10	18	14	50	71	38
West Brom	42	14	9	19	58	66	37
West Ham	42	12	12	18	51	60	36
Ipswich	42	10	11	21	40	63	31
Soton	42	6	17	19	46	67	29
C Palace	42	6	15	21	34	68	27
Sunderland	*42*	*6*	*14*	*22*	*30*	*68*	*26*
Sheff Wed	*42*	*8*	*9*	*25*	*40*	*71*	*25*

SECOND DIVISION

1965-66	1966-67	1967-68	1968-69	1969-70
Champions: Manchester City Also promoted: Southampton Relegated: Middlesbrough, Leyton Orient	Champions: Coventry City Also promoted: Wolverhampton Wanderers Relegated: Northampton Town, Bury	Champions: Ipswich Town Also promoted: Queen's Park Rangers Relegated: Rotherham United, Plymouth Argyle	Champions: Derby County Also promoted: Crystal Palace Relegated: Bury, Fulham	Champions: Huddersfield Town Also promoted: Blackpool Relegated: Aston Villa, Preston North End

THIRD DIVISION

1965-66	1966-67	1967-68	1968-69	1969-70
Champions: Hull City Also promoted: Millwall Relegated: Southend United, Exeter City, Brentford, York City	Champions: Queen's Park Rangers Also promoted: Middlesbrough Relegated: Swansea Town, Darlington, Doncaster Rovers, Workington	Champions: Oxford United Also promoted: Bury Relegated: Grimsby Town, Colchester United, Scunthorpe United, Peterborough United	Champions: Watford Also promoted: Swindon Town Relegated: Northampton Town, Hartlepool, Crewe Alexandra, Oldham Athletic	Champions: Orient Also promoted: Luton Town Relegated: Bournemouth, Southport, Barrow, Stockport County

FOURTH DIVISION

1965-66	1966-67	1967-68	1968-69	1969-70
Champions: Doncaster Rovers Also promoted: Darlington, Torquay United, Colchester United	Champions: Stockport County Also promoted: Southport, Barrow, Tranmere Rovers	Champions: Luton Town Also promoted: Barnsley, Hartlepools United, Crewe Alexandra	Champions: Doncaster Rovers Also promoted: Halifax Town, Rochdale, Bradford City	Champions: Chesterfield Also promoted: Wrexham, Swansea City, Port Vale

LEAGUE CUP

1965-66	1966-67	1967-68	1968-69	1969-70
West Bromwich Albion beat West Ham United 1-2 4-1	Queen's Park Rangers 3 West Bromwich Albion 2	Leeds United 1 Arsenal 0	Swindon Town 3 Arsenal 1	Manchester City 2 West Bromwich Albion 1

SCOTTISH CUP

1965-66	1966-67	1967-68	1968-69	1969-70
Rangers 1 Celtic 0, after 0-0	Celtic 2 Aberdeen 0	Dunfermline Athletic 3 Hearts 1	Celtic 4 Rangers 0	Aberdeen 3 Celtic 1

SCOTTISH FIRST DIVISION

1965-66
	P	W	D	L	F	A	Pts
Celtic	34	27	3	4	106	30	57
Rangers	34	25	5	4	91	29	55
Kilmarnock	34	20	5	9	73	46	45
Dunfermline	34	19	6	9	94	55	44
Dundee U	34	19	5	10	79	51	43
Hibernian	34	16	6	12	81	55	38
Hearts	34	13	12	9	56	48	38
Aberdeen	34	15	6	13	61	54	36
Dundee	34	14	6	14	61	61	34
Falkirk	34	15	1	18	48	72	31
Clyde	34	13	4	17	62	64	30
Partick	34	10	10	14	55	64	30
Motherwell	34	12	4	18	52	69	28
St J'stone	34	9	8	17	58	81	26
Stirling A	34	9	8	17	40	68	26
St Mirren	34	9	4	21	44	82	22
Morton	*34*	*8*	*5*	*21*	*42*	*84*	*21*
Hamilton	*34*	*3*	*2*	*29*	*27*	*117*	*8*

1966-67
	P	W	D	L	F	A	Pts
Celtic	34	26	6	2	111	33	58
Rangers	34	24	7	3	92	31	55
Clyde	34	20	6	8	64	48	46
Aberdeen	34	17	8	9	72	38	42
Hibernian	34	19	4	11	72	49	42
Dundee	34	16	9	9	74	51	41
Kilmarnock	34	16	8	10	59	46	40
Dunfermline	34	14	10	10	72	52	38
Dundee U	34	14	9	11	68	62	37
Motherwell	34	10	11	13	59	60	31
Hearts	34	11	8	15	39	48	30
Partick	34	9	12	13	49	68	30
Airdrie	34	11	6	17	41	53	28
Falkirk	34	11	4	19	33	70	26
St J'stone	34	10	5	19	53	73	25
Stirling A	34	5	9	20	31	85	19
St Mirren	*34*	*4*	*7*	*23*	*25*	*81*	*15*
Ayr	*34*	*1*	*7*	*26*	*20*	*86*	*9*

1967-68
	P	W	D	L	F	A	Pts
Celtic	34	30	3	1	106	24	63
Rangers	34	28	5	1	93	34	61
Hibernian	34	20	5	9	67	49	45
Dunfermline	34	17	5	12	64	41	39
Aberdeen	34	16	5	13	63	48	37
Morton	34	15	6	13	57	53	36
Kilmarnock	34	13	8	13	59	57	34
Clyde	34	15	4	15	55	55	34
Dundee	34	13	7	14	62	59	33
Partick	34	12	7	15	51	67	31
Dundee U	34	10	11	13	53	72	31
Hearts	34	13	4	17	56	61	30
Airdrie	34	10	9	15	45	58	29
St J'stone	34	10	7	17	43	52	27
Falkirk	34	7	12	15	36	50	26
Raiths	34	9	7	18	58	86	25
Motherwell	*34*	*6*	*7*	*21*	*40*	*66*	*19*
Stirling A	*34*	*4*	*4*	*26*	*29*	*105*	*12*

1968-69
	P	W	D	L	F	A	Pts
Celtic	34	23	8	3	89	32	54
Rangers	34	21	7	6	81	32	49
Dunfermline	34	19	7	8	63	45	45
Kilmarnock	34	15	14	5	50	32	44
Dundee U	34	17	9	8	61	49	43
St J'stone	34	16	5	13	66	59	37
Airdrie	34	13	11	10	46	44	37
Hearts	34	14	8	12	52	54	36
Dundee	34	10	12	12	47	48	32
Morton	34	12	8	14	58	68	32
St Mirren	34	11	10	13	40	54	32
Hibernian	34	12	7	15	60	59	31
Clyde	34	9	13	12	35	50	31
Partick	34	9	10	15	39	53	28
Aberdeen	34	9	8	17	50	59	26
Raith	34	8	5	21	45	67	21
Falkirk	*34*	*5*	*8*	*21*	*33*	*69*	*18*
Arbroath	*34*	*5*	*6*	*23*	*41*	*82*	*16*

1969-70
	P	W	D	L	F	A	Pts
Celtic	34	27	3	4	96	33	57
Rangers	34	19	7	8	67	40	45
Hibernian	34	19	6	9	65	40	44
Hearts	34	13	12	9	50	36	38
Dundee U	34	16	6	12	62	64	38
Dundee	34	15	6	13	49	44	36
Kilmarnock	34	13	10	11	62	57	36
Aberdeen	34	14	7	13	55	45	35
Dunfermline	34	15	5	14	45	45	35
Morton	34	13	9	12	52	52	35
Motherwell	34	11	10	13	49	51	32
Airdrie	34	12	8	14	59	64	32
St J'stone	34	11	9	14	50	62	31
Ayr	34	12	6	16	37	52	30
St Mirren	34	8	9	17	39	54	25
Clyde	34	9	7	18	34	56	25
Raith	*34*	*5*	*11*	*18*	*32*	*67*	*21*
Partick	*34*	*5*	*7*	*22*	*41*	*82*	*17*

SCOTTISH SECOND DIV

1965-66	1966-67	1967-68	1968-69	1969-70
Champions: Ayr United Also promoted: Airdrie	Champions: Morton Also promoted: Raith Rovers	Champions: St Mirren Also promoted: Arbroath	Champions: Motherwell Also promoted: Ayr United	Champions: Falkirk Also promoted: Cowdenbeath

SCOTTISH LEAGUE CUP

1965-66	1966-67	1967-68	1968-69	1969-70
Celtic 2 Rangers 1	Celtic 1 Rangers 0	Celtic 5 Dundee 3	Celtic 6 Hibernian 2	Celtic 1 St Johnstone 0

WORLD CUP 1970

Brazil keeps Trophy as flair overcomes fear

DESPITE the drawbacks of holding the World Cup finals in Mexico, the 1970 tournament was certainly the finest of the century. Brazil, who were the worthy winners, played fabulous free-flowing attacking football and had assembled probably the greatest side on earth. England, the holders, had strengthened their 1966 team, and their match with Brazil in the early stages, which was billed as the "real" final, lived up to expectations. And although the modern trend of containing, defensive football was prevalent all over the globe, there were a host of thrilling matches and the average number of goals per match actually increased over the previous two World Cups.

Mexico in June was never the ideal location. And when, at the behest of European television, the kick-off times were adjusted to noon when the heat and humidity were at their worst, it was feared that the players would simply wilt in the conditions. Amazingly, they didn't and the football was of the highest standard.

England, the only British team at the finals, still had the core of the side that had triumphed at Wembley. Six of that team played in Guadalajara and there were exciting new faces – Terry Cooper, Alan Mullery and Francis Lee to name but three. Experts were agreed that England's squad was, in fact, stronger than four years previously. Brazil, as well, had unearthed a new crop of talent – Jairzinho, Rivelino and Tostao.

The game was played in 98-degree heat – army training manuals of the day said that it was folly to undertake even the lightest exercise in temperatures above 85°F – and the England players got precious little sleep the night before the match as their hotel was surrounded by thousands of noisy fans all chanting for Brazil.

England were not fazed. Brazil were kept at bay in the first half by a save by Gordon Banks that defied belief. The match was only 10 minutes old when Jairzinho delivered a perfect centre to Pele. Banks was covering his near post when Pele forcefully headed the ball towards the opposite corner. Pele wheeled away convinced that he had scored but, somehow, Banks flung himself the width of the goal and with a breathtaking one-handed save turned the ball away with his fingertips.

But, in the second half Banks was powerless when Tostao swept past three defenders and passed to Pele, who instantly pushed the ball on for Jairzinho to score. Even then England were not finished and for much of the rest of the match it was all Brazil could do hold on to their lead. However, England wasted at least five good chances, the best producing a terrible miss by Jeff Astle.

Even though they lost 1-0 England still reached the quarter-finals. So after the "real" final came a repeat of the 1966 final, a match against West Germany in Leon. This time, Banks could do nothing for England. The night before the match he drank a bottle of beer that left him with such bad food poisoning that Peter Bonetti had to play in his place.

The enforced change did not seem to matter when England were leading 2-0 with 22 minutes remaining, thanks to goals from Mullery and Martin Peters. But Bonetti, diving to stop a drive from Franz Beckenbauer, let the ball under his body when it looked like he had the shot covered.

Helmut Schoen, the West German manager, had already made a substitution. The arrival of Jurgen Grabowski had brought fresh heart, and a fresh pair of legs to Germany. The England team started to flag. As Germany pressed for the equaliser, panic also started to set in on the England bench.

Sir Alf Ramsey was never a man happy with making substitutions. Two players, Cooper and Bobby Charlton, were clearly suffering from exhaustion. To most observers Cooper's problem was the more pressing as Grabowski was taking him apart. Inexplicably Colin Bell replaced Charlton and Ramsey left Cooper on the field. Then, to compound his error, Ramsey replaced Martin Peters with Norman Hunter, and disastrously the whole shape of the England team had been changed.

If the point of bringing on Hunter was to bolster a sagging defence, it backfired. In the 81st minute Uwe Seeler scored an extraordinary header following a defensive lapse by the tired Brian Labone. Psychologically England were now finished. In extra time Gerd Muller administered the coup de grace. The holders were out, and the dream final against Brazil – a mirage.

Few would have expected West Germany's semi-final against Italy to be as drama-laden and thrilling, particularly as the Italians were in the grip of the notoriously defensive catenaccio system. They had, in fact, got through the first stage by winning their opening game 1-0 and the shut up shop for the next two matches, settling for goalless draws against Uruguay and Israel.

They did much the same thing against Germany, sitting on a 1-0 lead they had taken in the seventh minute. Once again they thought they had done just enough, but up popped Karl-Heinz Schnellinger with a last-minute equaliser. Then the game really came to life in the space of 16 minutes in extra time. Muller gave Germany the lead, Italy equalised and then took the lead themselves, Muller levelled the scores again and a minute later Italy's Rivera scored the decisive goal in a 4-3 thriller to reach the final.

There they met Brazil, who had cruised past Uruguay in the other semi-final. It was in a sense the perfect match. As both teams had won the World Cup twice they were battling for outright possession of the Jules Rimet trophy, but more importantly it was viewed as a showdown for the soul of football. Brazil, with their flamboyant style of play, represented Latin flair and all that was good about the game. Italy, with their emphasis on negative thinking, were, despite the undoubted skills their players possessed, the epitome of Latin fear. To add edge to the contest it was the New World versus the Old.

There was only one winner. Italy's man-for-man marking system collapsed in the face of the Brazilian onslaught and a rampant Pele. Brazil took the lead in the 18th minute with a spectacular Pele header. Italy were somewhat fortunate to equalise eight minutes before half-time when a sloppy back-pass let Boninsegna round the keeper. In the second half Gerson's 66th minute goal from outside the penalty are opened the floodgates. Five minutes later, Gerson lifted a free-kick to Pele, who nodded the ball down into the path of the onrushing Jairzinho, who became the first player to have scored in every round of the World Cup.

The match had became a football fiesta. And Pele, the world's greatest player, graced the world final by conjuring up an incomparable goal four minutes from time. Jairzinho had found him with a perfectly weighted through pass, Pele then laid the ball off sublimely for Carlos Alberto to thunder it into the net. It was the result all neutrals had thirsted for: Brazilian brio had vanquished the Italian inquisition.

Brilliant Brazil: Banks with his brilliant save was one of the few people to stop Brazil, for whom Jairzinho scored in every round, Pele was irrepressible and Tostao was his perfect foil

FOR THE RECORD

FIRST ROUND

GROUP 1	P	W	D	L	F	A	Pts
Soviet Union	3	2	1	0	6	1	5
Mexico	3	2	1	0	5	0	3
Belgium	3	1	0	2	4	5	2
El Salvador	3	0	0	3	0	9	0

GROUP 2	P	W	D	L	F	A	Pts
Italy	3	1	2	0	1	0	4
Uruguay	3	1	1	1	2	1	3
Sweden	3	1	1	1	2	2	3
Isreal	3	0	2	1	1	3	2

GROUP 3	P	W	D	L	F	A	Pts
Brazil	3	3	0	0	8	3	6
England	3	2	0	1	2	1	4
Romania	3	1	0	2	4	5	2
Czech	3	0	0	3	2	7	0

GROUP 4	P	W	D	L	F	A	Pts
W. Germany	3	3	0	0	10	4	6
Peru	3	2	0	1	7	5	4
Bulgaria	3	0	1	2	5	9	1
Morocco	3	0	1	2	2	6	1

QUARTER-FINALS

West Germany 3 England 2
HT 0-1 Att. 24,000
Italy 4 Mexico 1
HT 1-1 Att. 24,000
Brazil 4 Peru 2
HT 2-1 Att. 54,000
Uruguay 1 Soviet Union 0 aet
HT 0-0 Att. 45,000

SEMI-FINALS

Italy 4 West Germany 3 aet
HT 1-0 Att. 80,000
Brazil 3 Uruguay 1
HT 1-1 Att. 51,000

THIRD PLACE PLAY-OFF

West Germany 1 Uruguay 0
HT 1-0 Att. 104,000

FINAL

Brazil 4 Italy 1
HT 1-1 Att. 107,000

Teams
Brazil Felix; Carlos Alberto, Brito, Piazza, Everaldo, Clodoaldo, Gerson, Jairzinho, Tostao, Pele, Rivelino
Italy Albertosi; Burgnich, Cera, Rosato, Facchetti, Bertini (sub: Juliano), Mazzola, De Sisti, Domenghini, Boninsegna (sub: Rivera), Riva

Leading goalscorers 10 Gerhard Muller (West Germany); 7 Jair Ventura Filho Jairzinho (Brazil); 5 Teofilo Cubillas (Peru); 4 Pele (Brazil), Anatoliy Bishovets (Soviet Union)
Total goals scored 95
Average per game: 2.97
Sendings-off None
Number of players used by finalists
16 Brazil; 17 Italy

● In the qualifier between the USA and Bermuda in Kansas City on November 3, 1968, both goalkeepers were carried off injured before half time. The first goalkeeper to be substituted in the finals was Steve Adamache of Romania, who came off with an injury after 29 minutes of the game against Brazil on June 10, 1970. He was replaced by Necula Raducanu.
● When Mario Zagalo managed Brazil to their 1970 triumph, he became the first man to play in and then manage a World Cup winning team. He was a member of the Brazilian sides which won the trophy in 1958 and 1962.

THE
1970-71
SEASON

Busby legacy breaks his successor

SIR MATT BUSBY'S decision to hand over the reins at Manchester United was finally confirmed on August 10 when Wilf McGuinness was appointed manager. The decision pitched the club into a season of turmoil.

Many of the United team looked on Busby as a father fig-ure. In contrast, they had very little respect for McGuinness. There was talk of a dressing-room revolt and of some of the senior members of the squad not being prepared to play for him.

By the standards expected at Old Trafford, United had a terrible first half of the season, only winning five of their 22 League matches before Christmas. The pressure mounted inexorably on McGuinness until, on December 28, he was demoted to reserve team trainer.

The humiliation was too much for him to take and, on February 27, he resigned, saying: "For 18 years I have been devoted to United. Now I must find a future away from Old Trafford."

Busby took over again temporarily, but he was still determined to retire. He thought he had found the ideal successor when, after a secret meeting at a petrol station in April, Jock Stein agreed to take the job. But Stein, perhaps fearful of having to work in the shadow of Busby, quickly had second thoughts, leaving United in the lurch once again.

It was hardly surprising that the upheavals took their toll on the players. And it was also hardly surprising that the person most affected was George Best. He had been missing training sessions with increasing frequency, and on January 10

McGuinness: no chance

the club suspended him for two weeks. Best was also fined a record £250 by the FA's disciplinary committee when he arrived 90 minutes late for a hearing.

The upheavals continued until well past the end of the season, when Frank O'Farrell was appointed manager and Busby joined the United board. But O'Farrell was soon to discover what Stein had feared – that Busby was an almost impossible act to follow.

Hateley keeps the flag flying

Full circle: the wandering Hateley finally returned home to Notts County

THE TIMES were a-changing for many of the players who had graced football for the last decade. And as the old stars bowed out a new generation came forward to fill their boots.

Sir Alf Ramsey, with one eye on the European championships, decided that it was time to start rebuilding the England team. Bobby Charlton, who made his 500th appearance for Manchester United the day before his 33rd birthday in October, was dropped from the side that beat East Germany in November. The same fate befell his brother, Jack, and England's long-serving goalkeeper Gordon Banks, who made way for Peter Shilton.

Two other England stars decided to retire, the former captain Jimmy Armfield and Jimmy Greaves, who became only the fourth person to score more than 350 goals in the League.

The much-travelled Tony Hateley was also entering the

twilight of his career, back where it first started with Notts County. Hateley returned to the club where he had started out in 1958 in a £20,000 deal with Birmingham in October. In total, Hateley had now been involved in transfers worth £400,000, with his share of the fees being in the region of £20,000. But Hateley showed that there was plenty of life left in his legs when he hit his 200th League goal on May 1.

Ted MacDougall, too, was on target. He scored 49 goals in the season for Bournemouth, 42 in the League and seven in the FA Cup, with six of them coming in the 8-1 demolition of Oxford City in the first round replay.

Trevor Francis, although a good deal younger, was equally prolific. In only his first season he ran up a sequence of 12 goals in eight League matches for Birmingham. They included all four against Bolton, the first time a 16-year-old had achieved this feat.

The impossible double act: George Best and Sir Matt Busby

Arsenal's Double defies critics

North Bank hero: Charlie George delights his fans with the winning goal at Wembley which secured the Double

WINNING the Double is more than extraordinary – after all, only Tottenham in 1961 had achieved it this century – but to win it in the manner Arsenal did was almost to defy belief. In September they had been thrashed by Stoke 5-0; by the end of February they were seven points behind Leeds; and in the FA Cup semi-final against Stoke they were 2-0 down after 30 minutes and only equalised, from a hotly-disputed penalty, in the dying moments of the match.

Yet Arsenal matched all of this adversity with a determination that eventually outlasted all of their opponents. Their 5-0 mauling by Stoke made them a closer-knit side as they closed ranks, particularly against the media who had branded Arsenal as boring and mechanistic.

Their dramatic let-off against Stoke in the FA Cup semi-final on March 27 (they won the replay 2-0 four days later) came in the midst of an awesome run. Between March 2 and May 3 Arsenal played 13 League matches and won 11, drawing one. The only loss was away to Leeds. In that time Arsenal won 1-0 on six occasions. That was the kind of competition they were.

Their final victory in that spectacular 13-match run was probably the sweetest. On May 3 Arsenal travelled to White Hart Lane and only their neighbours, and bitter rivals, Tottenham stood between them and the title. Arsenal either had to win or draw 0-0. (Because of the vagaries of goal average, any score draw would have given Leeds the championship).

With a capacity 50,000 inside, and as many locked out, the match went to the wire. Ray Kennedy headed Arsenal into the lead two minutes from time, but this was largely irrelevant, as a Spurs goal would have given the title to Leeds. Two minutes seemed an age as Spurs desperately attacked the Arsenal goal to deprive their foes of the coveted Double, but keeper Bob Wilson bravely denied Tottenham.

Five days later Liverpool were the obstacles at Wembley. Only four teams this century (Newcastle in 1905, Sunderland in 1913, Manchester United in 1957 and Tottenham in 1961) played in an FA Cup final and won the League title. All, apart from Tottenham, had had their hopes of the elusive Double dashed.

After a scoreless 90 minutes, Arsenal found themselves down 1-0 after two minutes of extra time thanks to Steve Heighway, and with a mountain to climb. Liverpool had one of the meanest defences in the League and had only conceded one goal in the Cup. But then they conceded two: the first a scrambled equaliser from Eddie Kelly and the second a scorching blaster from Charlie George, the darling of the North Bank, eight minutes from the end. Once again Arsenal had come from behind to triumph and their manager had achieved what even the legendary Herbert Chapman hadn't: the fabulous Double.

99

Chelsea complete London's coup

THE FIRST round of the European Cup Winners' Cup brought a feast of goals, with Cardiff demolishing Larnaca 8-0 at home and Chelsea powering past Aris Salonika 6-2 on aggregate.

Cardiff were the surprise package of the tournament.

They won just as emphatically in the second round, dispatching Nantes 7-2 on aggregate, and were rewarded with a money-spinning quarter-final against Real Madrid. The first match, in Cardiff on March 10, went down in Welsh folklore when Brian Clark scored the only goal of the game for the Second Division side. Cardiff, though, could not hang on to their advantage and lost the second leg 2-0.

Chelsea almost went out in the quarter-finals as well when they fell two goals behind in Bruges. But a resounding 4-0 victory at Stamford Bridge put them through to the last four, where they were drawn against Manchester City, the holders.

City could count themselves lucky to have got that far. They had only squeezed past Linfield on the away goals rule in the first round, and had needed a replay to beat Gornik in the quarter-finals after both matches finished 2-0.

Both Chelsea and Manchester

City were depleted by injuries. But the London club, even though they were missing Peter Bonetti, Peter Osgood and Ian Hutchinson, prevailed 1-0 in both legs to avenge their exit from the FA Cup at the hands of City.

Chelsea were back at full strength for the final against Real Madrid in Athens on May 19. Inspired by Charlie Cooke, they took the lead with a goal from Osgood. But a mistake by John Dempsey near the end allowed Real to equalise. Bonetti had to be at his brilliant best in extra time as Chelsea came under increasing pressure, and they were grateful to hang on for the replay two days later.

Dempsey made amends for his error by giving Chelsea the lead once again, rifling a shot in after his header had been parried. Osgood extended Chelsea's advantage, and even though Real scored a consolation goal the third trophy of the season was on its way to London.

Second time around: Chelsea needed a replay to beat Real Madrid

Colchester 3 Leeds 2: 'The most fantastic result you'll ever see'

EVERY YEAR there are headline making upsets in the FA Cup, but the fifth-round result from Layer Road on February 13 will certainly be remembered as one of the all-time shocks. Colchester, of the Fourth Division, with six players over the age of 30, beat mighty Leeds, stuffed with internationals such as Jack Charlton, Norman Hunter and Johnny Giles, 3-2. The result was so incredible that one newspaper called it: "The most fantastic result you'll ever see."

The hero of the afternoon – among an entire team of heroes – was the veteran Ray Crawford, who nine years earlier had spearheaded Ipswich to their only League title. Crawford, who had been in non-League football and on the dole a few months before he was rescued from obscurity by Colchester's manager Dick Graham, rocked Leeds in the 18th minute with a headed goal.

Six minutes later Crawford

collided with Gary Sprake, the Leeds goalkeeper, and both men tumbled to the ground. Quick-thinking Crawford showed he had lost none of his predatory skills by hooking the ball into the net with his left foot while still on the ground: 2-0. The half-time scoreline was received with incredulity around the country.

Amazingly, plucky Colchester made no effort to sit on their lead in the second half. Instead they continued to attack and harass their illustrious opponents. Their bravery was rewarded when Dave Simmons headed them into a 3-0 lead in the 54th minute. Ecstatic supporters rushed on to the pitch to congratulate him.

Inevitably, Leeds, the runaway League leaders, rallied and as the Colchester players tired snatched two goals from Hunter and Giles with 15 minutes remaining.

Leeds then threw everybody into attack and relentlessly bombarded the Colchester goal,

Upset of the century: Ray Crawford heads the first goal for Colchester

but Graham Smith, the keeper, rose to the occasion brilliantly and played like an international to frustrate Don Revie's star-studded team and earn a place in the sixth round, and history.

Jubilant fans hoisted Crawford on to their shoulders and paraded him around the ground as the dishevelled Leeds players slunk off in disbelief. The

reward for the Colchester players was a tie at Goodison against Everton in the quarter finals, and a free fortnight's holiday with their wives promised to them by Graham if they beat Leeds. At Goodison, inevitably, the bubble burst and they went down 5-0. Still, they had their famous victory to savour as they lazed on a beach in the summer.

Ibrox tragedy leaves 66 dead

The day after: officials inspect the mangled crush barriers of staircase 13 at Ibrox

FOR THE RECORD

■ The pools companies said that they would increase their stakes by about 20% when decimal currency was introduced. The increased stakes led to bigger payouts, and in April Albert Crocker won a world record £401,792.

■ Peter Bonetti made his 500th appearance for Chelsea on January 23.

■ The Football League rejected a £600,000 offer to sponsor the League Cup and all four countries turned down a £100,000 offer for the home championship.

■ Corinthian Casuals' reputation for sporting play took a knock when they conceded three penalties in their 5-0 defeat by Woking in the Isthmian League.

■ Midweek evening matches were suspended because of the power cuts brought about by the miners' strike. Clubs were also allowed to start their Saturday games at 2.15pm.

■ Joao Havelange, the president of the Brazilian Sports Confederation, was nominated for election as the president of Fifa in 1974.

■ Derek Dougan was elected chairman of the PFA.

■ Tranmere drew a record number of League matches, 22 out of 46 in the Third Division.

THE worst sporting disaster in Britain cast a pall over the New Year's celebrations in Scotland. The traditional Old Firm match between Rangers and Celtic drew the usual huge crowd to Ibrox Park on January 2, and with 80,000 people packed into the ground the conditions existed for the third tragedy to hit the stadium.

With a few minutes remaining Celtic led 1-0 and thousands of people were leaving the terraces to make their way home. Then Colin Stein scored a late equaliser and the remaining home supporters roared their approval.

The departing fans, alerted by the noise, turned and tried to rush back to see what the excitement was about. As they forced their way up staircase 13 they collided head-on with people still trying to leave the ground.

Although Ibrox had been designed to handle large crowds, the crush was simply too great. As wide as the staircase was, it could not cope with the sudden pressure and crush barriers started to buckle under the strain.

As the barriers gave way people slipped and fell head-long down the steep staircase. This started a domino effect and soon hundreds of people were swept away in the pandemonium. Panic quickly set in, making matters worse.

For a few brief moments it was thought that the accident was relatively minor. But it did not take long for the full horror to emerge. In all, 66 people died and more than 200 were injured. Many of the victims were suffocated by the sheer weight of other people lying on top of them.

The public was appalled that so many people had been killed and that, once again, their deaths had been caused by crush barriers giving way. Reginald Maudling, the Home Secretary, immediately announced that there would be a formal inquiry. The Wheatley Report called for much stricter crowd control at matches, and for football grounds to be subject to the same stringent safety rules as other places of public entertainment such as cinemas.

But the Safety of Sports Grounds Act was not introduced until 1975, and even then the legislation was not able to save the lives of countless other people who were to die at football matches.

Football ground disasters

1902	Twenty-five people died and more than 500 were injured when a stand collapsed under the weight of people who had come to watch the Scotland v England international at Ibrox Park.
1914	Seventy-five people were injured at Hillsborough when a wall collapsed during an FA Cup replay between Sheffield Wednesday and Wolverhampton.
1946	Thirty-three people died and 400 were injured when crush barriers collapsed at Burnden Park during the match between Bolton and Stoke.
1961	Two people died at Ibrox when crush barriers collapsed during Rangers' match against Celtic.
1964	The world's biggest football disaster. Three hundred people died and more than 500 were injured in a riot after a disputed goal was scored in Lima, Peru.

Dougan: players' choice

Fairs Cup Revie's only consolation

LEEDS gained some consolation for their domestic disappointments by becoming the fourth English club in a row to win the Fairs Cup. But, like their campaigns at home, it was a gruelling battle that lasted until the first week of June.

The semi-finals produced an all-English pairing and Leeds played two titanic matches against Liverpool. The first game, at Anfield, was decisive with Billy Bremner, who had been out of action for over a month with an injury, scoring the only goal of the two legs.

Leeds's strength was sapped further in the first leg of the final, against Juventus in Turin. Eddie Gray dislocated his shoulder and then torrential rain forced the match to be abandoned after 55 minutes.

Leeds showed great fortitude two days later when they came back from two down thanks to goals from Paul Madeley and Mick Bates, who came on as a substitute 15 minutes from the end and scored two minutes later.

The return match was just as testing. Allan Clarke gave Leeds an early lead but Juventus struck back with a goal from Anastasi. The Italians knew that they were still behind on the away goals rule and they had to score again.

Leeds started to look wearier and wearier as the game went on, but their defence remained resolute and Juventus were unable to find a way past the determined tackling. Somehow Leeds conjured up the will to survive the 90 minutes and collect some reward for a season of toil that had lasted not far short of a full year.

Winning the marathon: Mick Jones, the Leeds striker, battles with Tancredi of Juventus

The last lap: Allan Clarke celebrates the final goal in a gruelling Cup run that went on until June

Fans riot after ref's blunder

TWO TERRIBLE decisions by match officials and the hot-temperedness of Don Revie's Leeds players sparked off a riot that seriously damaged the sport's reputation and certainly changed the destiny of the League championship. All parties were to blame, but it was Leeds who paid the price.

On April 17, Leeds were two points clear of Arsenal, but had played two games more so they desperately needed to beat lowly West Bromwich Albion at Elland Road. With 28 minutes remaining and Leeds trailing 1-0, WBA's Tony Brown blocked a pass from Norman Hunter and hared after the ball as it rebounded into the Leeds half with Colin Suggett running in support.

The Leeds defence, the arch exponents of the offside trap, stopped and pointed out to the referee, Ray Tinkler, that his linesman had flagged Suggett as yards offside. Even Brown had stopped. Inexplicably Tinkler waved play on, claiming afterwards that Suggett was not interfering with play.

Brown, now in virtually an empty half, passed to Jeff Astle, who also looked clearly offside. Once again the Leeds defence ground to a halt and appealed to the linesman but he resolutely refused to raise his flag. Astle then calmly sidefooted the ball past Gary Sprake. There was instant uproar.

The entire Leeds team encircled Tinkler, pushing, shoving and arguing furiously. But the referee would not bend, whereupon nearly 40 irate Leeds fans invaded the pitch in pursuit of revenge against Tinkler. In the ensuing chaos the Leeds players had to protect Tinkler from the marauding fans, the linesman was hit by a stone, and it took the police nearly five minutes to restore order.

Thirty-two spectators were arrested. The match was resumed and Leeds managed to score, leaving the final result 2-1 to WBA. On the same day, Arsenal beat Newcastle 1-0 to take over the leadership of the First Division on goal difference.

Unsurprisingly, Revie and the Leeds club chairman, Percy Woodward, condemned the match officials and condoned the fans. To add grist to their mill, Alan Ashman, WBA's manager, also agreed the goal was offside. Television evidence hung both parties. Yes, West Brom's second goal was offside twice, but did that really justify the players' outburst and the consequent riot? The FA soon made their answer clear: Leeds were fined £750 and ordered to play their first four home games of the next season away from Elland Road.

But the cost to Leeds was even greater than the FA's punishment. Sixteen days after the Elland Road fracas, Arsenal stole home in the title race by one point – the point they could have had if referee Tinkler had followed Brian Clough's dictum: "If he's not interfering with play, what is he doing on the field?" Leeds finished the season with 64 points, the highest amount (under the two-points for a win rule) a club had ever accumulated without winning the championship.

Astle: punished

League Cup brings Rangers some cheer at last

Sweet sixteen: Johnstone was the youngest player in a Scottish Cup final

AT LAST Rangers had something to shout about: they had beaten Celtic 1-0 to win the Scottish League Cup. Admittedly it wasn't much to shout about as Celtic once again won the Double of the Scottish League and Cup, but when the silverware cupboard had become as bare as Ibrox's, something was better than nothing. Rangers had not won a major trophy for five years, a Rangers record made all the worse as Celtic in those years had been sweeping all before them, including the European Cup.

The League Cup victory, on October 24, also promised hope for Ibrox's future as the winning goal was scored by 16-year-old Derek Johnstone, the youngest player ever to appear in a Scottish final. But Rangers never capitalised on their early season success and after New Year and the tragedy of the Ibrox disaster only won a mere six League matches out of 16 to finish a sorry fourth in the First Division. However, in the Scottish Cup final they gave Celtic a real run for their money as another precocious Johnstone goal forced a replay which Celtic only won 2-1 thanks to a Hood penalty.

PELE
Simply the best

Garth Crooks

I WAS in Spain covering the World Cup campaign as a member of the BBC TV World Cup panel, a genuine thrill for me that helped to take my mind off being dropped from the England squad that was taking part in football's supreme tournament.

Italy had just secured their second triumph against an unpopular German team, and I was sitting in the lounge of the Porto Ramana hotel in Marbella still fantasising about an elusive goal that could have transformed me from a League player to one with full international status.

Suddenly, like a dream sequence in some great Hollywood movie, from the recesses of the hotel lobby emerged the greatest footballer of all time, the one player who had inspired all my dreams and aspirations. And this man walked over to me and said: "Excuse me. I am told you like playing tennis. Would you like to play?" Practically speechless and head spinning, I remember managing to mutter something barely audible and totally unintelligible to the demi-god, Pele.

The moment still ranks as one of the most precious in my life, to be conjured up for endless mental action replays, and crystallises exactly

Victimised: Pele during the 1966 World Cup

what Pele meant to me, and thousands of youngsters like me all over the world.

It was the perfect set-up. Without the sting. Alan Durban, the former Stoke City manager, had arranged something so special for me that I could never hope to express my gratitude. Durban understood the moment perfectly.

The boy later to be known throughout the world simply as Pele was baptised Edson Arantes do Nascimento in a small town called Tres Coraçes. Legend has it that he learned the fundamentals of the game in the backstreets of Brazil, with balls made of old rags stuffed in socks. But the game was already in his blood; his father Dondinho was a promising player before injury curtailed his career. The son not only had the inspiration in his genes, he was equally blessed with the resilience and resolve of great men. All these attributes would make an indelible mark on the history of the game.

In 1956, a packed Wembley Stadium saw England, inspired by Stanley Matthews, beat Brazil 4-2. It was Matthews' last great international performance, and as night fell on the career of one great player dawn was breaking on that of another. Pele was just 17, but even with his extraordinary talent he could never have envisaged the future ahead.

In 1958 Sweden were the World Cup hosts, determined to emulate Uruguay (1930) and Italy (1934) by becoming the third host nation to win the Jules Rimet Trophy. Pele, meanwhile, scored his first goal in the World Cup, in the quarter-final against Wales. He went on to complete a memorable hat-trick against France in the semi-final. His second goal was struck superbly with the outside of his right foot, flying into the roof of the net. But it was his third goal that was vintage. He caught a through ball on his thigh and before a Frenchman could assess the danger he volleyed an unstoppable shot past the stranded goalkeeper. The boy from Tres Coraçes had arrived.

A wet Rasunda stadium in Stockholm found Pele as precocious in the final against Sweden as in the earlier rounds. Brazil's innovative 4-2-4 formation suited the youngster, and in the 55th minute he flicked the ball over the head of Parling, leaving the embarrassed Swedish left-half swinging wildly at Pele's midriff. Pele not only kept his balance but also his composure, volleying the ball home to give Brazil their third goal. Yet it was Brazil's fifth goal which displayed Pele's athleticism and bravery. He nonchalantly back-heeled the ball to Zagalo and, running for the return pass, leaped above the defender to nod home his second goal of the match.

Tears of joy flowed down the face of the

prodigy as Brazil lifted the trophy for the first time. What the world had witnessed was not just a new philosophy of play but a player about to fuel the greatest sporting explosion since Joe Louis.

Brazil retained the trophy in Chile, the first team to do so since Italy before the war. Pele, however, missed much of that tournament, including the final, when he was injured in the early stages of the competition.

By 1964 the Brazilian team was respected worldwide, particularly in Britain. Fifa had decided to stage the 1966 World Cup in England and, somewhat fittingly, the hosts were invited to

Mesmeric: Brazil bewitched the world

take part in a tournament to mark Brazilian football's 50th anniversary. Brazil, not surprisingly, were in carnival mood with Pele leading the samba. England lost 5-1, leaving Alf Ramsey and the rest of Europe to go away and try to devise sophisticated methods of stopping this South American phenomenon.

A confident Brazilian team arrived in England in 1966 in search of a third consecutive World Cup. By this time Pele was an international superstar and, along with Cassius Clay, had become the most famous sportsman in the world.

Brazil's opening game against Bulgaria was a physical one. Regardless, the defending champions won 3-1 and left Goodison Park to a standing ovation. But what became apparent throughout the game was that Pele was a marked man. Injured in that match, he missed the following game, a classic against Hungary.

Meanwhile, members of the international media were anxious to know whether or not Pele felt he was being deliberately singled out for special treatment. His reply was noble: "We all play hard to win but no player goes out deliberately to hurt another." But the evidence clearly did not support it. The next game, against Portugal, saw Pele choke on those very words. Not only singled out, he was carried off with damaged knee ligaments. Brazil lost and Pele returned to Santos vowing never to return to the game's greatest tournament.

If this inglorious treatment of the sport's greatest hero led to the decision, England's winning performance also helped give the game a different complexion. Alf Ramsey's emphasis on efficiency temporarily rendered the Brazilian philosophy as a style now out of date. Pele, however, continued to add to his already glittering career at home and he scored his 1,000th goal while playing for Santos against Vasco da Gama in that cathedral of Brazilian football the Maracana stadium.

Rejuvenated, and after careful consideration, Pele decided to make himself available for the 1970 World Cup in Mexico, his fourth finals and, at 30, presumably his last chance to show off his skills on the world stage.

What took place in the heat and altitude of Guadalajara ignited the sport with Pele, at the heart of a mesmeric Brazilian side, fulfilling all his promise and inspiring fantasies among professionals and pundits the world over.

Immortalised by colour television, the superb rhythmic play of the South Americans is legendary with Pele providing the most spectacular, memorable moves to the unmistakable backbeat of the Brazilian drum. Five hundred million viewers thrilled to the sheer inventive audacity of Pele lobbing the Czech goalkeeper from the halfway line, only to miss the goal by inches. It was a move revered and since copied, only to remind us of the original genius.

And Britain revels in the memory of the England match. Jairzinho making it to the byline when only he thought it was possible, sending the perfect cross over to the far post for Pele, who seemed to suspend himself in mid-air for what

Finest hour: Brazil won the 1970 World Cup with a series of dazzling performances

appeared to be an eternity before heading the ball downwards, crying, as legend has it, "goal", only for both the move and the execution to be equalled by one of the most astonishing saves of all time from our own national hero Gordon Banks.

Pele scored four goals in the tournament, including the first goal of a victorious final which secured an unprecedented third World Cup, allowing Brazil to keep the Jules Rimet Trophy and inscribing them and Pele in football history.

Acknowledged as the footballing icon of his age, it was Pele who was the main catalyst in the endeavour to make football a truly international sport with his move to New York Cosmos and the instigation of the North America Soccer League. It is testament to his patronage and status within the sport that within a few years of his retirement the NASL died.

I never got to play football against this great ambassador of sport. Indeed, television and video have been my only opportunities to see him play. With one memorable, magical exception in 1969, when Santos played, gratifyingly, my old home team, Stoke City. Standing in the miserable, damp, vile weather with 24,000 other people packed into the Victoria Ground to watch Stoke lose 3-2 (Pele put a thunderous right-footer past Banks) was, however, every bit as thrilling for this 11-year-old kid as playing tennis with the living legend one afternoon in the sunny climes of Marbella.

Icon of his age: Pele's modesty made him football's greatest ambassador

Partick spoil Celtic's party

IN OCTOBER, Partick Thistle, an unfashionable mid-table side, pulled off one of the upsets of the decade when they overwhelmed their all-conquering neighbours Celtic to win the Scottish League Cup 4-1, their first trophy for more than 50 years.

The former European champions were stunned as Partick raced into a 4-0 lead within 37 minutes with goals from Alex Rae, Bobby Lawrie, Denis McQuaide and Jim Bone. When the half-time score was announced at grounds around the country it was greeted by disbelief, then derision before it was confirmed.

Celtic had their excuses: their captain Billy McNeill was out with an injury and their quicksilver winger Jimmy Johnstone was substituted early in the first half, but they could not deny that the ferocity of Partick's attacks in the opening minutes unsettled them, and ultimately cost them the Cup.

Their hopes of a second European Cup vanished at Parkhead in the semi-final. After two goalless draws with Inter Milan and a barren 30 minutes of extra time Celtic fell victim to the lottery of the penalty shoot-out. Dixie Deans missed his spot-kick while Inter scored all theirs and marched on to the final 5-4. Jock Stein, Celtic's manager, was inconsolable: "We don't consider we lost on football," he said, "but to a circus turn."

Their consolation was a League and Cup Double, their second in succession, and Deans made up for his European Cup gaffe in the Scottish Cup final, scoring a hat-trick as Celtic trounced Hibs 6-1.

Derby frolic as Leeds falter

ON the face it, the title race could be described as a thriller with an unexpected twist on the final page; in reality, it was more like musical chairs. Thus when the music stopped, Derby County, sitting on a beach in Majorca, were, to everybody's surprise, the League champions.

But in the early days of the season all the talk was of newly promoted Sheffield United, who overwhelmed Leeds 3-0, beat Arsenal's Double-winning side at Highbury and were top of the table. Four successive defeats in October ended their fairytale hopes. Manchester United, with George Best in ebullient form, established an eight-point lead before also slipping away.

By Easter the destiny of the title was finely balanced between four contenders: Derby, Leeds, Liverpool and Manchester City. Liverpool had crept into the race with a fabulous late surge, winning 13 and drawing two in a 15-match run between January and May. City were the first to crack, strangely enough after Malcolm Allison had bought the quixotic Rodney Marsh from QPR and unwittingly disrupted his side.

For Leeds there was more at stake than the championship, there was also the little matter of the Double to be won and the pain of the previous season to be erased. With a week to go to the Cup final the top of the First Division looked like this:

	P	Pts
Manchester City	42	57
Liverpool	40	56
Derby	41	56
Leeds	40	55

Only Liverpool, Derby and Leeds could win the title as Derby still had to play Liverpool and therefore it was mathematically impossible for Manchester City, who had played all their games, to become champions.

In midweek Leeds beat Chelsea and Derby seemed to have done them a favour by ending Liverpool's unbeaten run. Leeds were now in the driving seat. To win the Double all they had to do was to beat Arsenal in the final and not lose to Wolves at Molineux.

Their task was inexplicably made much harder by the League's decision that Leeds had to play their final League fixture on the Monday after the Cup final. Despite a personal plea from Don Revie to Alan Hardaker, the League secretary, there was to be no respite, the match would have to be played 48 hours after the final.

On the Saturday a goal from Allan Clarke in a sterile final gave Leeds the first half of the Double. But there were no celebrations. Within an hour of the final whistle the Leeds players were in their coach heading north for their date with destiny.

And once again fate dealt them a sorry blow. Two penalties, both for blatant handball, were rejected and Leeds went down 2-1. Meanwhile, at Highbury, Liverpool, facing a jaded and disappointed Arsenal, had the championship within their grasp. If Leeds lost (and their fans kept shouting to the players, "Leeds are losing") and they won, the title would go to Anfield. But they failed to score and the goalless draw handed the championship to Brian Clough and his Derby holidaymakers.

Leeds could claim that they had in fact lost the title the previous season. Because of the riot provoked by referee Ray Tinkler's controversial offside decision in the match against WBA, Leeds were ordered to play their first four home games away from Elland Road. In those four "home games" they dropped two points – exactly the same number they dropped in their genuine 17 home games.

Although they were the Cup winners for the first time any joy they felt was swept away by the loss of the title. "It was as if we had nothing," Clarke said. "We wanted that League championship so badly." For the second successive season it had escaped them by a single point.

Singular failure: Munro scores for Wolves to dash Leeds's title chances for the second season running

Newcastle, Hereford's stepping stone to big time

Look what we've done: Ron Radford and Ricky George scored the goals that brought down Newcastle, six times winners of the FA Cup

HEREFORD'S exploits in the FA Cup were undoubtedly instrumental in winning them a place in the League at the end of the season, even though they only finished runners-up in the Southern League.

Hereford had only enjoyed limited success in the Cup before, twice reaching the third round in 1958 and 1966. So reaching the third round again (by beating Northampton for the second year in a row), was an achievement in itself. When they were drawn against First Division Newcastle everybody expected their progress would be halted at St James's Park.

The match was postponed because of bad weather and when it was played nine days late Hereford produced the shock of the round by holding Newcastle 2-2. But there was a bigger shock to come.

The replay was also plagued by the weather and was postponed several times. When the match was finally played on February 5, Hereford's pitch resembled a swamp. But Newcastle could not blame the conditions for their defeat – they created enough chances to have easily beaten Hereford.

Fred Potter, the Hereford goalkeeper, had an outstanding game but he could not stop Malcolm Macdonald giving Newcastle the lead 10 minutes from time. Three minutes later though, Ron Radford ploughed his way through the mud to score a scorching equaliser with a shot from 30 yards. Newcastle flagged in extra time allowing Radford to set up Ricky George for an historic winner.

Because the two matches had taken so long to complete, Hereford had to play their fourth round match four days later. There was so much interest in the visit of West Ham to Edgar Street that forged tickets were discovered in the city the day before the match.

Hereford produced another minor miracle when they held the First Division side 0-0. Ron Greenwood, the West Ham manager, admitted: "We are lucky to still be in the Cup."

Hereford succumbed to a Geoff Hurst hat-trick in the replay but their brave efforts did not go unnoticed. At the League's annual meeting in June they received the same numbers of votes as Barrow, who were seeking re-election. But, just as they had done against Newcastle, Hereford triumphed in the replay, winning 29-20 in a second ballot.

FOR THE RECORD

■ Norman Burtenshaw, the referee, reported the entire Benfica team to Uefa when he was attacked after Arsenal won a friendly against the Portuguese side 6-2 at Highbury in August.

■ Crystal Palace's match against Nottingham Forest was delayed for five minutes when the Forest players disputed a goal scored by Palace. Steve Kember of Crystal Palace admitted that the ball had not gone into the net and it was disallowed.

■ Dave Sexton, the Chelsea manager, put Peter Osgood on the transfer list for "lack of effort" but then changed his mind a fortnight later.

■ Aston Villa were fined £3,000 and suspended until the end of the next season by the FA's disciplinary committee.

■ Brian Phillips, the former Mansfield player banned for life after the 1963 bribery scandal, had his sentence lifted under the new rule allowing banned players to appeal after seven years.

■ Tommy Docherty was appointed Scotland manager on September 12.

Osgood: unmovable feast

Docherty: movable feast

Rangers' triumph ends in disaster

POOR old Rangers. Just as they were poised to celebrate winning their first European trophy and lay the ghost of Celtic's 1967 European Cup triumph their victory was besmirched by the behaviour of their fans.

Some 20,000 had travelled to Barcelona for the European Cup Winners Cup final against Moscow Dynamo and were in the mood for a party. Their antics delayed the start of the match as they spilled over on to the field and the players had to leave three times before the match could commence.

Rangers played sweet football and by the 50th minute were 3-0 up with a goal from Colin Stein and two from Willie Johnston. Unfortunately each goal was greeted by a pitch invasion from the jubilant supporters. Rangers eased up in the second half and with three minutes remaining were hanging on at 3-2 to a slender victory. When the final whistle came thousands of relieved Rangers supporters invaded the pitch. Opinions differ as to who was to blame for what happened next.

The Spanish police believed they were confronted by a drunken, riotous mob and acted accordingly. The Scottish supporters believed Franco's fascist police came at them wielding clubs and batons and they were simply defending themselves. Whatever, a pitch battle ensued in which one man died and 150 were injured. Hundreds more were arrested and thrown into jail as the mayhem spread to the streets of Barcelona.

The sourness of Rangers' victory was made even more bitter when Uefa banned them from European competition for two years (subsequently reduced to one year). As Dynamo had demanded the match be replayed Rangers could consider that they got off lightly.

After Rangers' triumph, and disaster, they re-shuffled their management with Willie Waddell moving upstairs and Jock Wallace taking over the running of the team.

Wallace obviously thought that Johnston and Stein were disruptive influences in the Ibrox dressing room and had to be dispatched as soon as possible. Johnston was sold to West Bromwich in September for £135,000, and Stein went to Coventry in October for £90,000 plus another player.

After the pair had gone Wallace said: "We have sold two stars and found a team."

Blond bombshell: Stein, an old-fashioned centre-forward

Johnston: double strike

Keegan quick to make a mark for Liverpool and his country

WITH GEORGE BEST on the wane, have Liverpool unearthed British football's next superstar in Kevin Keegan? Early indications are that their £33,000 close-season signing from Scunthorpe has all the hallmarks of one the greats. Keegan, working in tandem with John Toshack, was one of the crucial elements that propelled Liverpool up the League table after the New Year when they were unbeaten in 15 League matches.

Keegan, another one of Bill Shankly's canny acquisitions, exploded into the First Division when he scored against Nottingham Forest on the opening day of the season. His ability so impressed the normally cautious England manager Sir Alf Ramsey that he quickly recruited him to the England Under-23 team.

Perhaps other First Division managers had overlooked Keegan because of his size. For at 5ft 8in he does not look the part of a striker, but despite his height he is powerful in the air and brave on the ground. And but for their inability to score in the final match of the season, Keegan would have had a championship medal in his first season.

Rising star: Keegan, another nugget unearthed by Bill Shankly

Referees' hard line goes soft

ON THE face of it, football's decision to enforce the laws of the game was eminently sensible. It would, so the pundits said, bring England in line with the rest of the world and herald a return to the age of sportsmanship. But a secret meeting on Sunday August 15 had far-reaching consequences that nobody could have dreamt of when the League and the FA instructed referees to start the crackdown.

Henceforth, tackling from behind was banned and even the most technical of offences would lead to automatic bookings. To remind the players of the rules, lists of all the misdemeanours that were subject to cautions were posted in every dressing-room.

The effect on the game was immediate and dramatic. By the following Saturday four players had been sent off and 120 had been booked. On September 4 alone 50 players were booked, taking the total to 292 after four weeks.

That prompted an immediate reaction from the players. After a seven-hour meeting, Derek Dougan, the PFA chairman, said: "The livelihood of our members has been put in jeopardy. We appreciate that something needed to be done, but we are getting away from commonsense and instead finding chaos and confusion."

The turning point came in October when Dougan successfully appealed against a booking he had received in August. The disciplinary committee decided that the booking would still stand, but it would not count against him.

That decision opened the floodgates. By the start of January, when there had already been more than 1,100 bookings, the FA had been inundated with hundreds of appeals. And it did not take long for the FA's disciplinary committee to be accused of applying double standards.

The problem was that although the referees were properly carrying out their instructions, the disciplinary committee seemed all too willing to let players off on appeal. Bob Lord, the Burnley chairman, said that referees should resign en masse because they were not getting any support from their masters. "Referees are made to look fools in the eyes of players," he said.

It was hardly surprising that the match officials became more and more perplexed and despondent. If they upheld the law they were criticised and, as in the case of John Thacker, who did not book anybody after 20 players were involved in a brawl during the match between Ipswich and Arsenal, they were also condemned for not being strict enough.

As the confusion mounted, the League argued that they should control the disciplinary process because it was their players who were affected. Eldon Griffiths, the Minister for Sport, also became involved because the government said that football was subject to the terms of the Industrial Relations Act.

A measure of compromise was finally reached by the end of the season, with referees applying a greater degree of discretion in the way they interpreted the rules. The League also won the introduction of a totting-up system, with penalty points for offences and an automatic two-match ban for players who collected 12 points.

FOR THE RECORD

■ Giacinto Facchetti played his 60th game for Italy in October, a national record.

■ Alvechurch finally beat Oxford City 1-0 in the fifth replay of their FA Cup fourth round qualifying match. In all they played for 11 hours, a record for the competition.

■ Chelsea beat Jeunesse Hautcharage by a record 21-0 on aggregate in the European Cup Winners Cup, including a 13-0 win at Stamford Bridge. Peter Osgood broke another record by scoring eight goals in the tie.

■ Leeds called off a £170,000 deal to buy Asa Hartford from West Bromwich when a medical showed that he had a possible hole in the heart. However Manchester City had no reservations and bought him in 1974. Hartford played for them 184 times and scored 22 goals.

■ David Webb took over in goal for an hour when Peter Bonetti injured his ankle during Chelsea's match with Coventry on December 18. Then on December 27 he played the entire match in goal because both of Chelsea's regular keepers were unfit. He did remarkably well as Chelsea drew the first match 1-1 and won the second 2-0 against Ipswich.

■ Europe's first all-weather football pitch opened in Islington, London, in January.

Tackles from behind, like John Loughlan's challenge on Wyn Davies, became subject to automatic bookings, but many players were let off on appeal

Ramsey writes the wrong scripts

Netzer: midfield maestro

Rock bottom: Neill condemns England to their second defeat in a row at Wembley

ENGLAND'S progress to the quarter-finals of the European championships was smooth enough, with five wins and a draw in group three. And when they were drawn against West Germany Sir Alf Ramsey was confident enough to write: "England will not only beat West Germany but will also go on to win the championship."

How wrong he was. The first leg, at Wembley on April 29, brutally exposed how much the two countries' fortunes had changed since they had met in the 1966 World Cup final. West Germany had developed a mighty side – Franz Beckenbauer as sweeper, Gunter Netzer in midfield and Gerd Muller up front – and they took England apart.

With 10 minutes left the score was 1-1, but that was highly flattering to England. Out-thought and totally out-played they conceded two more goals in the last six minutes. Ramsey was roundly criticised for his team selection and tactics and he compounded matters by picking an equally stolid side for the return leg in Berlin, which was drawn 0-0.

Ramsey's other predictions about the tournament were equally off-target. When he said that England would win he highlighted Italy, Yugoslavia and Hungary as the other likely semi-finalists. Of those three teams, only Hungary made it. Hungary eventually finished in fourth place and West Germany proved how far they had progressed by sweeping past Russia 3-0 in the final.

There was worse to come for Ramsey in the home internationals. He rang the changes for the match against Northern Ireland and the public that had been calling for new faces turned on him when England lost 1-0 to a Terry Neill goal. It was Northern Ireland's first victory against England since 1957 and the first ever occasion that England had lost two matches in a row at Wembley. England's sole consolation was a scrappy victory over Scotland at Hampden Park for a share of the title.

Maverick genius climbs the heights and plumbs the depths

GEORGE BEST'S tempestuous relationship with Manchester United hit rock bottom at the end of a roller-coaster season that had promised much but delivered only disappointment.

Things did not start well when Best was sent off in United's second match of the season, against Chelsea. However, he was cleared by the FA and celebrated in the next match by demolishing West Ham almost single-handed. His hat-trick included a goal that Trevor Brooking was moved to describe as "fantastic" – Best beat three defenders in quick succession and then turned Bobby Moore inside out with an incomparable dummy before hammering in his shot.

Best scored 11 goals in 10 League matches in the autumn and it looked as if he was back to his breathtaking best. The problem was that his off the field antics were taking an ever-increasing toll.

At the turn of the year he admitted: "I'm off form and I'm sick about the way I'm playing." Best promptly vanished and was dropped by Manchester United for missing an entire week's training. United ordered Best to move back into his old digs for the rest of the season, but that hardly curbed his carousing and the flow of goals dried up.

By the end of the season Best had managed to play in 40 of United's 42 League matches, and he was the club's leading scorer. But there was no doubt that he was cracking up fast.

The final straw came in May, when Best was dropped by Northern Ireland for not joining their squad before the home international against Scotland. Best claimed that he was a physical and mental wreck, and admitted that his drinking had become excessive.

He fled to Spain, refusing to talk to anybody. Best said that he was going to retire and, at the age of 26, it looked as if his career was over.

Mullery gets his own back

THE Uefa Cup final between Tottenham and Wolves provided two milestones in the history of English football: it was the first European final to be contested by two English clubs, and when Tottenham proved victorious they became the first British club to have won two different European competitions. Their first success had been in 1963 in the European Cup Winners Cup.

Martin Chivers had virtually engraved Tottenham's name on the new trophy (it replaced the old Fairs Cup) with two classic breakaway goals in the first leg at Molineux, and the 2-1 lead they took back to White Hart Lane left Wolves with a daunting task.

Alan Mullery made it even harder with an extraordinary header from a free kick taken by Martin Peters. Wolves refused to wilt and David Wagstaffe gave them a lifeline shortly before half-time with a thundering 20-yard shot that cannoned

Down but not out: Mullery is injured after scoring against Wolves

off the post. But Tottenham's midfield held and, with Pat Jennings resolute in goal, Spurs made history.

The Spurs players hoisted Mullery on to their shoulders and paraded him around the pitch. It was a fitting tribute to their 30-year-old captain. Two months before, his career seemed to be in tatters as he was ban-

ished on loan to Fulham, his former club.

A spate of injuries forced his return and in the semi-final of the Uefa Cup against AC Milan it was Mullery's long-range equaliser in the San Siro stadium that earned Spurs a place in the final. It was Mullery's swansong: in the summer he returned to Fulham permanently.

At long last, a real Cup for Stoke's hand-picked vintage crop

STOKE were one of the oldest teams in the League but in their lengthy history they had never been to Wembley. And it was thanks to two of their oldest players that they collected their first major trophy.

Stoke's appearance in the League Cup final was entirely thanks to the 34-year-old Gordon Banks. The semi-final against West Ham had finished level on aggregate and there were only three minutes left in extra time when Banks saved Geoff Hurst's penalty to keep Stoke's hopes alive.

The first replay ended goalless but there was plenty of drama early in the fourth meeting between the two teams. Bobby Ferguson, the West Ham keeper, was concussed and Bobby Moore had to take over in goal. Moore even managed to parry a penalty but was beaten by the follow-up shot.

Inspired, West Ham took the lead although Stoke were level by half-time. Terry Conroy

Saving grace: Banks keeps out Hurst's penalty with three minutes to go in the semi-final

scored just after the break and Stoke just hung on to win a pulsating match 3-2. Tony Waddington, the Stoke manager, said: "The game was out of this world. After this, Wembley could be

something of an anti-climax."

He was almost proved right. Although Conroy scored after five minutes Stoke looked no match for Chelsea. Peter Osgood equalised and Chelsea

continued to dominate. It was left to George Eastham, at 35 another of Stoke's veterans, to score his first goal in 18 months and give Stoke something to celebrate at long last.

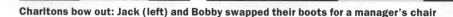

End of an era as the Charlton brothers retire

AN ERA came to a painful end when both Charlton brothers left the clubs that they had served so loyally and moved into management.

Before the season had even started Leeds announced that Jack was no longer their first-choice centre-half. They wanted him to spend his time watching their upcoming opponents, but Jack refused to accept that his career was over.

Bobby, too, was out of favour. On August 25 Manchester United demoted him to the second team, the first time he had played for the reserves in 10 years. With Old Trafford in turmoil he chose his words carefully: "There are things I could say about the situation here that I would regret later."

The parting of the ways was an emotional occasion. More than 60,000 people attended his testimonial match against Celtic, a record, and another 57,000 came to his last home match at Old Trafford. It was a fitting tribute for a man who had played for the club since 1956 and had won every honour in the game.

Celtic, too, provided the opposition for Jack's testimonial, with nearly 35,000 packing Elland Road. But his career ended on a flatter note as he was forced to limp off with a hamstring injury during Leeds's match at Southampton.

Both men had played more than 600 times for their clubs and their experience was not lost to the game: Bobby took over as manager at Preston North End and Jack took charge at Middlesbrough.

Charltons bow out: Jack (left) and Bobby swapped their boots for a manager's chair

O'Farrell: United's latest whipping boy

TWO things brought about Frank O'Farrell's downfall at Manchester United. One – United's terrible form – he had some influence over; the other – George Best – he could do nothing about at all.

Manchester United did not win in the League until their tenth match and spent the first third of the season on or near the bottom of the table. To compound their misery they were knocked out of the League Cup by Bristol Rovers, going down 1-0 at home.

O'Farrell had already spent a fortune bringing players to Old Trafford and his response to the crisis was to lash out another £200,000 on Bournemouth's ace striker Ted MacDougall. The fee was a record for a Third Division player.

Best, meanwhile, had made his peace with the club once again. Having fled to Spain in the summer, saying that his career was over and he intended to retire, he had returned home. But he was as wayward as ever,

and when he skipped training at the end of November O'Farrell dropped him. When he left Manchester without permission and was seen in a London nightclub he was put on the transfer list.

But within 10 days Louis Edwards, the United chairman, said that Best would resume training with the club, and everybody assumed that this meant he had been taken off the transfer list. O'Farrell was said to be deeply unhappy at the way Best was being treated and there was widespread specula-

Docherty: big spender

tion that the United manager was about to resign, particularly because United had just suffered their heaviest defeat in four years, 5-0 at Crystal Palace.

But before he got a chance to act United struck first. On December 19 the board announced that O'Farrell, his coach Malcolm Musgrove and the chief scout John Aston had all been fired. When O'Farrell asked why he had been dismissed he was told that it was because United were bottom of the table.

Within three days Tommy Docherty had been appointed on a salary that was said to be in the region of £15,000 a year. Not one for understatement, he said: "Only one word can sum up my feelings – fantastic. My aim has always been to be the best manager in football. At Old Trafford I will get the best chance of proving I have what it takes."

Like O'Farrell, Docherty decided to spend his way out of trouble. He clearly favoured Scottish players, buying George

Graham for £120,000, Alex Forsyth for £100,000 and Lou Macari for £200,000.

Even so it took him a while to record his first victory in the League, which did not come until mid-February. United did just enough to drag themselves clear of relegation. And despite the club's dismal performance the Old Trafford faithful did not appear to be disheartened – they attracted more than a million people to their 21 home League matches.

However, Manchester United's problems with Best would not go away. At first, Best, who quit yet again on the day that O'Farrell was sacked, said that he would never play for the club again. But he resumed training in late April, having reached an understanding with Docherty.

The club would overlook his off the field antics providing Best made up for any missed training sessions in his own time. But, like everything else at Old Trafford, it would not be long before it all ended in tears.

Allison finds life without Mercer starts badly and gets even worse

MALCOLM ALLISON'S time at Manchester City was every bit as turbulent as the upheavals at Old Trafford. And the drama started even before a ball had been kicked.

Allison's partnership with Joe Mercer came to a bitter end in the summer when Mercer was demoted and Allison was given sole charge of the team. This was more than Mercer could stomach and within days he had left to become the manager of Coventry in place of Gordon Milne.

Allison promised that City would play attractive football and named Leeds as their greatest challengers for the championship. But he was being wildly over-optimistic. City lost seven of their first 10 League matches and slid down the table almost as fast as United.

It was unheard of for both Manchester clubs to be propping up the rest of the division. And,

like at United, it was almost impossible to imagine City being put out of the League Cup by a minnow. Worse, the side that claimed their scalp were their near-neighbours Bury.

Allison was soon at loggerheads with his board. Despite his objections, they sold Ian Mellor to Norwich for £65,000. The board said that City needed the cash but Allison, not a man to mince his words, retorted: "My row with the directors has gone right to the heart of football's greatest problem.

"It has been about money – the need for it and the balancing of it against such assets as young players. My directors insisted we sold Mellor. They are responsible for the club and I am not going to resign."

When Mercer returned to Maine Road with Coventry the fans made their feelings about Allison clear. Mercer was cheered before the match and

was the model of diplomacy after Coventry won 2-1. "I don't regard it as putting one over on City. How can I when I know these lads so well?" Allison, though, could not resist having a sly dig at his former mentor. "Gordon Milne has done a very good job at Coventry," he said.

Allison certainly had a way with words. Three weeks after saying that he was not going to resign he was catching a train south. The morning's papers were full of reports that Crystal Palace were in no rush to appoint a new manager. But, within an hour of arriving in London, Allison was being presented to the press as the man to save Palace from relegation.

The long-suffering Maine Road faithful had the last laugh though. Manchester City finished the season comfortably in mid-table while Allison's Palace were consigned to the Second Division.

FOR THE RECORD

■ Bobby Moore celebrated his 100th international appearance by leading England to a 5-0 victory over Scotland at Hampden Park. The game, part of the Scottish FA's centenary celebrations, was England's biggest victory in Scotland since 1888.

Moore: centurion

■ Newspaper allegations that Wolverhampton players were offered bribes to lose their match with Leeds, which decided the League championship in 1972, were referred to the Director of Public Prosecutions. The Leeds chairman strongly denied the claims.

■ The High Court overturned the FA disciplinary committee's fine and ban for a foul on Ernie Machin because the hearing breached the rules of natural justice. The judge said Machin had been convicted of something he had never been charged with.

■ Jimmy Hill temporarily abandoned his job as a commentator to take over as a linesman when the official suffered an injury during the match between Liverpool and Arsenal at Highbury in September.

■ The referee collapsed and died of a heart attack during the match between Exeter and Stockport.

■ David Nish's £225,000 transfer from Leicester to Derby broke the British record for a full-back.

Going down: Allison's new club, Crystal Palace, were doomed, while his old club, Manchester City, survived

> *How could I avoid being Player of the Year playing behind our defence?*
>
> PAT JENNINGS
> Tottenham's goalkeeper

Jennings: Spurs' saviour

Clemence's homework pays off

In a league of their own: Liverpool parade the championship trophy

THE PUNDITS predicted a two-horse race for the championship: between Leeds and Manchester City. They were right about two clubs dominating the race for the title, but wrong about their identities. Liverpool went top on September 23, were harried all the way by Arsenal, who briefly took the top spot for a fortnight in February when they won 2-0 at Anfield, but in the end comfortably won the League with three points to spare.

Liverpool's foray into Europe was much more nerve-wracking. In the Uefa Cup semi-final in April they faced the holders, Spurs. Liverpool won the first leg at Anfield with an Alec Lindsay goal. At White Hart Lane, in a magnificent match,

Martin Peters scored twice for Spurs but a vital goal from Steve Heighway meant his team went through to the final against Borussia Moenchengladbach on the away goals rule. Both managers praised the quality of play and Bill Shankly promised to go for the Double.

The first leg of the final on May 11 was yet another tremendous match as Liverpool finished 3-0 winners with two goals from Kevin Keegan and one from Larry Lloyd. However, the Germans were unfortunate not to score: they hit the post and both sides missed a penalty.

Shankly, mindful of the semi-final against Spurs, was quick to point out the importance of not conceding a goal. Ray Clemence, who saved the

penalty, justifiably claimed the credit: "I watched Heynckes take a penalty in the semi-final on TV and decided to dive the same way. It was a reward for my homework."

And rewarded it was. Twelve days later Liverpool were thoroughly outplayed in the second leg, losing 2-0, but tenaciously clung on to their slender lead to win their first European trophy and complete a unique Double of League and European trophy in a single season, the first English team to achieve such a feat.

It did not escape Clemence, nor Shankly, that if he had not saved that penalty at Anfield the away goals rule that had favoured Liverpool at Tottenham would have given the Cup to Borussia Moenchengladbach.

Norwich's great escape rounds off a roller-coaster season

NEWLY PROMOTED Norwich found their first ever season in the First Division to be a heady cocktail of dismal failure, partial success and, ultimately, nerve-tingling survival.

Ron Saunders' team were sixth in the table on November 18 and then did not win another League match until they beat Chelsea 1-0

on April 14. Somehow they scuffled into the League Cup final on March 3, having eliminated Arsenal and Chelsea.

There, Tottenham, another London club, awaited the Norfolk club who had actually won the trophy in 1962 when the big boys ignored the fledgling competition. Sadly for Norwich it

was Spurs who became the first club to win the trophy twice. The final was a disappointing affair as the two midfields bogged each other down. Ralph Coates, a 22nd-minute substitute for John Pratt, scored the only goal 18 minutes from time.

Somehow Norwich managed to rescue their season in their

last five League matches, winning three and losing two to finish 20th and two points away from relegation. Crucially, in three days, they beat West Brom 1-0 at the Hawthorns and Crystal Palace 2-1, with a goal from Dave Stringer in injury time, to send both clubs into the Second Division.

Porterfield and Montgomery the two unlikeliest of Cup-winning lads

EACH season the FA Cup keeps true to its romantic image by producing a clutch of upsets as the little clubs tweak the noses of their betters. However, by the time of the final the form book has reasserted its authority and, so the theory goes, "normality" will prevail at Wembley. Unfortunately for Don Revie's mighty Leeds, Second Division Sunderland did not keep to the script.

Leeds, the Cup holders, were the hottest favourites in years. Eleven of their 12-man squad were internationals, they were in the final of the European Cup Winners Cup and had finished third in the First Division.

Sunderland, who had spent much of the season battling to avoid relegation to the Third Division, were a bunch of unknowns and the club had not played in a Cup final since 1937. The nation warmed to this modern-day battle of David and Goliath, not least because Leeds, with their abrasive and cynical methods of play, were the most unpopular side in the country. However, few outside of Wear-side actually believed it was possible.

There had been indications that Sunderland should not be lightly dismissed – they had imperiously dismissed Manchester City and Arsenal to reach the final – and they had some of the most vocal and fanatical fans in the country. Thus, on May 5, Wembley echoed to continuous renditions of "Ha'way the lads" and Leeds had their comeuppance.

The pattern of the match was settled in the first half-hour when Sunderland refused to be cowed by Leeds and even went close to scoring when Michael Horswill's 20-yard shot went narrowly wide. Then, in the 31st minute, Leeds's world turned upside down.

Billy Hughes's corner swung over to the far post – big Dave Watson failing to connect but he distracted two defenders – and Vic Halom's knee knocked it back across goal where it fortuitously fell to Ian Porterfield. The midfielder found the time to control the ball and shoot over David Harvey and score.

The goal seemed to knock the stuffing out of Leeds, but after half-time they attacked with a vengeance throwing both full backs into the attack. In the 65th minute they seemed to have the equaliser. Paul Reaney, the right back, crossed to the far post where Trevor Cherry, the other full back, came with a brilliant blind-side run to head the ball perfectly towards goal.

But Jim Montgomery instinctively dived and parried the ball only for it to fall to Peter Lorimer, five yards in front of an open goal. The man with the hardest shot in football took aim and fired. Incredibly Montgomery had scrambled up. He pushed the ball on to the underside of the bar and the danger was over.

Montgomery's historic double save had won the Cup. When the final whistle blew, Bob Stokoe, the Sunderland manager since December, hared across the pitch to embrace his match-winning goalkeeper amid scenes of uncontrollable joy.

FOR THE RECORD

■ The League's annual meeting in June decided to introduce three up and three down promotion and relegation for the top three divisions. Calls for four teams to be promoted and relegated were rejected.

■ The long-standing gulf between amateurs and professionals was finally closed when the FA Council decided to abolish the distinction from the start of the 1974 season. From then on all footballers, whether paid or not, would be described as players.

■ The Football League doubled their receipts from the pools companies with a £23m 13-year deal. Many clubs were angered by the deal because they thought that the League should have obtained more money.

■ England beat Scotland 3-2 at Morton in the first official women's international.

■ The Southern and Northern Premier Leagues unveiled plans to merge and form a national league with regional feeder leagues.

■ Ted Croker was appointed secretary of the FA on June 22.

And the FA Cup had added another chapter to its never-ending romantic history.

The moment that finished Leeds: Porterfield (far right) scores the winning goal

Stokoe: Midas touch

Leeds denied European trophy by Greek referee and Italian keeper

DON REVIE may have assembled one of the most gifted and professional club sides in Britain but once again major honours heartbreakingly eluded them. Eleven days after their humbling defeat in the FA Cup final they succumbed to AC Milan 1-0 in the European Cup Winners Cup final in Salonika.

But for once Leeds, notorious for their cynicism, could justly claim to have been robbed. They fell behind to a fourth-minute goal from a free-kick that the Greek referee, Christos Michas, should probably not have given. Chiarugi's free kick from 20 yards was deflected off the Leeds wall. Worse was to come.

Leeds, despite being deprived of Billy Bremner, Allan Clarke, Eddie Gray and Johnny Giles, comprehensively out-played the Italian side but simply could not score. Vecchi, Milan's goalkeeper, played outstandingly to beat out shot after shot. However, his heroics were aided by Michas's inept refereeing.

The catalogue of dubious decisions was extraordinary: Mick Jones was clearly brought down in the penalty area by Anquilletti right in front of the referee; Zignoli handled a cross from Peter Lorimer in the area and Jones was again felled in the box, this time by Zignoli. Even the Greek crowd were incensed by what they were watching and began to chant for the hapless Leeds team.

The game ended in fisticuffs when a frustrated Norman Hunter retaliated after a vicious foul by Rivera and, in the ensuing melee, Hunter and Sogliano were sent off. The crowd shouted: "Shame, shame," when the Italian players attempted to celebrate their victory.

With his season in tatters Revie must have rued the boast he made in March when he committed his team to a Treble: "We shall play our strongest team for everything we are involved in – championship, FA Cup, European Cup Winners Cup."

Victim of injustice: Hunter was sent off when his patience snapped in a terrible final

Nine years of Leeds's fluctuating fortunes

Year	League	FA Cup	League Cup	Europe
1965	2	final	3rd rnd	
1966	2	4th rnd	3rd rnd	Fairs Cup semi-final
1967	4	semi-final	4th rnd	Fairs Cup final
1968	4	semi-final	winners	Fairs Cup winners
1969	winners	3rd rnd	4th rnd	Fairs Cup quarter-final
1970	2	final	3rd rnd	Champions Cup semi-final
1971	2	5th rnd	2nd rnd	Fairs Cup winners
1972	2	winners	3rd rnd	Uefa Cup 1st rnd
1973	3	final	4th rnd	Cup-Winners' Cup final

Unlucky break: Harvey fails to reach Chiarugi's deflected free kick

Celtic's title record a close-run thing

CELTIC'S eighth consecutive championship – a record in Scottish League history – was not quite the canter it appeared to be at the start of the season.

For, as Celtic came out of the starting stalls with three consecutive wins, Rangers began with the worst start in their history and by the beginning of October were lying an embarrassing 13th in the table.

Then the Ibrox team mounted a fightback that bordered on the miraculous: winning 24 of their next 28 League matches and losing only one. However the task was always going to be too much and Celtic pipped Rangers to the title by a solitary point – albeit with a far superior goal difference. But Rangers' renaissance was not all in vain.

At Hampden on May 5 Rangers prevented Celtic from achieving the Double in a thrilling see-saw Cup final which they finally won 3-2.

Kenny Dalglish gave Celtic the lead in the 24th minute only for Derek Parlane to equalise 10 minutes later. Rangers then took the lead themselves immediately after the beginning of the second half. Alfie Conn, with a blistering burst of pace, completely bamboozled Billy McNeill and scored a memorable goal only to see it squandered when John Greig handled in the penalty area and George Connelly coolly slotted home the equaliser. In a frantic finish Derek Johnstone's header struck the post, rolled along the goalline and Tommy Forsyth stuck out a foot to score his first goal for Rangers and snatch the Cup.

Despite their League success, Celtic did not have much luck in the League Cup either, losing the final in December for the third consecutive year. This time it was Hibs – still smarting from the 6-1 hammering Celtic had given them in the previous year's Scottish Cup final – who did the damage. Pat Stanton put Hibs ahead on the hour and laid on a second for Jim O'Rourke. Dalglish got one back for Celtic with 20 minutes remaining, but to no avail.

Brave Banks unable to battle his way back after losing an eye in a head-on car crash

Forced to admit defeat: Banks's retirement was announced on the BBC

EVEN THOUGH he was 35, Gordon Banks was still regarded as the best goalkeeper in the country, and many people thought he was the best keeper of all time. He had just signed a long contract with Stoke and was still a key member of Sir Alf Ramsey's squad for the 1974 World Cup.

But his career was brought to an untimely end in October when his car collided head-on with a van and shards of glass from the shattered windscreen badly damaged his right eye. It seemed almost inconceivable that two sportsmen could be cut down in their prime by the same freak injury – it was only a few years since the celebrated England and Northamptonshire cricketer Colin Milburn had lost the sight in one eye in a car crash.

Banks refused to be beaten and said that he hoped to resume training in the New Year and continue playing by wearing contact lenses. He was picked for a representative match, but playing on the right wing. Stoke said that he would return to action in their summer tour of Australia and New Zealand, and Ramsey chose him for an FA XI to play in Gibraltar.

Sadly, all the optimism was in vain and Banks was forced to admit in August that he would never play again.

Spot on: Pele scores against Fulham at Craven Cottage

BOBBY MOORE
The perfect Englishman respected throughout the world

Steve Hutchings

BOBBY MOORE was the quintessential Englishman. While the rest of the team celebrated winning the World Cup in 1966 their captain could only think of one thing – collecting the trophy from the Queen. It wasn't the glory and drama of the moment that was on his mind. No, Moore was worried that his muddy hands would spoil the Queen's white gloves when he shook hands with her. So before stepping forward to receive the trophy Moore carefully wiped his hands clean on the velvet drapes lining the approach to the Royal Box. But that was Moore all over – quiet and unassuming even at the pinnacle of his career.

Moore was arguably the best defender of his generation, only rivalled by the subsequent emergence of Franz Beckenbauer. Yet, for such a great defender, he was always lacking in pace. He knew it was a failing and compensated for it with outstanding vision and forethought. Moore was hardly ever caught out because he always seemed to be in the right place at the right time.

He owed that knack to the two men who were most influential on his early days at West Ham – Malcolm Allison, who coached the young players, and Noel Cantwell, another of the senior pros. Moore asked Cantwell whether it was possible to be a great player if you were not quick enough. Cantwell, picking his words carefully to avoid damaging Moore's confidence, explained what it was that made Johnny Haynes such a respected striker. Haynes, he said, lacked pace. But even before he received the ball he knew where everybody was on the pitch. He knew instantly what he was going to do.

Starting out: began his career at West Ham

Moore heeded the advice, and England's final goal against West Germany in the World Cup final was a case in point. With seconds remaining, Moore had possession of the ball. Jack Charlton and Nobby Stiles screamed at him to blast it high into the crowd, safely out of reach of the Germans. But that was not Moore's style; not the way he thought the game should be played. In his mind's eye he knew where Geoff Hurst, his West Ham teammate would be. Quick as a flash he placed his clearance into space for Hurst to run on to and complete his hat-trick. Speed of thought was, truly, every bit as important as speed of action. It was the perfect vindication of everything he had learnt from Cantwell and Allison.

Moore virtually idolised both of them when he joined the Upton Park ground staff. Like a puppy, he followed them around everywhere, wanting to talk football all the time. They spent so much time talking in a cafe near the ground that the owner banished them to an upstairs room to make room for his other customers. And on his honeymoon in Majorca, Moore discovered that Allison and Cantwell were on holiday on the same island. He promptly decamped to their villa and spent the night talking football, leaving his wife far from delighted.

Moore's willingness to learn his trade enabled him to rise through the ranks at West Ham after arriving as just another youngster with puppy fat and no more than ordinary ability. Allison was so impressed by Moore's determination that he persuaded Ted Fenton, the West Ham manager, that he had the makings of a great player. Ironically, it was Allison who was not picked when Moore, on Cantwell's recommendation, made his first-team debut at 17.

Moore had already progressed to the England Youth team, coached by Ron Greenwood, who replaced Fenton at West Ham in 1961. Moore was a willing disciple of Greenwood's ideas of how football should be played, and he was soon promoted to captain. But off the field the two men's relationship was not quite so smooth.

Moore nearly missed the 1966 World Cup finals because he was arguing with Greenwood over a transfer and how much he was paid. Days before the tournament was due to start, Moore had still not signed a contract with West Ham so, according to FA rules, he was ineligible to play. Greenwood was summoned to the England team's hotel and the problem was circumvented by Moore signing a temporary contract.

Ramsey also had his run-ins with Moore. Despite his diffident, gentlemanly image, Bobby was one of the lads. A terrible insomniac, Moore often found it difficult to relax. A few beers in the evening helped him to unwind. Ramsey, with his old-fashioned notions of discipline, was not pleased to discover that Moore was one of a group of players to have broken a curfew, albeit by a matter of minutes. And Greenwood was incandescent with rage when Moore went out for a few drinks the night before West Ham were

BOBBY MOORE

Born April 12, 1941, Barking

PLAYING CAREER

West Ham United 1958-74

Joined the West Ham ground staff, and signed as a professional in 1958

Made his debut against West Ham United against Manchester United on September 8, 1958

Played 642 times (544 in the League) and scored 22 League goals

1964: Won the FA Cup. Elected Footballer of the Year, the youngest player to win the honour

1965: Won the European Cup Winners Cup

Fulham

Signed for Fulham on March 14, 1974. Played 150 matches (124 in the League) and scored one League goal

1975: FA Cup beaten finalist

Retired: May 14, 1977

Internationals Played for the England Youth (18 times) and Under-23 teams (eight times). Made his full international debut against Peru in May 1962. Appointed England captain May 20, 1963

Played a record 108 matches for England, captaining his country 90 times and scoring two goals

1966: Won the World Cup

1970: World Cup quarter-finals

Also played for San Antonio Thunder, Seattle Sounders and Team America

MANAGEMENT CAREER

Oxford City Manager 1979-81

Coached Eastern Athletic (Hong Kong) in 1983

Southend United Manager 1984-86

1967: Awarded an OBE

Died February 24, 1993

First honour: Moore captained West Ham to victory in the 1964 Cup final

Ultimate honour: the World Cup at Wembley

embarrassed by Blackpool in the FA Cup.

Unlike George Best and Jimmy Greaves, who revelled in the liberal 1960s, Moore knew how to conduct himself in a proper fashion. So he enjoyed a couple of lagers from time to time? But he never allowed a night out to affect his game and he never gave less than 100%. Ramsey knew that players had to left off steam from time to time and he was never going to let the rare minor indiscretions cloud his belief that Moore was the cornerstone of the England team.

After his first match in charge, a 5-2 defeat in France, Ramsey spent most of the journey home deep in discussion with Moore about what they were going to do next. Moore was appointed the captain of England in 1963, in only his 12th international. With Moore his loyal lieutenant, Ramsey was free to experiment with the rest of the team in his unceasing search for the right combination to win the World Cup.

A measure of Moore's importance to England can be gleaned by comparing him with Billy Wright, England's other great leader. Both men captained the team 90 times. Under Wright, England won 49 matches and conceded 135 goals. Under Moore, there were 57 victories and only 75 goals against.

Ever dependable: Moore won 108 caps

Perhaps the only mistake that Ramsey made was persevering with Moore a little bit too long. But who could blame him. Moore was seemingly unflappable, and at a time when football was becoming ever more defensively minded he still believed that there was more to defending than just stopping your opponent by any means. The bone-crunching tackle was not for him; rather the surgical strike that left Moore on his feet with the ball under control, ready to be stroked upfield to start the counter-attack.

Moore's determination to play the ball cleanly was, sadly, his and England's undoing in Katowice in a qualifying match for the 1974 World Cup. England trailed 1-0 (under pressure, Moore had deflected a free kick into his own net) when Moore, for once, was caught in possession and Poland scored again. The 2-0 defeat was the beginning of the end for both Ramsey and Moore.

Three more internationals took Moore past Bobby Charlton's record 106 caps, and Greenwood (having vetoed moves to Tottenham and Brian Clough's Derby) finally allowed him to leave West Ham. Moore wanted to go to Crystal Palace, to team up with his old mentor Allison. Instead, he was transferred to Fulham. There was one more trip to Wembley, for an FA Cup final – lost to his old club West Ham – before Moore retired in 1977.

Unsuccessful spells in management with Oxford City and Southend, and failed business ventures did nothing to diminish Moore's reputation. The global superstar from working-class east London never forgot the debt he owed football. He played again for England, against West Germany, to raise funds for the victims of the Bradford fire. And he returned to Wembley, his home from home, in 1986 to team up with Best in a match for Sports Aid.

His sudden death, from cancer, at 51, shocked everybody. Ken Bates, the outspoken Chelsea chairman, spoke for the country when he said: "He will never grow old in people's minds, in the same way that President Kennedy won't." Allison, for all his flamboyance, cried his heart out. Cantwell was inconsolable.

Pele, undoubtedly the world's greatest player, had no doubts about Moore's greatness. After Brazil had beaten England 1-0 in the 1970 World Cup finals Pele and Moore exchanged shirts as a mark of the respect that each man had for the other. When Pele heard of Moore's death he said: "Words cannot sum up the grief I feel for my great friend. He was one of the world's finest defenders and a great sportsman."

That was the key to Moore. Never mind that his critics said that he was one-paced. Never mind that Beckenbauer might have been a more accomplished player. At a time when so many idols had turned out to have feet of clay Moore will always be remembered for being the perfect gentleman.

As Reg Burr, the Millwall chairman, said: "Bobby's type of Englishness drew on the better side of our national character, on our sense of fair play and of dignity. People of all ages feel we have lost a link to a better, more decent time."

Bowing out: Moore ended his career in America

Clown makes fools of England

DESPITE a 90-minute onslaught by England in front of a packed Wembley crowd, their failure to do better than a 1-1 draw against Poland condemned them to World Cup oblivion. The hero of the night was Jan Tomaszewski, the Polish goalkeeper. He had been dubbed a "clown" by Brian Clough, TV pundit and Derby manager, before the match. However, his antics on October 17 made fools of England instead.

Tomaszewski was simply unbeatable: he used every single part of his body – fist, fingertip, leg, hand, torso and foot – to thwart England. The only thing that got past him all night was a penalty. Tomaszewski's inspired performance, part brilliance, part sheer luck, was compounded by England's misfortune – they hit every part of the woodwork – and the ability of defenders to miraculously clear off the line whenever the occasion demanded.

Domarski of Poland scored first, in the 57th minute, when Norman Hunter, picked instead of Bobby Moore, was caught in possession. Allan Clarke levelled the scores six minutes later from a generously awarded penalty. The Polish goal now came under permanent bombardment and Moore, on the bench, exhorted Sir Alf Ramsey to use one of his substitutes.

With five minutes remaining, Ramsey, who had never been comfortable with substitutions, relented. "Kevin, get stripped," he ordered. Kevin Keegan duly

Britain, an island of 55 million Poms, will be green with envy when Australia compete in the World Cup finals

Melbourne Newspaper

took off his tracksuit. "Not that Kevin, the other one." With 100 seconds left Kevin Hector made his England debut. And he still had the best chance of the match, but his header was inches wide.

So Poland would go to the World Cup finals in West Germany, and England had, for the first time, failed to qualify. It was a chastening experience for the nation and on a par with the humiliating defeat by Hungary in the same stadium 20 years earlier. Ramsey, who had played his last international in that match, understood the pain of such public failure only too well.

However, England had only themselves to blame for their misery. In their three-team group they had failed to beat Wales at Wembley in March, and had given a spineless performance in Chorzow in June, where Moore made an uncharacteristic blunder and they lost 2-0.

It would have changed the course of English football history if Hector's header had gone into the net

JIMMY GREAVES

Ramsey's 11-year record as England manager					
P	W	D	L	F	A
113	69	27	17	224	99

Clough deserts Derby

Clough: war of words

BRIAN CLOUGH'S big mouth and his battles with the Derby board produced an explosive showdown and one that, for once, he did not win.

Clough brought the behind the scenes warfare out into the open by making two blistering attacks. The first was on the FA, whom he condemned for their handling of Leeds's disciplinary record. In a newspaper article he said that Leeds should have been demoted and "the men who run soccer missed the most marvellous chance of cleaning up the game in one swoop".

Then, days before England's crucial World Cup qualifying game against Poland he accused some of his own players of being cheats. He claimed they were not giving 100 per cent for the club because they were more concerned with the international match.

Sam Longston, the Derby chairman, was horrified. He feared that his club would receive heavy punishment and could even be expelled from the League. So he told Clough to shut up and stop writing for

newspapers and appearing on television.

Clough was having none of it and thought he could call the club's bluff by resigning. But Derby stood firm and on October 17 Clough and his assistant Peter Taylor left. Derby appointed Dave Mackay, and the former player had a torrid time for the rest of the season, having to deal with revolts by the fans and his players – all of whom were intensely loyal to Clough.

Clough and Taylor soon agreed to take charge at Brighton, and their arrival trebled the attendance for the Third Division club's next home match. But it was not long before Clough was up to his old tricks.

Brighton were bundled out of the Cup 4-0 by Walton and Hersham and were then thrashed 8-2 by Bristol Rovers. Clough said that he was ashamed by the performances and accused his players of not knowing their own trade, lacking heart and shirking their moral responsibilities.

Then he fell foul of the Brighton board as well. Clough admitted that he was interested in a £400 a week offer from the Shah of Iran to take charge of his country's national side.

The Brighton board vetoed the move and said that Clough and Taylor had to honour their contracts. Clough's response was grudging: "Of course I wanted to go to Iran, but I'm staying at Brighton to do a job. I'm not saying I'm happy here."

And just how unhappy matters had become would soon become apparent.

End of the road: Tomaszewski foils yet another England attack

The violent and ugly side of the beautiful game

England's worst export: Tottenham fans go on the rampage in Rotterdam

Spurs shamed

The second leg of Tottenham's Uefa Cup final against Feyenoord in Rotterdam was overshadowed by rioting Spurs fans. Seventy people were arrested and more than 200 were injured in the disturbances.

Sydney Wale, the Tottenham chairman, made an impassioned plea to the crowd at half-time: "You hooligans are a disgrace to Tottenham and England. This is a football game, not a war."

It was to no avail and the Spurs board wrote to Feyenoord and the Rotterdam police apologising for the shameful behaviour. Spurs lost the final 4-2 on aggregate.

Cup disgrace

Three Atletico Madrid players were sent off in the first leg of the European Cup semi-final against Celtic. Four Atletico players and two Celtic players were also booked.

Atletico, managed by Juan Carlos Lorenzo, the man in charge of the 1966 Argentina World Cup side branded "animals" by Alf Ramsey, had six of their players banned for the return leg. They were also fined £14,000 by Uefa. Celtic lost the semi-final 2-0 on aggregate.

Birch thugs

In a sign of what was to come, hundreds of arrests were made at pre-season friendlies. Len Shipman, the League president, said the government should bring back the birch. "Ruthless action is imperative. Fines will not stop violence."

Players blamed

The Police Federation said that players' behaviour was also to blame for the troubles dogging the game. "When an England player in an international match is seen by millions of TV viewers getting himself sent off after attacking an opponent, what happens? He is picked again and only prevented from playing by a higher authority. Can we wonder at the behaviour of young hooligans?"

Referee ignored

Mike Doyle and Lou Macari refused to leave the pitch when they were both sent off after a fracas during Manchester United's ill-tempered match with Manchester City at Old Trafford on March 13.

Clive Thomas, the referee, took both teams off the pitch until his instruction was obeyed, and also booked four more players. The match was a 0-0 draw.

No nonsense: Clive Thomas stood his ground

121

Sir Alf made the scapegoat

SIX MONTHS after England's dismal elimination from the World Cup finals at the hands of Poland, the FA summarily dismissed Sir Alf Ramsey, the manager who had won them the World Cup in England eight years previously.

However, the failure in the 1970 World Cup in Mexico when England lost to West Germany 3-2 in extra time, with Ramsey being blamed for bringing on two substitutes, and the Poland debacle, where he was blamed for bringing on a substitute too late, made his sacking inevitable.

Ramsey, the first of the "modern" England managers, was never popular with the press or the FA mandarins. Indeed the two forces virtually colluded in his downfall. Fleet Street knives were out for him immediately after England's elimination and Sir Harold Thompson, the FA's vice-chairman, made sure they hit their mark.

Ramsey was given his marching orders on April 21 but the decision was not announced until 10 days later once they had found a suitable stand-in. Up stepped genial Joe Mercer, Coventry's general manager and the former manager of Manchester City, who was appointed to hold the fort as a caretaker manager.

"I do not want the job on a permanent basis," the smiling 59-year-old said. "I'll just hold the reins for a few weeks. I'll tell the players to go out and enjoy themselves." Mercer was in complete contrast to the diffident and stand-offish Ramsey, and, during his short tenure, it worked. England lost only one of seven matches.

By July the FA reverted to type and appointed Don Revie, of Leeds, and the outstanding English manager of the decade. The fun period was over and dour professionalism was once again the order of the day, of which Revie was the arch exponent.

Alan Hardaker, the secretary of the Football League and never one to mince his words, told the FA secretary: "You must be off your heads." He later amplified this comment: "Revie as England manager was a classic case of poacher turning gamekeeper."

England's greatest manager

Born: January 22, 1920 in Dagenham, Essex.

Signed for Southampton in April 1944 and made his first-team debut in October 1946. Played 90 matches and scored eight goals.

Joined Tottenham in May 1949 and played for them until 1954, scoring 24 goals in 226 matches. Second Division champions in 1950, First Division champions in 1951, and First Division runners-up in 1952.

Made his debut for England on December 1, 1948, against Switzerland at Highbury. Won 32 caps, including 29 consecutively. Scored three goals, all of them penalties.

Appointed the manager of Ipswich in 1955. Third Division South champions in 1957, Second Division champions in 1961 and First Division champions in 1962. Thus, he achieved the feat of winning the Second and First Divisions as both a player and a manager.

Became the manager of England in May 1963 and was dismissed in April 1974. Was the most successful England manager ever, only losing 17 matches out of 113 (with 69 wins and 27 draws).

Won the World Cup in 1966 and was knighted for services to football in January 1967.

Briefly managed Birmingham in the 1977-78 season.

Mentor and maestro: Ramsey and Moore discuss tactics in one their last matches together

Mercer: caretaker

Big-spending Docherty hits rock bottom at Manchester United after Best storms out and City condemn them to relegation

TOMMY DOCHERTY'S attempts to spend his way out of trouble and tame George Best both ended in disaster as Manchester United were relegated to the Second Division for the first time in 36 years.

Once again, their form in the League was abysmal and at Christmas their goalkeeper, Alex Stepney, was their joint leading goalscorer with two penalties. Then, in the New Year, the club finally parted company with George Best.

At first it seemed that Docherty had reached an understanding with his wayward genius and Best returned to the first team in October. However, their relationship reached breaking point just before United's third round FA Cup match against Plymouth.

Best missed a training session but thought he had kept his side of the bargain by making up the work in his own time. However, Docherty dropped him and Best's retort was: "If I can't get into a struggling team like Manchester United then it's time to quit." This time it really was the end of the line.

In the end, United were undone by one of their former

Getting his own back: Law's goal doomed United

stalwarts Denis Law, who had joined Manchester City after being released by Docherty during the close season. United needed to win both of their final two games of the season to stand any chance of staying up

They came unstuck in their penultimate match, at Maine Road. Francis Lee's run towards the penalty area appeared to be covered by the United defence but he threaded the ball into the six-yard box, where Law hit a cheeky back-heel into the corner of the net.

Ironically, Law, at the start of his career with United, had won a penalty against City in the 1962-3 season in a game that relegated City and kept United in the First Division.

Eight minutes from the end of the match the United fans went wild and invaded the pitch, forcing the referee to abandon the match. The League decided to let the score stand.

Revie's record run speaks for itself

AFTER the heartbreak of last season, when Don Revie speculated about going for an historic Treble and ended up with nothing, Leeds were not going to make any more rash promises. Instead, they let their football do the talking for them.

They won their first seven matches, swept past Sheffield United's record of 23 matches without defeat from the start of a season, and were within an ace of passing Burnley's all-time unbeaten record when they lost their 30th League match, 3-2 at Stoke on February 23.

That was one of only four defeats in the League that Leeds suffered all season and the other three came in consecutive matches in March. They lost to

Liverpool, their closest rivals, went down 4-1 to struggling Burnley, their worst home defeat since Don Revie had taken charge, and were then beaten 3-1 by West Ham. People started to wonder whether

Revie: kept quiet

Leeds's nerve was going to crack once again – particularly as Liverpool had closed the gap to four points with three games in hand.

But Leeds, free to concentrate on the League after their shock exit from the FA Cup at the hands of Bristol City in the fifth round, kept their resolve. It was Liverpool, still busy in the FA Cup, who slipped and handed the title to Leeds when they lost at home to Arsenal with two matches still to go.

With Leeds in the spotlight, Bristol Rovers' performance in the Third Division went virtually unnoticed. They almost matched Leeds's unbeaten run, not losing until their 27th match, at Wrexham on February 2.

Shankly bows out on a high note with yet another trophy

BILL SHANKLY crowned his glittering career with yet another trophy, the FA Cup, and then announced that he was bowing out at the summit because of the continual strain of being involved in top-flight football. There was a smooth handover of power as Liverpool promoted his assistant Bob Paisley, who had been with the club since 1939.

Liverpool's 3-0 victory over Newcastle in the FA Cup final was a wonderful demonstration of all that Shankly held dear. Although there was no score at half-time Liverpool smoothly moved up through the gears in the second half and were soon cruising to victory.

Tommy Smith's pinpoint cross picked out Kevin Keegan, who deftly controlled the ball and dispatched it with brio. Then John Toshack sliced the Newcastle defence open, Steve Heighway produced a clever change of direction and that was goal number two.

It was not Liverpool's style to ease up when they had the game under control. Their hallmark was precise passing, and Keegan's second, two minutes from time, was a wonderful culmination of a flowing move. It was a crushing end for Newcastle who had undergone an ordeal even to reach Wembley.

They were 2-1 down at home to Nottingham Forest in the sixth round when the visitors were awarded, and scored, a penalty in the second half. Pat Howard was sent off for arguing with the referee over the penalty and Newcastle fans invaded the pitch, stopping the game for nearly 10 minutes.

Despite being reduced to 10 men, Newcastle recovered to win 4-3 when play resumed. But Nottingham Forest successfully appealed against the result and the FA said that the match had to be replayed at a neutral venue. Malcolm Macdonald, the Newcastle striker, said: "My reaction is one of disgust but not surprise. I half expected a ridiculous solution and they came up with one."

It needed another 210 minutes of football in four days at Goodison Park before Newcastle finally prevailed, thanks to a single goal from Macdonald.

Shankly's achievements

Born: September 2, 1913 in Glenbuck, Ayrshire

Played for Carlisle United and Preston North End. Won the FA Cup with Preston in 1938.

Won five Scottish caps in the 1938-39 season.

Appointed the manager of Carlisle in 1949. Moved to Grimsby in 1951, Workington in 1953 and Huddersfield in 1956.

Became the manager of Liverpool in December 1959.

1962	Second Division champions.
1964	First Division champions.
1965	FA Cup winners.
1966	First Division champions, European Cup Winners Cup beaten finalists.
1969	First Division runners-up.
1971	FA Cup beaten finalists.
1973	First Division champions, Uefa Cup winners.
1974	FA Cup winners, First Division runners-up.

Shankly retired at the end of the 1973-74 season and was awarded the OBE.

Died: September 28, 1981 in Liverpool.

Bill Shankly was one of five brothers who played professional football. Bob Shankly was also a successful manager, taking Dundee to the Scottish championship for the first time in 1962.

The last hurrah: Shankly retired on a winning note

One way street: Keegan and Liverpool dominated Newcastle

Docherty's boys do the business

Leading light: the predatory Jordan was always Scotland's spearhead

TOMMY DOCHERTY may not have rescued Manchester United from relegation, but the two precious wins Scotland secured against Denmark under his stewardship the previous year virtually clinched Scotland's place in the World Cup finals in West Germany. By September all Willie Ormond's team had to do was beat Czechoslovakia once, either home or away.

But in the first match, at Hampden on the 26th, the Czechs drew first blood when, in the 33rd minute, Nehoda broke clear on the right and his speculative cross skated under the goalkeeper. Within seven minutes a Docherty stalwart, Jim Holton, the imposing Manchester United centre-half, had equalised, nodding in Tommy Hutchison's corner.

In the second half Scotland threw everything into attack. In the 70th minute, with the Czech defence under fearful pressure, a Billy Bremner free kick struck a post and it seemed the Czechs had survived yet another onslaught. But the ball broke to Willie Morgan (another Docherty player at United) and Joe Jordan, brought on to replace Kenny Dalglish six minutes earlier, became Scotland's hero as he met Morgan's centre to head home the winner.

It was the fourth time Scotland had qualified for the World Cup finals (though in 1950 in a fit of pique they refused to take up the invitation). The return match in Bratislava in October was irrelevant, although any disappointment they may have had by going down to a Nehoda first-half penalty was tempered by the news that England had been eliminated by Poland.

Stand-in keeps City at bay as Wolves find the right formula

WOLVERHAMPTON won the League Cup, their first major honour since they took the FA Cup in 1960, thanks in no small part to their reserve goalkeeper Gary Pierce.

Pierce had been deputising for Phil Parkes for several weeks and he produced a series of good saves in the second half just when the match was threatening to swing Manchester City's way.

Wolves dominated the first half and took the lead just before the interval when Kenny Hibbitt mis-hit a shot but still scored. But Manchester City came back strongly and Colin Bell's fierce shot gave Pierce no chance. Bell hit the woodwork again and that was the best chance Manchester City had.

From then on, Pierce kept them at bay and Wolverhampton's confidence slowly returned. In a match that got more exciting the longer it went on, John Richards scored the winner for Wolves with only six minutes remaining.

The post-match celebrations were spoiled by an act of petulance by Rodney Marsh. The moment the final whistle blew the Manchester City forward headed straight for the dressing-room, refusing to applaud the winning team or to go to collect his loser's souvenir tankard.

Golden reserve: Pierce makes another save to deny Lee

125

TOTAL FOOTBALL swept the tenth World Cup off its feet. With Pele gone and Brazil reneging on their birthright, the stage was set for Holland's Johann Cruyff and West Germany's Franz Beckenbauer to battle for the accolade of the world's greatest footballer. But for the billions watching around the globe the tournament was more than a titanic struggle between two individuals, it was the revelation of a whole new team game: Total Football.

However for West Germany and Holland, the two exponents of this method, it meant two different things. For Holland, blessed with remarkable talent, it meant that forwards were also defenders, and defenders forwards, with Cruyff the puppet-master pulling all the strings. Each member of the team had to be prepared to function as a multi-purpose player instead of being tied to their traditional role. The world gasped at this innovation. Others pointed out that at last they were doing their job: they were footballers.

West Germany's version was something entirely different. Their system had evolved out of catenaccio, the Italians' use of a sweeper behind the defensive back line to negate attacking moves. However this stiflingly defensive tactic was turned on its head by West Germany, who used their sweeper, the incomparable Beckenbauer, to explode out of his lair to launch devastating attacks. Paul Breitner, too, was nominally a defender but he was equally dangerous going forward, particularly in support of their two genuine wingers, Jurgen Grabowski and Uli Hoeness.

Little wonder then, in the Olympic stadium in Munich on July 7, these two great, revolutionary sides clashed in the World Cup final. If it wasn't the most amazing final of all time, it began with the most extraordinary piece of drama. Straight from the kick-off, Cruyff set off on another of his scintillating runs. His pace and ball control took him sweeping and twisting past the entire German team. Only Hoeness, frantically racing back to try to cover the danger, got anywhere near him. But Hoeness's last-ditch tackle was ill-timed and brought Cruyff down just inside the penalty area. Jack Taylor, the English referee unflinching under the

WORLD CUP 1974
Europeans dominate as West Germany triumph

Despite drawing with Brazil, Scotland were eliminated on goal difference

pressure of the home crowd, had no hesitation in awarding a penalty. Johann Neeskens duly scored from the spot. It was the fastest goal in a World Cup final and West Germany were behind without having touched the ball.

West Germany hardly got a look in for the next 20 minutes as well. The Dutch domination was total, and the German crowd gasped at the ease with which Cryuff's side strung together a host of pretty passes. But perhaps they thought it was going to be all too easy, because they failed to convert their arrogant superiority into more goals. West Germany clung on to Holland's coat tails and were rewarded for their perseverance after 25 minutes

when Taylor awarded another penalty when Jansen tripped Holzenbein. Germans in the crowd thought that justice had been done, although the decision was far less clear-cut.

Breitner scored from the spot and then Gerd Muller gave Germany the lead two minutes before half-time. He was a classic striker, and his goal proved the point. The pass from Bonhof was not quite on target and as Muller controlled the ball it ran away from him slightly. But, in a flash, he dragged it back and hit his shot past Jan Jongbloed.

And just to prove that the match was not entirely about outfield players, Sepp Maier gave a virtuoso performance in the second half. He

made one particularly good save from Johann Neeskens, after which Holland's momentum finally ebbed away. And Germany recaptured the World Cup they had first won in 1954. Coincidentally, having been the first team to win the World Cup after losing a match in the finals, 20 years later they repeated the "feat".

So in the end, football reigned supreme. But it was a close-run thing. The tenth World Cup was beset with problems. Fifa had unveiled a widely criticised new-look second phase that abolished the quarter-finals and semi-finals. They were replaced by two groups of four qualifiers from the first round, the winners of each group to contest the final. This was done to allow another eight revenue-generating matches to be staged. Not surprisingly there were fears that commercialism was ruining the game with off-the-field financial deals apparently more important that what took place on the pitch.

Concerns about security in West Germany in the wake of the 1972 Olympic massacre in Munich did not help matters, nor did Brazil – forsaking their adventurous style in favour of defensive European play. To boot, it seemed to rain all the time.

England and Sir Alf Ramsey, of course, were not present – thanks to a Polish goalkeeper. But Scotland's pride in being the only British representatives, the first time they had qualified since 1958 – was ultimately dented by their own naivety.

Their first match of the tournament, when they beat Zaire by only 2-0, was their downfall. A brave 0-0 draw with Brazil, a shadow of their former selves, followed. Billy Bremner was inspirational and was unlucky not to score, as were Joe Jordan and Peter Lorimer. In the meantime, though, Yugoslavia had demolished Zaire 9-0, a scoreline that hardly reflected their total domination of the match.

With the Yugoslavs holding such a huge goals advantage Scotland had to beat them. But Scotland slipped behind eight minutes from time and a late equaliser from Jordan was not enough to save them as Brazil beat Zaire 3-0 to edge Scotland out by a single goal, the first time the World Cup finals had used goal difference to separate teams.

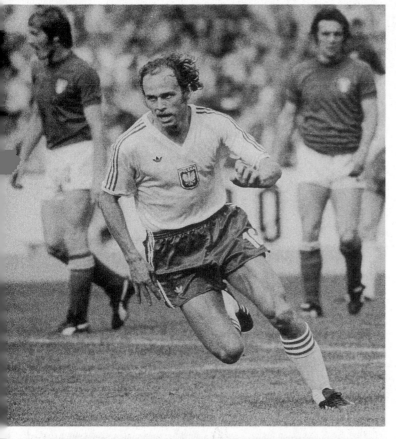

FOR THE RECORD

FIRST ROUND

GROUP 1	P	W	D	L	F	A	Pts
E. Germany	3	2	1	0	4	1	5
W. Germany	3	2	0	1	4	1	4
Chile	3	0	2	1	1	2	1
Australia	3	0	1	2	0	5	1

GROUP 2	P	W	D	L	F	A	Pts
Yugoslavia	3	0	2	0	10	1	4
Brazil	3	1	2	0	3	0	4
Scotland	3	1	2	0	3	1	4
Zaire	3	0	0	3	0	14	0

GROUP 3	P	W	D	L	F	A	Pts
Holland	3	2	1	0	6	1	5
Sweden	3	1	2	0	4	0	4
Bulgaria	3	0	2	1	2	5	2
Uruguay	3	0	1	2	1	6	1

GROUP 4	P	W	D	L	F	A	Pts
Poland	3	3	0	0	12	3	6
Argentina	3	1	1	1	7	5	3
Italy	3	1	1	1	5	4	3
Haiti	3	0	0	3	2	14	0

SECOND ROUND

GROUP A	P	W	D	L	F	A	Pts
Holland	3	3	0	0	8	0	6
Brazil	3	2	0	1	3	3	4
E. Germany	3	0	1	2	1	4	1
Argentina	3	0	1	2	2	7	1

GROUP B	P	W	D	L	F	A	Pts
W. Germany	3	3	0	0	7	2	6
Poland	3	2	0	1	3	2	4
Sweden	3	1	0	2	4	6	2
Yugoslavia	3	0	0	3	2	6	0

THIRD PLACE PLAY-OFF

Poland 1 Brazil 0
HT 0-0 Att. 79,000

FINAL

West Germnay 2 Holland 1
HT 2-1 Att. 77,833

Teams
West Germany Maier; Vogts, Schwarzenbeck, Beckenbauer, Breitner, Bonhof, Hoeness, Overath, Grabowski, Muller, Holzenbein
Holland Jongbloed, Suurbier, Rijsbergen (sub: De Jong), Haan, Krol, Jansen, Neeskens, Van Hanegem, Rep, Cruyff, Rensenbrink (sub: Van de Kerkhof)

Leading goalscorers 7 Grzegorz Lato (Poland); 5 Andrzej Szarmach (Poland), Johannes Neeskens (Holland); 4 Gerhard Muller (West Germany), Ralf Edstrom (Sweden), Johannes Rep (Holland)
Total goals scored 97
Average per game: 2.55
Sendings-off Raymond Richards (Australia) v Chile; Referee: Jafar Namdar (Iran).
Carlos Caszely (Chile) v West Germany; Referee: Dogan Babacan (Turkey).
Julio Montero-Castillo (Uruguay) v Holland; Referee: Karoly Palotai (Hungary).
Luis Edmundo Pereira (Brazil) v Holland; Referee: Kurt Tschenscher (West Germany).
Mulamba N'daye (Zaire) v Yugoslavia; Referee: Omar Delgado (Colombia).
Number of player used by the finalists
18 West Germany; 15 Holland

● Leslaw Cmikiewicz of Poland appeared in six matches yet totalled only 102 minutes' football. Each time he was a substitute and his longest stint was 33 minutes against Yugoslavia.

Strangely, Scotland were the only team in the tournament not to have lost a match, as West Germany lost to East Germany 1-0 in their first meeting since the countries had been divided after the Second World War.

England did gain some solace from the tournament. Poland, who as supposed minnows had eliminated them at Wembley from the finals, were the surprise package of the tournament, finishing in third overall place when they beat Brazil 1-0 in a bitter and bruising game.

Their match against West Germany, to decide which team would qualify the final, was played on a quagmire. They lost 2-1, but many believe the result would have been reversed had the playing surface been better. In Kazmiercz Deyna,

Bang on target: Lato of Poland was the tournament's leading scorer, Neeskins's penalty gave Holland an early lead but Muller's goal won the final for West Germany

Gadocha and Grzegorz Lato, Poland had three of the world's best players and Lato finished as the tournament's leading scorer.

However West Germany were worthy finalists (despite their slip-up against their comrades from across the Iron Curtain). And against Holland, West Germany had faced the other team of the tournament. It was the final the whole world wanted to see, much as in the 1970 World Cup finals the mouth-watering confrontation was between England and Brazil. But was the triumph of Total Football truly going to herald a new dawn?

It would fanciful to think that many other countries could copy the strategy of Total Football. As Rinus Michels, the Dutch team manager, pointed out: you need at least seven world-class players – one fewer and you are in trouble. And who, apart from Holland and West Germany, could boast seven world-class players? The next World Cup would give us a clue.

Keegan and Bremner shamed

Bremner: petty gesture

THE Charity Shield was supposed to provide a showpiece start to the season but the conduct of Billy Bremner and Kevin Keegan at Wembley on August 10 reduced the event to an all-time low.

The match was shown live on television for the first time and viewers saw an ill-tempered match between Leeds and Liverpool boil over after an hour when Bremner and Keegan traded punches. There was no doubt that they both deserved to be sent off but as they left the pitch they both petulantly tore off their shirts and threw them away.

The match finished 1-1 and Liverpool won the penalty shoot-out when the Leeds goalkeeper David Harvey took Leeds's sixth kick and lofted it over the bar. But everybody was more interested in what action the authorities would take rather than the result.

A disgusted spectator tried to have Bremner and Keegan charged with a breach of the peace, but a magistrate refused to issue a summons. The FA were nowhere near as lenient. Bremner and Keegan were each fined £500 and banned until the end of September, which meant that they would miss 11 matches.

Vernon Stokes, the chairman of the disciplinary committee, admitted that the punishment might not have been so severe if the match had not been played at Wembley and shown on television. This did not impress either club and Bob Paisley, the Liverpool manager, said: "People who don't know how to run the country are trying to run football, which they know even less about."

But Ted Croker was adamant that the right decision had been taken. "We are trying to make football more acceptable to a wider range of people. Players must learn that they cannot throw punches at each other."

Keegan: petty gesture

Leeds banned for four years after disallowed goal sparks riot

NOTHING, it appeared, was going right for Leeds. After a series of gruelling battles to reach the final of the European Cup their potential day of glory turned into a night of shame in Paris.

Leeds's uncompromising style had won them few friends on the continent. Both Leeds and Ujpest Dozsa were reduced to 10 men when Leeds won 2-1 in Hungary and Duncan McKenzie, who was sent off for retaliation, was banned for three matches by Uefa. Then, in the second leg of the semi-final, with Leeds trying to protect a one-goal advantage in Barcelona, Gordon McQueen was sent off for hitting a Spanish player.

Leeds, only the second English club to reach the final, had high hopes of beating Bayern Munich, the European Cup holders, on May 28. The final was also a physical match – Andersson was carried off after four minutes after a clash with Terry Yorath and Hoeness also limped off before half-time.

With Bayern forced to reshuffle their formation Leeds dominated most of the match. Their

Last tango in Paris: French riot police survey the wrecked Parc de Princes after the European Cup final

fans believed that two penalties should have been awarded against Beckenbauer, and when Lorimer had a goal disallowed for offside in the 66th minute a mob ran wild.

While French riot police tried to quell the unrest on the terraces first Roth and then Muller put the trophy beyond Leeds. Each goal was the signal for a further outbreak of fighting.

The disturbances continued throughout the night after the match and Uefa, thoroughly sick of the conduct of English hooligans, banned Leeds from Europe for four years.

All change at the top in Scotland

THE WINDS of change were sweeping through Scottish football, and Celtic fans were none too happy about it. First, the entire structure of the League format had been rewritten for the start of the next season. Second, their glorious run of nine successive League titles was brought to an end by their bitter rivals, Rangers.

After years of heated and lengthy argument the 37 clubs at last agreed on much-needed change. From next season there would be a three-division League. The first tier, the Premier Division, would comprise 10 clubs, the other two tiers, to be called the First and Second Divisions, would have 14 clubs in each

(Meadowbank were admitted to the League to balance the numbers). Promotion and relegation would be two up and two down.

The new format meant that the Premier Division clubs would play each other four times in the League. It was hoped that this would make the top division, in particular, more competitive and therefore more attractive. However, Celtic fans – with a whiff of paranoia – suspected the changes were introduced to hinder the continuance of their utter domination of trophies in the last decade.

Their fears probably had more to do with the swagger with which Rangers carried off the championship: seven points

clear of Hibs, the runners-up, and 11 points ahead of Celtic in third place.

Under the authoritarian and fitness-obsessed regime of Jock Wallace, their manager, and the cool elegance of Sandy Jardine, Rangers were worthy champions. They beat Celtic in both League matches, the second on January 4 taking them to the top of the table, whereupon Celtic seemed to have lost heart.

Still, by the standards of any other club, Celtic had a successful season winning both Cups. The Scottish Cup victory, 3-1 against Airdrie, was their 24th success and it also marked the retirement of their captain, Billy McNeill.

Chester's Cup run helps lift their League burden

At last: Ray Graydon broke Ron Saunders' duck

THE League Cup certainly lived up to its reputation as the second-best Cup in England as Second Division clubs blasted their betters from the First and managed to provide three of the four semi-finalists alongside Fourth Division Chester.

While the Second Division was to yield the eventual winner, little Chester's amazing run defied all logic. Alone of the 92 League clubs, Chester had never been promoted and when they began their campaign by beating Walsall 2-1 in the first round nobody could have dreamed of how far they were going to go. Second Division Blackpool and Third Division Preston also succumbed to give the men from Cheshire a home fourth-round tie against star-studded Leeds.

Two goals from John James and one from defender Trevor Storton rocked the Yorkshire side and gave Chester a thoroughly deserved victory. A goalless draw at St James's Park and another James goal at Sealand Road saw off Newcastle.

The semi-final, over two legs against Aston Villa, saw two dramatic matches. In the first, Chester, at home, were twice behind but snatched a 2-2 draw. In the second, Chester again fell behind, this time 2-0. The

Fourth Division side rallied to level the scores, but a Brian Little goal ended the fairytale.

Chester did get one consolation from their record-breaking run: when Lincoln lost at Southport on the last Tuesday of the season Chester took the fourth promotion place by four-hundredths of a goal and the burden of being the only club not to have won promotion was finally lifted.

Villa, their semi-final conquerors, went on to beat Norwich 1-0 in a dour final. The deadlock was finally broken 10 minutes from time when Ray Graydon successfully followed through after Kevin Keelan had parried his penalty.

Ron Saunders, Villa's manager, probably did not care too much about the quality of the football. It was the third successive year he had led a side to the League Cup final (Norwich in 1973, Manchester City in 1974) but the first he'd actually won.

THE
1974-75
SEASON

Wimbledon the pick of the pack in a season when the underdogs savaged their masters

THE bizarre trail of upsets that had characterised the League Cup somehow spilled over into the FA Cup, making it most certainly the season of the underdogs. Pride of place went to Southern League Wimbledon who lost in a fourth round replay, but non-League Altrincham, Leatherhead, Stafford Rangers and Wycombe Wanderers also seriously embarrassed supposedly superior opposition.

All five survived the first matches in the third round and went into the draw for the fourth round. Wimbledon beat First Division Burnley 1-0 at Turf Moor (the first time a First Division club had been beaten at home by a non-League club since the formation of the Third Division in the 1920s); Altrincham drew with Everton 1-1 at Goodison having led, but a nine-man Everton rallied to equalise with a penalty; Leatherhead stunned Brighton 1-0 at the Goldstone ground; Stafford drew 0-0 with Rotherham; and Wycombe also held Middlesbrough in a goalless draw.

Although Altrincham and Wycombe narrowly lost the replays, Stafford convincingly beat Rotherham away 2-0 and three non-League clubs had made it to the next round – an unheard of feat.

Wimbledon faced mighty Leeds at Elland Road, a daunting task for any side. To everybody's surprise they were equal to the occasion with Dickie Guy, their part-time goalkeeper and full-time clerk, the hero. Guy pulled off a succession of extraordinary saves – including a Peter Lorimer penalty – to deny Leeds in a thrilling goalless draw.

Wimbledon's luck did not hold in the replay – played at Selhurst Park to accommodate the huge number of fans fascinated by the little club's exploits – when a wayward Johnny Giles shot was deflected off Dave Bassett for the only goal.

Leatherhead had their heroics, too, at Filbert Street where they actually led 2-0 before Leicester decided enough was enough and dispatched the upstarts 3-2. Stafford also went down, 2-1 away to Peterborough, and the non-League challenge was extinguished. But not the challenge of the underdogs.

Seemingly encouraged by this orgy of giant-killing, League clubs in the lower divisions took up the mantle. First Division Spurs and Sheffield United were knocked out by Second Division Nottingham Forest and Aston Villa, and Third Division Walsall demolished Manchester United and Newcastle. Amid all this carnage, Second Division Fulham were quietly making progress towards their first FA Cup final.

Leeds dismiss Clough after 44 stormy days

Clough: stormy reign

BRIAN CLOUGH'S brief sojourn at Brighton ended in acrimony in July when he left the Third Division club to become manager of Leeds. Mike Bamber, the Brighton chairman, accused Leeds of going back on a compensation agreement and issued a writ against Clough, alleging breach of contract.

But that was nothing compared with the storm that engulfed Clough when he arrived at Leeds. Clough plunged into the transfer market, put established players on the transfer list and imposed authoritarian discipline at the club. When Leeds won only one of their first six League matches and slipped to 19th in the table Clough was continually barracked by the Leeds fans.

A newspaper claimed that there had been a dressing-room revolt and the players had passed a vote of no confidence in Clough. At first, Manny Cussins, the Leeds chairman, denied the report. But hours later Clough and his solicitor were summoned to a meeting at which Clough was sacked. He received a £44,000 pay-off on his five-year contract.

Clough's reign had lasted just 44 days. Cussins, who had described Clough as "the ideal manager" when he appointed him, said: "What has been done is for the good of the club. The club and the happiness of the players must come first."

Although the players claimed that they had had no part in Clough's dismissal, he was bitterly disappointed: "I think it is a very sad day for Leeds and for football." For once, the press agreed with him. Headlines accused Leeds of cowardice and one respected commentator said: "This disgraceful affair now more than ever raises the question: who is running professional football – the managers or the players?"

Jimmy Armfield, after much deliberation, agreed to take charge at Leeds. Clough returned to the game in January when he was appointed manager of Nottingham Forest. Yet again, he was quick to make his mark.

His first match in charge was the FA Cup third round replay against Tottenham. Despite being a struggling Second Division side, Forest produced one of the shocks of the round when Neil Martin's solitary goal brought them victory at White Hart Lane.

Clever Dick: Guy's saves were the inspiration for Wimbledon's FA Cup run

130

Disillusioned Nicholson quits over players' greedy demands

End of the road: "Players have become impossible. There is no longer respect."

BILL NICHOLSON resigned as the Tottenham manager in August, exasperated at the way money had come to control the game he loved. Spurs had equalled their worst ever start to a season by losing their first four League matches but that was not what persuaded Nicholson the time had come to go.

The problem was the increasing demands that players were making. Nicholson had been involved in an acrimonious contract dispute with Martin Chivers, who had publicly described the club's offer as "rubbish". Chivers was put on the transfer list and Nicholson's attempts to sign a replacement were thwarted by several players' demands for under-the-counter payments.

When Tottenham lost the fourth match, 2-1 at home to Manchester City with Chivers restored to the side, Nicholson had finally had enough after 38 years with the club as a player and manager.

He emphasised that Tottenham's poor start had nothing to do with his decision to leave – he would have gone at the end of last season had Tottenham won the Uefa Cup. Nicholson left nobody in any doubt what the problem was.

"Players have become impossible. They talk all the time about security but they are not prepared to work for it. I am abused by players. There is no longer respect," he said.

Both Nicholson and his chairman, Sidney Wale, confirmed that Tottenham had faced unwarranted demands in the past few seasons. They said that the "going rate" for players to join a London club was at least £7,000 and often a five-figure sum.

Both the board and a deputation of senior players, led by the captain Martin Peters, tried to convince Nicholson to stay, but he could not be talked round. Nicholson tried to persuade Johnny Giles to apply for the job, and then favoured the former Spurs hero Danny Blanchflower.

The Spurs fans were far from impressed when, of all people, the board appointed a former Arsenal captain. Nicholson was scathing about the Hull City and Northern Ireland manager: "I thought they'd appoint Danny," he said. "I don't even know Terry Neill."

Neill: surprise choice

Precocious Taylor runs rings round Fulham's wise old heads

FULHAM'S path to only the second all-London Cup final with West Ham had been less than smooth. The Second Division side had needed seven games to eliminate Hull and Nottingham Forest to reach the fifth round, and pipped Birmingham in the semi-final replay with just nine seconds remaining. By contrast West Ham swept to Wembley in a run reminiscent of their successful 1964 campaign.

Then their captain had been Bobby Moore, but this time Moore was on the opposite side and partnered by another veteran, and former England captain, Alan Mullery. But it was a youngster, 21-year-old Alan Taylor, who captured the headlines. The centre forward, who had been playing for Fourth Division Rochdale before Christmas and had cost a mere £40,000, burst Fulham's bubble with two devastating goals in the space of five minutes.

On the hour, Pat Holland set up Billy Jennings whose far-post shot was only pushed away by Peter Mellor, the Fulham goalkeeper. Taylor pounced and cracked the ball into the opposite side of the goal.

Minutes later, Holland was again in the thick of things. He struck a beautifully weighted pass to Graham Paddon who unleashed a ferocious shot. Once again the hapless Mellor was unable to hold the ball and, falling backwards, dropped it in front of the predatory Taylor.

Goal maker: Jennings's pressure on the Fulham defence created the opportunity for Taylor

> *Now we are going into Europe and I have only ever been abroad twice. And that was to Spain on my holidays*
>
> ALAN TAYLOR
> West Ham's FA Cup
> final hero

When the dust settled only Derby were standing

DAVE MACKAY put the tensions created by Brian Clough's departure from Derby behind him as he guided the club to their second championship in four years. And, as had happened previously, they won the title thanks to other teams' results.

Derby did not go to the top of the table until early April and the race was so close that five teams were still in contention. Stoke's defeat on April 12 ruled them out. A week later, even though Derby only drew, Everton's and Liverpool's losses ruled them out. Then, four days later, Ipswich could only draw at Manchester City. Thus, Derby became the First Division champions before they played their last match.

It was a fascinating climax to a title race that had been remarkably close all season and had witnessed some amazing fluctuations in fortunes. Newly-promoted Carlisle were one of the early pace-setters but nosedived straight back into the Second Division. Ipswich, the other front-runners in the autumn, failed to score in five consecutive League matches but only slipped from first place to third. Stoke signed Peter Shilton, went top, but then lost three matches in a row over Christmas. Everton had their turn in front, as did Liverpool . . . and so it went on.

Six different teams had topped the table by December and, in all, the lead changed hands a record 21 times. The only thing that was certain was that London's best were having one of their worst years ever. At one stage Chelsea, Arsenal, Tottenham and QPR filled four of the bottom five places. In the end only Chelsea went down, although Tottenham only escaped by beating Leeds on the last day of the season.

Macdonald head of the class

MALCOLM MACDONALD, restored to Don Revie's England side, wrote his name into the history books and lifted England's hopes of reaching the quarter-finals of the European championships when he scored all five goals when the national side demolished Cyprus at Wembley. Macdonald became the first player to score five goals in a Wembley international.

Revie, who in two previous internationals ignored the Newcastle centre forward, had been reluctant to pick him. Despite this, Macdonald rose to the occasion in his typical bulldog manner. Macdonald had got his name on the score sheet as early as the second minute when he headed in Alan Hudson's free kick, but by half-time the score was only 2-0, against the weakest team in the group.

Macdonald turned the match into a rout in the second half with three headed goals and emulated Willie Hall's feat against Ireland in 1938. This gave England a healthier goal difference in a group that had become a two-horse race with Czechoslovakia.

England, however, could well rue their goalless draw with Portugal at Wembley in November, particularly as Czechoslovakia thumped five past them in Prague and England could only muster a 1-0 win in the return with Cyprus in Limassol.

Bang on target: Macdonald scores against West Germany

Still going strong: A month later he grabbed all five against Cyprus

Quitting while he was ahead: Law retired rather than play in the reserves

■ Denis Law retired rather than play reserve team football for Manchester City. He said: "I always wanted to call it a day while I am still on the top."

■ The FA rejected a proposal to show instant action replays on giant screens during England's 100th international at Wembley, against West Germany, on March 12. They said it would undermine the referee's authority.

■ Notts County became the first team to play 3,000 matches in the League. They drew 2-2 with their local rivals Nottingham Forest on March 25.

■ Stan Bowles had to retake a penalty for QPR when a spectator threw a second ball on to the pitch at Luton. He scored both times.

■ Sir Stanley Rous was the first winner of the Sports Writers Association annual award for services to sport.

■ Jimmy Hill became the unpaid managing director of Coventry in April.

■ Wales's 3-1 victory in Luxembourg on May 1 was the first time they had ever won four European championship matches in a row.

■ Orient finished 12th in the Second Division despite having scored only 28 goals. They drew 20 of their 42 matches and finished with 42 points.

United back at first attempt

MANCHESTER UNITED bounced back into the First Division without too much difficulty a year after they had been relegated. Although they had established a five-point lead before the end of September, and were not beaten at home until February 1, they were never able to run away with the title.

Sunderland and Norwich kept up the pressure and Aston Villa came with a late charge. In the end, Norwich, like Manchester United, went straight back to the Division and Villa finished runners-up by three points.

The return to winning ways brought the fans flocking back to Old Trafford. More than 60,000 came to the match against Sunderland in November, the biggest attendance anywhere in the League since 1973. The only problem was that Manchester United suffered as much as anybody else from hooligans. The FA and League jointly agreed in December that all United's away matches should be all-ticket in an effort to combat the problem.

After their recent upheavals United enjoyed the period of calm, with a settled side and tranquillity behind the scenes. Frank Blunstone turned down the opportunity to become the manager of Chelsea because he wanted to stay at Old Trafford "for job satisfaction and loyalty".

DON REVIE
The ultimate pro who lost his way

Martin Searby

Master tactician: Revie planned exhaustively

NOBODY could have envisaged what a glittering future was in store for Leeds United when Don Revie was appointed player-manager in March 1961. They were a struggling Second Division club, £100,000 in debt with a decrepit ground, and the new boy won only once in the remaining nine games of the season.

He was lucky to get the job when Jack Taylor was sacked. Harry Reynolds, a director who was later to become chairman, wrote a letter recommending his ageing midfield star as the manager of Bournemouth, before realising that Revie might be as effective as anybody else available at the time. At the end of the season Reynolds must have been wondering if he had picked the right man for the job as Leeds barely escaped relegation to the Third Division.

But Revie was a shrewd footballer who first saw the way ahead when the Hungarians came to England in 1953 and were the first overseas team to win at Wembley, 6-3. When they followed that with a 7-1 annihilation in Budapest Revie quickly adapted the deep-lying centre-forward role of Nandor Hidegkuti, who scored a hat-trick in the first match. Revie played the role with such distinction at Manchester City that he was the Footballer of the Year in 1955.

Not the easiest of men to manage because of his own ideas, Revie started playing at Leicester City and went on to Hull, Manchester City and Sunderland before arriving at Leeds in November 1958. The four transfers amounted to £80,000, a record for those days, and made it clear that his talent was apparent to many, even if the underlying defects, which were to surface after his Elland Road days, were not.

Revie's first, and some might argue most crucial, move into the transfer market did not look all that sound when he paid £25,000 for a 5ft 4in 31-year-old midfield player from Everton. Within days of arriving, Bobby Collins wanted to leave. But Revie persuaded him to stay at Leeds, and Collins became the cornerstone of Revie's first team, leading them to promotion in 1964.

Collins collected the Footballer of the Year award the next season when Leeds came close to the League and Cup double, though ultimately missing both trophies, and Revie was rewarded with a then unheard of seven-year contract.

Billy Bremner, Jack Charlton, Willie Bell and Albert Johanneson were already in the team when Revie took over. But not the least of Revie's talents was the ability to plan ahead, appoint talented staff and delegate authority. While he was making the League side a force to be reckoned with Syd Owen, the coach, Maurice Lindley, Revie's assistant, and Les Cocker, the trainer, were inculcating Revie's ideas into young players who would become world names.

Norman Hunter, Paul Reaney, Paul Madeley, Peter Lorimer, Eddie Gray, Terry Cooper and the much, and often wrongly, maligned Gary Sprake started as juniors before becoming an inherent part of the club's history as, in the next 10 years, they won two League titles, the FA Cup, the League Cup, and the Fairs Cup twice.

It was on their first foray into Europe that fate dealt Leeds a blow which, at the time, looked crippling but, in the event, led to one of the most outstanding midfield duos of all time, the pairing of Johnny Giles and Bremner. In the first round of the Fairs Cup in Turin, Collins broke his thigh bone and Giles, the extraordinary Irishman who was the youngest person ever to play for the Republic, came in off the wing, where he had played since his move from Manchester United for a bargain £35,000 two years earlier.

Giles, who was capped 60 times, was a hugely gifted player with the ability to pass long and short, bend the ball, and unleash a tremendous shot. He was also no shrinking violet and players who tried to kick him often received more than they had bargained for in return. He was an extension of Revie's tactical acumen on the field and intuitively altered the course of events as if he was radio controlled.

Revie searched for discipline on the field, and he made sure his players knew how to negate opposition strengths. But Leeds were getting a reputation as "the nearly men": runners-up twice and fourth twice in the championship, and losing semi-finalists twice and runners-up in the FA Cup in the four years since their promotion.

But a goal from Cooper in the League Cup final against Arsenal, and one from Mick Jones in the Fairs Cup final against Ferencvaros put some silver on the sideboard.

The 1968-69 season was to prove a memorable nine months for Revie as only Manchester City and Burnley managed to beat his team, who swept to their first League title with six points to spare over Liverpool. Ironically, it was Leeds's

Strike force: Clarke struck up a telling partnership with Jones, Revie's first £100,000 signing

very success that alienated many football followers outside the Yorkshire city. Revie's insistence on rigorous defence meant Sprake kept 24 clean sheets and only 26 goals were conceded.

Leeds were perceived as a negative side, far removed from their great rivals on Merseyside and 16 of their matches contained only a solitary goal. The soccer public of that era expected more and it gave rise to all sorts of fanciful talk about "total football"; 25 years later Revie's tactics would have been widely applauded.

Revie's first £100,000 signing was Jones, the Sheffield United centre-forward who had already won two England caps. A bull of a striker, he did not really come into his own until Allan Clarke arrived from Leicester City two years later. The pair struck up a partnership which brought Leeds 188 goals in five seasons as they remained one of the top sides in the championship, in both domestic cups and in Europe. The "nearly" tag returned in 1970 when they lost to Celtic in the European Cup semi-final, conceded the League by fielding a reserve team against Derby County (for which they were fined £5,000), and lost the FA Cup final in a replay with Chelsea after the first draw in 42 years of Wembley finals.

Magic moment: Bremner and Charlton are introduced to Prince Philip at the 1972 Cup final

Two seasons later they beat Arsenal in the Centenary final, but 48 hours after Clarke headed the winner at Wembley they failed to beat Wolves and were again runners-up in the League as Derby took the title by one point.

With so many fine players now highly experienced after growing up in the Revie family, Leeds gained a wider acceptance with more outgoing, confident play. Most of the time the players didn't see "the boss" except on match days, when he would give his usual profound analysis of the opposition, and the team was on automatic pilot during the latter part of Revie's reign.

There were still huge disappointments: Sunderland beat them in the 1973 FA Cup final, and they lost of the European Cup Winners' Cup to AC Milan, which ended with the referee, Michas, banned for cheating, but Revie's last season proved to be his greatest triumph.

Leeds started the 1973-74 season with seven straight wins and did not lose a game until they went down at Stoke on February 23, eventually taking the title by five points from a tremendous Liverpool side.

In 1974 Revie left to take over the England

team. Although there was a European Cup final under his ultimate successor, Jimmy Armfield, the glory days were over, and as the aging team broke up unthinkable relegation was only six seasons ahead.

Perhaps Revie's greatest achievement was to reciprocate the fierce loyalty of his players who were constantly united under his banner for 13 years. On his death from motor neurone disease in 1989 to a man they paid tribute to the person they always saw as a father figure.

His tactics and strategy did not always win friends but who could doubt the efficacy of them? He had a shrewd eye for a player but was more interested in the character and ability to comply with his overall plan. That may have made Leeds negative in the early years but maturity brought the ability to perform within his basic structure.

He cast such a long shadow over Elland Road that one of the first things Howard Wilkinson did when he arrived 14 years later was to take down the blown-up pictures of Revie's men which still adorned the foyer. "That's all history," he said. But what a history.

Runaway champions: Leeds were not beaten until February on their way to the 1973-74 League title

THE REVIE YEARS

Born July 10, 1927, Middlesbrough

PLAYING CAREER
In his teens he played for Middlesbrough Swifts where Bill Sanderson, the manager, collected huge dossiers on the opposition
Leicester City 1946-49
Made his debut for Leicester City in war-time football aged 16
Hull City 1949-51
Manchester City 1951-56
Honours Footballer of the Year 1955
Sunderland 1956-58
Leeds United 1958-61
Internationals Six caps, 1955-57 (4 goals)

MANAGEMENT CAREER
Leeds United Manager 1961-74
Honours European Cup: Semi-final 1970
European Cup Winners Cup: Runners-up 1973
Fairs/Uefa Cup: Winners 1968, 1971; Runners-up 1967; Semi-finalists 1966; Fourth round 1969; Third round 1974
FA Cup: Winners 1972; Runners-up 1965, 1970 (after a replay), 1973; Semi-final 1967, 1968; Fifth round 1963, 1971, 1974; Fourth round 1964, 1966; Third round 1962, 1969
Second Division: Winners 1964
League Championship: Winners 1969, 1974; Runners-up 1965, 1966, 1970, 1971, 1972; Third 1973; Fourth 1967, 1968
League Cup: Winners 1968; Fourth round 1962, 1964, 1967, 1969, 1973; Third round 1963, 1965, 1966, 1970, 1972; Second round 1971, 1974
England Manager 1974-77
Died May 26, 1989

THE
1975-76
SEASON

Crackpot ideas wheeled out to crack down on hooliganism

ONE thing was getting to be certain. When the season kicked off the thugs on the terraces would be back, kicking each other and anybody else who got in their way.

But within weeks the violence took a frightening turn for the worse. So-called Chelsea fans, having failed to get their match with Luton abandoned by staging a pitch invasion when they were losing 3-0 and attacking the Luton goalkeeper, rampaged through the town and destroyed a train on the way back to London. On the same day, another train was halted at Crewe when hooligans set it on fire.

British Rail promptly stopped running football specials for the rest of the season and refused to sell cheap tickets until after 3pm on Saturdays. If fans wanted to travel, their club would have to charter a special train and be responsible for the damage.

Elsewhere, the reactions to violence were remarkably predictable. Don Revie, the England manager, called for the return of the birch, saying: "We have tried everything else, we might as well try this drastic deterrent." Eric Reed, the referee of the match between Chelsea and Luton agreed with him.

With a growing clamour for the introduction of identity cards, some people had more novel solutions. Dan Tana, the Brentford chairman, made a citizen's arrest of a troublemaker at one of his team's home matches. "Some louts used bad language," he said. "I was embarrassed so I nabbed the worst offender and handed him over to a policeman."

The Police Superintendents' Association even suggested that matches should be classified in the same way as films with fans under the age of 16 banned from "X-rated" games unless they were accompanied by an adult. Chelsea, with some of the worst problems, were not impressed with this bizarre proposal. "Who would decide which matches were selected?" Brian Mears, their chairman, asked.

West Ham attempt one escape act too many

Shell-shocked: Day conceded a hotly-disputed goal

WEST HAM made up for their indifferent domestic form by producing a series of inspired performances in the European Cup Winners Cup. But their travels were not without some strange moments.

In the second round they travelled to Armenia to play Ararat Erevan and were leading 1-0. Mervyn Day, their goalkeeper had hold of the ball and was about to throw it upfield when an Ararat player dived in and headed the ball out of his hands. Both men went down in a heap

and the ball trickled over the line. West Ham expected to be awarded a free kick for the foul on the goalkeeper but the West German referee allowed the equaliser to stand. That night West Ham's interpreter stunned his hosts at the post-match dinner by lecturing them on the importance of sportsmanship.

West Ham's finest performances came in the quarter-finals. Trailing 4-0 at half-time to Den Haag, they battled back to 4-2. Then, at Upton Park, they turned the tables, won 3-1 and went through on the away goals rule.

But West Ham could not pull off another great escape in the final, against Anderlecht in Belgium. Despite equalising twice they went down 4-2 to a vastly experienced side. Ironically, when West Ham had won the Cup Winners Cup in 1965 they had done it at "home" at Wembley. This time, too, the winners played in their own country.

> *Some of the players picked are donkeys. Give them a lump of sugar and they run all day and play bingo all night*
>
> ALAN BALL
> attacking Don Revie's choice of players for the England squad

Unimpressed: Mears scoffed at the police's ideas

Poor Newcastle founder on rock-solid Doyle

Opening shot: Barnes gives Manchester City the lead at Wembley in the League Cup final

BOTH Manchester City and Newcastle were back at Wembley for the second time in three years after having suffered setbacks there, and it was Newcastle who were to go home disappointed again.

The 30-year-old Mike Doyle was the cornerstone of Manchester City's 2-1 victory in the League Cup final. The veteran who had been to Wembley three times before was the backbone of City's defence and also created their first goal. At a well-rehearsed set piece he headed the ball down for Peter Barnes to score in the 12th minute.

Doyle looked to have City's defence well organised, but one moment of inattention allowed Alan Gowling in for a sweetly-taken equaliser. Dennis Tueart restored City's lead just after the interval with a spectacular overhead kick and that was the game all but over. Newcastle tried hard to get back on terms but Doyle's composure kept them at bay.

Bremner's shenanigans put him out in the cold

BILLY BREMNER, the captain of Scotland and Leeds, had his international career curtailed on September 8 when the Scottish selectors banned him and four other internationals from playing for their country for life. Bremner and the four players (Arthur Graham, Joe Harper, Pat McCluskey and Willie Young) were accused of incidents in a nightclub and then in the team's hotel in Copenhagen after Scotland's European championship qualifier against Denmark on September 3, which the Scots won with a Harper goal.

When the allegations occurred in the press, Bremner said: "I have heard about these rumours. They are nonsense. There was no row in the club, no fight, and no trouble about the bill. Anyway, what we do in our spare time is nothing to do with anybody else."

Despite his protestations, the Scottish selectors' committee relied on reports from officials and took their decision without calling on any of the five players to defend themselves. "I am staggered," Bremner said after the ban was announced, "I don't know if I shall be allowed to appeal."

Leeds also reprimanded Bremner, and warned him about his future conduct. For Bremner, 32 and capped 54 times for his country, his career in the top flight was effectively over and a year later he was transferred to Hull City in the Second Division.

Astounded: Bremner was banned for life by Scotland

137

THE
1975-76
SEASON

Bayern's third European title

BAYERN MUNICH confirmed their status as the No1 team in Europe when they beat St Etienne 1-0 in the European Cup final at Hampden in May. It was their third consecutive success and emulated Ajax's hat-trick of 1971-73.

St Etienne, the French champions, were formidable opponents although their classy international right-winger, Dominique Rocheteau, was recovering from a leg injury and only played as a substitute for the last eight minutes. But in midfielder Dominique Bathenay, the Argentinian centrehalf Osvaldo Piazza and the centre-forward Herve Revelli they had the resources to pose a serious threat.

Not that Bayern were a bunch of nonentities with Franz Beckenbauer at sweeper, Gerd Muller in attack and Karl-Heinz Rummenigge on the wing. The German champions had shown impressive form in reaching the final: Benfica were trounced 5-1 in Munich and Real Madrid 2-0.

The final lived up to expectations – St Etienne hit the bar twice in the first half – and was only settled by a single goal from Franz Roth in the 57th minute. From a free kick just outside the penalty area Roth pounced on the ball and blasted it past Ivan Curkovic, St Etienne's Yugoslav goalkeeper.

Bayern could have scored more than once, but Curkovic pulled off some remarkable saves – as did Sepp Maier at the other end. Rocheteau weaved his magic for the last few minutes but Maier was not going to allow the historic achievement to slip through Bayern's fingers.

Stokes sends Saints to heaven

Second best: Southampton emulate Sunderland's feat by overturning Manchester United

"SUNDERLAND" was the entire content of Tommy Docherty's team talk to his young Manchester United team before their FA Cup final against Second Division Southampton. Docherty's concern was self-explanatory: if Sunderland could pull off the Cup final shock of the century by beating Leeds in 1973, anything was possible. "It is the perfect warning to my lads," Docherty said. "To take nothing for granted."

Manchester United were in much the same predicament as Leeds had been three years previously: overwhelming First Division favourites against Second Division underdogs. There was more fearful symmetry: Leeds and Manchester United had finished third in the First Division with Sunderland and Southampton sixth in the Second Division. Unfortunately for Docherty and his tyros, the warning failed and symmetry triumphed, as Manchester United went down by exactly the same score – 1-0.

Bobby Stokes scored the all-important goal seven minutes from time, just as both legweary teams were mentally preparing themselves for the ordeal of extra time. Jim McCalliog, a former Manchester United player, executed a perfect through pass for Stokes, who despite thinking he might be offside, ran on with ball waiting for the whistle. The United defence froze. Alex Stepney, the goalkeeper, now the last line of hope, came out to cut off the angle, but Stokes nervelessly pushed the ball to the left past the diving Stepney.

United really had only themselves to blame, although if Sammy McIlroy's header in the 59th minute had gone in instead of hitting the top of bar it might well have been a different story. But for the team that had played such scintillating football throughout the season, and, just 10 days before this May Day confrontation, still had hopes of a League and Cup Double, it was a miserable performance.

The hallmarks of their football: pace and flair just were not there. Gordon Hill, one of their two orthodox wingers, played so badly he had to be taken off in the 66th minute. Lou Macari was similarly ineffectual. By contrast, Mike Channon and

Stokes: nerveless

Peter Osgood easily outshone their younger, and more illustrious, opponents. For the Southampton manager, Lawrie McMenemy, it was a moment to savour as his fans gave him an ovation. "It's not so long ago they were throwing things at me," he said.

Not even Celtic can halt Rangers

THE FIRST season of the revolutionary 10-club Premier Division in Scotland – initiated to make the League more competitive – resulted in a two-horse race for the championship: between Rangers and Celtic. After an initial burst by Rangers, Celtic led the table for much of the season until a dramatic collapse in April and May handed their rivals the title on plate.

Celtic had their problems with Jock Stein out of the manager's chair after his car crash in July and his assistant Sean Fallon having to deputise. But to win only one of the final seven League matches (losing four) with Rangers breathing down your neck is carelessness in the extreme.

Rangers, under the dictatorial control of Jock Wallace, went about the task of being the first Premier Division champions with military precision. Wallace

took the view that a winning settled side – whoever was in it – was the formula. So, once Wallace had found the winning formation he stuck to it. If that meant leaving Derek Parlane and Sandy Jardine on the bench, so be it.

Celtic's eclipse by Rangers had begun back in October when they lost the Scottish League Cup final to a second-half header from Alex MacDonald. By the end of the season the misery was piling on: they had failed to beat Rangers all season, losing two of their Premier matches by a single goal and drawing the other two. Then in May Rangers completed the Treble. And in style.

Derek Johnstone put Rangers ahead against Hearts after only 41 seconds. Johnstone had even made the chance by getting a free-kick from a Jim Jeffries foul. Johnstone soared above the Hearts defence to head

Johnstone: match winner

home. From then on it was one-way traffic. MacDonald extended the lead just before the interval and Johnstone secured the victory nine minutes from time. A Graham Shaw tap-in kept the score to 3-1.

Heavyweight clubs upstaged by lightweight rivals

THE FA Cup was obviously fated to be an upset year the moment the results of the first round came through: six League clubs had been beaten by non-League opposition and another four could only muster draws. Then, in the third round in January, the previous year's finalists, West Ham and Fulham, also fell by the wayside.

Meanwhile the heavyweight opposition were knocking each other out. Derby disposed of Liverpool, Everton and Newcastle before themselves succumbing to Manchester United in the semi-final. Wolves flattened Arsenal and Ipswich before Manchester United laid them low in a sixth round replay. And Stoke toppled Tottenham Hotspur and Manchester City, until they ran into Second Division Sunderland.

The carnage was such that the last 16 in the competition were seven clubs from the First Division, seven from the Second Division, one from the Third and one from the Fourth. And

Capital punishment: Crystal Palace beat Chelsea 3-2 en route to the semi-final

on it went. Bradford knocked out Norwich 2-1 with an 87th minute goal to become only the third Fourth Division club to reach the sixth round. Crystal Palace went one better and progressed to the semi-finals and became the fourth Third Divi-

sion club since the war to do so.

Their semi-final against Second Division Southampton at Stamford Bridge was disparaged by Manchester United's manager Tommy Docherty, whose team were facing Derby in the other semi-final. "This is

the first time that the Cup final will be played at Hillsborough," he said. "The other semi-final is a bit of a joke, really." For all the little clubs who had battled so hard on the road to Wembley, Southampton gave them the last laugh.

THE 1975-76 SEASON

Taylor and Lincoln fit like two peas in a pod

GRAHAM TAYLOR repaid his chairman's faith as Lincoln produced a record-breaking season to race away with the Fourth Division title. When Taylor's playing career was cut short by a hip injury in 1972 the Lincoln chairman appointed Taylor the manager of the club. Half of the board opposed the move, because of Taylor's lack of experience – at 28 he was the youngest manager in the League.

The journeyman defender took to management like a duck to water and fostered a remarkable spirit at the club. His insistence on developing links with the local community brought the crowds flocking back to Sincil Bank, and the supporters were rewarded by greatly improved performances.

"We concentrate on doing the simple things well," Taylor said. And Lincoln played remarkably well. They were unbeaten at home, only lost four games away, scored 111 goals and finished with a record 74 points.

Pressure increases on dithering Revie

THE FACT that Czechoslovakia, who qualified for the European championship quarter-finals instead of England, eventually triumphed in the final against West Germany, the world champions, was scant consolation to England and Don Revie. His failure, hard on the heels of Sir Alf Ramsey's failure to make it to the World Cup finals in 1974, meant that press and public were baying for his blood.

Revie's tenure, in place of the disgraced Ramsey, had begun brightly enough. England had beaten Czechoslovakia 3-0 at Wembley, West Germany 2-0, hammered Cyprus 5-0, and had won the Home international championship by demolishing Scotland 5-1. At the end of his first season, Revie's record was: P8, W5, D3, L0. So far, so good.

But was it? Along the way England drew 0-0 with Portugal at Wembley in a pitiful display against a packed Portuguese defensive midfield. Czechoslovakia thundered five past the hapless Portuguese. Moreover, it was clear that Revie was prone to dithering. In the eight matches only Dave Watson was an ever-present as Revie anxiously rotated 27 other players, unsettling the squad.

In Bratislava, England went ahead courtesy of Mick Channon, but still lost 2-1 to the Czechs. A handsome win in Lisbon was essential – the significance of the goalless draw at Wembley against Portugal finally sinking in – but in the end England were fortunate to scrape a 1-1 draw. Czechoslovakia completed the formalities by winning in Cyprus 3-0.

Flashpoint: Brian Flynn restrains a fan after Toshack's goal was disallowed at Ninian Park

To rub matters in, Wales – the only British country to do so – comfortably qualified for the quarter-finals, beating Hungary home and away in the process. Their opponents in the quarter-finals were Yugoslavia.

Wales lost the first leg 2-0 away and faced a stern task in the return leg at Ninian Park, made worse when Yugoslavia took the lead from a penalty. Ian Evans equalised just before half-time. Then 20 minutes into the second half the East German referee disallowed a Welsh goal, spectators invaded the pitch, beer cans were thrown and play was suspended for five minutes. When play was resumed, another Welsh goal was disallowed and a Terry Yorath penalty was saved. Four players were booked, the police had to escort the referee from the field, and Wales were ignominiously dumped out of the semi-finals.

The semi-finals, both played in Yugoslavia, threw up the intriguing possibility of a repeat of the 1974 World Cup final: Holland v West Germany. In the event Czechoslovakia easily disposed of Holland 3-1 after extra time (the Dutch goal coming from a fortuitous deflection) and West Germany somehow scrambled past Yugoslavia.

Spurred on by their partisan crowd, the hosts annihilated the normally rock-solid defence to hold an easy 2-0 lead at half-time. But complacency set in and, with two astute substitutions, the West Germans had levelled by full-time. In the extra period, Yugoslav despair at having squandered such an advantage set in and West Ger-

many ran in another two goals.

In the final, Czechoslovakia, now clearly on a roll, rattled in two goals and once again the West Germans were on the rack. Gerd Muller managed to pull one back before half-time. It was enough to put the world champions back into the game as the Czechs visibly tired. A dubious equaliser (it appeared the Czech keeper was fouled) forced yet another match into extra time, and, despite another Czech onslaught, there were no more goals.

In the penalty shoot-out, seven shots went in, then Uli Hoeness blazed his shot over the bar. Panenka, of Czechoslovakia, stepped up to take the kick that would win the trophy. The West German goalkeeper went the right way, but Panenka coolly lofted the ball over him.

Paisley gets it right as Liverpool thrive on their never-say-die spirit

BOB PAISLEY, in his second season in charge, collected his second trophy when Liverpool completed the double of the League and the Uefa Cup for the second time. And, as had happened in the League, Liverpool were taken right to the wire.

Liverpool's spirits were lifted in the semi-final when they went to the formidable Nou Camp and beat the Barcelona of Johann Cryuff and Johann Neeskens 1-0. A 1-1 draw at Anfield was enough to take them to the final against Bruges.

Everything looked lost when Bruges raced into a 2-0 lead at Anfield after just 12 minutes. Liverpool, though, came storming back in the second half with three goals in five minutes, a long-range effort from Ray Kennedy, a close-in shot from Case and finally a penalty from Keegan.

The second leg was every bit as gripping. Bruges took another early lead, which meant that although the scores were level they had the advantage on the away goals rule. Keegan quickly scored yet again, bending a shot past the goalkeeper from a free kick, and the battle was really on.

Bruges were relentless in their pursuit of the winning goal

Clemence: vital save

Case: vital goal

and Liverpool were forced to pull almost everybody apart from Keegan back into defence. Somehow Liverpool always seemed to be able to block the ball at the vital moment although there was one last scare to come when Clemence was forced to make a great save with just a few minutes to go.

So Paisley had silenced the

doubters who thought he would not be able to fill Bill Shankly's shoes. However, it was not a vintage season for Liverpool. Too often they were dependent on Keegan and John Toshack – or even David Fairclough, who seemed to work miracles every time he came off the bench. So much so that he earned himself the title "Super Sub".

QPR's run fizzles out short of the winning post

QPR's home victory over Liverpool on the first Saturday of the season was widely thought to be a flash in the pan; most commentators regarded it as two points dropped by Bob Paisley's Liverpool rather than a good result by Rangers.

How wrong they were. QPR were unbeaten in their first 10 matches and led the First Division at the end of September. Everybody seemed surprised by the unfashionable club's start, but it was not as unexpected as it appeared.

Dave Sexton had a formidable array of talent at his dis-

posal: Phil Parkes, Frank McLintock, David Webb, Don Masson, Gerry Francis, John Hollins, David Thomas, Don Givens and Stan Bowles. The majority were international players, and Francis had just been appointed the England captain.

But Sexton also had two problems. Stan Bowles was unsettled – constantly asking for a transfer because his wife was homesick for the north – and his team did not have the experience of having been involved in a close title race before.

A bad patch either side of

Christmas saw them slip to fifth in the table and it began to look as if they were going to be a flash in the pan after all. But Sexton steadied the ship and QPR had a remarkable second half of the season, winning 13 of their last 15 matches. The game that would come back to haunt them was a 3-2 defeat at Norwich in April.

Liverpool, though, were past masters of the close finish and they were never more than a point or two behind. QPR finished their programme 10 days before Liverpool and held a one point advantage which meant

that everything depended on Liverpool's final game, at Wolverhampton.

When Wolves took an early lead and were still ahead with 15 minutes left there were echoes of 1972, when Leeds had lost the title at Molineux. Liverpool, though, drew on all their reserves of experience and three late goals brought them a record ninth championship. QPR, despite their great finish, were left to reflect on what might have been had they not lost to Norwich, although second place was their highest ever finish.

THE 1976-77 SEASON

Wayward Macari accidentally changes course of history

LIVERPOOL could point to end of season fixture congestion for their downfall in the FA Cup final on May 21, but there was no denying that Manchester United were determined to lay

Aerial combat: Pearson and Case battle for supremacy

the ghost of their defeat by Southampton the year before.

Liverpool had had an easy passage to the final and were clear favourites to complete the second leg of their Treble. But Tommy Docherty's Manchester United, despite a slightly suspect defence, were capable of playing top-quality football.

With both sides equally matched the game was finely balanced for the first half. Although Liverpool appeared to have an advantage in midfield they went behind in the 50th minute when Stuart Pearson scored a somewhat fortunate goal.

His low shot should not have posed too many problems for a goalkeeper of Ray Clemence's calibre, but somehow Clemence let the ball slip under his body. The goal brought the game to life and within two minutes Liverpool had equalised when

Jimmy Case crashed a shot into the top corner.

If Manchester United's first goal was slightly lucky there was no doubt that their second, three minutes later, was a fluke. Even Jimmy Greenhoff, the scorer, admitted as much. His shot rebounded off a defender into the path of Lou Macari. With Macari having a clear chance of scoring, Greenhoff decided to get out of his way. But Macari mis-hit his shot, which was going well wide until it cannoned off the retreating Greenhoff and ballooned over Clemence's head.

For once, Liverpool's control of midfield could not bring them another goal. As Manchester United celebrated at the final whistle, Bob Paisley was left to console his players and try to lift their spirits at a moment when it seemed that their dream was about to turn into a nightmare.

One certainty for managers – getting the sack

IT WAS a bad time for managers. Among the most notable names to vacate the hot seat were Tony Waddington, who had been Stoke's manager since 1960; Bob Stokoe, who had guided Sunderland to their 1973 FA Cup triumph and promotion to the First Division last season; and Fulham's legendary Alec Stock.

As Johnny Giles pointed out when he quit West Bromwich Albion in April: "In the last 10 months 33 League clubs have changed managers. The directors have power without responsibility. The government should issue a health warning to managers: the only certain thing is the sack."

His former teammate at Leeds, Jack Charlton, who quit Middlesbrough the day after Giles at WBA, was also disenchanted with the game. But his discontent was aimed at Middlesbrough's lukewarm fans rather than his directors. Hav-

Giles: health warning

ing guided the North East club to the First Division in his first season in charge in 1974 and to the top of the table in October, he had seen attendances slump from around 25,000 to 14,000 in weeks as Middlesbrough gravitated to a comfortable mid-table position.

Early casualty: Stokoe and Sunderland part company

142

Hearts hit the self-destruct button

FOR the first time in their 103-year history proud Hearts were relegated. Yet inexplicably they reached the semi-finals of both the Scottish Cup and League Cup. Quite how their Cup form deserted them in the League is a mystery that Willie Ormond, their new manager having retired from his post as the national manager, will have to solve if Hearts are to immediately bounce back into the Premier Division.

Their start in the League, although indifferent – they drew seven, and won one of their first 10 matches – did not presage the horror that was to come by the season's end. In the next 21 matches Hearts effectively cut their own throats losing on 14 occasions. Although they won two and drew three of their last five games it was all too late, and they went down with Kilmarnock. Ayr United, the other candidates for relegation, had effectively rescued themselves with a dramatic burst of form in March and April.

At the other end of the table it was business as usual with Celtic crowned as champions, and Rangers occupying the runners-up spot. Celtic were runaway champions and it was obvious by the beginning of the year that nobody could realistically overhaul them. They eventually finished eight points ahead of Rangers, who had mounted a thrilling late run of six consecutive victories to steal second place.

They were less fortunate in the Scottish Cup final where they succumbed 1-0 to Celtic, allowing their rivals to complete the Double. Celtic's goal came as early as the 20th minute, when Derek Johnstone handled Kenny Dalglish's chip and Andy Lynch converted the penalty. The Rangers strike force was muted in the rain-sodden conditions, although Chris Robertson, who came on as a substitute, twice went close to scoring the equaliser.

It was a poor final though memorable for two historic footnotes. It was live on television, which many blamed for the poor attendance of 54,000 – the worst for over 50 years; and Alfie Conn, playing for Celtic, became the first player to win the Cup with both Old Firm sides. He had been on Rangers' Cup-winning side in 1973 when they beat Celtic 3-2. Two Old Firm Cup finals and each time on a different winning team!

Celtic also made another piece of history when they reached the League Cup final for the 13th consecutive year. Aberdeen spoiled the celebrations by winning the trophy 3-2 in extra time with a goal from David Robb. It was their first League Cup triumph since the season of 1955-56.

Villa's Little finally ends 330-minute stalemate

WEMBLEY was starting to feel like home from home for Ron Saunders. For the fourth time in five years he was back there for a League Cup final. His record so far was two losses (with Norwich in 1973 and Manchester City in 1974) and one win (with Aston Villa in 1975).

This time he left with a draw as Aston Villa were held 0-0 by Everton. The replay, four days later, also ended all square although Everton scored both goals – Roger Kenyon's own goal being cancelled out by Bob Latchford's scrambled effort in the 90th minute.

The second replay provided more excitement than both the previous games put together. Everton led with 10 minutes to go; Aston Villa equalised then took the lead a minute later; then two minutes after that Everton forced the game into extra time once again. Matters were finally resolved when Brian Little scored his second goal to give Saunders his second trophy after 330 minutes of largely unimpressive toil.

Evasive action: John Burridge ducks under Duncan McKenzie

Liverpool rise to the occasion

BOB PAISLEY had assembled a settled side at Liverpool, and his team appeared to be making serene progress towards a fabulous Treble of the League, the FA Cup and the European Cup.

Apart from one brief spell around Christmas, Liverpool were hardly troubled in the League. They only lost two of their first 16 games, and although they could never totally shake off the pursuing Ipswich and Manchester City, they took the title with a game to spare, thanks to a sequence that saw them only lose two matches from the start of February to the end of the season.

Bob Paisley, who had been given a job for life, faced his toughest challenge in lifting the team's morale after Liverpool were beaten by Manchester United in the FA Cup final. His players responded magnificently.

The European Cup final against Borussia Moenchengladbach in Rome on May 25, a mere four days after the FA Cup final, was widely acclaimed as the greatest game in recent history. Liverpool's performance was regarded as even more phenomenal than their victory over St Etienne in the quarter-final.

Liverpool trailed 1-0 to the French club after the first leg, and the return match was one of the most electrifying ever seen at Anfield. Kevin Keegan's lob after two minutes levelled the aggregate score, but St Etienne, roared on by their supporters' chants of "Allez les Verts", pounded the Liverpool goal. Both teams left the pitch to a standing ovation at half-time.

Bathenay scored for St Etienne and Ray Kennedy struck back, but Liverpool were facing elimination on the away goals rule. With the Kop mimicking the French fans by shouting "Allez les Reds" the stage was set for David Fairclough. With eight minutes to go, Liverpool's Super Sub ran half the length of the pitch, waltzed past two defenders and scored one of the best individual goals seen at Anfield.

Emlyn Hughes described the match as the most exciting he had ever played in, but it was nothing compared with the final. Liverpool played sublime football and took the lead with a goal from Terry McDermott. But Allan Simonsen equalised for Borussia early in the second half and then it was the Germans' turn to dominate.

It looked to be only a matter of time before the Liverpool defence gave way but the turning point was yet another brilliant save by Ray Clemence. The Germans started to lose heart and Liverpool came storming back. Steve Heighway's corner eluded the flailing Borussia goalkeeper and up popped Tommy Smith of all people to head a vital goal.

Liverpool were now rampant and Borussia were totally unable to contain Keegan. When he was chopped down by Berti Vogts in the 83rd minute, Phil Neal's penalty put the result beyond doubt. The disappointments of Wembley were forgotten as the Liverpool fans painted the town red. The celebrations lasted long into the night and nobody was complaining when the Liverpool fans found the team's hideaway and joyously threw several Liverpool players into the hotel swimming pool.

Mighty atom: Keegan gives Vogts the slip again

You'll never walk alone: the Kop moved lock, stock and barrel to Rome

Scots wreck Wembley

Tartan terrors: rampaging Scots tear down the goal

Treble chancers: Macdonald and Francis were hat-trick heroes

THE biennial invasion of Wembley by Scotland's travelling army of fans truly was an invasion. After the 2-1 defeat of England, hordes of drunken Scottish fans, bedecked in tartan scarves and caps, charged across the pitch to fete their victorious players

Then they turned their attention to the goalposts (tearing them down and ripping out the nets) and the Wembley turf (carving pieces out of it to take home as souvenirs). During the weekend of June 4, 132 Scots were arrested and some £18,000 of damage caused at Wembley with both goals broken, goalmouths bereft of turf, and terraces littered with thousands of broken bottles and discarded beer cans.

Although the victory was only their fifth on English soil since 1938 and meant that Scotland had retained the Home championship, it was hard to understand what had so excited the Scottish fans, aside from large amounts of alcohol.

It was not a memorable match as England were missing two key players, Kevin Keegan and Trevor Brooking. The Scots were deserving winners, with Danny McGrain, Kenny Dalglish and Lou Macari the outstanding players. Gordon McQueen had given them the lead three minutes before half-time when he headed home Don Masson's free-kick, Dalglish made it 2-0 in the 60th minute, and Mick Channon scored an 87th minute penalty to make the score somewhat more respectable.

Immediate calls were made to ban travelling Scottish fans from all England-Scotland matches at Wembley. Ted Croker, the FA secretary, went further and said: "The ground will be fenced in by November for the Italy match." Quite why he thought that the Scots would come to Wembley to see England v Italy in a World Cup qualifier was perplexing. Or was he just intending to punish English fans for Scottish transgressions?

Wimbledon reap benefit of heroic Cup exploits

WIMBLEDON were finally granted their just reward when they won election to the League at Workington's expense on June 17. The Southern League champions proved their credentials with another stirring performance in the FA Cup, which convinced the delegates at the League's annual meeting that their performances against Burnley and Leeds in 1975 were not a flash in the pan.

Once again Wimbledon showed that they were a match for anybody in the country. Although they reached the third round by beating two other non-League sides, they more than held their own against First Division Middlesbrough. After being restricted to a 0-0 draw at Plough Lane, the best that the Middlesbrough manager Jack Charlton could do was blame the playing surface. Charlton accused Wimbledon of deliberately neglecting their pitch and said: "We couldn't play football today. The replay will show whether Wimbledon are able to play – little or not."

The replay showed that Wimbledon could, indeed, play. Three days later they went down by a single goal at Ayresome Park, and that was a penalty.

Wimbledon were not going to let their new-found status go to their heads, though. The club had been run on a shoestring for a long time and Dickie Guy, their goalkeeper and the hero against Leeds, said that the players were still prepared to play as part-timers.

Traitor Revie deserts England

Bowles blazes dazzling trail across Europe

QPR's first foray into Europe, although it did not provide a trophy, was a more than a creditable success. Indeed Stan Bowles' scoring wizardry proved so bewitching that he finished, with 11 goals, as the Uefa Cup's leading scorer and broke the British record for a European tournament.

Bowles got off to a cracking start against Brann Bergen scoring a hat-trick in both legs of the first-round tie as QPR thrashed the Norwegian side 11-0 on aggregate. Bowles continued in cracking form knocking in another three goals against Slovan Bratislava in the next round.

With Derby and Manchester United knocked out of the Uefa Cup by AEK Athens and Juventus, QPR were the sole British representatives left in the competition and their third round opponents, Cologne, were no pushovers. But once again Bowles inspired the west London club and his brilliant final goal gave them a 3-0 lead to take to West Germany.

And they needed that extra cushion. At half-time QPR were 3-1 adrift and down to 10 men after Dave Clement's dismissal. Yet they held on to squeak through 4-4 on the away goals rule. Their luck ran out against AEK Athens.

A pair of 3-0 results, with Gerry Francis scoring two penalties in his first European match and Bowles his 11th goal, meant a penalty shoot-out. Both sides scored with four of their first five penalties but in the sudden-death stage David Webb's attempt was saved and QPR's adventure was over.

UNLIKE his predecessor, Sir Alf Ramsey, Don Revie didn't wait to be pushed out of his job as the England manager – he jumped. However the manner of his departure shocked the nation and the FA when they learnt from a newspaper that Revie had secretly, and deceptively, found himself another job before quitting his England post.

Ostensibly Revie had gone to Helsinki to watch Italy – England's opponents in a crucial World Cup qualifying match in November – play Finland while his England squad were enjoying a successful summer tour in South America. In reality Revie had gone to Dubai and negotiated a £340,000 tax free four-year contract to manage the United Arab Emirates. Revie's deception did not stop there.

Before he formally resigned, Revie privately approached the FA and, because of the "heartache" the job was causing him and his wife, offered "to save trouble and go" if they paid up the rest of his contract (£50,000) and gave him a £50,000 golden handshake. Because Manchester United had suddenly sacked Tommy Docherty and there was speculation that Revie might be offered the post, they asked Revie directly if he had another job lined up. Revie denied that he had, but the FA still spurned his offer.

Then on July 13, the day after the Daily Mail had exclusively revealed Revie's sudden decision to quit, the same paper revealed his deal with the UAE. The FA were outraged and charged Revie with acting deceitfully and damaging the image of football. Revie refused to attend the subsequent FA hearing and they promptly suspended him from any involvement with football under the FA's jurisdiction until he did so.

Revie was then given a 10-year ban for "bringing the game into disrepute", but in 1979 he successfully overturned this in the High Court because of the probable bias of Sir Harold Thompson, the FA chairman,

Take the money and run: Revie fled to the Middle East

during Revie's disciplinary hearing.

Although the whole affair stunned and dismayed the nation, Revie's decision to pack in the England job after three years was, in itself, no surprise. In that time he had managed England for 29 internationals, winning 14 and losing seven; failed to take them past the European championship qualifying stages and was, barring miracles, poised to see them fail to reach the World Cup finals in Argentina.

Revie, although an extremely successful manager with Leeds – winning two League titles, the FA Cup, the Fairs Cup and reaching the European Cup final – had painfully discovered the huge chasm between international and club management.

Brian Clough was immediately installed as the people's choice to replace him. But Clough, controversial, single-minded and outspoken was not exactly the FA's cup of tea. Diplomatically, they did decide to interview him and were taken aback with his performance – he almost convinced them to give him the job. Caution prevailed however and Ron Greenwood, the avuncular manager of West Ham, who had taken over as a caretaker manager after Revie's sudden departure, was confirmed as national manager in December.

Adulterous Docherty gets the sack

THE colourful and controversial career of Tommy Docherty took another bizarre twist when Manchester United sacked him as their manager on July 4, six weeks after he had led them to triumph in the FA Cup final. Docherty's fault lay not in what he had done on the pitch, but in his behaviour off it. Ten days earlier Docherty had publicly announced that he was leaving his wife and four children to live with Mary Brown, the wife of the United physiotherapist, Laurie Brown. It was a bombshell for a club renowned for its links with Catholicism.

Docherty had explained that this decision had been a difficult and painful one and that his relationship with Mrs Brown was not a casual one – their affair had been going on for some three years. If Docherty had hoped that by bringing his situation into the open he would kill press interest in his personal

> *I have been punished for falling in love. What I have done has got nothing at all to do with my track record as a manager*
>
> TOMMY DOCHERTY

life, he was very much mistaken. If anything it fanned the flames.

The popular press besieged Old Trafford and Docherty's home and the details of his love affair were all over the news pages. As the story raged on the support Docherty had received from the club ebbed away until Louis Edwards, the Manchester United chairman – 24 hours after he had said that Docherty's departure was nonsense – finally bowed to the inevitable.

Docherty was officially dismissed for transgressing the club's "moral code", but one

newspaper claimed that club wives had been instrumental in the sacking. Dave Sexton (who had been released by QPR at his own request) was a quiet, dependable and uncontroversial replacement.

Docherty, who had been the first manager since Sir Matt Busby to bring success to the club, had, in a way, brought this debacle on himself. If he hadn't, because of his outrageous quips and larger-than-life persona not been a household name, it is unlikely that the press would have taken such a passionate interest in something that is, after all, commonplace.

He soon bounced back and the man who had managed Chelsea, Rotherham, Aston Villa, Porto and Scotland, took over the reins at Derby County. The irrepressible Scot was once again confirming one of his one-liners: "I've had more clubs than Jack Nicklaus."

Dalglish steps into Keegan's boots

Smooth succession: Dalglish was Keegan's perfect replacement

NOBODY could understand it when Bob Paisley signed David Johnson from Ipswich just before the start of the season. Why, they wondered, did Liverpool need yet another player when they already had an abundance of riches?

The answer was quite simple, although for most of the season it was a well-guarded secret. Kevin Keegan wanted to move to Europe and one leading club, Real Madrid, had already approached Liverpool with a sizeable offer. Paisley, though, struck a bargain with Keegan: if Keegan stopped at Liverpool for one more season then the club would not stand in the way of him going abroad. As a result, Johnson was being bought as a potential replacement.

Liverpool kept their end of the bargain and the European Cup final was Keegan's swansong before he moved to SV Hamburg for a record £500,000. The deal made Keegan the highest paid English footballer of all time, but Paisley still had his

doubts: He said: "I wouldn't play a man for England if he is with a foreign club. We have to fight against this trend of losing our best players."

Paisley also had his doubts about Johnson. To allay his fans' fears about the loss of Keegan he spent the bulk of the money, £440,000 to buy Kenny Dalglish from Celtic days before the Charity Shield. The deal broke the transfer record between British clubs and as one star had been gone out another was about to be born.

147

JOHANN CRUYFF
Dutch conquistador still to vanquish the world

Steve Coppell

I REMEMBER the evening well, December 7 1966, huddled around a crackling radio with fading batteries. I was with a group of fellow Liverpool fans when the result came through from Holland: Ajax 5 Liverpool 1. Surely not. It must have been a mistake. Liverpool never lost 5-1 to anybody. What would Shankly say?

The next morning the newspapers revealed the thoughts of the great man. Liverpool were not beaten 5-1 by Ajax, they were beaten 5-1 by the fog! Shankly had been told that because Holland was flat the Dutch were used to playing in the fog and that explained the result. The return leg a week later would be a different story.

That game was the first time I saw Johann Cruyff, one of the best players I have ever seen. Right from the first whistle, I was transfixed by the way the 19 year old glided around the pitch and even at this early stage he was always pointing the way for others.

"Where did 'e come from?" was the most commonly used expression from the Anfield crowd that night. The final score was 2-2 (7-3 on aggregate) and without doubt I had witnessed not only the early days of a great footballing career, but also the embryo of an orchestrated, yet utterly fluid style of play which would make a significant impact on world football for the next two generations.

The zenith of Cruyff's playing career was a prolonged four-year spell in the early 1970s when he could apparently do no wrong. Domestic success was followed by three successive European Cup triumphs with Ajax. In 1974 he moved to Barcelona, who at that time were in lower mid-table. A few months later, after a 20-game unbeaten run, they were the Spanish champions. A couple of months after this, Cruyff was leading his country out in the World Cup final against West Germany.

Although Holland lost that final, at 27 Johann Cruyff had achieved more on the football field than he ever could have imagined. At this point in his career it seems financial reward, rather than success on the football pitch, took over. Cruyff had come from a modest background, so his concern over financial insecurity was understandable.

But his priorities were regrettable. Barcelona reportedly paid a £400,000 signing-on fee to bring him to Spain and every season after his transfer he was campaigning, striving and cajoling to win new contracts and a higher salary. Cruyff's brilliance captivated the huge Barça faithful, but unfortunately it was chimerical. Real Madrid, Barcelona's arch rivals, walked away with the subsequent two League titles.

Cruyff, the maestro of the Total Football strategy by which Holland had enthralled the world in 1974, also became a control freak. He became embroiled in the delirious politics of hiring and firing. Coaches and players fought, and lost, verbal wars with Cruyff until he surrounded himself with a coterie he could manipulate. Unfortunately, total control did not bring success, and a temperamental star who does not deliver the silverware has a short shelf-life, especially in Spain.

Having alienated the Catalan public, Cruyff then enraged the Dutch nation by refusing to play in the 1978 World Cup finals in Argentina. The man in control wanted to finish his career at the top and did not wish to risk his lofty position by going to South America. Many Dutch still feel today that Cruyff would have made all the difference. Without him Holland still reached the World Cup final for the second tournament in succession, and lost in extra time. If their greatest

---

Tactical genius: Cruyff was the maestro of Holland's total football strategy in the 1970s

JOHANN CRUYFF

Born April 25, 1947, Amsterdam

PLAYING CAREER

Ajax Amsterdam 1964-73
Joined Ajax in 1957 as a 10-year-old, and made his debut in 1964; played for Ajax until 1973, winning six League titles, four Cups, three European Cups

Barcelona 1973-78
Honours One League title and one Cup

LA Aztecs 1978-79

Washington Diplomats 1979-80

Levante 1981

Ajax Amsterdam 1982-83
Honours Two League titles, one Cup

Internationals Made his debut for Holland on September 7, 1966 v Hungary and scored once in a 2-2 draw in Rotterdam. Played for Holland until 1978, collecting 48 caps, and scoring 33 goals. Runner-up at the 1974 World Cup

Other honours European Footballer of the Year in 1971, 1973 and 1974

MANAGEMENT CAREER

Feyenoord Player-manager 1983-84
Honours One League title and one Cup

Ajax Amsterdam Manager 1986-88
Honours One European Cup Winners Cup and two Cups

Barcelona Manager 1988-
Honours One European Cup, one European Cup Winners Cup, four League titles and one Cup

player had deigned to grace the occasion, surely they would have won? Instead Holland are forever burdened with being known as the best team never to have won the World Cup.

The Indian sunset of his playing career took place at home in Holland where he won League championships first with Ajax and then Feyenoord. Inevitably a contract dispute brought about his unthinkable transfer from Ajax to rivals Feyenoord.

I was fortunate enough to be living in Holland during this period and I could savour his performances on a regular basis. He was brilliant and transformed an average Feyenoord side into champions. Incidentally, a young player in the side at this time was Ruud Gullit who, according to Cruyff's whims, alternated from sweeper to the right wing.

It would be easy to conclude that Cruyff was a brilliant footballer who was a mercenary megalomaniac. His decision to move into coaching proved that he was also a missionary of sorts. I have always felt that Dutch football was technically and tactically the most advanced in the world, but particularly suited to the Dutch mentality. Cruyff's teams took this distinction to another level again, and he had the will and the coaching ability to have this style adopted successfully by the very different mentality of the Catalan.

It is difficult to describe playing styles on paper but simply I would say English teams play structured, formal football almost rectangular, brick-wall style. German and Italian teams – with obvious character differences – are strong and difficult to beat. Their emphasis is on defence so both can be likened to a triangle with a very solid foundation.

Cruyff's teams defy description. They are rotational, flowing and changing, but the emphasis is on attack. Only two players have strict

Seeking his fortune: Cruyff was a cultivated, and inspirational, player for Barcelona

defensive responsibilities, everybody else is encouraged to attack. Yet he rarely uses a conventional centre-forward. Hence the controversy with first Lineker and more recently Stoichkov, both natural goal-scoring centre-forwards who, in the Cruyff style, had to attack from wide positions. In Cruyff's teams the players conform to the style, and the style wins.

He has coached both Ajax and Barcelona to European Cup Winners Cup triumphs. But the crowning of Cruyff was his four successive Spanish League titles (1990-94) and the capture of the European Cup in 1992, a trophy Barcelona had never won. Indeed it was only their third European Cup final. To the Catalans, Cruyff had delivered the Holy Grail, the trophy that Real Madrid from 1956 to 1960 had made their own personal property. At a stroke, Cruyff the coach had erased all his failings as a Barcelona player.

Now, he only has one thing left to win and that is the prize that eluded him as a player, the World Cup. It was not surprising that once again money thwarted his highest achievement. Once Holland had qualified for the World Cup finals in America the plan was for Cruyff to take over the national side from Dick Advocaat. But squabbles over his remuneration with the Dutch FA quickly scuppered that notion.

Given the quality of players at his disposal, and their already well-voiced support of him, Holland would have been among the favourites to win the trophy in 1994 and finally lose that unwelcome tag of being the Nearly Men of world football. But once again rows over money, an

issue that seems to have split Dutch teams time and again, resurfaced.

As a player, and as a coach, certainly at club level, Johann Cruyff has had the biggest influence over European football for the last 25 years. It will be interesting to see if he finds it in himself to conquer that last horizon: the World Cup.

Crowning glory: the European Cup in 1992

In the hot seat: Barcelona's manager

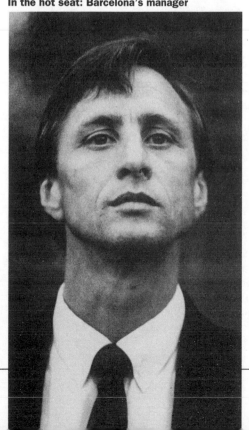

Chairmen call players' bluff in strike threat

MANY PLAYERS were still deeply unhappy about their lot, and days before the season started more than 100 of them in the Midlands voted in favour of industrial action over their dispute about freedom of contract. Within days, the PFA had received further support from other areas of the country.

Lawrie McMenemy, the Southampton manager, was dismissive of the threat. "The players will never go on strike," he said. "They are too apathetic." Other clubs were more alert to the danger and an extraordinary meeting of the League was called to try to prevent a showdown.

Prompted by Jimmy Hill, the clubs agreed a compromise although the players were not convinced because the League said it would not announce the details until later in the season. When the details finally emerged in April, players discovered that they were free to choose between clubs, providing the clubs involved agreed a transfer fee. If the clubs could not agree then the case would go to an independent tribunal.

The PFA were far from impressed. Cliff Lloyd, their secretary, said: "This is a long way from what we wanted. The position remains unchanged. Players are completely in the hands of the clubs."

John Lacy became one of the first players to put the new process to the test when he moved from Fulham to Tottenham in July. The tribunal ruled that the fee should be £200,000, £50,000 less than the sum Fulham had demanded.

Scotland's World Cup dream turns into a Welsh nightmare

SCOTLAND were the only country from the British Isles to qualify for the World Cup finals in Argentina, and they booked their tickets to South America at the expense of Wales. England predictably were edged out by Italy on goal difference, but that outcome was virtually certain before Don Revie's infamous desertion to the Middle East in July 1977.

Although Czechoslovakia were the other team in the Scotland-Wales group, it always looked as qualification was between the British pair after Wales had beaten Czechoslovakia 3-0 in March 1977. Then, when Scotland also beat the Czechs, 3-1, in September, they were in the driving seat. If they beat Wales away in October they were through, a draw would mean Wales would have to win in Prague in November to displace them from the finals, while a defeat would require Wales to draw against the Czechs.

The crucial match was played at Anfield because none of the Welsh stadiums met the requisite safety standards, but despite the disadvantage of playing a "home" game away, the Welsh were much the better side and looked the more likely to score. However with 12 minutes remaining the French referee awarded a penalty for a disputed handball. Don Masson converted and Scottish fans in the capacity crowd went delirious. Television replays however showed that the referee had got it wrong. Three minutes from time, a scintillating header from Kenny Dalglish put the result beyond doubt.

Mike Smith, the Wales manager, was crestfallen: "None of my players handled the ball. Words cannot describe how we feel losing a match after putting up such an historic fight."

On the same night England's slender hopes evaporated when they could only beat Luxembourg 2-0 away. Qualification now rested on beating Italy at

Man on the spot: Masson sealed Wales's fate

Wembley in November and praying Luxembourg could sneak a draw in Italy in December. Otherwise Italy would go through on goal difference, and so it proved. England won 2-0, but Italy trounced Luxembourg by 3-0.

England's failure rested not on the two matches with Italy, the two countries exchanged 2-0 victories, but their inability to run up big scores against the minnows of Luxembourg and Finland. The result that certainly damned them was the woeful 2-1 victory over Finland at Wembley in October 1976. Italy, a year later, hammered the Scandinavians 6-1 and took control of their destiny.

Italy's results will be more crucial than the number of goals England score

RON GREENWOOD
the England manager, two months before Italy qualified on goal difference

United kick off with an own goal

French fracas: United's fans shamed the club in Europe and incurred Uefa's wrath

MANCHESTER UNITED'S foray into Europe brought shame on the club before their first match had started on September 14. The Cup Winners Cup first round match against St Etienne had not kicked off when fighting erupted at the French ground. Riot police stormed the terrace and it was nearly half an hour before the unrest was quelled, although there were further skirmishes all night after the match had been drawn 1-1.

Uefa expelled Manchester United from the competition but the club argued that they were not to blame. They claimed that rival supporters had not been properly segregated, French fans had started the fighting and the riot police had over-reacted and made matters worse.

Manchester United were reinstated on appeal but ordered to play the second leg at least 300km from Old Trafford. Alan Hardaker, aware of the reputation of United's fans, said that the match could not be played in London, so it was switched to Plymouth.

The game passed off without incident and United won 2-0. Their Cup run was ended, though, by Porto in the next round. At least this time all the drama was on the field rather than off it.

Porto won the first leg 4-0. For a while it seemed that United might be able to climb a mountain at Old Trafford when they led 4-1 in the second leg. Needing another two goals they pressed forward, exposing their defence and letting Porto score again. The task was now beyond them and they went out 6-5 on aggregate.

Elton John forms harmonious duet with Taylor

ELTON JOHN was determined to put Watford on the map. Bobby Moore was said to be a candidate to manage his Fourth Division team, but the rock star turned to Graham Taylor instead.

The transformation that Taylor had worked at Lincoln had not gone un-noticed. Big-name teams were eyeing-up Taylor, and Elton John had to work hard to persuade Taylor to join the club.

But once he was installed at Vicarge Road, having told his multi-millionaire chairman that it would cost a mere £1m to get the team into the First Division, Taylor relished getting his teeth into the task.

His impact was immediate. He brought in Bertie Mee, who had led Arsenal to the Double in 1971, and set about turning the club upside down.

Watford adopted the long-ball game, with Luther Blissett as their target man, to deadly effect. Watford romped away with the Fourth Division title by 11 points and the combination of Elton John's money and Taylor's determination were obviously going to be a powerful force.

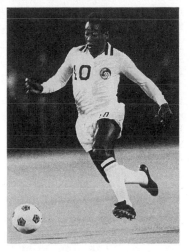
151

Villa's European odyssey runs aground in Spain

WHILE Liverpool were taking over Ajax's and Bayern Munich's mantle as the kings of Europe in the Champions Cup, English clubs were finding the Uefa Cup a harder nut to crack. This year it was Aston Villa's turn to fly the flag.

By the time the Birmingham club had reached the quarter-finals they had disposed of Fenerbace (6-0), Gornik Zabrze (3-1) and last year's runners-up, Athletic Bilbao (3-1). But then they ran into Barcelona who had knocked out Ipswich in the previous round on penalties.

A 2-2 draw at Villa Park left the Midlands side a mountain to climb at Nou Camp and despite a valiant rearguard battle the Catalan side won 2-1 to reach the semi-finals.

Forest go right to the top and never look back

NEWLY-PROMOTED Nottingham Forest wasted no time in making their mark in the First Division. Three wins in a row took them straight to the top of the table, a place that they occupied for almost all of the rest of the season.

The arrival of Peter Shilton from Stoke in September for £250,000 added extra strength to an already formidable defence. Forest were unbeaten at home in the League and only conceded a total of 24 goals.

By December the championship was already looking like a two-horse race, with Forest and Everton comfortably clear of the rest. And the title was effectively decided in the space of 48 hours – Everton were hammered 6-2 at home by Manchester United on Boxing Day and then lost 3-1 at Leeds the next day.

Forest finished the holiday programme five points clear and Brian Clough, their manager, was moved to quip: "The last time Nottingham were five ahead of anybody was in a cricket match." Everton did close the gap to a single point at one stage, but there was no stopping Nottingham Forest. They were unbeaten from mid-November to the end of the season and made sure of the club's first championship on April 18, with an incredible five matches still to play.

Clough became the first manager since the legendary Herbert Chapman to win the title with two different clubs. Clough and his assistant Peter Taylor were rewarded with a testimonial match against Derby. While Clough was his usual ebullient self Taylor was more modest, saying: "Our aim was to qualify for Europe but when we signed Shilton I knew we had a great chance of winning the title."

Shilton, however, was not involved in Forest's other triumph, in the League Cup final. Shilton was Cup-tied and Forest had sold their other first choice goalkeeper so Chris Woods, an 18-year-old reserve with no League experience, had to step into the breach against Liver-

Instant success: Forest won the title first time out

pool at Wembley. Woods's goal was peppered by the Liverpool forwards but he showed every bit as much composure as Shilton to keep the game scoreless after extra time.

Woods was equally unflappable in the replay but Forest owed their 1-0 victory to a poor decision by the referee Pat Partridge. There was no doubt that Phil Thompson brought down John O'Hare with a professional foul, but television replays showed that the incident took place outside the area and a penalty should not have been awarded.

After the match, Taylor was asked whether Forest deserved to have won given that the penalty should not have been given. "Who's got the Cup then?" he asked, quick as a flash, before striding away with the trophy in his arms.

Blyth Spartans the pathfinders in the year of the minnows

RIGHT FROM the start, everybody was calling the FA Cup the "Year of the Minnows". That was hardly surprising when six non-League clubs reached the third round for the first time since 1919.

All the minnows bar one fell by the wayside, leaving Blyth Spartans to carry the standard. Even their flag seemed to be about to be lowered in the fourth round at Stoke when they trailed 2-1 with less than 15 minutes to go, despite having taken the lead early in the game.

But helped by the woodwork they drew level. A free kick hit the post, a follow-up header hit the other post and the rebound was nudged in by Steve Carney. Then, from another free kick, Terry Johnston's volley made sure that they were the first non-League club to reach the fifth round since Yeovil in 1949.

Blyth were drawn against Third Division Wrexham, who had taken two First Division scalps – Bristol City 3-0 after a pulsating 4-4 draw, and Newcastle 4-1 in a replay. This time it was Wrexham's turn to come back from the dead, snatching an equaliser in the 88th minute and winning the replay 2-1. The second match attracted so much interest that Blyth switched the game to Newcastle's ground to accommodate a 42,000 crowd.

With so many of the big teams knocking each other out, the quarter-finals had a strange look to them with Second Division Millwall and Orient also in contention.

Wrexham went down 3-2 to Arsenal, Millwall were swept aside 6-1 by Ipswich and the underdogs' baton passed to Orient. They held Middlesbrough to a goalless draw at Ayresome Park and then Peter Kitchen continued his run of scoring in every round as they won the replay 2-1.

Kitchen, though was powerless against Arsenal in the semi-final and Orient bowed out 3-0. Even so, the succession of shocks went to show that it had not been hyperbole to call the season the "Year of the Minnows".

Robson masterminds Ipswich coup

Comeuppance: Osborne's goal taught Arsenal a lesson

FOR THE RECORD

■ Joe Jordan's £350,000 move from Leeds to Manchester United on January 6 was the biggest transfer deal between two English clubs. Four days later, Liverpool raised the record to £352,000 when they bought Graeme Souness from Middlesbrough. But even that record did not last long as Manchester United bought Gordon McQueen (below) for £495,000 in February.

IF Arsenal thought all they had to do was turn up at Wembley and their fifth FA Cup would be simply handed over to them, then they hadn't been following the knocks fate had been dishing out to favourites throughout the campaign. The "Year of Minnows" reached its logical conclusion when Ipswich duly lifted the FA Cup for the first time.

Although the final score was 1-0, it did not accurately represent Ipswich's domination. The country cousins from Suffolk out-played, out-thought and out-smarted the pride of London. Indeed they could easily have won by a hatful. Paul Mariner hit the bar, John Wark found the same post twice and Pat Jennings had to make a brilliant save to deny George Burley's header. It was, in fact, a 1-0 rout.

Apparently, Arsenal's humiliation had been hatched by the Ipswich backroom boys who had watched Arsenal three times before the final and deduced that the vast majority of Arsenal's attacks were initiated by Sammy Nelson at left-back. "Stop Nelson and you stop Arsenal," Bobby Robson, the

Smiles all round: Ipswich celebrate their first FA Cup

Ipswich manager, said to his players. Thus David Geddis was pulled out of midfield and instructed to close down the full-back. It worked like a dream.

However with 14 minutes remaining, Ipswich had not converted their tactical superiority into goals. Then Geddis swept past Nelson on the right wing and squared the ball low across the goal, Willie Young attempted to clear but put the ball straight to Roger Osborne who slammed it just inside the

upright. It was a vital strike.

The excitement of scoring the winning goal was too much for Osborne and he was taken off to thunderous applause. "I was physically and mentally drained," Osborne said. "I think the sun had got to me. I felt faint and asked to come off."

The Arsenal manager, Terry Neill, conceded that Ipswich deserved their victory but, ominously, went on to say: "We have learnt from this defeat and we will be back next season more determined than ever."

■ Bob Hatton (above) was presented with a silver salver before Blackpool's match on February 4 to mark the fact that he had already scored three hat-tricks this season. After the presentation he then scored another hat-trick against Blackburn. At the end of the season Everton's Bob Latchford collected a £10,000 prize offered by the Daily Express for scoring 30 goals in the League.

■ Leeds were banned from staging FA Cup ties at Elland Road for three years after a pitch invasion during their third round match against Manchester City. And Millwall's ground was closed for two matches after disturbances during their quarter-final against Ipswich.

Rangers reverse their fortunes to leave Aberdeen in their slipstream

Swansong: Greig stepped up from captain to manager

AFTER their humiliation the previous season when Celtic won the Double and Rangers nothing, the men from Ibrox enjoyed sweet revenge by going one better and captured all three trophies. Surprisingly, Celtic were not their main rivals – they never came to terms with the loss of Kenny Dalglish to Liverpool, and finished fifth and out of Europe. Instead it fell to the North East and Billy McNeill's Aberdeen, in his first season in charge, to give Rangers a run for their money.

But as the season began, Rangers looked anything but runaway winners. After two games they were propping up the table! Then Jock Wallace's team embarked on a breathtaking sequence of seven wins, one draw and no losses to march to the top of the Premier Division. Yet, just as Rangers seemed to be comfortably in charge of the title race, Aberdeen began to creep up on them. Their 4-0 defeat of Rangers at Pittodrie on Christmas Eve signalled the beginning of a charge that was to take the title race to the wire.

Aberdeen did not lose any of their remaining 17 matches (drawing five) and by April had overhauled Rangers to go top themselves, albeit briefly. It eventually all depended on the final games of the season, Rangers beat Motherwell 2-0 while Aberdeen could only draw at Hibernian, and Rangers had taken the title by two points.

The two leading clubs clashed yet again in the Scottish Cup final at Hampden on May 6 where Rangers confirmed their supremacy with a 2-1 victory that flattered McNeill's side, Aberdeen's goal coming four minutes from time. It was a wonderful end to the playing career of the Rangers' captain, John Greig, who three weeks later was installed as their new manager after Wallace had departed to take over at Leicester City.

Spurs scoop world to snatch Ardiles and Villa for £700,000

TWO WEEKS after Argentina had won the World Cup, Keith Burkinshaw, Tottenham's unassuming manager, announced to the press that he had signed two of their squad, Osvaldo Ardiles and Ricardo Villa. The hard-bitten newspapermen were stunned. Ardiles, probably the greatest midfielder in the world, had been the principal architect of Argentina's triumph, and Villa, who twice played as a substitute during the campaign, was a skilled, but tough, midfielder who also scored goals. For £700,000 it was a steal, and perhaps the transfer coup of the century.

After the World Cup everybody expected Argentina's squad to be snapped up by the top European countries, but that usually meant the free-spending Spaniards and Italians, not the English who had no real history of overseas players in their domestic game. Somehow Burkinshaw scooped the world. Even more surprisingly it had all been so easy.

Harry Haslam, the manager

Latin American connection: Villa, Burkinshaw and Ardiles transformed Tottenham's fortunes

of Sheffield United, had direct links with Argentina and alerted Spurs to the possibility of snapping up Ardiles cheaply – Sheffield United could not afford him – and he and Burkinshaw flew to Argentina. When Burkinshaw met Ardiles and his wife, Ardiles was more interested in the weather and the European sights than his salary. Within 20 minutes Ardiles had signed. Then, almost as an afterthought, Ardiles asked Burkinshaw if he liked Villa, because if he did, he would come to England as well.

Burkinshaw was flabbergasted. He rang the Spurs chairman to get permission to sign a second Argentinian, Villa came to see him the next day and in five minutes he had signed up as well. In all the double transfer negotiations had taken just 25 minutes and transformed Tottenham's prospects for the season.

They had just returned to the First Division after a season in the Second, but only by the narrowest of margins, on goal difference. Their modest squad had not looked likely to make an impact on the likes of Liverpool, Forest and Everton.

The press reaction spelled out their wonderment at Burkinshaw's audacity. It was described as "shattering new ground in the game", and The Guardian said: "It was as if the janitor had gone to buy a tin of paint and had come back with a Velasquez."

European campaign salvages Liverpool home-front losses

LIVERPOOL, by their standards, had a remarkably listless domestic season. Even though Kenny Dalglish had an immediate impact, and Alan Hansen had also arrived, they could only finish seven points adrift of Nottingham Forest in the League. The FA Cup was even worse. Liverpool went out 4-2 to Chelsea in the third round, prompting Bob Paisley to say: "My players had sawdust in their heads today." And reaching the final of the League Cup for the first time was scant consolation when they were beaten by Nottingham Forest.

But in Europe it was a completely different story – Liverpool still reigned supreme. Dynamo Dresden posed no threat, going down 6-3 on aggregate and Benfica held no terrors either in the quarter-finals. The Portuguese side had not been beaten in 46 matches and took an early lead in Lisbon. Despite torrential rain that threatened to turn the match into a lottery Liverpool stuck to their task. First Jimmy Case, then Emlyn Hughes brought Benfica's sequence to an end. Unhampered by the rain, Liverpool ran away with the second leg 4-1.

The semi-finals pitted Liverpool against their old adversaries Borussia Moenchengladbach. The two sides had met twice before in European finals and Liverpool had won on both occasions. Borussia sensed that, at last, their luck was changing when they won 2-1 at home, their second goal coming in the final minute. Just as Benfica had discovered though, Anfield was a different proposition. The match was one-way traffic with Liverpool scoring three times without reply.

Wembley had been chosen to stage the final, which gave Liverpool an enormous psychological advantage. And their opponents, Bruges, could still recall losing to Liverpool in the Uefa Cup final two years before.

Bruges, in awe of Liverpool and of the crowd, opted to play an ultra defensive game. They barely mounted an attack worthy of the name, just sitting back and absorbing the pressure. That was hardly the way to beat Liverpool, masters of biding their time and waiting for the right moment. It duly arrived in the 66th minute when Dalglish was given far too much space to run at the Bruges defence. As Jensen advanced Dalglish paused for an instant before chipping over the goalkeeper from close range.

Even then, Bruges showed little inclination to go on the attack and Liverpool were content to protect their lead. It was hardly the best of games but that did not matter to Liverpool. They were, after all, the first English club to retain the European Cup.

FOR THE RECORD

■ The Football League and the North American Soccer League reached an agreement about the transfer of players. Charlton, in a move described as "trail-blazing" by Alan Hardaker, established a permanent link with the New Hampshire team where both clubs would share players and profits.

■ Both Peter Bonetti and Ron Harris played their 700th first-team match for Chelsea on the same day, March 11.

■ Michel Hidalgo (below), the French national manager, escaped an attempted kidnap in Bordeaux on May 22.

■ Wigan were elected to the League in place of Southport on June 2. The two clubs received the same number of votes in the first round, but Wigan won 29-20 in the second round.

■ Denis Follows, the former FA secretary, was knighted in the Queen's birthday honours list.

■ The government gave £1m to the Sports Council to be used to develop facilities that would benefit the local community at 18 clubs.

■ The High Court upheld the FA's ban on 12-year-old Theresa Bennett (below) playing for a boys' team, stating that football was not covered by the Equal Opportunities Act.

Magic moment: Dalglish watches his chip beat Jensen to retain the European Cup at Wembley

ARGENTINA'S eventual triumph in the World Cup final after extra time at home in their capital city of Buenos Aires before their exultant and ecstatic fans on June 25 laid to rest 58 years of disappointment, betrayal, failure, slurs, and theft on the world stage. Argentina had always seen itself, not Brazil, as the home of South American football. So in 1930 the country was mortified when they blew the very first World Cup final to their bitter rivals Uruguay, in Montevideo. That was just the beginning of their World Cup travails.

First Italy began poaching their best players and making them Italian internationals (this went on until the 1960s). Three times they were rejected as the hosts, although Uruguay, Brazil, Chile and Mexico had got the nod. The first time they were snubbed they boycotted the tournament for 24 years. When they did return, their best result was to reach the quarter-finals against England in 1966, when their captain, Antonio Rattin, and his team were branded as "animals". Meanwhile Argentina were a dominant force in their continent, winning 13 of 31 South American championships.

Even when Argentina were finally allowed to host a World Cup it was far from certain that they would actually stage the competition. The country was wracked by unrest as left-wing guerillas fought the an oppressive military dictatorship, the national economy was a shambles and thought unlikely to be able to afford the event and there were repeated calls for the finals to be moved elsewhere, with Holland and Belgium the favourites to take over. But the rebels and the government agreed a truce (national pride on the football field being more important than who ran the country), stadiums were rebuilt and the tournament passed off smoothly.

More importantly, Argentina had, by beating Holland – runners-up in West Germany four years earlier – proved they were world masters. The pain of over a half-century of humiliation was erased in 120 minutes of vibrant football and on that hot June evening the populace went into night-long raptures.

The match had been thrilling, if badly refereed. Mario Kempes, playing the game of his life, gave

WORLD CUP 1978

On home soil Argentina come good at last

Argentina the lead in the 38th minute when he astutely touched home Leopoldo Luque's pass. Despite numerous Dutch attacks and missed chances – with both defences showing all the signs of the pressure created by the fervent crowd – Argentina clung on to their lead as the game entered its final phase.

In the 81st minute, Arie Haan sprung their offside trap with a through ball to Rene van de Kerkhof. His cross was headed in by the substitute, Dirk Nanninga. With seconds remaining, it appeared that Holland had stolen the game when Rob Rensenbrink's powerful and accurate long-range shot beat the goalkeeper only to rebound of the base of the left-hand post.

That was the last effective chance Holland had. In extra time Kempes popped up again with a powerful run from outside the penalty area to score a wonderful solo goal by beating three players, including Jan Jongbloed the goalkeeper. Ten minutes later Kempes, the leading scorer of the tournament, delivered the killing blow when, after another powerful run, he exchanged a one-two with Daniel Bertoni, who slotted the ball home. Holland had now joined Czechoslovakia and Hungary in a select club: two World Cup finals, no World Cup.

They had their excuses. There was no Johann Cruyff or Rinus Michels, and, as seems commonplace in the Dutch household, bickering was rife. Argentina, too, had their problems for, as usual, many of their stars were playing in Europe. Cesar Menotti, their chain-smoking national coach, wisely decided to focus his squad on home-based players such as Osvaldo

Ardiles, who was the midfield player of the tournament. In fact Kempes was the only overseas player in the winning team.

There were some in South America however that believed that Argentina should not even have been allowed to play in the final. The circumstances surrounding their victory over Peru were engulfed in controversy. After two matches in the second round group, Brazil and Argentina had the same number of points. Everything rested on the last two games, Brazil versus Poland and Argentina against Peru.

Inexplicably, Fifa did not insist that the two games were played simultaneously. So after Brazil had beaten Poland 3-1, Argentina kicked off knowing that they had to win by four goals to reach the final. Peru started well enough but caved in 6-0. The finger of suspicion was pointed firmly at the Peruvian goalkeeper Quiroga, who had been born in Argentina.

There were allegations that the Peruvian team had been bribed by the ruling Argentinian junta, and counter claims that Brazil had offered the Peruvians money to play well. For the Brazilians it was the last straw. They felt they had already been victimised in their first round match against Sweden. With the match level at 1-1, Zico drove a free kick into the net. But Clive Thomas blew for time while the ball was in mid-air and refused to allow the goal, condemning Brazil to face Argentina and Peru in the second round. To this day, the controversial Welsh referee still claims that his action was perfectly justified, as the rules are the rules.

Quite what justification Scotland

could conjure up for their abject performance in Argentina was difficult to fathom. Ally MacLeod's team arrived on a wave of Tartan sentiment and expectation. It was hailed as the greatest team to compete in the World Cup, and once again Scotland were the only British country to qualify – England being edged out on goal difference by Italy.

With players like Martin Buchan, Kenny Dalglish, Archie Gemmill, Joe Jordan, Lou Macari, Don Masson and Bruce Rioch in their squad, the Scots seemed to have good grounds for optimism. Moreover their group, with the exception of Holland, looked easy enough with Iran, playing in their first ever World Cup, and unfancied Peru in their third. Such complacency was to prove Scotland's undoing.

In their match against Peru, Jordan gave them the lead after 14 minutes, yet amazingly Scotland went to pieces and the veteran Teofilo Cubillas ran riot. He created the equaliser two minutes from half-time and scored two high quality goals in the space of seven minutes in the second half as Peru won 3-1.

If that wasn't bad enough, Scotland had to experience the shame of Willie Johnstone being sent home, and banned for a year from international football, for failing a random drugs test after the match. Johnstone protested his innocence, claiming the drugs were for hay fever but subsequently admitted they were stimulants that he also used in domestic, club football.

Scotland's nightmare was only beginning. Now they had to face the novices, Iran. Scotland's performance was utterly inept in the 1-1 draw. They could even count themselves lucky to have got on the scoresheet. Iran gifted Scotland an undeserved half-time lead when one of their players collided with his goalkeeper and the ball ended up in the net. It was the most bizarre, and softest of goals.

This left MacLeod's demoralised and vilified team with a mountain to climb: beat Holland by three goals or get on the plane home. When Holland took the lead with a Rob Rensenbrink penalty, the mountain had become even higher. This time Scotland rose to the challenge. Dalglish equalised just before half-time, Gemmill's penalty put them ahead and, with

Scottish tails up, Gemmill scored the goal of the tournament. He started his run outside the penalty area, beat three Dutch defenders and then confounded the keeper by chipping in under pressure. Was a miracle on the cards?

No, because four minutes later Johnny Rep soon stopped all this Scottish bravado and heroism with a thunderous 25-yard shot to leave the score 3-2 and secure Holland's place in the next round. So once again Scotland had their World Cup glory. As in 1974, when they were the only unbeaten team in the tournament, they comforted themselves with one thought: forget Peru and Iran, they had beaten the team that had been the thickness of a post from being world champions.

Cubillas: destroyed Scotland

Bettega: beat Argentina

Fever pitch: the home fans

Goal of the tournament: Gemmill's dribble stunned Holland

Local heroes: Luque, Kempes (two goals) and Bertoni (one goal) over-ran the Dutch in extra time

Rejuvenated Toshack calls up old guard

SWANSEA continued their march up the League, winning promotion to the Second Division a year after coming up from the Fourth Division. To add to the delight for John Toshack, their player-manager, he was also recalled to the Welsh team. He celebrated by scoring a hat-trick as Scotland were beaten 3-0 in the Home championships.

Toshack, while developing young players at the club, also turned to two of his former Liverpool teammates to bring experience to the side. Phil Boersma was signed from Luton for £35,000 and Ian Callaghan joined from Liverpool.

They bolstered a team that had already tasted success in the League Cup, beating Tottenham 3-1 at White Hart Lane to win the match 5-3 on aggregate.

Apart from one spell in February, when they went five matches without a win, Swansea were hardly ever out of the promotion race. Fittingly, they made sure of a place in the Second Division when Toshack scored the winning goal against Chester- field in the final match of the season.

Toshack: recalled

Latchford and Greenwood lead England out of the wilderness

Sterling effort: Keegan helps England get a 1-1 draw in Dublin

RON GREENWOOD'S prospects of his tenure as England manager being extended to include the 1982 World Cup finals in Spain clearly depended on England qualifying for the 1980 European championships, particularly as they had not qualified for the previous two World Cup finals. England's group was an intriguing one as it included the two Irelands, Bulgaria and Denmark, with the winner going through to the quarter-finals in Italy.

With so much pressure on him, Greenwood must have had near-apoplexy in their opening game against Denmark in Copenhagen in September. By the 23rd minute two headers from Kevin Keegan had put England 2-0 up. Then, in a three-minute spell, the Danes levelled the scores, their first goal coming from a penalty.

Shortly after the interval Bob Latchford restored the lead and Phil Neal made it 4-2 with five minutes left, only for the Danes to pull another goal back.

Despite frantic efforts by the home team, England clung on. A relieved Greenwood said: "I'm an advocate of attacking football – but that was carrying it to extremes."

A month later England had a creditable 1-1 draw with Eire in Dublin, and then in February they ran riot against Northern Ireland at a packed Wembley with a resounding 4-0 victory, Latchford scoring twice. And to cap Greenwood's first full season officially in charge, Bulgaria were given similar treatment in Sofia in June as England returned 3-0 victors.

Meanwhile the other countries were cutting each other's throats with Northern Ireland beating Bulgaria, but losing to Denmark, and Eire beating Denmark, but losing to Bulgaria. Thus, with half their qualifying games played, England were sitting comfortably at the top of their group, having won three, and drawn one of their four matches with an extremely healthy goal difference.

Latchford: hotshot

I've served more time than Ronnie Biggs did for the Great Train Robbery

MALCOLM ALLISON
appealing against his lifetime ban from the touchline

Stein puts patriotism before pounds

JOCK STEIN'S rich and rewarding managerial partnership with Celtic spanning 13 glorious years was brought to an inglorious end. After the disappointments of the previous season when Celtic finished fifth in the Premier Division, failed to win a trophy or even qualify for Europe while Rangers waltzed to the Treble, Celtic's directors wanted a younger man.

Stein, 56, had agreed in May to hand over the reins to Billy McNeill, his captain when Celtic had won the European Cup in 1967, and who had, in his first season in charge of Aberdeen, run Rangers close in the League and Scottish Cup.

Stein had been given to understand that the club he had served so well (one European Cup, 10 championships, eight Scottish Cups, six Scottish League Cups) would grant him a

McNeill: chosen man

directorship. Instead Celtic offered him the post of commercial director.

He saw it as an insult: that he would be effectively a glorified pools vendor. Consequently, on August 21 he went to England, to manage Leeds United who had never really recovered from

Brian Clough's disastrous 44-day reign in 1974.

Coincidentally, Stein lasted exactly the same number of days at Elland Road. But, unlike Clough, he did not leave under a cloud. Indeed Manny Cussins, the Leeds chairman implored him to stay and offered financial incentives to do so. However a bigger, and more patriotic carrot had been dangled in front of the Big Man: managing his country, something he had briefly done as a caretaker in 1965.

After the debacle of the national side in Argentina, Ally McLeod had resigned on September 26 and the Scottish Football Association, desperate to recover lost pride, naturally turned to their greatest-ever club manager and appointed him on October 4. He had much to do.

Shrewsbury flirt with the big time

GRAHAM TURNER, the newly arrived player-manager of Shrewsbury, certainly brought a breath of fresh air to the club. At the end of his first full season in charge the team had produced their best-ever performances in the League and in the FA Cup.

A 4-1 victory over Exeter in the final game of the season secured the Third Division championship, and promotion to the Second Division for the first time in the club's history, but most of the excitement in the town revolved around the

team's performances in the FA Cup.

Victories over Mansfield, Doncaster and Cambridge earned them a plum tie in the fourth round, at home to Manchester City. The First Division strugglers were swept aside 2-0 but Shrewsbury were left cursing the luck of the draw for the next round.

Instead of being paired with another of the glamour clubs they were presented with a trip to Aldershot. The Fourth Division team were clearly no

slouches either, having beaten Sheffield United in a replay.

Shrewsbury appeared to be down and out when they trailed 2-1 with less than a minute left to play until they snatched a very late equaliser and won the replay 3-1 in extra time.

That put Shrewsbury in the sixth round for the first time and they gave another First Division side, Wolverhampton a run for their money. Shrewsbury drew 1-1 at Molineux thanks to an Atkins penalty, before bowing at 3-1 at Gay Meadow.

Docherty: courting disaster

How television's Snatch of the Day became Swap of the Day

ITV SHOCKED everybody when they announced in November that they would be showing football on Saturday nights next season rather than the BBC. Match of the Day was established as a national tradition, while the ITV companies had to make do with highlights on Sunday afternoons. Everybody, the BBC included, assumed that the established order was not going to change.

So news of ITV's three-year deal with the Football League was greeted with incredulity. Not even all the clubs could believe that the "Snatch of the Day" had happened. Jimmy Hill, the Coventry managing director who was also a Match of the Day presenter, said: "It wasn't an honourable deal, it was railroaded through. The clubs didn't even know whose bid they were accepting."

The BBC had no intention of relinquishing the jewel in their sporting crown and so court action became inevitable. The BBC won a respite when the Office of Fair Trading banned the agreement because it broke the rules regarding restrictive practices.

A £10m four-year compromise, dubbed "Swap of the Day", was reached with the two networks sharing coverage – the

BBC would have Saturday football next season, and then the coverage would alternate.

This offer was thrown out by club chairman because they did not want to commit themselves to such a long-term deal. But, warned by Alan Hardaker that they faced the prospect of no coverage at all with the consequent loss of money, the clubs finally backed down at the League's annual meeting in June.

Dalglish: top man

Liverpool's mean machine rolls on

RECORDS came thick and fast as three clubs, Liverpool, Nottingham Forest and Everton, vied for the top spot in the First Division, all of them seemingly unbeatable.

Nottingham Forest surpassed Leeds's record of 34 consecutive matches without defeat in the League in October and did not have their run halted until December 9, when they went down at Liverpool. That ended a sequence of 42 League matches (21 wins and 21 draws) stretching back to November 1977.

Everton did not lose until their 20th League match of the season, at Coventry on December 23. But neither side could keep pace with Liverpool, even though Liverpool lost their first game relatively early in the season on October 28. Their 1-0 reverse at Everton was their first defeat in a local derby since 1971.

The thing that kept Liverpool in front was their incredible start to the season. They won six games in a row at the start, scoring 20 goals and conceding one, including a 7-0 destruction of Tottenham, the London club's

Happy anniversary: Paisley celebrated 40 years at Liverpool

record defeat in the League.

When Liverpool lost for the fourth and final time on April 16, Bob Paisley said: "We were absolute rubbish. The League is still wide open." Some chance. Liverpool coasted to the title with a record 68 points and a record low of 16 goals conceded, with Ray Clemence keeping 27 clean sheets. All of this was done by just 15 players, two of whom only made four appearances between them.

It was a breathtaking performance to mark Paisley's 40th year with the club. And when Liverpool made sure of a record

11th title on May 8 the ever-modest Paisley was more concerned for his players than himself. "The atmosphere was overpowering," he said. "I was worried that all the publicity about my anniversary might upset the players' concentration."

The tributes began to flock in. Kenny Dalglish, Liverpool's leading scorer, was voted Player of the Year; the club collected a £50,000 prize from The Sun for beating a target of 84 goals and Paisley, to nobody's surprise, was chosen as Manager of the Year.

Birtles scuppers Southampton after Clough reads the riot act

THE EARLY stages of the League Cup took their usual toll on the big clubs with no less that six First Division clubs going out to lesser opposition in the second round alone.

Liverpool, despite their rampant form in the League, were victims of the biggest upset, losing to Third Division Sheffield United. The "Liverpool old guard" at Swansea brought down Tottenham in a replay, and Arsenal were beaten by yet another Third Division side, Rotherham.

With so many of the big guns gone so quickly things were made considerably easier for the surviving big names. Nottingham Forest, after needing a replay to overcome Oldham, breezed past Oxford, Brighton

and Watford. Their only hard game was a 3-2 win at Everton in the fourth round.

Southampton's route to the final was considerably more difficult – Birmingham, Derby, a replay against Reading, Manchester City and a one-goal aggregate against Leeds in the semi-final.

Nottingham Forest looked remarkably shaky in the first half of the final and they trailed to a goal from David Peach. Brian Clough did not mince his words during the interval and Forest were transformed after the break.

Garry Birtles, a bargain buy from a local non-League side, quickly got the equaliser and Southampton did well not to concede another goal until the

Turning point: Birtles scores the equaliser for Forest

78th minute, when Birtles struck again. Birtles had two other efforts disallowed, both for offside, and a part in Forest's third goal, scored by Tony Woodcock.

Nick Holmes got a late conso-

lation but Southampton never looked like coming back. Winning the trophy for the second year running gave Forest the perfect fillip for the later stages of their other Cup campaign, in Europe.

Francis breaks £1m barrier

WHEN, in 1905, Alf Common was transferred from Sunderland to Middlesbrough for £1,000, there was a hue and cry about the sum of money Middlesbrough had forked out for one player. Seventy-four years later, the Nottingham Forest manager, Brian Clough, born in Middlesbrough, for whom he played before being transferred to Sunderland, provoked similar outrage when he paid £1m for Trevor Francis. Little wonder that the North East is regarded as the hotbed of English football.

Francis, like Common, was one of the most gifted players of his era. He had made his First Division debut for Birmingham when only 16, and in the subsequent eight years had scored 118 goals in 278 appearances, and played for England 12 times. Clough, having led Nottingham Forest out of the depths of the Second Division to the heights of the First Division championship, was ambitious that this success would endure. Hence the absurd outlay on Francis.

The transfer on February 9 doubled the previous record between British clubs, £500,000 paid by West Bromwich Albion for Middlesbrough's David Mills only the month before. To be fair to Clough the £1m price was set by Birmingham themselves. Firmly rooted to the bottom of the First Division table, they stared relegation in the face and knew they could not realistically hang on to their ambitious superstar.

Clough had to outbid Jimmy Hill's Coventry to get his man, and the Forest manager sweetened the deal with Francis by agreeing that he could spend his summers playing for Detroit Express in America.

The striking disadvantage of the deal from Forest's point of view was that it had come so late in the season that Francis would only be eligible for one match in the European Cup – the final. Clough's outrageous gamble would pay off, with Forest making the final, and Francis scoring the only goal.

Spiralling transfer fees in the domestic market

£1,000 Alf Common 1905
(Sunderland to Middlesbrough)

£5,000 Syd Puddefoot 1922
(West Ham to Falkirk)

£10,890 David Jack 1928
(Bolton Wanderers to Arsenal)

£20,000 Tommy Lawton 1947
(Chelsea to Notts County)

£50,000 Denis Law 1960
(Huddersfield to Man City)

£110,000 Alan Ball 1966
(Blackpool to Everton)

£500,000 David Mills 1979
(Middlesbrough to West Brom)

£1,150,000 Trevor Francis 1979
(Birmingham to Nottm Forest)

FOR THE RECORD

■ The FA banned Don Revie for 10 years for signing a secret deal with the United Arab Emirates while still the England manager, and trying to persuade England to pay him £50,000 compensation if he resigned. Revie decided to sue the FA because the sentence was "savage and out of all proportion".

■ Sammy Chapman, the former Nottingham Forest captain, won a test case in court which established that players received money from testimonial games free of tax.

■ The Charlton forwards Mick Flanagan and Derek Hales were sent off for fighting during their team's draw with Maidstone in the FA Cup.

■ Uefa said that England would only be allowed to enter three teams in the 1980-81 Uefa Cup.

Smiling all the way to bank: Francis and his wife celebrate the monumental deal with Clough

English clubs maintain the pressure on European rivals

WHILE winning the European Cup was becoming something of an English habit as Nottingham Forest added to Liverpool's triumphs in the previous two years, the Uefa Cup and the Cup Winners Cup were still proving elusive.

The English contingent went into the Uefa Cup with high hopes and these were duly rewarded in the first round as Arsenal thumped Locomotive Leipzig 7-1, with Frank Stapleton scoring five goals – including one for the opposition, West Bromwich Albion raced past Galatasaray 6-2 and Everton trounced Finn Harps 10-0. Manchester City had a fright against Twente Enschede: only qualifying because of an own goal.

Then luck went against Everton as they fell victims to the away goal rule while Arsenal benefited from it before being out-thought by the classy Red Star Belgrade in the third round. Meanwhile West Brom and Manchester City coasted serenely to the quarter-finals. Indeed City hammered the crack Italian side AC Milan 5-1.

However both were undone in the quarter-finals. Their only consolation was that they were both beaten by the eventual finalists. WBA lost to Red Star Belgrade 2-1 and City succumbed to Borussia Moenchengladbach 4-2. The German side eventually went on to beat Red Star 2-1 in the two-legged final.

It was much the same story for Ipswich Town in the European Cup Winners Cup, where Bobby Robson's team comfortably reached the quarter-finals before their European naivety was exposed. Holding a 2-1 lead from the first leg at Portman Road thanks to Eric Gates, Ipswich conceded a goal to Barcelona's Migueli at Nou Camp and were knocked out on the away goals rule.

Brady: seized the time

United's amazing revival buried by Brady's desperate last-gasp effort

AN UNNECESSARY blunder by Terry Neill, the Arsenal manager, five minutes from time turned a prosaic FA Cup final into one of the most explosive finishes seen at Wembley since Stanley Matthews' heroics in 1953. With five minutes remaining Arsenal were 2-0 ahead and coasting to their fifth FA Cup trophy when Neill pulled off David Price and put on Steve Walford. It utterly disrupted the Arsenal defence and, with a minute to go, Gordon McQueen and Sammy McIlroy had put Manchester United level. Extra time loomed.

But not for Liam Brady, the architect of Arsenal's two first-half goals. Now it was United's turn to fall victim to complacency, and then panic. Brady picked up the ball in his half and ran straight at the heart of the United midfield as they backed off, hoping to deny him space rather than commit themselves to the tackle.

Brady swung his sweet left foot one more time to find Graham Rix clear on the left wing. Meanwhile Alan Sunderland had made a blindside run on the right and arrived perfectly at the far post to connect with Rix's cross and snatch an unbeliev-

Nodding home: Stapleton scores Arsenal's second goal

able winner. United could barely draw breath before the referee blew the final whistle.

For Arsenal, it was the end of a long and arduous FA Cup campaign. Their third round struggle with Jack Charlton's Third Division Sheffield Wednesday had been little short of titanic. It took five matches (three of them at neutral Filbert Street in the course of seven days), involving 16 goals and 540 minutes of play before they could finally meet Notts County in the fourth round. So, what began as a marathon in Sheffield in January, ended as a sprint in London in May.

Manchester United surely had believed the omens were on their side when extra time was imminent. Their road to Wembley had already been paved with London clubs – Chelsea, Fulham and Tottenham falling to Dave Sexton's glittering array of stars. Then they had done the difficult bit: knock out the eventual League champions, Liverpool, after a replay in the semi-final.

Sexton described it as a cruel result: "When we got the two goals back we were thinking of the breather before extra time and lost concentration for a few vital seconds."

Fixture log-jam proves no obstacle to Celtic's dramatic charge

IT WAS a remarkable season by any standards. First, the leading three clubs, Celtic, Rangers and Aberdeen, all had new managers in Billy McNeill, John Greig and Alex Ferguson respectively. Second, the winter was so dire that not only did it play havoc with the early rounds of the Scottish Cup, it made interpreting the League tables with so many games in hand an impossible task. Never more so than at the final run-in.

Dundee United, under Jim McLean, took full advantage of this and led the Premier Division for much of the season, but how false was their position? On April 25 Dundee United had two League matches left,

against Celtic and Aberdeen, with 43 points accumulated. Celtic had seven games to play, two of them against Rangers, and had 36 points. Rangers had 35 points with seven games remaining, but also the Scottish Cup final against Hibs to play. Aberdeen also had 35 points but only five games left, one of them against Rangers. To the winner the spoils, but which was better: points in the bag or games in hand? And who would be the first to lose their nerve?

Dundee United cracked straightaway, losing to Celtic and drawing with Aberdeen, who too then caved in, losing to Rangers and only amassing five points from their five remaining

matches. Meanwhile Rangers were making heavy weather of disposing of Hibs in the Cup, the final going to a second replay. As the others faltered, Celtic had grasped the nettle.

Apart from losing to Rangers at Ibrox 1-0, they won all their remaining fixtures, but none more important than their final match of the season at Parkhead. Rangers, who still had two games in hand, needed at least a draw to prevent Celtic from taking the championship.

With just over 20 minutes remaining Celtic were in trouble, trailing to an Alex MacDonald goal and reduced to 10 men after John Doyle had been sent off. Then they mounted a cham-

pionship-winning recovery as Roy Aitken equalised and George McCluskey gave them the lead. Still Rangers weren't dead: Rob Russell levelled the scores to leave the title tilting Rangers' way.

In the last five minutes Rangers wilted under the green and white onslaught, and MacLeod put Celtic ahead for the second time. To make matters worse poor Colin Jackson put through his own goal to give Celtic a 4-2 victory and the Premier title.

Rangers' sole consolation was that, after two drab 0-0 draws with Hibs, they eventually prevailed 3-2 in the second replay of the Scottish Cup final.

Francis uses his head to give Clough Europe's major prize

Rare occurrence: Francis scored with a header the first time he played in Europe

NOTTINGHAM FOREST and Liverpool were undoubtedly two of the finest sides in Europe. Liverpool, the European Cup holders, were seeded in the competition but Forest, making their European debut were not. The draw that everybody feared and nobody wanted duly happened and the two teams were paired in the first round.

Both matches were thrilling, and either would have graced the final, so it was a shame that one team had to lose. Forest took a 2-0 lead at the City Ground when Liverpool, pushing forward to try to cancel out Garry Birtles' goal, let Colin Barrett finish off a slick counter-attack near the end.

Liverpool had come back from worse before as Brian Clough knew: "Two goals might not be enough at Anfield," he said. But this time Liverpool's touch deserted them. The woodwork was rattled several times but Liverpool were never going to pull off a miracle and the game finished 0-0.

Forest's semi-final against Cologne, the conquerors of Rangers, was every bit as enthralling as their contest with Liverpool. At home, Forest came back from two goals down after 20 minutes to lead 3-2 only to concede an equaliser to the Japanese substitute Yashiko Okudera, who scored within seconds of coming on.

Although Clough blamed Peter Shilton for two of the goals he was certain that Forest could still reach the final. "Only a fool would write us off," he said. He was right. Ian Bowyer's header in Germany capped a game that Clough described as his "finest hour".

The final, against Malmo was an even finer 90 minutes. Forest were without Archie Gemmill and Martin O'Neill, but Trevor Francis was eligible to play in the European Cup for the first time. And it was Forest's record signing who turned the match. He timed a long run from midfield to arrive at the far post at just the same moment as John Robertson's cross. The crowd were treated to something of a rarity, a headed goal from Francis.

Robertson, Francis and John McGovern dominated the second half and Forest, although not the equal of Liverpool in the League, showed that they were every bit as good in Europe.

Toast of England: Forest won the European Cup for the first time

163

THE
1979-80
SEASON

Transfer fees out of control as the market goes haywire

TREVOR FRANCIS'S £1m move to Forest last season opened the floodgates and big-money transfers became so commonplace that everybody thought that football had money to burn.

In August, Bob Paisley, the Liverpool manager, voiced many people's fears when he said: "There is a danger of the whole set-up going berserk and the game being ruined. People who sign contracts should honour them." The very next day, Ray Wilkins became the second most expensive footballer in Britain when he moved from Chelsea to Manchester United for £825,000.

A very few people did show the restraint that Paisley called for. Bob Stokoe resigned as the Blackpool manager because he did not think the club should have bought Brian Smith from Bolton. And Ron Harris, the veteran Chelsea player rejected a move to Luton, even though it would have earned him £15,000. "There are some things money can't buy," he said. "I have spent 19 years with Chelsea, the good times and the bad. There isn't a price on that."

Just about everybody else did have their price. The Francis record was broken on September 5 when Steve Daley joined Manchester City from Wolverhampton. The basic fee was £1,150,000, and the extra costs raised the final bill to £1,437,500. Manchester City

had spent more than £5m so far in the season, which had still hardly begun.

Worse, the Daley record only lasted three days. Andy Gray's move from Aston Villa to Wolverhampton upped the ante to £1,469,000. And it was not only the established stars who were commanding million-pound fees. In August Norwich rejected a £1m offer for the still unproven Kevin Reeves. By March the club, suffering from low attendances and declining income succumbed and Reeves joined Manchester City for £1m.

The madness was not only confined to the Football League. The transfer of Ian Redford from Dundee to Rangers broke the Scottish record. And Weymouth collected a non-League record £35,000 when they sold Graham Roberts to Tottenham. Even America got in on the act. The Tampa Bay Rowdies were said to have offered £1m for three Millwall players, although nothing ever came of the rumours.

Amid all the mayhem, one deal shone out. Lawrie McMenemy's luring of Kevin Keegan to Southampton for a mere £420,000 was definitely the bargain of the season.

Small fortune: Daley took Manchester City's spending to more than £5m

Where the money went – Deals in excess of £500,000

Player	Teams	Value*
Andy Gray	Aston Villa to Wolverhampton	£1,469,000
Steve Daley	Wolverhampton to Manchester City	£1,437,500
Kevin Reeves	Norwich to Manchester City	£1,250,000
Steve Archibald	Aberdeen to Tottenham	£900,000
Ray Wilkins	Chelsea to Manchester United	£825,000
Tony Woodcock	Nottingham Forest to Cologne	£650,000
John Gidman	Aston Villa to Everton	£650,000
Mike Flanagan	Charlton to Crystal Palace	£650,000
Peter Withe	Newcastle to Aston Villa	£500,000

*prices are based on press estimates

Going one better: Wolves spent £1.5m on Andy Gray

How McMenemy captured Keegan

ON FEBRUARY 11 Southampton manager Lawrie McMenemy pulled off a secret transfer coup to rival Keith Burkinshaw's capture of Osvaldo Ardiles and Ricky Villa 18 months earlier. McMenemy's star signing was Kevin Keegan. In both instances the tabloid press – who normally live off such stories – only discovered what was going on when it was formally announced.

In Keegan's case McMenemy had lured football reporters to a country hotel in Hampshire "to meet somebody who will play a big part in Southampton's future." Then he produced, like a rabbit out of a hat, Kevin Keegan. There were gasps of astonishment at McMenemy's conjuring trick.

Keegan, who had left Liverpool three years previously to ply his skills on the Continental stage with Hamburg, had twice been voted European footballer of the year (only the second player to have achieved this) and was one of the hottest properties around. When he had announced that he intended leaving Hamburg at the end of the season, it was assumed that a big Italian, or Spanish, club would lash out a fortune for his services and therefore no English club could compete. And,

This way forward: Keegan comes back to England from Germany

anyway, Liverpool had first refusal on his signature.

McMenemy saw it differently. He knew that transfers between EEC countries were restricted to £500,000 and therefore Keegan was affordable. He also believed that Keegan probably would not want to risk being overshadowed by Kenny Dalglish, his replacement at Anfield and who was now the current darling of the Kop, by returning to Anfield. So McMenemy set to work.

He checked that Keegan would prefer a move to England, particularly as he wished to be part of the England set-up before the 1982 World Cup. Trusting his instincts, McMenemy waylaid Keegan before

England's European championship qualifier against Eire on February 6. After a three-hour discussion, where McMenemy laid out Southampton's plans and ambitions, Keegan was convinced. Especially as he would be teaming up with his best friend in football, Mick Channon. Once it was clear he had Keegan in place Liverpool waived their option and Hamburg, resigned to losing him, settled for £420,000.

The significance of Keegan's decision to return home rather than stay abroad was not lost on Ron Greenwood, the England manager. "Kevin's availability is of the utmost importance to England," he said on hearing the news.

Shilton's blunder ends Forest's reign

NOTTINGHAM FOREST were starting to develop an Indian sign over Liverpool in Cup competitions as, once again, Forest brought about Liverpool's downfall in the League Cup.

Liverpool only had themselves to blame in both legs of the semi-final. In the first, at the City Ground, Ray Clemence brought down Garry Birtles in the last minute and John Robertson converted the penalty kick. Then, at Anfield, Liverpool conceded another penalty which was scored by Robertson. Despite David Fairclough's late goal, Forest reached the final for the third year running.

Their opponents at Wembley were Wolverhampton, who had to overcome two of the surprise teams in the competition. In the fifth round Wolves needed two replays to beat the Third Division highfliers Grimsby, who had already accounted for Second Division Notts County and First Division Everton.

Then they lost the first leg of the semi-final to Swindon before a 3-1 win at Molineux just gave them the verdict 4-3 on aggregate. Swindon themselves had taken two First Division scalps, Stoke and Arsenal after extra time in a replay.

Forest's hopes of winning the League Cup for the third time in

a row were dashed by a terrible blunder by the usually dependable Peter Shilton.

Peter Daniel lofted the ball into the Forest penalty area. David Needham appeared to have the cross covered but Shilton raced off his line and ran straight into his defender. Andy Gray was able to take advantage of the confusion and slip his shot between the two stranded Forest players.

Shilton claimed that he had called for the ball, but said that Needham probably had not heard him above the noise of the crowd. He admitted that the only goal of an otherwise sterile match was his fault.

Needham: defensive mix-up

THE
1979-80
SEASON

Harlow's bark was nearly as good as their bite

EVERY DOG, it is said, has its day and this year it was Harlow Town's turn to wag their tail in the FA Cup. The Isthmian League team had to come through five qualifying games, but once they reached the competition proper they really had the bit between their teeth.

The Essex team specialised in containing League opponents in the first match and then surprising them in the replay. In the second round Harlow drew at Southend and then beat them 1-0 three days later. In the third round, once again they came from behind to draw at Leicester and then prevailed 1-0 in the replay at Harlow Sports Centre.

Harlow were finally collared at Watford in the fourth round but not before they almost snatched another draw. Harlow led 1-0 at the interval but Watford bit back with four goals early in the second half. Harlow rallied with two more goals but this time the equaliser was beyond them.

Brooking profits from Arsenal's labours

WHEN Trevor Brooking won the FA Cup for West Ham with only the third headed goal of his career, Arsenal must have wondered if it had been worth all the blood, sweat and tears they had had to endure to reach the final for the third consecutive time, the first club this century to do so. After all, to lose to a 13th minute goal from a Stuart Pearson mis-hit shot that was deflected off Brooking's forehead was scant reward for the heroics Arsenal performed against Liverpool in the semi-final.

It was the most protracted semi-final in the history of the Cup, stretching over four games and 420 minutes of football, and was supposed to produce the eventual Cup winners.

Liverpool and Arsenal began with a 0-0 draw at Hillsborough on April 12, moved on to Villa Park and a pair of 1-1 draws before a change of venue, Highfield Road, Coventry, settled the tie with a Brian Talbot goal. It was May 1, nine days before the final and Arsenal still had two League games to play.

On the day, Arsenal were clearly suffering from their earlier labours and, of course, West Ham had had ample opportunity to analyse their Cup style during the semi-final replays. They took full advantage and, having gone ahead, simply closed them down, and became the third Second Division club in eight years to win the FA Cup. Their margin of victory would probably have been greater if Willie Young had not cynically brought down Paul Allen – the youngest player ever to appear in a final – just outside the area when he was clear.

Stoops to conquer: Brooking's header turned out to be Arsenal's undoing

166

Ferguson and Aberdeen finally end Old Firm's monopoly of the title

ALEX FERGUSON, in only his second season in charge of Aberdeen, pulled off the impossible. He broke the Old Firm duopoly of the League championship for the first time since Kilmarnock in 1965, and gave Pittodrie only their second championship in their 77-year history. But Ferguson's miracle was a damned close-run thing.

For nearly all of the season Celtic had led the table, and at one point had been 10 points clear of Aberdeen, although because of the weather and their League Cup run, they did have three games in hand. But come March Aberdeen mounted a relentless challenge, made all the more interesting because postponed fixtures meant they had to play Celtic twice in the League, away. Could Aberdeen steal the championship from Celtic at Parkhead? Unthinkable.

In the first match, on April 5, Drew Jarvie and Mark McGhee provided the goals to defeat Celtic 2-1. Now the jitters were beginning to show as Celtic went down 3-0 to Dundee United, although with six games to play Aberdeen still trailed by three points. Celtic then spectacularly crashed 5-1 at Dundee, who were already doomed to relegation, while Aberdeen beat Kilmarnock 3-1.

The crunch match – the game that would almost certainly determine the title – was on April 23 at Parkhead. A George McCluskey penalty gave Celtic the lead, but Steve Archibald, McGhee and Gordon Strachan silenced the Glasgow crowd to rack up a 3-1 win, taking Aberdeen to the top of the Premier Division for the first time that season.

On May 3, Aberdeen, in their penultimate fixture, travelled to Easter Road to play Hibs, while Celtic were playing their final fixture at Love Street against St Mirren. If Aberdeen won and Celtic drew then the championship would – barring mathematical miracles – belong to Aberdeen. Ferguson's team turned on the style and Hibs were duly routed 5-0.

Strachan: turning point

Meanwhile the visiting fans waited for news from Love Street where the match was running late. With minutes remaining, the game was still scoreless when the news went round that Celtic were being awarded a penalty. The referee consulted his linesman, awarded a free-kick outside the box and, shortly afterwards, blew the whistle. Instant jubilation. Aberdeen, providing they didn't lose by 10 goals at Partick Thistle on the following Tuesday (they drew 1-1) were the champions for the first time in 25 years.

Penalty misses in European final deepen Arsenal's season of gloom

"LUCKY old Arsenal," has been the taunt down the decades, and if ever that taunt was going to be forgotten, then May 1980 was the month that should have done it. Four days after losing the FA Cup final Arsenal travelled to the Heysel stadium in Brussels to meet Valencia in the European Cup Winners Cup final. It was Arsenal's 16th match in 46 days.

Valencia were formidable opponents: they were managed by Alfredo di Stefano and had Argentina's World Cup striker, Mario Kempes, and West Germany's Rainer Bonhof, in their team. Yet true to the modern tradition it was a final that both teams refused to either lose or win. After 120 minutes of counter-play, the winner would be decided by the lottery of a penalty shoot-out. It was the first time a European final would be settled this way.

Kempes took the first penalty and missed. Liam Brady then stepped up. If he scored then Arsenal would have the clear advantage and the pressure would be on the Spanish team. Brady, of all people, fluffed the opportunity. Now the pressure fluctuated back and forth. After eight successful penalties, the contest entered sudden death. Arias put Valencia 5-4 ahead. Graham Rix, 22, had to level the scores or Arsenal had lost. Pereira, the Valencia goalkeeper, moved as Rix shot, but the keeper had guessed right and saved the penalty.

Arsenal's misery was not over. There was still a Uefa Cup place up for grabs if they won both of their remaining League matches. Two days after the Heysel final they scrambled a 2-1 win at Wolves, but 48 hours after that match their last glimmering hope of rescuing something disappeared. They collapsed 5-0 at Middlesbrough.

Luck just had not rubbed Arsenal's way, despite all their efforts, bravery and determination. As a footnote to a season of failure, they set two incredible records: they were the first English side to play 70 competitive matches in a single season, and they were the first club – who had not lost a game in the competition – to fail to win a European trophy having reached the final.

Rix: heartbroken

Victory for Revie does him no good

DON REVIE's courtroom battle against the FA in December did little to enhance the image of English football.

Revie, banned for 10 years for walking out of the England manager's job to take a highly-paid post in the United Arab Emirates, won the argument that the penalty that had been imposed was an unfair restraint of trade. But during the two-week court case he hardly enhanced his reputation.

Revie's barrister grilled Sir Harold Thompson, the chairman of the FA, about the way Revie had been found guilty of bringing the game into disrepute. But Revie fared little better when he was cross-examined about his motives.

The court found in Revie's favour, with Mr Justice Cantley saying that Thompson had shown a "likelihood of bias" when he was the chairman of the FA inquiry into Revie's conduct. As a result, the 10-year ban had to be overturned.

But Mr Justice Cantley said that he made the ruling "with great regret". He said: "The way Mr Revie resigned presented a sensational and outrageous example of disloyalty, breach of duty, discourtesy and selfishness."

Ted Croker, the FA secretary, said that the judge's ruling had shown that the FA were justified in charging Revie with bringing the game into disrepute. Although, technically, there was nothing to stop the FA taking further action they were not going to pursue the case because they did not want to appear to be vindictive.

England's honour in tatters

ENGLAND, who had comfortably qualified for the European championships in Italy, had high hopes. Kevin Keegan had even said when he signed for Southampton in February that they would win the competition. By the end of a tedious tournament – bar the final – England's reputation was in tatters, both on the field and, more importantly off it.

It might all have been so different if Belgium had not equalised in England's opening match in Turin on June 12. Ray Wilkins had sprung Belgium's offside trap in the 32nd minute, but then Ceulemans equalised six minutes later and fighting broke out on the terraces between Italian and English fans.

The crowd was some 15,000, of which a large number were England supporters somewhat the worse for drink. When the Italians began taunting them about the equaliser, scuffles broke out, seats were torn up and serious fighting ensued behind the England goal. The Italian police stepped in smartly and dispersed the fracas with batons and tear gas.

Unfortunately the gas spread to the pitch and play was held up for five minutes as the players, eyes streaming, fought to regain their breath. Although Tony Woodcock seemed to have grabbed the winner in the 73rd minute – it was ruled offside – the match had effectively been ended by the crowd trouble. More than 70 fans were taken to hospital, and the next day Uefa fined the FA £8,000.

A dark cloud now hung over the event. Italy, their players and officials still reeling from the scandal of bribery allegations against AC Milan and other clubs, did not help matters by playing the most sterile football ever seen at a major tournament.

Their single goal in three matches – against England – was a result of a lacklustre tackle by Phil Neal on Graziani. Fortunately the host nation's spinelessness cost them a place in the final when Belgium outdid them at their own craven game,

Star turn: Schuster brightened the tournament

Flashpoint: England fans rioted after Belgium's goal

secured a 0-0 draw and eliminated them having scored more goals.

The one bright spot in the entire event was Belgium's match with West Germany, who had introduced the youngsters Bernd Schuster, 20, the revelation of the tournament, and

Hans Peter Briegel, 24, into an already impressive side. West Germany's 2-1 victory confirmed them as the pre-eminent European side, but it took a goal three minutes from time headed home by Horst Hrubesch – his second in the match – to shake off the Belgian challenge.

Canny Paisley looks to the future

EMLYN HUGHES had left Liverpool before the season started, and some of the other players were starting to show their age. That apart, nothing much had changed at Liverpool.

After a couple of early setbacks they did the one thing that they were best at – not lose. Sixteen games without defeat took them to the top of the table, and once they had got there in December they were not going to be dislodged. Liverpool's progress was not quite as smooth as last season but they still won the title with a game in hand.

Paisley, meanwhile had his eye on the future. During the summer he heeded the advice of one of his scouts and spent £300,000 on a striker who had only played 33 times in the Fourth Division for Chester – Ian Rush.

Plucked from obscurity: Rush had only played 33 matches

Forest overcome every obstacle to stay on top of Europe's summit

BRIAN CLOUGH was far from happy with some of his players' efforts in the League. After a defeat by Bolton he fulminated: "I know what their approach is to their wages, cars, houses, agents and newspaper columns. I want to know what their attitude to football is, because that's where everything else stems from."

But Clough could have no complaints about his players' attitude in the European Cup. Each round set them a harder task and each time his team responded with more determination.

At least this time the draw kept Nottingham Forest and Liverpool apart in the first round. But Liverpool surprisingly fell at the first hurdle for the second successive year when they badly underestimated the threat posed by Dynamo Tbilisi, losing 3-0 in Russia.

Forest had few problems, apart from the distances they had to travel, against Oester Vaxjo of Sweden and Arges Pitesti of Romania in the first two rounds. The hard work really started in the quarter-finals.

Dynamo Berlin left the City Ground with a 1-0 advantage but Forest were quick to wipe that out in East Berlin, scoring three goals in the first half with Trevor Francis scoring twice and John Robertson adding a penalty.

With Ajax, Real Madrid and Hamburg the other semi-finalists there were not going to be any easy games. This time Forest did not falter at home and the Francis and Robertson (with yet another penalty) double act was in fine form. Their two goals enabled Forest to withstand a 1-0 defeat at Ajax.

In the final, against Hamburg, Forest were severely hampered. Francis had torn an Achilles tendon and could not play, Peter Shilton limped through the game with a pain-killing injection in his pulled calf muscle, and Stan Bowles had walked out on the club.

With the disruption of his team, Clough, not surprisingly, decided a cautious approach was needed on May 28. He packed the Forest midfield to counter the threat posed by Kevin Keegan and chose to play on the break.

The tactics worked to perfection in the 20th minute when Robertson finished a quick counter-attack with a thunderous shot from outside the area that went in off the post. Forest then shut up shop with Shilton, despite his injury, determined not to make another mistake as he had done in the League Cup final.

So the European Cup returned to England for the fourth year in succession and Forest became only the second English club after Liverpool to retain the trophy. Clough, after his earlier complaints about his players, was delighted: "The odds were stacked against us but it was the best 90 minutes we ever had. It was absolutely marvellous."

Robertson: broke deadlock

169

LEAGUE TABLES AND RESULTS 1970 – 1980

	1970-71	1971-72	1972-73	1973-74	1974-75
WORLD CUP				West Germany 2 Holland 1	
EUROPEAN CHAMPIONSHIP		West Germany 3 USSR 0			
EUROPEAN CUP	Ajax 2 Panathinaikos 0	Ajax 2 Inter Milan 0	Ajax 1 Juventus 0	Bayern Munich 4 Atletico Madrid 0, after 1-1	Bayern Munich 2 Leeds United 0
EUROPEAN CUP WINNERS CUP	Chelsea 2 Real Madrid 1, after 1-1	Rangers 3 Dynamo Moscow 2	AC Milan 1 Leeds United 0	Magdeburg 2 AC Milan 0	Dynamo Kiev 3 Ferencvaros 0
FAIRS CUP – UEFA CUP (1971)	Leeds United beat Juventus 2-2 1-1 on away goals	Tottenham Hotspur beat Wolverhampton Wanderers 2-1 1-1	Liverpool beat Borussia Moenchengladbach 3-0 0-2	Feyenoord beat Tottenham Hotspur 2-2 2-0	Borussia Moenchengladbach beat Twente Enschede 0-0 5-1
FA CUP	Arsenal 2 Liverpool 1	Leeds United 1 Arsenal 0	Sunderland 1 Leeds United 0	Liverpool 3 Newcastle United 0	West Ham United 2 Fulham 0

FIRST DIVISION

1970-71

	P	W	D	L	F	A	Pts
Arsenal	42	29	7	6	71	29	65
Leeds	42	27	10	5	72	30	64
Tottenham	42	19	14	9	54	33	52
Wolves	42	22	8	12	64	54	52
Liverpool	42	17	17	8	42	24	51
Chelsea	42	18	15	9	52	42	51
Soton	42	17	12	13	56	44	46
Man Utd	42	16	11	15	65	66	43
Derby	42	16	10	16	56	54	42
Coventry	42	16	10	16	37	38	42
Man City	42	12	17	13	47	42	41
Newcastle	42	14	13	15	44	46	41
Stoke	42	12	13	17	44	48	37
Everton	42	12	13	17	54	60	37
Huddersf'd	42	11	14	17	40	49	36
Nottm F	42	14	8	20	42	61	36
West Brom	42	10	15	17	58	75	35
C Palace	42	12	11	19	39	57	35
Ipswich	42	12	10	20	42	48	34
West Ham	42	10	14	18	47	60	34
Burnley	*42*	*7*	*13*	*22*	*29*	*63*	*27*
Blackpool	*42*	*4*	*15*	*23*	*34*	*66*	*23*

1971-72

	P	W	D	L	F	A	Pts
Derby	42	24	10	8	69	33	58
Leeds	42	24	9	9	73	31	57
Liverpool	42	24	9	9	64	30	57
Man City	42	23	11	8	77	45	57
Arsenal	42	22	8	12	58	40	52
Tottenham	42	19	13	10	63	42	51
Chelsea	42	18	12	12	58	49	48
Man Utd	42	19	10	13	69	61	48
Wolves	42	18	11	13	65	57	47
Sheff Utd	42	17	12	13	61	60	46
Newcastle	42	15	11	16	49	52	41
Leicester	42	13	13	16	41	46	39
Ipswich	42	11	16	15	39	53	38
West Ham	42	12	12	18	47	51	36
Everton	42	9	18	15	37	48	36
West Brom	42	12	11	19	42	54	35
Stoke	42	10	15	17	39	56	35
Coventry	42	9	15	18	44	67	33
Soton	42	12	7	23	52	80	31
C Palace	42	8	13	21	39	65	29
Nottm F	*42*	*8*	*9*	*25*	*47*	*81*	*25*
Huddersf'd	*42*	*6*	*13*	*23*	*27*	*59*	*25*

1972-73

	P	W	D	L	F	A	Pts
Liverpool	42	25	10	7	72	42	60
Arsenal	42	23	11	8	57	43	57
Leeds	42	21	11	10	71	45	53
Ipswich	42	17	14	11	55	45	48
Wolves	42	18	11	13	66	54	47
West Ham	42	17	12	13	67	53	46
Derby	42	19	8	15	56	54	46
Tottenham	42	16	13	13	58	48	45
Newcastle	42	16	13	13	60	51	45
Birmingham	42	15	12	15	53	54	42
Man City	42	15	11	16	57	60	41
Chelsea	42	13	14	15	49	51	40
Soton	42	11	18	13	47	52	40
Sheff Utd	42	15	10	17	51	59	40
Stoke	42	14	10	18	61	56	38
Leicester	42	10	17	15	40	46	37
Everton	42	13	11	18	41	49	37
Man Utd	42	12	13	17	44	60	37
Coventry	42	13	9	20	40	55	35
Norwich	42	11	10	21	36	63	32
C Palace	*42*	*9*	*12*	*21*	*41*	*58*	*30*
West Brom	*42*	*9*	*10*	*23*	*38*	*62*	*28*

1973-74

	P	W	D	L	F	A	Pts
Leeds	42	24	14	4	66	31	62
Liverpool	42	22	13	7	52	31	57
Derby	42	17	14	11	52	42	48
Ipswich	42	18	11	13	67	58	47
Stoke	42	15	16	11	54	42	46
Burnley	42	16	14	12	56	53	46
Everton	42	16	12	14	50	48	44
QPR	42	13	17	12	56	52	43
Leicester	42	13	16	13	51	41	42
Arsenal	42	14	14	14	49	51	42
Tottenham	42	14	14	14	45	50	42
Wolves	42	13	15	14	49	49	41
Sheff Utd	42	14	12	16	44	49	40
Man City	42	14	12	16	39	46	40
Newcastle	42	13	12	17	49	48	38
Coventry	42	14	10	18	43	54	38
Chelsea	42	12	13	17	56	60	37
West Ham	42	11	15	16	55	60	37
Birmingham	42	12	13	17	52	64	37
Soton	*42*	*11*	*14*	*17*	*47*	*68*	*36*
Man Utd	*42*	*10*	*12*	*20*	*38*	*48*	*32*
Norwich	*42*	*7*	*15*	*20*	*37*	*62*	*29*

1974-75

	P	W	D	L	F	A	Pts
Derby	42	21	11	10	67	49	53
Liverpool	42	20	11	11	60	39	51
Ipswich	42	23	5	14	66	44	51
Everton	42	16	18	8	56	42	50
Stoke	42	17	15	10	64	48	49
Sheff Utd	42	18	13	11	58	51	49
Middlesbro	42	18	12	12	54	40	48
Man City	42	18	10	14	54	54	46
Leeds	42	16	13	13	57	49	45
Burnley	42	17	11	14	68	67	45
QPR	42	16	10	16	54	54	42
Wolves	42	14	11	17	57	54	39
West Ham	42	13	13	16	58	59	39
Coventry	42	12	15	15	51	62	39
Newcastle	42	15	9	18	59	72	39
Arsenal	42	13	11	18	47	49	37
Birmingham	42	14	9	19	53	61	37
Leicester	42	12	12	18	46	60	36
Tottenham	42	13	8	21	52	63	34
Luton	*42*	*11*	*11*	*20*	*47*	*65*	*33*
Chelsea	*42*	*9*	*15*	*18*	*42*	*72*	*33*
Carlisle	*42*	*12*	*5*	*25*	*43*	*59*	*29*

	1970-71	1971-72	1972-73	1973-74	1974-75
SECOND DIVISION	Champions: Leicester City Also promoted: Sheffield United Relegated: Blackburn Rovers, Bolton Wanderers	Champions: Norwich City Also promoted: Birmingham City Relegated: Charlton Athletic, Watford	Champions: Burnley Also promoted: Queen's Park Rangers Relegated: Huddersfield Town, Brighton & Hove Albion	Champions: Middlesbrough Also promoted: Luton Town, Carlisle United Relegated: Crystal Palace, Preston North End, Swindon Town	Champions: Manchester United Also promoted: Aston Villa, Norwich City Relegated: Millwall, Cardiff City, Sheffield Wednesday
THIRD DIVISION	Champions: Preston North End Also promoted: Fulham Relegated: Reading, Bury, Doncaster Rovers, Gillingham	Champions: Aston Villa Also promoted: Brighton & Hove Albion Relegated: Mansfield Town, Barnsley, Torquay United, Bradford City	Champions: Bolton Wanderers Also promoted: Notts County Relegated: Rotherham United, Brentford, Swansea City, Scunthorpe United	Champions: Oldham Athletic Also promoted: Bristol Rovers, York Relegated: Cambridge United, Shrewsbury Town, Southport, Rochdale	Champions: Blackburn Rovers Also promoted: Plymouth Argyle, Charlton Athletic Relegated: Bournemouth, Tranmere Rovers, Watford, Huddersfield Town
FOURTH DIVISION	Champions: Notts County Also promoted: Bournemouth, Oldham Athletic, York City	Champions: Grimsby Town Also promoted: Southend United, Brentford, Scunthorpe United	Champions: Southport Also promoted: Hereford United, Cambridge United, Aldershot	Champions: Peterborough United Also promoted: Gillingham, Colchester United, Bury	Champions: Mansfield Town Also promoted: Shrewsbury Town, Rotherham United, Chester
LEAGUE CUP	Tottenham Hotspur 2 Aston Villa 0	Stoke City 2 Chelsea 1	Tottenham Hotspur 1 Norwich City 0	Wolverhampton Wanderers 2 Manchester City 1	Aston Villa 1 Norwich City 0
SCOTTISH CUP	Celtic 2 Rangers 1, after 1-1	Celtic 6 Hibernian 1	Rangers 3 Celtic 2	Celtic 3 Dundee United 0	Celtic 3 Airdrie 1

SCOTTISH FIRST DIVISION

1970-71

	P	W	D	L	F	A	Pts
Celtic	34	25	6	3	89	23	56
Aberdeen	34	24	6	4	68	18	54
St J'stone	34	19	6	9	59	44	44
Rangers	34	16	9	9	58	34	41
Dundee	34	14	10	10	53	45	38
Dundee U	34	14	8	12	53	54	36
Falkirk	34	13	9	12	46	53	35
Morton	34	13	8	13	44	44	34
Motherwell	34	13	8	13	43	47	34
Airdrie	34	13	8	13	60	65	34
Hearts	34	13	7	14	41	40	33
Hibernian	34	10	10	14	47	53	30
Kilmarnock	34	10	8	16	43	67	28
Ayr	34	9	8	17	37	54	26
Clyde	34	8	10	16	33	59	26
Dunfermline	34	6	11	17	44	56	23
St Mirren	*34*	*7*	*9*	*18*	*38*	*56*	*23*
Cowdenb'th	*34*	*7*	*3*	*24*	*33*	*77*	*17*

1971-72

	P	W	D	L	F	A	Pts
Celtic	34	28	4	2	96	28	60
Aberdeen	34	21	8	5	80	26	50
Rangers	34	21	2	11	71	38	44
Hibernian	34	19	6	9	62	34	44
Dundee	34	14	13	7	59	38	41
Hearts	34	13	13	8	53	49	39
Partick	34	12	10	12	53	54	34
St J'stone	34	12	8	14	52	58	32
Dundee U	34	12	7	15	55	70	31
Motherwell	34	11	7	16	49	69	29
Kilmarnock	34	11	6	17	49	64	28
Ayr	34	9	10	15	40	58	28
Morton	34	10	7	17	46	52	27
Falkirk	34	10	7	17	44	60	27
Airdrie	34	7	12	15	44	76	26
East Fife	34	5	15	14	34	61	25
Clyde	*34*	*7*	*10*	*17*	*33*	*66*	*24*
Dunfermline	*34*	*7*	*9*	*18*	*31*	*50*	*23*

1972-73

	P	W	D	L	F	A	Pts
Celtic	34	26	5	3	93	28	57
Rangers	34	26	4	4	74	30	56
Hibernian	34	19	7	8	74	33	45
Aberdeen	34	16	11	7	61	34	43
Dundee	34	17	9	8	68	43	43
Ayr	34	16	8	10	50	51	40
Dundee U	34	17	5	12	56	51	39
Motherwell	34	11	9	14	38	48	31
East Fife	34	11	8	15	46	54	30
Hearts	34	12	6	16	39	50	30
St J'stone	34	10	9	15	52	67	29
Morton	34	10	8	16	47	53	28
Partick	34	10	8	16	40	53	28
Falkirk	34	7	12	15	38	56	26
Arbroath	34	9	8	17	39	63	26
Dumbarton	34	6	11	17	43	72	23
Kilmarnock	*34*	*7*	*8*	*19*	*40*	*71*	*22*
Airdrie	*34*	*4*	*8*	*22*	*34*	*75*	*16*

1973-74

	P	W	D	L	F	A	Pts
Celtic	34	23	7	4	82	27	53
Hibernian	34	20	9	5	75	42	49
Rangers	34	21	6	7	67	34	48
Aberdeen	34	13	16	5	46	26	42
Dundee	34	16	7	11	67	48	39
Hearts	34	14	10	10	54	43	38
Ayr	34	15	8	11	44	40	38
Dundee U	34	15	7	12	55	51	37
Motherwell	34	14	7	13	45	40	35
Dumbarton	34	11	7	16	43	58	29
Partick	34	9	10	15	33	46	28
St J'stone	34	9	10	15	41	60	28
Arbroath	34	10	7	17	52	69	27
Morton	34	8	10	16	37	49	26
Clyde	34	8	9	17	29	65	25
Dunfermline	34	8	8	18	43	65	24
East Fife	*34*	*9*	*6*	*19*	*26*	*51*	*24*
Falkirk	*34*	*4*	*14*	*16*	*33*	*58*	*22*

1974-75

	P	W	D	L	F	A	Pts
Rangers	34	25	6	3	86	33	56
Hibernian	34	20	9	5	69	37	49
Celtic	34	20	5	9	81	41	45
Dundee U	34	19	7	8	72	43	45
Aberdeen	34	16	9	9	66	43	41
Dundee	34	16	6	12	48	42	38
Ayr	34	14	8	12	50	61	36
Hearts	34	11	13	10	47	52	35
St J'stone	34	11	12	11	41	44	34
Motherwell	34	14	5	15	52	57	33
Airdrie	34	11	9	14	43	55	31
Kilmarnock	34	8	15	11	52	68	31
Partick	34	10	10	14	48	62	30
Dumbarton	34	7	10	17	44	55	24
Dunfermline	34	7	9	18	46	66	23
Clyde	34	6	10	18	40	63	22
Morton	34	6	10	18	31	62	22
Arbroath	34	5	7	22	34	66	17

	1970-71	1971-72	1972-73	1973-74	1974-75
SCOTTISH SECOND DIV	Champions: Partick Thistle Also promoted: East Fife	Champions: Dumbarton Also promoted: Arbroath	Champions: Clyde Also promoted: Dunfermline Athletic	Champions: Airdrie Also promoted: Kilmarnock	Champions: Falkirk Runners-up: Queen of the South
SCOTTISH LEAGUE CUP	Rangers 1 Celtic 0	Partick 4 Celtic 1	Hibernian 2 Celtic 1	Dundee United 1 Celtic 0	Celtic 6 Hibernian 3

	1975-76	1976-77	1977-78	1978-79	1979-80
WORLD CUP			Argentina 3 Holland 1		
EUROPEAN CHAMPIONSHIP	Czechoslovakia 2 West Germany 2; Czechoslovakia won 5-3 on penalties				West Germany 2 Belgium 1
EUROPEAN CUP	Bayern Munich 1 St Etienne 0	Liverpool 3 Borussia Moenchengladbach 1	Liverpool 1 FC Bruges 0	Nottingham Forest 1 Malmo 0	Nottingham Forest 1 SV Hamburg 0
EUROPEAN CUP WINNERS CUP	Anderlecht 4 West Ham United 2	SV Hamburg 2 Anderlecht 0	Anderlecht 4 FK Austria 0	Barcelona 4 Fortuna Dusseldorf 3	Valencia 0 Arsenal 0; Valencia won 5-4 on penalties
UEFA CUP	Liverpool beat FC Bruges 3-2 1-1	Juventus beat Athletic Bilbao 1-0 1-2 on away goals	PSV Eindhoven beat Bastia 0-0 3-0	Borussia Moenchengladbach beat Red Star Belgrade 1-1 1-0	Eintracht Frankfurt beat Borussia M'gladbach 2-3 1-0 on away goals
FA CUP	Southampton 1 Manchester United 0	Manchester United 2 Liverpool 1	Ipswich Town 1 Arsenal 0	Arsenal 3 Manchester United 2	West Ham United 1 Arsenal 0

FIRST DIVISION

1975-76
	P	W	D	L	F	A	Pts
Liverpool	42	23	14	5	66	31	60
QPR	42	24	11	7	67	33	59
Man Utd	42	23	10	9	68	42	56
Derby	42	21	11	10	75	58	53
Leeds	42	21	9	12	65	46	51
Ipswich	42	16	14	12	54	48	46
Leicester	42	13	19	10	48	51	45
Man City	42	16	11	15	64	46	43
Tottenham	42	14	15	13	63	63	43
Norwich	42	16	10	16	58	58	42
Everton	42	15	12	15	60	66	42
Stoke	42	15	11	16	48	50	41
Middlesbro	42	15	10	17	46	45	40
Coventry	42	13	14	15	47	57	40
Newcastle	42	15	9	18	71	62	39
Aston Villa	42	11	17	14	51	59	39
Arsenal	42	13	10	19	47	53	36
West Ham	42	13	10	19	48	71	36
Birmingham	42	13	7	22	57	75	33
Wolves	42	10	10	22	51	68	30
Burnley	42	9	10	23	43	66	28
Sheff Utd	42	6	10	26	33	82	22

1976-77
	P	W	D	L	F	A	Pts
Liverpool	42	23	11	8	62	33	57
Man City	42	21	14	7	60	34	56
Ipswich	42	22	8	12	66	39	52
Aston Villa	42	22	7	13	76	50	51
Newcastle	42	18	13	11	64	49	49
Man Utd	42	18	11	13	71	62	47
West Brom	42	16	13	13	62	56	45
Arsenal	42	16	11	15	64	59	43
Everton	42	14	14	14	62	64	42
Leeds	42	15	12	15	48	51	42
Leicester	42	12	18	12	47	60	42
Middlesbro	42	14	13	15	40	45	41
Birmingham	42	13	12	17	63	61	38
QPR	42	13	12	17	47	52	38
Derby	42	9	19	14	50	55	37
Norwich	42	14	9	19	47	64	37
West Ham	42	11	14	17	46	65	36
Bristol C	42	11	13	18	38	48	35
Coventry	42	10	15	17	48	59	35
Sunderland	42	11	12	19	46	54	34
Stoke	42	10	14	18	28	51	34
Tottenham	42	12	9	21	48	72	33

1977-78
	P	W	D	L	F	A	Pts
Nottm F	42	25	14	3	69	24	64
Liverpool	42	24	9	9	65	34	57
Everton	42	22	11	9	76	45	55
Man City	42	20	12	10	74	51	52
Arsenal	42	21	10	11	60	37	52
West Brom	42	18	14	10	62	53	50
Coventry	42	18	12	12	75	62	48
Aston Villa	42	18	10	14	57	42	46
Leeds	42	18	10	14	63	53	46
Man Utd	42	16	10	16	67	63	42
Birmingham	42	16	9	17	55	60	41
Derby	42	14	13	15	54	59	41
Norwich	42	11	18	13	52	66	40
Middlesbro	42	12	15	15	42	54	39
Wolves	42	12	12	18	51	64	36
Chelsea	42	11	14	17	46	69	36
Bristol C	42	11	13	18	49	53	35
Ipswich	42	11	13	18	47	61	35
QPR	42	9	15	18	47	64	33
West Ham	42	12	8	22	52	69	32
Newcastle	42	6	10	26	42	78	22
Leicester	42	5	12	25	26	70	22

1978-79
	P	W	D	L	F	A	Pts
Liverpool	42	30	8	4	85	16	68
Nottm F	42	21	18	3	61	26	60
West Brom	42	24	11	7	72	35	59
Everton	42	17	17	8	52	40	51
Leeds	42	18	14	10	70	52	50
Ipswich	42	20	9	13	63	49	49
Arsenal	42	17	14	11	61	48	48
Aston Villa	42	15	16	11	59	49	46
Man Utd	42	15	15	12	60	63	45
Coventry	42	14	16	12	58	68	44
Tottenham	42	13	15	14	48	61	41
Middlesbro	42	15	10	17	57	50	40
Bristol C	42	15	10	17	47	51	40
Soton	42	12	16	14	47	53	40
Manchester	42	13	13	16	58	56	39
Norwich	42	7	23	12	51	57	37
Bolton	42	12	11	19	54	75	35
Wolves	42	13	8	21	44	68	34
Derby	42	10	11	21	44	71	31
QPR	42	6	13	23	45	73	25
Birmingham	42	6	10	26	37	64	22
Chelsea	42	5	10	27	44	92	20

1979-80
	P	W	D	L	F	A	Pts
Liverpool	42	25	10	7	81	30	60
Man Utd	42	24	10	8	65	35	58
Ipswich	42	22	9	11	68	39	53
Arsenal	42	18	16	8	52	36	52
Nottm F	42	20	8	14	63	43	48
Wolves	42	19	9	14	58	47	47
Aston Villa	42	16	14	12	51	50	46
Soton	42	18	9	15	65	53	45
Middlesbro	42	16	12	14	50	44	44
West Brom	42	11	19	12	54	50	41
Leeds	42	13	14	15	46	50	40
Norwich	42	13	14	15	58	66	40
C Palace	42	12	16	14	41	50	40
Tottenham	42	15	10	17	52	62	40
Coventry	42	16	7	19	56	66	39
Brighton	42	11	15	16	47	57	37
Man City	42	12	13	17	43	66	37
Stoke	42	13	10	19	44	58	36
Everton	42	9	17	16	43	51	35
Bristol C	42	9	13	20	37	66	31
Derby	42	11	8	23	47	67	30
Bolton	42	5	15	22	38	73	25

	1975-76	1976-77	1977-78	1978-79	1979-80
SECOND DIVISION	Champions: Sunderland Also promoted: Bristol City, West Bromwich Albion Relegated: Oxford United, York City, Portsmouth	Champions: Wolverhampton Wanderers Also promoted: Chelsea, Nottm F Relegated: Carlisle United, Plymouth Argyle, Hereford United	Champions: Bolton Wanderers Also promoted: Southampton, Tottenham Hotspur Relegated: Blackpool, Mansfield Town, Hull City	Champions: Crystal Palace Also promoted: Brighton & Hove Albion, Stoke City Relegated: Sheffield United, Millwall, Blackburn Rovers	Champions: Leicester City Also promoted: Sunderland, Birmingham City Relegated: Fulham, Burnley, Charlton Athletic
THIRD DIVISION	Champions: Hereford United Also promoted: Cardiff City, Millwall Relegated: Aldershot, Colchester United, Southend United, Halifax Town	Champions: Mansfield Town Also promoted: Brighton & Hove Albion, Crystal Palace Relegated: Reading, Northampton Town, Grimsby Town, York City	Champions: Wrexham Also promoted: Cambridge United, Preston North End Relegated: Port Vale, Bradford City, Hereford United, Portsmouth	Champions: Shrewsbury Town Also promoted: Watford, Swansea City Relegated: Peterborough United, Walsall, Tranmere Rovers, Lincoln City	Champions: Grimsby Town Also promoted: Blackburn Rovers, Sheffield Wednesday Relegated: Bury, Southend United, Mansfield Town, Wimbledon
FOURTH DIVISION	Champions: Lincoln City Also promoted: Northampton Town, Reading, Tranmere Rovers	Champions: Cambridge United Also promoted: Exeter City, Colchester United, Bradford City	Champions: Watford Also promoted: Southend United, Swansea City, Brentford	Champions: Reading Also promoted: Grimsby Town, Wimbledon, Barnsley	Champions: Huddersfield Town Also promoted: Walsall, Newport County, Portsmouth
LEAGUE CUP	Manchester City 2 Newcastle United 1	Aston Villa 3 Everton 2, after 0-0 and 1-1	Nottingham Forest 1 Liverpool 0, after 0-0	Nottingham Forest 3 Southampton 2	Wolverhampton Wanderers 1 Nottingham Forest 0
SCOTTISH CUP	Rangers 3 Hearts 1	Celtic 1 Rangers 0	Rangers 2 Aberdeen 1	Rangers 3 Hibernian 2, after 0-0 0-0	Celtic 1 Rangers 0

SCOTTISH PREMIER DIVISION

1975-76
	P	W	D	L	F	A	Pts
Rangers	36	23	8	5	60	24	54
Celtic	36	21	6	9	71	42	48
Hibernian	36	18	7	11	55	43	43
Motherwell	36	16	8	12	57	48	40
Hearts	36	13	9	14	39	45	35
Ayr	36	14	5	17	46	59	33
Aberdeen	36	11	10	15	49	50	32
Dundee U	36	12	8	16	46	48	32
Dundee	36	11	10	15	49	62	32
St J'stone	36	3	5	28	28	79	11

1976-77
	P	W	D	L	F	A	Pts
Celtic	36	23	9	4	79	39	55
Rangers	36	18	10	8	62	37	46
Aberdeen	36	16	11	9	56	42	43
Dundee U	36	16	9	11	54	45	41
Partick	36	11	13	12	40	44	35
Hibernian	36	8	18	10	34	35	34
Motherwell	36	10	12	14	57	60	32
Ayr	36	11	8	17	44	68	30
Hearts	36	7	13	16	49	66	27
Kilmarnock	36	4	9	23	32	71	17

1977-78
	P	W	D	L	F	A	Pts
Rangers	36	24	7	5	76	39	55
Aberdeen	36	22	9	5	68	29	53
Dundee U	36	16	8	12	42	32	40
Hibernian	36	15	7	14	51	43	37
Celtic	36	15	6	15	63	54	36
Motherwell	36	13	7	16	45	52	33
Partick	36	14	5	17	52	64	33
St Mirren	36	11	8	17	52	63	30
Ayr	36	9	6	21	36	68	24
Clydebank	36	6	7	23	23	64	19

1978-79
	P	W	D	L	F	A	Pts
Celtic	36	21	6	9	61	37	48
Rangers	36	18	9	9	52	35	45
Dundee U	36	18	8	10	56	37	44
Aberdeen	36	13	14	9	59	36	40
Hibernian	36	12	13	11	44	48	37
St Mirren	36	15	6	15	45	41	36
Morton	36	12	12	12	52	53	36
Partick	36	13	8	15	42	39	34
Hearts	36	8	7	21	39	71	23
Motherwell	36	5	7	24	33	86	17

1979-80
	P	W	D	L	F	A	Pts
Aberdeen	36	19	10	7	68	36	48
Celtic	36	18	11	7	61	38	47
St Mirren	36	15	12	9	56	49	42
Dundee U	36	12	13	11	43	30	37
Rangers	36	15	7	14	50	46	37
Morton	36	14	8	14	51	46	36
Partick	36	11	14	11	43	47	36
Kilmarnock	36	11	11	14	36	52	33
Dundee	36	10	6	20	47	73	26
Hibernian	36	6	6	24	29	67	18

	1975-76	1976-77	1977-78	1978-79	1979-80
SCOTTISH FIRST DIVISION	Champions: Partick Thistle Also promoted: Kilmarnock Relegated: Dunfermline Athletic, Clyde	Champions: St Mirren Also promoted: Clydebank Relegated: Raith Rovers, Falkirk	Champions: Morton Also promoted: Hearts Relegated: Alloa, East Fife	Champions: Dundee Also promoted: Kilmarnock Relegated: Montrose, Queen of the South	Champions: Hearts Also promoted: Airdrie Relegated: Arbroath, Clyde
SCOTTISH SECOND DIV	Champions: Clydebank Also promoted: Raith Rovers	Champions: Stirling Albion Also promoted: Alloa	Champions: Clyde Also promoted: Raith Rovers	Champions: Berwick Rangers Also promoted: Dunfermline Athletic	Champions: Falkirk Also promoted: East Stirling
SCOTTISH LEAGUE CUP	Rangers 1 Celtic 0	Aberdeen 2 Celtic 1	Rangers 2 Celtic 1	Rangers 2 Aberdeen 1	Dundee United 3 Aberdeen 0, after 0-0

THE 1980-81 SEASON

End of home championship

As an international tournament the home championships had been in the doldrums for years. In the first half of the century, before the four home nations embraced Fifa and entered the World Cup, there was a degree of validity in the importance of the event. Indeed in the 1950 and 1954 World Cups it was designated as a qualifying tournament in its own right with the top two countries qualifying for the finals. But by the 1980s the international fixture list both for club and country was extremely crowded what with European competitions, European championships and World Cup qualifying tournaments. As a consequence the gloss had gone off the championship and only the fixture between Scotland and England attracted sizeable crowds.

And that was another problem. The biennial invasion of the rowdy Scots to Wembley had become more than an irritant – particularly when the Tartan army invaded the pitch at Wembley and demolished the goalposts in 1977. Thus in September the FA announced that there would be no tickets available for spectators from Scotland for the 1981 match in England. The Scottish Supporters' Club unsuccessfully challenged this in the courts citing the Race Relations Act. Then the riots during the Maze hunger strike caused both England and Wales to refuse to play in Belfast. The championship was abandoned despite Scotland having fulfilled all their fixtures. It was the death-knell and the championship was finally killed off in 1984, its centenary year.

Wind of change much needed

As the decade started Britain was deep in the grip of recession – inflation was still high and unemployment had passed 2m and was still rising – and football was not immune to the country's financial woes. Attendances were declining and there was a growing number of people within the game who realised that football needed to act before the rot really set in.

So on August 11, just before the season started, the Secretaries, Coaches and Managers Association published their detailed analysis of the problem: "Soccer – the fight for survival. A blueprint for the future." It was a wide-ranging review that combined the best of thinking from the elder statesmen and the brightest young minds – the members of the study group were Alan Dicks, Ken Friar, Harry Haslam, Bill Nicholson, Ron Saunders, Graham Taylor and Terry Venables.

Many of their proposals went to the heart of issues that were to dog football for the next decade. But, as always, chairmen seemed to be more concerned with the interests of their of own club rather than the overall good of the game.

Two days of talks were held in October and an extraordinary general meeting was called on February 9. By then many of the proposals had been rejected (reducing the number of clubs in the top two divisions and regionalising the Third and Fourth Divisions; cutting the size of the majority needed to get decisions taken) and others had been deferred for further discussion (appointing one person to have overall charge of the running of football; introducing professional referees).

Football hooligans? Well there are 92 club chairmen for a start

Brian Clough

But some progress was made. At the least the clubs managed to agree to award three points for a win next season, increase the voting power of Third and Fourth Division clubs, and limit the number of matches played on Friday and Sunday.

The issue of Sunday football was the perfect illustration of why somebody was needed to settle disputes between the Football League and the Football Association. Because of the three-day week, the Football League decided to allow games to be played on a Sunday for the first time since 1974. But when Port Vale sought permission from the FA to stage a Cup match on a Sunday they were refused, with the FA re-stating its opposition to Sunday play.

And it wasn't only off the field that football had its troubles. Violence at grounds was also becoming commonplace. When Terry Curran of Sheffield Wednesday was sent off at Oldham on September 6 visiting fans ran amok. The match was held up for half an hour and the incident reduced Jack Charlton, the Wednesday manager, to tears. On the same day, a young Middlesbrough fan died when his head was smashed in outside Ayresome Park after the match with Nottingham Forest. And West Ham were forced to play the second leg of their European Cup Winners' Cup match against Castilla behind closed doors because of the outrageous behaviour of their so-called fans in Madrid.

With spectators increasingly unable to afford to go to watch matches, and ever more worried for their safety if they did, it was little wonder that the wise men's fears were justified. By the end of the season attendances had slumped by 2.7m to 21.9m, costing about £6m in lost gate receipts. The transfer market slumped and many clubs were forced to sell star players at a loss to raise money.

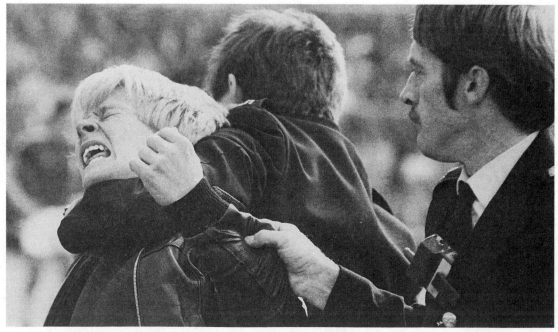

The unacceptable face of football: one of 13 arrests which marred Sheffield Wednesday's match at Oldham

Allison extravagance costs City dear

Champagne Charlies: John Bond and Malcolm Allison, two managers who squandered Manchester City's millions

THE BIG-SPENDING, high-living Malcolm Allison duly got his comeuppance the second time around at Maine Road when he was sacked as manager in December by Manchester City yet again. But this time he left the club in a financially parlous state having spent over £4m on players, some of them non-descripts.

Allison had formed a flamboyant managerial partnership with Joe Mercer in the late 1960s and the pair put City – always in the shadow of their more illustrious neighbours, United – firmly on the Manchester map when they won the League championship, the FA Cup, the European Cup Winners' Cup and the League Cup. When Mercer left to be the general manager of Coventry City in 1973, Allison had taken sole charge but the golden era quickly came to a sudden end and he left after eight months.

But by January 1979 the cigar-smoking, champagne Charlie was back in favour at Manchester City and he went on a spending spree that was to leave English football gasping. In came little known "stars" such as Steve Daley for £1.5m from Wolves, Mick Robinson for £750,000 from Preston North End, Kevin Reeves for £1m from Norwich. And with Brian Clough emulating him at Nottingham Forest the transfer market went haywire. In just over a year Allison had bought 10 players for more than £4m and sold nine – nearly all established stars – for £2.5m. And it did not work. By October and after 12 games of the season City had a paltry four points and a huge overdraft. Exit Allison, enter John Bond of Norwich.

Amazingly the whole process started again as Bond sold seven players (including Daley at a loss of £1m) and lashed out £1.2m for Trevor Francis from Forest. But even Francis did not stay long and was soon off to Italy for £1m, another loss. But as Bond wheeled and dealed in the market that Clough and Allison had inflated, it collapsed on him and City were the losers as Bond spent £3m, only recouping £1.8m. In his first season Bond had lifted City from the foot of the First Division into a comfortable mid-table place and to the FA Cup final. Yet, inexplicably, the former manager of fiscally responsible Norwich had caught the Allison bug in Manchester and City were never quite the same.

Steve Daley: £1m loss

Kevin Reeves: £1m purchase

Dundee Utd's Cup heroics

ALTHOUGH Alex Ferguson's Aberdeen started the season like a runaway train (only losing one League match in their first 22) before grinding to a halt, the team that stood out was Jim McLean's Dundee United. Under their perfectionist, long-serving manager they reached two Cup finals, winning one. The one they captured, the League Cup in December, was particularly sweet. For a start it was their neighbours and fierce rivals, Dundee of the First Division, that were the victims in the first all-Dundee final. And even better it was played at Dens Park, their rivals' ground and, of course, by retaining the trophy at their expense they proved that last year's victory over Aberdeen had not been a flash in the pan.

Dundee United came close to making it a double five months later in the Scottish Cup final against Rangers. McLean's team, one of the most attractive in the Scottish League, were not overawed by the big boys from Glasgow. After all they had dispensed with Celtic, easy Premier Division champions, 3-2 in the semi-final replay. They knew they could hold their own, and so it proved with Rangers outplayed in a 0-0 draw. Though to be fair, Rangers did miss a last-minute penalty. Last-minute Cup dramatics were nothing new to Rangers. They had flirted with elimination in the fourth round against lowly St Johnstone of the First Division and only a last-gasp goal enabled them to escape with a 3-3 draw. However in the Cup final replay they rediscovered their swagger and cruised through 4-1.

Villa finally the right one

WHAT a difference a few days makes. On Saturday May 9, Ricardo Villa, who had spent much of his time in the shadow of Osvaldo Ardiles, had played one of his most inconspicuous games for Tottenham. The entire Spurs team had been ineffective and, a goal down with only 10 minutes to go, the FA Cup was inexorably slipping away from them.

Keith Burkinshaw, the Tottenham manager, took Villa off and the midfield player tearfully trudged towards the sidelines aware that all of Argentina was watching his humiliation. He was so disconsolate that he wanted nothing more to do with the match. But as he reached the mouth of the tunnel he stopped for one last look back at Wembley.

Tottenham had been awarded a free kick just outside Manchester City's penalty area and Glenn Hoddle was standing over the ball. Tommy Hutchison, who had given City the lead in the first half, knew that Hoddle could bend free kicks so he pulled out of the wall to cover the danger.

Even though he should have stayed put, Hutchison had guessed correctly. Hoddle curled the free kick and Hutchison was in just the right place – if you were a Tottenham fan. Hoddle's shot ricocheted off Hutchison's shoulder past a diving Joe Corrigan, who almost certainly would have saved it otherwise.

Villa, still spurning the bench, headed for the dressing room. But if he was upset then Hutchison, only the second man to score for both sides in an FA Cup final, was mortified. Burkinshaw could have disciplined Villa for his display of petulance, but the Tottenham manager had no hesitation in naming an unchanged side for the replay on the following Thursday. Villa repaid his faith by giving Tottenham an early lead, but City struck back with a stunning volley from Steve Mackenzie and a penalty from Kevin Reeves. Garth Crooks slid a rebound past Corrigan and at long last a final that had started so woefully the Saturday before was coming to life. There were still almost 15 minutes left, and the Cup final's first penalty shoot-out was looking a distinct prospect, when Villa received the ball in midfield.

Spurning the safe, simple square pass, Villa headed towards the penalty area. At first, he did not appear to pose any great threat to City as he moved that way, then this. But Villa was blessed with great strength and he repeatedly rode the defence's challenges, leaving Tommy Caton, Ray Ranson and Nicky Reid flat-footed. As Villa weaved his magic Corrigan was alive to the danger. Corrigan raced off his line but Villa kept his balance, slipped the ball through the goalkeeper's legs and scored an outstanding solo goal.

As the crowd roared its approval Villa's joy knew no bounds. He wheeled away in triumph, the previous disappointment forgotten in the euphoria. "It's great after last Saturday," he said. "I don't know how many players I beat but the thrill was terrific when the ball went into the net. I say thank you to the manager."

Burkinshaw repaid the compliment. "He was pleased that I had so much faith in him. But how can you leave out a player of his quality." That quality won the match single-handed and once again it was the year of the one – the year of destiny that Tottenham fans and the club so faithfully believe in. They were rewarded with a trophy in 1901, 1921, 1951, 1961, 1971, and now in 1981.

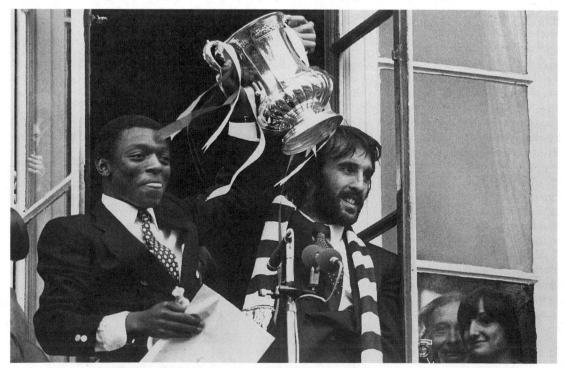

Year of destiny: Garth Crooks and Ricardo Villa parade the FA Cup, yet another trophy won in a year of One

Hero and villain: Tommy Hutchison scores for the "right" team to give Manchester City the lead in the Cup final

Strike one: Ricardo Villa scores the first of his two goals in the replay four days later

Crystal Palace's latest craze: musical chairs with their never-ending hot-seat shuffles

CRYSTAL PALACE, who had been hailed under the managership of Terry Venables as the "Team of the Eighties," had the most disastrous of seasons. They were relegated from the First Division having accumulated a bare 19 points from 42 matches; the ownership of the club changed hands in farcical fashion and they changed managers so frequently it appeared that there was a revolving door to the hot seat at Selhurst Park.

First Venables quit in October to take over Tommy Docherty's job at QPR and was replaced by Ernie Walley on a temporary basis. Within two months Walley was given permanent status and installed with Malcolm Allison, who had been sacked by Manchester City, as

joint managers. It did not last long, and Allison was soon made the sole manager. But meanwhile there was another farce being enacted in the boardroom. In December it emerged that Ernie Clay, the Fulham chairman, was negotiating to take over the shares held by Raymond Bloye, the Palace chairman. There was speculation that Ron Noades, the Wimbledon chairman, was one of many other interested parties. Noades denied this and called the rumours "a joke." By the end of January Noades and his partners had bought 75% of the holding in Palace but Noades still continued to run Wimbledon. In February the League chairmen passed a resolution that no club official could be

involved in the affairs of another club. So Noades announced he was going to sell his shares in Wimbledon, only to change his mind the next day but claim that he would have no say in the affairs of Wimbledon.

With Noades in charge of Palace the managerial hot-seat shuffle re-started as Dario Gradi, the Wimbledon manager, replaced Allison. However Gradi could not stop the inevitable slide into the Second Division, and even there Palace continued their downward spiral with seven losses and a draw in their first 13 League matches. Gradi was promptly sacked in November and Steve Kember was back in charge, the fifth manager Crystal Palace had had in the space of 13 months.

Noades: the Palace Don

European success Ipswich's only consolation as Villa snatch title

IPSWICH TOWN, under the shrewd management of Bobby Robson, were chasing a treble of League championship, FA Cup and Uefa Cup before they fell victim to fixture congestion. Never out of the top three in the First Division they led from August through to the middle of October, regained top spot in January and then faltered in the final eight games. They only won two of their games in that sequence, including beating Aston Villa, the eventual champions 2-1 at Villa Park, and they lost in the FA Cup semi-final to Manchester City.

But in the Uefa Cup they did achieve some consolation, knocking out Cologne and St Etienne before beating AZ 67 Alkmaar 5-4 on aggregate in the final. Robson had put together a wonderfully skilful passing side that he built around the two Dutchmen, Frans Thijssen and Arnold Muhren. And with the goalscoring capacity of Paul Mariner, Alan Brazil, Eric Gates and John Wark – all of whom reached double figures and scored 59 goals between them – only the burden of expectation and the weight of matches stopped Robson's team sweeping all before them.

By contrast, Villa, under Ron Saunders, had a much easier ride. Surprisingly they were beaten three times by Ipswich, yet perhaps their defeat by Ipswich in the third round of the FA Cup was a blessing in disguise. With only the championship to play for, and miraculously avoiding a spate of injuries or suspensions (they only used 14 players in the entire campaign) they carried off their first League title for 71 years.

The road to the championship: Peter Withe scores for Villa against Middlesbrough

Something to shout about: 50,000 fans applaud Bobby Robson's team outside Ipswich town hall

Muhren congratulates Wark

Liverpool prove the masters of foreign fields yet again

Still going strong: Souness, Dalglish and Hansen hold the European Cup aloft in Paris

I've always said there's a place for the press but they haven't dug it yet

TOMMY DOCHERTY

FOR A WHILE, it looked as if the start of the 1980s was going to mark the beginning of the decline of Liverpool from the great heights of the previous decade. They lost 1-0 to Fourth Division Bradford in the second round of the League Cup before going through on aggregate, went out of the FA Cup in the fourth round at Everton, and drew far too many matches in the League, particularly away.

Liverpool's indifferent performances in the League meant that they only finished fifth, their worst placing in 16 years. And they needed two attempts to beat West Ham and collect the League Cup that had always eluded them in the past.

But Liverpool had not lost their touch entirely, and it seemed that they were saving their best performances for the European Cup, and particularly the home legs. Oulu of Finland were swept aside 10-1 with Graeme Souness and Terry McDermott both scoring hat-tricks, Aberdeen were beaten 4-0 and CSKA Sofia, who had put out Nottingham Forest, the holders, conceded five goals with Souness getting another hat-trick. But Bayern Munich were among those who thought that Liverpool were not the side that they were before. When they drew the first leg of the semi-final 0-0 at Anfield they wrote Liverpool off as an unimaginative side and confidently predicted that they would reach the final.

Bayern, though, had overlooked Liverpool's trademark; their strength in depth. Injuries forced Liverpool to start two reserves, Richard Money and Colin Irwin, in the return match. And when an unfit Kenny Dalglish limped off early in the match he was replaced by another understudy, Howard Gayle.

The Germans had not planned on facing players they had not heard of and this, combined with their over-confidence, was their undoing. They were run ragged and the veteran Ray Kennedy tucked away the decisive goal seven minutes from time. Bayern equalised in the dying seconds, but Liverpool went through on the away goals rule.

The final in Paris on May 27 was widely expected to be a scintillating match with Liverpool facing Real Madrid, six times winners of the competition. But the game did not live up to the anticipation, and the first half was a scrappy, niggling affair. The second half was little better, although it gradually became apparent that the remorseless play of Liverpool was grinding Real down.

With eight minutes remaining it was Ray Kennedy who, once again, proved to be decisive. His throw in released Alan Kennedy, whose powerful run took him past a feeble tackle from Cortes, the Real right back. Alan Kennedy had been forced wide and Agustin, the goalkeeper, was quick off his line to close down the angle. But Kennedy kept his cool and forced the ball through the narrowest of gaps between Agustin and the near post.

Although it was not the best of games it confirmed Liverpool's and Bob Paisley's greatness. Liverpool became only the fourth team to win the European Cup three times, and Paisley was the first ever manager to do the hat-trick.

He was dynamic. If you lost a game you lost to rubbish. If you won, you had beaten a great team

ROGER HUNT
on Bill Shankly

Shankly: his deep-rooted affection for the game was infectious and it rubbed off on players and public alike

Shankly, the darling of the Kop, dies

BILL SHANKLY died on September 28 in a Liverpool hospital after a heart attack two days earlier from which the doctors had confidently predicted he would recover. He was the darling of the Kop, the man who had dragged Liverpool out of the Second Division and turned them into one of the greatest clubs in the country. His legacy would mean they would go on to be one of greatest clubs in the world.

His lifelong love affair with football had begun 67 years earlier when he had been born into a footballing family in a mining village in Ayrshire. Two of his uncles and all four of his brothers were, or became, professional footballers. Bill would be a Scottish international and win the FA Cup with Preston. The second world war would interrupt his career just, at 25, when he was at his peak. After the war he returned to Preston and played with Tom Finney, whom he idolised. Soon he turned to management with clubs in the lower divisions before Second Division Liverpool appointed him their manager in 1959.

Liverpool had been relegated in 1954 and although they were always narrowly missing out on promotion the board seemed content to jolly along as a successful Second Division club. Shankly did not see it that way but his ambitions were con-stantly thwarted by the refusal of the directors to spend money on new players. The arrival of an equally ambitious director changed all that and in 1961 Shankly promptly went out and bought Ian St John and Ron Yeats. The next year they were promoted. By 1964 Liverpool were League champions.

Over the next 10 years Shankly's Liverpool would win the championship twice more, the FA Cup twice and the Uefa Cup. He rebuilt his team twice, often unearthing staggering talent such as Emlyn Hughes, Ray Clemence, John Toshack, Steve Heighway and the apple of his eye – Kevin Keegan. The odd blunder was made in the transfer market, often due to his stubborn refusal to admit his mistakes, but by and large he made several spectacular raids.

Europe seemed to have been his Achilles heel. He was naturally xenophobic, hated flying and travelling in general, and was distrustful of most things foreign – in particular their football and their footballers. The European Cup semi-final against Inter Milan in 1965, his first foray into continental competition, confirmed all his worst fears, and certainly embittered him. In the San Siro, with Liverpool holding a comfortable 3-1 lead, the Italian fans jeered his team on to the field and pelted them with bottles and smoke bombs. The Spanish referee then allowed two Inter goals – one from a blatant foul on the goalkeeper and one from an indirect free-kick – and disallowed a perfectly good Liverpool one. The tie was lost and so were any lingering doubts about foreigners in Shankly's mind.

And yet Shankly bestrode the 1960s. His deep-rooted affection for the game was infectious and it rubbed off on his players and public alike. An eccentric, he became legendary for his wit and instant quips to ingenuous interviewers in that inimitable rasping voice. The most famous of course was: "Football is not a matter of life and death – it's much more important than that."

His retirement in 1974 immediately after winning the FA Cup came as surprise to everybody. He was 60 and going out at the top, but football was Shankly's life. He had no outside interests, and when Liverpool failed to offer him a directorship or a clear role in the club he felt let down. So much so he would travel to other clubs, other matches where his wit and knowledge were greeted with open arms. His memorial service was attended by tens of thousands as Liverpool flocked to mark the passing of a man who transformed their lives.

Shankly leads out the Preston team in his final season as a player

Toshack the miracle worker rewarded as Swansea take the First Division by storm

SWANSEA CITY'S meteoric rise continued apace as they shot to the top of the First Division only four seasons after playing in the Fourth. Under the inspired managership of John Toshack they took 22 points from their first 10 matches to lead the title race on October 17.

But as the season continued Toshack could not match the consistency of his former club Liverpool, and Swansea soon slipped back. However, they twice regained first place, first over Christmas and then, after a run of seven wins and two draws, again briefly in March. They faded to finish sixth but that, though, was their lowest placing of the season. It was a remarkable performance by a team that had been put together relatively cheaply.

But, among the smaller clubs, what goes up will sooner or later come down again. The bubble burst very quickly and by the start of the 1986 season Swansea were back in the Fourth Division, the heady days of 1981 but a brief memory.

QPR discover it's not so fantastic on plastic

QUEEN'S PARK RANGERS spent the summer tearing up their pitch and replacing it with artificial turf. They saw it as a shrewd investment that would enable Loftus Road to stage other events during the week and bring in more money to the Second Division club.

Their first home match against Luton, themselves soon to experiment with an artificial pitch, created much interest. The press seemed to agree that the new surface was a good idea, with the *Daily Star* saying "it's fantastic on plastic."

But it did not take long for the novelty to wear off. Players were soon moaning about the pace and bounce of the pitch, and there were fears that it was causing more injuries. And after Blackburn lost 2-0 on October 3 they complained to the Football League: "We felt the surface was not suited to good football." Three weeks later, Leicester also complained about the pitch after losing 2-0.

The FA, who were ambivalent about the idea, also had a confrontation with QPR. In November the club said they would withdraw from the FA Cup because they were only going to be allowed to use the pitch on a one-year trial. But the FA made concessions and QPR withdrew the threat.

Although Luton, Oldham and Preston went on to try artificial pitches and various efforts were made to curb the excessive bounce the experiment that the *Daily Star* dubbed "the most important this century" soon fizzled out and before the end of the decade grass was once again growing at Loftus Road.

FOR THE RECORD

■ The Football League introduced three points for a win, a decision that was criticised by Alan Durban, the Sunderland manager, on the opening day of the season. After his side had drawn 3-3 at Ipswich he said: "It is outrageous that clubs should lose two points each for drawing after giving a superb exhibition like that."

■ The British transfer record was broken when Bryan Robson (below) moved from West Bromwich to Manchester United for £1.5m on

October 1. The West Brom manager had said "he leaves over my dead body," and the chairman had said he was not for sale "at any price."

■ Bob Lord, the Burnley chairman for 26 years and a former leading light of the Football League, died on December 8, aged 73.

■ Chelsea's fans caused such a disturbance at Derby on November 28 that the FA ordered all their away matches from January 1 to the end of the season to be all-ticket. The ban was lifted in February, just before Chelsea challenged it in the High Court.

■ Sepp Blatter, a former amateur footballer and general secretary of the Swiss Ice Hockey Federation, was elected general secretary of Fifa on January 15.

■ Bad weather during December and January created a backlog of fixtures. The postponed fixtures did not help many clubs facing cashflow problems, and the Fulham manager Malcolm Macdonald suggested that matches should be played during the summer.

■ The Football League management committee proposed to do away with the Fourth Division and replace it with three regional sections of the Third Division. The plan was rejected by Third and Fourth Division clubs in October.

■ The Football League ordered referees to send players off for committing professional fouls next season.

■ Bristol Rovers, in dispute with their landlords, announced plans to share Bristol City's ground in November. But their fans objected so strongly that they resolved the dispute over their rent and stayed at Eastville.

Novelty turn: QPR's artificial surface made its debut against Luton Town on September 1, 1981

Jimmy Hill leads rebel tour to South Africa

SOUTH AFRICA were desperate to bring high-class sport to their shores and encouraged by a tour of rebel English cricketers they planned a visit by a group of British footballers.

Mindful of international sanctions, Ted Croker, the secretary of the FA, warned that any players who got involved could be putting their career at risk, and Tottenham refused to let Osvaldo Ardiles join the party for fear of prejudicing his transfer to Paris St Germain.

Croker was furious when he discovered that one of the organisers of the trip was Jimmy Hill, the Coventry chairman. "Hill is acting irresponsibly," he said. "It is not South Africa's interest he has at heart." But the tour went ahead in July, with the rebels drawing two matches and winning one. The FA set up a special investigation but took no further action.

England qualify despite Norway debacle

THE radio commentator could not contain himself. "We are the best in the world. We have beaten England. Lord Nelson, Lord Beaverbrook, Sir Winston Churchill, Sir Anthony Eden, Clement Attlee, Henry Cooper, Lady Diana. We have beaten them all. Maggie Thatcher can you hear me? Maggie Thatcher, your boys took a hell of a beating. Norway have beaten England at football."

It was little wonder he was so excited. Norway, everybody's perennial underdogs, had just beaten England 2-1 in Oslo in a Group Four qualifying match for the World Cup. Ron Greenwood, the England manager, said: "We let them play for five minutes and they scored two goals."

It looked as if the defeat on September 9 could cost England their place in the finals. England had already dropped three points to Romania and lost to the equally unfancied Switzerland. They still led the group but only had one match left. Romania, one point behind with two matches in hand, and Hungary, three points behind with three matches in hand, looked set to take the two places on offer in Spain. And Norway and Switzerland were still in with chances.

Fortunately for England every one of the remaining results went in their favour. Romania drew with Hungary and then lost at home to Switzerland. Hungary brushed aside Switzerland and Norway to make sure of their place. Then Romania were held to a goalless draw in Switzerland, which almost put paid to their chances. Thanks in no small part

Norwegian nightmare: Hallvar Thoresen scores the winning goal in the World Cup qualifying match in Oslo

to their 4-0 drubbing of Norway in the very first match of the group, England knew that a draw with Hungary at Wembley on November 18 would suffice. Hungary, because they had already qualified, looked as if they did not care too much about the result and the only goal of the match from Paul Mariner was enough for England to sneak through to Spain. They were joined by Scotland and Northern Ireland, who both eased their way past Sweden, Portugal and Israel in Group Six. It was the first time since 1958 that Britain had had more than one representative in the finals and it was only goal difference that stopped the home nations making a clean sweep.

The Republic of Ireland finished their campaign with a stirring 3-2 home victory over France on October 14. But they could only sit and watch as France won their last two

Sneaking home: Mariner scored the vital goal against Hungary at Wembley

matches to take the second qualifying place in Group Two and eliminate Holland, the beaten finalists in 1978, in the process.

Wales could claim to be even unluckier in Group Three. The match that proved to be their undoing was also on October 14, at Swansea. The floodlights failed, temporarily stopping the match and unsettling Wales, who dropped a crucial point to Iceland in a 2-2 draw.

Aberdeen and Forfar surprise everybody to give Old Firm a close run for their money

BILLY MCNEILL's Celtic began the season extraordinarily. In the Scottish League Cup in August they faltered alarmingly against St Mirren, losing on the opening day, and then slipped against St Johnstone as well to miss the final stages.

Yet in the League they were in scintillating form: winning their first seven games. In fact they led the table from start to finish. So dominant was their lead that when they met Aberdeen on January 30 everybody assumed it would be the championship decider, and with Celtic triumphant, were already writing their name on the roll of honour. As it turned out, it was the championship decider, but not in the way anybody would have guessed.

It was now Aberdeen's turn to

McNeill: close shave

hit top form and brush aside all opposition. From February 20 to May 15 they won 16 League matches, losing one and drawing one. By the final weekend Celtic's massive lead had been whittled down so much that they were mightily relieved to win

their final match against St Mirren, particularly as Aberdeen had enjoyed a 4-0 goal spree against Rangers at Pittodrie. Aberdeen's consolation was 4-1 victory over Rangers in the Scottish Cup final.

Not all the drama was confined to the Premier Division clubs. Little Forfar Athletic, of the Second Division, were the Cup kings of the season. They reached the quarter-finals of the Scottish League Cup and the semi-finals of the Scottish Cup, having disposed of Hearts, Hamilton and Queen's Park – all of the First Division – en route to a tilt at mighty Rangers. Unfazed by the Ibrox club, Forfar almost pulled off the impossible and Rangers were grateful to escape to a replay in which their class inevitably told.

Liverpool easily run away with the League

BOB PAISLEY started the season by continuing to rebuild Liverpool. Ray Clemence, one of the last players left from the Shankly era was transferred to Tottenham, and Jimmy Case and Ray Kennedy were soon to leave Anfield.

The new-look team took a while to settle and as the New Year started Liverpool were in an unfamiliar position, a lowly 12th in the First Division. But unlike other clubs, they did not suffer too badly from fixture congestion caused by the bad weather in December and January because they went out of the FA Cup in the fifth round and the European Cup in the quarter-finals.

That freed Liverpool to concentrate on the League and by the beginning of March they had climbed to sixth place. After a defeat by Brighton on March 6 they won 11 League matches in a row and did not lose any of their final 16 games.

It was their 13th championship (with a record 87 points, thanks to the introduction of three points for a win) and Paisley said: "I'm proudest of this one because there was so much

to do." An indication of the shrewdness of his rebuilding was that Liverpool only used 16 players in the League throughout the season.

The League Cup final on March 13 was a battle between Liverpool past and Liverpool present. Tottenham led in the

11th minute and their breakaways continually tested Bruce Grobbelaar. But Clemence was finally beaten in the last minutes of the match. Clemence conceded two more goals in extra time and the League Cup was back at Anfield for the second year running.

Extra special: Liverpool snatched an amazing victory in extra time in the League Cup final against Tottenham

Dougan: Wolves' saviour

Bristol City, Wolves go bust

FOOTBALL reaped the whirl-wind of its financial foolishness as the money ran out with a vengeance. The first club to feel the pinch were Bristol City, who had overstretched themselves in the First Division and could not afford their wage bill as the team slid back down the League.

City had lost almost £500,000 the previous season when they were relegated from the Second Division, and by the end of October they were £700,000 in debt (with £120,000 tax outstanding) and losing £3,000 a week. In the week before Christmas two of their directors resigned in order to make way for two local businessmen who promised to raise £500,000 to save the club. But with City wallowing at the foot of the Third Division it was still not enough.

Early in the New Year Bob Houghton resigned as manager and said: "There is nothing more I can do." With losses reaching more than £4,000 a week accountants were called in to try to save the club.

Their solution was drastic; give eight players, whose wages were costing a staggering £250,000 a year, immediate free transfers. The players used the PFA to try to improve City's offer of compensation but the writing was on the wall on January 26 when the club's chairman said Bristol City would go out of business in a fortnight if agreement was not reached.

Finally, on February 3, the "Ashton Gate Eight" bowed to the inevitable and allowed their contracts to be cancelled clearing the way for the Robins to be reborn from the ashes, although too late to prevent relegation to the Fourth Division.

Wolves, who were relegated from the First Division, went even closer to the brink. Rash spending on players and a £10m bill for the new stand at Molineux left them more than £2.5m in debt at the end of the season. Then, in early June, Chesterfield issued a writ for an outstanding instalment of a transfer fee. Within a fortnight the Wolves chairman had resigned because "it was impossible for the present board to continue to run the club."

Doug Ellis took over and claimed that the club had been saved with 24 hours to spare, but the problems would not go away and the Official Receiver was called in early in July. Both the League and the Receiver set a deadline for rescue attempts and five consortia battled to raise the money before the end of the month.

In the end Wolves were saved with just three minutes to spare by a group led by Derek Dougan, their former star player. With attendances continuing to fall these were not isolated incidents and many other clubs were forced to make drastic economies just to stay afloat.

Aston Villa's novices land the European Cup

ASTON VILLA, the European novices with a novice manager, astounded the continent and probably themselves when they lifted the European Cup. Everybody was especially surprised as they beat the West German champions Bayern Munich, who could boast Paul Breitner in midfield and Karl-Heinz Rummenigge in attack. The European Cup had now been won for six years in succession by an English club.

But who would have thought it would have been Villa? Liverpool, who had won the trophy three times in the previous five seasons, were defending the Cup and Aston Villa's European experience was confined to two Uefa Cup campaigns in 1975-6 and 1977-8. In the first they could not get past the first round, in the second they reached the quarter-finals. And Ron Saunders, the manager who had guided them to their first League title since 1910, walked out in February over a contractual disagreement leaving Tony Barton, his assistant, in his first managerial post. Although the League champions, Villa were hardly a side composed of household names: Jimmy Rimmer was in goal, Allan Evans in defence, Gordon Cowans, Des Bremner and Dennis Mortimer in midfield, Tony Morley on the left wing, Gary Shaw and Peter Withe in attack. Fortunately their path to the final had not been stuffed with star sides either: Valur Reykjavik of Iceland; Dynamo Berlin of East Germany, whom they beat on away goals; Dynamo Kiev and then Anderlecht of Belgium, who had succumbed by a single goal.

The final in Rotterdam on May 26 should have been a one-sided affair particularly when Rimmer had to go off injured after only eight minutes. The replacement keeper, Nigel Spink, 23, had only played one first team game for Villa. He will never forget his second as

Super sub: Spink comes off the bench to inspire Aston Villa

he played out of his skin and muzzled the predatory Rummenigge. In the 67th minute Morley created a goal of delightful virtuosity from the left wing. He bamboozled the German right-back, took the ball to the byline and crossed to Withe who scored off the post. It was the only goal, and Villa had proved that inexperience can win the day.

FA Cup scant reward for Tottenham

TOTTENHAM'S centenary year looked to be an *annus mirabilis*. By March they were in the semi-finals of the FA Cup, the final of the League Cup, the semi-finals of the European Cup Winners' Cup and had enough games in hand to capture the League championship.

Then virtually everything went wrong. They lost the League Cup final after extra time (their first defeat in 16 Cup finals, including replays) to Liverpool having led for 87 minutes. A bruising encounter with Barcelona was lost over two legs by a single goal. And a stunning late run of unstoppable form by Liverpool, coupled with a ridiculous fixture backlog – in April and May Tottenham had a colossal 18 fixtures to complete – extinguished their championship aspirations. Worse, on the eve of the FA Cup semi-final against Leicester, Argentina invaded the Falkland Islands and war with Britain looked virtually certain. This placed a great strain on Osvaldo Ardiles and Ricardo Villa, Tottenham's two Argentine aces.

During the semi-final Ardiles was continually booed by the Leicester fans and he left Britain the next day to join Cesar Menotti's defending World Cup side with his future at Spurs in grave doubt. Yet despite the intolerable pressure he was under he made certain that Tottenham would reach their second successive FA Cup final by engineering a magnificent goal. In the 56th minute he received Glenn Hoddle's short corner, eluded a defender and drove a low centre into the penalty area for Garth Crooks to crash home. A spectacular own goal completed Leicester's misery. Tottenham's opponents were to be Second Division QPR, managed by the former Spurs player Terry Venables.

Then, on the eve of the final, history once again conspired to deal Tottenham another blow as the British Task Force approached the Falklands. Diplomatically it didn't seem possible that an Argentinian could take part in one of Britain's great sporting occasions when at any moment there could be news of British fatalities. So Keith Burkinshaw, the manager, and Ricky Villa, the hero of the 1981 final, conceded that he should not play. Villa watched the final on TV at home.

Not that there was much to watch. A long season had taken its toll, the disappointments and the tense political situation only made matters worse. A deflection from Hoddle put Tottenham ahead, but then a Terry Fenwick set-piece goal meant a replay. So five days later they met again at Wembley. Spurs were unchanged, but QPR were now without their captain Glenn Roeder, suspended for a League infringement, and their striker, Clive Allen, who had been injured in the first match. A sixth penalty from Hoddle won a lacklustre final.

So Spurs had won their seventh FA Cup, emulating Aston Villa's record, and repeating their feat of exactly 20 years ago. But the celebrations were short-lived: Ardiles did not return to Britain after the World Cup, signing instead for Paris St Germain on July 5.

■ **Bobby Robson (above), who had worked wonders at unfashionable Ipswich, was appointed England manager on July 7.**

■ **Diego Maradona joined Barcelona on May 28. They paid a world record £4.2m to Boca Juniors and Argentinos Juniors.**

■ **A fan was stabbed to death after Arsenal's match with West Ham on May 1. The game was held up for more than 10 minutes because of crowd trouble and Terry Neill, the Arsenal manager, said: "It makes you wonder what sort of parents produce mindless morons like this." It was the second football fatality of the season – a fan had also been killed after Tottenham's match against Manchester United on November 21.**

■ **Kevin Keegan was made an OBE in June.**

■ **Alan Mullery resigned as Charlton's manager on June 1 and became Crystal Palace's sixth manager in 20 months three weeks later.**

■ **Jimmy Frizzell, the Oldham manager, was sacked in June after spending 23 years at the club as a player and manager.**

■ **Hereford had a bad season. The directors' wives offered to take over the cleaning duties to save money for the struggling club. And the team was hit so badly by a flu bug that they banned all their players from coming to Edgar Street in late September.**

■ **Wolverhampton finally cancelled the contract of Peter Knowles on June 5. He had walked out of the club in 1969 to become a Jehovah's Witness.**

Penalty: Tony Currie brings down Graham Roberts and Glen Hoddle converts the winning spot kick in the replay

WORLD CUP 1982

Cynical Italy turn out to be genuine heroes

IT WAS as if there were two Italys playing in the 1982 World Cup finals in Spain. The first cynically chiselled out three draws to qualify for the second phase by the slenderest of margins. The second gloriously exploded on to the world stage and captured the World Cup for the third time.

Italy Mk I began cautiously, with a goalless draw with Poland and a fortunate 1-1 draw against Peru. Their third match against Cameroon, who had refused to be cannon fodder for the rest of the group, would decide who accompanied Poland into the next phase. Cameroon's lack of sophistication and inability to translate possession into goals left them needing to win, despite having drawn their first two matches. The Italians, much more experienced at this level, duly eked out another draw, 1-1, and qualified by virtue of having scored one more goal than their African rivals.

Although Italy Mk I cannot be forgiven for the sterility of their first three games, the tactic of playing not to lose (something they are supposed to be past masters at) was foisted upon the first phase by the political decision of Joao Havelange, the Fifa president, to increase the number of participants. He had done this to reward the Third World countries that had voted him into power by expanding the number of finalists from a sensible and manageable 16 to an overblown and unwieldy 24. Thus, the first phase comprised six groups of four, with the top two in each group qualifying for the next phase i.e. 36 matches were needed to eliminate 12 teams.

With the phoney war over, Enzo Bearzot, their manager, unleashed Italy Mk II and Paolo Rossi with a vengeance. One after another the world's big guns were silenced. Italy's transformation in the second round was a sight to be seen. They were in the same group as Diego Maradona's Argentina and Brazil – who with Eder, Falcao, Junior, Socrates and Zico playing dream football – had rediscovered all the joyous flair that had endeared them to the world in the era of Pele. Against all odds, Italy beat them both.

The match against Brazil was extraordinary. Rossi put Italy ahead in the fifth minute, Socrates equalised seven minutes later only to see Rossi restore Italy's lead in the 25th minute. Brazil, pushing forward exuberantly, levelled the scores again when Falcao dribbled across the penalty area, spotted a gap, and beat Dino Zoff with a stupendous shot. If the score had remained 2-2 then Brazil would have reached the semi-finals but, characteristically, they eschewed any thought of closing the game down. To their cost. Six minutes after the equaliser Rossi completed his hat-trick to the dismay of

Strike force: Armstrong's goal (top) took Northern Ireland into the second round for the first time and Robson was quick off the mark against France

neutral fans all over the world.

Poland, Italy's opponents in the semi-final, were without their key player, Zbigniew Boniek, and succumbed 2-0, both goals coming from Rossi who had clearly discovered a rich vein of form. In the final, in Madrid on July 11, Italy met West Germany and many people thought that their bubble would burst.

In fact, it was the Germans who came down to earth. Even though Antonio Cabrini missed a penalty in the first half there was no stopping Rossi. He put Italy ahead in the 56th minute with a diving header, which established him as the tournament's leading scorer with six goals, and created a goal for Marco Tardelli 13 minutes later. Alessandro Altobelli added a third in the 80th minute and the best that West Germany could muster was a consolation goal from Paul Breitner two minutes later.

Although Italy had begun the tournament in such a craven way, their triumph was well deserved. In successive matches they had beaten Argentina (the world champions), Brazil (the favourites), Poland (who finished third) and West Germany (the European champions). Never mind that these were the only four matches they won in the whole of 1982 – when it mattered Italy beat the best the world could offer.

In the cynicism stakes, West Germany were the real champions. After an amazing 2-1 reverse at the hands of Algeria, everything hinged on West Germany's final game in the first phase. Because Algeria had played the day before, both West Germany and Austria knew that if West Germany won 1-0 both countries would qualify at Algeria's expense. West Germany duly scored early in the game, and for the rest of the match neither team made any effort whatsoever. It was one of the most blatant examples of cheating that anybody had ever encountered. Algeria complained long and loud about the "Great Gijon swindle" but Fifa ignored their protests.

Then, in the semi-final against France, West Germany behaved equally badly. Harald Schumacher, the West German goalkeeper, felled Patrick Battiston with an evil challenge and the French defender was carried off unconscious. Schumacher escaped unpunished and West Germany were even awarded a goal kick. From that moment, everybody wanted West Germany to lose. They appeared to have got their comeuppance when they trailed 3-1 in extra time but the loss of Battiston was a mortal blow to the French. They conceded two goals in five minutes and West Germany won the first ever penalty shoot-out in the finals 5-4. West Germany's qualification for the semi-final had not exactly been impressive either. They engineered a stultifying 0-0 draw against England and beat Spain 2-1. This left Spain with only honour to play for in the final match of their second-phase group against England. For the hosts a draw would be a moral victory, England needed to win by two goals to edge out West Germany.

Ron Greenwood, the England manager, had problems with his squad. Two key players, Kevin Keegan and Trevor Brooking, had been injured and not yet played in the tournament, but both were potential match-winners. It was thought that both players could probably last about 30 minutes, so Greenwood had a choice: play them from the start, or have the option of bringing them on as a double substitution. To the chagrin of the English press, he chose the latter.

Thus it was that, after 60 minutes, with the match scoreless, Keegan and Brooking arrived on the pitch. Within minutes both of them had missed good chances. But the damage had been done in the first hour. England's inability to pierce the Spanish defence had given the host country heart and, as the minutes

ticked away, they became more confident. Greenwood's caution meant that England were eliminated unbeaten, having conceded only one goal in the tournament, but had thrown away a semi-final place.

It had all looked so different in the opening game against France on June 16. Bryan Robson's 27-second goal in their 3-1 defeat of France was the springboard for England's untroubled qualification for the second phase. Only Brazil progressed with a better record.

England could blame Northern Ireland and Gerry Armstrong for having to face Spain at all. Armstrong's second-half goal, an instinctive strike after Luis Arconada, the Spanish goalkeeper, could only push away Billy Hamilton's cross, gave Northern Ireland an upset 1-0 victory against the host country. The no-hopers surprisingly topped the group and joined France and Austria in their second phase group instead of Spain.

Although Northern Ireland did not win a game in the second phase they at least progressed further than Scotland, who were in their third successive World Cup finals. Drawn in a difficult group with Brazil and the Soviet Union, the Scots put on a brave show, drawing with the Soviet Union and briefly leading against Brazil before being routed 4-1. Scotland went out on goal difference and maintained their unenviable record of never having gone beyond the first round of a World Cup finals despite having qualified five times.

FOR THE RECORD

FIRST ROUND

GROUP 1	P	W	D	L	F	A	Pts
Poland	3	1	2	0	5	1	4
Italy	3	0	3	0	2	2	3
Cameroon	3	0	3	0	1	1	3
Peru	3	0	2	1	2	6	2

GROUP 2	P	W	D	L	F	A	Pts
W. Germany	3	2	0	1	6	3	4
Austria	3	2	0	1	3	1	4
Algeria	3	2	0	1	5	5	4
Chile	3	0	0	3	3	8	0

GROUP 3	P	W	D	L	F	A	Pts
Belgium	3	2	1	0	3	1	5
Argentina	3	2	0	1	6	2	4
Hungary	3	1	1	1	12	6	3
El Salvador	3	0	0	3	1	13	0

GROUP 4	P	W	D	L	F	A	Pts
England	3	3	0	0	6	1	6
France	3	1	1	1	6	5	3
Czech	3	0	2	1	2	4	2
Kuwait	3	0	1	2	2	6	1

GROUP 5	P	W	D	L	F	A	Pts
N. Ireland	3	0	2	0	2	1	4
Spain	3	1	1	0	3	3	3
Yugoslavia	3	1	1	1	2	2	3
Honduras	3	0	2	1	2	3	2

GROUP 6	P	W	D	L	F	A	Pts
Brazil	3	3	0	0	10	2	6
Soviet Union	3	1	1	1	6	4	3
Scotland	3	1	1	1	8	8	3
New Zealand	3	0	0	3	2	12	0

SECOND ROUND

GROUP A	P	W	D	L	F	A	Pts
Poland	2	1	1	0	3	0	3
Soviet Union	2	1	1	0	1	0	3
Belgium	2	0	0	2	0	4	0

GROUP B	P	W	D	L	F	A	Pts
W. Germany	2	1	1	0	2	1	3
England	2	0	2	0	0	0	2
Spain	2	0	1	1	1	2	1

GROUP C	P	W	D	L	F	A	Pts
Italy	2	2	0	0	5	3	4
Brazil	2	1	0	1	5	4	2
Argentina	2	0	0	2	2	5	0

GROUP D	P	W	D	L	F	A	Pts
France	2	2	0	0	5	1	4
Austria	2	0	1	1	2	3	1
N. Ireland	2	0	1	1	3	6	1

SEMI-FINALS
Italy 2   Poland 0
HT 1-0 Att. 50,000
West Germany 3   France 3
West Germany won 5-4 on penalties
HT 1-1 Att. 63,000

THIRD PLACE PLAY-OFF
Poland 3   France 2
HT 2-1 Att. 28,000

FINAL
Italy 3   West Germany 1
HT 0-0 Att. 90,000

Teams
Italy Zoff, Cabrini, Scirea, Gentile, Collovati, Oriali, Bergomi, Tardelli, Conti, Rossi, Graziani (sub: Altobelli)
West Germany Schumacher, Kaltz, Stielike, K-H Forster, B Forster, Breitner, Breigel, Dremmler (sub: Hrubesch), Rummenigge (sub: H Muller), Littbarski, Fischer

Leading goalscorers 6 Paolo Rossi (Italy); 5 Karl-Heinz Rummenigge (West Germany); 4 Zbigniew Boniek (Poland); Zico (Brazil)

Total goals scored 146
Average per game: 2.81

Sendings-off Lasislav Vizek (Czechoslovakia) v France; Referee: Paolo Casarin (Italy).
Gilberto Yearwood (Honduras) v Yugoslavia; Referee: Gaston Castro (Chile).
Mal Donaghy (Northern Ireland) v Spain; Referee: Hector Ortiz (Paraguay).
Americo Gallego (Argentina) v Italy; Referee: Nicolae Rainea (Romania).
Diego Maradona (Argentina) v Brazil; Referee: Mario Rubio Vazquez (Mexico).

Number of players used by finalists
15 Italy; 16 West Germany

Contrasting fortunes: Battiston is scythed down by Schumacher (left) and Rossi scores Italy's first goal in the final

Paisley quits on highest note

Paisley: promising wing-half

ON March 26 Bob Paisley climbed the 39 steps at Wembley and held the League Cup aloft. It was a fitting finale for one of the most successful managers Europe has ever seen. In his nine-year reign at Anfield the former Durham miner and bricklayer had won 13 trophies, and this was his third consecutive League Cup.

His track record was mind-boggling. Within weeks Paisley was celebrating another League title, his sixth, comfortably achieved. At one point Liverpool were 16 points ahead of second-placed Watford and they simply strolled home, eventually finishing 11 points clear. Paisley had announced in August that he would be retiring at the end of the season and he kept his word on May 14. Nine days later Joe Fagan, another stalwart of the famous Anfield Boot Room, was appointed as his successor.

Fagan was 62, the oldest manager to make his debut in the history of the Football League. But then smooth succession from within was the Liverpool way. When Bill Shankly retired in 1974 Paisley had been rustled up from the Boot Room as his successor. And like Fagan he, too, had been coerced into the job.

Paisley was born on January 23, 1919 in a Durham mining village. He enjoyed phenomenal success as a schoolboy footballer and as an amateur with Bishop Auckland. By 1939 he was a professional with Liverpool where he fell under the spell of Matt Busby, who became his mentor.

The second world war interrupted the career of this highly promising wing-half, though he did win a League championship with Liverpool in 1947 and only missed the 1950 FA Cup final because of injury. He retired as a player in 1954 but, amazingly in those days, had taken a course in physiotherapy and had a keen interest in training techniques. By 1959 he was appointed Liverpool's full-time trainer. It was a decision that would change his life and transform Liverpool FC.

With the arrival of Shankly later the same year the pair were about to launch Liverpool on an odyssey of success that nobody could ever have dared script. Paisley became Shankly's right-hand man, his hatchet man and his miracle worker.

Paisley was a genius at diagnosing the seriousness of an injury, how to treat it and how long to allow before the player was brought back. These skills were to prove invaluable as Liverpool were honed into the fittest squad in the land and other managers would marvel at how few injuries their players received.

As a manager, Paisley soon showed his astuteness did not stop with the magic sponge. Ray Kennedy, the Arsenal striker Shankly had purchased just before he resigned, had not fitted in at Anfield until Paisley converted him into a midfield player. It was Paisley who broke transfer records when he brought Kenny Dalglish down from Scotland to replace Kevin Keegan and lured Graeme Souness from Middlesbrough.

It was Shankly who transformed Liverpool from a semi-successful Second Division side into a European powerhouse, but it was his sidekick, Paisley, who ensured that all of the promise of the 1960s and 1970s was fulfilled and that the Anfield legacy would be successfully passed on to future generations of Liverpool managers.

Paisley's nine great seasons

1975	First Division runners-up
1976	Uefa Cup winners; League champions
1977	European Cup winners; League champions; FA Cup finalists
1978	European Cup winners; First Division runners-up; League Cup finalists
1979	League champions
1980	League champions
1981	European Cup winners; League Cup winners
1982	League champions; League Cup winners
1983	League champions; League Cup winners

Continuing the tradition: Paisley hands over the reins to Fagan, another product of the famous Boot Room

Crazy days at Charlton

WHEN Mark Hulyer took control of Charlton the fans hoped that it would mark the start of a revival for the Second Division side. Instead, they saw their club reduced to a laughing stock by a season of off-the-field farce.

Hulyer was a street-wise young businessman who had purchased Charlton from the Gliksten family, who had run the club for half a century. Within months of becoming chairman Hulyer set The Valley buzzing by offering Barcelona £250,000 for Allan Simonsen.

The delighted fans could hardly believe it – Charlton were buying the Danish international forward who was a former European Footballer of the Year and paying him £82,000 a year for two years. The problem was that nobody else could believe it either, least of all Barcelona.

Officially, the deal was done on October 8. But a week later Barcelona, wanting to make sure that they got paid, said that they would not release Simonsen until they received a bank guarantee for £100,000. Almost daily it seemed that the deal was off, then it was back on again,

then it was in yet further doubt.

Simonsen finally made his League debut for Charlton on November 13, scoring a goal in the 3-2 defeat by Middlesbrough. But that was far from the end of the mess. Charlton were struggling near the bottom of the division and on November 22 their manager, Ken Craggs, said that he had been assured by Hulyer that his job was safe. The very next day he was promptly sacked.

It was not long before Charlton realised that they could barely afford the wages they had offered Simonsen. In February they admitted that the entire affair had been a costly mistake. Within weeks Simonsen had made the last of his 16 appearances for the club and had returned to Denmark.

There was worse still to come. In June, Leeds United issued a winding-up notice because they were owed £35,150 by Charlton. It was also revealed that the club had tax debts of £145,000. The High Court told Charlton to pay the money or close, and the club was only allowed to continue when Hulyer reached an agreement with the Inland Revenue.

Great Dane: Ken Craggs welcomes Allan Simonsen to The Valley

Maxwell's madness thwarted

Chairman curbed: Maxwell was shown the door by two sets of fans

ROBERT MAXWELL had been hailed as a hero for saving Oxford United from the brink of bankruptcy. But when he bought a controlling interest in Reading on April 16 he was reviled.

Maxwell caused uproar when he unveiled his grand plan – merge the two clubs into a single team, the Thames Valley Royals. Although the Oxford board unanimously approved the proposal both sets of supporters were not prepared to see their team die. The Oxford fans staged a sit-in on the pitch and a black coffin was paraded around Reading. Maxwell, for once, did not get his way. The Reading chairman and two other directors resigned on May 13 which allowed Roger Smee, who had previously tried to take over the club, to become chairman. With Smee, a former Reading centre-forward, in charge Maxwell was thwarted. He finally lost the battle on June 22 when he was out-voted at an extraordinary general meeting.

FOR THE RECORD

■ Eight players got on the score sheet as Swansea hammered Sliema 12-0 in the European Cup Winners' Cup first round on September 15. Swansea then hit another five goals without reply in the second leg in Malta.

■ The 390,451 people who passed through the turnstiles in England on September 19 was the smallest total attendance for a Saturday in September since the war. The figure was more than 15% down on the corresponding week in the previous season.

■ Graham Taylor, the Watford manager, was put in charge of the England youth team on November 3.

■ Peter Taylor returned to Derby County as their manager on November 8. He put one over his old boss, Brian Clough, when Derby beat Nottingham Forest 2-0 in the third round of the FA Cup.

■ Jimmy Dickinson, the former Portsmouth player and manager and England international, died on November 9, aged 57.

Alcoholism v
Communism

Banner at Scotland v Soviet Union
game

Military-style thugs destroy little northern club's big day

FOR little Ilkeston Town of the Northern Counties East League, the FA Trophy third round match against Enfield on February 27 should have been the greatest day in the club's history. They had fought their way through three qualifying rounds and had then beaten two Alliance Premier League teams to set up a third round match at home to Enfield, one of the strongest sides in non-League football.

With 15 minutes remaining Enfield had an unassailable 5-1 lead. Then, in what resembled a carefully-planned military operation, hundreds of young hooligans wearing matching green berets invaded the pitch.

The referee was forced to abandon the game, which was awarded to Enfield. There had also been crowd trouble when Ilkeston had won at Barnet in the previous round and the FA ordered an immediate inquiry.

The investigation lasted almost a month and Ilkeston were cleared of any responsibility for the incidents on March 23. In a worrying sign of how far hooliganism was spreading its tentacles throughout the country it was discovered that the gang had nothing to do with the town and had deliberately travelled from Derby just to make trouble.

Scholar takes over at Spurs

A STUNNING COUP by Irving Scholar, a multi-millionaire tax exile resident in Monte Carlo, saw the old, patrician board of directors of Tottenham Hotspur swept away in December and a bustling group of young Turks installed in their place. Scholar and his allies were able to take control of Spurs for little more than £500,000 because of grave doubts about the club's financial viability. Despite having played at Wembley four times in the year and generating a turnover in excess of £3m, profit was a paltry £200,000. Worse, the new West Stand looked like costing nearly twice its original estimate of £3.5m.

Such mismanagement by the old board, led by chairman Arthur Richardson, led to much grumbling among the shareholders but nobody thought that Tottenham were vulnerable to a takeover from outside the board. But political ineptitude and sheer complacency led to their downfall. Richardson had become the Tottenham chairman in 1980, ousting the long-serving Sydney Wale, after a bitter battle in the boardroom. Wale, a significant shareholder, never forgave him.

Richardson believed he was impregnable. Under Tottenham's articles of association all share transfers had to be accepted by the board. So, while Richardson knew that Scholar was buying up shares, he simply refused to register them. What he had not realised was that Scholar was also buying up proxies with the shares. By the beginning of December Wale decided to throw in his lot with the new guard and sold his shares to Scholar, giving him and his allies a majority. Scholar promptly called an extraordinary general meeting and Richardson and his fellow directors resigned. The way was now clear for a new team to take charge at Tottenham. Scholar promised modern management, diversification and a financially secure club.

Scholar: outfoxed old guard

England reject a smash hit at Newcastle

KEVIN KEEGAN'S illustrious career seemed to be in decline after the World Cup. Age was taking its toll on his bad back and before the start of the season Southampton sold him to Second Division Newcastle.

Then Bobby Robson, in his first match in charge, dropped the England captain for the European championship qualifying match against Denmark in Copenhagen. Keegan was deeply hurt that Robson did not tell him before the squad was announced and he said that he never wanted to play for his country again. When England only drew 2-2 on September 22 Robson was roundly condemned. The England manager was spat at when he went to Newcastle to watch a League match; the St James's Park faithful could not understand why their new-found idol had been overlooked.

Ron Greenwood had once described Keegan as the "most modern of modern footballers".

And although Robson thought Keegan was past his best there were many people who thought that, even at 31, he was still the leading forward in England. Keegan scored on his debut for Newcastle and in each of the next two League matches. He hit a rich vein of form and when he hammered four goals past Rotherham on October 2 speculation mounted about him being recalled by England.

But Keegan was adamant that his international career was over. Instead he would devote his energies to helping Newcastle back into the big time.

Keegan: successfully returned to the north-east

Aberdeen and Dundee United upstage Old Firm

GLASGOW's traditional hold on the honours in Scotland was rudely shattered by two clubs from the north east: Aberdeen and Dundee United. Alex Ferguson's Aberdeen captured the Scottish Cup and the European Cup Winners' Cup, while Jim McLean's Dundee United snatched the League championship by a solitary point. Only the League Cup went to Glasgow when Celtic beat Rangers 2-1.

Aberdeen's triumph in Europe was only the third time a Scottish club had won a European trophy and they did it with a swagger – losing only once in any leg of the competition. To get to the final in Gothenburg Aberdeen had to overcome the formidable Bayern Munich in the quarter finals. An impressive defensive display in Germany ended in a 0-0 draw, but with 15 minutes remaining at Pittodrie the Germans were leading 2-1 and seemed certain to go through. Alex McLeish's headed equaliser put Aberdeen back in the match, but unless they scored the winner Bayern would still qualify by virtue of away goals. The improbable was about to happen. Just after the restart up popped John Hewitt, the 20-year-old substitute, to make the score 3-2. Pandemonium. The semi-final was less dramatic. Aberdeen trounced Waterschei of Belgium 5-1 at home making the 1-0 away defeat irrelevant.

The conditions in Sweden on May 11 were atrocious, heavy rain and wind making the pitch virtually unplayable and only 17,804 spectators braved the elements for the final against Real Madrid. Aberdeen led after seven minutes with a thunderous goal from Eric Black.

But the heavy ground conspired against them. McLeish's attempted back pass stopped in the water and a desperate Jim Leighton conceded a penalty when he brought down Santillana, who had pounced on the loose ball. Juanito duly converted to level the scores. The Spanish club were somewhat lucky to have gone into extra time, but then with eight minutes left justice was done when up popped substitute Hewitt – yet again – to head the precious winner.

The Scottish Cup final against Rangers 10 days later was a dour affair, Aberdeen once again winning in extra time with Eric Black scoring the only goal four minutes from time.

Dundee United's first ever League title was the stuff of fiction. It was the classic tale of the tortoise and hare. Celtic led the table until the last month of the season, then Dundee United, with six consecutive victories, stole through to pip Celtic by one point.

Eric Black gives Aberdeen the lead against Real Madrid with an unstoppable shot

Smiling heroes: Black, Hewitt and Cooper happy to have won the European Cup Winners' Cup in Gothenburg

FOR THE RECORD

■ The rule requiring players to be sent off for committing a professional foul meant that 120 players were dismissed by November 28. However, the attempt to eliminate cheating was weakened when the FA referees' committee rescinded the rule in July.

■ Police in south Yorkshire were told to arrest players whose behaviour on the pitch was likely to incite crowd trouble.

■ George Graham was appointed manager of Millwall on December 6. Three months later he was imposing his authority, ordering six players to report for extra training because he thought that anybody who had lost their first-team place should work twice as hard to get it back.

■ Osvaldo Ardiles returned to Tottenham from Paris St Germain on December 29.

■ Celtic's 2-1 win at Rangers on January 1 was their first victory away from home on New Year's Day for 62 years.

■ Malcolm Struel, the Swansea chairman, was rebuked in February for calling the Welsh FA "bumbling amateurs".

THE
1982-83
SEASON

> *He's not only a good player, but he's spiteful in the nicest sense of the word*
>
> Manchester United manager
> RON ATKINSON
> on Norman Whiteside

Another Chester report simply gathers dust

THE favourite response to a problem was to spend a lot of time talking about it and then do very little. So it was hardly surprising that Sir Norman Chester's report, The State of Football, soon sunk without a trace.

Football had plenty of problems and Sir Norman was the ideal choice to come up with some answers because he had conducted a similar investigation in 1968. That report had been well received but its recommendations were largely ignored. Fifteen years later, with football facing a crisis, his second attempt to bring about reform fared little better.

Clubs knew they had to do something to reverse the decline in attendances and cut their ever-increasing losses, but they could not agree on anything.

John Smith, the Liverpool chairman, wanted to create a Super League and, backed by Arsenal and Tottenham, wanted it limited to just 16 teams. But other clubs feared that the few would get richer at the expense of everybody else. Football wanted more money from television, who were not prepared to pay, and neither side could agree on shirt advertising which meant that sponsorship deals were at risk.

Sir Norman must have won-

dered why he bothered publishing his report on March 28. Although its suggestions were, once again, eminently sensible (reducing the size of the First Division; splitting the Third and Fourth Divisions into four regions; allowing home clubs to keep the gate money and changing the League's constitution to make it easier to reach decisions) they were, once again, rejected out of hand.

Within a month most clubs had made it clear that they did not support his proposals. As the bickering went on it was clear that everybody was prepared to put their own interests above the good of the game as a whole.

Watford's glittering first prize: second place

Going straight for goal: Gerry Armstrong tries to reach a long ball lofted into the box, Watford's trademark

ALTHOUGH Liverpool had sewn up the championship in April, Watford were having their title race with Manchester United. First prize: second place. And on May 14 Watford triumphed with the sweetest of 2-1 victories over Liverpool at Vicarage Road. Watford were runners-up, one point ahead of Manchester United.

It was a truly remarkable achievement. Seven years earlier Watford were a modest mid-table Fourth Division club with no history and little ambition. Then Elton John took over the club, injected his own money and appointed Graham Taylor as the manager with Bertie Mee as his assistant. Within two years Watford had escaped the clutches of the Fourth Division and they were on their way.

Over the next five years Taylor, with Elton John's enthusiastic support, assiduously worked his way towards the First Division, discovering such talented players as John Barnes and Luther Blissett. But not without controversy. Using the techniques of "match analysis" pioneered by Wing Commander Charles Reep at Wolves in the 1950s, Taylor perfected a "direct" method of play that was criticised by purists as simply "long ball," i.e. hoofing the ball up in the air, harrying the defence and profiting from any errors. It certainly wasn't pretty, but it did get results.

Brighton rock the big boys

FIVE DAYS before their fourth round FA Cup-tie against Manchester City, Brighton's chairman, Mike Bamber, predicted his club would go all the way in the competition. Bravado it may have been, but come May 21 when Brighton marched out on to the Wembley turf to face Manchester United in the final who would have argued against his prophecy? Certainly not Liverpool. The team who would go on to be the runaway League champions and League Cup winners were widely touted for the treble. And in the fifth round they were hosting lowly Brighton who were sliding inexorably into the Second Division and had never progressed beyond this round.

No problem surely? But Liverpool and the pundits had reckoned without Jimmy Case, still smarting after being sold while still in his prime. Brighton, under the management of the flamboyant Jimmy Melia, led at half-time, Liverpool equalised but then a late goal from Case finished off his former teammates. To add insult to injury, Phil Neal then missed a penalty.

Norwich and Sheffield Wednesday were duly disposed of in the next rounds and the

Melia: always a showman

Brighton chairman's boast did not seem so fanciful after all. However, Brighton had to play the final against Manchester United without Steve Foster, their inspirational captain and centre-half. He was suspended because of a booking in a League match, and despite taking his case all the way to the High Court was forced to sit on the sidelines as Brighton enjoyed the biggest day in their history.

And enjoy it they did. As the underdogs, and already rele-gated from the First Division, they had nothing to lose. So for much of the first half they played composed and relaxed football and put United out of their stride. Brighton's lead at the interval, courtesy of Gordon Smith's 14th-minute header, was well deserved. However, Manchester United soon got a grip on their game and with 17 minutes left, goals from Frank Stapleton and Ray Wilkins appeared to have sealed Brighton's fate as the natural order re-asserted itself. But then that man Case intervened again. His corner, three minutes from time, was pulled back to Tony Grealish who stabbed the ball into the path of Gary Stevens and the final was all square.

In extra time Brighton should have won the Cup just before the end when Mick Robinson set up Smith with a great chance. But just as the nation thought Brighton had pulled off a miracle Smith hesitated and Gary Bailey saved the day. The bubble had burst. In the replay, five days later, and despite the return of Foster, Brighton were swept away 4-0 by an imperious United who were in no mood to flirt with humiliation again.

Brighton lapped: after a shock in the first match Manchester United trounced them in the replay

KEVIN KEEGAN
Heart of oak with a touch of steel

Deryk Brown

H E WAS a natural finisher. He had pace, and could run almost as fast with the ball as without it. He more than jumped his height. He could use his low centre of gravity to ferret into space when none seemed to exist. And he was tough. Kevin Keegan's most notorious sending-off was with Billy Bremner in the Charity Shield. His most costly sending-off came early in his time in West Germany, when he flattened an opponent and was banned for two months. That nearly wrecked his German adventure as soon as it had begun.

But Keegan's charisma and skills were such that he could break the rules – more significantly, teams were ready to play for him and around him. Perhaps at Liverpool this would mean a nod-down from Toshack, or one of those low diagonal forward balls that Keegan so loved to run on to.

And seldom has there been a more intelligent footballer. Overall, it showed in the fact that Keegan always made the right decision. He joined Liverpool just as they were replacing Leeds United as Britain's best. Liverpool's team-play in the 1970s was superb, and Keegan needed a team, not a collection of ball-jugglers.

On leaving Liverpool he chose not Italy, where he would surely have burnt himself out, but West Germany. He retired as a player at the right time, the biggest name in Geordieland since Jack Milburn. Then, instead of trying to manage Barnsley or Bradford City, he went into exile, De Gaulle like, as though he knew that one day the call to greatness would come.

The call came in February 1992. Keegan returned to manage Newcastle, standing 23rd in the Second Division. They beat Bristol City 3-0 the next Saturday, the gate of 29,263 being almost double that of the previous match. One remembers Keegan's press conference afterwards. Failure had never occurred to him.

Keegan had seen enough failure around him.

He was a man of the 1970s, that era when players wore their hair long. Sometimes they even permed it. They grew bushy sideburns and sported kipper ties and outrageous flared trousers. They were a chirpy, jack-the-lad lot. But they could not build on the World Cup win of 1966. Too many players under-achieved. For instance, Worthington, Currie, Bowles, Beattie and Hudson. Keegan was in a Doncaster pub-disco that dreadful June day in 1970 when England collapsed out of the World Cup to West Germany. He was on the substitutes' bench at Wembley in October 1973 when a Polish goalkeeper called Tomaszewski somehow held England to a 1-1 draw that meant elimination from the finals of 1974. And although England beat Italy 2-0 at Wembley in November 1977, with Keegan scoring, it was not enough to stop the Italians going to Argentina the next year at our expense.

When England did reach the World Cup finals in Spain in 1982, Keegan had back trouble. His tournament lasted 27 minutes as a substitute as England limply drew 0-0 with Spain and were eliminated. It was his last cap. Keegan had worshipped Shankly and liked and respected Don Revie, but there was to be no marriage with Bobby Robson. He dropped Keegan from his squad. Keegan responded in his next match for Newcastle, scoring four goals for the only time in his career.

Soon Keegan retired to the Costa del Sol, where he never went on the beach and never drank champagne (he doesn't like the stuff). He

Little man who made the big time: Keegan scores for Liverpool against Derby

KEVIN KEEGAN

Born February 14, 1951, Armthorpe, South Yorkshire

PLAYING CAREER

Scunthorpe 1967-71
120 League appearances, 18 goals

Liverpool 1971-77
230 League appearances, 68 goals
Honours European Cup: Winners 1977
Uefa Cup: Winners 1973, 1976
FA Cup: Winners 1974; Finalists 1971, 1977
League Championship: Winners 1973, 1976, 1977; Runners-up 1974, 1975
Footballer of the Year 1976

SV Hamburg 1977-80
Honours European Cup: Finalist 1980
West German championship 1979
European Footballer of the Year 1978, 1979
West German Footballer of the Year 1978

Southampton 1980-82
68 League appearances, 37 goals

Newcastle United 1982-84
78 League appearances, 48 goals

Internationals England debut 1972
63 appearances, 21 goals
Captain 29 times

MANAGEMENT CAREER

Newcastle United Manager 1992 to present
Honours First Division: Winners 1993

played golf, he followed the turf. When Tyneside telephoned, the Messiah was ready.

Those 1970s frizzy perms made Keegan and his contemporaries look more like poodles than bulldogs. But Keegan was an English bulldog. Proud to follow the flag. Heart of oak. Never say die. That is why we have always admired him so much.

Keegan travelled to Liverpool one Monday in May 1971. With him was Ron Ashman, his manager at Scunthorpe, the clubs having agreed a transfer fee of £33,000. Ashman was keen to tie up this small fortune for Scunthorpe; Keegan had been told by his father, a miner, not to sell himself cheaply.

Keegan was down-page news at Liverpool, who were five days away from an FA Cup final against Arsenal. The offices at Anfield were temporarily in a hut at the end of a car park. Keegan sat on a dustbin for half an hour before meeting the manager, Bill Shankly.

Keegan's spirits lifted as soon as he heard Shankly talk. This strange Scotsman entranced him. And Shankly was impressed when the 5ft 8in youngster stripped for his medical. "Aye, son, have you ever thought of being a boxer?" purred Shanks. "What a physique son. Have you ever done weights?" Incidentally, Shankly's instincts were right. Keegan had tried boxing in his youth in Doncaster.

Shankly offered Keegan £45 a week. Keegan, remembering his father's orders, looked unimpressed, while Ashman, seeing his £33,000 recede, turned white. Keegan said he earned £35

Making his mark: Keegan at Newcastle

Keegan, scoring against Scotland, had his international career cut short by Bobby Robson

at Scunthorpe plus a £10 win bonus, whereupon Shankly clinched the deal by offering him £50 a week.

On the drive home Ashman reproached Keegan, whose wage was only £30. Keegan, defensively, said that at least he had told the truth about the £10 bonus. "Yes," retorted Ashman, "but whenever did you get a win bonus at Scunthorpe?" And they burst out laughing.

Thus began the rise and rise of Kevin Keegan, the little man who made the big-time. He was not as gifted as some of his contemporaries. But he could move a mountain or two.

Keegan was born in Doncaster on St Valentine's Day 1951. During his six years at Liverpool they won the European Cup once, the Uefa Cup twice, the League championship three times, and the FA Cup once, and Keegan was Footballer of the Year in 1976. He moved to SV Hamburg in June 1977. In his second season he was their top scorer as they won the Bundesliga for the first time in 19 years. He was European Footballer of the Year in 1978 and 1979. He signed for Southampton in July 1980, then played his last two seasons for Newcastle, retiring in May 1984 after leading them to promotion to the First Division. Years later, of course, he returned to Gallowgate as manager to have an even more inspirational effect. He won 63 England caps, scoring 21 goals and captaining the side 29 times. At first, England was different. "When I ran nobody moved out of the way. It was not like Liverpool at all," Keegan said after his international debut in Cardiff in November 1972.

It is quite a record for a little lad once turned away by Coventry City. Why is it so good? Some would say that Keegan was lucky, and Jack Charlton once observed that if Keegan fell into the River Tyne he would surface with a salmon in his mouth. Some would say that he had a genius for PR, and the Southampton players used to say that when Keegan was late for the team bus he was walking the town looking for somebody who did not have his autograph.

Luck and PR, certainly. But much more.

Although Keegan was not as talented as, say, Kenny Dalglish, the man who took his No7 shirt at Liverpool (who was?), he had many virtues. For a start, his self-belief was a mile high. A more enthusiastic, committed footballer you could not find. Shankly inspired in the dressing room, Keegan did so on the field.

Excelling in exile: Keegan led Hamburg's revival

THE
1983-84
SEASON

Charlton reprieved

NOTHING seemed to be going right for Charlton. No sooner had they survived one winding-up petition for tax debts at the end of last season than they were back in court again.

The problem was that when Mark Hulyer, the chairman, bought the club from Michael Gliksten, ownership of The Valley remained with one of Gliksten's companies. And Charlton could no longer afford the rent.

Gliksten went to court on October 17, claiming that he was owed more than £500,000. Other creditors, fearful that the edifice would come tumbling down, persuaded the court to postpone a final decision.

The lawyers had a field day as the case dragged on, but it looked as if the game was finally up in February 13. Apart from Gliksten, the Inland Revenue and the Customs and Excise were owed money and Charlton's debts exceeded £1m.

They managed to win another reprieve because Chief Francis Nzeribe, a Nigerian arms dealer, was said to be about to buy the club. That deal came to nothing and a fortnight later a winding-up order was duly issued, Hulyer resigned and Charlton's match with Blackburn was postponed.

On March 8, though, Charlton became the latest in an ever-growing list of clubs to cheat death. The local council offered £250,000 sponsorship, a consortium put up the rest of the money and the court approved the formation of a new company just 25 minutes before Charlton were due to lose their League status.

Fagan's triumphant debut

ANY DOUBTS there were about Joe Fagan stepping into Bob Paisley's shoes were soon dispelled. Liverpool lost the Charity Shield 2-0 to Manchester United, but after that they just marched serenely on.

By the start of November they were top of the First Division and apart from one very brief period in March they stayed there for the rest of the season. Liverpool thus became only the third club after Huddersfield and Arsenal to win the League three years in a row.

They owed much of their success to the goalscoring abilities of Ian Rush. He scored five against Luton, four against Coventry and a hat-trick against Aston Villa as he hit 32 goals in the League and 45 in all. Liverpool's progress in the League Cup was far less assured. They needed three matches to beat Fulham and were held 2-2 at Anfield by Walsall in the semi-final. The final was the first time Liverpool had met Everton at Wembley and everybody in the city was captivated by the occasion.

Heavy rain took the edge off the occasion and the two teams ground out a 0-0 draw. But it did not dampen the crowd's enthusiasm and as the players made their lap of honour after extra time the stadium resounded to chants of: "Merseyside, Merseyside!" A 1-0 victory in the replay at Maine Road left Liverpool on target for a treble of trophies in the European Cup. And the harder the challenge the better Liverpool responded. Some of Liverpool's finest performances of the season came away from home in second leg matches in the European Cup. Athletic Bilbao were beaten 1-0 in the second round, Benfica 4-1 in the quarter-final and Dynamo Bucharest 2-1 in the semi-final, with Rush getting both goals.

But the final, on May 30, was Liverpool's toughest of all. They had to face Roma in the cauldron of the Olympic stadium in Rome. Liverpool showed no signs of nerves and Phil Neal gave them the lead after 15 minutes, albeit somewhat luckily.

On song: Rush becomes Liverpool's highest scorer in a season

Winning ways: Liverpool captured the European Cup for the fourth time

> *Our methods are so easy, sometimes players don't understand them at first*
>
> JOE FAGAN
> Liverpool manager

Pruzzo equalised just before half-time and Roma piled on the pressure. Liverpool did not crack but nor could they score, even in extra time. The penalty shoot-out, at the Italian fans' end of the ground, raised the game to fever pitch.

Neal would normally have led off for Liverpool. But at the last moment Steve Nicol stepped forward and blazed the ball over the bar. Di Bartolomei gave Roma the lead, gently placing the ball in the centre of the goal as Grobbelaar guessed wrongly and dived. The Liverpool fans were subdued.

Neal kept Liverpool in the hunt and then the match was level again as Conti, too, fired over the top. Souness and Righetti traded goals and the ever-dependable Rush was also on target. Graziani hammered his attempt but the ball clipped the crossbar and flew over the top. It was now the Roma fans' turn to fall silent.

Everything depended on Alan Kennedy. He coolly placed the ball just inside the post and Liverpool had won the European Cup again. "I was really confident," he said. "I took a penalty in training and put it in the same spot. Just like that."

Hooliganism unchecked on the domestic front and English fans also wreak havoc throughout Europe

No sooner had football resumed than its biggest enemy – the hooligans – renewed their offensive. The second Saturday of the season, September 3, brought trouble at both ends of the country, with disturbances at Ayresome Park during Middlesbrough's match with Leeds and seven policemen injured in running battles with Chelsea fans in Brighton.

Official inquiries cleared all four clubs of any blame and it appeared that the authorities were powerless as more clashes were reported almost every week. Worryingly, it soon became apparent that hooliganism was no longer a purely domestic issue. When Tottenham beat Feyenoord 2-0 in the second round, second leg of the Uefa Cup on November 2 more than 30 people were injured in Rotterdam and Spurs were fined nearly £8,000 by Uefa. And little Luxembourg were left wishing that they had not been drawn in the same European championship qualifying group as England on the night of November 16. Luxembourg had unpleasant memories of England's last visit in 1977 and they had made elaborate plans involving the police forces of four countries.

But the disappointment of failing to reach the finals drove the England fans wild. They ran riot in the city centre and caused thousands of pounds of damage. Only 13 arrests were made, but nine of the offenders were fined and sentenced to up to four months in jail.

And the so-called fans were not content to fight each other either. When Notts County beat Bristol City in the FA Cup on January 10 the referee was hit by a missile during a pitch invasion and complained about the lack of protection he had received from the police.

Pitch invasions were a popular tactic and more than a hundred people were injured when fans of West Ham, who lost 3-0, made two attempts to get their FA Cup match against Birming-

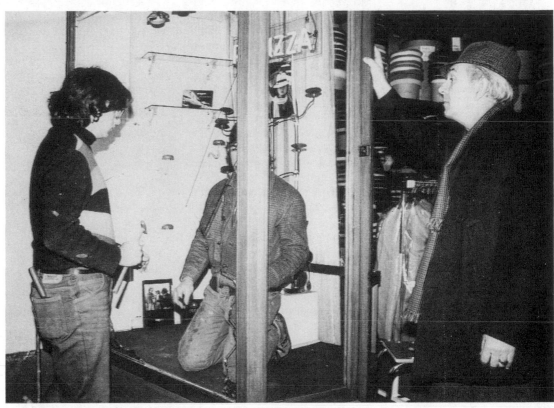

Disgraceful aftermath: thousands of pounds of damage was caused to shops in Luxembourg

Massed ranks: the security forces could not keep England fans under control

ham abandoned on February 18. West Ham were threatened with a two-year ban from the competition, but had the decision reversed on appeal.

All this trouble had been noted with growing concern by Uefa, whose general secretary, Hans Bangerter, threatened to ban British clubs from Europe unless the government stopped hooligans travelling abroad. Little did he know that the apocalypse was soon to come.

FOR THE RECORD

■ The Scottish FA proposed a three-way tournament involving England and a leading overseas side to replace the defunct home international championship.

■ The total attendance on August 27 was the lowest ever for the first day of a season, although First Division crowds were larger than last season.

■ Tottenham's 3.8m shares were snapped up within minutes of going on sale on September 6. The offer was oversubscribed by more than four times. The shares were first quoted on the Stock Exchange on October 13, and more than 1.5m were traded in the first 20 minutes.

■ Simon Garner of Blackburn and Tony Caldwell of Bolton both scored five goals on September 10. It was the first time two players had scored five times on the same day for nearly two decades.

■ Sir Denis Follows, a former secretary of the FA, died on September 17, aged 75.

■ Pat Jennings made his 100th appearance for Northern Ireland against Austria on September 21.

Miller: inspirational

Aberdeen double up again

ABERDEEN continued to be the dominant team in Scotland. Having achieved a Double of European Cup Winners' Cup and Scottish Cup the previous season, they proceeded to achieve the "real" Double of League championship and Scottish Cup. Their inspiration was Willie Miller, aided by the likes of Gordon Strachan, Doug Rougvie and Alex McLeish, and guided by the wily management of Alex Ferguson.

The League championship really was a procession. By mid-October they were top and by the end of the season they were seven points clear of Celtic, having won 25 and lost four of their League matches. In the Scottish Cup final on May 19 Celtic were the obstacle to Aberdeen gaining their first "real" Double. Eric Black put Aberdeen ahead in the first half before an ugly incident changed the course of the match. Celtic's Roy Aitken lunged at Mark McGhee and was sent off. Aitken was the first player to be sent off in a Scottish Cup final since 1929.

Having been largely outplayed in the first half, now 10 Celtic players were determined to battle till they dropped. With four minutes to go Paul McStay scored the equaliser and the game went into extra time. Here the advantage of 11 fit men over 10 tired ones told and McGhee scored a cracking winner. And another piece of history was enacted: Aberdeen became only the second club this century to

McGhee: winning goal

lift the Scottish Cup in three successive years.

The one real blot on their season was in the defence of their European Cup Winners' Cup. Having sailed into a semi-final against Porto all they needed to do at Pittodrie was overturn a Portuguese 1-0 lead from the first leg. But Aberdeen were too blasé and lost 1-0 instead.

Goicoechea scythes down Maradona

DIEGO MARADONA had his season cut short by a terrible tackle by Andoni Goicoechea. The Barcelona forward's ankle was shattered by the Bilbao full-back on September 26, and it was immediately predicted that Maradona would be out of action for at least three months.

Barcelona fans, furious at the way their star had been scythed down, tried to storm the Bilbao players' hotel. The Spanish FA were not happy about the incident either, and three days later they acted to ban Goicoechea, dubbed "the Butcher of Bilbao", for 18 matches.

Home nations miss their cue on the European stage

NONE of the Home Nations qualified for the finals of the European championships in France in June, although England, Northern Ireland and Wales came exceedingly close. Scotland were never in the hunt. For Bobby Robson in his first campaign as England manager it was bitterly disappointing as they failed by a single point.

Two results in their five-team group (with only one country to qualify) were England's undoing. They failed to beat Greece at Wembley and then lost at home to Denmark. Both were remarkable results as earlier they had thrashed Greece 3-0 away and taken a point in Denmark, the eventual qualifiers.

The home match against Denmark, on September 21, was the key game in the group as the Danes knew defeat would almost certainly end their hopes of qualifying. However, instead of playing for the draw as expected, they clearly set out to win, playing composed possession football with Michael Laudrup and Allan Simonsen the dominant players. A 39th minute penalty, conceded by Phil Neal when he handled a Laudrup cross and converted by Simonsen, settled the match and Denmark topped the group for the first time. And, apart from a 1-0 defeat by Hungary, they never looked back.

Northern Ireland were the surprise packet of the qualifying stages. Their five-team group was supposed to be a pushover for West Germany, the World Cup runners-up and reigning European champions. But Northern Ireland inflicted two 1-0 victories, home and away, upon West Germany to throw the group wide open. It went down to the wire with the Germans needing to beat Albania at home in their last game on November 20 to qualify, which they did with only 10 minutes to spare, and got through only on goal difference.

Wales, too, did themselves proud, and a victory against Yugoslavia in Cardiff on December 14 would have sent them on their way to France. Instead a 1-1 draw meant that everything hinged on the final match between Yugoslavia and Bulgaria in Split on December 12. A draw would have put Wales through, any victory would do for the Yugoslavs, but a win by Bulgaria could have been sufficient for them to leapfrog into first place. In a dramatic match Bulgaria led after 28 minutes, Yugoslavia equalised two minutes later and then took the lead in the 52nd minute.

The match then swung Bulgaria's way as they grabbed an equaliser on the hour and pressed for the winner. With seconds remaining the scores were tied and it looked as if Wales were through. Then the Yugoslav defender Radanovic headed a winning goal and suddenly they were out.

Britain left holding two winning tickets in penalty lottery

BRITISH CLUBS had their finest night in European competition on March 21. All six clubs involved in the three competitions reached the semi-finals. In the Champions' Cup: Liverpool and Dundee United; in the Cup Winners' Cup: Manchester United and Aberdeen; and in the Uefa Cup: Spurs and Nottingham Forest. And when the draws kept all six apart there was the prospect of three all-British finals.

Unfortunately only Liverpool and Tottenham made it to their respective finals, where Liverpool won in a penalty shoot-out. Amazingly so did Spurs in the two-legged final against Anderlecht. At White Hart Lane, Tottenham's goalkeeper, Tony Parks produced two scintillating saves to give Spurs their third European trophy.

Fame is the spur: Steve Archibald shoots against Hadjuk Split in the Uefa Cup semi-final

Maxwell covets United

THE ABORTIVE attempt to merge Oxford and Reading into the Thames Valley Royals did nothing to dampen Robert Maxwell's desire to own more football clubs. Even though Maxwell owned Oxford and was thus prevented by the League's rules from involvement in any other club he wanted to be bigger and better than everybody else. So less than two months after Oxford had knocked Manchester United out of the League Cup Maxwell turned his greedy eye towards Old Trafford. Maxwell used his newspaper, the *Daily Mirror*, to unveil a £10m bid for Manchester United on February 3.

One of the headlines on the report claimed that the deal would be completed in a week. Although Manchester United fans were incredulous, a deal very nearly was done. Martin Edwards, the chairman, and his brother owned the bulk of the club between them and they were tempted by the offer.

They indicated that if Maxwell raised his bid to £15 a share then they would sell. But Maxwell was not prepared to pay any more and the nego-

tiations ended on February 13. Not to be out-done, Maxwell switched his attention to Derby on March 1. The struggling Second Division club lacked the glamour and status of Manchester United but they were desperately in need of money.

Derby were £1.5m in debt, banned from the transfer market because they still had not paid for players they had bought, and facing a winding-up petition from the Inland Revenue. A judge refused a petition to allow Maxwell to take over the club, but not even that could stop him. By the end of the summer Peter Taylor, the Derby manager, had been sacked and Maxwell had leased the Baseball ground from the local council and installed his son Ian as the Derby chairman.

Just because I'm a professional it doesn't mean I'm not a human being

MICK MILLS
upset at the abuse he received on not joining Sunderland

■ Injury-struck Watford advertised in The Times for professional footballers "… men or women … preference given to applicants with two arms and two legs in working order."

■ Alan Smith lost three teeth during Leicester's 2-2 draw with Stoke on September 24. They were retrieved from the pitch and replaced in hospital.

■ The second round of the League Cup saw the competing clubs seeded for the first time.

■ Ken Bates, the Chelsea chairman, called an extraordinary meeting on September 26 to remove Dave Mears and Viscount Chelsea from the board. He was angry that Mears had sold Stamford Bridge to Marler properties.

■ Tottenham Hotspur beat Nottingham Forest 2-1 on October 2 in the first of 10 live matches due to be shown on television.

■ John Greig resigned as the Rangers manager on October 28. He was replaced by Jock Wallace of Motherwell.

Hands across the terraces: Ken Bates at Stamford Bridge

Platini ends France's agony

IN THE finals of the European championships Michel Platini conclusively demonstrated that he was one of the world's greatest players. He led France, the host nation, to victory not only with dazzling skills and vision – he also scored nine of their 15 goals.

Dizzy Swansea on the slide

Turbulent year: Toshack left, returned and was then sacked

SWANSEA'S downward spiral was happening almost as quickly as their previous climb to the heights. Newly relegated from the First Division they dropped straight out of the Second Division, failing to win an away match all season and never being placed higher than 20th in the table.

Their struggles on the field were matched by the problems off it. The chairman and vice-chairman resigned on October 16 and Doug Sharpe took over a club that was more than £1.5m in debt. Sharpe's first job in charge was to stave of the bankers, who demanded that Swansea raised nearly £500,000 in a few weeks.

John Toshack, the manager,

resigned within a fortnight and although Doug Livermore took over temporarily Swansea had difficulty in finding a permanent replacement. Colin Appleton turned them down, so Toshack was re-appointed on December 21. But there was little he could do to stop the rot. Every player was up for sale in an attempt to raise money and three of them, including the veteran striker, Bob Latchford, were given free transfers to cut the wage bill.

The former forward even made a comeback as a sweeper in a rare victory on December 31. But when he refused to resign on March 5 he was sacked and left Swansea for the second and final time.

France had shown in the World Cup in Spain two years earlier that they were a side of great attacking flair but were still haunted by the memories of their catastrophic defeat at the hands of West Germany in the semi-final in Seville. France's fluent football had given them a two-goal lead in extra time but, inexplicably, instead of shutting up shop they went in pursuit of more goals. Instead they conceded two goals and lost the penalty shoot-out. In the European championships they also played with a swagger, rifling their way into a semi-final with Portugal in Marseille. It proved to be as dramatic as the World Cup. Once again the match went into extra time, but now France fell behind – for the first time in the match – to a goal from Jordao in the 97th minute. Now the French had to show tenacity. With six minutes remaining Domergue levelled, and then, with the dreaded penalty shoot-out looming, Platini fired a Tigana cross into the Portuguese net barely a minute from the end. Their opponents in the final were Spain, who had knocked out Denmark 5-4 in a penalty shoot-out.

The final in Paris on June 27 was to be the acid test. France had never won a major tourna-

ment: they had been humiliated by Brazil in the semi-final of the 1958 World Cup. The nation held its breath while the sporting press, especially L'Equipe, raked over the ashes of such disappointing defeats. The fears transmitted themselves to the players and suddenly the elan disappeared from their game and at the interval the match was goalless. But in the 16th minute of the second half fate, for once, blessed France. A curling free kick from Platini on the edge of the area was falling neatly into the arms of Luis Arconada, but bizarrely the Spanish goalkeeper allowed it to slip out of his hands and into the net. Spain simply fell apart.

With six minutes to go France were down to 10 men when Le Roux was sent off for his second bookable offence. Spain, sensing their opportunity, mounted attack after attack. Seconds before the final whistle, with virtually the whole of the Spanish team in the French half, Tigana cleared the ball over their heads and into the path of the onrushing Bellone. His chip over Arconada settled matters.

It had been a poor final, but the right team were European champions, and the right man, Platini, the man of the tournament.

France's finest hour: Platini lifts the European championship cup

Form book finally ends minnows' majestic haul

BOURNEMOUTH set the theme for a topsy-turvy year in the FA Cup in the Third Round on January 7 when the Third Division club knocked out Manchester United, the holders, 2-0. It was the first time that Bournemouth had reached the Fourth Round in 24 years. Telford continued the shocks with 4-1 victory at Rochdale to became the first non-League club for three seasons to make the Fourth Round. In all, nine First Division clubs fell at the first hurdle (admittedly five of them against First Division opponents).

So it went on. In the Fourth Round, Brighton, last season's Cup finalists but now of the Second Division, proved last year's FA Cup elimination of Liverpool was no fluke by doing it again, this time at the Goldstone ground. With the big guns dropping like flies, the way was open to the minnows. And it was little Plymouth Argyle who came through on the rails.

On March 14 Plymouth beat Derby 1-0 in a Sixth Round replay with an Andy Rogers goal direct from a corner. They were only the sixth Third Division club to have reached the semi-finals of the FA Cup. There they met "super" minnows Watford who, although they had finished First Division runners-up the previous season, had never captured a major honour and were enjoying only their second season in the top flight.

Thus, despite the presence of 20,000 Argyle fans – nearly four times their average attendance – at Villa Park on April 14, the West Country club succumbed to a George Reilly goal in the second half. Everton, Watford's opponents at Wembley on May 19, were appearing in their first final since 1968 but their eighth overall. History, and form, finally asserted itself and Watford were swept away 2-0 as Everton collected their fourth FA Cup trophy.

■ Kenny Dalglish scored his 100th League goal for Liverpool on November 26. He became the third player to score 100 goals in the Scottish and English Leagues.

■ Seven Notts County players were booked at the same time on December 27 when the defensive wall did not retreat 10 yards at a free kick.

■ Jason Dozzell, aged 16 years and 57 days, became the youngest goalscorer in First Division history when he came on as a substitute and scored for Ipswich on February 4.

■ Arsenal, 16th in the First Division, sacked Terry Neill on December 16. Don Howe was put in charge of the team temporarily, and appointed full-time on April 28.

■ Chris Withe of Bradford and Willie Naughton of Preston both scored direct from corners in the two teams' match on January 2.

■ Clubs were so short of cash that only nine players moved on March 22, the day of the transfer deadline. The total of the fees was less than £300,000.

Changing the guard at Palace: Coppell becomes their eighth manager

■ Cambridge broke a record run of 31 matches without victory on April 28. However they had already been relegated from the Second Division.

■ Crystal Palace sacked Alan Mullery on May 14. They appointed Dave Bassett but he returned to Wimbledon after four days, saying he had made a mistake.

■ Steve Coppell became Palace's eighth manager in under four years on June 3.

■ Terry Venables accepted an offer of £150,000 a year to become the Barcelona coach on May 24.

■ Tommy Docherty became a manager for the 17th time when he took charge of Wolves on June 8.

Finishing touch: Andy Gray scores Everton's second goal against Watford

Changing his mind at Palace: Bassett quits after four days

These people are society's problems and we don't want your hooligans at our sport

FA secretary
TED CROKER
to Margaret Thatcher after the
Luton-Millwall riot

Millwall riot sparks blazing hooligan row with Thatcher

HOOLIGANISM had been a running sore for over a decade, but although extensively reported in the media few people had actually witnessed it first hand. Then, on March 13, Millwall fans ran amok at Luton during an FA Cup quarter-final. Crucially, the riot was shown live on television and the entire nation, including Margaret Thatcher, the Prime Minister, watched in horror.

Hundreds of Millwall fans ripped up plastic seats, hurled some of them on to the pitch and used the rest as shields, weapons and batons as they engaged in a full-scale battle with 200 police-men. Nearly all of the television audience had probably never seen anything like it before.

The referee had to take the players off the pitch for 25 minutes while the police dealt with the mob. Luton did eventually win 1-0 to go through to meet Everton in the semi-final, but that was largely ignored as the riot made headlines worldwide.

To cap the riot on the pitch, the Millwall hordes rampaged through the town, causing thousands of pounds of damage to shops, houses and cars. And they wrecked the train back to London. Forty-seven people, including 31 policemen, were injured. The day after the mayhem at Luton, the Uefa executive awarded the 1988 European championships to West Germany. Bert Millichip, the FA chairman, claimed that England's application failed because of the riot.

On March 28, Thatcher conducted an hour-long ministerial meeting on hooliganism and, unhappy with football's failure to tackle the violence, summoned football's chiefs to Downing Street to explain themselves. Whereupon they did themselves, and football, no favours. On April 1, of all days, Ted Croker, the FA's secretary, told the Prime Minister: "These people are society's problem and we don't want your hooligans at our sport." The net effect of this complacency was that the government passed a bill banning the sale of alcohol at football grounds and set in motion plans for a national identity card system.

Some clubs did respond to the crisis. Despite howls of protests from the other clubs, Luton banned away fans from Kenilworth Road. And Chelsea, another club notorious for hooliganism, tried to tackle the problem, albeit in a muddled and haphazard way.

Ken Bates, their controversial chairman, banned a section of the press from Stamford Bridge for reporting hooliganism at Chelsea, erected an electrified fence to prevent pitch invasions and announced he was starting an ID card scheme.

The fence fell foul of the Greater London Council and was never switched on and the ID system was abandoned as unworkable. The press were eventually readmitted when Bates discovered it was impossible to stop them reporting from the terraces.

But although Bates was misguided, his heart was in the right place. In July the FA, incredibly, cleared Millwall of any blame for the Luton riot.

Pitched battle at Kenilworth Road: police struggle to control hundreds of Millwall fans

Terrace of shame: the trail of destruction left by the mob who had ripped up seats

half an hour after the first, as the Liverpool fans weighed in with rocks, fists, beer cans and fireworks. The belated police intervention only made matters worse as police beat the panicking fans with batons to clear the terrace while fans lay dying. Amazingly, the match went ahead after a one hour 25 minute delay although West German television had the sensitivity to pull the plugs. And many of the fans in the stadium and the players were unaware of the scale of what had occurred. In England the television commentary swung from discussion and news about the mounting death toll to normal commentary on the game.

Although it almost went unnoticed, Liverpool lost 1-0 to a hotly contested penalty conceded by Gary Gillespie outside the area, and converted by Michel Platini. After the dust settled, everybody blamed each other as nobody would take responsibility. Politically it eventually brought down the Belgian government. In football, punishment was more swift. Within days the FA withdrew all English clubs from European competition for a year. It was not enough. Uefa banned all English clubs from European competition indefinitely, with Liverpool receiving an extra three-year ban to apply when English clubs were let back in. Fifa banned all English clubs worldwide, but in July reduced this to Europe, including Scotland, Ireland and Wales.

In Downing Street, Margaret Thatcher, the Prime Minister, was appalled at the scenes she had watched on television and the international damage it would do to Britain. Her efforts to force football to put its house in order were redoubled and the identity card scheme, which football claimed was unworkable, became the linchpin of her solution to hooliganism.

Shamefully, four of the six English clubs who had qualified for European competition (Everton, Manchester United, Norwich and Southampton) went to the High Court to get the ban lifted. They claimed it was unfair on them as they had

Dundee United left with nothing

DUNDEE UNITED did not win anything but, in a season where the honours were spread between Glasgow and Aberdeen, they certainly were in with a shout in all the competitions. Despite a poor start to the League – taking only nine points from their first 10 games – they rallied, beating Aberdeen twice in 10 days, to finish third to Aberdeen and Celtic for the second year in succession.

Dundee United's 1-0 defeat of Aberdeen at Pittodrie on December 22 ended a run of 24 home League matches without defeat. And which was the previous team to have a won League match at Pittodrie?

Dundee United in September 1983. Dundee United also put paid to Aberdeen's hopes of a fourth successive Scottish Cup when they beat them 2-1 in a semi-final replay at Tynecastle in April.

But despite these sterling performances against the runaway champions – Aberdeen led from start to finish and won the Premier League with a record number of points – it was the Old Firm that left Tayside without any Scottish silverware. Dundee United lost the League Cup final to Rangers by a solitary goal from Iain Ferguson and then the 100th Scottish Cup final to Celtic 2-1, having scored

the opening goal themselves.

In a season of remarkable performances by this canny side ably led by Jim McLean and Walter Smith, Dundee United saved probably their best for the third round Uefa Cup ties against Manchester United. In a thrilling match at Old Trafford in the first leg they were 1-0 down at half-time to a Strachan penalty before two goals from Hegarty and Sturrock meant that Manchester United went to Tannadice all square at 2-2. However, a McGinnis own goal spoilt the party and Dundee United went out 5-4 on aggregate in another wonderfully contested match.

A Juventus fan uses a plank to attack the barbed-wire perimeter fencing

Anti-climax: Juventus fans witness the return of the Cup at Turin airport

not been party to the events at Heysel. Liverpool took separate legal action. Only Spurs refused to be involved. The ban was upheld, the judge agreeing that

everything should be done, and be seen to be done, to ensure that such a tragedy never happened again. Sadly the football authorities did not heed him.

39 killed in Heysel stampede

THE disaster at Bradford 18 days earlier and the mayhem at Luton in March had not prepared anybody for the criminal tragedy at the Heysel stadium in Brussels on May 29. The occasion, the European Cup final between Liverpool and Juventus, was the climax of the season, but just as we were about to enjoy the summit of European football the game reached its nadir.

Before the match even started Liverpool fans charged Juventus fans, who attempted to run away to safety. But an old wall collapsed and in the ensuing panic the Italians fell over each other and some were crushed to death. Thirty-eight people died that day (one more died in hospital later) and more than 400 were injured. The appalling scenes were watched by a global television audience dumbstruck with horror and incomprehension. How could such a thing have happened? Sadly, the answer is easy and a damning indictment of every aspect of the way football was run.

The stadium, a run-down, antiquated dinosaur, should never have been chosen as the venue for such an important and volatile match. And the corner of Z terrace was a death trap with two adjacent walls at one end providing no safe means of exit. Ticket control was non-existent and many Italian fans easily acquired tickets for the neutral Z section. It was into this section that the Liverpool fans charged when they easily broke out of their restricted X and Y terraces. Security and policing were pitiful. Liverpool fans, once inside, were able to hand their tickets over the wire to others outside. Some simply crawled in under the fence. The police precautions, such as they were, had not even anticipated that violence might occur before the kick-off. There was no attempt to search spectators for weapons or to prevent alcohol being brought into the ground. Many of the fans were drunk, and many had sticks, bottles and iron bars. There was no closed circuit television and the emergency services were woefully inadequate.

The failure of the Belgian police to have properly researched patterns of English hooliganism was incredible. No English police force would ever have made the dreadful mistakes the Belgians did, they would have spotted the problem much earlier and dealt with it; for all the warning signs were there.

The first Liverpool charge, after the usual bout of taunts and insults, happened at 6.30pm as eight policemen looked on. The fatal charge was the third,

Failing to segregate fans and allowing Italians into neutral sections created the conditions for mayhem

Debris of a disaster: stewards survey Z terrace, where the wall had collapsed on terrified Juventus fans

56 perish in Bradford inferno

death toll could have been in the thousands. Still, it was the worst sporting disaster ever to occur in England.

The cause of the fire was eventually diagnosed as years of accumulated rubbish under the 76-year-old stand, which was almost certainly set alight by a discarded cigarette or dropped match. That the rubbish had been ignored for so long was a damning indictment of how football clubs viewed safety and the welfare of their paying customers.

On the very same day hooliganism raised its ugly head and claimed a life. A wall collapsed, killing a young boy, and 96 policemen were injured when Leeds fans rioted at a match in Birmingham. The two incidents, 100 miles apart, were a sorry reminder of the state in which English football now found itself.

The aftermath: Judge Popplewell inspects the charred remains of the wooden main stand

TV money foolishly rejected

FOOTBALL seemed to think that television had bottomless pockets. So, on January 17, with the contract to show matches being renegotiated, club chairmen turned down £16m over four years. They were certain that they could get more money.

But the men who ran the game did not realise that their product had been devalued by the years of hooliganism. A bad winter and a large number of postponed matches had also affected clubs' cashflow.

Despite a warning from the Football League about the financial consequences of their rejecting the deal, the clubs refused to change their mind when they met again on Febru-ary 14. With the television companies adamant that they were not going to raise their offer, the prospect of a television black-out was looming.

Finally both the BBC and ITV ran out of patience. On May 2, they gave football a one-month deadline to reach agreement. Even then, the clubs were prepared to cut off their nose to spite their face.

The 1985-86 season duly started without any television coverage as the talks dragged on. In the end, though, football had to give in. And their intransigence had cost them a fortune. When agreement was finally reached football was forced to settle for a mere £1.3 m.

Strachan: tug-of-war transfer

Celebration ends in tragedy –

IF HOOLIGANISM was the most visible blot on football's tattered reputation, the state of our stadiums was the other. Many were antiquated, decaying and unsafe. Just how unsafe became tragically clear on May 11 at Valley Parade, the last day of the League season, when Bradford City were playing Lincoln and were celebrating their Third Division championship and promotion to the Second Division. Just before half-time a fire started in the wooden main stand. Within minutes the blaze spread all along the stand and the celebrating fans were caught in a death trap. Many escaped on to the pitch, but 56 people died and hundreds suffered burns, some very serious.

The pitch had provided the only safe means of exit and if the spectators had been caged in (one of the methods used to curb hooliganism) then the

Death trap at Valley Parade: terrified fans flee on to the pitch, their only safe means of exit, to try to escape the flames

Telford and York take the whole country by storm

TELFORD took the giant-killing honours with a Cup run that took them all the way to the fifth round, with League opposition at every stage and a draw that was not kind to them. The Gola League side travelled to Third Division Lincoln in the first round, held them to a draw and then won the replay. The second round sent them to another Third Division club, Preston, who were despatched 4-1.

At least Telford were given a home tie in the third round. But instead of one of the glamour clubs they had to face yet another Third Division team. Bradford, who topped the table, were sent packing 2-1.

Even then Telford did not get any reward, being sent to one of the Fourth Division's pacesetters, Darlington. Another replay was needed before Telford got a chance to cash in with another trip, to Everton.

Telford finally met their match at the First Division leaders, but they were not disgraced in a 3-0 defeat and went home considerably richer than when they had started their trek around the country.

The greatest upset of the competition came in the fourth round. Arsenal had wobbled at the previous stage, needing two matches to get past Hereford. Their luck ran out at Bootham Crescent on January 26, when Keith Houchen scored the only goal, a penalty, to give Third Division York an historic victory. It was the seventh time since the war that Arsenal had been knocked out of the Cup by a team from a lower division.

Merseyside pendulum swinging Everton's way

HOWARD KENDALL had been steadily building a good side since his arrival at Goodison Park, and Everton at last were ready to emerge from the shadow of their great rivals Liverpool.

The first hint of what was about to come came in the Char-ity Shield when Everton won 1-0 with Bruce Grobbelaar conceding an own goal. By the end of October it was clear how far the pendulum had swung. Everton won 1-0 at Anfield and moved into fourth place while Liverpool slipped down to 18th.

Apart from a brief period over Christmas and the New Year, Everton were never out of first place from the start of November to the end of the season. And from December 26 to May 8 they strung together a remarkable sequence, winning six matches in a row, drawing two, and then running up 10 consecutive victories. The title was theirs on May 6, with five matches still to play.

The key to their success was the relentless pressure that the team exerted. Even when an opponent had the ball, he was given little time to do anything. Peter Reid was Everton's mainspring in midfield, and his industry deservedly brought him a first full cap for England and the acclaim of his fellow professionals, who chose him as their player of the year.

Everton's easy ride in the League was matched by their progress in the European Cup Winners' Cup. They did not meet a side of note until the semi-finals, but Bayern Munich were polished off 3-1 at home and Rapid Vienna were overrun 3-1 in the final in Rotterdam on May 15.

Everton had a majestic treble in their sights. But the Bradford inferno cast a pall over the FA Cup final on May 18. Even when Kevin Moran became the first man to be sent off in a final Everton could not press home their advantage. A man short, Manchester United battled on gamely to win a muted match 1-0 in extra time.

Moran fouls Reid to become the first person sent off in an FA Cup final

The many sides of Anton Johnson

ANTON JOHNSON was finally banned for life from any involvement with football clubs. The only surprise on February 11 was that it had taken the Football League so long to catch up with him. Johnson, a self-proclaimed millionaire who favoured a full-length wolfskin coat, dark glasses, big cigars and a Rolls-Royce, had broken just about every rule in the League's book since he had become involved in football in 1979.

The first club to suffer from his questionable dealings were Rotherham. When Johnson bought the club it was profitable. He left them deep in debt and the subject of League investigations over illegal payments.

Johnson also used a Guernsey-based company to take over Bournemouth while he was still involved with Rotherham. The use of this company allowed him to conceal his involvement in two clubs at the same time, which was not allowed under League rules. Amazingly, by 1983, Johnson was able to boast: "I have helped in the purchase of a dozen clubs."

Bournemouth, too, rued the day that Johnson became involved. But unfortunately other clubs seemed to fall for the brash claims (most of which were unfounded) of an inveterate self-publicist.

When Johnson breezed into Southend in 1983 he was hailed as the saviour of an almost bankrupt club – particularly when he was instrumental in appointing Bobby Moore as chief executive.

Soon, though, everything went sour as Southend, too, discovered discrepancies in their finances. Johnson was questioned by the police and the League finally acted, sending in a team of accountants to examine the books. They discovered such a tangle of questionable transfers and missing money that they were left with no option but to ban Johnson.

Johnson: banned

205

BOBBY ROBSON
Before Taylor, England were fine – but nobody noticed

Chris Nawrat

IT WOULD have been forgivable if, in the dark days of 1993, Bobby Robson had gloated over, or even taken some satisfaction in, the plight of Graham Taylor. His successor as the England manager had been bequeathed a team of world-class players, a team that had reached the World Cup semi-finals, yet Taylor had somehow perpetrated the impossible.

For only the third time since England had deigned to enter the World Cup in 1950 they had failed to qualify for the finals. Only Sir Alf Ramsey (in 1974) and Don Revie (in 1978) had committed such a gaffe. Ramsey was sacked, Revie fled to the riches of the Arabian deserts. Taylor, to his credit, eventually fell on his sword. And Robson, to his credit, kept his vow of silence.

It was a remarkable act of self-restraint. Robson, it should be remembered, had been the most vilified England manager ever. The tabloid press

took a macabre delight in twisting the knife every time England had a poor result: "Plonker"; "In the name of God go"; "In the name of Allah go" (after a 1-1 draw away to Saudi Arabia); "England Mustafa New Boss" and "Desert Prats", were just some of the headlines during Robson's tenure. The hate campaign reached its nadir with revelations about extra-marital sexual liaisons.

Somehow Robson weathered all the storms whipped up by the media. They wounded him, upset him, but he stood firm. "It's the most difficult part of my life," he said. "It's very hurtful and you know it's going to hurt your family. I try not to read the papers too much. If it's abusive, I don't read it."

When Graham Taylor suffered much the same tabloid abuse, with much more justification as England suffered the embarrassment of defeat at the hands of the United States and conceding an

eight-second goal to San Marino, Robson kept his own counsel. He could have said that after Ramsey, he was the best manager England ever had. He didn't. He could even have pointed out that, technically, Ramsey never actually qualified for the World Cup finals. (In 1966 England were the hosts, and in 1970 they qualified as the defending champions).

So let history say it for him. Under Robson England qualified for two successive World Cup finals. In 1986 England were top of their qualifying group, unbeaten with a goal difference of 19. In 1990 England were again unbeaten, second in their group without having conceded a goal – the only country to keep a clean sheet.

Then, when Robson's teams were on the world stage, they reached the quarter-finals and semi-finals respectively. By contrast, Scotland, having qualified seven times, have yet to get past

Hair's breadth from glory: Robson motivating his players before the shoot-out with West Germany

BOBBY ROBSON

Born February 18, 1933, Sacriston, County Durham

PLAYING CAREER
Fulham 1950-56
Signed in 1950 (152 games, 68 goals)
West Bromwich Albion 1956-62
Transferred for £25,000 (239 games, 56 goals)
Fulham 1962-67
Transferred for £20,000 (193 games, nine goals)
Internationals
Made his debut for England in November 1957 v France, and scored twice in the 4-0 victory. Received 20 caps and scored four goals

MANAGEMENT CAREER
Vancouver Royals Manager 1967-68
After an acrimonious break-up with the club he returned to Fulham
Fulham 1968-69
Appointed November, sacked January
Ipswich Manager 1969-82
Won the FA Cup in 1978; the Uefa Cup in 1981; League runners-up in 1981 and 1982
PSV Eindhoven Manager 1990-92
Won two League titles
Sporting Lisbon Manager 1992-93
Porto Manager 1994-
League champions 1995
England
Manager of England July 1982 to July 1990
Record P 95 W 47 D 38 L 10 F 154 A 60

Moment of glory: Bobby Moore and Alf Ramsey get their hands on the World Cup

Journeyman: Greenwood had limited success

the first round. And who did Robson's teams lose to in 1986 and 1990? Argentina (courtesy of Maradona's cheating handball) and West Germany (via a penalty shoot-out), both of which went on to win the tournament. After Taylor's clangers, Robson's term of office now looks positively masterful.

History, of course, will not be so generous as to kindly overlook two disastrous European championship campaigns, 1984 and 1988, under Robson's management. In the first England failed to qualify, edged out by Denmark – a country not yet regarded as any kind of football power. In the second England stormed through to the finals in West Germany only to fall flat on their faces. They lost to Jack Charlton's Republic of Ireland, Holland and the Soviet Union to finish bottom of their group.

Strangely, a similar fate befell Graham Taylor in the European championships in Sweden in 1992, for which England had qualified without losing a match. Two goalless draws, no wins and only one goal. Once again this left England propping up the table. Robson, of course, bounced back. Taylor went under.

Quite why one England manager succeeds where another fails is a conundrum to which the mandarins of Lancaster Gate would dearly love to know the answer. Their appointment policy over the past 30-plus years shows no line of consistency whatsoever. If we ignore Walter Winterbottom (who never had control over team selection), Joe Mercer (who was a seven-match caretaker) and Terry Venables (who will not be truly tested until the European championships in 1996), England have had five managers: Sir Alf Ramsey, Don Revie, Ron Greenwood, Bobby Robson and Graham Taylor.

Of these five, three had been England internationals (Ramsey, Revie and Robson); three had been established First Division players (Ramsey, Revie and Robson); two were managers who had won the League championship (Ramsey and Revie); and three were managers who had won other trophies (Revie, Greenwood, Robson).

Using just those bare statistics, Ramsey, England's most successful manager, has the best credentials. Despite never having managed a championship-winning team, Robson, with 20 caps, just edges out Revie, with six, by virtue of greater international experience as a player. Greenwood is way behind, with Taylor nowhere. Yet Revie was a disaster and Greenwood moderately successful.

Any analysis of the individual men's personalities gives little away as well. Robson and Taylor were ditherers? In his first eight matches Revie used 27 different players with only one ever-present. Taylor was frightened of flair players? They all were. Taylor dropped Paul Gascoigne and Chris Waddle (but persisted with John Barnes), but then Robson retired Kevin Keegan and Glenn Hoddle – whom Greenwood had hardly picked – Revie played Tony Currie just once and Ramsey discarded Jimmy Greaves.

And just to confuse the matter, there was one thing they all had in common: they had built their club successes on a tightly-knit camaraderie, a sort of family. Which is precisely the one thing

Ignominy: Taylor's team fell to earth

you cannot do in international management.

The job of England manager, which has often been described as being more onerous than the Prime Minister's, has been much misunderstood, particularly by its occupants. Ramsey was fortunate: the media were less intense in the 1960s; the pressure to succeed was not as compelling and the players were less demanding.

By the 1990s Taylor reaped the whirlwind that had (just) failed to sweep Robson away. The media pressure on the man in the hot seat borders on the unbearable. "You go into a press room and there's 250 journalists from all different countries," Robson told the author Johnny Rogan. "You've got 50 tape recorders on your desk and that's just the front row. There's five or six camera crews all filming live so if you stumble on a word it's all on tape. If Alf Ramsey moved into that now, he wouldn't believe it compared to what he had."

Taylor innocently thought that because he was brought up in a journalistic family he could sweet-talk his way past the press. He was wrong. Robson knew what the bottom line always was: "It's about results. You know what the job is? Winning."

The art of winning is arcane. Twice in the World Cup finals Robson lost the services of Bryan Robson, his captain fantastic, because of injuries. Robson is convinced that if, in the 1990 finals, he had been able to field a midfield of Bryan Robson, David Platt and Gascoigne, not only would they have beaten West Germany in the semi-final, Argentina would have fallen in the final and England would be the defending world champions.

Such a sweet outcome in Italy four years ago would have meant that Robson would have gone down in history as England's greatest manager and, of course, Graham Taylor would never have had to resign. He would have inherited an even better team from Robson, one that had automatically qualified for the 1994 World Cup finals. By such paper-thin scripts are destinies shaped.

Super League on the agenda

FOOTBALL finally gave in and accepted television's much-reduced offer midway through the season, but this did not stop the clubs' continual bickering. The arguments merely shifted to another power struggle.

Leading clubs wanted a greater say in how the game was run and talk of a breakaway Super League was rife. Even though Canon said they were not going to renew their backing of the League, and a group of sponsors warned the game that it had to get its act together before the money ran out, the wrangling went on.

Eventually the leading clubs got their way in April, although not until they had taken the Super League issue to the brink. The Second Division, fearful of losing their share of the television money, conceded that their voting rights should be reduced, and it was agreed that the First Division would shrink to 20 clubs over the next two seasons. To ease the realignment of the divisions, play-offs would be introduced.

At least the clubs realised that they were not going to be able to bully the television companies into submission. When the television contract came up for negotiation again in June, a £6.2m two-year agreement was reached in a matter of days.

Scotland, too had its share of the arguments. Unlike England, an agreement with television was in place in time for the start of the season. But within months there were arguments about the way the money was divided. By February nine of the 10 Premier League teams had joined forces and were threatening to set up their own league.

N Ireland and Scotland off to Mexico amid controversy

ALL the British teams bar Wales and the Republic of Ireland qualified for the World Cup finals in Mexico, England qualifying for the first time since 1970, coincidentally when the finals were also held in Mexico. England's cause was definitely helped by having Northern Ireland in the same Group. Billy Bingham's men beat Romania home and away while England could only draw both their matches with Romania.

Northern Ireland's qualification was not without a whiff of controversy. By November 13 an undefeated England had already qualified when they had thrashed Turkey 5-0 the month before, but Northern Ireland needed a point at Wembley to edge out Romania.

To British eyes an inspired 40-year-old Pat Jennings, who had not played League football for a year, in his 113th international (a world record), played a blinder to deny England in a goalless draw. To the Romanians it was a fix. But having lost twice to Northern Ireland themselves, it was more like sour grapes.

Wales were the team who had just cause for complaint for not being on the plane to Mexico. In the final match of the Group they had to beat Scotland at Ninian Park to qualify for a play-off against Australia or New Zealand, both minnows.

Wales were 1-0 ahead at half-time and the Scots were despondent. As the second half wore on Jock Stein, Scotland's manager, sensed the Welsh had settled for preserving their slender lead and Davie Cooper was sent on for Gordon Strachan. The Scots were immediately revitalised.

However the goal that levelled the scores and eliminated the Welsh should never have happened. With 10 minutes to go a dubious handball in the Welsh penalty area was adjudged by the French referee to be a penalty to Scotland. Cooper scored from the spot. Stein the maestro had pulled another masterstroke.

Sadly the match will be remembered for the death of the 62-year-old Stein, the most successful manager in Scottish history. Seconds before the final whistle he collapsed in the stadium's tunnel and died of a heart attack. Alex Ferguson, the successful manager of Aberdeen, stepped in as caretaker manager for the two-legged play-off against Australia (which Scotland won) and the finals in Mexico.

Cooper: vital penalty

Wembley wizard: Jennings kept England at bay to ensure Northern Ireland's World Cup qualification

United's flying start comes down to earth

MANCHESTER UNITED got off to such a flying start that people were soon assuming that they would run away with the First Division. United won their first 10 games to go nine points clear of Liverpool, and had Tottenham's long-standing record of 11 wins at the start of a season in their sights.

But a draw with Luton cost them the honour which, instead, went to Reading with 13 successive victories. But while Reading duly ran away with the Third Division, United's challenge faltered. They clung to the top of the First Division for the first half of the season, but they were dropping too many points and their early advantage was slowly whittled away.

Liverpool were reshaping their side and people were questioning whether Kenny Dalglish could make the transition from player to player-manager. There was even talk of this being London's year, with Chelsea and West Ham going well.

But it was Everton who showed first with an outstanding 2-0 victory at Anfield in February that put them in the driving seat. It looked as if Everton were going to go one better than their neighbours for the second year running.

But you wrote off Liverpool at your peril. And the turning point came when Dalglish restored himself to the team. He had dropped himself early in the season and played very little since, prompting speculation that he was on the verge of giving up playing altogether.

Liverpool had seven matches left and they needed to win every one of them to stand any chance of catching up. Everton faltered, drawing at Nottingham Forest and losing at Oxford, and Liverpool pounced. Inspired by Dalglish they won all seven matches, only conceding one goal. Fittingly, it was Dalglish who scored early in Liverpool's last match, a far from easy trip to Chelsea, to take the title to Anfield for the sixteenth time.

Everton, too, had a tough last match at home to West Ham to decide who took second place. But West Ham's fixture backlog (10 games in under a month) caught up with them, and Everton easily prevailed in one of the most exciting finishes to the season for years.

Dalglish: came back to secure Liverpool's sixteenth title

Scotland mourns Stein, a colossus of the game and the people's hero

JOCK STEIN, the manager of the Scotland national team and a football colossus, collapsed from a heart attack and died in the tunnel at Ninian Park on September 10. It was seconds before the end of Scotland's match against Wales which all but qualified Stein's team for the 1986 World Cup finals. The tragedy numbed the players and the whole of Scotland.

Stein was the most successful manager in Scottish history. Although a Protestant, he became the manager of Celtic, where he had been captain the 1950s, and guided them to capture the European Cup in 1967, the first British side to do so.

Under Stein's stewardship Celtic won 10 League titles, eight Scottish Cups and six League Cups between 1965 and 1978 before a car accident almost cost him his life. Before his tenure at Parkhead, he had managed Dunfermline from 1960 to 1964, winning the Scottish Cup in 1961. He spent 10 months at Hibs before joining Celtic.

After his accident Stein was briefly the Leeds manager before returning to Scotland later that year to manage the national side and take them to the 1982 World Cup finals in Spain.

Stein was born on October 5, 1922 in the Lanarkshire mining town of Burnbank, a fervent football community which has produced many top players. And two other legendary managers, Matt Busby and Bill Shankly, hailed from just a few miles away. Like Busby and Shankly, Stein was a man of the people and never forgot his roots.

Stein: Celtic's guru

THE
1985-86
SEASON

Wimbledon tough it out

WIMBLEDON'S remarkable rise continued apace, but the unfashionable team were making themselves few friends along the way. In August, Wimbledon were fined £3,000 by the FA because of their players' bad disciplinary record – they collected more than 250 disciplinary points in the previous season, the third time that they had topped this figure.

And in December the police warned the team about their behaviour, with allegations that Wimbledon players had made provocative gestures to the home crowd during a match at Barnsley's Oakwell ground. Then, in July, Wimbledon were fined a further £3,500 because, once again, of the number of players they had had booked and sent off.

Dave Bassett, the Wimbledon manager, was quick to defend his team, arguing that they were being unfairly penalised for their direct style of play. And though Wimbledon's approach was not pretty it was certainly more than effective.

They were unbeaten in their last 16 League matches, and the arrival from neighbours Millwall of John Fashanu, the club's record signing (albeit for a mere £125,000), provided the goals to propel Wimbledon into the First Division for the first time in their history.

Contrary to public opinion, I don't tell my players to kick the opposition in the nuts

DAVE BASSETT
Wimbledon manager

Venables hires Lineker in answer to Barcelona's Spanish inquisition

TERRY VENABLES had a topsy-turvy season with Barcelona. In March the Catalan club, despite having won the Spanish League the previous season, announced that Venables's contract would not be renewed at the end of June and the speculation was that he would be replaced by Howard Kendall. Unhappy with all the rumours, Venables responded by saying he intended to take a year off from the game. However, Arsenal made some not so discreet inquiries about his services which led to their coach, Don Howe, quitting in a huff.

Barcelona quickly changed their minds when Venables steered them to only their second European Cup final against the Romanian army side Steaua Bucharest, and confirmed Venables as their coach for the following season.

The final, in Seville in May, was a dreadful affair. The Spanish side, playing in their own

Team spirit is an illusion you only glimpse when you win

STEVE ARCHIBALD
of Barcelona

country, were under tremendous pressure to win and were the clear favourites. Yet on the night they froze. The Romanians went into their shell and stonewalled the Spanish for 120 minutes, and both sides failed to score.

In the penalty shoot-out the players' nerves were so frayed that only two of the seven penalties were scored, Steaua Bucharest surprisingly winning 2-0 to become the first east European side to lift the European Cup.

Not surprisingly Venables swooped during the World Cup finals to purchase a striker, and one that could also take penalties. Gary Lineker, of England and Everton, and the tournament's top scorer with six goals, joined Barcelona in July. It was believed that Lineker had cost the club in excess of £5.7m, with £4.2m going to Everton and £1.5m to the player.

Anxious moments for Venables and his assistant Alan Harris: under pressure at Nou Camp

'Rangers will sign Catholics' – Souness

RANGERS stunned everybody when they announced that Graeme Souness, then with Sampdoria, was to replace Jock Wallace as their player-manager. But there was a further shock in store at the press conference in April to announce his arrival. Souness pledged that the Glasgow club would now sign Catholics.

The statement created a furore in Glasgow where for 113 years the city had been divided by religious bigotry. Indeed, Rangers seemed to have an unwritten policy against fielding a Catholic player. Celtic, by contrast, had no such qualms about Protestants. Indeed Jock Stein, himself a Protestant, having been once asked who he would sign if offered a choice between two players of equal merit, one a Protestant and one a Catholic, replied: "The Protestant, because I know Rangers would never sign the Catholic."

But now, according to the former Liverpool player, all that was to change. "The best players will be signed, no matter what they are," Souness said. "It is not a thorny question as far as I

am concerned. How could I possibly have taken on this if I could not have signed Catholics? I am married to one and share my life with one. I could not have returned to Italy and told my wife I had the job, but there was a problem with Catholics."

Souness also vowed to go on a spending spree to find the best players and make Rangers one of the leading clubs in Britain. "I see this club as second only to Manchester United in Britain and bigger than Liverpool, Arsenal, Tottenham and anyone else."

However he was aware of the enormity of the task – Rangers had not won the title for nine years – and said: "To say I have been thrown in at the deep end is an understatement. I am envious of what Kenny Dalglish has done at Anfield and I want to follow in his footsteps. I believe I have taken on a harder job than he did because Liverpool were already a winning side."

Souness still had to see out the Italian season at Sampdoria before taking charge at Ibrox. Thirty-three in May, Souness cost Rangers some £400,000 in transfer fee and compensation.

Souness: "Thrown in at the deep end is an understatement"

■ One Chelsea fan was jailed for life and another sentenced to eight years on November 8. They were convicted of incidents that took place after Chelsea's game with Manchester United the previous December.

■ Thirteen players were sent off on December 14, a record for the Football League. Four players were sent off in Scotland on the same day.

■ An official receiver was appointed at Swansea on December 20, when the Inland Revenue was granted a winding-up order. But the club won a stay of execution and the court allowed them to continue playing for the rest of the season.

■ Bryan Robson, making his comeback after a lengthy injury, was sent off in Manchester United's fourth round FA Cup match at Sunderland.

■ The Popplewell report into safety at sports grounds, commissioned in the wake of the Bradford fire, was published on January 16.

■ Arsenal shareholders complained about four of their players having been convicted for drink-driving offences in the past 18 months.

Unhappy return: Bryan Robson (centre) was sent off in his comeback match

Hearts pipped at the last post

IT WAS the cruellest of seasons for Hearts. The Edinburgh club took advantage of postponed matches to top the Premier Division on December 21 and tenaciously clung to the pole position until the very last Saturday with a 27-game undefeated run from October until May.

Then, away to modest Dundee, where a draw would have given them their first Premier Division title, they lost 2-0. Celtic, who had not been on top since the autumn, romped home 5-0 at St Mirren to steal the title on goal difference.

Aberdeen, who started well in the Premier Division, leading from October to mid-December, inexplicably slipped away, eventually finishing fourth. But the two Cups were a completely different story as they captured both. The League Cup was particularly sweet as it was the only domestic trophy that Alex Ferguson, their manager, had not previously won and Aberdeen did it without conceding a single goal. In the Scottish Cup Aberdeen compounded Hearts' misery at losing the championship by walloping them 3-0 in the final.

211

Bad weather and too many competitions cause chaos

THE FREEZING weather that gripped Europe in February reopened the debate about whether British football should have a mid-season break. But not everybody was in favour. When Millwall's FA Cup replay with Southampton was postponed for a second time George Graham, the Millwall manager, complained that football was getting too soft. "The pitch was fit enough for play," he said.

It was not long before the fixture lists were reduced to chaos. Matters were not helped by the invention of the Screen Sports Super Cup and the Full Members Cup, ostensibly to create more money-spinning matches. Critics accused the League of greed, and half of the clubs in the First and Second Divisions refused to enter the Full Members Cup. Those that took part saw little benefit and Coventry's match against Millwall drew just 1,086 spectators

Yet, at the same time, the Football League was insistent that the season had to finish on time to allow England to prepare for the World Cup. However, on April 1, the League finally had to concede that matches would have to be played after May 3, the original deadline.

Even then, many clubs suffered, particularly Darlington. Three days after the season should have ended their footsore team played their eighth match in 13 days and their second on successive nights – and they still had another two games to go.

Liverpool win Mersey final to double Dalglish's delight

THE CITY of Liverpool had never seen anything like it. They were used to the rivalry between Liverpool and Everton, but with both teams disputing the League title and both teams in the FA Cup final as well, the city went football crazy.

For weeks, the city was decked out in red and blue. And when Liverpool just pipped Everton in the League it only added to the excitement. Could Liverpool join the elite few who had done the Double? Or would Everton gain their revenge. It really did seem as if Liverpool was the centre of the footballing universe.

Tickets for the Wembley final were prized possessions. Some reports said that £6 standing tickets were changing hands for £100, others put the price at nearer £1,000. But for most fans their tickets were priceless, not to be sold at any price.

And the game lived up to its billing, thanks to the master marksmen who had done so much for their teams. Gary Lineker struck first, tucking the rebound in after Bruce Grobbelaar could only parry his rasping shot. Everton were immediately inspired and played like a side possessed. Grobbelaar's goal was under siege and there was little Kenny Dalglish could do about it. Ian Rush, though, had other ideas.

Fed perfectly by Jan Molby, he ghosted through the Everton defence and round Bobby Mimms to put Liverpool back into the match. And five minutes later Rush combined with Molby again to set up Craig Johnston. Now it was Liverpool's turn to dominate and Everton's turn to suffer incessant pressure. With six minutes left Rush lashed another shot past Mimms to put the result beyond doubt.

It was the perfect end to Dalglish's first season as manager, and perfect proof that, despite what some pre-season doubters had thought, he was the right man to continue the great tradition started by Bill Shankly. And as Liverpool paraded the Cup around Wembley their supporters acknowledged the fact. Before they left the stadium they sang a moving tribute to the man who made it all possible – Shankly.

Perfect ending: Rush scored two goals and made one more in the thrilling FA Cup final

Rous, great reformer, dies

SIR STANLEY ROUS, the grand old man of British football died on July 18 at the age of 91.

Rous, the son of a grocer, began his love affair with football at an early age. He started his village's team while he was still at school and went on to play in goal for Lowestoft. But it was as an official rather than as a player that he made his mark.

After the first world war Rous became the senior sports master at Watford Grammar School and still found time to become a top-flight referee. He was a linesman at the 1926 Cup final and also took charge of the 1934 final. Rous's officiating was also respected throughout Europe, where he was the referee for 36 international matches.

Rous was one of six candidates to become secretary of the Football Association in 1934, and he was surprised to be appointed. But it soon became clear that the FA had made the right choice. In no time at all, Rous had rewritten the rules of the game and revolutionised the way that the linesmen and referee controlled matches, introducing yellow and red cards.

Rous's patient diplomacy was responsible for the home nations rejoining Fifa in 1947, and his tireless work for both Fifa and Uefa led to him being elected president of Fifa in 1961. But Rous was more than just an efficient administrator; one profile described him as "a man who resides at the mountain top, his views wide and all-embracing, his horizons limitless. Football is his game and the world his playing pitch."

Rous's work in modernising the game earned him respect wherever he went, and when he "retired" in 1974 he was immediately elected as an honorary life president of Fifa. He continued to be a keen spectator at football matches until just before his death, and hundreds of dignitaries from around the world attended a gala dinner to celebrate his 90th birthday.

Denis Follows, who succeeded him as the FA secretary, summed up Rous's contribution to world football when he said: "The secretary is the servant of the association and we all know what happened; the servant became the master."

Dalglish: the record-breaker who instantly made his mark as a manager

■ Kenny Dalglish won his 100th cap for Scotland on March 26.

■ Oxford United, in their first season in the First Division, won their first major trophy when they upset QPR 3-0 in the League Cup final on April 20.

■ Fifa lifted its ban on English clubs playing friendlies in Europe but, in May, Uefa decided not to readmit English clubs to the three European competitions.

■ Tottenham sacked Peter Shreeve and his assistant John Pratt on May 13. Three days later, David Pleat was appointed manager.

■ George Graham was appointed Arsenal manager in place of Don Howe on May 14.

■ Chris Woods moved from Norwich to Rangers on July 1 for £600,000, the British record fee for a goalkeeper. Rangers continued their spending spree when they signed Terry Butcher for £725,000, a Scottish record, later in the month.

■ Andy Roxburgh, who had never managed a club, was surprised to be named Scotland manager on July 16.

■ The Inland Revenue were granted a winding-up order against Middlesbrough on July 30.

■ There were two big transfers in the close season when Ian Rush was sold to Juventus for £3m and Gary Lineker joined Barcelona. The fee for Lineker was £4.2m and he got a £1.5m signing-on fee, spread over six years.

Spending spree: Rangers made Woods Britain's most expensive keeper

THE THIRTEENTH World Cup confirmed Diego Armando Maradona as the greatest player on earth. Sadly for the most popular sport on the globe it also confirmed him as the greatest cheat. Worse, the most blessedly gifted footballer since Pele was unrepentant, and boasted about his sin, calling it "the hand of God".

Maradona's disgrace was perpetrated in the quarter-final match against England. In the 51st minute Maradona and Peter Shilton, England's goalkeeper, rose together in the penalty area to meet a misdirected, lofted clearance from Steve Hodge. Maradona failed to get his head to the ball so he deliberately used his hand, flipper-like, to propel the ball over Shilton and into the England net. Instantly the Argentinian superstar danced away, arms aloft to celebrate his "goal". Inexplicably, the linesman did not raise his flag, and the Tunisian referee, Ali ben-Naceur, gave a goal despite Shilton's vehement protestations.

Everybody in the stadium and the billions watching on television knew what Maradona had done. Even he knew himself. That was what gave such offence, particularly when he tried to shrug off what had happened when the world's press interrogated him. "It was a little bit of Maradona's head, a little bit of the hand of God." Balderdash. It was all the hand of Maradona. But given the adulation he received in South America he probably thought that he *was* a god, and the rest of us poor, foolish mortals.

The England team were punch-drunk by the referee's decision. Thus, four minutes later, when Maradona did display his divine talent they literally stood by in astonishment. From a position wide on the right, and in his own half, Maradona took off to score a stupendous solo goal as he waltzed his way through virtually the entire England team. Peter Beardsley, Peter Reid, Gary Stevens, Terry Butcher and Terry Fenwick were all bamboozled before Maradona contemptuously put the ball past Shilton. As an Italian journalist remarked: "England were still in a state of shock, like a man who has just had his wallet stolen."

To their credit, England rallied, despite the manifest injustice done to them. With nine minutes remain-

WORLD CUP 1986
Maradona blasphemed his God-given talent

Hand of God: Maradona's cheating tarnished Argentina's triumph

ing John Barnes, who had come on as a substitute for Trevor Steven to add firepower to England's attack, in true winger's fashion ran straight at the Argentinian defence, rounded the full-back and pulled back the perfect cross for Gary Lineker to head home. Six minutes later Barnes, with a similar scintillating run, broke the Argentine defence yet again, but this time Lineker could not quite reach the cross for justice to be done.

England's path to the quarter-finals had not been a smooth one. Bryan Robson, their captain, had been carrying an injury whose full extent had not been known. England began their campaign by losing a scrappy game 1-0 to Portugal. Their bad start bordered on the cat-

astrophic in their second game when Robson dislocated his shoulder, Ray Wilkins was sent off for petulantly throwing the ball at the Paraguayan referee five minutes before half-time, and England could only draw 0-0 with Morocco. Ironically, this forced Bobby Robson, the England manager, to reshape his team, particularly in midfield, and it worked to his advantage.

The revamped team with Reid, Steven and Hodge in place trounced Poland 3-0 with a Lineker hat-trick to comfortably qualify for the next round, where Lineker, with another two goals, and Beardsley with one, easily eliminated Paraguay to set up the fateful clash with Argentina.

Northern Ireland and Scotland, the other British representatives, were unable to make it past the first phase. Northern Ireland always had an uphill task in a group that contained Brazil and Spain. Their only point came from a 1-1 draw with Algeria.

Scotland, too, were in a powerful group, nicknamed the group of death. But, unlike England, they were not able to reorganise in the face of adversity. Scotland had, in fact, inadvertently reshaped their team before the tournament started, by dropping Alan Hansen. Kenny Dalglish, his Liverpool teammate, miffed at Hansen's omission, then realised that he was carrying an injury.

Scotland lost their first match 1-0 to Denmark and then enjoyed their best game against West Germany where, shades of 1982 against Brazil, they briefly led courtesy of a goal from Gordon Strachan. In their final match, they could only draw 0-0 with a violent Uruguayan team who had a player sent off in the first minute. Had Scotland beaten the 10 men they would have reached the second round as one of the third-placed teams.

Fifa had been tinkering with the structure of the competition yet again, and had decided to abandon a second phase played on a group basis in favour of reinstating the knockout element after the first round. But the only way of reducing 24 teams to 16 was by allowing the four best third-placed teams from the first round to qualify.

Not only did this make this first round even more meaningless than in 1982 – now 36 matches would only eliminate eight countries – it also created anomalies. There could be no complaint about Belgium and Poland qualifying in third place with three points. But both Bulgaria and Portugal finished with two points and a goal difference of minus two. Bulgaria qualified because they finished third in their group, Portugal went home because they were fourth in their group. Worse, Uruguay finished with an inferior record to Portugal's (two points but a goal difference of minus five) but still qualified because they finished in third place.

Not that Uruguay lasted long. Argentina dispatched them in the second round 1-0 en route to a final showdown with West Germany,

Mixed fortunes: Strachan scored Scotland's only goal; Lineker was the tournament's leading scorer and Pumpido denies Rummenigge in the final

FOR THE RECORD

FIRST ROUND

GROUP A	P	W	D	L	F	A	Pts
Argentina	3	2	1	0	6	2	5
Italy	3	1	2	0	5	4	4
Bulgaria	3	0	2	1	2	4	2
South Korea	3	0	1	2	4	7	1

GROUP B	P	W	D	L	F	A	Pts
Mexico	3	2	1	0	4	2	5
Paraguay	3	1	2	0	4	3	4
Belgium	3	1	1	1	5	5	3
Iraq	3	0	0	3	1	4	0

GROUP C	P	W	D	L	F	A	Pts
Soviet Union	3	2	1	0	9	1	5
France	3	2	1	0	5	1	5
Hungary	3	1	0	2	2	9	2
Canada	3	0	0	3	0	5	0

GROUP D	P	W	D	L	F	A	Pts
Brazil	3	3	0	0	5	0	6
Spain	3	2	0	1	5	2	4
N. Ireland	3	0	1	2	2	6	1
Algeria	3	0	1	2	1	5	1

GROUP E	P	W	D	L	F	A	Pts
Denmark	3	3	0	0	9	1	6
W. Germany	3	1	1	1	3	4	3
Uruguay	3	0	2	1	2	7	2
Scotland	3	0	1	2	1	3	1

GROUP F	P	W	D	L	F	A	Pts
Morocco	3	1	2	0	3	1	4
England	3	1	1	1	3	1	3
Poland	3	1	1	1	1	3	3
Portugal	3	1	0	2	2	4	2

SECOND ROUND

Mexico 2 Bulgaria 0
HT 1-0 Att. 114,000
Belgium 4 Soviet Union 3 aet
HT 0-0 Att. 32,000
Brazil 4 Poland 0
HT 1-0 Att. 45,000
Argentina 1 Uruguay 0
HT 1-0 Att. 26,000
France 2 Italy 0
HT 1-0 Att. 70,000
West Germany 2 Morocco 0
HT 1-0 Att. 19,000
England 3 Paraguay 0
HT 1-0 Att. 98,000
Spain 5 Denmark 0
HT 1-0 Att. 38,000

QUARTER-FINALS

France 1 Brazil 1
France won 4-3 on penalties
HT 1-1 Att. 65,000

West Germany 0 Mexico 0
West Germany won 4-1 on penalties
HT 0-0 Att. 44,000
Argentina 2 England 1
HT 0-0 Att. 114,000
Belgium 1 Spain 1
Belgium won 5-4 on penalties
HT 0-0 Att. 45,000

SEMI-FINALS

West Germany 2 France 0
HT 1-0 Att. 45,000
Argentina 2 Belgium 0
HT 0-0 Att. 110,420

THIRD PLACE PLAY-OFF

France 4 Belgium 2 aet
HT 2-1 Att. 21,000

FINAL

Argentina 3 West Germany 2
HT 1-0 Att. 114,590

Teams
Argentina Pumpido; Cuciuffo, Brown, Ruggeri, Olarticoechea, Batista, Giusti, Enrique, Burruchaga (sub: Trobbiani), Maradona, Valdano
West Germany Schumacher; Jakobs, K-H Forster, Briegel, Brehme, Eder, Berthold, Matthaus, Magath (sub: D Hoeness), Rummenigge, Allofs (sub: Voller)

Leading goalscorers 6 Gary Lineker (England); 5 Emilio Butragueño (Spain), Careca (Brazil), Diego Maradona (Argentina); 4 Preben Elkjaer-Larsen (Denmark), Igor Belenov (Soviet Union), Jorge Valdano (Argentina), Alessandro Altobelli (Italy)

Total goals scored 132
Average per game: 2.54

Sendings-off Michael Sweeney (Canada) v Hungary; Referee: Jamal Al Sharif (Syria). Ray Wilkins (England) v Morocco; Referee: Gabriel Gonzalez (Paraguay). Basil Gorgis (Iraq) v Belgium; Referee: Palacio Jesus Diaz (Colombia). Miguel Bossio (Uruguay) v Denmark; Referee: Antonio Ramirez Marquez (Mexico). Jose Batista (Uruguay) v Scotland; Referee: Joel Quiniou (France). Frank Arnesen (Denmark) v West Germany; Referee: Alexis Ponnet (Belgium). Thomas Berthold (Mexico) v West Germany; Javier Aguirre (Mexico) v West Germany; Referee: Palacio Jesus Diaz (Colombia).

Number of players used by finalists
18 Argentina; 17 West Germany

who had been getting stronger as the tournament progressed. However Franz Beckenbauer, their coach, kept insisting that they weren't good enough to win the tournament. In the first hour it looked as if he was right as Argentina, the hot favourites, established a seemingly impregnable 2-0 lead.

Lothar Matthäus, who had been given the job of marking Maradona, gave Argentina their first goal when he brought him down from behind. Jorge Burruchaga floated the free-kick into the area and José-Luis Brown outjumped Schumacher on the far post. The second was equally clear cut. Enrique put Jorge Valdano away on the right and, once again, Schumacher was found wanting. Despite Beckenbauer's doubts about his team, they then showed great resolve to get back on level terms. Rudi Völler flicked on a cor-

ner for Karl-Heinz Rummenigge in the 73rd minute. Nine minutes later, in a similar move, it was Völler's turn to finish off a corner with a header.

But Argentina and Maradona were not to be denied. Two minutes later, the Argentine captain split the West German defence with a pass giving Burruchaga oceans of space to stroke home the winner.

So Maradona and Argentina

won the World Cup. History will not quite remember it that way. For sure, the record books will show Argentina, captain Diego Armando Maradona, as the 1986 World champions. But people will not put great store by that triumph. Nor will they recall that Maradona was especially brilliant. Their abiding memory will be that he was a cheat. That should haunt Maradona for the rest of his days.

Atkinson out, Ferguson in

MANCHESTER UNITED'S terrible start to the season did not take long to cost Ron Atkinson his job. During Atkinson's time in charge United had never finished lower than fourth in the League, but only three wins from 13 matches left them 19th in the table.

The final straw came when United were humbled by Southampton in a third round replay in the League Cup on November 4. After the 4-1 defeat Atkinson admitted that he had hit rock bottom in his five-year tenure at Old Trafford and said: "We need to get some First Division respectability and I still believe that is possible with the staff we have got. I thought we would get a result at Southampton but things didn't work out. That's history now."

But within two days Atkinson was history in the most expensive sacking in English football. Tommy Docherty, perhaps still bitter at having to leave Old Trafford under a cloud, was quick to dance on Atkinson's grave. He said: "The sacking of Ron Atkinson is the best thing that could happen to Manchester United and it didn't come a day too soon. I don't like to see any manager get the sack, but I can't say I feel sorry because I hate the man.

"His downfall has been all of his own doing. I dislike him because of his flash personality. And to my mind it's that sort of attitude which has finally got him the sack."

Atkinson was replaced by Alex Ferguson, the successful Aberdeen manager who had previously rejected offers from Rangers, Arsenal and Tottenham, but admitted: "The Old Trafford job was one I simply could not turn down."

The change cost United more than £1m in compensation to Atkinson, his coach Mick Brown and Aberdeen, plus a £400,000 contract for Ferguson.

But despite inheriting an ageing team, Ferguson was upbeat about the future. "The League title has got to be the players' objective and they could even do it this season," he said. "I have never thought in terms of being second or third. My job is to win every game here. That's the way I intend to attack the job, and I'm sure the players do not need to be told what the target is."

Despite losing his first match in charge, Ferguson soon won the respect of the players: "He put his finger on things quickly and made a very good impression – he was a breath of fresh air," Kevin Moran said.

United recovered to finish in 11th place, but Ferguson knew he still had a lot of work to do if he was going to mount a serious challenge for the League title. At the end of the season he told the board that they needed nine new players to win the championship.

Atkinson: the most expensive sacking in English football

Liverpool fans in court

THE HEYSEL tragedy continued to haunt English football as the case involving 26 Liverpool fans dragged through the courts.

The fans first appeared before magistrates in September, but the proceedings against them were adjourned twice. Finally, the presiding magistrate said that there was a case to answer and that they should be extradited to Belgium to face charges of involuntary manslaughter.

But the fans appealed to the High Court and succeeded in having the ruling overturned on a technicality, when Lord Justice Watkins said that the correct procedures had not been followed. MPs were outraged. Alf Dubs, Labour's home affairs spokesman, said it was a "disgraceful" decision. "We have been made to look fools and the Belgians will think we

are not serious about tackling the problem."

But the Belgians were not deterred by the setback. Represented by the Director of Public Prosecutions, they appealed to the House of Lords. On June 30, the fans, who had been on bail, were taken into custody. And a fortnight later five Law Lords unanimously allowed the appeal and said that the fans should be returned to Belgium.

Lord Bridge of Harwich said it was "absurd" to insist on strict adherence to a treaty signed in 1902 when such a grave crime was involved. This time it was the fans' families who were outraged. They claimed that the decision was political and also unfair as Juventus fans would escape punishment because there was no extradition treaty between Belgium and Italy.

Ferguson: had rejected offers from Rangers, Arsenal and Spurs

Souness brings success, strife and Sassenachs

GRAEME SOUNESS'S first season as the manager of Rangers was probably the most extraordinary in the history of the Ibrox club. At the end of it Rangers had won their first League championship for nine years, but not without mishaps and controversy along the way.

Souness had made his debut as player-manager in the League on August 9, away to Hibernian. Unfortunately the fiery Scot was involved in a full-scale brawl and was sent off. Nine players were booked as Rangers lost 2-1. Rangers were promptly fined £5,000, and Hibernian £1,000, by the Scottish FA.

Rangers' unhappy start continued through to the end of November as they won only 11 matches out of 19, and at one stage they were nine points behind the League leaders, Celtic. And on January 31 Rangers appeared to have a hit an all-time low when little Hamilton knocked them out of the Scottish Cup 1-0 at Ibrox, of all places.

However it may have been a blessing in disguise as Rangers were able to concentrate on the League where they had been whittling away Celtic's lead. Between November 29 and the last game of the programme on May 9 Rangers only lost one League match – to Celtic at Parkhead. Eventually Rangers won the title comfortably, six points ahead of their Old Firm rivals.

Dramatic though this turnaround was, even more surprising were Souness's forays into the transfer market. For once Scotland, which for more than a hundred years had witnessed an exodus of their best players to England, saw the trend reversed as Rangers lured no fewer than six Englishmen north of the border (Colin West from Watford, Chris Woods from Norwich, Terry Butcher from Ipswich, Neil Woods from Doncaster, Graham Roberts from Spurs and Jimmy Phillips from Bolton).

And in the close season he added Trevor Francis from Atalanta and Mark Falco of Spurs to bring the number up to a record eight. Souness may not have yet fulfilled his pledge to sign Catholics, but he was signing the next worst thing – Sassenachs.

Opening shot: Souness is sent off as George McCluskey of Hibs is carried off

Heading in the opposite direction: Souness with Roberts, one of the many Englishmen he signed

FOR THE RECORD

■ Middlesbrough, in the hands of the Official Receiver, had to play their first home match of the season at Hartlepool because they were locked out of Ayresome Park. The club was rescued when a new consortium agreed to pay all the outstanding debts.

■ Manchester United fined seven of their players a total of £12,000 for being late for dinner on the club's pre-season tour of Denmark.

■ Harry Haslam, the former Luton and Sheffield United manager, died on September 11, aged 65.

■ Aston Villa sacked Graham Turner on September 14, the day after the first team had been thrashed 6-0 by Nottingham Forest and the reserves had been walloped 7-0 by Manchester United.

■ There was another fire at Bradford on September 20, when Leeds fans overturned a fish and chip stall which caught alight.

■ Fulham suffered their record defeat on September 23, 10-1 at the hands of Liverpool in the League Cup.

THE
1986-87
SEASON

Harvey: replaced Kendall

Everton win the pass-the-parcel contest but suddenly lose Kendall

DESPITE the vain attempts of the likes of Tottenham, Wimbledon, Nottingham Forest and Arsenal to vie for the League title, once again it became a private Merseyside duel. And for the second time in three years Everton won the League championship, and yet again at a canter – nine points ahead of Liverpool. So for the third year in succession the two Merseyside clubs had occupied the top two positions in the First Division championship.

Not that this was quite clear when the season started with the First Division leadership changing hands like a game of pass the parcel. Tottenham Hotspur were the first to hold pole position before giving way to Wimbledon

at the beginning of September.

Purists howled at the thought of biff and bang merchants even contemplating the championship, but then Forest took top spot and stayed in the top three until the New Year before faltering. Arsenal also had their share of title pretensions – leading from mid-November to the end of January.

But come the New Year the Liverpool giants stretched their legs and put together a string of form that left all the others in their wake. Kenny Dalglish's Liverpool went 12 League matches without defeat, winning 10, to gallop their way to top place. But five defeats in their final nine matches realistically killed off their last

hopes of the championship.

Everton's run was even more remarkable: of their last 29 League matches they only lost four, slowly moving from mid-table to the front. Howard Kendall, their manager, had admirably proved the old adage that the First Division title race is a marathon, not a sprint.

Then, in June, Everton fans were shocked to learn that Kendall, who had guided their club to the European Cup Winners' Cup, two League titles and the FA Cup in six years, was leaving to coach Spanish club Athletic Bilbao. Colin Harvey, Kendall's assistant coach and midfield colleague in Everton's 1970 championship-winning side, took over as manager.

Mergers bypassed as Londoners unite to stay divided

MERGER MANIA swept London but the boardroom plans were soon scotched by rival fans, who were united by their common desire to see their teams saved.

The first two clubs to contemplate an amalgamation were Wimbledon and Crystal Palace. The idea was prompted by Wimbledon suffering a low level of support and a ground that was little changed from the club's days in the Southern League. Sam Hammam, Wimbledon's Lebanese managing director, saw the formation of a south London "super club" based at Selhurst Park and the sale of Plough Lane as a logical step forward.

But when the news broke in February both sets of fans were violently opposed to the idea. Wimbledon's fans staged a pitch invasion and Ron Noades, the Crystal Palace chairman, admitted that he had received death threats. Chris Wright, the leader of the Palace Action Group, even went so far as to say: "If Sam Hammam buys Palace he will think the streets of Beirut are quiet compared to what will happen in SE25."

The plan was short-lived, and

We will not be moved 1: QPR fans protest against the proposed merger with Fulham

called off by Noades when more than 90% of the Palace fans voted against the idea in a ballot in the club's programme.

On February 28 there were also simultaneous protests at QPR and Fulham, where both matches were held up for 20 minutes. The target of the fans' ire was a proposed shotgun wedding between the two clubs.

Like Hammam, David Bulstrode of Marler Estates, who owned Fulham, said that he was going to merge the club with QPR and move to Loftus Road. Jim Gregory, the QPR chairman who had sold out to Bulstrode, was promptly greeted with banners that read "Jim 'Judas' Gregory sold the QPR family for 30 pieces of silver –

traitor", and "Marler – football's Aids virus."

The Football League's management committee was forced to call an emergency meeting, which decided to block the merger. But in the end Bulstrode decided to save them the trouble by calling the move off himself and selling Fulham to a consortium led by Jimmy Hill.

Brave Luton ban away fans

ON THE face of it, Luton Town's decision to ban away fans from matches at Kenilworth Road seemed an excellent idea. In the 1984-85 season not only had there been the appalling scenes when Millwall fans invaded their pitch, fought with police and ran amok through the town, there had also been 190 arrests and 96 casualties throughout the season. The toll went down to 102 in 1985-86. However once the ban was imposed in 1986-87 there was not one single arrest made inside or outside the ground. But there was an almighty row.

The argument against the ban on away fans was three-fold. First, it penalised the innocent as well as the guilty. Second, it deprived the game of its atmosphere and third, it also deprived the away team from valuable vocal support. Luton's counter to this was that it made the game safer, the local residents were not plagued by hooliganism and the club saved a fortune in policing costs.

The Football League's opening salvo was to instruct Luton to lift the ban for League Cup matches. David Evans, the chairman, refused. The scheme, using identity cards, got underway four days later with a home match against Southampton. Unfortunately there were problems with the computerised turnstiles and many supporters missed Luton's fourth-minute opening goal. Critics gloated.

The row blew up in September when Luton insisted that Cardiff City supporters would not be allowed into their ground for their forthcoming League Cup match, notwithstanding a League regulation that stipulated the home club had to provide 25% of the available tickets for away supporters. Luton were expelled from the competition. Luton then said they would play behind closed doors as this would not breach League regulations. By October 6, after a meeting of all 92 clubs, the League suggested the match should be played at a neutral venue, but Luton refused and withdrew from the competition.

We will not be moved 2: David Evans stands firm over the ban on away fans

Two days later the FA muddied the waters still further by announcing that Luton could compete in the FA Cup without away supporters but only if they allowed other clubs to ban their supporters as well. Upset with this decision, there were idle murmurings that various League clubs would boycott the FA Cup.

By December tempers were frayed on all sides and Luton offered a partial relaxation of their ban: 500 tickets would be offered to certain clubs, increasing to 1,000 if there was no trouble. But when Luton drew Liverpool at home in the FA Cup tempers almost boiled over. The BBC came to the rescue and screened the game live on a Sunday.

Now the fracas turned into a farce. Liverpool were held to a goalless draw and Luton contrived to miss the replay at Anfield when their plane was unable to take off. Kenny Dalglish, the Liverpool manager, demanded an inquiry. When Luton did play a fortnight later they thrashed Liverpool 3-0 and Dalglish complained they should not even have been in the competition, having missed the original replay. The gods struck again when Luton were drawn to play QPR – at home. Fortunately for all concerned Luton lost the replay and the row subsided.

On June 4, despite the support of the Bedfordshire police for the scheme, Luton quietly announced they would discontinue their ban on away supporters and a brave, but foolhardy, attempt to tackle hooliganism ended.

219

The mighty fall sad victims to first play-offs

THE FIRST end of season play-offs in modern history brought only grief to two formerly mighty clubs, both of whom sunk to depths they had never reached before.

Sad Sunderland slipped into the Third Division for the first time in their history despite beating Gillingham 4-3 at Roker Park in front of their biggest crowd of the season. But that result, in the second leg, left the score 6-6 on aggregate and Sunderland went down on the away goals rule.

Bob Stokoe, their caretaker manager, immediately quit, despite having only been in charge for less than a month. Stokoe, who was brought in as caretaker manager to try to stave off relegation when Lawrie McMenemy left, said: "The most important thing is not my future, but that of Sunderland. I was brought in to help them survive and we have just failed. I've put in my heart and soul, but I think it's fate in some ways."

Phil Neal, the Bolton player-manager, was also fated to see his club slip into the Fourth Division for the first time in its history. Neal did stay with his club, though he decided to give up as a player. "The legs won't go any more," he said.

There was happier news, though, for Charlton, who kept their place in the First Division after beating Leeds in a replay; Swindon, who returned to the Second Division after nearly 20 years, again after a replay, and Aldershot, who won promotion to the Third Division against Wolverhampton.

Dundee United's trophy cupboard still bare

DUNDEE UNITED won many friends, but sadly no trophies. They became the first Scottish side to reach the final of the Uefa Cup, and with the big guns knocking each other out progressed smoothly to the Scottish Cup final against St Mirren. Under the inspirational management of Jim McLean they played neat, tidy, attractive football, and although their League aspirations had faded shortly after the New Year, they surely expected one piece of silverware.

By comparison with the Scottish Cup, their path to the Uefa Cup final had been strewn with giants. They eliminated Hadjuk Split 2-0, then Barcelona – under Terry Venables and last year's European Cup finalists – 3-1, which included a memorable 2-1 victory in the Nou Camp.

Their away performance in the second leg of the semi-final was perhaps even more remarkable. Having been held 0-0 at Tannadice they swept past Borussia Moenchengladbach 2-0 to reach the final against Gothenburg. A battling performance – particularly from their goalkeeper Billy Thompson – saw them lose only 1-0 in Sweden, but in the second leg they were never allowed to recover from Gothenburg's first-half goal and eventually lost 2-1.

Paul Hegarty: One of Jim McLean's stalwarts in a frustrating season

Three days earlier, despite being favourites, they had lost a lacklustre Scottish Cup final to St Mirren in extra time. It was the first time that St Mirren had won the Cup since 1959. And so to everyone's surprise, Dundee United's cupboard was bare.

Torquay's bizarre escape as police dog bites a player

AUTOMATIC relegation from the Fourth Division made for a nail-biting finish on the last day of the season. And, in a bizarre twist to the tale, Torquay escaped the drop thanks to one of their players being bitten by a police dog.

With just eight minutes remaining Torquay trailed Crewe 2-1, and their biggest crowd of the season were resigning themselves to the drop. Jim McNichol went down injured and Ginger, a police dog, forgot his training and rushed on to the pitch. He sunk his teeth into the helpless Torquay defender and

the referee was forced to halt the game for five minutes while McNichol received treatment to the wounds.

The stoppage threw Torquay a lifeline and with just seconds remaining in injury time Paul Dobson scored an equaliser. The 2-2 draw was enough to condemn Lincoln, who lost 2-0 at Swansea, to the GM-Vauxhall Conference on goal difference. Their place was taken by Scarborough.

Lew Pope, the Torquay chairman, said: "I'm going to buy Ginger the biggest steak in Torquay."

Dobson: life-saving equaliser

Coventry break Spurs' perfect record

COVENTRY, who had never appeared in an FA Cup final in their 104-year history, confounded Tottenham who had never lost any of their seven finals. Very much the underdogs, Coventry fought bravely and gamely to twice come from behind to eventually triumph 3-2 in extra time. But although it was a match full of drama and courage, it was also a match strewn with errors.

Tottenham had opened the scoring in the second minute when Chris Waddle picked up a woefully inadequate clearance and produced one of his dazzling bursts to cross the ball high to the far post. In darted Clive Allen to glance his 49th goal of the season. But, within seven minutes, Coventry, the poor relations of the expensively-assembled London side, were level. A cross from Gregory Downs was not cleared by either Ray Clemence or Steve Hodge and the nippy Dave Bennett whipped the ball away and thumped it home.

Defensive frailty was the culprit again four minutes from half-time when Hoddle's free-kick sailed over the stranded Steve Ogrizovic for the hapless Brian Kilcline to put through his own net as Gary Mabbutt thundered in. Yet Coventry never gave up and 18 minutes after the break had forced another equaliser when Bennett's cross eluded the Spurs defence and Keith Houchen headed home. And so to extra time.

This was to prove exceptionally cruel to Gary Mabbutt. In his attempt to clear Lloyd McGrath's cross he merely deflected the ball into his own net after six minutes. Thus a Tottenham side that included Osvaldo Ardiles and Glenn Hoddle surrendered their historic record.

It was a remarkable triumph for a modest, provincial club and just reward for the canny management duo of George Curtis and John Sillett. Forget that they had only finished tenth in the League, now it was Coventry that had never lost an FA Cup final.

From villain to hero: Kilcline scored an own goal but still collected the Cup

FOR THE RECORD

■ Notts County, one of the founder members of the Football League, became the first club to complete 3,500 matches when they beat Port Vale on February 7.

■ Uefa's executive committee voted 8-3 to continue the ban on English clubs playing in Europe for another year.

■ The Football League agreed to allow two substitutes to be used next season.

■ Clive Allen broke Jimmy Greaves's record when he scored his 44th goal of the season for Tottenham on April 7. He was voted footballer of the year by the Football Writers' Association. Teammate Ray Clemence also entered the record books with his 1,099th senior game on April 18, passing Pat Jennings's British record.

■ Swindon lost 2-1 to Notts County on August 31, their first defeat in the League in nine months and their first home loss in a year. Soon afterwards, they suffered their heaviest defeat for 24 years, 6-2 to Blackpool.

■ A British XI drew 3-3 with an International XI in Belfast on December 3 in a match to mark Pat Jennings's retirement after 119 games for Northern Ireland.

■ Queen of the South leased their car park to a property company for 125 years. The rent was greater than the club's annual gate receipts.

Hot shot: Clive Allen, Footballer of the Year, finished with 49 goals

DIEGO MARADONA
The demi-god who proved to have hands of clay

John Duncan

IF ONLY Steve Hodge had belted the ball into touch. If only Peter Shilton had gone for his punch with more conviction. If only it was possible to remember Diego Maradona for the second goal he scored against England in the World Cup quarter-final of 1986 and not the first.

But temptation was not something Maradona was used to resisting. Rising with Shilton he disguised his deception with practised skill, his crime exposed only by constant replay, his guilt hinted at by a momentary worried backwards glance at the referee. But however it was achieved the result will always stand, a fact of modern football that Maradona, the brightest star of an era where results and the riches that come with them meant everything, knew well.

Kindhearted souls might say that Maradona never had a chance, that he was the world's greatest player at a time when greed was good, that he was the victim of a burgeoning media market whose appetite could never be satiated. The best player and perfect representative of a discredited decade.

Diego Armando Maradona's first exposure to the potential of his own talent came at the age of seven, when he began juggling oranges with his feet on a late-night Argentinian variety show. Born in 1960 to a poor family, he used the same skills entertaining the crowd in the half-time intervals of League matches.

He was signed by Argentinos Juniors at the age of 10, played a full season aged 16 in 1976 and helped the side earn promotion to the First Division. He was picked for the national team at the age of 17, but was dropped at the last minute from the Argentine squad for the 1978 World Cup. In 1981 he went to Boca Juniors (40 matches, 28 goals) who naturally enough won the title, before setting out on the world stage in 1982 having secured a move to Barcelona. He was still only 22 years old.

The world lay at Maradona's left foot. Two goals against Hungary in the first stages of the World Cup finals marked a few hatchet-men's cards. In the quarter-final groups he was struck in the face as he tried to turn the brutal Claudio Gentile, who escaped without punishment. Against Brazil he was constantly provoked until he was eventually shown the red card for his retribution, a chest high, studs raised assault.

Hand of God? The controversial goal

Perhaps this was the point when Maradona decided that skilfully executed cheating paid. His World Cup was over. The brutality was not.

Andoni Goicoechea, aka the Butcher of Bilbao, has a boot in a glass case in his living room. He doesn't need a plaque. Everybody who visits knows that this was the tool which Goicoechea used to destroy the ankle ligaments of Maradona in September 1983. That left the then Barcelona player with three steel pins in his leg. In one way or another, everybody wanted a piece of the best player in the world.

It was Terry Venables who rescued Maradona. With every 100-peseta thug in the Spanish League out to cripple him, virtually bankrupt, brash and unpopular in Barcelona despite his 22 goals in 36 games, Venables sold him to Napoli and saved his career.

On July 5, 1984, 60,000 people turned up to see Maradona in Napoli colours for the first time in a training session. The desperate southern Italian club, second-raters throughout their 58-year history, had got their man by agreeing to allow Maradona to pursue any external commercial interests he wanted.

The investment provided excellent returns. Maradona cost 13 billion lire; during his seven years at the club Napoli made profits of 200 billion lire. After whetting Neapolitan appetites Maradona returned to the international spotlight for the 1986 World Cup in Mexico.

Rarely can a single player have dominated a tournament as thoroughly. Argentina were an otherwise ordinary side, prodded to victory by the goals, crosses and powerful bursting runs of one man.

"Arsenal could have won the 1986 World Cup with Maradona," Bobby Robson said at the time. The crosses for all three goals against South Korea, a left-foot shot steered past Galli against Italy, the most perfect of crosses for

Out of favour: Maradona was jeered by the crowd after Argentina lost the World Cup final

Argentina's second goal against Bulgaria.

"The best one-footed player since Puskas," Sir Stanley Matthews said in Mexico. "In 1986," Franz Beckenbauer, the West German manager said, "there were moments when he reached the level of Pele."

Mexico's heat and altitude suited Maradona perfectly. Invisible for long stretches, he emerged from hiding to turn a game in an instant with a breathtaking piece of skill. Or skullduggery. Dismal, unadventurous England were holding out in the quarter-finals until Maradona attacked at the heart of their defence, the ball was lifted skywards by Hodge and Maradona punched the ball past Shilton.

"A little bit the hand of God, a little the head of Diego," he said in Spanish afterwards. The phrase gains a lot in translation. Five minutes later he gathered the ball inside his own half, brushed off Beardsley and Reid, ghosted past Butcher and Shilton and scored. It was one of the best World Cup goals ever. But it will never be his most famous.

The semi-final. Maradona burst into the area to reach a through ball (left-footed) before three converging Belgians. 1-0. He twisted past three more to shoot (left-footed). 2-0. In the final, West Germany were forced to employ Lothar Matthäus, their most creative midfielder, to snuff him out. With Maradona quiet and a 2-0 lead squandered, Maradona received a loose bouncing ball on the halfway line, twisted backwards and (left-footed), with two Germans within a yard of him, sent Burruchaga through to score the goal which won the Cup.

The Italian championship duly arrived, Maradona inspired, in 1987. Naples went berserk for five days. A Neapolitan graveyard was daubed with the slogan: "You don't know what you missed." The next day the slogan had been overwritten. "Don't be so sure we missed it."

Happier days: A jubilant Maradona after the defeat of England in the 1986 World Cup finals

---

DIEGO MARADONA

Born October 30, 1960, Lanus, Buenos Aires

PLAYING CAREER
Argentinos Juniors 1976-80
116 matches, 28 goals
Boca Juniors 1981-82
40 matches, 28 goals
Honours Argentinian championship 1981
Barcelona 1982-84
36 matches, 22 goals
Honours Spanish Cup: Winners 1983
Napoli 1984-91
186 matches, 81 goals
Honours Uefa Cup: Winners 1989
Italian League championship 1987, 1990
Italian Cup: Winners 1987
Seville 1992-93
26 matches, 5 goals
Newell's Old Boys 1993-
Internationals Argentina debut 1977
Honours World Cup: Winners 1986; Finalist 1990

But the wave of euphoria quickly crashed on the treacherous shores of self-destruction. Intoxicated and suffocated by ever increasing adulation and press attention, Maradona could never show his face during the day. Bravado became arrogance and he took to Napoli's seedy nightlife with a vengeance. Napoli's indulgence of his whims (he once stayed fishing with his father in Argentina after the Italian season had begun) left him to slide unchecked into disrepute.

He found it increasingly hard to get up in the mornings so Napoli had to train in the afternoons. Maradona drifted into the milieu of the Camorra and a disappointing 1988 left Napoli's 1989 title expectations low. But with the club enjoying a commanding lead at the top of Serie A the illegal betting operations of the Mafia were in line for huge losses, having underestimated Napoli's chances at 5-1.

Mysteriously, Maradona's form and the lead evaporated, with Napoli's first European triumph in the Uefa Cup barely appeasing the suspicions of a city where corruption is endemic. The title came again in 1990, but Maradona's time in Italy was coming to a close.

With Maradona overweight, suffering from a huge blood clot on his foot, and forced to have cortisone deposits from previous painkilling injections surgically scraped from his ankle, Argentina stuttered to the second round of the World Cup in Italy. Outplayed and outclassed by the luckless Brazil in the knockout stages, Maradona summoned a late effort with three Brazilians marking him and sent Caniggia through for the 80th-minute winner.

He did little as his side scraped through on penalties against Yugoslavia, before imploring Neapolitans to support Argentina in the semifinal. "Napoli no es Italia." It was a big mistake. Argentina beat the hosts on penalties but Italian supporters had their revenge on Maradona in the final, greeting his tears after a brutal and dull final against West Germany with derision.

Napoli fell out of love with Maradona and the 1990-91 season saw a long messy divorce. A succession of fines, failure to travel abroad with the team, announcements of retirement, a court case detailing his connection with drugs and prosti-

tutes, before finally, on March 17, 1991, the decree nisi. Maradona failed a dope test, traces of cocaine were found, and he was banned from the game for 15 months.

Napoli fought for custody insisting he returned after his ban, but instead the Argentinian opted for a brief inglorious spell at Seville, before returning to Argentina to star for an underachieving Argentinian side, Newell's Old Boys.

But there were still more twists in the tale. After Argentina were humiliated 5-0 in Buenos Aires in a World Cup qualifier there was a clamour for Maradona to be recalled to the national side. Although 33, overweight, unfit and having been sacked by Newell's Old Boys for refusing to train, his country still believed in the myth of Maradona the miracle worker.

The adoring Argentina public got their way. Maradona returned for the two play-off games against Australia and his left foot seemed as sweet as ever as Argentina qualified for the finals in America. Now Maradona went into overdrive and incredibly shed nearly two stone in three months. When he stepped out in the Foxboro stadium in Boston on June 21 for Argentina's opening game against Greece he seemed to have rolled back the years.

His passing was as immaculate as ever and his goal against the Greeks was a thing of sublime beauty. But, as ever, the beast was lurking beneath the surface. After his country's second match Maradona was given a routine dope test – which he spectacularly failed and the roof caved in all over again.

The Argentine Football Federation promptly banished him from the tournament and Fifa banned him from any involvement in football. Maradona fled home to Argentina in disgrace yet again. This time his career was well and truly over. Even the flawed genius, although protesting his innocence, recognised this and announced his retirement.

If only Maradona had not been so stupid and foolish; if only he had been able to resist temptation; if only … but sadly the kid who had fought his way out of the gutter and reached the dizzy heights had finally plumbed the depths of ignominy.

THE
1987-88
SEASON

Liverpool 1987-1988					
P	W	D	L		Pts
40	26	12	2		90
(3 points for a win, with 21 clubs)					

Leeds 1973-1974					
P	W	D	L		Pts
42	24	14	4		62
(2 points for a win, with 22 clubs)					

We know Ian Rush lets his goals do the talking, but so far he hasn't spoken very much

GIANNI AGNELLI
Juventus president

Liverpool storm to the title

FORGET Ian Rush, languishing at Juventus, Liverpool had John Aldridge. And what a replacement! When the dust settled on the season Liverpool had won the championship with nine points to spare, broken myriad records en route and the Rush look-alike had proved he was a look-alike in the scoring department: 26 goals in the League (to finish top scorer) and four in the Cups. Not bad for a Merseyside lad who had graduated from South Liverpool FC to Newport County to Oxford United . . . to Liverpool FC.

As usual, Liverpool began their League campaign slowly. But, before anybody had quite realised it, they were building an unbeaten run of phenomenal proportions. By December 19 Kenny Dalglish's side had gone 19 League games without defeat from the beginning of the season, their best start to a First Division season since 1949-50. On Boxing Day they broke their own record and were 10 points clear of Nottingham Forest.

The records kept tumbling. On January 31 their FA Cup

Perfect replacement: Aldridge finished top scorer in the League

fourth round victory at Aston Villa was their ninth consecutive game without conceding a goal. On March 16 they completed 29 games without defeat, emulating the record set by Don Revie's Leeds in 1973-74. Four days later came their Waterloo as Everton, the defending champions, prevented their bitter rivals from taking pole position in the history books in a

match as keenly contested, and as stirring, as any Cup final.

Ironically, the goal that undid them was scored by Wayne Clarke, the younger brother of Allan Clarke who was a key member of the Leeds side in their fabulous, unbeaten run 14 years earlier. Liverpool were to lose only one more League game, before clinching their 17th League title on April 23.

Rangers grab the headlines, Celtic the Double

HARDLY a day went by without either Graeme Souness or Rangers hitting the headlines in the English, as well as the Scottish, press. Unfortunately this was frequently for all the wrong reasons as Souness and his players kept getting themselves into hot water.

The season was barely a few weeks old before Souness had been sent off for a foul against the Celtic striker Billy Stark in Rangers' 1-0 defeat at Parkhead. He also hurled insults at the referee. It was the third time he had been sent off in little over a year. The Scottish FA punished the player-manager with a five-match ban.

In the next Old Firm clash on October 17 a goalmouth fracas of unbelievable proportions led to Terry Butcher and Chris Woods, of Rangers, and Frank McAvennie, of Celtic, all being

shown the red card. The Strathclyde police stepped in this time and charged the trio, along with Graham Roberts of Rangers, with disorderly conduct likely to provoke a breach of the peace. All four players pleaded not guilty.

Video evidence was used during their trial and both Woods and Butcher were found guilty and fined £500 and £250 respectively. Roberts escaped with a not proven verdict and only McAvennie was found not guilty. Within days there were rumours that the three Rangers players – all English – wanted to leave Ibrox and return to the south. In May, after a dressing-room argument with Souness, Roberts was granted a transfer and by August the former Tottenham player had joined Chelsea.

Despite the bad publicity,

Souness was his usual busy self in the transfer market and seemed to have no problem luring English stars to Ibrox. Ray Wilkins (£200,000) joined from Paris St Germain, and Mark Walters (£575,000) of Aston Villa was snatched from under the noses of Everton. Ian Ferguson was added to Souness's impressive squad from St Mirren for £850,000, a record between Scottish clubs, as was Richard Gough (£1.5m) from Spurs, a record between English and Scottish clubs.

Despite the transfer frenzy, Rangers had little silverware to show from the season. In October they captured the Scottish League Cup in a thrilling 3-3 draw with Aberdeen by winning the first-ever penalty shoot-out in the final, 5-3. Then their season fell apart. Terry Butcher broke his leg in the 1-0 home

McAvennie stands up to Woods

defeat by Aberdeen and missed the rest of the campaign. And to add insult to injury, Celtic cantered to the Double.

All change at White Hart Lane

THE COMINGS and goings at Tottenham made it resemble a railway station rather than a football club as White Hart Lane experienced a season of total upheaval. First to depart was Richard Gough, their centre-half. The homesick Scot was transferred to Rangers for £1.5m in October.

Next was David Pleat, the manager, 18 months after he had arrived. *The Sun* newspaper had revealed in June that police had questioned him about kerb crawling when he was the Luton manager. The Spurs board were unhappy about the affair but stood by him. But then in October the same newspaper revealed that he was yet again caught in a vice swoop and Pleat was finished at Tottenham.

Terry Venables, the former

Spurs player who had quit Barcelona in September after a string of bad results, was persuaded to take up the post – but not until December when he had finished his holiday in Florida – and Osvaldo Ardiles was appointed caretaker player-coach. On the field Tottenham were having a nightmare. Their 3-0 home defeat by Wimbledon on October 31 was their fifth successive loss and there was a clamour for Venables to cut short his vacation.

By November 23 Spurs had gone seven games without a win and Venables took up his post a week early. Unfortunately Tottenham's tale of woe continued with an embarrassing 2-1 defeat in the Fourth Round of the FA Cup by Third Division Port Vale. Tottenham's season was

in tatters – they had slipped from second in the table in September and eventually finished 13th – and was only enlivened by more arrivals and departures.

Ardiles went on loan to Blackburn minutes before the March 24 transfer deadline and Ray Clemence, their goalkeeper, announced he would retire at the end of the season. Meanwhile Venables went on a £6.5m spending spree capped by the signing of Paul Gascoigne in July for £2m from Newcastle. Gascoigne, at 21 and as yet uncapped by England, was Britain's first £2m player.

Other signings included Terry Fenwick, Bobby Mimms, Paul Stewart and Paul Walsh. For the long-suffering Spurs fans it finally looked as if Venables had the club back on the rails.

Sacked: David Pleat

Appointed: Terry Venables (right) and Alan Harris

Merthyr send Atalanta home punch drunk

LITTLE Merthyr Tydfil enjoyed the greatest night in their history when they humbled Atalanta 2-1 in the first round of the European Cup Winners' Cup on September 16.

The collection of part-timers from the Southern League Midland Division knocked the Italian Second Division team out of their stride right from the start of the match and Kevin Rogers gave them the lead after 35 minutes. Although Atalanta equalised quickly, Merthyr kept up the pressure and Ceri

Williams scored a deserved winner in the 82nd minute.

Williams said: "I'll probably wake up tomorrow with a hangover. I have to leave for work at 6am, but that won't stop me celebrating." Williams was not the only person suffering a bad head the next day. An Italian reporter wrote that his town was "suffering from a hangover of Alpine proportions".

But Merthyr's celebrations were short-lived. Atalanta scored twice in five minutes (although Merthyr claimed that

the first goal was offside) in the second leg. Merthyr hurled themselves forward in search of the equaliser and Williams went heart-stoppingly close with a 20-yard volley but the dream result was not to be.

Merthyr's honourable performance showed once again that the underdogs could have their day. In the League Cup, Reading overturned Chelsea and Southend, despite having the worst defensive record in the League, ousted another First Division side, Derby.

There were even more shocks in the FA Cup. Non-League sides Yeovil and Sutton despatched Cambridge and Peterborough, and Sutton took Middlesbrough to a third round replay. However, the season's giant-killing honours went to Third Division Port Vale, who toppled Tottenham 2-1 in the fourth round.

Macdonald's Huddersfield humiliated

MALCOLM MACDONALD left Maine Road a shell-shocked man on November 7. He had only been in charge of struggling Huddersfield for less than a month and he had just seen his team, bottom of the Second Division, annihilated 10-1 by Manchester City.

"Yes, I think you could say that it was perhaps my most humiliating day within football," Macdonald said. "I am shell-shocked as is everybody else connected with the club. We started off so well in the first quarter of an hour and could easily have scored a couple of goals, that was the silly thing about it. Once Manchester City went in front for some reason we just went totally to pieces. It was altogether just a total shambles."

Jimmy Frizzell, the Manchester City general manager, put it another way. Asked whether he had discussed the match with Macdonald, he said: "No. I've nae got many teeth and I would'nae like tae lose those I have."

City rewrote the record books that day; the biggest winning margin in their history, Huddersfield's worst defeat ever and the first time three players had scored a hat-trick in the same match for 25 years. And they went on to hammer Plymouth 6-2 a few days later, with Tony Adcock scoring another hat-trick.

By the end of the season, with Huddersfield firmly rooted to the bottom of the table, 14 points adrift with a goal difference of minus 59, Macdonald had resigned in despair.

Wimbledon ace Liverpool

"GAME, set and match to Wimbledon". That was just one of a host of headlines the day after one of the biggest upsets in the history of the FA Cup final. Liverpool, runaway League champions, and odds-on favourites to complete their second Double in three years, stumbled and fell over little Wimbledon, who 11 years previously had been a Southern League side. It was either a fairy-tale or a nightmare, depending on your point of view.

The hero of the day was without a doubt Dave Beasant, Wimbledon's goalkeeper and captain. His penalty save in the second half deprived Liverpool of the equaliser they needed to get back into a game that was fast slipping away from them. The villain was Brian Hill, the referee, who blew for a free kick when he should have played advantage and awarded a goal. Bravely, he admitted as much after the game.

That decision almost certainly turned the match. In the 35th minute Peter Beardsley was fouled by Andy Thorn but still managed to find the net. The goal did not stand and Liverpool were awarded a free kick instead. The injustice clearly unsettled their composure and, while they were still arguing with the referee about his decision, Lawrie Sanchez headed home a Dennis Wise free-kick. It was to be the only score.

The fates had certainly decreed that it was not going to be Liverpool's day. In the 61st minute John Aldridge stepped up to take his 12th penalty of the season, having successfully converted the previous 11. Beasant dived the full width of the goal to deny him. It was the first time a penalty had ever been missed in a Wembley Cup final. For the next 30 minutes Wimbledon's resolute defence defied the Liverpool bombardment and Beasant became the first goalkeeper to captain a Cup-winning side.

Strangely it was Beasant's last game for the club. Within three weeks he was transferred to Newcastle for £850,000, a British record for a goalkeeper.

Beasant was the first goalkeeper to captain a Cup-winning side

Match winner: Beasant's penalty save broke Liverpool's heart

Forest just keep hold of Clough in lengthy tug-of-war with Wales

WALES'S failure to qualify for the European championship cost Mike England his job after nearly eight years and brought a new twist to the club versus country debate.

When England was sacked in February there were rumours that Wales might turn to Brian Clough. Intense speculation reached a fever pitch when Clough said that he was prepared to leave Nottingham Forest if they stopped him running the Welsh team on a part-time basis. Both Clough and his chairman, Maurice Roworth, had talks with the Welsh FA but, in the end, Forest refused to allow Clough to take the job and he did not quit.

Wales struggled to come up with an alternative. Swansea refused to let Terry Yorath divide his time between two teams; the veteran Bob Paisley was mentioned in passing; Tottenham would not let Terry Venables be approached; David Williams, the Norwich coach, took charge for one match but his club blocked any further involvement; Clough threw his hat back in the ring and Roworth vetoed the idea again.

In little more than two months Wales had gone full circle so they went back to Yorath. He was appointed, at first for three matches and, finally, permanently in July, but still only on a part-time basis.

Mike England: sacked by Wales

Greedy Maxwell turns his attention to Watford

IF THERE was one thing that Robert Maxwell loved it was wheeling and dealing. Owning Derby, where he was the chairman, and Oxford, where his son was in charge, and still having shares in Reading was not enough to sate his appetite for power.

Maxwell wanted more. So, in November, he reached a £2m agreement with Elton John to buy Watford as well. But as far as the Football League was concerned that was one deal too many. The League refused to sanction the sale, which prompted a vitriolic outburst from Maxwell.

He dubbed the League's management committee the "mismanagement committee" and said: "What we have is a professional game dominated by incompetent, selfish, bungling amateurs. It is time those who love the sport woke up and kicked them out."

Philip Carter, the League's president, wasted no time in hitting back. He said: "He's a bare-knuckle fighter lashing out in all directions because he can't get his own way. His comments are unfortunate and deplorable. I thought he was attempting to

Like a candle in the wind: Elton John's liaison with Maxwell did not last long

use bully-boy tactics. He has made many outrageous statements."

Relations between the two men hardly improved when the League won a temporary injunction stopping Maxwell's company buying Elton John's shares but abandoned the court case four days later. Then a secret deal between Maxwell

and Carter, in which Maxwell could buy Watford in exchange for selling his interest in Oxford, unravelled as well.

Maxwell lost his temper yet again and Carter, accused of going back on a signed agreement by the Derby board, had his presidency of the League called into question.

The storm only blew over on

December 20 when Maxwell abandoned his plans for Watford and agreed to sell his shares in Reading. And the League, who had admitted that their rules may not have been able to stop Maxwell had he persevered, quickly reinforced their regulations restricting people having an interest in more than one club.

Dutch paint a masterpiece as England prove to be fakes

HOLLAND's 2-0 defeat of the Soviet Union in the final of the European championships at long last laid to rest the ghosts of Dutch football. Twice they had reached the World Cup final, in 1974 and 1978, and lost – first to West Germany and then to Argentina. Now they had finally succeeded in a major tournament, and with brio.

Their 2-1 victory over West Germany in the semi-finals – their first for 32 years – was sweet revenge for their 1974 disappointment and surely consoled Rinus Michels, their manager, for his dispiriting loss 14 years earlier. And their football – centred around the fabulous talents of Marco Van Basten, Ruud Gullit and Frank Rijkaard – was reminiscent of the Total Football played by the Holland team of the 1970s.

In Van Basten, Holland possessed the man of the tournament and his performance in the final was electric. In the 33rd minute he headed a cross neatly into the path of Gullit who nodded a perfect goal past the Russian goalkeeper, Dassayev. Twenty minutes later Van Basten produced the goal of the tournament when he latched on to Arnold Muhren's deep cross and thundered an unstoppable volley past the hapless keeper. But just as it seemed that Holland would coast to victory, shades of past failures re-emerged.

Hans Van Breukelen, the Dutch keeper, foolishly gave away an unnecessary penalty six minutes after Van Basten's strike and all the old fears of snatching defeat from the jaws of victory came flooding back. Particularly as Holland had lost to the Soviet Union 13 days earlier in a group match. Fortunately for Van Breukelen he managed to save Belanov's penalty and the danger had passed.

For Bobby Robson's England the tournament was an unmitigated disaster. After all the worries about whether they would qualify at all for the finals in West Germany, they had done so in style. Having travelled to Belgrade needing a point against Yugoslavia, they came home convincing 4-1 victors.

But in the finals they were cruelly exposed and lost all their three matches.

The most humiliating defeat was at the hands of the Republic of Ireland, managed by Jack Charlton, who had once been rejected as the England manager. The Republic were somewhat fortunate to have qualified at all, Scotland effectively doing the work for them by unexpectedly beating Bulgaria in Sofia in the last of the qualifying matches. The Irish team, largely composed of Football League players many of whom were only "Irish" because of parents or grandparents born in the Republic, played a canny spoiling game that utterly confounded England.

Ray Houghton's fifth-minute header, after blunders by Kenny Sansom and Gary Stevens left John Aldridge clear to fire in a cross, knocked England back on their heels. Inept performances from England's forwards, most noticeably John Barnes and, inexplicably, Gary Lineker, combined with a string of spectacular saves from Pat Bonner, the Irish keeper, sealed England's fate.

Further defeats at the hands of the Soviet Union and Holland meant that Robson's team had to slink home with their tails between their legs. Ireland, by contrast, drew with the Soviet Union, only lost 1-0 to Holland, narrowly missed out on a place in the semi-finals and came back national heroes.

Gullit: fabulous talents recreated the age of Total Football

Bonner: string of saves

Shearer, at 17, was the youngest hat-trick scorer in the First Division

More hooliganism keeps clubs out of Europe

BOBBY ROBSON'S humiliation at the European championships was made a hundred times worse for England off the field. The disgraceful scenes of English fans running amok undoubtedly condemned English clubs to at least another year in the wilderness.

Within days, the FA had withdrawn their application for English clubs to be readmitted to Europe. They knew that there was no chance of the ban being lifted because Uefa had already made it clear that they were not going to consider the matter until the tournament had finished.

The arrest of 381 English fans in Germany made for a grim end to a season that had been lawless before the opening day. The first taste of things to come occurred in early August, before a ball had even been kicked in anger. A ferry was forced to return to England when Manchester United and West Ham fans, both heading for pre-season friendlies on the continent, started fighting in the middle of the North Sea, terrifying the other passengers.

Then Scarborough should have celebrated their first ever game in the League on August 15. But there was so much disorder that the start of the second half was delayed by more than 10 minutes as police struggled to regain control. Eighteen fans were jailed for their part in the affray and Wolves, the visiting team, were fined £5,000 and ordered to make their away matches all-ticket.

The police and courts were also kept busy by players, who could hardly be said to be setting the best of examples. As well as court cases stemming from the battle of Ibrox, police had to stop the fighting between Lincoln and Barnet players in a GM-Vauxhall Conference match. Andy Brannigan of Arbroath was convicted of assault for breaking a player's leg, and Chris Kamara of Swindon was found guilty of causing grievous bodily harm to Jim Melrose of Shrewsbury.

The FA banned Kamara for the rest of the season and its chairman, Bert Millichip, said football was able to keep its house in order without the need

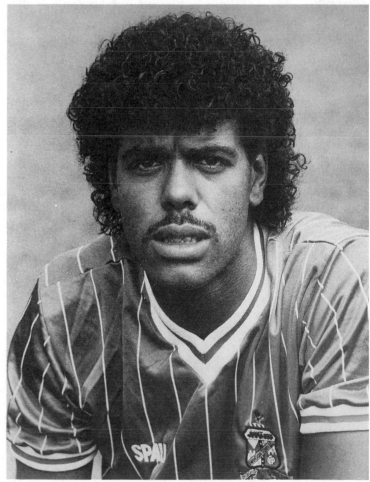
Punished: Kamara was banned for the rest of the season

for police involvement. However, in a season when more than 100 players were sent off before the end of November, proposals to deduct points from clubs with a poor disciplinary record received short shrift from the Football League.

Coventry make history the wrong way round at Sutton

THE third round of the FA Cup always produces some upsets but January 7 produced a truly memorable shock. With all the clouds hanging over the game, there was evidence aplenty that romance was alive and kicking.

Sutton United had drawn the First Division highflyers Coventry at home. The mid-table GM-Vauxhall Conference team were the usual eclectic mix; an insurance executive, a bricklayer, a Cambridge graduate, a member of the Jamaican international side, and a manager with a penchant for the finer points of English literature.

And the portents were there. Last season Sutton had taken Middlesbrough to a third round replay and had only lost by one goal after extra time. Then, Barrie Williams, their manager, had quoted Shakespeare to inspire his team. This time he chose Kipling's "everlasting teamwork of every bloomin' soul."

And it was undoubtedly Sutton's more cohesive teamwork that made Coventry wilt at Gander Green Lane. Tony Rains, the Sutton captain, struck first with a header from a corner in the 42nd minute. "We worked on it this morning, and I missed," he admitted.

Coventry equalised early in the second half but Matthew Hanlan restored Sutton's lead after two minutes. It was another set piece from a corner and, again, it had not worked in the morning training session.

Coventry besieged the Sutton goal, and twice had shots cleared off the line in the last few minutes, but they had no complaints. Their manager, John Sillett, admitted: "It will be worse when we open the papers and realise we made history the wrong way round."

Sutton's historic victory, only the sixth time a non-League club had knocked out a First Division side since the Second World War, duly captured all the headlines, putting Bradford's 1-0 victory over Tottenham into the shade.

But not even Williams' inspiration could lift Sutton in the fourth round against Norwich, when the giant-killers were themselves killed off. Two goals in two minutes were the start of an 8-0 rout.

Words of wisdom: Rains was inspired by his manager quoting Kipling

Clough gives troublemakers a taste of their own medicine

BRIAN CLOUGH found a novel way to deal with fans invading the pitch after Nottingham Forest's 5-2 defeat of QPR in the quarter-finals of the League Cup on January 18.

The Forest manager, a longtime campaigner against hooliganism, rushed off the bench, grabbed two fans, clipped them round the ear and hauled them off the pitch. People watching the incident on television did not quite know what to make of it; some thought he was a hero for tackling the louts but others thought he was wrong to descend to their level.

The next day Clough admitted that he had been in the wrong, even though he had acted for the best of reasons. Honour was restored when he apologised to the two fans and they, in turn, apologised to the club for running on to the pitch.

Gotcha: Television shows Clough collaring one of the fans invading the pitch

The Forest fans made their feelings clear when they cheered Clough before the start of Forest's next home game.

The FA, though, took a dimmer view, fining Clough £5,000 and banning him from the touchline for the rest of the season. Once again, the Forest fans showed what they thought, cheering Clough as he took his place in the stand.

Seconds out: Jones and Davis come out fighting

WIMBLEDON brought a new meaning to pre-season friendlies in their warm-up game on the Isle of Wight on August 14. Vinnie Jones, who epitomised their fighting spirit, did not take long to get in the swing of things when he laid out a Shanklin defender, an offence that cost him his place in the Charity Shield team.

There was worse to come as the brawling on the field got to be nearly as bad as the violence off it. The season was less than a month old when Paul Davis of Arsenal flattened Glenn Cockerill, breaking the Southampton player's jaw. Cockerill decided not to press charges, but the FA hit Davis with a £3,000 fine and a nine-match ban. Arsenal's reaction was to ban television cameras from their ground because ITV film of Davis throwing the punch was used by the disciplinary hearing.

The police were, however, involved after an ill-tempered match between Rangers and Aberdeen in October. Terry Butcher, incensed at a tackle that put Iain Durrant out of action for the rest of the season, kicked down the door of the referee's dressing-room. Although the police took no further action, the Scottish FA decided to fine Butcher £500.

The following month Wimbledon were back in the headlines for all the wrong reasons when John Fashanu allegedly punched Viv Anderson after Manchester United lost 2-1 in the League Cup.

Anderson hardly did his cause any good when, in his autobiography, he came out strongly in favour of professional fouls. But hopes that the FA were taking a tougher line on misconduct were dashed when Fashanu only received a three-match ban and £2,000 fine, and Anderson was banned for one match and fined £750.

Mark Dennis, too, was perceived to have got off lightly when he was charged with bringing the game into disrepute for the sixth time. He received the minimum ban of three matches, plus a £1,000 fine.

Crowds line the street to mourn Newcastle's Jackie Milburn

Gotcha: Davis was hit with a £3,000 fine and a nine-match ban

All hell breaks loose as Rangers sign a Catholic

GRAEME SOUNESS and Rangers stunned all of Scotland when they actually did the unthinkable: on July 10 they signed a Catholic, Mo Johnston. Souness had vowed he would when he took the helm at Ibrox three years previously, but so far his major excursions into the transfer market had been to lure Englishmen north of the border.

Johnston's transfer was controversial twice over. Aside from being a Catholic, he was a former Celtic player who had agreed to rejoin them from Nantes on May 12 for £1.2m. And Celtic had even paraded him before the Scottish Cup final. Miraculously Souness had managed to incense both sets of rival fans in Glasgow.

Bigoted Rangers' supporters demonstrated outside Ibrox and burnt scarves, programmes and tickets in protest. Over at Parkhead, Celtic's management could not believe what had happened. Johnston, the 27-year-old Scottish international striker they had sold to Watford, having agreed to join Celtic then refused, had been instructed by Fifa's general secretary, Sepp Blatter, to stick to his verbal agreement. Johnston claimed that he had not signed a contract.

The £1.5m transfer brought Souness's dealings to £11m. To Protestant bigots he was a traitor. To the cynics the surprise was that Johnston was not English.

The day football killed itself

Football is irrelevant now, nobody is even asking after the other scores

KENNY DALGLISH
immediately after
the Hillsborough disaster

You'll never walk alone: the goal at the Kop end draped with flowers and mementoes

Lest we forget: Grobbelaar and Nicol at the requiem mass in Liverpool Cathedral

BRITAIN'S worst sporting tragedy occurred at one of football's showpiece events: the FA Cup semi-final, and millions around the world watched in horror as 95 spectators, including women and children, were killed and hundreds injured.

However, unlike the Heysel disaster, hooliganism was not responsible, this time the blame had to be laid squarely at football's door. For despite the deaths that had occurred at Ibrox in 1971 and Bradford and Heysel in 1985, England's stadiums were still death traps and football's administrators had done little, if anything, to deal with the problem.

Thus, at 2.50pm on April 15 at the all-ticket match between Liverpool and Nottingham Forest at Hillsborough the police allowed between 3,000 and 4,000 Liverpool fans, restless at the length of the queues and anxious about the approaching kick-off, to rush into the Leppings Lane End of the stadium.

In the surge that ensued thousands of the spectators were crushed against the perimeter fencing behind the Liverpool goal and, in the panic, were unable to escape. At the time most people were unaware of the scale of the disaster, believing that it was just a case of rowdyism. After six minutes the referee stopped the match as fans tore down advertising hoardings to use as makeshift stretchers and the full horror of the scene became apparent.

The catalogue of errors that led to this was legion. Liverpool had been allocated 24,000 tickets when their average attendance was 40,000 whereas Forest had been given 30,000 when their average was 17,000. There was a breakdown in communications with the emergency services and ambulances and medical equipment arrived late because they were not informed of the scale of the problem. And so on.

But the principal reason for the tragedy lay in the attitude football had to its stadiums. Instead of treating them as places of entertainment, they were more like prisons with fans on the terraces caged in, as if they were all hooligans. This was compounded by the woefully inadequate emergency medical facilities and poor communication between the police and stewards.

The day after Hillsborough, The Sunday Times roundly condemned all the football authorities, accusing them of complacency, and called for modern, all-seat stadiums to replace the death-traps that spectators had to endure. "Clubs that do not do so do not deserve to be in first-class football," the newspaper said. "Otherwise football will continue to be a slum sport played in slum stadiums and these tragic events will be repeated."

An inquiry was set up, under Lord Justice Taylor, and eventually his report was to echo these thoughts and recommend mandatory all-seat stadiums for clubs. But for the 95 dead and the hundreds of other victims it was too late.

Atkinson kicks off merry-go-round

SOME of the biggest names in management went through a topsy-turvy season in which they experienced the highs and lows of the game in rapid succession.

Ron Atkinson looked to be headed for the big time when he moved from West Brom to take charge of Atletico Madrid. But he quickly discovered that Spanish football club presidents are a fickle bunch, and none more so than the explosive Jesus Gil.

Third place in the League was not good enough and, despite having a two-year contract worth more than £500,000, Atkinson was fired after just 96 days. He was replaced in the hot seat by Colin Addison, who had moved from West Brom with him. Addison fared a little better, managing to stay at the club until the end of season.

As Atkinson was returning home, Malcolm Allison was heading to Europe to try to revive his career with the struggling Portuguese club Farense. But his reign was even shorter, a mere two months. Allison, though, still had big ambitions, even though he ended up at a little club, Fisher Athletic. He boasted that he would take the GM-Vauxhall Conference team into the League.

Jock Wallace, too, was on his way back to England from the continent. Amazingly, in January, Colchester, then bottom of the Fourth Division, managed to lure the former Rangers manager out of retirement in Spain. His was ultimately the only success story, although it took him a while to get to grips with the ailing club.

It took Wallace a month to end a sequence of 18 matches without a win, but in mid-April Colchester still looked like favourites for the drop. Somehow though, he worked a little bit of magic and the last five games were all won as Colchester scrambled their way to safety.

How the mighty have fallen: Allison went from the heights of Farense to the depths of Fisher Athletic

Moynihan: stubborn

Identity card row threatens clubs' swift return to Europe

THE DOOR finally started to open to allow English clubs back into Europe when Uefa's executive committee said that they were prepared to lift the ban for the start of the 1990-91 season. However, their decision in April was conditional upon government approval.

Although Colin Moynihan, the Minister for Sport, said that while he would try to have Liverpool readmitted to Europe at the same time as other English clubs, he was still insistent that identity cards must be in force for the start of next season.

When football said that it could not afford a national scheme the government threatened to impose a levy on transfer fees. And when the draft legislation was published football was shocked. Graham Kelly said the proposals were "horrendous" and Jack Dunnett, the League president, said the proposals could cost more than £30m. Even the referees wrote to Moynihan rejecting the idea.

FOR THE RECORD

■ Brighton's first choice goalkeeper, Perry Digweed, did not turn up for the match against Scunthorpe on September 10 because nobody remembered to tell him he was playing.

■ Oxford fired Mark Lawrenson, their manager, for complaining about the sale of Dean Saunders by Kevin Maxwell. Saunders went to Derby, run by Robert Maxwell, for £1m.

■ Derby signed two Czech internationals who had fled from their home country and were granted political asylum in England. But Fifa refused to let them play for a year because they had left Czechoslovakia without permission.

■ Tottenham broke the British sponsorship record when they signed a £1.1m three-year arrangement with Holsten. But before the season was over Norwich topped this figure with a £1.5m deal with Asics.

■ Philip Carter, the Everton chairman, became the first Football League president to be voted out of office. David Dein of Arsenal also lost his place on the management committee on October 18 because of the bias the two men had supposedly shown in the negotiations with television. Carter was replaced by Jack Dunnett, the first man to hold the post twice.

■ John Hall increased his efforts to take over Newcastle by raising his offer to £1,000 a share in October. The battle for control raged all season, and the local council offered to mediate when Gordon McKeag, the club chairman, said he had received death threats.

■ Ipswich caused a stir by signing Sergei Baltacha from Dynamo Kiev for £200,000 on December 8. He scored on his first-team debut the next month.

■ Tottenham had two points deducted by the League for calling off their opening day match because building work was still in progress at White Hart Lane. The decision was overturned on appeal and replaced by a £15,000 fine.

But the government was unmoved, with Moynihan accusing football of ignoring offers from companies who were prepared to run a membership scheme at no charge. With neither side prepared to budge it was clear that there was still a long way to go before England's isolation would be ended.

233

Tottenham reshuffle their pack

THE to-ings and fro-ings at Tottenham just kept on happening, with a series of spectacular transfers after the season had finished.

Talk of Gary Lineker returning to England had swirled around the country in November. Johan Cruyff, the Barcelona coach, was said to have offered Lineker to Manchester United for £2.5m. United said they could not afford that much, Arsenal said they were not interested, and Rangers, with their reputation for spending enormous sums on English players, were then installed as the favourites.

Within a week the price had risen, with Aston Villa reportedly being told that Lineker would cost them £3m, with £2m going to Barcelona as the transfer fee and £1m going to Lineker to make up for what he would have earned in Spain.

Just as quickly as it had started the speculation died down, at least until April. Lineker was dropped and Terry Venables went to Barcelona to talk to the player he had taken to Spain in the first place. Venables succeeded in bringing Nayim to White Hart Lane on loan but he had to wait a little longer to land the star prize.

Lineker rejected a better offer from Monaco before committing himself to Tottenham in June in a £1.5m deal that included Nayim. But Venables soon recouped the money, with enough to spare to pay Lineker's £5,000 a week wages for several years, when he sold Chris Waddle to Marseille for £4.5m, a British record.

And Venables's rebuilding process did not stop there. His final move of a hectic month was to allow the long-serving Ossie Ardiles to go to Swindon as their player-manager.

Going: Waddle went to Marseille for £4.5m, a British record

Coming: Lineker turned down Monaco to return to England

Stevens' blunder cost Rangers a clean sweep

RANGERS utterly dominated the season and only a crass error by Gary Stevens denied them an historic treble. After three games of the season Rangers went to the top of the Scottish Premier League with a 5-1 victory over Celtic at Ibrox. Thirty-three games later they were still there as League champions, without ever having been dislodged or really threatened.

The poor early-season form of Celtic, who finished third, left them with far too much to do – and only Aberdeen, the run-

ners-up by six points – offered much of a challenge. Rangers' strength lay in the expensively purchased pool of players at Souness' disposal.

Rangers' first trophy, the League Cup, had been acquired much earlier, on October 23, when they duly disposed of Aberdeen 3-2 in a thrilling final. Aberdeen had twice drawn level before, in extra time, Ally McCoist delivered the coup de grace in injury time.

The Cup final was less of a spectacle, but extremely gratify-

ing to Celtic. Four minutes from half-time Joe Miller pounced on a silly backpass by Stevens for the only goal of the game. The Rangers players wept openly on the pitch as the fabulous treble eluded the best team in Scotland.

There was one consolation for Graeme Souness. After a takeover by the multi-millionaire David Murray, he became a member of the Rangers board with a 10% stake in the club, estimated as being worth £600,000.

Murray: bought Rangers

Title won with very last kick

Final play: Michael Thomas scored the most dramatic goal in League history to snatch the title

THE LAST week of the season – extended to May 26 because of the Hillsborough disaster – was as dramatic as anything that could have been scripted by Hollywood. Liverpool, who in February had been 19 points behind Arsenal, simply had to beat Everton in the Cup final, beat West Ham at home and not lose by two goals to Arsenal at Anfield to become the first side to win the Double twice. Daunting as it sounds, Liverpool took to their tasks with relish.

The Cup final, on May 20, was an emotional affair as the two Merseyside clubs mourned the Hillsborough dead. The rival fans mingled before and during the match, maintained a minute's silence and sang You'll Never Walk Alone with Gerry Marsden.

Winning the FA Cup had become an obsession at Anfield as all at the club saw it as a token, but important, tribute to the Hillsborough victims. And John Aldridge, with a fourth-minute goal, seemed to have won it for them. But, with seconds remaining, Everton equalised when Bruce Grobbelaar failed to clear a shot and Stuart McCall nipped in.

Ian Rush, who had been brought on for Aldridge, restored their lead in the fourth minute of extra time with a classic striker's goal. Eight minutes later McCall volleyed a clearance straight into the back of the net and it was all square again.

Within two minutes Everton's hopes were dashed. Rush, who had been struggling all season, got the neatest of headed flicks on to John Barnes's cross and the first half of the Double was complete. West Ham were duly thrashed 5-1 two days later and only Arsenal, who had not won at Anfield for 14 years, remained.

Thus, on May 26, the League championship came down to the last match of the season. And to cap this most extraordinary of seasons it was a match between the first and second sides in the table – only the second time in the 101-year history of the Football League that this had happened.

The Match of the Century certainly lived up to its billing: it was like chess on speed. George Graham chose to play a sweeper system to deny Liverpool the space they needed to make full use of Barnes, and Kenny Dalglish used Aldridge and Rush (replaced by Beardsley) to probe the Arsenal defence. The pace was relentless and both sides strove for the ultimate prize. At half-time the match was scoreless and Liverpool were 45 minutes away from the Double.

But seven minutes into the second half Alan Smith scored a disputed goal from an indirect free-kick when a linesman briefly raised his flag and the nerve-tingling drama was going to go to the wire.

With 90 minutes gone, and the 40,000 crowd whistling like fury, Lee Dixon cleared the ball from deep in the Arsenal defence to Smith, who lobbed it into the path of the onrushing Michael Thomas. He evaded two challenges and, having waited for Grobbelaar to commit himself, flicked the ball past him to score the most dramatic goal in League history.

LIVERPOOL
Red machine ran as smooth as clockwork

Garth Crooks

LIVERPOOL were always difficult; on and off the field. I remember, as a Tottenham player, one incident after a match when both sets of players were having a "friendly" drink together that made this crystal clear.

"Glenn Hoddle's not good enough to get in our side," were the words that stopped the conversation dead in its tracks. There was no doubt who the offender was. Graeme Souness, who as a player was an uncompromising brute. His charming smile and his off-the-field politeness were the nets in which he would ensnare you.

The jibe spun a sober Tottenham contingent around on their heels. Cold stares waited impatiently for some form of elaboration in the hope that it might reduce the rising temperature in the bar. Souness left the area in the conspicuous manner in which he arrived. I soon realised that the intimidation we had witnessed was all part of the Anfield roadshow.

It all started under the charismatic Bill Shankly – the master of intimidation. Few managers possess it – he invented it. Not long after Liverpool had been dubbed the Red Army, a term used to give clarity to the type of environment to which you were about to be exposed, Shankly had retired and Liverpool had passed on the leadership to Bob Paisley with no apparent join.

It seemed as though Paisley only needed time to become familiar with Shankly's filing system to add to the family silver. The next 10 years saw

Start of an era: the 1965 Cup final

Paisley transform Liverpool from a formidable club side to one of the most dynamic clubs in Europe, completing his first championship and Uefa Cup double in his second season.

Yet at this stage few could appreciate or predict what Shankly had started. The sheer emotion generated by the Anfield crowd was indicative of him. Those scenes of the mercurial Scot, hands aloft in the centre circle receiving homage as though he were the Messiah are legendary. Even against mediocre sides it was impossible to get into the ground after 2pm on a Saturday, such was the euphoria.

Match officials would forget which decision they had made and why they had made them when caught in the Anfield cauldron. Visiting teams knew that under no circumstances could their defenders afford to be clumsy in the vicinity of the penalty area, for fear of the famous Anfield cry of "handball!" or "penalty!" It never ceased to amaze me how the players and fans could achieve that infamous Anfield appeal in total unison; meanwhile, match officials responded instinctively as though they had been struck by lightning.

Yet whenever players and officials came on to the pitch for the traditional pre-match walkabout you knew, at that precise moment, there was nowhere on earth they would rather be.

The Kop were famous among the pros for churning out lyrics, Lennon and McCartney style, but with a more cruel twist than their virtuoso compatriots. I remember when I played for Manchester United. "Whose up Mrs Brown? Whose Up Mrs Brown?" sung to the famous Cockney tune of Knees up Mother Brown, was the chorus that greeted us during one particular walkabout.

The object of derision was Tommy Docherty, the former manager of Manchester United who had just been dismissed by his employers because of an affair with the wife of the club's physiotherapist, Laurie Brown.

The sentiments sent my blood cold. This was not due to the fact that I was particularly friendly with Docherty. It was due to the unmerciful way the Kop used humour and verse as a poisoned cocktail to deal with their adversaries.

This satirical sword had the potential to inflict tremendous psychological damage to the opposition. But, as the famous emblem hanging over the tunnel stated: "This is Anfield". Before you got to their generals, you had to deal with the infantry.

Driving force: Dalglish

THIRTY GOLDEN YEARS

1959: Bill Shankly appointed the Liverpool manager

1962: Second Division champions

1964: First Division champions

1965: FA Cup winners

1966: First Division champions, European Cup Winners Cup beaten finalists

1969: First Division runners-up

1971: FA Cup beaten finalists

1973: Uefa Cup winners, First Division champions

1974: FA Cup winners, First Division runners-up, Bill Shankly retires and Bob Paisley takes charge

1975: First Division runners-up

1976: Uefa Cup winners, First Division champions

1977: European Cup winners, First Division champions, FA Cup beaten finalists

1978: European Cup winners, First Division runners-up, League Cup beaten finalists

1979: First Division champions

1980: First Division champions

1981: European Cup winners, League Cup winners

1982: First Division champions, League Cup winners

1983: First Division champions, League Cup winners, Bob Paisley retires and Joe Fagan takes over

1984: European Cup winners, First Division champions, League Cup winners

1985: European Cup beaten finalists, First Division runners-up, Joe Fagan retires and Kenny Dalglish is appointed player-manager

1986: FA Cup winners, First Division champions

1987: First Division runners-up, League Cup beaten finalists

1988: First Division champions, FA Cup beaten finalists

1989: FA Cup winners, First Division runners-up

For the past 30 years Liverpool have carefully appointed their generals. Keegan, Toshack and Hughes were the players on whom Shankly bestowed his dream. Paisley gratefully capitalised on the sound foundations built by Shankly, winning his first European championship in 1977 against the West German champions Borussia Moenchengladbach. Liverpool, through their carefully selected appointees, had discovered the secret to success, guarding it jealously with the mask of footballing simplicity.

A feature that has raised eyebrows in the world of football has been the enormous lengths Liverpool have gone to to ensure a player is of the right psychological make-up. Much of their success is due to getting this part of the purchase right.

Keegan's departure to Hamburg forced Liverpool to replace him with what they considered to be the best around. Having spent an entire season monitoring his attitude, Kenny Dalglish was their choice and a superb one it was too. In his first season Dalglish scored the winner to secure Liverpool's second European Cup triumph with a superbly taken goal against Bruges.

After championships in 1979 and 1980, Paisley became the first British manager to win three European Cups when Liverpool beat Real Madrid 1-0 in Paris. Three consecutive League championships and League Cups followed and, between 1986 and 1990, a further three championships, including the League and Cup double. Liverpool had become the most formidable team in Europe.

I had witnessed the cohesive force that made Liverpool special. On tour, their emphasis on team spirit bordered on paranoia – strangers were not welcome. Night after night the entire team would congregate in the lobby, singing traditional team songs passed down from previous Liverpool sides; pulling funny faces as hotel guests watched, astonished to see star players like Hansen and Lawrenson, Dalglish and Souness join in the merriment as their international images went up in smoke. The point was clear – one in, all in – there were no stars.

This same spirit ran through Anfield like a dose of salts and was clearly evident in 1985 and again in 1989 when disaster struck. A catalogue of administrative failures resulted in insufficient segregation during the 1985 European Cup final between Liverpool and Juventus at the Heysel Stadium. Persistent charging by opposing fans caused a wall to collapse, killing 39 people. Liverpool fans were singled out, held responsible and their team banned from Europe. What Liverpool had not realised was that Uefa had just cut their lifeline.

The shock of that decision turned into excruciating pain four years later when, in 1989, during the FA cup semi-final against Nottingham Forest, a cloud descended over the entire city, as 95 men, women and children were crushed to death. The city, its players and families closed ranks and mourned their dead.

Something spiritual happened to the club that day, setting Liverpool FC and their city apart

Still going strong: Liverpool made a habit of winning trophies at home and abroad

from the rest of the country. Amid cries for the FA Cup to be abandoned the city insisted, in honour of its dead, that the competition continue. The club rose like a phoenix out of the ashes as they attempted to become the first club to win the famous League and Cup double twice. It was befitting that Liverpool and Everton should have both walked out together to contest the 1989 FA Cup final.

Liverpool's victory over Everton was like a sedative to the club and, providing that they were winning, it continued to be so. Yet one sensed that the burden they were carrying was too much.

Six days later Arsenal played Liverpool at Anfield, needing a two-goal victory to clinch the championship. The ground was, once again, the hotbed it always was and Liverpool were on for an historic double. However, Arsenal had other ideas. With seconds to go Michael Thomas snatched the second goal for Arsenal and with it the League championship. Suddenly 1989 would be remembered for all the wrong reasons.

Kenny Dalglish's transition from player to manager was indicative of the club's astuteness. However, it often seemed that the hope of at

least half of the city fell on to the shoulders of their beloved team.

Pressurised and frustrated, Dalglish announced his retirement from the game only to return six months later as the manager of Blackburn Rovers. It was at this point that the cracks in the Shankly dynasty became visible.

For Hillsborough to strike so soon after Heysel was a devastating blow to a club that found itself having to adjust to the staple diet of domestic football. Not only was the club weak, it was vulnerable. The appointment of Graeme Souness as manager in 1990 highlighted their insecurity. Souness's attitude at Rangers was bullish to say the least. A peacetime prime minister may have been much better suited rather than one always ready for war.

Notably, the singing of the traditional songs accompanied by the stupid faces are no longer witnessed in the hotel lobbies, or anywhere else. The same players that were once not good enough to play for Liverpool are now wearing the famous red shirt and, sadly, it appears that the Liverpool dynasty is, at the moment, on hold, desperately in need of another Shankly.

Smooth succession: Moran, Paisley and Fagan were all products of the famous Boot Room

THE 1989-90 SEASON

Swindon suffer heavy losses after betting scandal exposed

SWINDON, under the inspirational leadership of Ossie Ardiles, were pushing hard for promotion to the First Division when the roof fell in on their world.

Out and down: Hillier, the Swindon chairman, was convicted of fraud

The FA announced that it was investigating claims that the Swindon chairman, Brian Hillier, and manager, Lou Macari, had bet against their team before they lost an FA Cup match to Newcastle in 1988. Hillier admitted that the bet had been made, but said it was only insurance to cover money that Swindon would lose by not reaching the next round.

Both Hillier and Macari were found guilty of bringing the game into disrepute in February. Hillier was banned from football for six months (a sentence subsequently increased to three years), the club was fined £7,500 and Macari was fined £1,000. Within a week Macari, who by then was the manager of West Ham, had resigned from Upton Park.

The FA's investigation of Swindon also unearthed alarming evidence of unlawful payments to players and the manipulation of transfer fees. On May 1, Hillier, Macari, Colin Calderwood, the club captain, and Vince Farrar, Swindon's former chief accountant, were arrested. Hillier, Macari and Farrar were all charged with tax offences and released on bail.

Amid all the off the field turmoil, Ardiles had taken Swindon to the play-offs, where they beat Sunderland to win a place in the First Division for the first time in the club's history. But when Swindon admitted 36 breaches of League regulations on June 7, their punishment was harsh.

The League promoted Sunderland in their place, and relegated Swindon to the Third Division, giving their place in the Second Division to Tranmere. Swindon were horrified and appealed. They won some respite when the League restored them to the Second Division, a decision that infuriated Tranmere.

Hillier, Macari and Farrar were sent for trial at Winchester crown court. The case lasted five weeks and Macari was acquitted, but both Hillier and Farrar were convicted: Hillier of conspiracy to defraud the Inland Revenue and Farrar of conspiracy and false accounting. Farrar received a six-month suspended sentence and Hillier was jailed, initially for a year although the sentence was halved on appeal.

Macari: fined £1,000

Hapless Hartlepool take a hammering but refuse to lie down

PITY poor Hartlepool. They lost their first three games of the season, conceding 10 goals and failing to score even one. Then things went from bad to even worse in September.

A trip to Stockport turned into a nightmare. Hartlepool were three goals down by half-time and sunk 6-0, with Brett Angell scoring four of the goals.

Just to prove that it was not a freak result they caved in 6-0 again a fortnight later, this time at home to Doncaster, for whom Lee Turnbull got a hat-trick.

The rot continued into November when hapless Hartlepool went to Aldershot. It was the same old story: 3-0 down at half-time, beaten 6-1 and another hat-trick conceded to

Steve Claridge. Not surprisingly, Hartlepool, with only two wins to their name, were bottom of the Fourth Division.

Bobby Moncur, their manager, had had more than enough humiliation and he offered to resign. He was talked out of it by the club's chairman. But a fortnight later, after Hartlepool had gone out of the FA Cup in the

first round 2-0 at home to Huddersfield, and lost again in the League, he finally quit.

Things looked up a bit after Christmas, when Hartlepool even managed to win two matches in a row. They took their revenge on Stockport 5-0 and managed to finish the season a respectable 12 points clear of relegation.

Heroics guarantee World Cup trips

DESPITE the odd hiccup along the way, England, Scotland and the Republic of Ireland qualified for the World Cup finals in Italy, all finishing runners-up in their groups.

Wales and Northern Ireland fared less well. Wales had a good excuse, they were in with West Germany and Holland, but two home draws did not help their cause. Northern Ireland's faint hopes were dashed in Dublin in October when Jack Charlton's Republic side beat them 3-0. Two goals from John Aldridge in Malta in November ended any doubts. It was the first time the Republic had qualified for the finals and followed on from their success in qualifying for the European championships two years earlier.

England virtually clinched their Italian berth with a stirring 0-0 draw in Sweden (the group's other qualifiers) in September. The hero of the night was England's captain, Terry Butcher, who played on despite having 10 stitches inserted during the half-time interval. The newspapers next day all carried gory photographs of Butcher with a blood-stained shirt and bandage round his head.

A month later, in Poland, another hero emerged, the goalkeeper Peter Shilton. He made four magnificent saves to keep the game scoreless and guarantee England's qualification.

Scotland lived on their nerves throughout the campaign and a feeble 3-0 defeat by France had left them needing a point at Hampden against Norway if they were to edge out France. Ally McCoist brilliantly scored the goal they needed to give them a cushion when he flicked the ball over Eric Thorsvedt. And they needed the cushion. With a minute left Scottish goalkeeping blunders returned to haunt them as Jim Leighton misjudged a speculative, long-range shot and the Norwegians equalised.

In the draw in December, England were seeded and would play all of their matches in Cagliari, on the island of Sardinia. This conveniently meant any hooligan problems would, initially, be kept off the mainland. Unfortunately the other countries in England's group were the Republic, Egypt and Holland. This raised fears of clashes with Dutch hooligans. Once again Scotland drew the short straw: Brazil, Sweden and Costa Rica.

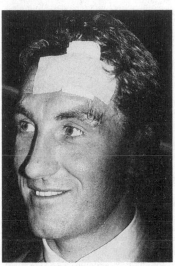

Butcher: bloody battler

Tug of war: the close attentions of a Polish defender are sufficient to distract Barnes, who headed just wide of the post

Palace turn the tables on Liverpool

LIVERPOOL were red-hot favourites to sweep past Crystal Palace in the FA Cup semi-final at Villa Park on April 8. After all they were the Cup holders, top of the First Division and had thrashed Palace 9-0 at Anfield in September when eight different players had scored, a League record. By contrast Palace were deep in the relegation mire. But then Wimbledon had been massive underdogs in the 1988 final against Liverpool.

And this was a different Palace: only six players who had been humiliated in the autumn took the field in Birmingham. In particular Steve Coppell had broken the record for a goalkeeper when he paid Bristol Rovers £1m for Nigel Martyn.

After a quarter of an hour the match seemed to be following the script as Ian Rush put Liverpool ahead. Then they lost Rush and Gary Gillespie because of injury and in the second half Palace tore into them. Mark Bright equalised within seconds of the re-start and Gary O'Reilly put them ahead with 20 minutes remaining.

The pendulum swung Liverpool's way with McMahon's equaliser and a Barnes penalty. The drama was not over however: Andy Gray headed the equaliser two minutes from time. Extra time was to see Liverpool off as Alan Pardew headed in a corner to send Palace into their first final.

The second semi-final was as startling with Manchester United held 3-3 by plucky Oldham and then going through 2-1 in the replay. Could Palace pull it off again in the final? With seven minutes remaining it seemed so. The introduction of the partially fit Ian Wright 20 minutes from time, when United were 2-1 ahead, proved to have been a Coppell masterstroke.

Within three minutes Wright shredded the United defence for the equaliser. Two minutes into extra time Wright produced another gem for the lead. But, unlike Liverpool, United refused to buckle, pouring forward in search of the equaliser. Chance after chance was missed, until Hughes finally scored to take the Cup final into its fourth replay in a decade.

Like Brighton in 1983, Palace had missed the boat. The replay, five days later, was a scrappy affair. Alex Ferguson, United's manager, dropped his goalkeeper Jim Leighton for the on-loan Les Sealey. Lee Martin scored the only goal in a match mostly memorable for a series of niggling incidents. United's triumph meant they had emulated Tottenham and Aston Villa's record of seven FA Cups.

Just in time: Wright came on to score the equaliser for Palace

Rough and tumble: Andy Gray and Danny Wallace tangle for the ball in the drawn FA Cup final at Wembley

United bamboozled by Knighton's bid

Room of his own: Knighton lords it in his castle

THE MANCHESTER UNITED faithful were amused on the opening day of the season when Michael Knighton made a surprise entrance on to the Old Trafford pitch. The property owner, decked in Manchester United training kit, blew kisses, saluted the crowd, juggled the ball and fired shots into an empty net.

It transpired that Martin Edwards, United's majority shareholder, had agreed to sell his shares to Knighton in exchange for £10m cash and £10m to spend modernising the stadium. Knighton, then, was now the owner of Manchester United.

The intended deal attracted the attention of a generally hostile press who poured scorn on the new "owner". Knighton claimed that the newspapers were hounding him and were unjustly misrepresenting his future intentions for Manchester United. Some of the most vitriolic criticism was found in the Daily Mirror whose proprietor, Robert Maxwell, some suspected, harboured designs of his own concerning the future ownership of United.

The whole affair became intolerable for United and Knighton. In October Knighton decided to withdraw his offer. Knighton's received a non-executive seat on the board and the episode was over.

Taylor orders safety first

LORD JUSTICE TAYLOR produced a sweeping condemnation of English football in his final report on the Hillsborough disaster, which was published on January 29. He was widely praised for the thoroughness of his investigation and for consulting everybody involved in football, from fans to the people who ran the national game.

Taylor lamented the fact that his was the ninth report on safety this century yet grounds were still incredibly squalid. He said football was blighted by old and crumbling stadiums with poor facilities, and lacked proper leadership. Although he condemned hooliganism, he pointed out that fans were fenced in and treated like prisoners of war.

In all he made 76 recommendations, the most important of which were that all-seat stadiums should be introduced to First and Second Division grounds by 1994 and the rest of the League by 1999. He also said that a national identity card scheme was unworkable and dangerous, because it would create a crush of fans outside of grounds.

Football immediately accepted all of his points as did the government, which gave up its long-running battle to enforce membership cards. Taylor's proposals were incorporated into the Football Spectators Act, which established a Football Licensing Authority to make sure the changes were carried out.

But it was not long before football was complaining about the cost of implementing the changes. The authorities said the total bill would top £100m, and many smaller clubs could be forced out of business.

The government was insistent that football had to find the money itself. However, in the Budget on March 20 they did relent slightly by cutting the amount of betting duty levied on the football pools by 2.5%, on condition that the money was used to finance ground improvements.

241

THE
1989-90
SEASON

Hearts thwarted in audacious takeover of Hibs

HEARTS, who had finished third and qualified for Europe, put forward in June a radical proposal: a merger with their Edinburgh rivals, Hibernian. Hearts' £6.12m bid for the Easter Road club was a calculated attempt to form one strong Edinburgh club to break the Glasgow duopoly.

Hearts had a point. In the 45 years since the Second World War, there had been only 12 occasions when a club other than Rangers or Celtic had won the championship. And the last time Hibs had won the title was in 1952, Hearts 1960.

But this bold and ambitious plan was doomed from the outset. The fans mounted protests and marches with banners proclaiming "Hands off Hibs". The Hibs board voted unanimously to reject the offer. The Hibs supporters even campaigned for people who held accounts with the Bank of Scotland (who were backing the Hearts bid) to close them. So in July Hearts bowed to the inevitable and pulled out.

Hot-head Souness sets Rangers on fire

RANGERS began the season in dreadful fashion, winning only two of their first eight League matches, and were bottom of the table for three consecutive weeks after four games. But Graeme Souness's team turned that round in dramatic fashion and by mid-December they headed the Premier League table and stayed there to the end of the season, comfortably taking the title seven points clear of Aberdeen.

Off the pitch, however, Souness did not have such an easy time of it. In December he had a heated altercation with the Hearts captain, Dave McPherson, after Rangers had beaten them 2-1 at Tynecastle. The police reported the incident to the Scottish FA. Souness's complaint was that players were deliberately exaggerating fouls in order to get players sent off. Then in May he was fined a record £5,000 for breaking a touchline ban imposed earlier. The ban was also extended until the end of the 1991-92 season.

This was Souness's third touchline ban, each of them stemming from his failure to adhere to the first ban in 1989. However, Souness was caught bang to rights as video evidence clearly showed him shouting to his players from the tunnel in February.

While Rangers had difficulty controlling their fiery manager, Celtic, their cross-town rivals, had difficulty controlling their form. Leading the table at the end of October, they eventually slumped to fifth and were edged out of Europe by Dundee United. It was the first time that Celtic had missed European

Top dogs: Ally McCoist parades Rangers' 40th championship trophy at Ibrox

qualification for nine years.

Not that Celtic had particularly enjoyed their campaign in the European Cup Winners' Cup, going out in the first round 6-6. Trailing 2-1 to Partizan Belgrade from the away leg, they contrived to score five goals at Parkhead – four of them from their Polish striker Darius Dziekanowski – and concede four, the last coming within 90 seconds of the final whistle. The 5-4 score meant the Yugoslavs went through on the away goals rule.

There were goals galore at Parkhead in September, but at Hampden in May Celtic and Aberdeen managed to play 120 minutes of stultifying, goalless football in the Scottish Cup final. However, because of the imminent World Cup, the Scottish FA had decreed there was to be no replay so the final went to a penalty shoot-out for the first time.

It then took 20 penalties before there was a result. Celtic missed their first, Aberdeen their fourth. With 18 kicks taken neither keeper had yet touched the ball, but on Aberdeen's 10th attempt the Dutch keeper, Theo Snelders, acrobatically deflected Anton Rogan's kick. Brian Irvine coolly slotted home and Celtic had triumphed 9-8. More of such nonsense would be seen in Italy in the World Cup finals.

Tabloid vendetta drives Robson out

THE tabloid papers' constant sniping at Bobby Robson finally drove to him resign as England manager and move abroad to coach PSV Eindhoven.

The speculation about Robson's future started in March, with a report that he would have to win the World Cup to stand any chance of keeping his job. More fuel was added to the fire when another paper claimed that sources in the FA said that it had already been decided that Graham Taylor would be the next England manager.

Eindhoven had approached Robson through an intermediary in April and said that the job in Holland was his if he wanted it. Robson's response was that his first loyalty was to England, and he was not prepared to talk to anybody until the World Cup was over. But Bert Millichip, the FA chairman, could not give Robson any assurances about his future, so he gave Robson permission to talk to Eindhoven.

Even then, despite the fortune he was offered, Robson wanted to stay with England.

I was just a victim of the tabloid newspaper war. I had watched this cancer spread over the eight years I had been in the job. It was ugly and damaging, and so often the reports were untrue

But at a second meeting with Millichip the FA did not offer to extend his contract. So, on what Robson described as "one of the saddest days of my career", he told the FA he would be leaving after the World Cup.

It did not take long for the news to leak out of the FA and Robson woke on the morning of May 24 to find his house besieged by reporters. At the press conference to confirm his departure Robson lashed out at the tabloid press, accusing them of printing scurrilous rumours. He left for Italy bitter at the treatment he had received over the years from the media and

Robson: embittered

knowing that he had his work cut out to stop the events of the past few weeks affecting his team's morale.

30 seconds of madness that seemed to last the whole season

TELEVISION viewers watched in amazement as the match between Arsenal and Norwich on November 4 degenerated into an all-out brawl. Norwich, who led 2-0 at half-time, were unhappy that Arsenal were awarded a penalty in the last seconds of the match. When Lee Dixon scored, to give Arsenal a dramatic 4-3 victory, the scuffling started.

Within seconds, almost all the players were involved in the fracas and police had to restore order. Amazingly, the referee, George Tyson, said that he was not going to take any action. The FA were not as lenient. Describing the incident as "30 seconds of madness", they fined Norwich £50,000 and Arsenal £20,000.

The FA were soon collecting another £20,000 each from West Ham and Wimbledon. They were involved in another mass brawl during their League Cup match on November 22, which West Ham won despite having Julian Dicks sent off.

Two days later, a pair of managers were also in trouble. John Bird of York and Ray McHale of Scarborough were both sent off for squaring up to each other and trying to trade punches. That indiscretion brought them both a three-month touchline ban.

And just when it looked as if England had convinced the rest of the world that it had its hooliganism problem under control, all the good work was undone when Leeds fans ran amok in Bournemouth on the last day of the season.

There were 120 arrests for rioting, looting and assault before, during and after the Second Division match on May 5. The local police were furious, saying that they had

Flash point: O'Leary manhandles Bowen and the fighting soon spread

warned the League not to stage the game on a bank holiday weekend. The chief constable of Dorset said police should be given the power to change fixture lists, and the League admitted that they were wrong not to heed the police advice.

LEAGUE TABLES AND RESULTS 1980 – 1990

	1980-81	1981-82	1982-83	1983-84	1984-85
WORLD CUP		Italy 3 West Germany 1			
EUROPEAN CHAMPIONSHIP				France 2 Spain 0	
EUROPEAN CUP	Liverpool 1 Real Madrid 0	Aston Villa 1 Bayern Munich 0	Hamburg 1 Juventus 0	Liverpool 1 AS Roma 1; Liverpool won 4-2 on penalties	Juventus 1 Liverpool 0
EUROPEAN CUP WINNERS CUP	Dynamo Tbilisi 2 Carl Zeiss Jena 1	Barcelona 2 Standard Liege 1	Aberdeen 2 Real Madrid 1	Juventus 2 Porto 1	Everton 3 Rapid Vienna 1
UEFA CUP	Ipswich Town beat AZ Alkmaar 3-0 2-4	IFK Gothenburg beat SV Hamburg 1-0 3-0	Anderlecht beat Benfica 1-0 1-1	Tottenham Hotspur beat Anderlecht 1-1 1-1 (4-3 on penalties)	Real Madrid beat Videoton 3-0 0-1
FA CUP	Tottenham Hotspur 3 Manchester City 2, after 1-1	Tottenham Hotspur 1 Queen's Park Rangers 0, after 1-1	Manchester United 4 Brighton & Hove Albion 0, after 2-2	Everton 2 Watford 0	Manchester United 1 Everton 0

FIRST DIVISION

1980-81

	P	W	D	L	F	A	Pts
Aston Villa	42	26	8	8	72	40	60
Ipswich	42	23	10	9	77	43	56
Arsenal	42	19	15	8	61	45	53
West Brom	42	20	12	10	60	42	52
Liverpool	42	17	17	8	62	42	51
Soton	42	20	10	12	76	56	50
Nottm F	42	19	12	11	62	44	50
Man Utd	42	15	18	9	51	36	48
Leeds	42	17	10	15	39	47	44
Tottenham	42	14	15	13	70	68	43
Stoke	42	12	18	12	51	60	42
Man City	42	14	11	17	56	59	39
Birmingham	42	13	12	17	50	61	38
Middlesbro	42	16	5	21	53	61	37
Everton	42	13	10	19	55	58	36
Coventry	42	13	10	19	48	68	36
Sunderland	42	14	7	21	52	53	35
Wolves	42	13	9	20	43	55	35
Brighton	42	14	7	21	54	67	35
Norwich	*42*	*13*	*7*	*22*	*49*	*73*	*33*
Leicester	*42*	*13*	*6*	*23*	*40*	*67*	*32*
C Palace	*42*	*6*	*7*	*29*	*47*	*83*	*19*

1981-82

	P	W	D	L	F	A	Pts
Liverpool	42	26	9	7	80	32	87
Ipswich	42	26	5	11	75	53	83
Man Utd	42	22	12	8	59	29	78
Tottenham	42	20	11	11	67	48	71
Arsenal	42	20	11	11	48	37	71
Swansea	42	21	6	15	58	51	69
Soton	42	19	9	14	72	67	66
Everton	42	17	13	12	56	50	64
West Ham	42	14	16	12	66	57	58
Man City	42	15	13	14	49	50	58
Aston Villa	42	15	12	15	55	53	57
Nottm F	42	15	12	15	42	48	57
Brighton	42	13	13	16	43	52	52
Coventry	42	13	11	18	56	62	50
Notts C	42	13	8	21	61	69	47
Birmingham	42	10	14	18	53	61	44
West Brom	42	11	11	20	46	57	44
Stoke	42	12	8	22	44	63	44
Sunderland	42	11	11	20	38	58	44
Leeds	*42*	*10*	*12*	*20*	*39*	*61*	*42*
Wolves	*42*	*10*	*10*	*22*	*32*	*63*	*40*
Middlesbro	*42*	*8*	*15*	*19*	*34*	*52*	*39*

1982-83

	P	W	D	L	F	A	Pts
Liverpool	42	24	10	8	87	37	82
Watford	42	22	5	15	74	57	71
Man Utd	42	19	13	10	56	38	70
Tottenham	42	20	9	13	65	50	69
Nottm F	42	20	9	13	62	50	69
Aston Villa	42	21	5	16	62	50	68
Everton	42	18	10	14	66	48	64
West Ham	42	20	4	18	68	62	64
Ipswich	42	15	13	14	64	50	58
Arsenal	42	16	10	16	58	56	58
West Brom	42	15	12	15	51	49	57
Soton	42	15	12	15	54	58	57
Stoke	42	16	9	17	53	64	57
Norwich	42	14	12	16	52	58	54
Notts C	42	15	7	20	55	71	52
Sunderland	42	12	14	16	48	61	50
Birmingham	42	12	14	16	40	55	50
Luton	42	12	13	17	65	84	49
Coventry	42	13	9	20	48	59	48
Man City	*42*	*13*	*8*	*21*	*47*	*70*	*47*
Swansea	*42*	*10*	*11*	*21*	*51*	*69*	*41*
Brighton	*42*	*9*	*13*	*20*	*38*	*68*	*40*

1983-84

	P	W	D	L	F	A	Pts
Liverpool	42	22	14	6	73	32	80
Soton	42	22	11	9	66	38	77
Nottm F	42	22	8	12	76	45	74
Man Utd	42	20	14	8	71	41	74
QPR	42	22	7	13	67	37	73
Arsenal	42	18	9	15	74	60	63
Everton	42	16	14	12	44	42	62
Tottenham	42	17	10	15	64	65	61
West Ham	42	17	9	16	60	55	60
Aston Villa	42	17	9	16	59	61	60
Watford	42	16	9	17	68	77	57
Ipswich	42	15	8	19	55	57	53
Sunderland	42	13	13	16	42	53	52
Norwich	42	12	15	15	48	49	51
Leicester	42	13	12	17	65	68	51
Luton	42	14	9	19	53	66	51
West Brom	42	14	9	19	48	62	51
Stoke	42	13	11	18	44	63	50
Coventry	42	13	11	18	57	77	50
Birmingham	*42*	*12*	*12*	*18*	*39*	*50*	*48*
Notts C	*42*	*10*	*11*	*21*	*50*	*72*	*41*
Wolves	*42*	*6*	*11*	*25*	*27*	*80*	*29*

1984-85

	P	W	D	L	F	A	Pts
Everton	42	28	6	8	88	43	90
Liverpool	42	22	11	9	68	35	77
Tottenham	42	23	8	11	78	51	77
Man Utd	42	22	10	10	77	47	76
Soton	42	19	11	12	56	47	68
Chelsea	42	18	12	12	63	48	66
Arsenal	42	19	9	14	61	49	66
Sheff Wed	42	17	14	11	58	45	65
Nottm F	42	19	7	16	56	48	64
Aston Villa	42	15	11	16	60	60	56
Watford	42	14	13	15	81	71	55
West Brom	42	16	7	19	58	62	55
Luton	42	15	9	18	57	61	54
Newcastle	42	13	13	16	55	70	52
Leicester	42	15	6	21	65	73	51
West Ham	42	13	12	17	51	68	51
Ipswich	42	13	11	18	46	57	50
Coventry	42	15	5	22	47	64	50
QPR	42	13	11	18	53	72	50
Norwich	*42*	*13*	*10*	*19*	*46*	*64*	*49*
Sunderland	*42*	*10*	*10*	*22*	*40*	*62*	*40*
Stoke	*42*	*3*	*8*	*31*	*24*	*91*	*17*

	1980-81	1981-82	1982-83	1983-84	1984-85
SECOND DIVISION	Champions: West Ham United Also promoted: Notts County, Swansea City Relegated: Preston North End, Bristol City, Bristol Rovers	Champions: Luton Town Also promoted: Watford, Norwich City Relegated: Cardiff City, Wrexham, Orient	Champions: Queen's Park Rangers Also promoted: Wolverhampton Wanderers, Leicester City Relegated: Rotherham United, Burnley, Bolton Wanderers	Champions: Chelsea Also promoted: Sheffield Wednesday, Newcastle United Relegated: Derby County, Swansea City, Cambridge United	Champions: Oxford United Also promoted: Birmingham City, Manchester City Relegated: Notts County, Cardiff City, Wolverhampton Wanderers
THIRD DIVISION	Champions: Rotherham United Also promoted: Barnsley, Charlton Athletic Relegated: Sheffield United, Colchester United, Blackpool, Hull City	Champions: Burnley Also promoted: Carlisle United, Fulham Relegated: Wimbledon, Swindon Town, Bristol City, Chester	Champions: Portsmouth Also promoted: Cardiff City, Huddersfield Town Relegated: Reading, Wrexham, Doncaster Rovers, Chesterfield	Champions: Oxford United Also promoted: Wimbledon, Sheffield United Relegated: Scunthorpe United, Southend United, Port Vale, Exeter City	Champions: Bradford City Also promoted: Millwall, Hull City Relegated: Burnley, Orient, Preston North End, Cambridge United
FOURTH DIVISION	Champions: Southend United Also promoted: Lincoln City, Doncaster Rovers, Wimbledon	Champions: Sheffield United Also promoted: Bradford City, Wigan Athletic, Bournemouth	Champions: Wimbledon Also promoted: Hull City, Port Vale, Scunthorpe United	Champions: York City Also promoted: Doncaster Rovers, Reading, Bristol City, Aldershot	Champions: Chesterfield Also promoted: Blackpool, Darlington, Bury
LEAGUE CUP	Liverpool 2 West Ham United 1, after 1-1	Liverpool 3 Tottenham Hotspur 1	Liverpool 2 Manchester United 1	Liverpool 1 Everton 0, after 0-0	Norwich City 1 Sunderland 0
SCOTTISH CUP	Rangers 4 Dundee United 1, after 0-0	Aberdeen 4 Rangers 1	Aberdeen 1 Rangers 0	Aberdeen 2 Celtic 1	Celtic 2 Dundee United 1

SCOTTISH PREMIER DIVISION

1980-81

	P	W	D	L	F	A	Pts
Celtic	36	26	4	6	84	37	56
Aberdeen	36	19	11	6	61	26	49
Rangers	36	16	12	8	60	32	44
St Mirren	36	18	8	10	56	47	44
Dundee U	36	17	9	10	66	42	43
Partick	36	10	10	16	32	48	30
Airdrie	36	10	9	17	36	55	29
Morton	36	10	8	18	36	58	28
Kilmarnock	*36*	*5*	*9*	*22*	*23*	*65*	*19*
Hearts	*36*	*6*	*6*	*24*	*27*	*71*	*18*

1981-82

	P	W	D	L	F	A	Pts
Celtic	36	24	7	5	79	33	55
Aberdeen	36	23	7	6	71	29	53
Rangers	36	16	11	9	57	45	43
Dundee U	36	15	10	11	61	38	40
St Mirren	36	14	9	13	49	52	37
Hibernian	36	11	14	11	38	40	36
Morton	36	9	12	15	31	54	30
Dundee	36	11	4	21	46	72	26
Partick	*36*	*6*	*10*	*20*	*35*	*59*	*22*
Airdrie	*36*	*5*	*8*	*23*	*31*	*76*	*18*

1982-83

	P	W	D	L	F	A	Pts
Dundee U	36	24	8	4	90	35	56
Celtic	36	25	5	6	90	36	55
Aberdeen	36	25	5	6	76	24	55
Rangers	36	13	12	11	52	41	38
St Mirren	36	11	12	13	47	51	34
Dundee	36	9	11	16	42	53	29
Hibernian	36	7	15	14	35	51	29
Motherwell	36	11	5	20	39	73	27
Morton	*36*	*6*	*8*	*22*	*30*	*74*	*20*
Kilmarnock	*36*	*3*	*11*	*22*	*28*	*91*	*17*

1983-84

	P	W	D	L	F	A	Pts
Aberdeen	36	25	7	4	78	21	57
Celtic	36	21	8	7	80	41	50
Dundee U	36	18	11	7	67	39	47
Rangers	36	15	12	9	53	41	42
Hearts	36	10	16	10	38	47	36
St Mirren	36	9	14	13	55	59	32
Hibernian	36	12	7	17	45	55	31
Dundee	36	11	5	20	50	74	27
St J'stone	*36*	*10*	*3*	*23*	*36*	*81*	*23*
Motherwell	*36*	*4*	*7*	*25*	*31*	*75*	*15*

1984-85

	P	W	D	L	F	A	Pts
Aberdeen	36	27	5	4	89	26	59
Celtic	36	22	8	6	77	30	52
Dundee U	36	20	7	9	67	33	47
Rangers	36	13	12	11	47	38	38
St Mirren	36	17	4	15	51	56	38
Dundee	36	15	7	14	48	50	37
Hearts	36	13	5	18	47	64	31
Hibernian	36	10	7	19	38	61	27
Dumbarton	*36*	*6*	*7*	*23*	*29*	*64*	*19*
Morton	*36*	*5*	*2*	*29*	*29*	*100*	*12*

	1980-81	1981-82	1982-83	1983-84	1984-85
SCOTTISH FIRST DIVISION	Champions: Hibernian Also promoted: Dundee Relegated: Stirling Albion, Berwick Rangers	Champions: Motherwell Also promoted: Kilmarnock Relegated: East Stirling, Queen of the South	Champions: St Johnstone Also promoted: Hearts Relegated: Dunfermline Athletic, Queen's Park	Champions: Morton Also promoted: Dumbarton Relegated: Raith Rovers, Alloa	Champions: Motherwell Also promoted: Clydebank Relegated: Meadowbank Thistle, St Johnstone
SCOTTISH SECOND DIV	Champions: Queen's Park Also promoted: Queen of the South	Champions: Clyde Also promoted: Alloa	Champions: Brechin City Also promoted: Meadowbank Thistle	Champions: Forfar Athletic Also promoted: East Fife	Champions: Montrose Also promoted: Alloa
SCOTTISH LEAGUE CUP	Dundee United 3 Dundee 0	Rangers 2 Dundee 1	Celtic 2 Rangers 1	Rangers 3 Celtic 2	Rangers 1 Dundee United 0

	1985-86	1986-87	1987-88	1988-89	1989-90
WORLD CUP	Argentina 3 West Germany 2				West Germany 1 Argentina 0
EUROPEAN CHAMPIONSHIP			Holland 2 USSR 0		
EUROPEAN CUP	Steaua Bucharest 0 Barcelona 0; Bucharest won 2-0 on penalties	Porto 2 Bayern Munich 1	PSV Eindhoven 0 Benfica 0; PSV won 6-5 on penalties	AC Milan 4 Steaua Bucharest 0	AC Milan 1 Benfica 0
EUROPEAN CUP WINNERS CUP	Dynamo Kiev 3 Atletico Madrid 0	Ajax 1 Lokomotiv Leipzig 0	Mechelen 1 Ajax 0	Barcelona 2 Sampdoria 0	Sampdoria 2 Anderlecht 0
UEFA CUP	Real Madrid beat Cologne 5-1 0-2	IFK Gothenburg beat Dundee United 1-0 1-1	Bayer Leverkusen beat Espanol 0-3 3-0; Leverkusen won 3-2 on penalties	Napoli beat VFB Stuttgart 2-1 3-3	Juventus beat Fiorentina 3-1 0-0
FA CUP	Liverpool 3 Everton 1	Coventry City 3 Tottenham Hotspur 2	Wimbledon 1 Liverpool 0	Liverpool 3 Everton 2	Manchester United 1 Crystal Palace 0, after 3-3

FIRST DIVISION

1985-86

	P	W	D	L	F	A	Pts
Liverpool	42	26	10	6	89	37	88
Everton	42	26	8	8	87	41	86
West Ham	42	26	6	10	74	40	84
Man Utd	42	22	10	10	70	36	76
Sheff Wed	42	21	10	11	63	54	73
Chelsea	42	20	11	11	57	56	71
Arsenal	42	20	9	13	49	47	69
Nottm F	42	19	11	12	69	53	68
Luton	42	18	12	12	61	44	66
Tottenham	42	19	8	15	74	52	65
Newcastle	42	17	12	13	67	72	63
Watford	42	16	11	15	69	62	59
QPR	42	15	7	20	53	64	52
Soton	42	12	10	20	51	62	46
Manchester	42	11	12	19	43	57	45
Aston Villa	42	10	14	18	51	67	44
Coventry	42	11	10	21	48	71	43
Oxford	42	10	12	20	62	80	42
Leicester	42	10	12	20	54	76	42
Ipswich	*42*	*11*	*8*	*23*	*32*	*55*	*41*
Birmingham	*42*	*8*	*5*	*29*	*30*	*73*	*29*
West Brom	*42*	*4*	*12*	*26*	*35*	*89*	*24*

1986-87

	P	W	D	L	F	A	Pts
Everton	42	26	8	8	76	31	86
Liverpool	42	23	8	11	72	42	77
Tottenham	42	21	8	13	68	43	71
Arsenal	42	20	10	12	58	35	70
Norwich	42	17	17	8	53	51	68
Wimbledon	42	19	9	14	57	50	66
Luton	42	18	12	12	47	45	66
Nottm F	42	18	11	13	64	51	65
Watford	42	18	9	15	67	54	63
Coventry	42	17	12	13	50	45	63
Man Utd	42	14	14	14	52	45	56
Soton	2	14	10	18	69	68	52
Sheff Wed	42	13	13	16	58	59	52
Chelsea	42	13	13	16	53	64	52
West Ham	42	14	10	18	52	67	52
QPR	42	13	11	18	48	64	50
Newcastle	42	12	11	19	47	65	47
Oxford	42	11	13	18	44	69	46
Charlton	42	11	11	20	45	55	44
Leicester	*42*	*11*	*9*	*22*	*54*	*76*	*42*
Man City	*42*	*8*	*15*	*19*	*36*	*57*	*39*
Aston Villa	*42*	*8*	*12*	*22*	*45*	*79*	*36*

1987-88

	P	W	D	L	F	A	Pts
Liverpool	40	26	12	2	87	24	90
Man Utd	40	23	12	5	71	38	81
Nottm F	40	20	13	7	67	39	73
Everton	40	19	13	8	53	27	70
QPR	40	19	10	11	48	38	67
Arsenal	40	18	12	10	58	39	66
Wimbledon	40	14	15	11	58	47	57
Newcastle	40	14	14	12	55	53	56
Luton	40	14	11	15	57	58	53
Coventry	40	13	14	13	46	53	53
Sheff Wed	40	15	8	17	52	66	53
Soton	40	12	14	14	49	53	50
Tottenham	40	12	11	17	38	48	47
Norwich	40	12	9	19	40	52	45
Derby	40	10	13	17	35	45	43
West Ham	40	9	15	16	40	52	42
Charlton	40	9	15	16	38	52	42
Chelsea	*40*	*9*	*15*	*16*	*50*	*68*	*42*
Portsmouth	*40*	*7*	*14*	*19*	*36*	*66*	*35*
Watford	*40*	*7*	*11*	*22*	*27*	*51*	*32*
Oxford	*40*	*6*	*13*	*21*	*44*	*80*	*31*

1988-89

	P	W	D	L	F	A	Pts
Arsenal	38	22	10	6	73	36	76
Liverpool	38	22	10	6	65	28	76
Nottm F	38	17	13	8	64	43	64
Norwich	38	17	11	10	48	45	62
Derby	38	17	7	14	40	38	58
Tottenham	38	15	12	11	60	46	57
Coventry	38	14	13	11	47	42	55
Everton	38	14	12	12	50	45	54
QPR	38	14	11	13	43	37	53
Millwall	38	14	11	13	47	52	53
Man Utd	38	13	12	13	45	35	51
Wimbledon	38	14	9	15	50	46	51
Soton	38	10	15	13	52	66	45
Charlton	38	10	12	16	44	58	42
Sheff Wed	38	10	12	16	34	51	42
Luton	38	10	11	17	42	52	41
Aston Villa	38	9	13	16	45	56	40
Middlesbro	*38*	*9*	*12*	*17*	*44*	*61*	*39*
West Ham	*38*	*10*	*8*	*20*	*37*	*62*	*38*
Newcastle	*38*	*7*	*10*	*21*	*32*	*63*	*31*

1989-90

	P	W	D	L	F	A	Pts
Liverpool	38	23	10	5	78	37	79
Aston Villa	38	21	7	10	57	38	70
Tottenham	38	19	6	13	59	47	63
Arsenal	38	18	8	12	54	38	62
Chelsea	38	16	12	10	58	50	60
Everton	38	17	8	13	57	46	59
Soton	38	15	10	13	71	63	55
Wimbledon	38	13	16	9	47	40	55
Nottm F	38	15	9	14	55	47	54
Norwich	38	13	14	11	44	42	53
QPR	38	13	11	14	45	44	50
Coventry	38	14	7	17	39	59	49
Man Utd	38	13	9	16	46	47	48
Man City	38	12	12	14	43	52	48
C Palace	38	13	9	16	42	66	48
Derby	38	13	7	18	43	40	46
Luton	38	10	13	15	43	57	43
Sheff Wed	*38*	*11*	*10*	*17*	*35*	*51*	*43*
Charlton	*38*	*7*	*9*	*22*	*31*	*57*	*30*
Millwall	*38*	*5*	*11*	*22*	*39*	*65*	*26*

	1985-86	1986-87	1987-88	1988-89	1989-90
SECOND DIVISION	Champions: Norwich City Also promoted: Charlton Athletic, Wimbledon Relegated: Carlisle United, Middlesbrough, Fulham	Champions: Derby County Also promoted: Portsmouth Relegated: Sunderland, Grimsby Town, Brighton & Hove Albion	Champions: Millwall Also promoted: Aston Villa, Middlesbrough Relegated: Sheffield United, Reading, Huddersfield Town	Champions: Chelsea Also promoted: Manchester City, Crystal Palace Relegated: Shrewsbury Town, Birmingham City, Walsall	Champions: Leeds United Also promoted: Sheffield United, Sunderland Relegated: Bournemouth, Bradford City, Stoke City
THIRD DIVISION	Champions: Reading Also promoted: Plymouth Argyle, Derby County Relegated: Lincoln City, Cardiff City, Wolverhampton Wanderers, Swansea	Champions: Bournemouth Also promoted: Middlesbrough, Swindon Town Relegated: Bolton Wanderers, Carlisle United, Darlington, Newport County	Champions: Sunderland Also promoted: Brighton & Hove Albion, Walsall Relegated: Rotherham United, Grimsby Town, York City, Doncaster Rovers	Champions: Wolverhampton Wanderers Also promoted: Sheffi Utd, Port Vale Relegated: Southend United, Chesterfield, Gillingham, Aldershot	Champions: Bristol Rovers Also promoted: Bristol City, Notts County Relegated: Cardiff City, Northampton Town, Blackpool, Walsall
FOURTH DIVISION	Champions: Swindon Town Also promoted: Chester City, Mansfield Town, Port Vale	Champions: Northampton Town Also promoted: Preston North End, Southend United, Aldershot *Scarborough replaced Lincoln*	Champions: Wolves Also promoted: Cardiff City, Bolton Wanderers, Swansea City *Lincoln replaced Newport*	Champions: Rotherham United Also promoted: Tranmere Rovers, Crewe Alexandra, Leyton Orient *Maidstone replaced Darlington*	Champions: Exeter City Also promoted: Grimsby Town, Southend United, Cambridge United *Darlington replaced Colchester*
LEAGUE CUP	Oxford United 3 Queen's Park Rangers 0	Arsenal 2 Liverpool 1	Luton Town 3 Arsenal 2	Nottingham Forest 3 Luton Town 1	Nottingham Forest 1 Oldham Athletic 0
SCOTTISH CUP	Aberdeen 3 Hearts 0	St Mirren 1 Dundee United 0	Celtic 2 Dundee United 1	Celtic 1 Rangers 0	Aberdeen 0 Celtic 0; Aberdeen won 9-8 on penalties

SCOTTISH PREMIER DIVISION

1985-86

	P	W	D	L	F	A	Pts
Celtic	36	20	10	6	67	38	50
Hearts	36	20	10	6	59	33	50
Dundee U	36	18	11	7	59	31	47
Aberdeen	36	16	12	8	62	31	44
Rangers	36	13	9	14	53	45	35
Dundee	36	14	7	15	45	51	35
St Mirren	36	13	5	18	42	63	31
Hibernian	36	11	6	19	49	63	28
Motherwell	36	7	6	23	33	66	20
Clydebank	36	6	8	22	29	77	20

1986-87

	P	W	D	L	F	A	Pts
Rangers	44	31	7	6	85	23	69
Celtic	44	27	9	8	90	41	63
Dundee U	44	24	12	8	66	36	60
Aberdeen	44	21	16	7	63	29	58
Hearts	44	21	14	9	64	43	56
Dundee	44	18	12	14	74	57	48
St Mirren	44	12	12	20	36	51	36
Motherwell	44	11	12	21	43	64	34
Hibernian	44	10	13	21	44	70	33
Falkirk	44	8	10	26	31	70	26
Clydebank	*44*	*6*	*12*	*26*	*35*	*93*	*24*
Hamilton	*44*	*6*	*9*	*29*	*39*	*93*	*21*

1987-88

	P	W	D	L	F	A	Pts
Celtic	44	30	10	4	78	24	70
Hearts	44	23	16	5	74	32	62
Rangers	44	26	8	10	85	34	60
Aberdeen	44	20	17	7	55	26	57
Dundee U	44	15	15	14	51	50	45
Dundee	44	18	7	19	71	63	43
Hibernian	44	12	19	13	41	43	43
Motherwell	44	13	10	21	37	56	36
St Mirren	44	10	15	19	41	64	35
Falkirk	*44*	*11*	*11*	*22*	*42*	*74*	*33*
Dunfermline	*44*	*9*	*10*	*25*	*45*	*81*	*28*
Morton	*44*	*3*	*10*	*31*	*27*	*100*	*16*

1988-89

	P	W	D	L	F	A	Pts
Rangers	36	26	4	6	62	26	56
Aberdeen	36	18	14	4	51	25	50
Celtic	36	21	4	11	66	44	46
Dundee U	36	16	12	8	44	26	44
Hibernian	36	13	9	14	37	36	35
Hearts	36	9	13	14	35	42	31
St Mirren	36	11	7	18	39	55	29
Dundee	36	9	10	17	34	48	28
Motherwell	36	7	13	16	35	44	27
Hamilton	*36*	*6*	*2*	*28*	*19*	*76*	*14*

1989-90

	P	W	D	L	F	A	Pts
Rangers	36	20	11	5	48	19	51
Aberdeen	36	17	10	9	56	33	44
Hearts	36	16	12	8	54	35	44
Dundee U	36	11	13	12	36	39	35
Celtic	36	10	14	12	37	37	34
Motherwell	36	11	12	13	43	47	34
Hibernian	36	12	10	14	34	41	34
Dunfermline	36	11	8	17	37	50	30
St Mirren	36	10	10	16	28	48	30
Dundee	*36*	*5*	*14*	*17*	*41*	*65*	*24*

	1985-86	1986-87	1987-88	1988-89	1989-90
SCOTTISH FIRST DIVISION	Champions: Hamilton Academical Also promoted: Falkirk Relegated: Ayr United, Alloa	Champions: Morton Also promoted: Dunfermline Athletic Relegated: Brechin City, Montrose	Champions: Hamilton Academical Runners-up (not promoted): Meadowbank Thistle Relegated: East Fife, Dumbarton	Champions: Dunfermline Athletic Runners-up (not promoted): Falkirk Relegated: Kilmarnock, Queen of the South	Champions: St Johnstone Runners-up (not promoted): Airdrie Relegated: Albion Rovers, Alloa
SCOTTISH SECOND DIV	Champions: Dunfermline Athletic Also promoted: Queen of the South	Champions: Meadowbank Thistle Also promoted: Raith Rovers	Champions: Ayr United Also promoted: St Johnstone	Champions: Albion Rovers Also promoted: Alloa	Champions: Brechin City Also promoted: Kilmarnock
SCOTTISH LEAGUE CUP	Aberdeen 3 Hibernian 0	Rangers 2 Celtic 1	Rangers 3 Aberdeen 3; Rangers won 5-3 on penalties	Rangers 3 Aberdeen 2	Aberdeen 2 Rangers 1

WORLD CUP 1990

Penal code puts football in the dock

IF the finals of the World Cup are supposed to be football's showcase then the 1990 tournament in Italy was an unmitigated disaster. The statistics tell the story: in 52 matches 115 goals were scored but there were 164 cautions and 16 dismissals. In the last seven matches, from the quarter-finals to the final, only two were decided by goals scored from the run of play, the rest were won either by penalties or by a penalty shoot-out. Football had become a travesty of itself.

However, in the midst of all this depressing cynicism, England did rather well and progressed to the semi-finals – their best performance since 1966, and at the end of the tournament were given the Fair Play award. Their success was something of a surprise, particularly to the press.

In the 18 months prior to the finals Bobby Robson, the England manager, had been the victim of a sustained witch-hunt in the tabloids that would have destroyed lesser men. Even the quality newspapers contributed to the hysteria and hardly a single reporter gave England a prayer. So biased were the journalists that, even as England came within a whisker of reaching the World Cup final, they were still carping about the team and its performance. Meanwhile back home millions watched England's success on television with rapture.

And the Republic of Ireland's. Jack Charlton's odd assortment of Irish and Football League players did spectacularly well to reach the quarter-finals in their very first appearance in the World Cup finals. Admittedly, given their playing resources, their style frequently resembled an average First Division side but their only defeat was to Italy, one of the favourites, in the quarter-final and that was to a single goal from Toto Schillaci.

Sadly Scotland maintained their usual record: for the seventh time they failed get past the first phase; they experienced yet another embarrassing defeat, 1-0 to Costa Rica; and a stirring display against Brazil almost got them into the second round until a late goal put them on the plane home.

England began with the normal hiccups, drawing against the Republic of Ireland and Holland, the European champions, and only qualified for the second round by scraping a 1-0 victory over Egypt. The victory over Belgium that took them to the quarter-finals was inspired by Paul Gascoigne, arguably the player of the tournament. In the last minute of extra time he picked up a ball just outside the England penalty area and ran straight at the heart of the Belgian midfield. Desperate not to concede a goal, the Belgians conceded a free-kick instead. Gascoigne grabbed the ball, looked up, and then put it over the Belgian defence for David Platt to steal in and volley the ball home.

Cameroon, England's quarter-final opponents, were the shock side of the tournament. In the opening match they had stunned Argentina, the defending champions, by beating them 1-0 despite being reduced to nine men. They didn't lie down in front of England either. Platt had put England ahead midway through the first half, but 15 minutes into the second half Roger Milla, Cameroon's star player despite being 38, was brought down and Kunde converted the penalty. Four minutes later Cameroon went ahead and England seemed incapable of finding the equaliser. With nine minutes remaining, England seemed destined to experience their most embarrassing result since they were beaten by the United States in 1950.

However Cameroon gave away a foolish penalty which Gary Lineker coolly struck home, and in extra time they repeated their mistake, brought Lineker down in the penalty area again, and the Spurs striker put England into the semi-final against West Germany in Turin.

And inevitably Lineker was England's saviour again. The Germans had fortuitously taken the lead in the 59th minute when Andreas Brehme's free-kick was deflected over Peter Shilton by Paul Parker. Ten minutes from time Parker made amends by supplying the cross for Lineker to equalise and take the match into extra time.

With no more goals – although both teams hit the post – the tie was decided on penalties, as had the other semi-final the previous day. West Germany scored from their four attempts but Chris Waddle and Stuart Pearce both missed and England were eliminated 4-3.

Strangely the abiding memory of the match will probably not be those two costly misses but Gascoigne's tears. The young Spurs midfielder had already been booked earlier in the tournament and when he was booked again – for talking back to the referee after a foul – he burst into tears as he realised he would automatically miss the final.

Not that he would have missed much. West Germany's opponents were Argentina, but not the free-flowing, attack-minded Argentina of 1986 and 1978. This was a cynical and ruthless Argentina orchestrated by their captain, the fading Diego Maradona, into a team that played something that had only a passing reference to football as the world understands it.

Their progress to the final was a tactician's delight and a football purist's nightmare. They had played six games and won only two. They qualified for the second round as one of the four third-placed teams with the best records. In the quarter-finals and semi-finals, against Yugoslavia and Italy, they only won through on penalty shoot-outs. The physical side of Argentina's play deprived them of three key players for the final, Caniggia, Olarticoechea and Giusti – all ineligible because of bookings or dismissals.

The final, in Rome on July 8, summed up the whole tournament. It was a tedious bore where the Argentinians were clearly playing for the penalty shoot-out and the Germans were waiting for the Argentinians to misbehave and be penalised by the referee. West Germany's gamesmanship proved superior.

In the 68th minute Jurgen Klinsmann was routinely tackled by Monzon. However the German's theatrics were convincing enough for the Mexican referee to dismiss the Argentinian. Five minutes from time Rudi Voeller collapsed in a heap in the penalty area after a challenge from Sensini and a generous penalty was awarded which Brehme converted. It was the only goal of the game.

Ten minutes earlier Calderon had similarly been brought down in the German area, but without reward. To round off the match, and the tournament, three minutes from time Dezotti was sent off when trying to get the ball from Kohler, who was obviously time-wasting. In the ensuing bedlam Maradona was booked for dissent.

There is little doubt that the spectre of the penalty shoot-out haunted this tournament and ultimately turned it into a horror show. Fifa may argue that it is the only feasible way to break a deadlock and that the paying spectators expect to see a result. However, as the tournament unfolded it was transparent that the intention of certain teams was simply to prevent the other side scoring and gamble on the penalty decider. It is interesting to note that in the knock-out phases of the World Cups from 1954 to 1970, where there were no penalty shoot-outs, there was not a single draw in 40 matches.

Leading lights: Milla (Cameroon), Schillaci (Italy), Gascoigne (England), Klinsmann (Germany) and Maradona (Argentina)

Turning points: Lineker scores the equaliser in the semi-final and Brehme's penalty gives West Germany the World Cup

FOR THE RECORD

FIRST ROUND

GROUP A	P	W	D	L	F	A	Pts
Italy	3	3	0	0	4	0	6
Czech	3	2	0	1	6	3	4
Austria	3	1	0	2	2	3	2
United States	3	0	0	3	2	8	0

GROUP B	P	W	D	L	F	A	Pts
Cameroon	3	2	0	1	3	5	4
Romania	3	1	1	1	4	3	3
Argentina	3	1	1	1	3	2	3
Soviet Union	3	1	0	3	4	4	2

GROUP C	P	W	D	L	F	A	Pts
Brazil	3	3	0	0	4	1	6
Costa Rica	3	2	0	1	3	2	4
Scotland	3	1	0	2	2	3	2
Sweden	3	0	0	3	3	6	0

GROUP D	P	W	D	L	F	A	Pts
W Germany	3	2	1	0	10	3	5
Yugoslavia	3	2	0	1	6	5	4
Colombia	3	1	1	1	3	2	3
UA Emirates	3	0	0	3	2	11	0

GROUP E	P	W	D	L	F	A	Pts
Spain	3	2	1	0	5	2	5
Belgium	3	2	0	1	6	3	4
Uruguay	3	1	1	1	2	3	3
South Korea	3	0	0	3	1	6	0

GROUP F	P	W	D	L	F	A	Pts
England	3	1	2	0	2	1	4
R of Ireland	3	0	3	0	2	2	3
Holland	3	0	3	0	2	2	3
Egypt	3	0	2	1	1	2	2

SECOND ROUND

Cameroon 2   Colombia 1 aet
HT 0-0 Att. 50,026
Czechoslovakia 4   Costa Rica 1
HT 1-0 Att. 47,673
Argentina 1   Brazil 0
HT 0-0 Att. 61,381
West Germany 2   Holland 1
HT 0-0 Att. 74,559
Republic of Ireland 0   Romania 0
Republic of Ireland won 5-4 on
penalties Att. 31,818
Italy 2   Uruguay 0
HT 0-0 Att. 73,303
Yugoslavia 2   Spain 1 aet
HT 0-0 Att. 35,500
England 1   Belgium 0 aet
HT 0-0 Att. 34,520

QUARTER-FINALS

Argentina 0   Yugoslavia 0
Argentina won 3-2 on penalties
Att. 38,971
Italy 1   Republic of Ireland 0
HT 1-0 Att. 73,303
W Germany 1   Czechoslovakia 0
HT 1-0 Att. 73,347
England 3   Cameroon 2 aet
HT 1-0 Att. 55,205

SEMI-FINALS

Argentina 1   Italy 1
Argentina won 4-3 on penalties
HT 0-1 Att. 59,978

West Germany 1   England 1
West Germany won 4-3 on penalties
HT 0-0 Att. 62,628

THIRD PLACE PLAY-OFF

Italy 2   England 1
HT 0-0 Att. 51,426

FINAL

West Germany 1   Argentina 0
HT 0-0 Att. 73,603

Teams

West Germany Illgner, Berthold (sub: Reuter), Kohler, Augenthaler, Buchwald, Brehme, Hassler, Matthaus, Littbarski, Voller, Klinsmann

Argentina Goycochea; Ruggeri (sub: Monzon), Simon, Serrizuela, Sensini, Basualdo, Burruchaga (sub: Calderon), Troglio, Lorenzo, Maradona, Dezotti

Leading goalscorers 6 Salvatore Schillaci (Italy); 5 Tomas Skuhravy (Czechoslovakia); 4 Michel (Spain), Roger Milla (Cameroon), Gary Lineker (England), Lothar Matthaus (West Germany)

Total goals scored 115
Average per game: 2.21

Sendings-off Andre Kana Biyik (Cameroon) v Argentina.
Benjamin Massing (Cameroon) v Argentina; Referee: Michel Vautrot (France).
Eric Wynalda (United States) v Czechoslovakia; Referee: Kurt Roethlisberger (Switzerland).
Vladimir Bessonov (Soviet Union) v Argentina; Referee: Erik Fredriksson (Sweden).
Eric Gerets (Belgium) v Uruguay; Referee: Sigfried Kirschen (East Germany).
Peter Artner (Austria) v United States; Referee: Jamal Al Sharif (Syria).
Khaleel Ganim Mubarak (United Arab Emirates) v Yugoslavia; Referee: Shizuo Takada (Japan).
Yoon Deuk-yeo (South Korea) v Uruguay; Referee: Tullio Lanese (Italy).
Rudi Voller (West Germany) v Holland; Referee: Juan Carlos Loustau (Argentina).
Frank Rijkaard (Holland) v West Germany.
Ricardo Gomes (Brazil) v Argentina; Referee: Joel Quiniou (France).
Refik Sabanadzovic (Yugoslavia) v Argentina; Referee: Kurt Roethlisberger (Switzerland).
Lubomir Moravcik (Czechoslovakia) v West Germany; Referee: Helmut Kohl (Austria).
Ricardo Giusti (Argentina) v Italy; Referee: Michel Vautrot (France).
Pedro Damian Monzon (Argentina) v West Germany; Referee: Edgardo Codesal Mendaz (Mexico).
Gustavo Abel Dezotti (Argentina) v West Germany.

Number of players used by finalists
17 West Germany; 20 Argentina

● No captain has ever lifted the World Cup trophy twice. Diego Maradona skippered the 1986 winners and was captain of the 1990 runners-up. Karl-Heinz Rummenigge has led two losing teams in the finals.

Arsenal march steadily to the title despite their trials and tribulations

Faeroes from zero to hero

THERE are upsets and shocks most seasons, but then along came the sensational Faeroe Islands. The islands in the far north of the Atlantic, a semi-autonomous part of Denmark with a population of barely 50,000, were playing their first ever competitive international.

The team of fishermen and farmers had to play their home match against Austria in Sweden because the islands only had artificial pitches, which were not allowed in the qualifying stages of the European championship.

Everybody expected the part-timers to be the whipping boys of Group Four. But, on September 12, in front of a mere 1,544 spectators, they embarrassed Austria 1-0 with a goal from Nielsen in the 61st minute. Nobody could believe it, least of all the Austrian manager Josef Hickersberger, who returned home and promptly resigned.

Anybody who thought the result was a fluke only had to go to Belfast in May. Northern Ireland took the lead just before half-time but the Faeroese fought back to earn a 1-1 draw and prove that they were anything but a joke side.

In Group Seven, England looked far from convincing as they drew twice with the Republic of Ireland and only just managed to win in Turkey with a scrambled goal from Dennis Wise on his debut. So the international honours belonged to Wales, who finished the season firmly atop of group five with three wins and a draw from four matches, including a creditable 1-0 victory over West Germany in Cardiff on June 5.

Bad blood: McClair tackles Adams in the match that erupted into a 21-man brawl

ARSENAL ultimately won the League at a canter with a record-breaking performance, but their season was not without its ups and downs. And for much of the time it looked as if the downs were going to outnumber the ups.

There was a shameful start to the campaign at Old Trafford when the match on October 20 dissolved into a brawl. The only one of the 22 players on the pitch not involved in the fighting was David Seaman, and it was the second time in as many seasons that Arsenal had been involved in such disgraceful scenes.

Retribution was swift. Arsenal fined George Graham and five players two weeks' wages, the FA fined both clubs £50,000 for bringing the game into disrepute, and Arsenal were docked two points and Manchester United one.

Then Arsenal were walloped 6-2 at home by Manchester United in the League Cup. And, just before Christmas, to add to the misery at Highbury, Tony Adams was jailed for nine months, with five months suspended, for drink-driving.

In between all these distractions, Arsenal were putting together a remarkable run of form in the League. They surpassed their best ever start to the season, and were not beaten in the League until February 2,

when they lost their 24th match to Chelsea. It was the only League match they were to lose all season, a performance that has only been bettered by Preston's 22 matches without defeat to win the first ever title back in 1888-89.

The final turning point came on March 3, when Arsenal won at Anfield. With Liverpool in disarray after the sudden departure of Kenny Dalglish, the bookmakers were soon refusing to accept any more bets on Arsenal winning the title. They ended the season seven points clear, even though the two points they had deducted meant that they had not led the table until January.

Super League on the cards

FOR a few brief months it looked as if club chairmen had finally managed to reach some sort of agreement on the future of the game. In August they agreed to return to a 22-team First Division and expand the League to 94 clubs, and a deal with ITV and BSB meant that there would be 115 live matches on television.

But nothing ever changed. No sooner had the season started than the bickering resumed. As the rows rumbled on, nobody could really work out exactly what it all meant, other than, as usual, the League and the FA were at each other's throats and the clubs were fighting among themselves over money.

At the heart of the matter was the question of who should run the national game. The dispute finally boiled over in April when the FA announced plans for an 18-team Super League, to start in the 1992-93 season.

The idea was that this would help the national side by cutting the number of matches played during the season. But the FA could not even agree among itself, with some people arguing that there should still be 22 clubs in the top flight because this produced more money-spinning fixtures.

Not surprisingly, the League was aghast, and its president, Bill Fox, accused the FA of trying to hijack the First Division.

But the League was forced to admit that it was powerless to stop any breakaway, although it threatened clubs with heavy fines if they did jump ship.

Finally, in June, the League told the FA to abandon its plans or face court action. The clubs responded by formally giving notice of their intention to resign from the League, so the case duly went to court.

The League lost its case, bringing the advent of the Premier League closer. But the only thing that was really clear at the end of a season of skirmishes was that there would be still more turmoil the following season before the matter was finally resolved.

Dalglish cracks under the pressure

KENNY DALGLISH was a man of few words as a manager, and he left the rest of the country speechless as well when he announced that he was resigning as Liverpool manager.

Dalglish's decision, on February 22, seemed to be inexplicable. The player that Anfield had idolised had maintained Liverpool's great tradition, winning the Double in his first season in charge and guiding Liverpool to three League titles and two FA Cups during his six-year reign. And Liverpool were once again on top of the First Division and had just played a

pulsating 4-4 draw with Everton in the FA Cup fifth round replay.

The Liverpool board had no inkling of what was about to happen when it gathered for a routine meeting. One by one they did their best to persuade Dalglish to stay. But at the end of an emotional meeting that lasted all day he was insistent, the constant striving for success had created pressures that he could no longer bear.

Ronnie Moran was appointed caretaker manager, but he said that he did not want the job permanently. Graeme Souness was

the obvious favourite, but he said he was not interested: "I would never contemplate leaving Ibrox." John Toshack, of Real Sociedad, and George Graham, of Arsenal, also ruled themselves out.

So Liverpool tried Souness once again. This time, lured by a five-year contract worth £350,000 a year, he agreed to join Liverpool on April 16. The Kop were delighted and Rangers were unhappy at losing their leading light. David Murray, their chairman, said: "I think he is making the biggest mistake of his life."

Liverpool stunned: a grim-faced Dalglish announces his resignation

Souness: lured back

If he has resigned because of the pressures, the rest of us have no chance

HOWARD WILKINSON

249

THE
1990-91
SEASON

Maradona the most hated man in Italy

Maradona: disgraced exile

DIEGO MARADONA's stormy spell in Italy ended in disgrace when he fled the country in the wake of a drugs and sex scandal.

The Napoli forward's antics had already so alienated his club's supporters, and the rest of the country, that he was voted the most hated man in Italy. In the poll in December the Argentinian received a worse rating than even Saddam Hussein.

Maradona's response was to threaten to quit if his club did not allow him to leave at the end of the season. In the end, though, matters came to a head when Maradona was linked with a vice ring and then tested positive for cocaine after a League match.

Facing suspension by the Italian FA, and the prospect of being sent to jail, Maradona decided that he had overstayed his welcome and returned to Argentina on April 2.

250

Rangers snatch League in an ultimate High Noon shoot-out

WALTER SMITH was a very relieved man on May 11, the very last day of the season. And extremely grateful to his English centre forward Mark Hateley. His two goals at Ibrox saw off Aberdeen's late dash for the title and confirmed Rangers as champions. The finale was as extraordinary as Arsenal's triumph in the English League two years earlier when they snatched the championship from Kenny Dalglish's Liverpool.

Coincidentally it was Dalglish who accidentally put Smith in the most awkward of situations, having to beat the League leaders in the last match for the title. It was Dalglish's shock resignation at Liverpool in February that led to Graeme Souness's own shock resignation from Rangers on April 16 to take over the helm at Anfield. Rangers had only four League matches remaining.

At Christmas Rangers had looked certain League champions. But a bad spell from the end of February to the beginning of April – when they won only two games in six – had seen Aberdeen creep up on them.

Then a 3-0 defeat at Motherwell in the penultimate game saw them lose pole position for the first time since December, and by the narrowest of margins. Aberdeen and Rangers were level on points and level on goal difference. However, the north-east club got the nod by virtue of having scored two more goals!

The deciding match was billed as a High Noon shoot-out and was an exciting affair as Rangers pulled out all the stops in front of their anxious fans. Hateley's double strike rewarded them as Aberdeen went down 2-0.

The Scottish Cup final a week later also proved to be a thrilling affair. Motherwell had rocked everybody by knocking out Aberdeen away and then disposing of Celtic in a replay having twice been behind. Dundee United, their opponents, had had a much easier run although they only scraped past East Fife when a late goal in extra time earned them a replay. And then they won that in extra time.

The drama of the earlier rounds was relived at Hampden Park. Motherwell went ahead against the run of play in the first half, but by full-time the sides were level at 3-3. Then just as it looked as if the final would go to a replay up popped Kirk in the final minute to give Motherwell their first Scottish Cup since 1952.

Finishing touch: Hateley's two goals gave Rangers the title

Smith: baptism of fire

We're back with a bang as Hughes and United proudly conquer Europe

Captain fantastic: Bryan Robson led United to victory in Rotterdam

MANCHESTER UNITED made it a triumphant return for English clubs to European competition when they beat mighty Barcelona in Rotterdam 2-1 to lift the European Cup Winners Cup. It was also a night of delicious ironies. Mark Hughes, who had been deemed a failure at Barcelona, scored both United's goals. Alex Ferguson, the manager who had brought him back to Old Trafford three years earlier, also equalled Johan Cruyff's record of winning the competition with different clubs. Ferguson's Aberdeen had taken the trophy in 1983, beating Real Madrid in the final.

United had rocked Barcelona back on their heels from the kick-off by mounting attack after attack. By the 68th minute the Catalan defence seemed shell-shocked and when Steve Bruce headed a Bryan Robson free kick goalwards, Hughes had a simple tap-in.

Six minutes later the Welsh international was on target again when he escaped his marker, went wide of Busquets, the goalkeeper, and thumped the ball past him from the tightest of angles.

In the 80th minute a Ronald Koeman speciality, from a free kick, reduced the arrears, but despite a nervous 10 minutes United clung on to win their second European trophy.

Woeful Worthing walloped

FEBRUARY was not a good month for Worthing. Already struggling in the Vauxhall League First Division they conceded 23 goals in less than a week, going down 10-0 at Whyteleafe in the League and losing 13-0 at Carshalton in the Loctite Cup.

Their manager, Joe Boon, was remarkably philosophical, saying: "The defeat at Carshalton was not as bad as it sounds. But we gave away five bad goals."

His chairman, John Mayer, was also resigned to the club's fate. "We have spent all our money on improving our ground, and there's nothing left to pay the players. Our sponsors have pulled out, and we get gates of only 150," he said.

Not surprisingly, the club finished rock bottom of the Division, 23 points adrift with only two wins and four draws from 42 matches and a goal difference of minus 129, having conceded 157.

Familiar territory: the Worthing goalkeeper is beaten yet again

251

THE
1990-91
SEASON

Derby trigger mad transfer merry-go-round

THE END of the season brought a frenzy of activity in the transfer market, with a series of spectacular sales during the summer.

Derby, who were desperate to reduce their wage bill after being relegated to the Second Division, set the ball rolling when they sold Mark Wright and Dean Saunders to Liverpool in quick succession in July. Wright moved for £2.2m on July 12 and Saunders followed him two days later for a British record £2.9m. Graeme Souness was obviously determined to rebuild his team as he quickly sold Peter Beardsley to Everton for £1m and Steve Staunton to Aston Villa for £1.1m, and used some of the money to bring Mark Walters to Anfield from Rangers for £1.25m.

In between times, Nottingham Forest bought Teddy Sheringham for £2m; Celtic signed Paul Elliott for £1.4m and Tony Cascarino for £1.1m; Manchester United signed Paul Parker for £2m; Manchester City spent £2.5m for Keith Curle and collected £1.3m for Mark Ward; and transfer tribunals ordered Leeds to pay £1.6m for Rod Wallace and £1.3m for Tony Dorigo.

But all of these deals were eclipsed by Aston Villa. Having spent £1.6m to bring Dalian Atkinson back from Spain they recouped all the money and plenty more as well with the sale of David Platt to Bari. The British record was raised even higher by the £5.5m price tag and it seemed that for a few heady weeks that money was no object in the multi-million pound pursuit of success.

Platt: British record

Superstition works for Spurs

WITH the very existence of the club in doubt throughout the season, Tottenham experienced drama and crisis on the pitch as well. Driven by superstition – the year ended in a '1' when Tottenham historically had won the FA Cup – and the desperate financial mess they were in, Spurs put together a successful Cup run that bordered on pure fiction.

Paul Gascoigne, pure genius and childish scoundrel, was the lead character. Going into the semi-final he had scored five crucial goals and against Portsmouth and Notts County had virtually single-handedly retrieved victory from certain defeat. Then, on Sunday April 14, Tottenham faced Arsenal in first semi-final to be held at Wembley. With millions watching around the globe, Gascoigne had a ready-made world stage on which to make his mark.

And in the fifth minute Gascoigne demonstrated why Lazio were prepared to pay £8.5m for him when he took one of most audacious free kicks ever seen. From fully 35 yards out Gascoigne thundered a dipping, swerving shot that flew past the Arsenal wall and evaded the groping fingers of David Seaman.

Then, six minutes later, he combined with Paul Allen on the right wing with a breathtaking exchange of passes that caught the Arsenal defence at

Daft as a brush: Gascoigne self-destructs in the Cup final

sixes and sevens. Allen's cross was met by Gary Lineker's toe. The match was effectively over. Arsenal pulled one back in the second half, but Lineker restored the two-goal lead when he ran at the Arsenal defence, Tony Adams lost him, and Seaman, uncharacteristically, failed to halt the danger.

Although Gascoigne was only half-fit – he had had a stomach operation a month earlier – and he only played for an hour, he was the winning inspiration for Spurs. He chased everything, harried and injected the vital urgency that lifted Spurs past their north London rivals, whose hopes of the Double were now dashed.

In the final, on May 18 against Nottingham Forest, Gascoigne again made his mark – but this time as the villain, not the hero. From the kick-off he had played like a maniac. He had badly fouled Gary Parker in the opening minutes and was fortunate not to be booked.

In the 15th minute he committed an horrendous scything tackle on Gary Charles just outside the Spurs penalty area. Gascoigne was left writhing in agony and had to be taken off with an injured knee. Once again he was fortunate not to receive harsher punishment from the referee.

But his team were punished. From the resultant free-kick Stuart Pearce shot through the

Tottenham wall to take the lead. Television evidence showed that the gap had been created by Forest's Lee Glover pushing Gary Mabbutt aside, but the goal stood.

Tottenham's misfortunes continued as the match went on: Lineker had a goal disallowed for offside that TV proved was legitimate; he then missed a penalty having been brought down in the area by Mark Crossley, the Forest keeper, who was neither cautioned nor sent off.

However, Paul Stewart rectified things with a well-taken equaliser in the 55th minute and the final drifted into extra time. Bizarrely, Brian Clough, who had never won the FA Cup, did not come on to the pitch to advise, exhort or comfort his young players. Instead he chatted to a policeman. By contrast, Terry Venables was visibly encouraging and counselling his team in the centre of the pitch.

Inevitably, this day of craziness continued to the end. The unfortunate Des Walker headed into his own net attempting to clear a flicked-on corner and handed Spurs their eighth FA Cup, a record. Much had been at stake, and although Gascoigne's injury threw into doubt his lucrative transfer to Italy, Spurs could now look forward to a Charity Shield appearance and a European campaign. It was news that would please their creditors.

Tottenham's nightmare ended by dream ticket

AFTER a year of uncertainty, Tottenham were finally rescued on June 22 when Terry Venables, the manager, and Alan Sugar, the Amstrad giant, formally took over the club for £7.2m. They were called the Dream Ticket and it appeared the nightmare of Tottenham FC, which had debts of some £20m, going out of existence was finally over.

The nightmare had started in September when it was revealed that Irving Scholar, the then chairman, had conducted secret negotiations with Robert Maxwell, the newspaper tycoon, to take over ailing Spurs. The debt was put at £12m.

Scholar had agreed with Maxwell that he would put £13.2m into the club. Worse, Scholar had borrowed £850,000 from Maxwell to make the final payment to Barcelona for the transfer of Gary Lineker, and he had not informed the rest of the Spurs board about his negotiations.

These extraordinary goings-on forced the Stock Exchange to investigate Spurs as they were a publicly quoted company. Six weeks after they began their scrutiny, the Exchange suspended all dealings in Tottenham's shares and Scholar was forced to resign as chairman.

Just before Christmas it was revealed that Venables was attempting to put together a consortium to take over the club, but finding suitable backers was proving difficult. As the months wore on there were rumours and counter rumours about the future of the club.

In March Lazio of Rome confirmed they had offered £8.5m for Paul Gascoigne and it appeared that, given their financial straits, Tottenham would have to bow to the inevitable.

Throughout the season Maxwell's interest in Spurs waxed and waned, but just as the Dream Ticket seemed set to clinch the deal he made a last-minute bid that almost came off. However Scholar, the majority shareholder, was persuaded by Sugar and Venables to sell to them and the predatory Maxwell was seen off.

It was an historic moment: successful businessman and successful manager in partnership at a leading football club. Their first task was to clear the debt and balance the books. Sugar warned the relieved fans that it would be some time before Tottenham ventured into the transfer market as a buyer.

Forced out: Irving Scholar's secret talks precipitated the crisis

Dynamic duo: Terry Venables and Alan Sugar snatched control of Tottenham from under the nose of Robert Maxwell

PAUL GASCOIGNE
The naughty boy
who has never grown up

Louise Taylor

PAUL GASCOIGNE

Born May 27, 1967, Gateshead
PLAYING CAREER
Newcastle United 1984-88
92 League appearances (9 as a substitute),
  21 goals
Tottenham Hotspur 1988-92
91 appearances (1 as substitute)
19 goals in the League, 8 in the League Cup,
  6 in the FA Cup
Honours FA Cup: Winners 1991
Lazio 1992–1995
Rangers 1995–
Internationals England debut June 1989 v
  Denmark in Copenhagen (as a substitute)
Honours World Cup: Semi-final 1990

PAUL GASCOIGNE is England's troubled talent. If he plays well everybody rejoices, if he reaches for the self-destruct button the country is concerned. And with good reason, for Gascoigne rarely does things by halves.

On song in Lazio's or England's midfield, he challenges critics to describe him as anything other than the greatest British footballing talent of his generation. But they know that nobody is more capable of blowing – and really blowing – golden opportunities than Gascoigne.

After treating Tottenham fans to a virtuoso performance in the 1991 FA Cup semi-final against Arsenal – who could forget his glorious 35-yard goal from a right-footed free kick – the Wembley stage seemed set for a splendid swan-song in the final against Nottingham Forest. A new life in Rome with Lazio beckoned, but two lunatic tackles in the first half put it very much on hold.

The second reckless lunge, at Gary Charles, left Gascoigne facing complicated cruciate ligament surgery on his right knee. The best prognosis was a year out of football, and everybody knew his suffering was totally self-inflicted.

Five months on, the convalescent, still wanted by Lazio, was enjoying some play time on his native Tyneside. He watched his former Newcastle teammates take on Derby from the packed St James's Park terraces. His knee survived the madcap jostling at the Gallowgate end, but emergency surgery was needed after an incident in a nightclub well after chucking-out time in the nearby pubs. Once again, Gascoigne had taken one risk too many.

As he did in a training session in April 1994, when he broke his right leg in two places with a reckless tackle. Once again, Gascoigne's mercurial career was put on hold. Lazio had welcomed their great Geordie hope in the summer of 1992. Whether through arrogance, ignorance or nonchalance, Gascoigne arrived embarrassingly overweight and unfit. The Italians were insulted, just like the television reporter whose microphone he would belch into and the physiotherapist whose treatment table he would urinate upon. Then there were the photographers he punched.

Soon, Lazio would be irritated and exasperated by Gascoigne's turbulent relationship with his on-off girlfriend Sheryl Kyle, a glamourous divorcee and a mother of two. Trust Gascoigne to fall for a woman to whom he is physically attracted to the point of obsession but whose dislike of football and jealousy provokes frequent rows of soap-opera scale. No sooner did they kiss and make up than it all seemingly ended in tears again.

Talking of tears, Gascoigne became a cult figure, an icon even, when he started crying after being booked during England's match against Germany in the semi-finals of the 1990 World Cup. The country sobbed with him, devastated that the discovery of the tournament would be suspended for the final.

In the event, England lost on penalties and the referee, Jose Wright, confirmed that the caution that made the tears flow was as much for backchat as a foul on Thomas Berthold. When you are one yellow card away from missing the World Cup final, winding-up the referee represents self-destruction written in 6ft-high capitals.

Even so, Gascoigne's performances against Holland and Belgium had been world class. He had done much to redeem Bobby Robson's bruised reputation as the England manager. It was all a long way from 1982 when a puppy-fat padded 15-year-old had been rejected by Robson after a trial with Ipswich. Later, Robson would recognise "Paul's flair, imagination and spontaneity".

A year and two CSEs (grade four English and environmental studies) after his trial at Ipswich, Gascoigne signed for Newcastle. It was every Dunston boy's dream come true.

But not Colin Suggett's. The Newcastle coach at the time recalls a hyperactive, impossibly cheeky, overweight teenager who compulsively guzzled Mars bars and McDonalds. The "alcoholic refuelling" would come later – in those days Gascoigne was flat on his back after three shandies.

Suggett advised Jack Charlton to release this disruptive influence. But Gascoigne charmed the manager out of it before bewitching St James's Park with his body swerves, free kicks and radar passing. Few players possessed half as many tricks.

Perhaps part of Gascoigne's problem is the extraordinary ease with which he mastered the

Over the top: Gascoigne's reckless challenge at Wembley almost ended his career

England expects: Gascoigne, so often a match winner, leads an attack against Turkey

Heartbreak: the 1990 World Cup semi-final

game. Perhaps it explained his compulsion to flirt with danger – as on the day he arrived at Lazio's training ground doing 80mph on a motorbike and not wearing a helmet.

Gascoigne's capacity to disarm would see him putting an arm around Margaret Thatcher and getting his next England manager, Graham Taylor, drunk on brandy. Taylor, like most managers to cross Gascoigne's path, frequently had his patience pushed to the limit. Stories of the prodigy's penchant for binges and puerile pranks with Jimmy "Five Bellies" Gardner and his other Geordie muckers abound.

But the bottom line for managers is that matches must be won and Gascoigne is a match winner. As Glenn Roeder, the Watford manager and a friend of Gascoigne's put it: "Paul's only Achilles heel is pace. He has perfect balance, vision, a football brain, awareness of what is going on around him, a fantastic first touch, and dribbling and shooting skills."

Most footballers are lucky to have one or two such gifts. And Gascoigne is also sufficiently muscular and sufficiently mean to look after himself. But if Gascoigne is a man on the pitch he all too often reverts to childhood off it.

Until his involvement with Kyle, he could not sleep unless the lights and the television were left on. Added to an apparent inability to be alone, this indicates incredible insecurity. Perhaps the brain haemorrhage his father suffered when Gascoigne was 11, or the trauma of seeing Steven Spraggon, his best friend's brother, killed by a car when he was 12 explains this.

In some respects Gascoigne can still behave like a 12-year-old. He relishes cutting the toes off teammates socks and makes cappuccino coffees with shaving foam. Personally chaotic, he frequently forgets his passport and admits to not knowing how much his bank account contains. It is a brand of unworldliness reserved for pop stars and top footballers.

Like so many gifted men, Gascoigne constantly demands reassurance. Terry Venables, the manager who brought him to Tottenham, appreciates this. "I used to talk to Paul on a friendly basis, to let him know I was thinking of him. He is the type of guy who needs to know you are concerned about him.

"You have to find the root of his problems. He may have come to me with a sore thumb and asked why he was feeling bad. The real reason wouldn't be the sore thumb. I always tried to get behind the superficial problems."

Some people say that Venables was too soft on Gascoigne at Tottenham. But, so far, he is the one person to have man-managed Gascoigne with any degree of success. The installation of his old mentor as the England manager could well be one of the best things to have happened to Gascoigne. As could his surprise transfer to Glasgow Rangers for £5m.

Although adored by Lazio fans, Gascoigne had a fits-and-starts career with the Roman club and his antics did not endear him to its management. His return to Britain was inevitable but the choice of club came as a shock. The chance to play in the European Cup and the proximity of his family in Newcastle certainly made up his mind.

Italian adventure: Gascoigne has been through turbulent times while playing for Lazio

Birmingham fans run riot

St Andrews witnessed the worst disturbances seen at an English football match for several years when the Third Division match between Birmingham and Stoke on February 29 was halted by a pitch invasion.

The incident was sparked by Stoke scoring a late and controversial equaliser. When Birmingham then had a shot cleared off the line hundreds of their fans swarmed on to the pitch, and one of them attacked the referee, Roger Wiseman.

Samesh Kumar, the Birmingham chairman, appealed to the fans to calm down and when he was ignored it was announced that the match would not continue. But, 20 minutes later, when police had cleared the ground, the remaining 35 seconds of the game were played.

Terry Cooper, the Birmingham manager, was horrified by the events and threatened to quit. He said: "I have to ask: 'Do you really want to be a manager of a club like this?' I don't know what the FA will do. If they dock points that's a season down the drain."

Birmingham's cause was hardly helped by Kumar, who said that one the reasons for the disturbance was "some scandalous decisions" made by Wiseman. That outburst led to him being charged with misconduct by the FA. The club were fined £50,000 and ordered to play two matches behind closed doors.

Wiseman, too, had had enough. Three weeks after the match he withdrew from the list of referees, citing the mental stress that he was under as the reason.

Careless United hand Leeds the championship on a plate

The Manchester United faithful had waited 25 years for their eighth League championship and throughout the season they were always the clear favourites to lift the title. Then in one fateful spell over Easter they hit relegation form, not championship form, when they only won four out of their last 14 League matches and handed the title to Leeds, who had dogged them throughout the campaign.

Not that Leeds were unworthy champions; after all, they were unbeaten at home and only lost four League matches. Howard Wilkinson had built a resilient side, which with the flair of Gordon Strachan – ironically a Manchester United cast-off – and in the last third of the season Eric Cantona, the French international, were virtually impossible to contain.

United had got off to a flying start, unbeaten in their first 12 League matches, but Leeds would never lie down, and were United's nemesis all season. The two sides built up a huge lead over the chasing pack and then seemed to be constantly swapping top place each week.

Their intertwining reached comic levels in January when they were drawn against each other in both Cups and had to play a League match as well. These three fixtures were scheduled over 11 days and billed as "The Battle of the Titans". United won both Cup games (and went on to win the League Cup) but in hindsight probably did their chief rivals a favour.

In football parlance, they left Leeds no choice but to concentrate on the League.

Which they did and United didn't. On April 16, Manchester United were on top of the table, two points clear of Leeds with a game in hand. Then on April 18 they drew with lowly Luton and over the next nine days their title aspirations turned into dust.

They lost 2-1 to Nottingham Forest at home, squandered their game in hand by falling 1-0

Turning the tables: Strachan masterminded Leeds's late charge to the title

In the bag: Leeds celebrate their first championship since 1974

to relegated West Ham and then lost 2-0 at Anfield on April 26. On the same day Leeds won 3-2 at Sheffield United by virtue of an own goal by Brian Gayle. A week before the end of the season, the impossible had happened: the championship had not gone to Old Trafford, but returned to Elland Road for the first time since 1974 and the days of Don Revie.

Dalglish is Blackburn's star turn

BLACKBURN ROVERS pulled off a spectacular coup when, barely an hour before their match against Plymouth on October 12, they announced that Kenny Dalglish was their new manager.

Dalglish had been lured out of retirement by Jack Walker, a lifelong Blackburn fan who had spent millions of pounds of his personal fortune on the club. The former Liverpool manager said: "Obviously, seven months ago football was not the most important thing in my life. I'd had enough and needed to recharge my batteries. But the time is right to come back. People will ask why I should have come to Blackburn, but they've impressed me as a club with ambitions to get into the Premier League."

Walker wanted nothing but the best for his beloved club, and for him money was no object. Dalglish was given a three-year contract worth £1m and told he had at least £10m immediately available to strengthen the team.

The club was immediately revitalised and from January to mid-March topped the Second Division. But then a disastrous

New broom: Dalglish swept Blackburn into the Premier League

run of six defeats looked as if it would end Walker's dream of Premier League football for the moment. They only just made the play-offs, where they squeezed past Derby 5-4 on aggregate to face Leicester in the decider at Wembley. There, Mike Newell's penalty put them back in the top flight for the first time since 1966.

Dalglish wasted no time in putting Walker's money to work, and in July he broke the British transfer record when he bought Alan Shearer from Southampton for £3.6m. That brought Dalglish's spending to more than £6m and made it perfectly clear he was determined that Blackburn were going to be among the country's best.

Premier League feud ends in peace

THE long-running battle over the Premier League finally came to an end, but not before everybody involved had spent yet another season in interminable wrangling.

The season did not start well, with the Football League in total disarray over what to do. Any hope of there being any constructive debate was soon dashed when clubs threatened to isolate the Premier League and Sir Bert Millichip, the FA chairman, responded by threatening to suspend the entire League. And the players said they would consider a strike if they did not get a big enough say in how the game was run.

The fateful decision to go ahead with the Premier League was finally taken by the FA

Council on February 20. That should have been the end of the matter but the PFA revived their strike threat.

So the arguments dragged on until the end of April, when the PFA won a 50% increase to £1.5m in the share of the money they received from television. That, finally, should have been the end of the matter.

But television and money added a further twist to the tale. On May 18 the FA announced a record-breaking deal with the BBC and Sky, worth £304m over five years. Sky would show 60 live matches a season on Sundays and Mondays, and the BBC would show highlights on Saturdays and during the week. However, ITV, complaining about the way deal had been done,

went to court and it was a further month before the dispute was settled.

Amazingly, at the end of all the in-fighting, very little appeared to have really changed. The First Division would become the Premier League, with 22 clubs due to reduce to 20 by 1995. The Second, Third and Fourth Divisions thus confusingly became the First, Second and Third Divisions.

There would be other cosmetic changes: the Premier League would allow a third substitute on the bench, and half-time would be extended to 15 minutes. The only thing that did seem to be different was the colour of the shirts the referees would wear: green in the Premier League and purple elsewhere.

The magic touches of Hateley and McCoist do the trick for Rangers

RANGERS eventually swept all before them, winning the Scottish Cup and the championship by nine points. But halfway through the season things did not look so clear cut.

In September Rangers had lost the semi-final of the League Cup 1-0 to Hibs – who went on to win their first trophy for 19 years – and were trailing to Hearts in the League. However, it proved to be just another sluggish start for the Ibrox club. From November 30 to the end of the season Rangers strung together a fabulous run, winning 20 of 24 League matches and only losing once.

Their large squad of international players was an obvious advantage, but the prolific scoring of Mark Hateley and Ally McCoist made Rangers virtually unbeatable. Between them they notched up a breathtaking 54 League goals, McCoist becoming the first Scot to win Europe's prestigious Golden Boot. And in July Rangers had another boost when Trevor Steven returned from Marseille for £2.4m. He had joined the French club only the previous August for a fee of £5m, a Scottish record.

By contrast, Celtic had a terrible season. They were knocked out of the League Cup on penalties by Airdrie, of all people, and beaten 1-0 in the semi-final of the Scottish Cup by Rangers, who were down to 10 men.

Then, in the last match of the season, Celtic needed only to draw with Hibs to finish runners-up and so qualify for the Uefa Cup ahead of Hearts. They lost 2-1, their first defeat in 17 League matches, and Hearts beat Falkirk 2-0 to snatch second place by one point. The gods did smile on Celtic in the end though: because of the expansion of the number of countries wishing to enter the competition Uefa granted Scotland an extra place and Celtic were reprieved.

Midas touch: McCoist was the first Scot to win the Golden Boot

Souness bungles publicity after heart surgery

GRAEME SOUNESS had always been the epitome of a professional – never smoking, hardly drinking, and keeping himself fit. So, hours after they had drawn with Portsmouth in the FA Cup semi-final on April 6, the Liverpool team were stunned when they were told that their 39-year-old manager had been taken to hospital because he needed an immediate triple heart bypass operation.

While he was recuperating, his judgment, for once, deserted him. Souness allowed the Sun to take pictures of him kissing his girlfriend as he recovered in hospital. Tactlessly, the photographs were published on the same day as a memorial service for the fans who had died at Hillsborough.

The people of Liverpool had never forgiven the Sun for its tasteless reporting of the tragedy, and were furious that Souness had dealt with the very paper that was still hated on Merseyside. There were continued calls for Souness to be sacked.

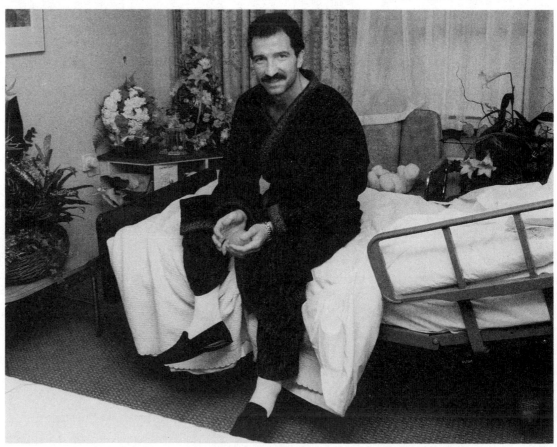

On the way back: Souness recovers in hospital after a successful triple heart bypass operation

Brilliant McManaman's switch puts Sunderland's lights out

THE DAY before the FA Cup final Graeme Souness defied the doctors and left hospital after his heart operation. It was just the fillip Liverpool needed.

Souness received a stirring welcome at Wembley, but Ronnie Moran, his assistant, was still in charge of the team to play Sunderland. And the massed fans from Wearside sensed that they might be able to pull off another famous upset.

Second Division Sunderland had already collected three First Division scalps: West Ham, Chelsea and Norwich in the semi-final. And Liverpool had looked far from convincing in the competition. They were taken to replays by Bristol Rovers and Ipswich and only just scraped past Portsmouth in the semi-final, which went to a penalty shoot-out.

The introduction of a shoot-out if the replay finished level had already accounted for several other clubs. Manchester United became the first First Division team to be eliminated this way when they went out to Southampton in the fourth round.

Sunderland harried Liverpool right from the kick-off, preventing them from getting fully into their stride, and deserved to be level at half-time. Both teams missed good chances, and Liverpool claimed that they should have been awarded a penalty just before the interval.

It was then that Moran made the switch that was to transform the match. Steve McManaman had only come into the side the day before, when John Barnes failed a fitness test, and at half-time Moran switched him from the left flank to the right.

Within two minutes of the restart he had burst down the right touchline, withstood a push in the back from a defender and lifted the ball into the penalty area. Michael Thomas waited for the ball to bounce and then unhesitatingly unleashed a brilliant volley. Tony Norman stood no chance of stopping the shot and Liverpool were ahead.

With McManaman continuing his incisive runs Liverpool soon settled into their smooth passing game. Thomas was the provider of the second goal, whipped in by Rush in the 67th minute, and Moran finally allowed himself a jig of delight on the touchline.

However, his greatest day ended on an odd note. It had been decided that tradition would be overturned and the losers would go up to the royal box first. Somebody, though, forgot to put the medals in the right order. So when a dejected Sunderland team trooped up the steps they were presented with the winners medals and they had to swap them afterwards with Liverpool, who were given the losers medals.

McManaman: the inspiration

Hail the conquering hero: Rush scores Liverpool's second goal at Wembley

Lineker goes to spread the word in Japan

BLACKBURN were not the only club prepared to spend big money in the pursuit of success. And perhaps the least expected move came in November when Grampus Eight, of the burgeoning Japanese League, signed Gary Lineker. The deal meant that Lineker would leave Tottenham at the end of the season, but it was not a happy time for him. His baby son was taken ill and diagnosed as having a rare form of leukaemia.

Lineker's teammate Paul Gascoigne was also back in hospital, but his suffering was all of his own making. Gascoigne was involved in a fracas in a Newcastle nightclub and damaged his knee again, putting back his recovery by several months and casting another cloud over his move to Lazio.

But it was not all doom and gloom at White Hart Lane. The club were able to announce that their debts had been cut from £21m to £5m and their finances were back under control, clearing the way for their shares to be re-listed on the Stock Exchange.

Lineker: learning Japanese

Taylor hits rock bottom in England's European fiasco

European misadventures: Taylor and McMenemy did not like their trip to Sweden

THE European championships saw Graham Taylor's career as the England manager hit rock bottom. Despite struggling to qualify, England had travelled to Sweden with confidence; they were in the weaker of the two groups and their captain Gary Lineker, with 48 international goals, seemed certain to equal and surpass Bobby Charlton's record of 49.

Three matches later, England had drawn two, lost one, Lineker had not scored a single goal and, to rub salt in the wound, had been substituted 29 minutes from the end of the final match against Sweden which England had to win to qualify for the semi-finals.

Bafflingly, Taylor had chosen to end Lineker's international career – he had announced he would retire after the championships – in a most humiliating way. Worse, Taylor's gamble failed as Sweden won 2-1 to leave England at the bottom of their group.

If it had not been for Lineker England would not have been there in the first place. A series of indifferent performances against the Republic of Ireland and Turkey in the qualifying group had meant that England needed a point against Poland in Poznan on November 13 if they were to pip Jack Charlton's Irish team for the trip to Sweden.

With 15 minutes remaining England were trailing to a first-half 40-yard goal from Szewczyk that had been deflected by Gary Mabbutt. Then Lineker won a corner from which he conjured an amazing volley to snatch a precious equaliser.

England were not alone in their misery. Italy and Spain had failed to qualify and war-torn Yugoslavia were excluded in line with UN sanctions over human rights. Denmark replaced them at 11 days notice, and proved to be the revelation of the tournament. In their first match – against England – the Danes achieved a creditable 0-0 draw, and might even have won.

Strangely, the usual European superpowers, France, Holland and Germany, all came unstuck as the tournament unfolded. Germany were extremely fortunate to reach the semi-finals. They beat Scotland 2-0 despite being outplayed, and then the Scots did them a huge favour by beating CIS 3-0.

France were as dismal as England, failing to win a single match. Holland, who had won their group convincingly, were Denmark's opponents in the semi-finals. The Dutch, twice behind, rallied to snatch a 2-2 draw. But, after a goalless 30 minutes of extra time, stuttered in the penalty shoot-out. Peter Schmeichel saved Holland's second kick, from Marco van Basten, and when nobody else missed, put Denmark into the final against Germany, the world champions.

Nobody really gave the Danes a chance; after all, they were only the substitutes for Yugoslavia and they had been hit by injuries. But in the 18th minute John Jensen stunned the Germans by taking the lead. Despite German pressure the Danes played a cool game of defence and counter attack and achieved the seemingly impossible when Kim Vilfort scored from a Christiansen header 12 minutes from time. Denmark, 2-0 victors over Germany, and European champions? As Schmeichel said: "We still don't understand what we have done."

Keegan just staves off relegation after Newcastle kick Ardiles out

OSSIE ARDILES should have known better than to listen to his chairman. It always seems that managers of struggling clubs get the sack just after being told that their job is safe.

And there was no doubt that Newcastle were struggling. By the start of February they were 23rd in the Second Division. Ardiles, who had been brought to the club to return them to the big time, was under increasing pressure as Newcastle faced up to the prospect of going down to the Third Division for the first time in their history.

But on February 2, Sir John Hall, the Newcastle chairman, was unequivocal: "Let's kill off once and for all the rumours that his job is on the line. If he leaves it will be of his own volition."

Three days later Ardiles was sacked and replaced by Kevin Keegan. Hall insisted that he had meant every word of what he had said and everybody assumed that the decision to sack Ardiles had been forced on the club by their backers, Newcastle Breweries.

Keegan won his first match in charge, 3-0 against fellow strugglers Bristol City. But it was not long before it looked like things were going to turn sour for the former Newcastle idol as well.

After Newcastle's victory over Swindon on March 14, Keegan rushed from the ground and headed for Heathrow, prompting speculation that he had resigned. Hall promptly announced that he was putting up £1/2m of his own money to buy players to strengthen the debt-laden team. All Keegan would say, cryptically, about his relationship with the club was: "I don't understand it. It's not like it said in the brochure."

It looked as if Keegan's arrival and Hall's money were too little to late, particularly when Newcastle were thrashed 6-2 at Wolverhampton. With

Keegan: great escape

two matches to go Newcastle were still in line for relegation but then successive victories over Portsmouth and Leicester enabled them to beat the drop. Hall, who by now had taken con-

- Peter Shilton left Derby to become player-manager at Plymouth on March 2.

- Aldershot, who had struggled to stay afloat all season, finally went out of business on March 25.

- Chris Waddle returned to England when he moved from Marseille to Sheffield Wednesday for £1m in June.

- The world record transfer fee was raised to £11.5m when AC Milan bought the Yugoslav midfield player Dejan Savicevic from Atletico Madrid. It was further increased to £13m when Gianluigi Lentini moved from Torino to AC Milan on July 1.

- South Africa were unanimously re-elected to Fifa on July 3 after 18 years in the wilderness.

- Coca-Cola took over as sponsors of the League Cup, signing a £2.25m two-year deal in July.

- Daniel Yorath, the son of the Wales manager, died suddenly just before he was due to start an apprenticeship with Leeds.

trol of the club was satisfied and Keegan was rewarded with a three-year contract.

About face: three days after being reassured that his job was safe Ardiles was summarily sacked by Newcastle

*Something special
has gone out of every
footballer's life*

DAVID PLATT

Moore: the epitome of fair play

Happier days: Moore at the height of his career with the World Cup trophy at Wembley in 1966

ON FEBRUARY 24 English football lost one of its greatest players and important role models when, at the age of 51, Bobby Moore OBE passed away, nine days after announcing that he was suffering from cancer.

Immediately the tributes poured in – from all over the world. For, although Moore would be best remembered for captaining England to the World Cup in 1966, he was also a wonderful ambassador for the game and represented all that was sporting and fair.

As a defender he was scrupulously clean, but brilliantly effective. His ability to read a move and intercept the ball was breathtaking; to an attacker it was as if you had had your pocket picked without knowing how or why.

Pele said of him: "Moore was my friend, the finest, the most honourable defender I ever played against." The duel between the two in the 1970 World Cup finals was one of the finest examples of physical and cerebral chess ever seen on a field.

Moore spent the bulk of his club career at West Ham (544 appearances) before transferring to Fulham (124) in 1974. At West Ham, despite perennial struggles against relegation, he helped mastermind the East End club to the first trophies in their history, the FA Cup in 1964 and the European Cup Winners' Cup in 1965, coincidentally both at Wembley. Fate of course decreed that a year later he would climb the same 39

The tributes poured: "He will never grow old in people's minds" — Ken Bates

steps to lift yet another trophy, this time the ultimate prize, the World Cup.

Moore's death stunned the nation and reminded them of the past and what was lost. As Ken Bates, the Chelsea chairman, said: "He will never grow old in people's minds, in the same way that President Kennedy won't. Camelot has always seemed real because we remember Kennedy as a young man and it's going to be the same with Bobby Moore."

England repeatedly shoot themselves in the foot

THE WRITING was on the wall for Graham Taylor and England's hopes of qualifying for the 1994 World Cup after a series of embarrassing results.

In October, at Wembley, England dropped a precious point to Norway, who had established themselves as the front-runners in group two by thrashing San Marino 10-0, when they allowed Rekdal to equalise Platt's 55th minute goal with 14 minutes left.

Then, despite two encouraging results (a 4-0 roasting of Turkey and a 6-0 annihilation of San Marino) in April England let slip a two-goal lead, once again at Wembley, against Holland for another draw. Holland's equaliser came from the spot five minutes from time after Des Walker had foolishly given away a penalty.

But worse was to come. In Chorzow, in May, only Ian Wright's 84th-minute equaliser saved England from a potentially lethal defeat by Poland.

Taylor blamed the players and said they were "running around like headless chickens".

Four days later in Oslo, Taylor made four changes and a wholesale tactical switch only to be humiliated 2-0 by Norway. In fact, the scoreline flattered England as they played utterly inept football. There were widespread calls for Taylor's head as English football seemed to have reached its nadir.

It hadn't. On June 9, in Boston, it reached rock bottom.

Famous in Anglo-American history for the Tea Party in 1773 that led to the colony throwing off Imperial rule, Boston threw another party that sent shivers down England's spine.

"There can't be a lower point for any manager, and yes, it is a national disgrace," Taylor said. "This result is now in the history books – I suppose it will haunt me from now on." Without a doubt "USA 2 England 0" will be forever inscribed on Graham Taylor's heart.

Yankee Doodle Dandies: the Americans were euphoric at inflicting a humbling defeat on England

Foxboro, Massachusetts, was no better place for England to play a road game than it was 218 years ago

MICHAEL GEE
of the Boston Herald, referring
to Battle of Bunker Hill

FOR THE RECORD

■ Peter Shilton was sent off for the first time in his career on August 28, in his 971st League game.

■ Hereford set an unenviable record when they had four players sent off in their match against Northampton on September 6.

■ Barclays announced in October that they would not be renewing their sponsorship of the League.

■ Ian Rush passed Roger Hunt's record of 286 goals for Liverpool on October 18. And Guy Whittingham broke Portsmouth's record with 42 in the League and 44 in all.

■ Chelsea secured their future in December when a bank bought Stamford Bridge and granted them a 20-year lease.

■ Adrian Blake, the Kingstonian goalkeeper, was hit by a coin thrown from the crowd and had to be substituted during the FA Cup first round replay with Peterborough, who led 3-0 at the time and went on to win 9-1. The FA ordered the match to be played again behind closed doors and Peterborough won 1-0.

■ Ted Croker, the former secretary of the FA, died on Christmas Day, aged 68.

Video nasty gets Vinnie a clip round the ear

WHEREVER Vinnie Jones went trouble seemed to follow. This time he got into hot water in the film studio for his appearance in a video, Soccer's Hard Men.

In the video, Jones said: "If you are going over the top on me you have got to put me out of the game because I'll be coming back for you, whether it's in the next five minutes or next season."

Sam Hammam, the Wimbledon chairman, branded Jones a "mosquito brain" and the rest of the country condemned a tape that seemed to glorify the worst aspects of behaviour on the pitch.

Although Jones apologised, the FA handed down a record £20,000 fine and a six-month ban suspended for three years in

November. Hammam, though, thought the FA had gone over the top and accused them of applying double standards, singling out Jones for punishment while being more lenient with other offenders.

Even after this incident Jones could not stay out of trouble. Summoned to Lancaster Gate on March 29 because he had exceeded 40 disciplinary points, he failed to turn up at the appointed hour and was banned indefinitely.

Jones claimed that he had got the time of the hearing mixed up, and made sure he arrived early for the rescheduled case a fortnight later. A four-match ban was imposed and, not before time, the FA told Jones to "grow up".

Jones: "mosquito brain"

THE
1992-93
SEASON

It's quite difficult dealing with Mr Flashman because if you speak your mind he tends to sack you

EDWIN STEIN
the Barnet assistant manager
sacked a mere three times

Clough leaves the helm as Forest's ship sinks

Barnet rise above the strife

MAIDSTONE, struggling in the Third Division with small crowds and huge debts, had their first match of the season called off and were given until the following Monday to guarantee that they would be able to fulfil all of their fixtures. Unable to come up with the necessary backing, they resigned from the League on August 17.

And it was not long before speculation was swirling around another Third Division club, Barnet. Within days of Maidstone's demise, the north London club were banned from the transfer market because they had not paid their players' wages.

Two months later the issue was still not resolved and it took the intervention of both the League and the PFA to head off a threatened walk-out by most of the squad. Barnet's shaky financial position was hardly helped when they were fined £50,000 for breaches of League regulations.

Things had got so bad by late March that, when salary cheques had bounced once again, the Cardiff chairman gave the Barnet players £1,000 to tide them over after the two clubs met at Ninian Park. And the League, with their fine still unpaid, finally ran out of patience and threatened to expel Barnet.

That prompted Stan Flashman, the controversial Barnet chairman, to resign, citing "health reasons". But, as his parting shot before he left, he sacked his manager, Barry Fry, for the eighth time.

Fry, who had already been dismissed and reinstated earlier in the season, was offered his job back by the new chairman. Hardly surprisingly, he opted to join Southend instead, saying: "Being manager of Barnet was like living with a double-decker bus on your head. When I left it was like it had been driven off."

Amazingly, despite having to have their wages paid by the PFA yet again, the players seemed to be unaffected by the financial turmoil. They finished third in the Third Division to claim the last automatic promotion place.

Bowing out: Clough salutes the Forest fans for the final time

BRIAN CLOUGH finally bowed to the inevitable and announced his retirement on April 26. "Old Big 'ead" had spent 18 years calling the shots at Nottingham Forest, but it had been painfully apparent all season that Clough was starting to lose his grip.

Forest had had a terrible start to the season, losing six of their first seven matches and only winning three games before Christmas. Despite trying to play some attractive football, they never looked like being able to drag themselves clear of relegation.

Clough had signed a one-year extension to his contract in November, but behind the scenes a storm was brewing. The board was split into pro and anti-Clough factions, and Clough was shocked by newspaper allegations about his alleged excessive drinking.

Finally, just after being made a Freeman of Nottingham, the 58-year-old Clough said that he would retire at the end of the season. The fans flocked to the City ground to pay their last respects on May 2, a match that Forest lost to Sheffield United to condemn them to the First Division.

Even the United fans saluted the man who many people thought was the greatest manager never to lead England. "Clough for England," they chanted without any hint of irony.

It was a sad end for a man who had taken Forest from the obscurity of the Second Division to the heights of the League title and two successive European Cups.

But Clough could not resist one last wisecrack. "I didn't expect today to be so emotional, but I ain't going to miss the job at all," he said.

Parting shot: Flashman quit as the chairman and sacked Fry yet again

United's championship at last

ALEX FERGUSON did not want a repeat of last season, when Manchester United let the title slip from their grasp. So when his team hit a patch of poor form, drawing five matches in a row and losing the next two, he decided it was time for a foray into the transfer market.

He pounced on November 26, signing the mercurial Eric Cantona from Leeds for £1.2m, a price that was widely regarded as a bargain. The deal marked a turning point in the fortunes of both clubs – Leeds struggled for the rest of the season while United got steadily better.

Cantona was soon scoring goals for Manchester United as they set off in pursuit of Norwich, who had opened up a clear gap at the top of the table. And it was a lack of goals that was to prove Norwich's undoing as they finished the season in third place, having conceded four more goals than they managed to score.

As Norwich slipped back, the battle between United and Aston Villa was intense. The spectre of another late failure was revived when United went four matches without a win in

Silver lining: Ferguson's title success lifted last year's cloud

March. But Ferguson was not going to make the same mistake twice.

United won their last seven matches while Villa were the team that faltered. They handed the title to United on May 2 when they lost to Oldham. Ferguson was playing golf at the time and the news was broken to him by another golfer, who went up to the United manager on the last green and said: "Excuse me Mr Ferguson, you are the champions."

The celebrations at United's home match against Blackburn the next day were enormous. Old Trafford had waited for this moment since 1967 and the legendary Sir Matt Busby was there to applaud Ferguson, the first manager to win a league title in both Scotland and England.

Morrow crocked as Arsenal crack both Cups

STEVE MORROW'S first appearance in a Wembley final was a dream that turned into a nightmare.

The full-back was still struggling to become established in the Arsenal side and had already spent several spells on loan to lower division clubs. And he probably only owed his place in the team to play Sheffield Wednesday in the League Cup final to injuries to more established players.

But Morrow did an excellent job in helping to stifle the threat posed by Chris Waddle, John Sheridan and John Harkes. Although Harkes gave Wednesday the lead in the ninth minute, Arsenal were level before half-time when Paul Merson volleyed the ball powerfully past Chris Woods.

With Arsenal starting to dominate the midfield, Merson hit a cross that was not cleared properly. Morrow popped up to give Arsenal a 2-1 victory. After the match, Tony Adams hoisted Morrow aloft to celebrate the young player's vital first goal for his club.

Then disaster struck. Morrow fell awkwardly from his captain's shoulders and there was a sickening crack as he hit the ground and broke his arm.

The injury cost Morrow a chance of a return to Wembley when the two clubs met again in the FA Cup final on May 15. The final was a muted affair, with Ian Wright giving Arsenal the lead and David Hirst scoring an equaliser in the second half.

The replay was little more attractive. Wright gave Arsenal

the lead but Waddle took the match into extra time. With a penalty shoot-out looming Andy Linighan, who had never been popular with the Arsenal fans, headed the winner a minute before time to silence his critics.

Norwich were not complaining either. The strike by their former player put Arsenal into the European Cup Winners Cup, handing the last Uefa Cup place to Norwich, the first time they had played in Europe.

There was also a first for Arsenal, who became the first English side to win both Cups in the same season. It was also historic for George Graham, who became the first person to win the League and both Cups as a player and a manager – all six honours coming with Arsenal.

Morrow: fall guy

Bribery scandal wipes out Marseille's triumphs

WHEN Basile Boli scored the only goal of the match as Marseille beat AC Milan in the European Cup final all of France celebrated. They were the first French team to bring home the trophy from a competition that the French had been instrumental in creating in the 1950s.

So the scandal that engulfed Marseille was even more shocking to France. The first rumblings had been heard before the final on May 26, with allegations surfacing that Marseille had bribed Valenciennes players to go easy in a League match the week before. Marseille won 1-0 to secure the title.

At first, Marseille denied the charge. But, in July, their midfield player Jean-Jacques Eydelie confessed that he had acted as a go-between for payments to three Valenciennes players. His admission opened the floodgates and implicated Marseille's general secretary, Jean-Pierre Bernes, the right-hand man of their president, the flamboyant Bernard Tapie.

Fifa and Uefa demanded action, but the French federation said that they could do nothing until the investigations were complete. As the case dragged on through the summer Uefa did not want the reputa-tion of the European Cup harmed so they excluded Marseilles from defending their crown days before they were due to play AEK Athens in the first round.

Tapie went to court to get the decision overturned but dropped the case when Fifa warned that France was running the risk of exclusion from all international competition.

The French federation finally decided to suspend Bernes and three players, and strip Marseille of their League title. But Marseille's real punishment was the amount of money they would lose by being excluded from Europe.

A club that had made a fortune, and was able to spend a fortune on players and wages, suddenly found itself on the financial rocks and having to sell players just to survive. Tapie said that £15m was needed and that he was going to resign as soon as his successor could be found.

Europe eludes Rangers

Fighting draw: Rangers came back from a 2-0 deficit against Marseille

FOR ONCE, Rangers' foray into Europe came close to fulfilling the form they constantly demonstrated in Scotland. They easily qualified for the Champions League of the European Cup, and in doing so had the added pleasure of eliminating Leeds United, the English champions, by comfortably beating them 2-1 home and away in the unofficial "British championship". However, Leeds were extremely fortunate to be playing the Scottish champions at all.

In the previous round, having lost 3-0 away to Stuttgart, Leeds had fought back tenaciously at Elland Road to win 4-1 and had seemingly been knocked out on away goals. Then it transpired that the German side had inadvertently fielded four foreign players, one more than is permitted, and Leeds were awarded the tie 3-0. In the ensuing replay at Barcelona, Leeds won 2-1.

In Group A of the Champions League, where the four teams met each other home and away, Marseille were Rangers' biggest hurdle. And after 75 min-utes of the home match against the French champions Rangers trailed 2-0 and seemed to be dead and buried. But goals from McSwegan and Hateley earned them a draw and a fighting chance of reaching the European Cup final for the first time. Marseille and Rangers sailed past Bruges and CSKA Moscow, the other clubs in the Group, to set up a winner-takes-all match in France on April 7.

Once again Rangers exhibited sterling courage to come back from a goal down, but the draw was never going to be enough. In the last match Marseille beat Bruges in Belgium to clinch a place in the final against AC Milan, where the French club unexpectedly won 1-0.

There was consolation for Rangers in Scotland where they swept everything before them with imperious power. They won the Premier League title for the fifth consecutive season, won both Cups by beating Aberdeen 2-1 twice to complete the Treble and broke numerous records en route. But still the Holy Grail of the European Cup eludes them.

Rearguard action: Tapie withdrew his case when Fifa upped the stakes

Venables and Sugar: a tale of two sweethearts who fell out of love

ON MAY 14, the day before the FA Cup final, it was apparent that Tottenham's so-called dream ticket of Alan Sugar and Terry Venables that had snatched the club out of the grasp of Robert Maxwell two years earlier had turned into a nightmare. In a sensational move, Sugar, the chairman, had Venables voted off the board and sacked as Tottenham's chief executive.

Sugar's dramatic coup stunned everybody. On the face of it, the break-up between the two men who had been hailed as saviours seemed inexplicable, particularly as the club's financial plight seemed to have been turned around in September when a trading profit of £2.9m, compared to the previous £3.1m loss, had been announced.

However, the source of the bad blood between Sugar and Venables soon leaked out. According to Sugar: "Venables behaved as if I was some kind of rich lunatic, a rich nutter who had put his money in and was supposed to sit over there and mind his own business."

It was Sugar's unease about Venables' encroachment on the commercial side and the character of some of the people he had employed at the club that provoked the rift. In particular, Sugar was disturbed by Venables' association with Eddie Ashby, an undischarged bankrupt with a string of failed companies behind him, who Venables had hired as "general manager" and who had been involved in the sale of Paul Gascoigne to Lazio. Venables' refusal to get rid of Ashby precipitated Venables' dismissal.

Venables did not take his sacking lightly and went to the High Court to seek reinstatement. Tottenham fans rallied to his cause as Sugar was seen as the villain of the piece. There were demonstrations outside the court with placards such as: "T yes, Sugar no", and Sugar's life was made a misery with anonymous abusive phone calls and death threats. Even a boycott of Tottenham's matches the following season was planned by the supporters.

However, two things turned Sugar's position around. First, the allegations in court in June that Brian Clough, the Nottingham Forest manager, had wanted a "bung" from Tottenham during the Teddy Sheringham transfer. And second, the astute appointment later that month of Osvaldo Ardiles as manager. Ardiles, a World Cup winner with Argentina in 1978, and a Spurs immortal, was just the palliative the angry Spurs fans needed, and the discontent melted away.

As did Venables' court action when the judge ruled that Sugar's decision to sack Venables was within his powers and he refused to force Sugar to reinstate him.

Venables: losing battle

Acrimonious divorce: Alan Sugar won the war of words in the High Court to decide who ran Tottenham

BRIAN CLOUGH
The maestro who bowed out on a low note

Alex Spillius

WHAT is our lasting memory of Brian Clough? Of a nonconformist genius, or of a sad, apparently alcoholic man in a green tracksuit top unable to summon his once mighty powers? Any answer will say something about the respondent, about whether he or she leans towards optimism or pessimism. Towards fond, selective recollection or realism. Probably most of us would mix a bit of both.

But what a pity the question can even be asked. Had it been put before the beginning of the 1992-93 season responses would have been unequivocally positive. Apart from maybe those who had felt the rough end of Clough's egoism in person. For the public he was a joy: eccentric, provocative, witty and wondrously gifted. The idioms of Clough's teams were style, flair and irrepressibility, and they even won things. To the supporters and many citizens of Derby and Nottingham his status edged on divinity.

Some favourite Clough moments. On a television panel during the 1986 World Cup Mick Channon was bleating on: "We've got to get bodies in the box. The French do it, the Brazilians do it, the Italians do it..." Clough interrupted: "Even educated fleas do it." (The remark was even funnier as Channon didn't have a clue what Clough was referring to – the Louis Armstrong song, Let's Do It.) Clough on politicians: "There are more hooligans in the House of Commons than at a football match." And on signing the striker Nigel Jemson: "I haven't seen the lad, but my coaches have and he also comes highly recommended by my greengrocer."

Clough became a fixture in the public mind during a TV discussion before England's 1-0 defeat by Poland in 1973 – which had extinguished England's hopes of qualifying for the World Cup finals the following year – when he called the Polish goalkeeper, Jan Tomaszewski, a "clown". Despite the fact that Tomaszewski disproved him with a string of miraculous saves, from then on the nation knew who Brian Clough was, which can be said of very few in football.

The man was outrageously controversial and we loved him for it. Even those who did not share his left-wing views would have been impressed by his chest-beating support for Labour when most football men were blandly Conservative. Later, stories emerged about fish and chips for striking miners, of spontaneous donations to charity and of chocolates and flowers for players' wives.

As a manager he was unrivalled at making a silk purse out of a sow's ear, of turning ordinary players into stars. His footballers have often had trouble pinpointing his power over them: partly it was inspired by fear, partly by respect for his quickness of mind and partly by his encouragement to play the game the natural way. His best teams had the perfect balance of powers: the straightforwardness of Larry Lloyd in defence, the industry of Ian Bowyer in midfield, the trickery of John Robertson on the wing, the deft improvisation of Trevor Francis in attack. At times he had money to spend – but only after he had earned it for Forest with trophies – though many of his expensive purchases failed: Justin Fashanu, Gary Megson and Asa Hartford among others.

Clough, with his partner Peter Taylor, brought inconceivable success to not one but two provincial cities with weak football traditions, and their record deserves reciting: one League championship with Derby; promotion from the Second Division with Nottingham Forest, followed by two League Cups, one League championship and, incredibly, two European Cups. (Strangely, the FA Cup always eluded Clough). When the final whistle blew after the second European triumph, over Hamburg, Clough, unpredictable as ever, didn't jump for joy but calmly rose from the bench with the look of a man who had finished a quietly satisfying day at the office.

It was no coincidence that after Taylor's acrimonious departure in 1982 Clough and Forest went on to win just two more League Cups, a comparative decline. Forest continued to delight, but Clough was never able to acquire a striker to match Francis, and his team, like the man, were highly entertaining but soft-centred. Also for the first time since those disastrous 44 days as manager of Leeds in 1974, Clough was left to soldier on alone. It wasn't just Taylor's

Exciting prospect: Clough was a prolific scorer in his brief career with Sunderland

Going down: Clough stares relegation in the face

diligence as a coach that was missed; the bitterness of their falling out debilitated Clough, crushingly saddened by a man who was once his best friend, but prevented by his pride of effecting a rapprochement.

After Taylor left it seemed Clough was cruising and somewhat waywardly at that. He seemed to lose the ambition to build a team with a genuine chance of regaining the championship – though League Cups were easy. He began an exclusive column for the Sun, an odd move for a Labour supporter. In 1977 he had been passed over for the England job in favour of Ron Greenwood; perhaps his comment a few years earlier that "I would like the supreme job of dictating football" had not helped. Clough was not called "Old Big 'Ead" for nothing, and the grey men of Lancaster Gate were not prepared to handle such an arrogant maverick. By the time Bobby Robson succeeded Greenwood, Clough was too much of an outsider – but it still hurt.

Clough had never endured adversity stoically. His playing career was tragically ended at the age of 27 by an horrendous injury after scoring 251 goals in 274 games for Middlesbrough and Sunderland. Clough never felt comfortable around injured players ever again. Although he won just two England caps, the frequent comparisons made at the time with Jimmy Greaves were valid.

Crowning glory: Forest won the European Cup in 1979 and retained it in 1980

Clough had great things ahead of him.

Taylor, who had befriended Clough at Middlesbrough, later recalled the three months Clough spent out of work immediately after he was sacked as Sunderland's youth team coach in 1965: "If it had been any longer, he'd have gone to pot. He was a no-hoper: jobless, boozing heavily and on his way out." The way back was offered by Fourth Division Hartlepools, where Clough became manager. With hindsight, his behaviour as described by Taylor was an omen of his problems in the twilight of his career.

Clough's magic as a manager did not disappear overnight, rather it faded as as his behaviour went from amusing to bewildering. In 1989 he hit a supporter who was invading the pitch, then literally kissed and made up in front of the TV cameras. More and more often he coped with the gremlins by being more outrageous and pecking TV interviewers became almost commonplace. Clough went through a phase of forbidding physios to treat players on the field. Darren Wassall came off during a reserve game complaining of an injured hand. Clough spat on the defender's injured limb and told him: "There, that's better." A distraught Wassall soon left Forest for Derby.

During the 1992-93 season Clough had clearly lost his way. Wassall, Des Walker and Teddy Sheringham were sold without replacements being found. As Forest struggled unhappily into bottom place, Robert Rosario, a striker with a one-in-eight strike rate, was signed, and Nigel

Clough, his son, was inexplicably moved to centre-back. Clough Snr's retirement at the end of the season was inevitable, but the announcement was messily brought forward by revelations in two Sunday tabloids about his drinking problems.

After 18 years Clough left amid tears and an affection reserved for a loved one, though his team were relegated by a distance. But then Clough was surely always going to go with a bang as well as whimper.

Controversy still dogged him after he had quit the game. A television documentary alleged he had acquired 2,000 League Cup final tickets which had found their way on to the black market and that he had demanded cash payments for Forest to appear in testimonials. In the High Court during the Terry Venables-Alan Sugar case it was also alleged that he liked a "bung" when buying and selling players.

Any mud that stuck after these allegations will surely fall off in time, and the memory will grow sweeter. Nothing will take Clough's record away from him, while the legacy of fine football he left at Forest will, with wise guardianship, outlast his lifetime. In the post-war pantheon of managers, he is up there with Matt Busby, Stan Cullis, Bill Nicholson, Bob Paisley, Alf Ramsey, Don Revie, Bill Shankly and Jock Stein. All are treasured for different reasons, but more than anything else Cloughie will be recalled with a smile, as an original; and life, let alone football, has few enough of them.

OLD BIG 'EAD'S ACHIEVEMENTS

Born March 21, 1935, Middlesbrough

PLAYING CAREER
Middlesbrough 1953-61
213 League appearances, 197 goals
Scored 100 goals in the League in fewer games than anybody else
Sunderland 1961-65
61 League appearances, 54 goals
Leading scorer in the Football League in the 1957-58 season (40 goals) and in 1958-59 (42 goals)
Leading scorer in the Second Division in 1959-60 (39 goals)
Internationals Played for England Under-23 (three times), England B (once) and appeared in two full internationals

MANAGEMENT CAREER
Hartlepools United Manager 1965-67
Aged 29, he was the youngest manager in the League
Derby County Manager 1967-73
Honours League Championship: Winners 1972
Second Division: Winners 1969
Brighton and Hove Albion Manager 1973-74
Leeds United Manager July 20, 1974-September 1, 1974 (44 days in charge)
Nottingham Forest Manager 1975-93
Honours European Cup: Winners 1979, 1980
FA Cup: Finalists 1991
First Division: Winners 1978; Runners-up 1979
League Cup: Winners 1978, 1979, 1989, 1990; Finalists 1980
Promoted from the Second Division in 1977

Double act: Clough and Taylor revived Forest's fortunes before their bitter split

THE
1993-94
SEASON

Toshack quits Wales after only 47 days

THE writing was on the wall for Terry Yorath when Wales just missed out on qualifying for the World Cup finals yet again. Determined to do better in the European championship, Wales turned to John Toshack.

However, the way Toshack replaced Yorath split Welsh football. Toshack agreed to run the national team while still managing Real Sociedad. Toshack was unaware of the furore until his first match in charge. During Wales's 3-1 defeat by Norway he was jeered by the fans, who chanted Yorath's name.

Toshack promptly quit after just 47 days in charge, complaining bitterly about the politicking, which he described as a "dirty war". He said he had been misled about Yorath's departure. "I have realised some things I did not know before and I have no intention of continuing. I want to wash my hands of the whole affair."

Exit Taylor, enter Venables

NOT since the dark days of the 1970s, when England twice failed to qualify for the World Cup finals, had the international side plumbed such depths. When Graham Taylor's team faced Holland in Rotterdam in October a draw would probably have secured their passage to America. Instead they went down 2-0 and left themselves with virtually no chance of qualifying.

Taylor and England had their excuses: Ronald Koeman should have been sent off when he brought down David Platt when he was in a clear goal-scoring position just outside the penalty box. However the German referee, Karl Assenmacher, decided otherwise. And Koeman, to add insult to injury, promptly went on to score the killing first goal from a free kick.

England's qualification now demanded that they won by seven goals away to San Marino and Holland lost to Poland. Mathematically possible, but in reality a pipe-dream. The pipe-dream became a nightmare in November when San Marino embarrassingly took the lead after eight seconds. It was only their second goal in the group. England eventually won 7-1 and Holland duly dispatched Poland to grab the second qualifying place behind the group leaders Norway.

Within days Taylor did the honourable thing and fell on his sword. But who was to succeed him? Steve Coppell instantly became the favourite and just as quickly ruled himself out: "I don't want the job and I don't envy who gets it." Suddenly it seemed that the managership of England was a poisoned chalice. Don Howe, Kevin Keegan and John Lyall were just some of the putative candidates who did not want to be in the frame.

Dave Bassett, the Sheffield United manager, wondered: "Who will the FA pick next? Probably Walt Disney." Roy Hodgson, Switzerland's manager, was also thought to be on the short-list. But he promptly kicked the idea into touch: "You have got to be joking. Even the Pope would have second thoughts about taking the England job."

In desperation the FA turned to Jimmy Armfield to head-hunt the new England boss. Despite his acrimonious feud with Alan Sugar and the questions surrounding his business dealings, Terry Venables was Armfield's, and the public's, choice. Indeed there was nobody else left to turn to.

Venables started out on the right foot by recalling Peter Beardsley and picking a crowd-pleasing team who duly beat the European champions Denmark 1-0 at Wembley in March. A 5-0 thrashing of Greece, and a goal-less draw with Norway, when England were unlucky to have a goal disallowed, followed in May. Suddenly life after Taylor did not seem so bad.

The first nail in England's coffin: Ronald Koeman takes advantage of the referee's leniency to punish England

Busby goes to heaven

SIR MATT BUSBY, the man who had single-handedly created the legend of Manchester United, died on January 20 at the age of 84. Busby had revelled in the fans delight when United won the title last season, their first championship since he had been in charge in the club's glory days in the 1960s.

Alex Ferguson, the United manager who had done so much to restore United's fortunes, said: "He was the outstanding man of them all – even Bill Shankly and Jock Stein sought his advice and experience."

It was a fitting tribute to a man who, like Shankly and Stein, was a product of the close-knit Scottish mining community that had spawned three of the greatest managers of all time.

Busby had played for Manchester City before the war and when he left the army he took charge of an ailing Manchester United. The struggling team were deep in debt and the ground was a bomb-damaged ruin. With no money to spend, Busby pulled on his tracksuit and concentrated on developing the talent at the club.

He turned the club around so quickly that they won the FA Cup in 1948 and the League in 1952, their first championship in more than 40 years. But Busby knew that his side was ageing, and with United languishing at the bottom of the table he replaced almost half of his team overnight with untried reserves.

The Busby Babes were born and they grew up fast, with successive League titles in 1956 and 1957. Tragically, the heart was torn out of the team by the Munich air disaster in 1958, when eight United players were killed and Busby was lucky to escape with his life.

Miraculously, Busby rebuilt United again, winning the FA Cup in 1963 and the championship in 1965 and 1967. His crowning glory came in 1968 when he finally laid the ghosts of Munich to rest with the defeat of Benfica at Wembley in in the European Cup final.

Spurs fall on hard times

THE TROUBLES that bedevilled Tottenham would just not go away. The feud between Alan Sugar and Terry Venables dragged on throughout the year and almost cost Spurs their place in the Premier Division.

During the two men's battles, evidence of financial irregularities came to light. Tottenham thought they were doing the right thing by reporting the cases to the FA, but their openness rebounded on them.

The transgression involved undeclared loans that were never intended to be repaid, and other payments to players. The FA regarded this as a serious breach of their rules and established a special commission to investigate.

At the end of a lengthy inquiry, Tottenham, who had admitted 34 charges of making irregular payments, were horrified when they were fined £600,000, banned from the FA Cup for a year, and told they would begin next season with 12 points deducted.

Sugar pointed out that the people responsible were no longer at the club and that the loss of points and the exclusion from the FA Cup would mean

Sugar: shocked and horrified

that the people who would really suffer were the fans.

Tottenham appealed and, after a degree of horse-trading, the 12-point penalty was reduced to six, with the fine increased to £1.5m and the FA Cup ban left in place. Sugar said: "I find it quite shocking really. If any other Premier League club has got anything to disclose to the authorities it is going to be a brave man that comes forward now. Looking on the positive side, we are not going to be relegated. We have lost two games and that's all. Arsenal had points deducted once and went on to win the League."

. . . but find rich pickings

TOTTENHAM'S response was swift and devastating. In 48 hours at the end of July they signed two World Cup stars, Ilie Dumitrescu from Romania for £2.6m and Jurgen Klinsmann from Germany for £2m. The two transfers astonished football.

It was a coup reminiscent of 1978, when Keith Burkenshaw, then the Spurs manager, snapped up the two Argentine World Cup stars Riccardo Villa and Osvaldo Ardiles for £750,000. Now, Ardiles, the Tottenham manager, was grabbing similar headlines.

With Klinsmann aboard, Tottenham have, with Teddy Sheringham, a £4.1m strike force that matches Blackburn's Alan Shearer and Chris Sutton, assembled at twice the price.

"Inside England, the prices are really stampeding; they don't reflect the quality of players in general," Ardiles said. "Abroad, the price reflects the player's ability more." He was not the only British manager to be that astute.

In the close season, a flock of overseas players moved to British clubs. Rangers were the biggest purchasers, bringing the Frenchman Basile Boli from Marseilles for £2.7m and the Dane Brian Laudrup from Fiorentina for £2.2m. Forest and Arsenal were not far behind; Forest signed the Dutchman Bryan Roy from Foggia for £2.5m and Arsenal bought the Swede Stefan Schwarz from Benfica from £1.75m.

Brian Robson, newly installed as the Middlesbrough manager, snapped up Jaime Moreno for a paltry £250,000 – the first Bolivian to play in English football.

Brady, Jordan and Macari walk Celtic plank

WHILE RANGERS just marched imperiously on, Celtic were steadily falling apart. The crisis was brought to a head on the eve of the club's annual meeting in October – Liam Brady walked out on the club and his assistant Joe Jordan followed a day later.

They had been hailed as saviours when they took charge 18 months before but their attempts to revive the club's fortunes had been bedevilled by internal politics.

The board turned to another Celtic hero, Lou Macari. His first game in charge delighted the fans, a 2-1 victory over Rangers. The suffering supporters soon had more to cheer about when the board they hated were swept aside by a consortium led by Fergus McCann.

However, the mood of optimism was short-lived. By the end of yet another barren season McCann had acrimoniously sacked Macari and controversially replaced him with Tommy Burns, the Kilmarnock manager.

Milan's dream final is Barcelona's nightmare

IT WAS the dream final that everybody wanted, Barcelona versus Milan for the European Cup. Everybody expected a thrilling match between two evenly-matched teams, and the spectators duly got a feast of football. What they did not to expect to see was a 4-0 demolition of Johann Cruyff's multi-million pound side.

The match was virtually over by half-time after Daniele Massaro gave Milan a 2-0 lead. His fellow striker Dejan Savicevic ran the Barcelona defence ragged and two minutes into the second half he audaciously lobbed the backpedalling Andoni Zubizarreta from outside the penalty area. Marcel Desailly, who had won the European Cup with Marseille the year before, added to Barcelona's misery in the 58th minute.

The Spanish press hailed Milan's victory as an historic defeat for Barcelona, who had been taught a lesson as Milan's hegemony was confirmed. Cruyff's response was to sign a new contract with Barcelona and begin dismantling his squad. Zubizarreta was packed off to Valencia, Michael Laudrup went to Real Madrid and Julio Salinas joined Deportivo La Coruña.

By a late twist of fortune, Barcelona already knew they would have an opportunity to redeem themselves in the European Cup. They had already snatched the Spanish League title at the last gasp. Deportivo needed to win their last match to take the championship but with

Eclipsed: Romario, a World Cup star, failed to shine in the European Cup

the score 0-0 Miroslav Djukic missed a penalty in the last minute. It was the second year in a row Barcelona had taken the title in the very last match of the season.

Nightmare goal ends Rangers' dreams of glory

IT SHOULD have all been so easy. Rangers had won the championship for the sixth year in a row, retained the League Cup and only Dundee United stood between them and a second successive clean sweep of the Scottish honours. And Dundee United were hardly the most difficult opponents. They had finished mid-table in the League, only winning 11 matches, and had lost the last six Cup finals they had appeared in.

But Rangers were undone by one of the most bizarre goals ever seen at Hampden Park. Dave McPherson attempted a suicidal back pass which forced Ally Maxwell, the Rangers goalkeeper, to rush his clearance.

He miskicked the ball, which flew straight to Christian Dailly, the Dundee United forward. Dailly's shot trickled towards the net but, amazingly, rebounded off the far post. Craig Brewster could not believe his luck and he raced in to score the easiest goal of his life.

If there was ever a club where something strange was going to happen it had to be Dundee United. Ivan Golac was hardly the archetypal manager. His idea of the right way to prepare for a big match was to take his players out for a drink and a walk round the park to admire the trees.

Unorthodox as the technique was, Dundee United's 1-0 vic-

Finishing touch: Craig Brewster salutes his manager

tory prompted Walter Smith, the Rangers manager, to threaten a root and branch clear-out of his team. And within weeks he had signed Basile Boli and Brian Laudrup.

Cantona conjures up Double despite a month of madness

Killing blow: Cantona sends Kharine the wrong way to score his first penalty

ON the surface, Manchester United's progress to the Double seemed to be serene. But at one point, after an incredible period of turmoil, they looked as if they would finish the season having won nothing.

After losing to Chelsea in September they seemed to be almost unstoppable in the League. By January they had opened up a 16-point gap over Blackburn and most people would have handed them the title there and then.

When they were beaten by Chelsea at Old Trafford in March, their first defeat at home for 17 months, their unbeaten run in the League was a record 34 matches. It was the start of a month of madness.

The team seemed to lose its collective head with four players sent off in the space of five matches. Eric Cantona was dismissed twice in successive games, Peter Schmeichel got his marching orders in the quarter-finals of the FA Cup and Andrei Kanchelskis was shown the red card in the League Cup final.

Aston Villa won 3-1 at Wembley to end United's hopes of becoming the first English side to complete the treble, a feat Alex Ferguson had accomplished in Scotland with Aberdeen. And with so many of their key players suspended, United were almost eliminated from the FA Cup by Oldham, one of the weakest teams in the Premier Division. With seconds remaining, Oldham were about to pull off the upset of the season but Mark Hughes conjured up a brilliantly taken goal to force the tie into a replay.

All the time, Blackburn had been closing the gap in the League. They had whittled away United's advantage so effectively that the two clubs were only separated by goal difference. But, showing the hallmarks of true champions, Ferguson steadied his team's jangling nerves. United moved into overdrive and it was Blackburn's turn to falter. United retained the title with a match to spare and finished seven points ahead of Blackburn.

United met Chelsea, their nemesis in the League, in the FA Cup final. In the first half it looked as if Chelsea were going to be the victors yet again. After the interval, however, United raised their game. Helped by two penalties scored by Cantona, the second a very questionable award because the offence appeared to be committed just outside the area, Chelsea were swept away 4-0.

Having won the Double for the first time in the club's history, only one challenge remains for Ferguson – to emulate Matt Busby and win the European Cup. Particularly because this year's campaign ended in disaster when United were ignominiously bundled out of the European Cup by Galatasary.

The Turkish side drew 3-3 at Old Trafford and drew the ill-tempered second leg 0-0 to go through on away goals. The ugly side of Cantona came to the fore when he started a brawl in the tunnel and claimed that the referee had been bought.

Scandal: Maradona failed drug test

IT WAS a bombshell as great as the Ben Johnson scandal at the 1988 Olympics. Diego Armando Maradona, the greatest player since Pele, had failed a routine drug test and was expelled from the World Cup finals in the United States.

At first Maradona protested his innocence saying that the drug that had been found in his urine sample after the match against Nigeria was simply a cold cure. While it is true that ephedrine, the banned substance, is present in common cold cures, Dr Michel d'Hooghe, Fifa's medical expert, took great pains to refute Maradona's defence.

The doctor explained that a full analysis had revealed that Maradona had been taking five banned drugs and if Maradona had been taking medicine for a cold there were better products. "We did not find one pill containing the five products so we suppose it must be a cocktail," he said.

When the Argentine Football Federation learnt of the news they acted swiftly and threw Maradona out of the tournament. Fifa banned Maradona from any involvement in football and decided to review the situation once the World Cup was over. But there was little sympathy for Maradona. "He broke the rules and that is the end of it," Guido Tognoni of Fifa said. "It would not matter if it was only a small dose. You cannot be half pregnant. You either are or you aren't."

Not for the first time Maradona fled to Argentina in disgrace. The affair was horribly reminiscent of 1991, when he had tested positive for cocaine after a League match in Italy and had been banned from football for 15 months. Facing prosecution on charges of possessing and distributing cocaine, and involvement in a vice ring in Naples, he had sneaked out of the country just before a warrant was issued for his arrest. No sooner had he returned home than he was arrested in Buenos Aires for taking cocaine.

When the news of the latest scandal broke Maradona had claimed: "I did not take drugs. I have never needed stimulants for showing my skill." He suggested that he was a victim of conspiracy and said: "Fifa beat me over the head without any compunction."

However two days later Maradona admitted that he had "forgotten to tell" the team doctor that he was taking pills. "I took those pills as if they were aspirin," he said. "Thousands of players do it but the cost is always higher when Maradona does it."

To everybody's surprise Maradona quickly returned to the World Cup to commentate for an Argentinian television station on his country's second-round match against Romania. With their playmaker gone, his former teammates were also heading home after their 3-2 defeat and Maradona accepted the inevitable and announced his retirement.

The Buenos Aires newspaper, La Prensa, summed up the whole sorry mess: "Maradona will never show his magic again. The biggest soccer star of modern times slammed the door on his sporting life, leaving us in a fog of scandal."

Maradona: disgraced game again

Tragedy: Escobar killed

Escobar: a £500,000 reward was offered for the conviction of his killers

WHEN Andres Escobar unluckily scored an own goal as Colombia lost to the United States it was an expensive mistake. The defeat made it virtually certain that Colombia, one of the pre-tournament favourites, would not reach the second round of the World Cup finals. But nobody could ever have imagined that he would pay for the mistake with his life.

Nine days later Escobar had returned home and was leaving a restaurant in Medellin with his fiancee. He was attacked by three men, one of whom said: "Thanks for the own goal" before repeatedly shooting Escobar in the chest and face. As each bullet hit his body, the attackers shouted: "Goal".

Escobar died instantly and there was outrage in Colombia.

At his funeral 100,000 Colombians cried for "justice" as they filed weeping past his open coffin. A year later Humberto Munoz Castro was convicted and sentenced to 43 years in jail.

Andy Townsend, the Republic of Ireland midfielder, spoke for everybody at the World Cup when he said: "It makes you wonder what it is all about. When lives are being taken because of football it makes you wonder if it is all worthwhile."

The tournament, already rocked by the Maradona scandal, had to come to terms with an even greater tragedy. An American television commentator said: "We thought we were going to watch another sports tournament. But instead we are seeing all of life, the good, the bad, and the very ugly."

Kidderminster are the first to put the big boys on the block

To boldly go: Humphreys took Kidderminster into the fifth round

KIDDERMINSTER had never reached the third round of the FA Cup before, and their greatest day was given even more spice when they were drawn against their near-neigbours Birmingham. To add to the excitement, Kidderminster's manager, Graham Allner, had been signed as a schoolboy by Birmingham but then rejected.

Birmingham took the lead in the ninth minute and were rampant for much of the match. But they wasted their chances, including missing a penalty. Kidderminster only managed a handful of attacks, but they made them tell. Goals from Cartwright and Purdie earned the GM-Vauxhall conference team a home tie against Preston.

This time Kidderminster had the best of the play and a goal from Humphreys ensured that they were one of the few non-League sides to have ever reached the fifth round, where they bowed out 1-0 to West Ham.

The fourth round proved to be an amazing graveyard for the big-name, big-money clubs. Cardiff beat Manchester City and then there were two days of mayhem in the replays. Blackburn, second in the Premier League and with a team valued at £12.9m, lost 1-0 at home to Charlton (£290,000). Arsenal (third, £8.8m) were trounced 3-1 by Bolton (£1.4m) at Highbury in extra time; Newcastle (fourth, £6.9m) lost 2-0 at Luton (£250,000) and Leeds (seventh, £9.9m) lost 3-2 in extra time at home to Oxford (£935,000). In total, £38.5m of Premier League talent had been made to look very foolish by less than £3m of players from the lower divisions.

Arsenal sing the same old song and still hit the right winning note

GEORGE GRAHAM, who had won every domestic honour with Arsenal, finally collected his first European trophy as a manager. He had played in Arsenal's only other European triumph, the 4-3 defeat of Anderlecht in the 1970 Fairs Cup final.

This time Graham inspired his below-strength team to beat Parma, the holders and favourites, 1-0 in the European Cup Winners Cup in Copenhagen. It was a classic Arsenal performance of resolute defence and containing football. Indeed, before the game kicked off, prescient fans sung the club's new anthem "One-Nil to the Arsenal".

In the 20th minute Alan Smith provided the one when he latched on to a failed overhead clearance. The nil came from Arsenal's immaculate back four, in which their captain Tony Adams was outstanding. Bob Wilson, watching Adams at breakfast on the morning of the game, said: "He strolled in like John Wayne. His face was fixed like a mask and it never broke again until the final whistle. You could see him thinking 'This is the day of battle.' He devotes himself to Arsenal. He is their rock."

One-Nil: Smith scores the goal to give Arsenal their European triumph

WORLD CUP 1994
Beauty beat the beast, thanks to Brazil and Fifa

FOOTBALL is about romance and dreams, or it is nothing. After the horrors of 1990 it seemed destined for nothing. But in 1994, despite the disgrace of Diego Maradona failing a drug test and the tragedy of Andres Escobar's murder, the beautiful game was born again. The midwives were Fifa, who used their legislative powers to privilege adventurous play. And, to everybody's satisfaction, Brazil delivered.

They had to. A generation had passed since Pele, Tostao, Rivelino, Gerson et al had last brought the ultimate trophy to the land of the samba. Destiny decreed that Brazil 1994 – Romario, Bebeto, Jorginho, Aldair et al – had finally to fulfil their roles as heirs apparent. They did, in style. Not the 1970 style, eschewing defence and simply relying on scoring more goals than their opponents. This was a modern Brazil: flair was tempered with a competitive and organised strategy that disappointed their attack-crazy fans at home, but won fans worldwide. They coasted serenely to the dream final against Italy.

By contrast their opponents had ridden their luck to have progressed so far. Italy were the worst of the third-placed teams to qualify for the second round. Indeed, their record was worse than the United States and Saudi Arabia. They were seconds away from being eliminated by Nigeria in the second round before Roberto Baggio baled them out. Their luck held again in the quarter-final against Spain, when Julio Salinas missed an easy opportunity and then, with seconds left, the referee missed Mauro Tassotti breaking Luis Enrique's nose in the Italian penalty area.

Sadly for a tournament characterised by exciting football, Italy retreated into their craven shell for the showpiece occasion frequently having their entire team camped in their own half. Frightened to take on the ebullient Brazilians at their own game, Italy played for the breakaway, extra time and the lottery of penalties. They got their comeuppance. After 120 minutes, the greatest show on earth came down to a penalty shoot-out and it was their very own genius, Roberto Baggio, who blasted his shot over to give Brazil an unprecedented fourth World Cup.

Generation game: the Cup returned to Brazil after 24 years

It was a fitting finale: Italian fear had fallen to Brazilian courage and the soul of football was alive and well. Billions of people breathed again, the beautiful game was in safe hands.

Fifa must get much of the credit for this resurrection. They introduced three points for a win in the first round; outlawed the tackle from behind; insisted on a liberal interpretation of the offside rule; forced "injured" players off the field to avoid time-wasting and instructed referees to follow these new guidelines or be banished from the tournament. By and large, the revolution worked. Admittedly some referees were over zealous in their application of the coloured cardboard, but then they, too, got their own red card.

Self-professed experts had dismissed Fifa's initiative as something concocted by meddling bureaucrats. How wrong they were. For the first time forwards were able to ply their trade without fear of defenders scything them down.

True, there were myriad yellow and red cards (227 and 15). But, equally true, attacking football was to the fore precisely because of the fear of punishment. This was not Fifa taking a sledge-hammer to crack a nut – this was taking a scalpel to excise a cancer.

Apart from the final, only two other matches ended in 0-0 draws, and 141 goals were scored. The Americans, who were written off as football dunces, were gripped by the excitement and the spectacle – the 52 matches were watched by 3,567,415 spectators at an average of 68,604 per game. Two billion people watched the final on television and the organisers made a profit of $20m on a $4bn turnover. And this was the tournament that the prophets of doom said was going to be a disaster.

England, along with Northern Ireland, Scotland and Wales, failed to qualify. This was the first time since the Home countries had entered the World Cup in 1950 that all four were absent. The Republic of Ireland, managed by Jack Charlton – a World Cup winner for England in 1966 – were left to carry the flag for the British Isles.

Ireland were duly, and unsurprisingly, adopted by the English media as "our" team. No fewer than 20 of the 22-man squad were playing in the English League (the other two played in Scotland), and were so Irish that the majority of them probably thought brogue was a kind of shoe you bought in posh shops. By and large, it was a journeyman squad of English pros, with Irish grandmothers, who battled hard but were found wanting on the world's biggest stage.

The manager didn't help. Charlton, a dour centre-half for Leeds in the 1960s and 1970s, cut much the same figure as an international manager in the 1980s and 1990s. In a World Cup that was a beacon for the game, Ireland were the only team to play boring, negative football. And Charlton gave the worst possible example to his players. He bitched about the rule changes. He bitched about the supply of water for his players in the desperate heat and humidity in America in the summer. He even argued about a delayed substitution when the paperwork was cocked up. So much so that he received a touchline ban and a £10,000 fine from Fifa.

To the English media, and his similarly fawning fans in Ireland, Jack was standing up to the Fifa mandarins. In reality he was being the same curmudgeonly so-and-so as Don Revie had been in Leeds' dark days. All mouth and no trousers. In the spring, Fifa had invited all the coaches at the World Cup to a briefing where every rule change and procedure for the tournament would be discussed and explained. Who didn't turn up? Charlton. Little wonder Fifa took a dim view of his constant complaints.

Charlton also never realised what tournament he was in. As the other coaches and countries quickly adapted and played attacking football, Charlton's Ireland were Leeds' stick-in-the-muds, trying to win games without really trying to score. Thus, having beaten Italy 1-0 in the opening game, they supinely lost to Mexico 2-1. They rescued themselves with a goalless draw with Norway only to be overrun 2-0 by Holland in the second round.

Sweet and sour: Romario (above left) and Roberto Baggio were the players of the tournament. But it was a disconsolate Baggio who lost the Cup

Their "proud" record under Charlton beggars belief: in two World Cups they have won only two matches out of nine – one of them in a penalty shoot-out – and scored a miserly four goals. Eamon Dunphy, a perennial thorn in Charlton's flesh, summed up their performance in America neatly: "At a tournament notable for its quality, Ireland stood out as beggars at the banquet."

Others relished the feast. Notably the United States who beat Colombia, one of the pre-tournament favourites, to qualify for the second phase where they only went down 1-0 to Brazil. But it was the forgotten states of the post-Communist Balkans that provided the real World Cup fireworks. Bulgaria and Romania did a little more than emerge from Stalinist backwaters, they exploded on to the world scene. Romania reached the quarter-finals. Bulgaria, who had never won a match in five World Cup finals, were inspired by Hristo Stoichkov into the semi-finals.

For the 1998 World Cup in France FIFA must continue with their experiments on the laws of the game, if only to reduce the number of penalty shoot-outs. Since they were introduced in 1982, when there was one, they have mushroomed. But they must look at the cause – not the effect. Instead of tinkering with sudden death extra time, they should change the rules to increase the number of goals scored per match.

FOR THE RECORD

FIRST ROUND

GROUP A	P	W	D	L	F	A	Pts
Romania	3	2	0	1	5	5	6
Switzerland	3	1	1	1	5	4	4
United States	3	1	1	1	3	3	4
Colombia	3	1	0	2	4	5	3

GROUP B	P	W	D	L	F	A	Pts
Brazil	3	2	1	0	6	1	7
Sweden	3	1	2	0	6	4	5
Russia	3	1	0	2	7	6	3
Cameroon	3	0	1	2	3	11	1

GROUP C	P	W	D	L	F	A	Pts
Germany	3	2	1	0	5	3	7
Spain	3	1	2	0	6	4	5
S Korea	3	0	2	1	4	5	2
Bolivia	3	0	1	2	1	4	1

GROUP D	P	W	D	L	F	A	Pts
Nigeria	3	2	0	1	6	2	6
Bulgaria	3	2	0	1	6	3	6
Argentina	3	2	0	1	6	3	6
Greece	3	0	0	3	0	10	0

GROUP E	P	W	D	L	F	A	Pts
Mexico	3	1	1	1	3	3	4
Ireland	3	1	1	1	2	2	4
Italy	3	1	1	1	2	2	4
Norway	3	1	1	1	1	1	4

GROUP F	P	W	D	L	F	A	Pts
Holland	3	2	0	1	4	3	6
Saudi Arabia	3	2	0	1	4	3	6
Belgium	3	2	0	1	2	1	6
Morocco	3	0	0	3	2	5	0

SECOND ROUND

Spain 3   Switzerland 0
HT 1-0 Att. 53,141
Italy 2   Nigeria 1 aet
HT 0-1 Att. 54,367
Germany 3   Belgium 2
HT 3-1 Att. 60,246
Bulgaria 1   Mexico 1
Bulgaria won 3-1 on penalties
HT 1-1 Att. 71,030
Holland 2   Ireland 0
HT 2-0 Att. 61,355
Brazil 1   United States 0
HT 0-0 Att. 84,147
Sweden 3   Saudi Arabia 1
HT 1-0 Att. 60,277
Romania 3   Argentina 2
HT 2-1 Att. 90,469

QUARTER-FINALS

Italy 2   Spain 1
HT 1-0 Att. 53,644
Bulgaria 2   Germany 1
HT 0-0 Att. 72,416
Brazil 3   Holland 2
HT 0-0 Att. 63,998
Sweden 2   Romania 2
Sweden won 5-4 on penalties
HT 0-0 FT 1-1 Att. 81,715

SEMI-FINALS

Italy 2   Bulgaria 1
HT 2-1 Att. 77,094
Brazil 1   Sweden 0
HT 0-0 Att. 84,569

THIRD PLACE

Sweden 4   Bulgaria 0
HT 4-0 Att. 83,716

FINAL

Brazil 0   Italy 0
Brazil won 3-2 on penalties

Teams

Brazil Taffarel; Jorginho (Cafu), Aldair, Marcio Santos, Branco, Mazinho, Mauro Silva, Dunga, Zinho (Viola), Romario, Bebeto
Italy Pagliuca; Mussi (Apolloni), Baresi, Maldini, Benarrivo, Berti, Albertini, D Baggio (Evani), Donadoni, R Baggio, Massaro
Referee S Puhl (Hungary)

Penalty shoot-out

Italy Baresi missed, Albertini scored, Evani scored, Massaro saved, R Baggio missed
Brazil M Santos saved, Romario scored, Branco scored, Dunga scored

Leading goalscorers 6 Hristo Stoichkov (Bulgaria), Oleg Salenko (Russia); 5 Romario (Brazil), Roberto Baggio (Italy), Jurgen Klinsmann (Germany); 4 Martin Dahlin (Sweden), Gabriel Batistuta (Argentina), Florin Raducioiu (Romania), Kennet Andersson (Sweden)

Total goals scored 141
Average per game: 2.71

Sendings-off Marco Etcheverry (Bolivia) v Germany; Referee: A Brizio Carter (Mexico).
Nadal (Spain) v South Korea; Referee: P Mikkelsen (Denmark).
Ioan Vladoiu (Romania) v Switzerland; Referee: N Jouini (Tunisia).
Luis Cristaldo (Bolivia) v South Korea; Referee: L Mottram (Scotland).
Gianluca Pagliuca (Italy) v Norway; Referee: H Krug (Germany).
Sergei Gorlukovich (Russia) v Sweden; Referee: J Quiniou (France).
Rigobert Song (Cameroon) v Brazil; Referee: A Brizio Carter (Mexico).
Tsanko Zetanov (Bulgaria) v Argentina; Referee: N Jouini (Tunisia).
Leonardo (Brazil) v United States; Referee: J Quiniou (France).
Fernando Clavijo (United States) v Brazil.
Gianfranco Zola (Italy) v Nigeria; Referee: A Brizio Carter (Mexico).
Emil Kremenliev (Bulgaria) v Mexico; Referee: Jamal al-Sharif (Syria).
Luis Garcia (Mexico) v Bulgaria.
Stefan Schwarz (Sweden) v Romania; Referee: P Don (England).
Jonas Thern (Sweden) v Brazil; Referee: J Torres Cadena (Colombia).

● An Albanian lost his wife when, short of money, he gambled her on the result of the Argentina versus Bulgaria match. He then complained to the police when his wife left him for the winner of the bet.

● *"Either you mean what you say or you crack jokes, and Fifa never crack jokes."* Guido Tognoni on the disciplinary crackdown.

Gerry wakes up the dreamers

IT CERTAINLY was a roller-coaster season for Tottenham. Although weighed down by the threat of losing six League points and exclusion from the FA Cup, their aspirations were boosted by the instant success of their three foreign stars, Jürgen Klinsmann, Ilie Dumitrescu and Gica Popescu and their extraordinary appetite for goals. Under Osvaldo Ardiles, Spurs opened the season with an all-out attacking side that seemed to operate on a policy of "we'll score more than you do".

It was certainly crowd-pleasing as the Famous Five (Klinsmann, Sheringham, Anderton, Barmby and Dumitrescu) notched up scores like 4-3. Unfortunately the 1990s were not as forgiving as the 1950s. Ardiles' inability to organise his defence was humiliatingly exposed when Notts County knocked Spurs out of the League Cup 3-0 in October. Ardiles was promptly sacked and Gerry Francis, who had fallen out with QPR when they attempted to bring in Rodney Marsh as general manager, replaced him.

Francis turned the team around within weeks. He settled the defence and forced the players through a tough fitness regime. The difference on the pitch was remarkable as Tottenham swiftly moved up the table. They moved up even faster when Alan Sugar's expensive battery of lawyers managed to have the six-point penalty and the exclusion from the FA Cup over-turned on appeal.

It was an embarrassing climb-down for the FA and many thought that Tottenham's name was now on the Cup. And as Klinsmann's goals guided them to a semi-final against Everton, including beating Liverpool at Anfield, most commentators anticipated a dream final against Manchester United. However, Everton refused to follow the script and sent Spurs packing 4-1.

To cap a season that had, at one stage, promised so much but delivered so little, Spurs failed to qualify for Europe, Klinsmann decided to join Bayern Munich and Popescu went to Barcelona to replace Ronald Koeman.

Brief honeymoon: Klinsmann lingered a year, but Ardiles was sacked

Rideout's flair leaves United with nothing

IT WAS a dispiriting season for Manchester United. The team that had so confidently won the Double the year before were expected to blossom and add more silverware to their collection. Instead they ended the season with a bare trophy cabinet.

United's failure in the FA Cup final was perhaps the most wounding reverse. Six days earlier they had lost the championship to Blackburn by a solitary point when they failed to beat West Ham at Upton Park. But at Wembley they were facing an Everton side that had flirted with relegation right up to the end of April.

Everton, with Joe Royle in charge, had showed their Cup mettle in the semi-final when they had obliterated Spurs, so United had no reason to feel complacent. From the kick-off it was obvious that this was to be a keenly-contested final.

Despite wave after wave of United attacks it was Everton who broke the deadlock. In the 30th minute Anders Limpar and Paul Rideout quickly counter-attacked from deep in Everton's half to catch the United midfield and defence napping. Although there were four blue shirts against two red, it required an inspired piece of football from Paul Rideout to make their advantage count.

When Graham Stuart's shot hit the crossbar Peter Schmeichel was caught in no-man's land. But before he had time to react to the rebound Rideout had nodded the ball past him. Despite a stirring second-half performance from Ryan Giggs, who had been brought on during the break, United could not find a way past a determined Everton defence.

Neville Southall played one of the best games of his career in the Everton goal. A double save

Blue heaven: Everton celebrate their defeat of the Cup holders

in the 76th minute from Paul Scholes epitomised United's misery. First he stopped a point-blank shot, then he somehow got his legs in front of Scholes' follow-up.

United had their excuses for losing the Cup final. After all they were without Eric Cantona, who was suspended until October; Andrei Kanchelskis, who had fallen out with Ferguson, and Andy Cole, who was Cup-tied. But this was not the first time they had failed to match the big occasion.

In the autumn they had been swept away in the European champions League by losing 4-0 to Barcelona and 3-1 to Gothenburg.

The loss of Cantona for the final three months of the season certainly did not help United's chances as they chased a second Double. But losing key players at critical times is no excuse, it happens to all teams at some point. United's season ended barren because when the serious questions were asked, they were at a loss for the answers.

Rovers snatch fantasy League

BLACKBURN ROVERS' success in lifting the League title after 81 years fulfilled every romantic's dream and every schoolboy's fantasy. That a founding member of the Football League, whose heyday petered out after the First World War, could turn the tide of history was a fairytale come true. That it was done by a long-suffering fan who dug deep into his pockets and made it work bordered on the miraculous.

For much of the 1980s Rovers had battled away in the then Second Division, constantly just missing out on promotion. Enter Jack Walker, 59, a local businessman and loyal supporter who had sold his steel works for £365m. In 1991 he recruited Kenny Dalglish, who had inexplicably walked out on Liverpool seven months earlier, as the new Rovers manager and, hey presto, they won promotion.

Then Dalglish and Walker got down to the real business: the championship. Walker did his bit by bankrolling serious forays into the transfer market and paying for a spanking new stadium. In total Dalglish spent something like £30m on players, breaking the British transfer record twice with Alan Shearer (1992, £3.6m) and Chris Sutton (1994, £5.5m). Both players proved to be well worth the money, Shearer finishing the 1995 season with 37 goals, and Sutton 21.

This spearhead, supported by the week-in, week-out consistency of the likes of Colin Hendry, Tim Sherwood, Hen-

Priceless asset: Shearer's golden touch delivered 37 invaluable goals

ning Berg and Graham Le Saux (total cost around £2m) saw off Manchester United's attempt to become the fourth club to win the title three years in succession. But it was a close thing.

Blackburn, after a sluggish start with only eight points from their first four games, surged to the top of the Premiership in November and from then on it was a two-horse race with only United in contention. Amaz-

ingly it went right to the wire as Blackburn faltered in the closing stages. On the very last day of the season Manchester United had to win at West Ham and hope that Blackburn failed to beat Liverpool at Anfield. Liverpool duly beat Rovers with a goal in the dying seconds, but an indomitable West Ham side held United to a 1-1 draw and Rovers had finally sneaked the championship by a point.

FOR THE RECORD

- Crystal Palace experienced a unique season. They reached the semi-finals of the FA and League Cups and were relegated from the Premier Division, thus managing to finish in the last four of all three major tournaments.

- Ted Drake, the former Arsenal and England striker, died at the age of 82. As a manager, Drake led Chelsea to their only League title in 1954-55.

- Davie Cooper, the former Scotland and Rangers winger, died in March from a brain haemorrhage at the age of 39.

- Bernard Tapie, the disgraced former president of Marseilles, was sentenced to two years in jail for corruption and tampering with witnesses in the wake of the attempted bribery of Valenciennes players in a French League match just before the European Cup final in 1993. Tapie's former club went into receivership with debts of more than 250m francs.

- Overseas players scored a unique double when English football writers chose Tottenham's Jürgen Klinsmann as the Player of the Year and Scottish writers chose Brian Laudrup, Rangers' Danish international. Laudrup was the first foreign player to win the Scottish award.

- Fulham's Terry Hurlock became the first player to accumulate 61 disciplinary points in the 21-year history of the system.

- A Bolton fan was fined £60 and banned for three months in March after admitting throwing a turnip in front of Graham Taylor, the Wolves manager. In the same month, a Manchester City fan was banned from bringing dead chickens into the ground. He used to celebrate City goals by swinging them around his head.

- British Steel withdrew their sponsorship of Middlesbrough when they discovered that only 2,000 tonnes of British steel were used in the construction of the club's new £16m stadium. The other 18,000 tonnes were imported from Germany.

- Nantes' 32-match unbeaten run in the French League came to an end when they were beaten 2-0 by Strasbourg. Paris St Germain previously held the record with 26 matches unbeaten.

- Malaysia banned 58 players in April after they admitted being involved in match fixing.

Yes? No? Yes! Sutton's toe-poke proves decisive as Blackburn beat Liverpool 3-2 in October

279

Thugs take to foreign fields

Yob mentality: English hooligans flaunt the Nazi salute in Dublin. The match was abandoned after 28 minutes

IN THE season of sleaze the last thing English football needed was an outbreak of football-related violence, particularly as the introduction of closed-circuit television, all-seater stadiums and more sophisticated police intelligence had stopped the hooligans in their tracks. But not abroad.

When England played the Republic of Ireland in a "friendly" in Dublin in February a neo-Nazi group, Combat 18, exploited the naivety of the Irish police to wreck the match. Using the pretext of the peace talks with the IRA, they whipped up an atmosphere of hate before the kick-off with Nazi salutes and chants of "No surrender to the IRA".

When David Kelly put Ireland ahead in the 12th minute they seized their opportunity. Seats were ripped up in the upper tier of the west stand in Lansdowne Road and hurled on to the mostly Irish supporters below. The match was abandoned as hundreds of spectators spilled on to the pitch to escape the trouble.

Despite repeated warnings from the English police, the Garda had kept too low a profile and known hooligans had been allowed into Ireland. Tickets were easily available and segregation became impossible.

A fortnight later the Belgian police adopted an entirely different approach when Chelsea played Bruges in the European Cup Winners Cup. They turned water cannons on fighting fans, rounded up 1,000 ticketless Chelsea supporters, detained them until the match was over, and then deported the lot.

Sadly the lesson did not travel to Spain. When Chelsea played Zaragoza in the next round tickets were sold to all-comers and the inevitable happened after Chelsea conceded a third goal. Fortunately the Spanish police, in riot gear, quelled the mayhem.

Consolation for Old Firm, misery for New Firm

RANGERS duly won the one that mattered, their 45th League title. And with eight successive championships under their belt they were one more title away from emulating Celtic's record of nine in a row from 1965 to 1974. But for the Ibrox management the rest of the season was a nightmare. Early elimination from the European Cup, the League Cup and the Scottish Cup emphasised that although they dominate the Scottish Premier Division, they are no Cup side.

Celtic, despite back-room rows between their manager, Tommy

Laudrup: crucial for Rangers

Burns, and their chairman, Fergus McCann, finally managed to end their six-year trophy drought when they beat Airdrie with a goal from Pierre van Hooijdonk to win the Scottish Cup. Airdrie were no mean opponents. In fact, they were the form Cup side of the season and that defeat was only their second in 14 Cup matches.

For Aberdeen and Dundee United, the teams dubbed the New Firm in the 1980s, it was a torrid year. Aberdeen's League position was so perilous that Willie Miller, once their most popular and successful player, was dismissed as manager and replaced by Roy Aitken. But even Aitken's attempts to

steady the sinking ship seemed doomed as Aberdeen stared relegation – for the first time in their history – in the face. Being knocked out of the Scottish Cup by lowly Stenhousemuir was a further embarrassment and Aberdeen just avoided the final ignominy of the drop by beating Dunfermline in the play-offs.

Dundee United, the Cup winners the previous season, were not so fortunate despite a change in manager. Ivan Golac left in March and was replaced by Billy Kirkwood, but the rot was set and United were relegated for the first time since 1932. They were replaced by Raith Rovers, who also won the Scottish League Cup.

Nayim's bolt from the blue stuns Seaman and Arsenal

IT CAME like a bolt of lightning. With less than 30 seconds to go in extra time of the European Cup Winners Cup final, with the scores level at one apiece, David Seaman had two things on his mind as the Zaragoza attack crossed the half-way line. Be in a position to defend against a wicked cross, and get mentally prepared for the penalty shoot-out. Nayim had other ideas.

Suddenly, from 50 yards, he unleashed a parabolic right-foot shot so deadly accurate that the back-pedalling Seaman, despite getting a hand to it, was powerless to stop it. Don't blame the goalkeeper, praise the goalscorer. L'Equipe, the French sports daily, rated it as the best goal in the last 10 years in any competition in the world.

For Seaman, and Arsenal, it was devastating. This time there was no chance of coming back. Arsenal's march to the final in Paris had been a nerve-jangling saga that had drawn on all their grit and endeavour. They had battled past Auxerre by winning 1-0 away, having drawn 1-1 at Highbury. They had gone on to conjure a remarkable result in Sampdoria when Ian Wright and Stefan Schwarz twice pulled them back from the brink of defeat. Seaman then put the icing on the marzipan by saving three penalties in the shoot-out.

But Arsenal's bid to become the first club to retain the trophy was thwarted by Mohamed Ali Amar, a Spaniard born in North Africa, whose soubriquet, Nayim, means "lucky". Cruelly, for four years he had been a Tottenham player under Terry Venables. Nayim and Paul Gascoigne had practised such "impossible" goals on the Spurs' training pitch. Long after the final was over Nayim reminded journalists of the spectacular 35-yard free-kick that Gascoigne had scored against Arsenal in the 1991 FA Cup semi-final. The goalkeeper that day? David Seaman.

Seaman saved three penalties in the semi-final in Italy only to be caught out in the final in France

Kluivert and Ajax find a chink in Milan's armour to bring their European dreams crashing down

MILAN's domination of European club football stuttered when they lost 1-0 to the young Turks of Ajax in Vienna. It was Milan's fifth European Cup final in seven years (winning three) and Fabio Capello's ageing team were seeking to emulate Real Madrid's record of winning the trophy six times.

Billed as one of the great showdowns, the match was more of a chess game with both sides happy to keep possession and probe for the counter attack. After 85 minutes the deadlock was broken when Frank Rijkaard, a former Milan player, found Kluivert with just enough space in the penalty area to lose his two markers and the Ajax player coolly slotted the ball past Rossi.

Does Ajax's victory suggest they will be the new Milan? Francisco Gento, who played in all of Madrid's six triumphs, thought not: "They play well as a team, but have only two or three smart players. This is not the beginning of an epoch."

Happy returns: Danny Blind brandishes Ajax's fourth European Cup

THE
1994-95
SEASON

Season of shame

NOVEMBER

Bruce Grobbelaar, Southampton's goalkeeper, is accused of match-fixing.

Paul Merson, the Arsenal striker, admits he has abused alcohol and drugs and is addicted to gambling.

JANUARY

Eric Cantona, Manchester United's French forward, assaults a Crystal Palace fan after being sent off.

FEBRUARY

Hundreds of Chelsea fans invade the pitch at Stamford Bridge after losing to Millwall in the FA Cup.

England's "friendly" against the Republic of Ireland in Dublin is abandoned because of rioting English fans.

Arsenal sack their manager, George Graham, after a Premier League investigation alleges that he received £425,000 from two transfer deals.

Belgian police deport more than 800 Chelsea fans before, and after, their European Cup Winners Cup tie.

MARCH

Chris Armstrong, Crystal Palace's striker, tested positive for cannabis.

Dennis Wise, the Chelsea captain, is given a three-month jail sentence for attacking a taxi driver. The conviction was quashed on appeal.

Grobbelaar, Aston Villa's John Fashanu and Wimbledon's Hans Segers are arrested by police investigating allegations of match-fixing.

APRIL

A Crystal Palace fan is crushed to death by a coach before the FA Cup semi-final against Manchester United at Villa Park when rival fans fight outside a pub.

Four days later, in the replay, both managers appeal to the crowd for peace but Roy Keane is sent off for stamping on Gareth Southgate. The FA fine him £5,000 for bringing the game into disrepute.

MAY

Ray Parlour is fined £800 in Hong Kong for an assault on a taxi driver while on tour with Arsenal.

The year sleaze threatened

A sorry mess from Cantona to Roy Keane

IT MAY have been a string of bizarre coincidences but, sadly, the 1994-95 season will be remembered for the wrong reasons: the year that football mirrored John Major's ailing government and slid into an ooze of sleaze. The scandal sheet (see panel) lists a variety of misdemeanours, mostly unconnected, but the overall picture was of a game seriously out of control.

Not that anybody quite realised that when the match-fixing allegations against Bruce Grobbelaar – the most serious since the 1960s – first surfaced in November. But within weeks that bombshell turned out to be the first salvo in a blitz of seismic proportions. One of the most shocking incidents was the insane kung-fu assault that Eric Cantona perpetrated on Matthew Simmons, a Crystal Palace supporter who had leapt from his seat and rushed to the perimeter of Selhurst Park to harangue the dismissed Manchester United star with a string

Storm at the Palace: mayhem ensues after Cantona's assault on a spectator who hurled abuse at him

of obscenities and gestures as he trudged off the pitch.

The incident was captured by television cameras and was front-page news for days as United banned Cantona for the rest of season. The FA extended the ban to the end of September, and then a magistrate sentenced Cantona to two weeks' imprisonment. Judicial sense finally prevailed and the jail sentence was overturned on appeal, with Cantona ordered to perform 120 hours' community service instead, teaching football to Manchester kids.

Somehow *l'affaire Cantona* seemed to have opened the floodgates as scandal followed scandal. Even hooliganism

reared its ugly head, first abroad and then at home when a 35-year-old Crystal Palace fan, Paul Nixon, died in a pub car park before United's FA Cup semi-final tie against Crystal Palace. Bad blood over the Cantona incident 11 weeks earlier was blamed for sparking the fracas in Birmingham.

Despite the opprobrium heaped on the hapless French star, Cantona did not quite fit in with the others implicated in the season of sleaze. He did at least have some sort of justification – he simply, and foolishly, lost his temper in the face of provocation. By contrast, Roy Keane's behaviour in the semi-final replay four days after the death of that Palace fan was in a different league.

He knew he was supposed to be on his best behaviour. Yet in a match where both managers had pleaded for peace in football before the kick-off, Keane decided to take the law into his own hands and mercilessly stamped on Gareth Southgate after the Crystal Palace defender had caught him with a late tackle. What was he thinking of? Certainly not the good of the game.

Addiction: Merson tells his sad tale

Lager lout: Merson used to drink 14 pints of lager a night

PAUL MERSON became the first Premier League player to confess to taking drugs when he told the Daily Mirror in November that he had been hooked on cocaine for the past year, often spending £150 a night on the drug. He also revealed he was an alcoholic and addicted to gambling – drinking 14 pints of lager a night and running up gambling debts of £108,000.

Having bared his soul in the press, the Arsenal striker threw himself on the mercy of the FA and George Graham, his manager, begging for "one last chance".

Fortunately for Merson, both the FA and his club heeded his pleas and agreed to give him his "last chance" if he underwent a

six-week course at a private drug and drink rehabilitation clinic. The 26-year-old readily complied and also voluntarily enrolled in Gamblers Anonymous. Another part of his treatment was to visit schools warning children of the dangers of alcohol and drugs.

After Merson successfully completed his £2,000-a-week treatment he said: "I have completely changed, I have started to grow up. It was the hardest six weeks I have known. I am an alcoholic, I can never drink again." Merson's rehabilitation was also translated to the football field as he swiftly returned to the Arsenal team, helping them reach the European Cup Winners Cup final.

to destroy the very soul of the game

Bungs: FA ban sacked Arsenal boss

ARSENAL sacked George Graham, one of the most successful managers in their history, when an inquiry by the Premier League concluded that he had received payments from transfers. The inquiry found that Graham, who had won six trophies in eight years, had received a total of £425,000 when John Jensen and Pal Lydersen were signed from the Danish club Brondby in 1991 and IK Start, a Norwegian club, in 1992. Both transfers involved the Norwegian agent Rune Hauge.

Graham's defence was that he had regarded the money as an "unsolicited gift" and had, in any case, repaid the money, plus £40,000 in interest, to Arsenal in December 1994 when he learnt that it was not a gift. However, the investigators could not agree with Graham's version of events: "We have great difficulty in accepting that Mr Graham did not know that the payments derived directly from the transfer fees paid by Arsenal."

Graham claimed that he had been the victim of "a kangaroo-court judgment". However in July a FA commission banned him from football for 12 months and ordered him to pay part of the costs of the case.

The rumours about Scandinavian transfers handled by Hauge had swirled around the game for a couple of years and the full story was originally uncovered by a Danish journalist, Henrik Madsen. The discrepancies in the transfer payments only came to light because Hamburg, who had sold Jensen to Brondby, had not received their 25% of the stated transfer fee of £1.57m. Instead they had only got 25% of the £900,000 that Brondby had actually received from Hauge.

Bad luck turned out to be Graham's undoing. Arsenal were drawn against Brondby in the European Cup Winners Cup

Another one that got away: Cole scores a hattrick in a match that Grobbelaar was allegedly given £40,000 to fix

Graham: backhander blunders

and when the two sets of directors met the discrepancy between the two sums was confirmed. The Inland Revenue also began to take an interest and when Graham was questioned about the tax implications of his dealings with Hauge he was advised by counsel to return the money, which he did. But it was too late.

Match fixing: Grobbelaar sparks police probe

IT IS the most damaging accusation of all and goes right to the soul of any sport: match-fixing. In November The Sun ran a six-page exposé of Bruce Grobbelaar and provided television, the FA and the police with video evidence to back up their story. The secretly recorded video purportedly showed the Southampton goalkeeper discussing with his former friend and fellow soldier Chris Vincent how he had thrown matches for cash.

The Sun claimed that Grobbelaar had been given £40,000 by a syndicate of Asian businessmen to throw Liverpool's match at Newcastle in November 1993, Liverpool lost 3-0, a 20-1 long shot. The paper also alleged that the former Liverpool goalkeeper joked about how he had lost out when he made two "unintentional" saves against Manchester United in January 1993. "Do you know how much money I lost?" he was reported as saying, "£125,000."

Vincent, who had been involved with Grobbelaar in failed business ventures in their native Zimbabwe, allegedly persuaded him to accept a £2,000 payment as a retainer to be paid every fortnight towards throwing a match later in the season. Grobbelaar protested his innocence and issued a libel writ against the newspaper. The FA charged him with bringing the game into disrepute but said they would take no action until the police had completed their investigations.

In dawn raids in March, Hampshire police arrested Grobbelaar, John Fashanu of Aston Villa, the Wimbledon goalkeeper Hans Segers, Fashanu's girlfriend and a Malaysian businessman. They were detained overnight after 20 officers raided four addresses, seizing documents and property, and were eventually released on police bail.

Rumours about Segers had started circulating after the disclosures in November, and centred on the last match of the 1993-94 season when, after leading 2-0, Wimbledon lost 3-2 to Everton, who thus narrowly avoided relegation. Segers was widely blamed for the final goal. Fashanu claimed he was only roped in because he had attempted to act as a mediator between Grobbelaar and Vincent over their failed business.

Speculation also centred on Far East gambling syndicates, in particular those based in Malaysia, where the rigging of matches was so commonplace that punters had turned their attention to betting on English League games.

ERIC CANTONA
L'Enfant Terrible

Chris Nawrat

Cantona won three successive League titles

THERE WAS just the merest hint of a smile on Eric Cantona's stoic face when he faced the media after a judge had quashed his jail sentence in March 1995. "When seagulls follow a trawler it is because they think sardines will be thrown into the sea," the great enigma announced to the cameras and scribblers. He never said another word and he left his questioners speechless. What did he mean? they clamoured. Did he mean anything? Thus, with one deft brushstroke, Eric artistically reclaimed himself from the snapping pack, and left them trailing in his wake, *sans* sardines. It was a classic Eric performance: out-fox the opposition with the impossible to comprehend. Ask any defender what Eric can do to you and they will tell you much the same story. The man is just impossible.

But that was on his curriculum vitae when he arrived from France to ply his trade in England. As was his genius. When you buy Cantona, you buy all of him – the tantrums and the tantalising ability. Manchester United bought a man who managed to get sent off twice in four days of madness in March 1994 as they faltered in their quest for the championship, but re-emerged to grasp that title and score twice in the Cup final to seal United's first Double.

The Manchester United manager has stood by Cantona throughout all his troubles, and with good reason. The Frenchman brought him two successive League titles, the first ending a 26-year drought. He also sees a side of Cantona that the public do not. Alex Ferguson describes him as "the best player I have ever worked with" and goes on to extol his supreme professionalism: "He is the first to arrive for training and the last to leave, and the work he puts into it is phenomenal, especially the help he gives other players. That's not all, he's the one who will stand all day signing autographs for kids and the first to volunteer to visit a hospital or a school." A model professional and a model schizophrenic?

Not since George Best and the Swinging Sixties has a player been so idolised in England, not even that other rascal Paul Gascoigne. And, like that devil-may-care pair, Cantona has received as much opprobrium as adulation. But where Gascoigne and Best were mostly infamous for their off-the pitch activities, Cantona's infamy was confined to the game. Brushes with referees, managers and officialdom; cynical fouls on opponents; punch-ups with teammates; frequent sendings off . . . this was the dark side of Cantona.

It was a dark side that exploded into the public glare in January 1995 at Selhurst Park, when Eric saw red and took the law into his own hands. The incident split the nation. Few people condoned Cantona's kung-fu

Comrades in arms: the strike force of Cantona and Jean-Pierre Papin swept Marseille to the title

ERIC CANTONA

Born May 24, 1966, Paris

PLAYING CAREER

Auxerre 1983-88
81 League matches, 23 goals. On loan to Martigues in 1985-86. Highest League position fourth in 1987. Fined for giving his goalkeeper a black eye and suspended for three months after a dangerous tackle.

Marseille 1988-89
22 League matches, 5 goals. Signed for £2m, a French record. Immediately won the League and Cup Double. Suspended indefinitely after kicking a ball into the crowd and throwing his shirt at a referee after being substituted. Loaned to Bordeaux.

Bordeaux 1989
11 League matches, 6 goals. Transferred for constantly missing training.

Montpellier 1989-90
33 League matches, 10 goals. Signed for £300,000. Won the French Cup. Suspended for 10 days after a fight with a teammate, throwing his boots in his face.

Marseille 1990-91
18 League matches, 8 goals. Signed by Franz Beckenbauer, Cantona had a dream start on his return, scoring 7 goals in the first 12 games of the season, but was then out for three months because of injury. Cantona never hit it off with Raymond Goethals, who replaced Beckenbauer.

Nimes 1991-92
17 League matches, 2 goals. Banned for three games for throwing the ball in a referee's face. Suspended for two months after attacking an opponent. Decided to retire after calling each member of a disciplinary committee "idiot" to their face.

Leeds United 1992
28 League matches, 9 goals; 5 European Cup

attack on a foul-mouthed yobbish spectator, but the country was divided over his punishment. The rent-a-quote right and the rabid tabloids demanded his head; the more discerning agreed with a long suspension and a heavy fine and hoped that the French genius would once again grace an English football field – and in the familiar No 7 shirt of Manchester United.

Let's go back to the summer of 1992 to see the bright side of Eric Cantona. To a glorious August afternoon when, basking in the glory of having brought Leeds their first championship for 18 years, Cantona scored a magical hat-trick in the Charity Shield to beat Liverpool 4-3 in a thrilling match. Each goal demonstrated Cantona's coolness when in the thick of the action.

The first was a thumping right-foot shot between two defenders from virtually the penalty spot; the second was another right-footer when, having headed down Gary McAllister's free-kick, Cantona instinctively latched on to a rebound from Rodney Wallace's chest; and, for variation, Cantona scored the third with his head, soaring above Mark Wright to leave Bruce Grobbelaar chasing shadows. The cries of "Ooh! Aah! Cantona!" from adoring Leeds fans rang round Wembley. By November the chant had been taken up by the Old Trafford faithful and by May he had fulfilled their wildest dream, the long-awaited championship. Cantona was on song for his country too, playing in four World Cup qualifiers and scoring four times. But then the red mist descended yet again.

Perhaps in all the millions of words that have tried to tease out the secret of this temperamental superstar one thing has been overlooked. For although born in a Paris suburb and brought up on the outskirts of Marseille, Cantona isn't quite French. In fact, he possesses a potent genetic cocktail that is quite explosive. His paternal grandfather was a Sardinian who emigrated to Marseille in 1955 and his maternal grandfather was an officer in the Spanish Republican army who fought against Franco, eventually seeking exile in southern France.

With that mix of fiery and passionate blood coursing through his veins, it is not surprising that Eric Cantona is regarded as both a hot-head and a genius. The French version of Spitting Image plays on his antecedents: Cantona's puppet is called Picasso and he paints red cards and gives them to himself.

Cantona's own interest in philosophy and the arts, in particular the French symbolist poet Rimbaud, was much trumpeted when he first arrived in England, and his own artistic efforts are quite revealing. His paintings are dramatic, expressionist canvases of bold, primary colours and his writings are quite heady stuff. For example: "An artist, in my eyes, is someone who can lighten up a dark room. I have never, and will never, find any difference between the pass from Pele to Carlos Alberto in the final of the World Cup in 1970 and the poetry of the young Rimbaud who stretches 'cords from steeple to steeple and garlands from window to window'. There is in each of these human manifestations an expression of beauty which touches us and gives us a feeling of eternity."

Pretentious? Maybe. But Cantona has designed his very demeanour to set himself apart from your average pro. He moves ramrod straight, like a soldier, with his collar turned up. And although he looks and dresses the part there is something that is not quite right, it's as if he conforms, but insolently. For his first court appearance he turned up without a collar and tie, having spent most of the small hours at

---

I am going training. I need to be fit for my next game

ERIC CANTONA

London nightclubs. His favourite player used to be Johann Cruyff, now it is Diego Maradona ("He's a genius who couldn't have had it any other way").

Everything about Cantona says this is a man with attitude, a man who will not let any personal injustice go unpunished, a man marked by his émigré Latin parentage. It is as if he is following Rimbaud's maxim that "to arrive at the unknown one must make oneself an outcast". It is something he has religiously done throughout his career. But then he would – he has always been steadfastly his own man.

Cantona's defence to all of his accusers and critics is what he achieves on the football pitch: his sublime feints, shimmies, delicate little backheels, exquisitely timed passes, and goals scored with the panache of a maestro. "He's lit up my football watching and that's what it's all about," George Best has said of the *enfant terrible*. "I would pay to watch Cantona." And in a game obsessed by money, that is the bottom line.

That's my boy: Cantona's goals inspired Manchester United to their first Double

---

matches; 2 goals. Only signed for Leeds because Trevor Francis, Sheffield Wednesday's manager, wanted him to do an extra week's trial. Howard Wilkinson snapped him up for £900,000. Inspired Leeds to their first championship since 1974. Became a cult figure with the fans at Elland Road but was too much to handle for Wilkinson, who dismayed his supporters by selling Cantona for £1.2m to arch-rivals Manchester United.

Manchester United 1992-
77 League matches, 39 goals; 7 FA Cup matches, 5 goals; 6 European Cup matches, 2 goals. The flowering of Cantona: the League championship in 1993, the Double a year later and the PFA Player of the Year in 1994, the first overseas player to be so honoured.
Fined £1,000 by the FA for spitting at hostile fans at Elland Road. Sent off in a European Cup-tie in Turkey in 1993 for accusing a referee of cheating and scuffling with the police – banned by Uefa for four European games.
Banned for five domestic games in 1994 after being sent off twice in four days. Also arrested and handcuffed by security guards at the World Cup after a row with an official. Sent off in a pre-season friendly and banned for three games.
Sent off against Crystal Palace in 1995 and attacked fan who was taunting him. United suspended him for the rest of the season and fined him £20,000. The FA extended the ban until September 30 and fined him a further £10,000. A Croydon magistrate sentenced him to two weeks' jail but this was reduced to 120 hours community service on appeal.

Internationals Debut in 1987, scoring in a 2-1 defeat by West Germany. 45 caps. Banned from the national side in 1988 after calling the manager, Henri Michel, "a bag of shit". When Michel was replaced by Michel Platini, Cantona's ban was rescinded. Aime Jacquet, the next manager, made him the national captain but Cantona was sacked after the Crystal Palace incident.

THE
1995-96
SEASON

Juventus lay the ghost of Heysel to rest

THE OMENS were not good for Juventus in the European Cup final. Ajax were hot favourites to win and repeat their three successive victories of the 1970s.

For Juventus, last year's beaten Uefa Cup finalists, it was a trophy they desperately needed to win. They had lost their first two European Cup finals by a single goal and then, when they did win, in 1985 against Liverpool in Heysel, 39 fans had been tragically killed before the kick-off. It was an empty victory, tarnished by blood and tears.

Their desire to win was evident from the start and, in the 12th minute, Fabrizio Ravanelli scored a goal born from this determination. Frank de Boer had attempted to head the ball back to his keeper, Edwin van der Sar, but Ravanelli darted past and slotted the ball home.

De Boer compensated for his error four minutes before half-time. This time it was the turn of Angelo Peruzzi, the Juventus keeper, to commit a gaffe when he could only pat de Boer's swerving free-kick on to the back of one of his defenders. Jari Litmanen seized on the mistake.

The second half became tedious as fear seemed to grip both sides, although Juventus had good chances to win in the closing minutes. Extra time was much the same. The penalty shoot-out gave Peruzzi the chance to make up for his costly error in the first half.

He did so in style, stopping Ajax's first penalty from Edgar Davids, and the fourth from Sonny Silooy to give Juventus a 4-2 penalty victory and a "real" European Cup triumph.

Demolition job: Juventus players celebrate their thrashing of Rangers on the way to winning the European Cup

Europe runs rings round Britain

BRITISH CLUBS did not enjoy the best of times in Europe, with only Nottingham Forest making any real progress.

Blackburn were cruelly exposed in the European Champions League. The low point came in Moscow with the unedifying sight of Graeme Le Saux and David Batty brawling during the match against Spartak Moscow. Rangers did little better in their group, getting hammered by Juventus – the Italians' 4-0 victory was Rangers' heaviest home defeat in more than three decades of European competition.

Celtic fared just as badly, going down 3-0 to Paris Saint Germain, the eventual winners of the Cup Winners' Cup, for their worst-ever result at home in Europe.

There was little to cheer on Merseyside either. Liverpool became the first English team to lose to a Danish side when they were hustled out of the Uefa Cup by the part-timers of Brondby. And Everton had

Craig Short sent off as they succumbed to Feyenoord.

Manchester United suffered the acute embarrasment of a first-round elimination by the unheralded Georgians of Rotor Volgograd, and Leeds were blown away 8-3 on aggregate (yet another worst-ever performance) by PSV Eindhoven, leaving only Nottingham Forest to fly the flag.

When Forest returned from Germany only 2-1 behind after the first leg of their Uefa Cup quarter-final with Bayern Munich, Steve Stone really should have known better than to say that their opponents were nothing special.

Forest played much the better football in the first half of the second leg but wasted a series of chances and had a goal disallowed. By half-time Bayern were 2-0 up and from then on it was one-way traffic as they coasted to a 5-1 win on the night and a 7-2 victory on aggregate.

To compound the suffering, Uefa then stripped England of a

place in the Uefa Cup because of the half-hearted attitude that had been taken to the InterToto Cup before the start of the season. Tottenham and Wimbledon were banned from Europe for fielding under-strength teams, but the ban was overturned on appeal.

Klinsmann: tormented Forest

Paisley, Liverpool's nice guy with the winning touch, dies

Paisley: decade of success

BOB PAISLEY, the former Liverpool manager, died on February 14, aged 77. His place in the pantheon of English football was best summed up by the former Liverpool captain Emlyn Hughes, who said: "When you talk of the greats you think of Sir Matt Busby, Jock Stein and Bill Shankly. If he is not among them he should be above them because none of them achieved what he did in the domestic game."

Paisley's achievements were truly remarkable, 20 trophies – three European Cups, one Uefa Cup, one European Super Cup, six League championships, three League Cups and six Charity Shields (one shared) – in less than a decade. They were even more remarkable because Paisley had, at first, not wanted to take charge at Anfield.

When Shankly announced his retirement in 1974, Paisley had tried to persuade him to stay on. Paisley reluctantly became manager, thinking he would be a stop-gap appointment and telling his players he did not fancy the job.

Everyone assumed that he would never be able to emerge from the shadow of Shankly, but they were quickly proved wrong by the former bricklayer from County Durham.

Paisley, a diffident man who always seemed happiest when wearing one of his trademark cardigans, claimed there was no secret to his success. However, there was no doubt that he had a prodigious eye for talent.

It was Paisley who took the foundations that Shankly had established and seamlessly added on the skills of Kenny Dalglish, Alan Hansen, Phil Neal, Graeme Souness and Ian Rush. He bought Dalglish to replace Kevin Keegan because he was "a Liverpool type".

That was typical of Paisley, who personified the ethos of the Boot Room. As a young wing-half, he won the FA Amateur Cup with Bishop Auckland before signing for Liverpool just before the start of the Second World War. He played 252 League matches before retiring in 1954 and joining the coaching staff as an assistant trainer. Paisley rose through the ranks, establishing a reputation as a skilled physiotherapist, to become Shankly's assistant.

Paisley was voted manager of the year a record six times, prompting Brian Clough to remark that he proved the fallacy of the myth that nice guys win nothing. When Paisley announced his retirement in 1983, a measure of the respect of his players was that the team insisted that he should be the one to climb the steps at Wembley to collect the League Cup.

> ## Nobody has the right to win anything they haven't earned
> BOB PAISLEY
> after his first European
> Cup triumph in 1977

■ An irate Wimbledon fan confronted Sam Hammam, the team's owner, after Leeds won 4-2 at Selhurst Park in September. The fan demanded a refund on his season ticket and was stunned when Hammam promptly obliged, handing over a handful of cash and tearing up the ticket.

■ Samba fever swept Teesside when Middlesbrough signed the 22-year-old Brazilian international Juninho (below) in October for £5m. Bryan Robson then signed two more Brazilians, the veteran full-back Branco and the midfielder Emerson.

■ An Italian referee abandoned a Second Division match in the 89th minute resulting in a punter just failing to win a 12 billion lire fortune on the pools.

■ Alan Shearer became the first player to score 30 goals in an English season in three successive years.

■ Manchester United, losing 3-0 at Southampton in April, abandoned their grey strip at half time and switched to blue and white striped kit. Alex Ferguson said the reason was that his players could not see each other.

■ Sam Hammam (below) announced in November that Wimbledon were considering moving to Dublin. The club said they could not afford to stay in London because they did not have their own ground and only drew small crowds. Irish clubs, fearful of the impact on their own small attendances, objected.

■ The Halifax Referees' Society called a one-week strike in December in protest at the number of attacks on their officials. More than 50 matches in three leagues had to be postponed.

■ Football suffered the worst disruption caused by weather since 1963. A total of 55 matches were postponed in England and Scotland on January 27.

■ Two days after the season ended, Barry Fry, the Birmingham manager, joined the merry-go-round at St Andrew's. Fry had signed 61 players in his three-year tenure. Thirty-six hours before he was sacked, he had been assured by David Sullivan that his future was safe. Fry was replaced by Birmigham hero Trevor Francis.

Rangers draw clear of Celtic

RANGERS' march to their eighth successive league championship wasn't the procession many had predicted as a rejuvenated Celtic harried them all the way. Indeed, if Tommy Burns's team had converted some of their 11 draws into victories, the trophy would have returned to Parkhead for the first time since 1988.

Paul Gascoigne, despite the odd brush with officialdom, proved to be the influential player that Smith had hoped he would be, and his 19 goals from midfield were duly rewarded when he was voted Scottish Player of the Year. Brian Laudrup and Gordon Durie were two other key influences in Rangers' triumphs. And it was this pair that dominated the Scottish Cup final.

Hearts went into the match buoyed by having two successive defeats of Rangers under their belts and by half-time were trailing by only one goal. Then an elementary blunder by Frenchman Gilles Rousset, when he fumbled a Laudrup cross and let it slip through his legs, opened the floodgates. Durie, with a hat-trick, and Laudrup, with two goals, ran riot and Hearts were demolished 5-1. It was Rangers' 14th Double and the biggest winning margin in a Cup final for 24 years.

Aberdeen won a dour Scottish League Cup final 2-0 against Dundee. Still, it was their first trophy since 1990 and, given that last season they were one match away from relegation, it is unlikely that the manner of victory bothered their manager, Roy Aitken. This was the last match to be played in front of the historic 92-year old-South Stand.

Upsetting the apple-cart: Bosman went to the European Court of Justice

Transfer market is thrown into chaos by Bosman verdict

THE FINAL twist in a long-running dispute between a Belgian player and his former club shook European football to its foundations. The prophets of doom claimed that it heralded the greatest revolution in English football since the abolition of the maximum wage.

Jean-Marc Bosman had been signed by RFC Liége for £66,000 in 1988. Two years later, when his contract expired, he was offered a new deal, but with his wages cut by 60%. Bosman said that he would rather move to Dunkerque. Liége responded by demanding a transfer fee in excess of £250,000, more than twice the sum that the French club were prepared to pay.

Bosman, left in limbo, began a court case claiming that he was the victim of restraint of trade. He fought all the way to the European Court of Justice which, in a preliminary ruling in December, found in his favour.

The court said that existing transfer regulations were in breach of European Union law governing the free movement of workers between member states. The court also said restrictions on the number of foreign players a team could field in European competitions were also unlawful.

Football was horrified. Smaller clubs, whose lifeline was developing young players and selling them on feared that their main source of income would be wiped out at a stroke, and the Professional Footballers' Association predicted that many of its members would be put out of work by an influx of foreign players.

While Uefa threatened to defy the court, England took the lead. Within a week, the Premier League accepted the ruling and told its clubs that they were free to field as many European nationals as they saw fit.

Rick Parry, the Premier League chief executive, then engaged in some astute diplomacy. He suggested that the British system, where an out of contract player is automatically granted a free transfer if he is not offered a new deal on at least the same terms as the old one, could be a model for the rest of Europe.

His patient lobbying paid off when the court confirmed that their ruling only applied to out of contract European nationals moving between member states of the European Union.

So deals between British clubs were not affected, nor was the transfer of players to and from countries outside the European Union. Agents, though, were still predicting a bonanza for players.

They said clubs would use the money they would otherwise have spent on transfer fees to pay signing-on bonuses and higher wages to attract out of contract players. And they raised the spectre of a player going from one English team to another via a temporary transfer to a European club to exploit the court's ruling.

It seemed likely that the only people who were certain to benefit would be lawyers as more test cases got taken to court.

Parry: diplomatic solution

England choose Hoddle as new coach

Next in line: Venables congratulates his successor

ONCE Terry Venables had made it clear that there was no going back on his decision not to continue as England coach after the European championships, the hunt was on for his successor.

The tabloids that had been excoriating Lancaster Gate for letting Venables go, promptly switched their attention to speculating on who would replace him.

The FA, although mindful that England's first qualifying match for the 1998 World Cup was only a few months away, refused to be rushed. They called in Jimmy Armfield, who had been their special adviser when Venables was appointed, to assist them again.

As the weeks dragged on, a host of names entered the frame – Steve Coppell, Alex Ferguson, Gerry Francis, Kevin Keegan, Howard Kendall, Bryan Robson and Howard Wilkinson to name but a few. One by one they were ruled out, either because they were unwilling to accept the poisoned chalice, or because of their club commitments, or because they were little more than the product of fevered tabloid imaginations.

Finally, in May, the die was cast. After taking several days to consider the offer, and despite efforts by Chelsea to keep him, Glenn Hoddle accepted a four-year contract, worth an estimated £300,000 a year.

Armfield hinted that Robson, Venables' assistant, had been considered first. But there was a widespread feeling that the FA had been running out of options and Hoddle, said to be unhappy with the unrest at Stamford Bridge and with only a month left to run on his contract with Chelsea, was the obvious, and perhaps the only, choice.

The irony of appointing Hoddle was not lost on a lot of people. A player widely respected throughout England and the continent had been chosen. Yet this was the same player who had only won 53 caps, having often found himself out of favour with the national side.

Hoddle, diplomatically, merely said: "I've had a burning ambition to do this since I was very young. It's the only job, in England or abroad, which I would have left Chelsea for."

Chelsea appointed Ruud Gullit as player-manager in place of Hoddle.

Leicester shrug off McGhee's walk-out

LEICESTER CITY lost their second manager in 12 months when Mark McGhee walked out on the club in December to take charge at Wolverhampton.

Martin George, the Leicester chairman, was furious. He had refused Wolverhampton, who had just parted company with the former England manager Graham Taylor, permission to talk to McGhee. And George also twice refused to let McGhee, who had quit Reading to join Leicester, talk to Wolverhampton.

George offered McGhee a £1,000 a week pay rise to stay and fumed: "I would not have expected a club of the stature of Wolves to make an approach in the first place knowing it would be rejected out of hand." McGhee, though, was unmoved and left saying: "I'm prepared to face the flak which will be thrown at me, but I can leave with a clear conscience."

Leicester turned to Martin O'Neill but, at first, it looked as if their season was going from bad to worse. O'Neill, the former Wycombe manager, lost his first nine matches in charge as Leicester slipped out of the First Division play-off race.

But seven wins from their last 10 matches was enough to earn Leicester a place in the play-offs. In the play-off final at Wembley they met Crystal Palace, who had been relegated from the Premiership with them the season before.

Crystal Palace took an early lead but Garry Parker equalised with a penalty in the 77th minute. Extra time was almost over when Leicester brought on their reserve goalkeeper Zeljko Kalac ready for a penalty shoot-out. But Kalac was never called into action as, with seconds remaining, Steve Claridge's mis-hit shot took Leicester straight back to the top flight.

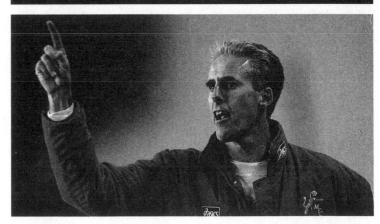

■ **Mick McCarthy (above), the Millwall manager and former Irish international, replaced Jack Charlton as the manager of the Republic of Ireland.**

■ **Louis Kilcoyne, the president of the Football Association of Ireland, was ousted by a vote of no-confidence in March when the Association was riven by a dispute over the sale of tickets for the 1994 World Cup.**

■ **Javier Clemente, the coach of the Spanish national side, lost track of the number of substitutes he had already used during a friendly against Norway in April. When one of his players came off injured with 15 minutes to go, Clemente was forced to send on Jose Molina, his substitute goalkeeper, to play on the left wing. Molina, on a remarkable debut, then went close to scoring a goal.**

■ **Bad luck comes in threes... Blackburn signed Garry Flitcroft from Manchester City for £3m in March. He was sent off after playing three minutes for his new club as Blackburn lost 3-0 to Everton, and was given a three-match ban.**

■ **Robert Chase finally stepped down as chairman of Norwich after a vitriolic campaign by the clubs' fans, who complained that he kept on selling the team's best players.**

THE 1995-96 SEASON

Cantona completes the double Double

Finishing touch: Cantona crashes Rush's deflection into the net to win the FA Cup

GIVEN THE season he'd had, it was inevitable that Eric Cantona would score the winning goal in the Cup final and so secure Manchester United's second Double. Alex Ferguson and his young side thus carved themselves a unique place in history: the only club, and the only manager to have won a double Double.

Cantona's strike was perfect in every sense. It came five minutes from time, and it was executed with all the skill of a maestro. Liverpool's goalkeeper, David James, punched David Beckham's corner away only to see it deflected off Ian Rush. The ball fell just outside the box, where Cantona was lurking. He pounced instantly and volleyed the ball through the crowded penalty area and into the net. And that was that, 1-0 and good night.

Cantona's 19th goal of the season was the one bright spot in an otherwise dire final. Inexplicably, Liverpool, who had played bright, attractive football all season and who had beaten and drawn with United in the League, simply froze. United were not much better as both sides seemed content to play cat and mouse with each other.

United had ridden their luck just to make the trip to Wembley for the third year in succession. Against Manchester City, when they were 1-0 down, they were awarded a penalty the United players hadn't even claimed. In the sixth round Southampton had a perfectly good goal by Neil Shipperley disallowed, and in the semi-final against Chelsea Craig Burley gifted them a goal with a lofted back pass.

> *I don't think Manchester United will have too many problems winning the title. You never get any decisions against them here.*
>
> GERRY FRANCIS
> after a 1-0 defeat at Old Trafford in March.

Venables quits over contract wrangle

LIKE MOST England managers, Terry Venables had a tough time of it. But unlike his predecessors, in particular Graham Taylor and Bobby Robson, Venables was not vilified for the performances of his teams. The media onslaught came about because of his acrimonious split from Tottenham and Alan Sugar, other business dealings that went wrong and several court cases.

The announcement that Venables was to step down as the England coach after the European championships came in January. In reality the die had been cast in mid-December when, in a court case that he lost, a judge described Venables' evidence as "wanton" and "not entirely credible". On December 16 in a Birmingham hotel, coincidentally the eve of the draw for Euro 96, Venables had a showdown with his principal opponent inside the FA. Noel White, the chairman of the international committee, had made his views on Venables plain.

Venables was seeking a renewal of his contract to take him up to the 1998 World Cup. Although he was backed by Graham Kelly and Sir Bert Millichip, White was adamant. Renewal of Venables' contract would be discussed after the Europan championships.

He told the FA that with so many court cases to come, not least Sugar's libel suit over Venables' recent autobiography, his position would be untenable and would disrupt England's World Cup campaign. Despite Kelly's pleas, Venables would not budge.

Venables felt he had been hounded out and talked of "an orchestrated campaign" against him. Kate Hooey, a Labour MP, had raised the matter in Parliament. Hooey, along with *The Daily Mirror*, the *Daily Telegraph* and the BBC programme, *Panorama*, are the prime suspects. However, Venables has always hinted that there is somebody in the background who is pulling their strings. Paranoia? We shall see.

Ferguson's young guns excel as Newcastle let title slip

Double delight: Cantona was the main reason Ferguson's team won the FA Cup and the Premiership trophy

ONCE AGAIN the championship went right down to the wire, but this time it was Manchester United who picked up the Premiership title, their third in four years. Newcastle, the unlucky side to miss out, had only themselves to blame. In January they had held a seemingly unassailable 12-point lead over Alex Ferguson's team, but a string of poor away results – they only won seven matches all season – saw that lead disappear.

The man principally responsible for United's storming comeback was Eric Cantona. He was, without a shadow of doubt, the reason they won the League and, fittingly, was voted Player of Year. The rehabilitation of Cantona was extraordinary by any standards. Here was a man vilified for his kung-fu attack on a spectator, who had to serve a nine-month suspension, and whose career was at a crossroads.

He rose to the challenge admirably. In his first match back in the No 7 shirt in October, he coolly slotted home a penalty to earn United a draw against Liverpool. Crucial goals from Cantona continued to be the hallmark of a dramatic season,

not least the winner at St James's Park – Newcastle's only home defeat.

United had begun the season in some disarray. Mark Hughes had gone to Chelsea, Paul Ince to Internazionale and Andrei Kanchelskis was in the midst of an acrimonious transfer to Everton. On the opening day they were also without Ryan Giggs, Andy Cole and Steve Bruce. They lost 3-1 to Aston Villa. Bravely, Ferguson was

Asprilla: controversial signing

gambling on the young players he was blooding in the first team. Alan Hansen, on BBC television, ridiculed Ferguson's strategy: "You can't win anything with kids." He was to be proved spectacularly wrong.

Phil and Gary Neville, Nicky Butt, David Beckham, and Paul Scholes successfully graduated with first-class honours. "Fergie's Babes" was the inevitable label slapped on them by the media. But Ferguson's managerial acumen wasn't entirely faultless. Cole had a poor season, and, at £7m, appeared to be a costly mistake.

There were similar criticisms of Kevin Keegan. In February he signed the Colombian Faustino Asprilla from Parma for £7m and brought him on as a substitute against Middlesbrough just hours after he got off the plane. Asprilla fashioned a goal almost immediately and turned the match around. But had Keegan disturbed the balance of his side? Subsequent results suggested so. After that match Newcastle had a nine-point lead with a game in hand. When the curtain went down they trailed the champions by four points.

EURO 96
Football comes home

Germany's sheer efficiency gave them their third European championship when they became the first side in Euro 96 to come from behind and win a match without recourse to a penalty shoot-out. Their 2-1 defeat of the Czech Republic in the final at Wembley was always the likely outcome after Germany had disposed of England in a semi-final that was eerily reminiscent of the 1990 World Cup semi-final. *Vorsprung durch technik* won the trophy for Germany. That, the thickness of a post and the bizarre golden goal rule.

This was not the Germany of 1990, 1974, 1970, nor indeed of 1966, despite all the nostalgic renditions of "Football's coming home, thirty years of hurt never stopped us dreaming", the song that was the nation's very vocal voice for a month. This was, by Germany's standards, an average side which, apart from Jürgen Klinsmann, had no genuine world-class players. The Czech Republic, their opponents, were even less blessed.

The Czechs' first game in the tournament had been against Germany and they were blown away 2-0. The bookmakers promptly offered 200-1 against them winning the tournament. However, they stunned everybody in their next match by beating Italy 2-1. Now, another Uefa rule change gave them the upper hand in what was called the "Group of Death".

Under the new regulation, teams finishing level on points would first be separated by the result between them. This meant that in the final first-round matches, Italy v Germany and the Czech Republic v Russia, Italy would have to score more points, rather than goals, than the Czech Republic. The Italians couldn't rise to the challenge and drew 0-0. The Czechs, having been 2-0 up, snatched a last minute goal to draw 3-3.

Italy's elimination in the first phase was the big shock of the tournament. It shouldn't have been; it mirrored what they'd done two years earlier in the World Cup. Once again they finished third in their group with four points, but this time there were no second chances for finishing third.

Italy had got to the 1994 World Cup final riding their luck. Or, more particularly, relying on

Moment of hope: Shearer's header against Germany in the semi-final

Roberto Baggio. But Baggio wasn't in England. Arrigo Sacchi, the Italian coach, had decided to omit him, Gianluca Vialli and Giuseppe Signori from the squad. And just to show he was Il Duce, Sacchi "rested" five players for the game against the Czech Republic.

The Czechs had learnt the lessons of survival after they escaped the Group of Death, strangling everything that came in their path. Portugal fell in the quarter-final when a wonderfully scooped goal from Karel Poborsky in the second half left their goalkeeper flat-footed and forlorn.

The third "flair" side to fall to the arch exponents of strangulation – and wait for the counter-attack – were France. It was the most dire match of the championship, but the Czechs won 6-5 on penalties to meet Germany in the final.

For England, meeting Germany in the semi-final was the "real" final, as it probably was for Germany. England were also on a roll, even though the preamble to the tournament had been a PR disaster.

For reasons best known to themselves, the FA had taken the national squad to China and Hong Kong for pre-championship friendlies. After the last match some of the players had gone for a night out and had been photographed with their shirts torn and spirits being poured down their throats. On the flight home two TV sets were broken and the players were accused of vandalism.

The uproar and media frenzy went on for days. When England drew 1-1 with Switzerland in their opening match – a harsh penalty going against Stuart Pearce – the tabloids went into overdrive. England's performance in their next match, against Scotland, gave them food for thought. And the match after that made them eat their words.

The Scots had done remarkably well in their first match, holding Holland 0-0, but the game against England was the big one – their "final". With 12 minutes to go and 1-0 down, Scotland were awarded a penalty. A brilliant save by David Seaman from Gary McAllister not only dashed their hopes, but within seconds, Paul Gascoigne had scored a virtuoso goal to complete Scotland's misery.

With support for England growing, the country was ripe for the next twist in the tale. Holland were one of the favourites and a team that oozed organisation and skill. England tore them apart 4-1, Alan Shearer and Teddy Sheringham scoring twice. Unfortunately for Scotland, the late goal that England conceded in the 78th minute meant that the Scots were edged out of the quarter-finals by the Dutch. This preserved their perfect record of never having qualified for the second phase of the finals of any major tournament they have reached.

Media frenzy of a different kind now ensued. First it was jingoism, then it was xenophobia. It started with the quarter-final against Spain and became hysterical in the semi-final against Germany. *The Daily Mirror* was an example. It began by printing a front-page apology for all the nasty things it had printed about Gascoigne, it continued by photographing its football reporters in the stocks, and ended with attacks on "Krauts".

England got by the Spanish for two reasons. A linesman (wrongly) decided Julio Salinas was offside when he scored, and David Seaman saved brilliantly from Miguel Nadal in the penalty shoot-out.

And on to Germany. England drew first blood within three minutes with Shearer's fifth goal of Euro 96. Stefan Kuntz equalised 13 minutes later. The two teams battled for the next 77 minutes with neither side giving any quarter.

The first eight minutes of extra time were some of the most extraordinary to have ever happened in a football match. Darren Anderton hit the post; Seaman spectacularly saved from Andreas Moller; the referee disallowed a Kuntz "goal"; and Gascoigne was a toe away from scoring.

The drama heightened as the dreaded nightmare of penalties dawned. Who was going to be the Stuart Pearce of 1996? Not the Forest full-back. Nor Shearer, Platt, Gascoigne, or Sheringham. No, this time the monkey jumped on to poor Gareth Southgate's back. Moller scored his penalty and Germany were through 6-5. Thirty years of hurt?

In the actual final, the Czechs, who 20 years before had beaten the Germans in a penalty shoot-out to win the European championship, played a canny game, even going ahead in the 59th minute with a penalty awarded for an offence that television replays proved was outside the box. Berti Vogts then made an inspired substitution, bringing on Oliver Bierhoff. With 17 minutes to go he rose at the far post to level the match. Then, in the fifth minute of extra time, Bierhoff latched on to a ball

Moment of despair: Southgate

from Klinsmann, turned, and struck a powerful shot. The ball took a slight deflection off Michal Hornak's heel and the Czech goalkeeper, Petr Kouba, could only parry the ball into the net.

It was the first golden goal of the tournament. Or was it? Much like England's third goal in 1966, Germany's golden wonder is open to debate. Was Kuntz – clearly offside – interfering with play? The linesman thought so. The Italian referee not. Whatever, it was an anti-climatic ending to a tournament that had promised so much.

With two quarter-finals and both semi-finals going to penalty shoot-outs, the introduction of the golden goal instead of straightforward extra time was a proven failure before the final. The idea behind it – sudden-death overtime as in American sports – was to encourage teams to attack, rather than gamble on the penalty shoot-out.

If anything, it had the opposite effect. Teams, knowing that one goal would end the match, were, with the notable exception of the England–Germany match, even more defensive. Under the old system, if you conceded a goal in the fifth minute of extra time you had 25 minutes to get it back. With the golden goal, you were out. Or, like the Czechs, you had lost the championship.

So, six years on from the sterility of the 1990 World Cup and its plethora of penalty deciders, the

Moment of triumph: Klinsmann

FOR THE RECORD

GROUP A

England	1	Switzerland	1
(Shearer)			
Holland	0	Scotland	0
Switzerland	0	Holland	2
Scotland	0	England	2
		(Shearer, Gascoigne)	
Scotland	1	Switzerland	0
(McCoist)			
Holland	1	England	4
		(Shearer 2, Sheringham 2)	

	P	W	D	L	F	A	Pts
England	3	2	1	0	7	2	7
Holland	3	1	1	1	3	4	4
Scotland	3	1	1	1	1	2	4
Switzerland	3	0	1	2	1	4	1

GROUP B

Spain	1	Bulgaria	1
Romania	0	France	1
Bulgaria	1	Romania	0
France	1	Spain	1
France	3	Bulgaria	1
Romania	1	Spain	2

	P	W	D	L	F	A	Pts
France	3	2	1	0	5	2	7
Spain	3	1	2	0	4	3	5
Bulgaria	3	1	1	1	3	4	4
Romania	3	0	0	3	1	4	0

GROUP C

Germany	2	Czech Rep	0
Italy	2	Russia	1
Czech Rep	2	Italy	1
Russia	0	Germany	3
Russia	3	Czech Rep	3
Italy	0	Germany	0

	P	W	D	L	F	A	Pts
Germany	3	2	1	0	5	0	7
Czech Rep	3	1	1	1	5	6	4
Italy	3	1	1	1	3	3	4
Russia	3	0	1	2	4	8	1

GROUP D

Denmark	1	Portugal	1
Turkey	0	Croatia	1
Portugal	1	Turkey	0
Croatia	3	Denmark	0
Croatia	0	Portugal	3
Turkey	0	Denmark	3

	P	W	D	L	F	A	Pts
Portugal	3	2	1	0	5	1	7
Croatia	3	2	0	1	4	3	6
Denmark	3	1	1	1	4	4	4
Turkey	3	0	0	3	0	5	0

QUARTER-FINALS

England	0	Spain	0
(England won 4-2 on pens)			
Att: 75,440			
Germany	2	Croatia	1
Klinsmann 21 (pen)		Suker 51	
Sammer 58		Att: 43,412	
France	0	Holland	0
(France won 5-4 on pens)			
Att: 37,465			
Czech Rep	1	Portugal	0
Poborsky 53		Att: 26,832	

SEMI-FINALS

Germany	1	England	1
Kuntz 16		Shearer 3	
(Germany won 6-5 on pens)			
Att: 75,862			
Czech Rep	0	France	0
(Czech Rep won 6-5 on pens)			
Att: 43,877			

FINAL

Germany	2	Czech Rep	1
Bierhoff 73, 95		Berger 59 (pen)	
Att: 73,611			

Leading scorers:
5 Shearer (England); 3 Klinsmann (Germany), Laudrup (Denmark), Stoichkov (Bulgaria), Suker (Croatia).

Booked: 153. **Sent off:** 7.

Total goals scored 61
Average per game 1.97

hoary old chestnuts were back on the brazier. And what did the armchair pundits offer: decide the match on the number of corners; withdraw a player from each side at five minute intervals; play endless sudden-death extra time. All of these so-called solutions have the same fatal flaw: they are not football. Any team that wanted to rack up a huge number of corners could easily do so; reducing the number of players could easily end up as farce; as for endless overtime . . . continue until midnight, or one team keels over from exhaustion?

All these "experts" derided Fifa in 1995 when they suggested two radical changes that would solve the problem without damaging the integrity of the game. Enlarge the size of the goals and/or confine offside to the space between the two penalty areas. If the first change had happened England would have reached the final. If the second, Spain would have played Germany instead of England. The problem that beset Euro 96 – 61 goals in 31 matches, less than two a game – is that modern football is now so competitive that there is not enough potential for scoring goals from open play, a trend which needs to be reversed to avoid the penalty shoot-out.

LEAGUE TABLES AND RESULTS 1990-1996

	1990-91	1991-92	1992-93	1993-94	1994-95
WORLD CUP				Brazil 0 Italy 0; Brazil won 3-2 on pens	
EUROPEAN CHAMPIONSHIP		Denmark 2 Germany 0			
EUROPEAN CUP	Red Star Belgrade 0 Marseille 0; Belgrade won 5-3 on penalties	Barcelona 1 Sampdoria 0	Marseille 1 AC Milan 0	AC Milan 4 Barcelona 0	Ajax 1 AC Milan 0
EUROPEAN CUP WINNERS CUP	Manchester Utd 2 Barcelona 0	Werder Bremen 2 Monaco 0	Parma 3 Antwerp 1	Arsenal 1 Parma 0	Real Zaragoza 2 Arsenal 1 (aet)
UEFA CUP	Inter Milan beat AS Roma 2-0 0-1	Ajax beat Torino 2-2 0-0; Ajax won on away goals	Juventus beat Borussia Dortmund 3-1 3-0	Inter Milan beat Casino Salzburg 1-0 1-0	Parma beat Juventus 1-0 1-1
FA CUP	Tottenham Hotspur 2 Nottingham Forest 1	Liverpool 2 Sunderland 0	Arsenal 2 Sheffield Wednesday 1, after 1-1	Manchester United 4 Chelsea 0	Everton 1 Manchester United 0

FIRST DIVISION – PREMIER DIVISION (1992–93)

1990-91

	P	W	D	L	F	A	Pts
Arsenal	38	24	13	1	74	18	83
Liverpool	38	23	7	8	77	40	76
C Palace	38	20	9	9	50	41	69
Leeds Utd	38	19	7	12	65	47	64
Man City	38	17	11	10	64	53	62
Man Utd	38	16	12	10	58	45	59
Wimbledon	38	14	14	10	53	46	56
Nottm F	38	14	12	12	65	50	54
Everton	38	13	12	13	50	46	51
Tottenham	38	11	16	11	51	50	49
Chelsea	38	13	10	15	58	69	49
QPR	38	12	10	16	44	53	46
Sheff Utd	38	13	7	18	36	55	46
Soton	38	12	9	17	58	69	45
Norwich	38	13	6	19	41	64	45
Coventry	38	11	11	16	42	49	44
Aston Villa	38	9	14	15	46	58	41
Luton	38	10	7	21	42	61	37
Sunderland	*38*	*8*	*10*	*20*	*38*	*60*	*34*
Derby	*38*	*5*	*9*	*24*	*37*	*75*	*24*

1991-92

	P	W	D	L	F	A	Pts
Leeds Utd	42	22	16	4	74	37	82
Man Utd	42	21	15	6	63	33	78
Sheff Wed	42	21	12	9	62	49	75
Arsenal	42	19	15	8	81	46	72
Man City	42	20	10	12	61	48	70
Liverpool	42	16	16	10	47	40	64
Aston Villa	42	17	9	16	48	44	60
Nottm F	42	16	11	15	60	58	59
Sheff Utd	42	16	9	17	65	63	57
C Palace	42	14	15	13	53	61	57
QPR	42	12	18	12	48	47	54
Everton	42	13	14	15	52	51	53
Wimbledon	42	13	14	15	53	53	53
Chelsea	42	13	14	15	50	60	53
Tottenham	42	15	7	20	58	63	52
Soton	42	14	10	18	39	55	52
Oldham	42	14	9	19	63	67	51
Norwich	42	11	12	19	47	63	45
Coventry	42	11	11	20	35	44	44
Luton	*42*	*10*	*12*	*20*	*38*	*71*	*42*
Notts C	*42*	*10*	*10*	*22*	*40*	*62*	*40*
West Ham	*42*	*9*	*11*	*22*	*37*	*59*	*38*

1992-93

	P	W	D	L	F	A	Pts
Man Utd	42	24	12	6	67	31	84
Aston Villa	42	21	11	10	57	40	74
Norwich	42	21	9	12	61	65	72
Blackburn	42	20	11	11	68	46	71
QPR	42	17	12	13	63	55	63
Liverpool	42	16	11	15	62	55	59
Sheff Wed	42	15	14	13	55	51	59
Tottenham	42	16	11	15	60	66	59
Man City	42	15	12	15	56	51	57
Arsenal	42	15	11	16	40	38	56
Chelsea	42	14	14	14	51	54	56
Wimbledon	42	14	12	16	56	55	54
Everton	42	15	8	19	53	55	53
Sheff Utd	42	14	10	18	54	53	52
Coventry	42	13	13	16	52	57	52
Ipswich	42	12	16	14	50	55	52
Leeds	42	12	15	15	57	62	51
Soton	42	13	11	18	54	61	50
Oldham	42	13	10	19	63	74	49
C Palace	*42*	*11*	*16*	*15*	*48*	*61*	*49*
Middlesbro	*42*	*11*	*11*	*20*	*54*	*75*	*44*
Nottm F	*42*	*10*	*10*	*22*	*41*	*62*	*40*

1993-94

	P	W	D	L	F	A	Pts
Man Utd	42	27	11	5	80	38	92
Blackburn	42	25	9	8	63	36	84
Newcastle	42	23	8	11	82	41	77
Arsenal	42	18	7	7	53	28	71
Leeds	42	18	16	8	65	39	70
Wimbledon	42	18	11	13	56	53	65
Sheff Wed	42	16	16	10	76	54	64
Liverpool	42	17	9	16	59	55	60
QPR	42	16	12	14	62	61	60
Aston Villa	42	15	12	15	46	50	57
Coventry	42	14	14	14	43	45	56
Norwich	42	12	17	13	65	61	53
West Ham	42	13	13	16	47	58	52
Chelsea	42	13	12	17	49	53	51
Tottenham	42	11	12	19	54	59	45
Man City	42	9	18	15	38	49	45
Everton	42	12	8	22	42	63	44
Soton	42	12	7	23	49	66	43
Ipswich	42	9	16	17	35	58	43
Sheff Utd	*42*	*8*	*18*	*16*	*42*	*60*	*42*
Oldham	*42*	*9*	*13*	*20*	*42*	*68*	*40*
Swindon	*42*	*5*	*15*	*22*	*47*	*100*	*30*

1994-95

	P	W	D	L	F	A	Pts
Blackburn	42	27	8	7	80	39	89
Man Utd	42	26	10	6	77	28	88
Nottm F	42	22	11	9	72	43	77
Liverpool	42	21	11	10	65	37	74
Leeds	42	20	13	9	59	38	73
Newcastle	42	20	12	10	67	47	72
Tottenham	42	16	14	12	66	58	62
QPR	42	17	9	16	61	59	60
Wimbledon	42	15	11	16	48	65	56
Soton	42	12	18	12	61	63	54
Chelsea	42	13	15	14	50	55	54
Arsenal	42	13	12	17	52	49	51
Sheff Wed	42	13	12	17	49	57	51
West Ham	42	13	11	18	44	48	50
Everton	42	11	17	14	44	51	50
Coventry	42	12	14	16	44	62	50
Man City	42	12	13	17	53	64	49
Aston Villa	42	11	15	16	51	56	48
C Palace	42	11	12	19	34	49	45
Norwich	*42*	*10*	*13*	*19*	*37*	*54*	*43*
Leicester	*42*	*6*	*11*	*25*	*45*	*80*	*29*
Ipswich	*42*	*7*	*6*	*29*	*36*	*93*	*27*

	1990-91	1991-92	1992-93	1993-94	1994-95
SECOND DIVISION–FIRST DIVISION (1992–93)	Champions: Oldham Athletic Also promoted: West Ham United, Sheffield Wednesday, Notts County Relegated: West Bromwich Albion, Hull City	Champions: Ipswich Town Also promoted: Middlesbrough, Blackburn Rovers Relegated: Plymouth Argyle, Brighton & Hove Albion, Port Vale	Champions: Newcastle United Also promoted: West Ham United, Swindon Town Relegated: Brentford, Cambridge United, Bristol Rovers	Champions: Crystal Palace Also promoted: Nottingham Forest, Leicester Relegated: Birmingham, Oxford, Peterborough	Champions: Middlesbrough Also promoted: Bolton Relegated: Swindon, Burnley, Bristol City, Notts County
THIRD DIVISION–SECOND DIVISION (1992–93)	Champions: Cambridge United Also promoted: Southend United, Grimsby Town, Tranmere Rovers Relegated: Crewe Alexandra, Rotherham United, Mansfield Town	Champions: Brentford Also promoted: Birmingham City, Peterborough United Relegated: Bury, Shrewsbury Town, Torquay United, Darlington	Champions: Stoke City Also promoted: Bolton Wanderers, West Bromwich Albion Relegated: Preston, Mansfield Town, Wigan Athletic, Chester City	Champions: Reading Also promoted: Port Vale, Burnley	Champions: Birmingham Also promoted: Huddersfield Relegated: Cambridge Utd, Plymouth, Cardiff, Chester, Leyton Orient
FOURTH DIVISION–THIRD DIVISION (1992–93)	Champions: Darlington Also promoted: Stockport, Hartlepool, Peterborough, Torquay Elected to the League: Barnet	Champions: Burnley Also promoted: Rotherham Town, Mansfield Town, Blackpool Elected to the League: Colchester	Champions: Cardiff City Also promoted: Wrexham, Barnet, York City *Wycombe W replaced Halifax Town*	Champions: Shrewsbury Also promoted: Chester, Crewe, Wycombe	Champions: Carlisle Also promoted: Walsall, Chesterfield
LEAGUE CUP	Sheffield Wed 1 Manchester Utd 0	Manchester United 1 Nottingham Forest 0	Arsenal 2 Sheffield Wednesday 1	Aston Villa 3 Manchester United 1	Liverpool 2 Bolton 1
SCOTTISH CUP	Motherwell 4 Dundee United 3	Rangers 2 Airdire 1	Rangers 2 Aberdeen 1	Dundee United 1 Rangers 0	Celtic 1 Airdrie 0

SCOTTISH PREMIER DIVISION

1990-91

	P	W	D	L	F	A	Pts
Rangers	36	24	7	5	62	23	55
Aberdeen	36	22	9	5	62	27	53
Celtic	36	17	7	12	52	38	41
Dundee U	36	17	7	12	41	29	41
Hearts	36	14	7	15	48	55	35
Motherwell	36	12	9	15	51	50	33
St J'stone	36	11	9	16	41	54	31
Dunfermline	36	8	11	17	38	61	27
Hibernian	36	6	13	17	24	51	25
St Mirren	36	5	9	22	28	59	19

1991-92

	P	W	D	L	F	A	Pts
Rangers	44	33	6	5	101	31	72
Hearts	44	27	9	8	60	37	63
Celtic	44	26	10	8	88	42	62
Dundee U	44	19	13	12	66	50	51
Hibernian	44	16	17	11	53	45	49
Aberdeen	44	17	14	13	55	42	48
Airdrie	44	13	10	21	50	70	36
St J'stone	44	13	10	21	52	73	36
Falkirk	44	12	11	21	54	73	35
Motherwell	44	10	14	20	43	61	34
St Mirren	*44*	*6*	*12*	*26*	*33*	*73*	*24*
Dunfermline	*44*	*4*	*10*	*30*	*22*	*80*	*18*

1992-93

	P	W	D	L	F	A	Pts
Rangers	44	33	7	4	97	35	73
Aberdeen	44	27	10	7	87	36	64
Celtic	44	24	12	8	68	41	60
Dundee U	44	19	9	16	56	49	47
Hearts	44	15	14	15	46	51	44
St J'stone	44	10	19	15	51	66	39
Hibernian	44	12	13	19	54	64	37
Partick	44	12	12	20	50	71	36
Motherwell	44	12	12	20	46	61	36
Dundee	44	11	12	21	48	68	34
Falkirk	*44*	*11*	*7*	*26*	*60*	*86*	*29*
Airdrie	*44*	*6*	*17*	*21*	*35*	*70*	*29*

1993-94

	P	W	D	L	F	A	Pts
Rangers	44	22	14	8	74	41	58
Aberdeen	44	17	21	6	58	36	55
Motherwell	44	20	14	10	58	43	54
Celtic	44	15	20	9	51	38	50
Hibernian	44	16	15	13	53	48	47
Dundee U	44	11	20	13	47	48	42
Hearts	44	11	20	13	37	43	42
Kilmarnock	44	12	16	16	36	45	40
Partick	44	12	16	16	46	57	40
St J'stone	*44*	*10*	*20*	*14*	*35*	*47*	*40*
Raith	*44*	*6*	*19*	*19*	*46*	*76*	*31*
Dundee	*44*	*8*	*13*	*23*	*42*	*57*	*29*

1994-95

	P	W	D	L	F	A	Pts
Rangers	36	20	9	7	60	35	69
Motherwell	36	14	12	10	50	50	54
Hibernian	36	12	17	7	49	37	53
Celtic	36	11	18	7	39	33	51
Falkirk	36	12	12	12	48	47	48
Hearts	36	12	7	17	44	51	43
Kilmarnock	36	11	10	15	40	48	43
Partick	36	10	13	13	40	50	43
Aberdeen	36	10	11	15	43	46	41
Dundee U	*36*	*9*	*9*	*18*	*40*	*56*	*36*

	1990-91	1991-92	1992-93	1993-94	1994-95
SCOTTISH FIRST DIVISION	Champions: Falkirk Also promoted: Airdrie Relegated: Clyde, Brechin City	Champions: Dundee Also promoted: Partick Thistle Relegated: Montrose, Forfar Athletic	Champions: Raith Rovers Also promoted: Kilmarnock Relegated: Meadowbank, Cowdenbeath	Champions: Falkirk Runners-up (not promoted): Dunfermline (*League reorganised*)	Champions: Raith Relegated: Ayr, Stranraer
SCOTTISH SECOND DIV	Champions: Stirling Albion Also promoted: Montrose	Champions: Dumbarton Also promoted: Cowdenbeath	Champions: Clyde Also promoted: Brechin City	Champions: Stranraer Runners-up (not promoted): Berwick	Champions: Greenock Morton Also promoted: Dumbarton Relegated: Meadowbank, Brechin
SCOTTISH THIRD DIV					Champions: Forfar Also promoted: Montrose
SCOTTISH LEAGUE CUP	Dunfermline 2 Hibernian 0	Hibernian 2 Dunfermline 0	Rangers 2 Aberdeen 1	Rangers 2 Hibernian 1	Celtic 2 Raith Rovers 2 (Raith win 6-5 on penalties)

Czech Rep. 1 Germany 2 (aet)

Ajax 1 Juventus 1 (Juventus won 4-2 on penalties)

Paris St Germain 1
Rapid Vienna 0

Bayern Munich beat Bordeaux 2-0 3-1

Manchester United 1
Liverpool 0

	P	W	D	L	F	A	Pts
Man Utd	38	25	7	6	73	35	82
Newcastle	38	24	6	8	66	37	78
Liverpool	38	20	11	7	70	34	71
Aston Villa	38	18	9	11	52	35	63
Arsenal	38	17	12	9	49	32	63
Everton	38	17	10	11	64	44	61
Blackburn	38	18	7	13	61	47	61
Tottenham	38	16	13	9	50	38	61
Nottm F	38	15	13	10	50	54	58
West Ham	38	14	9	15	43	52	51
Chelsea	38	12	14	12	46	44	50
Middlesbro	38	11	10	17	35	50	43
Leeds	38	12	7	19	40	57	43
Wimbledon	38	10	11	17	55	70	41
Sheff Wed	38	10	10	18	48	61	40
Coventry	38	8	14	16	42	60	38
Soton	38	9	11	18	34	52	38
Man City	38	9	11	18	33	58	38
QPR	38	9	6	23	38	57	33
Bolton Wan	38	8	5	25	39	71	29

Champions: Sunderland
Also promoted: Derby County, Leicester City
Relegated: Millwall, Watford, Luton Town

Champions: Swindon Town
Also promoted: Oxford United, Bradford City
Relegated: Carlisle United, Swansea City, Brighton, Hull City

Champions: Preston NE
Also promoted: Gillingham, Bury, Plymouth Argyle

Aston Villa 3
Leeds 0

Rangers 5
Hearts 1

	P	W	D	L	F	A	Pts
Rangers	36	27	6	3	85	25	87
Celtic	36	24	11	1	74	25	83
Aberdeen	36	16	7	13	52	45	55
Hearts	36	16	7	13	55	53	55
Hibernian	36	11	10	15	43	57	43
Raith	36	12	7	17	41	57	43
Kilmarnock	36	11	8	17	39	54	41
Motherwell	36	9	12	15	28	39	39
Partick	36	8	6	22	29	62	30
Falkirk	36	6	6	24	31	60	24

Champions: Dunfermline
Also promoted: Dundee United
Relegated: Hamilton, Dumbarton

Champions: Stirling
Also promoted: East Fife
Relegated: Forfar, Montrose

Champions: Livingston
Also promoted: Brechin City

Aberdeen 2
Dundee 0

Bibliography

Those wishing to read more about the events we chronicle should find these books, among the many we consulted, to be particularly useful.

100 GREAT BRITISH FOOTBALLERS Trevor Brooking; Queen Anne Press; 1988

A GAME OF TWO HALVES edited by Stephen F Kelly; Mandarin; 1992

A HISTORY OF BRITISH FOOTBALL Percy M Young; Arrow Books; 1973

A STRANGE KIND OF GLORY Eamon Dunphy; Heinemann; 1991

ALEX FERGUSON, 6 YEARS AT UNITED Mainstream Publishing; 1992

ALL PLAYED OUT Pete Davies; Heinemann; 1990

AGAINST THE ODDS Bobby Robson with Bob Harris; Stanley Paul; 1990

AN EVERTON DIARY Peter Reid with Peter Ball; Queen Anne Press; 1988

AN ILLUSTRATED HISTORY OF BALL GAMES Nigel Viney and Neil Grant; William Heinemann; 1978

AND THE SPURS GO MARCHING ON Phil Soar; Hamlyn; 1982

ANUARIO DEL FUTBOL El Pais; 1994

ARSENAL OFFICIAL HISTORY Phil Soar and Martin Tyler; Hamlyn; 1989

ASSOCIATION FOOTBALL, VOLUMES 1-4 edited by AH Fabian and Geoffrey Green; Caxton; 1960

ASSOCIATION FOOTBALL AND ENGLISH SOCIETY 1863-1915 Tony Mason; Harvester Press; 1980

BACK PAGE FOOTBALL Stephen F Kelly; Macdonald Queen Anne Press; 1988

BEHIND CLOSED DOORS Irving Scholar; Andre Deutsch; 1992

BOBBY MOORE Jeff Powell; Everest; 1976

BOBBY MOORE, A TRIBUTE edited by David Emery; Headline; 1993

BOBBY MOORE, THE LIFE AND TIMES OF A SPORTING HERO Jeff Powell; Robson Books; 1993

BOOK OF WORLD FOOTBALL Brian Glanville; Dragon; 1972

BOYS OF '66 Martin Tyler; Hamlyn; 1981

CHAMPIONS OF EUROPE Brian Glanville; Guinness; 1991

CLOUGH Tony Francis; Stanley Paul; 1989

CUP FINAL EXTRA Martin Tyler; Hamlyn; 1981

DALGLISH Stephen F Kelly; Headline; 1992

DON'T SHOOT THE MANAGER Jimmy Greaves with Norman Giller; Boxtree; 1993

EVERYMAN'S DICTIONARY OF DATES revised by Audrey Butler; J M Dent; 1987

FAMOUS SPORTING FIASCOS Stephen Winkworth; Sphere Books; 1984

FOOTBALL! Nicholas Mason; Temple Smith; 1974

FOOTBALL AGAINST THE ENEMY Simon Kuper; Orion; 1994

FOOTBALL AND THE DECLINE OF BRITAIN James Walvin; Macmillan; 1986

FOOTBALL IS MY PASSPORT Billy Wright; Stanley Paul; 1957

FOOTBALL PLAYERS' RECORDS 1946-92 Barry J Hugman; Tony Williams; 1992

FOR THE GOOD OF THE GAME John Harding; Robson Books; 1991

FULHAM'S GOLDEN YEARS Ken Coton; Ashwater Publishing; 1992

GAMES AND SETS, THE CHANGING FACE OF SPORT ON TELEVISION Steven Barnett; BFI Publishing; 1990

GAZZA AGONISTES Ian Hamilton; Penguin; 1993

GLASGOW RANGERS PLAYER BY PLAYER Bob Ferrier and Robert McElroy; Crowood; 1990

GLENN HODDLE, AN AUTOBIOGRAPHY Pelham Books; 1982

GLORY GLORY Bill Nicholson; Macmillan; 1984

GLORY GLORY MAN UNITED Bryan Robson; Collins Willow; 1992

HEART TO HEART Mike Aitken and Wallace Mercer; Mainstream; 1988

HEROES AND VILLAINS Alex Fynn and Lynton Guest; Penguin; 1991

HOOLIGANS ABROAD John Williams, Eric Dunning and Patrick Murphy; Routledge & Kegan Paul; 1984

HOTBED OF SOCCER Arthur Appleton; Rupert Hart-Davis; 1960

HOWARD KENDALL'S EVERTON SCRAPBOOK Souvenir Press; 1986

ILLUSTRATED ENCYCLOPAEDIA OF BRITISH FOOTBALL Phil Soar; WH Smith; 1990

JOCK STEIN Ken Gallacher; Stanley Paul; 1988

JUST LIKE MY DREAMS John Lyall; Penguin; 1990

LIVERPOOL Matthew Graham; Hamlyn; 1985

LIVERPOOL IN EUROPE Stephen F Kelly; Collins Willow; 1992

LIVERPOOL IN EUROPE Steve Hale and Ivan Ponting; Guinness; 1992

MANCHESTER UNITED: THE BETRAYAL OF A LEGEND Michael Crick and David Smith; Pelham Books; 1989

MORE CELTIC GREATS Hugh Keevins; Sportsprint; 1990

MORE RANGERS GREATS Dixon Blackstock; Sportsprint; 1991

MORE THAN A MATCH Lee Chapman; Random House; 1993

NEWS OF THE WORLD FOOTBALL ANNUALS Invincible Press

OUT OF TIME Alex Fynn and Lynton Guest; Simon & Schuster; 1994

PAUL GASCOIGNE, THE INSIDE STORY Jane Nottage; Collins Willow; 1993

PEARS CYCLOPAEDIA Christopher Cook; Pelham; 1990

PELE: MY LIFE AND THE BEAUTIFUL GAME Pele with Robert L Fish; New English Library; 1977

PERSONNA YEAR BOOK OF SPORTS Robert Martin; Pelham; 1969

PLAYFAIR WINNERS ANNUAL 1991-92 Edward Abelson; Queen Anne Press; 1991

PUFFIN BOOK OF FOOTBALL Brian Glanville; Puffin Books; 1970

ROTHMANS FOOTBALL YEAR BOOKS Queen Anne Press

SCOTTISH FOOTBALL Kevin McCarra;Polygon; 1984

SICK AS A PARROT Chris Horrie; Virgin; 1992

SOCCER Derek Henderson; Hamlyn; 1980

SOCCER, A PANORAMA Brian Glanville; Eyre and Spottiswoode; 1969

SOCCER FIRSTS John Robinson; Guinness Publishing; 1986

SOCCER SHORTS Jack Rollin; Guinness Publishing; 1988

SPORT IN BRITAIN, A SOCIAL HISTORY Tony Mason; Cambridge University Press; 1989

SPORTS QUOTES OF THE EIGHTIES Peter Ball and Phil Shaw; Mandarin; 1990

STANLEY MATTHEWS David Miller; Pavilion; 1989

SUNDAY TIMES: THE SPORTING DECADE -1980s Chris Dighton; Macdonald Queen Anne Press; 1990

SUNDERLAND AND THE CUP Arthur Appleton; Frank Graham; 1974

THE 1991 INFORMATION PLEASE SPORTS ALMANAC edited by Mike Meserole; Houghton Mifflin, Boston

THE BOOK OF SPORTS QUOTES Jonathan Green and Don Atyeo; Omnibus; 1979

THE COURAGE BOOK OF GREAT SPORTING TEAMS compiled by Chris Rhys; Stanley Paul; 1985

THE COURAGE BOOK OF SPORTING HEROES compiled by Chris Rhys; Stanley Paul; 1984

THE DAILY TELEGRAPH FOOTBALL CHRONICLE Norman Barrett; Carlton; 1993

THE DONS Jack Webster; Stanley Paul; 1990

THE DOUBLE AND BEFORE Danny Blanchflower; Four Square; 1961

THE ENCYCLOPAEDIA OF SPORT edited by Charles Harvey; Sampson Low, Marston and Co; 1959

THE EUROPEAN CHAMPIONSHIP John Robinson; Marksman; 1988

THE FOOTBALL ENCYCLOPAEDIA edited by Frank Johnston; Associated Sporting Press; 1934

THE FOOTBALL FACT BOOK Jack Rollin; Guinness Publishing; 1990

THE FOOTBALL LEAGUE 1888-1988 Bryon Butler; Macdonald Queen Anne Press; 1987

THE FOOTBALL MAN Arthur Hopcraft;

Sportspages; 1988

THE FOOTBALL MANAGERS Johnny Rogan; Macdonald Queen Anne Press; 1989

THE GLORY GAME Hunter Davies; Mainstream; 1990

THE GLORY, GLORY NIGHTS Colin Gibson and Harry Harris; Cockerel Books; 1986

THE GOLDEN AGE OF FOOTBALL Peter Jeffs; Breedon Books; 1991

THE GOOD, THE BAD AND THE BUBBLY George Best; Pan; 1990

THE GUINNESS BOOK OF SOCCER FACTS AND FEATS Jack Rollin; Guinness Superlatives; 1990

THE GUINNESS DICTIONARY OF SPORTS QUOTATIONS Colin Jarman; Guinness; 1990

THE GUINNESS FOOTBALL ENCYCLOPAEDIA edited by Graham Hart; Guinness; 1993

THE GUINNESS FOOTBALL FACT BOOK Jack Rollin; Guinness Publishing; 1993

THE GUINNESS INTERNATIONAL WHO'S WHO OF SPORT Peter Matthews; Ian Buchanan and Bill Mallon; Guinness; 1993

THE GUINNESS RECORD OF THE FA CUP Mike Collett; Guinness; 1993

THE GUINNESS RECORD OF WORLD SOCCER Guy Oliver; Guinness; 1992

THE HILLSBOROUGH STADIUM DISASTER The official report by Lord Justice Taylor; HMSO; 1990

THE HUTCHINSON ENCYCLOPAEDIA Guild Publishing; 1988

THE ILLUSTRATED FOOTBALLER Tony Ambrosen; Breedon Books; 1989

THE LEEDS UNITED STORY Jason Tomas; Arthur Barker; 1971

THE NEW SCOTTISH FOOTBALL FACT BOOK compiled and edited by Forrest HC Robertson; Sports Data Services; 1985

THE OFFICIAL HISTORY OF THE FOOTBALL ASSOCIATION Bryon Butler; Macdonald Queen Anne Press; 1991

THE ONLY GAME Roddy Forsyth; Mainstream; 1990

THE OXFORD COMPANION TO SPORTS AND GAMES edited by John Arlott Oxford University Press; 1975

THE SIXTIES REVISITED Jimmy Greaves & Norman Giller Queen Anne Press; 1992

THE SOCCER TRIBE Desmond Morris; Jonathan Cape; 1981

THE SPORTSPAGES ALMANACS Matthew Engel and Ian Morrison; Simon and Schuster

THE STORY OF THE WORLD CUP Brian Glanville; Faber and Faber; 1993

THE SUNDAY TIMES CHRONICLE OF TWENTIETH CENTURY SPORT Chris Nawrat, Steve Hutchings and Greg Struthers; Hamlyn; 1992

THE SUNDAY TIMES SPORTS BOOK John Lovesey, Nicholas Mason and Edwin Taylor; World's Work; 1979

THIS ONE'S ON ME Jimmy Greaves; Coronet; 1979

THREE SIDES OF THE MERSEY Rogan Taylor and Andrew Ward; Robson books; 1993

TOTTENHAM HOTSPUR PLAYER BY PLAYER Ivan Ponting; Guinness; 1993

TRAUTMANN Alan Rowlands; Breedon Books; 1990

WAR GAMES THE STORY OF SPORT IN WORLD WAR TWO Tony McCarthy; Queen Anne Press; 1989

WEST BROMWICH ALBION, THE FIRST HUNDRED YEARS G A Willmore; Readers Union; 1979

THE HAMLYN ILLUSTRATED HISTORY OF LIVERPOOL Stephen F Kelly; Hamlyn 1996

Acknowledgements

The publishers would particularly like to thank the staff of the Times Newspapers Picture Library and Dawn Wyman of the Hulton Deutsch Collection for their invaluable help in providing pictures for this book. Every effort has been made to trace copyright-holders but if errors or omissions are brought to our attention we shall be pleased to correct them in future editions of the book.

Action Images 113 top, 229 top, 266 bottom

Allsport 37 bottom, 207 top left, 224 bottom, 249 top, 280, 285, Shaun Botterill 256 bottom, 263 top, 272 bottom, 282 bottom, 283 top, Clive Brunskill 280 top, 281 bottom, 276 Simon Bruty 241 bottom, David Cannon 278 bottom, Chris Cole 274 bottom, Phil Cole 271 centre, Jan Collsioo 97 bottom left, Nick Potts 271 top, Pressens Bild 37 top, 37 centre, 73 bottom left, 97 bottom right, Gary Prior 278 top, Ben Radford 277 bottom, 281 top, Anton Want 275 top

Associated Press 33 bottom right, 44 left, 53 top, 53 bottom left, 70 bottom, 76 bottom, 93 bottom, 168 bottom, 180 top, 195 top, 205 bottom

Associated Sports Photography/ George Herringshaw 129, 158 bottom right, 165 bottom, 169 bottom, 259 left, Nigel French 261 top

Tony Bartelo 264 bottom

Caledonia Newspapers Limited 76 top, 79 bottom, 217 bottom

Calyx Photo Services 229 bottom

Colorsport 29 top right, 29 bottom, 33 top, 36 top, 51 top, 66 bottom right, 67, 68, 71 top, 86 bottom, 99, 102 top, 102 bottom, 103 left, 109, 110 left, 119 bottom left, 119 bottom right, 121 bottom, 125 top, 126, 127 top, 127 centre, 142 bottom left, 145 right, 146, 148, 149 bottom left, 149 bottom right, 157 top left, 157 top right, 157 centre left, 157 centre right, 157 bottom left, 157 bottom right, 158 top, 168 top, 184 top, 184 bottom, 185 left, 185 right, 206, 213 top left, 214, 215 top, 215 centre, 215 bottom, 247 top left, 247 top right, 247 centre top left, 247 centre top right, 247 centre bottom, 247 bottom, 255 bottom, 270, 271 bottom, 272 top, 273 bottom, 274 top, 275 bottom, 277 top, Andrew Cowie 273 top, Colin Elsey 178 top, Olympia 36 bottom, Varley 97 centre

Copyright Assignments (Norwich) Bryn Colton 264 top

County Press, Wigan 123 top, 125 bottom, 134 bottom, 145 left, 160 left, 172, 192

Alan Cozzi 265 bottom

Tony Edenden/Sportsfocus 220 top

Colin Elsey 77 right

Empics Neal Simpson 256 top, 284 bottom, 284 top

FIFA 13 centre top, 13 centre bottom, 13 bottom, 24 top, 24 bottom, 25 top, 25 centre left, 25 centre right, 25 bottom

Fotosports International 128 bottom, 138 bottom, 150, 167 bottom

Global Sports Photos 179 top

Barry Greenwood 241 top

Hailey Sports Photographic 189 bottom, 209 left, 219 right

Steve Hale 228 right

Tommy Hindley/ Professional Sport 221 right, 233 top

Hulton Deutsch Collection 6 top, 6 bottom, 8 top, 8 bottom, 9 bottom, 10 top, 13 top, 14 left, 15 bottom, 16 top, 16 bottom, 17 top, 17 bottom, 22 top, 22 bottom left, 22 bottom right, 26 top, 27 centre left, 27 bottom left, 27 bottom right, 29 top left, 31 top, 31 bottom left, 33 bottom left, 35 right, 38 bottom, 40, 41 top left, 44 right, 45 right, 46 bottom, 47 bottom, 50 bottom, 52, 53 bottom right, 54 top, 54 bottom, 55 top left, 56 top, 57 top, 57 right, 58 left, 59 right, 60, 61 top, 63 bottom right, 64 top, 65 top, 66 bottom left, 69 bottom, 70 top, 71 bottom, 73 centre, 73 bottom right, 80 right, 82, 83 left, 83 right, 84 top, 85 top, 85 bottom, 87 top, 89 bottom left, 89 bottom right, 92 bottom, 97 top, 98 top right, 98 bottom, 100 top, 100 bottom, 103 right, 107 bottom left, 113 bottom, 115 left, 116 top, 118, 119 top left, 120 bottom, 124 left, 124 right, 132, 133 top right, 135 top, 137 top, 138 top, 142 top, 144 bottom, 151 left, 152 top left, 152 bottom left, 154 bottom, 160 bottom right, 162 left, 163 top left, 163 bottom, 166 top, 166 bottom, 175 top, 175 centre, 177, 178 bottom, 186 top, 236 bottom, Rob Gallagher 254, 255 top left

ITV 230 bottom

Stewart Kendall/Sportsphoto Agency 196 left, 228 left, 268 right

Kicksports Foto 230 top

M. Larkin 39 bottom right

Mark Leech 147 bottom, 169 top, 180 bottom, 196 right, 218 top, 231 left, 234 left, David Davies 193 bottom left

Liverpool Daily Post and Echo 237 top

London Express News Service 201 bottom

London News Service Mark Morris 259 right, Paul Vincete 257 bottom

Eamon McCabe 145 centre

Mercury Press Agency 249 left

Monitor Press Features 69 top

North London Photo Service 141 left

Photographic News Agencies 38 top, 46 top, 62

Picture Services A. Harris 63 bottom left, S. Martin 27 centre right

Press Association 9 top, 61 bottom

left, 61 bottom right, 64 bottom, 66 top, 69 centre, 761 centre, 73 top, 73 centre top, 75, 77 left, 81 top, 84 bottom, 90 top, 93 top, 104 left, 106 bottom, 108 top right, 110 right, 111 bottom, 112 bottom, 114 right 115 right, 117 top, 122 left, 123 bottom, 130 top, 130 bottom, 133 top left, 143 left, 155 top right, 160 top right, 162 right, 165 top, 176 bottom left, 181 bottom, 183 top, 186 bottom, 193 top, 194 top, 200 top, 217 top, 218 bottom, 219 left, 221 left, 226 top, 231 right, 237 bottom, 239 top, 262 top, Fiona Hanson 238 left

Press Association/Reuter 12, 18 bottom, 21 bottom right, 32, 33 centre, 34 bottom, 39 top, 45 left, 47 top, 48 right, 49 bottom, 55 top right 56 bottom, 57 bottom left, 58 right

Press Portrait Bureau 15 top, 39 bottom left

Professional Sport Ltd 197 bottom

Pro-Shot 258 top

Duncan Raban/All-Action Photographic 213 top right, 216 top

Raymonds, Derby 74 centre, 74 bottom

Reuter 250 top

Scotsman Publications 23 bottom, 181 top

Sport & General 21 bottom left, 63 top, 65 bottom, 108 bottom, 182 bottom, 190, D. Bennett 164 right

Sportapics 213 bottom

Sporting Pictures (UK) 136 right, 140, 147 top, 151 bottom right, 153 bottom right, 163 top right, 173 bottom left, 173 bottom right, 176 top, 198 top, 209 right, 210 left, 227 top, 250 centre, 269 bottom

Syndication International/Hulton Deutsch 26 bottom, 34 top, 59 left, 74 top, 78 bottom, 79 top, 86 top, 98 top left, 102 right, 103 right, 103 top, 103 bottom, 144 top, 152, 159 bottom, 161, 164 left, 187 bottom, 189 top, 191 top left, 194 bottom, 199 bottom left, 202, 204 top, 223, 224 top, 225 right, 232 top, 232 bottom, 234 top right, 263 bottom, 268 left, 269 top **Bob Thomas Sports Phtotography** 143 right, 149 top, 155 top left, 159 top, 167 top, 176 bottom right, 188 bottom, 191 top right, 193 bottom right, 203 bottom, 219 right, 211 left, 222 top, 225 left, 228 right

Times Newspapers Picture Library 7 top, 7 bottom, 10 bottom, 18 top, 19 bottom, 20, 21 top, 28, 35 left, 41 top right, 41 bottom, 48 left, 50 top, 78 top, 81 bottom, 87 bottom, 90 bottom, 91 top, 92 top, 101 top, 107 top, 107 bottom right, 111 top, 112 top left, 112 top right, 116 bottom, 117 bottom, 119 top right, 120 top, 121 top, 122 bottom right, 126 left, 151 top right, 153 top right, 154 top, 173 top, 179 bottom, 182 top, 191 bottom, 207 top right, 227 bottom, 239 bottom, 240 top, 242, 243 top, 243

bottom, 250 bottom, 251 top, 252 bottom, 253 top, 255 top right, 258 bottom, Frank Baron 204 bottom, 205 top, Roy Beardsworth 257 top, Martin Beddall 253 bottom, David Davies 249 right, Ted Ditchburn 261 bottom, T. Dixon 114 left, Stewart Fraser 101 bottom, Greenwood 27 top, Harris 30, 31 bottom right, Warren Harrison 174 Frank Herrmann 131 top, 154 bottom, Tommy Hindley 187 op, P. Jay 211 right, D. Jones 133 bottom, Karadia 203 top, H. Kerr 134 top, Tom Kidd 266 top, Paul Lewis 199 top, F. McKechnie 234 bottom, Denzil McNeelance 233 bottom, John Manning 188 top, Dud Miller 200 bottom, Risley 19 top, 23 top, Hugh Routledge 207 bottom, 235, 248, 260 bottom, 267 top, Peter Simpson 201 top, Chris Smith 212, 222 bottom, 236 top, 240 bottom, 252 top, Ian Stewart 139 top, 199 bottom right, 208 bottom, 226 bottom, 260 top, 265 top, Tom Stoddart 216 bottom, Travis 131 bottom, Simon Walker 267 bottom, Warhurst 49 top, 55 bottom, Mike Wilkinson 208 top, Ian Wright 142 bottom right

UPI 51 bottom, 80 left, 88, 89 top, 91 bottom, Roy Letkey 197 top, Jeff Widener 195 bottom, Roland Witschel/DPA 198 bottom

United Sports Picture Agency 175 bottom

Universal Pictorial Press & Agency 14 right, 108 top left, 158 bottom left, 220 bottom, 262 bottom

Varley Picture Agency 135 bottom

Dave West 251 bottom